Fodor's

TEXAS

1st edition

Where to Stay and Eat
for All Budgets

Must-See Sights
and Local Secrets

Ratings You Can Trust

Fodor's Travel Publications   New York, Toronto, London, Sydney, Auckland
www.fodors.com

FODOR'S TEXAS

Editors: Debbie Harmsen (lead editor), Michael Nalepa

Editorial Production: Linda K. Schmidt, David Satz
Editorial Contributors: Maria Burwell, Paul Eisenberg, Shannon Kelly, Molly Moker, Jennifer Paull, Suzanne Robitaille.
Writers: Tony Carnes, Stewart Coerver, Tyra Damm, Jessica Norman Dupuy, Jennifer Edwards, Wes Eichenwald, Lisa Miller, Tim Moloney, Larry Neal, Michael Ream, Roger Slavens, Kevin Tankersley
Maps & Illustrations: Maps.com *cartographers*; Bob Blake, Rebecca Baer, and William Wu *map editors*
Design: Fabrizio LaRocca, *creative director*; Guido Caroti, Siobhan O'Hare, *art directors*; Tina Malaney, Chie Ushio, Ann McBride, *designers*; Melanie Marin, *senior picture editor*; Moon Sun Kim, *cover designer*
Cover Photo: (Big Bend National Park): Rob Howard/Corbis
Production/Manufacturing: Angela McLean

COPYRIGHT

1st edition

ISBN 978-1-4000-0719-6

ISSN 0743-3378

SPECIAL SALES

This book is available at special discounts for bulk purchases for sales promotions or premiums. Special editions, including personalized covers, excerpts of existing books, and corporate imprints, can be created in large quantities for special needs. For more information, write to Special Markets/Premium Sales, 1745 Broadway, MD 6-2, New York, New York 10019, or e-mail specialmarkets@randomhouse.com.

AN IMPORTANT TIP & AN INVITATION

Although all prices, opening times, and other details in this book are based on information supplied to us at press time, changes occur all the time in the travel world, and Fodor's cannot accept responsibility for facts that become outdated or for inadvertent errors or omissions. So **always confirm information when it matters,** especially if you're making a detour to visit a specific place. Your experiences—positive and negative—matter to us. If we have missed or misstated something, **please write to us.** We follow up on all suggestions. Contact the Texas editor at editors@fodors.com or c/o Fodor's at 1745 Broadway, New York, NY 10019.

PRINTED IN THE UNITED STATES OF AMERICA
10 9 8 7 6 5 4 3 2 1

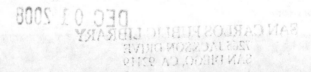

Be a Fodor's Correspondent

Your opinion matters. It matters to us. It matters to your fellow Fodor's travelers, too. And we'd like to hear it. In fact, we need to hear it.

When you share your experiences and opinions, you become an active member of the Fodor's community. That means we'll not only use your feedback to make our books better, but we'll publish your names and comments whenever possible. Throughout our guides, look for "Word of Mouth," excerpts of your unvarnished feedback.

Here's how you can help improve Fodor's for all of us.

Tell us when we're right. We rely on local writers to give you an insider's perspective. But our writers and staff editors—who are the best in the business—depend on you. Your positive feedback is a vote to renew our recommendations for the next edition.

Tell us when we're wrong. We're proud that we update most of our guides every year. But we're not perfect. Things change. Hotels cut services. Museums change hours. Charming cafés lose charm. If our writer didn't quite capture the essence of a place, tell us how you'd do it differently. If any of our descriptions are inaccurate or inadequate, we'll incorporate your changes in the next edition and will correct factual errors at fodors.com immediately.

Tell us what to include. You probably have had fantastic travel experiences that aren't yet in Fodor's. Why not share them with a community of like-minded travelers? Maybe you chanced upon a beach or bistro or B&B that you don't want to keep to yourself. Tell us why we should include it. And share your discoveries and experiences with everyone directly at fodors.com. Your input may lead us to add a new listing or highlight a place we cover with a "Highly Recommended" star or with our highest rating, "Fodor's Choice."

Give us your opinion instantly at our feedback center at www.fodors.com/feedback. You may also e-mail editors@fodors.com with the subject line "Texas Editor." Or send your nominations, comments, and complaints by mail to Texas Editor, Fodor's, 1745 Broadway, New York, NY 10019.

You and travelers like you are the heart of the Fodor's community. Make our community richer by sharing your experiences. Be a Fodor's correspondent.

Happy traveling in the Lone Star State!

Tim Jarrell, Publisher

CONTENTS

MAPS

ABOUT THIS BOOK

Our Ratings

Sometimes you find terrific travel experiences and sometimes they just find you. But usually the burden is on you to select the right combination of experiences. That's where our ratings come in.

As travelers we've all discovered a place so wonderful that its worthiness is obvious. And sometimes that place is so experiential that superlatives don't do it justice: you just have to be there to know. These sights, properties, and experiences get our highest rating, **Fodor's Choice**, indicated by orange stars throughout this book.

Black stars highlight sights and properties we deem **Highly Recommended**, places that our writers, editors, and readers praise again and again for consistency and excellence.

By default, there's another category: any place we include in this book is by definition worth your time, unless we say otherwise. And we will.

Disagree with any of our choices? Care to nominate a place or suggest that we rate one more highly? Visit our feedback center at www.fodors.com/feedback.

Budget Well

Hotel and restaurant price categories from ¢ to $$$$ are defined in the opening pages of each chapter. For attractions, we always give standard adult admission fees; reductions are usually available for children, students, and senior citizens. Want to pay with plastic? **AE, D, DC, MC, V** after restaurant and hotel listings indicate if American Express, Discover, Diners Club, MasterCard, and Visa are accepted.

Restaurants

Unless we state otherwise, restaurants are open for lunch and dinner daily. We mention dress only when there's a specific requirement and reservations only when they're essential or not accepted—it's always best to book ahead.

Hotels

Hotels have private bath, phone, TV, and air-conditioning and operate on the European Plan (aka EP, meaning without meals), unless we specify that they use the Continental Plan (CP, with a Continental breakfast), Breakfast Plan (BP, with a full breakfast), or Modified American Plan (MAP, with breakfast and dinner), or are all-inclusive (including all meals and most activi-

ties). We always list facilities but not whether you'll be charged an extra fee to use them, so when pricing accommodations, find out what's included.

Many Listings

★	Fodor's Choice
★	Highly recommended
⊠	Physical address
✛	Directions
⌂	Mailing address
☎	Telephone
🖷	Fax
⊕	On the Web
✉	E-mail
🎫	Admission fee
☉	Open/closed times
Ⓜ	Metro stations
▭	Credit cards

Hotels & Restaurants

🏨	Hotel
🛏	Number of rooms
♨	Facilities
⑩	Meal plans
✕	Restaurant
⚊	Reservations
⌇	Smoking
⑭	BYOB

Outdoors

🏌	Golf
⛺	Camping

Other

℃	Family-friendly
⇨	See also
⊠	Branch address
☞	Take note

1

Experience Texas

WORD OF MOUTH

"Everything in Texas is bigger—leave that little bitty camera at home and bring along a film and sound crew."

—Scarlett

FROM THE EDITORS

You may have heard the expression "Texas is like a whole 'nother country," and frankly, it is. Both of us have Midwestern roots, but we also both have ties to Texas; ties that began when we went to college in Texas (Mike went to Rice, Debbie went to Baylor), and deepened with family connections (Mike's in-laws and wife are from Fort Worth, while Debbie's parents retired to the Hill Country, and her sister lives in the Valley).

We both go back often to Texas and have things we cherish about it, like the BBQ, the bluebonnets, and the laid-back attitude. But we also remember our first introduction (some might call it indoctrination) to "the Great State," during our college years. We met Texans who had the Lone Star flag spread across an entire wall of their apartment; saw plenty of pickup trucks and guys walking across campus in their cowboy boots and, yes, sometimes cowboy hats, too; and heard expressions like "We're *fixin'*" to do this or that and countless *y'all*s (and it doesn't matter if it's directed at many people or just one). We also started to like country music and don't regret it one bit (we reckon y'all might like it, too, if you get out on the dance floor and try the Texas two-step with your *pardner*).

And for this book we've found a terrific team of writers *(⇨ About Our Writers at the end of the book)* who are passionate about Texas and have traveled over its many miles of deserts, forests, park land, beaches, and urban areas to do research for this first-edition book. They've visited the restaurants, toured or stayed at the hotels, checked out the attractions and rated them accordingly (though as we note in our About This Book earlier, everything in here is a place we recommend; some we just went so ga-ga over—and we think you will, too—that we had to give it a star).

Texas has so much culture and variety, it truly does have something for everyone. If you want an urban experience, Texas's four (five, if you count Fort Worth separately, which you should) amazing large cities, each unique and each charging ahead with development, are primed to greet you with a wealth of attractions. If you want to get out into Texas's wide-open spaces, there's plenty to choose from: the Hill Country, West Texas, and the Panhandle will let you rope cattle at a dude ranch, hike through the Chisos Mountains of Big Bend National Park, or meander through Larry McMurtry country in Archer City. In East Texas and North-Central Texas, you can view fall foliage or hunt for antiques. And in the Rio Grande Valley and along the coast, you can dive into the Gulf of Mexico, go bird-watching, or just relax on a beach.

And wherever you go, they'll be plenty of good cookin'—from barbecue to Tex-Mex to the state ice cream, Blue Bell—and country music to indoctrinate, err, *introduce* you to the Great State. Y'all have a great time in Texas!

—The Editors

WHAT'S NEW IN TEXAS

River Walk Gets More Mileage

If you've meandered along San Antonio's famed, and fabled, River Walk, dined along the river's shores, or taken a cruise past it, pretty soon, your "Been there, done that" words will not encompass the full experience. The currently 3-mi-long River Walk through Alamo City's downtown is expanding to 13 mi, stretching both north and south. The developed walk will connect downtown with Brackenridge Park and its attractions by early 2009, as well as the Spanish missions in the southern part of town by 2012. The $216 million project provides for landscaping, more than 20,000 planted trees, and additional pedestrian bridges and walkways.

Dallas Cowboys' Football Palace

The Dallas Cowboys are moving from their historic Texas Stadium in Irving to new digs in Arlington that even for Texas make the word big seem way too small. The stadium, set to open in June 2009, will hold 80,000 for most games, but seating can be expanded for big events—like the 2011 Super Bowl, which Dallas will host. Video screens that are *60 yards long* will run between the 20-yard lines, suspended 110 feet above the field. Even the Statue of Liberty could fit inside it—with the retractable roof closed.

Artsy Austin Takes It up a Notch

Art shouldn't be locked away at night in a museum where no one can enjoy it, and for that matter, it shouldn't be separated away by itself anyway but integrated with daily life. At least that's the thinking behind the new 21C towers that will soon be going up in downtown Austin. A contemporary art museum–hotel with restaurants and spa, plus a separate tower with residences, the 3.5-acre 21C Austin is being modeled after the 21C museum-hotel that debuted in Louisville, Kentucky, in 2006, where, as the *New York Times* described it, "every employee is a de facto docent." The $200 million project breaks ground in Austin's Waller Creek area (east downtown) in early 2009.

The Next Napa?

Texas has become the fifth-largest wine-producing state in the country, its vineyards contributing more than $1 billion annually to the state economy and producing a number of award-winning wines. Texas's varied climate allows vineyards to grow a wealth of varietals, with each region producing a distinct wine. Though the state has eight wine regions, the Panhandle and Central Texas tend to have the most "destination wineries." Each year, 5 million visitors journey along the Texas Wine Trail running through the heart of Texas in the scenic Hill Country west of Austin. They come for the tastings, seminars, demonstrations, cooking classes, entertainment, and tours of the region's 22 wineries, some of which even have bed-and-breakfasts. October is Texas Wine Month, with related events throughout the state all month long. There's even a winery inside Dallas-Fort Worth International Airport (La Bodega Winery, at terminals A and D).

Houston's New Downtown Park

In spring 2008 the Bayou City officially opened Discovery Green, a sparkling new 12-acre, Wi-Fi-enabled public park that's destined to become one of Downtown Houston's star attractions. Just a stone's throw from the Astros' Minute Maid Park, the Rockets' Toyota Center, and the George R. Brown Convention Center, Discovery Green features gardens, trails, a lake, picnic areas, fountains, performance spaces, and two restaurants created by the Schiller Del Grande Restaurant Group (of Café Annie and Taco Milagro fame).

Fencing in the Border?

The U.S. Department of Homeland Security is in the process of building portions of a fence along the Mexico/U.S. border. There's a battle over it, with critics contending that it could hurt the local economy, damage bird- and wildlife-migration patterns, and not be effective enough to warrant the cost and disruption. In March 2008 the El Paso City Council voted against giving Homeland Security access to the land to repair the current fence or to build nearly 57 mi of new fence. A bill passed by Congress, however, grants Homeland Security some leeway to accomplish the construction anyway.

Nolan Ryan Tapped as Rangers President

Texas sports legend Nolan Ryan, a Hall of Fame pitcher for the Texas Rangers as well as a player for the Astros, became the Texas Rangers' president in February 2008. The 61-year-old, who played for the Rangers from 1988 to 2004, is baseball's all-time leader in strikeouts (5,714) and no-hitters (7). He owns two minor-league teams, one in Round Rock and one in Corpus Christi.

Texas Gets Bigger

Everything's big in Texas, and its large cities just keep getting bigger. Four of the country's 10 fastest-growing metropolitan areas are in Texas, according to Census Bureau statistics released in late March 2008. Looking at figures from July 2006 to July 2007, the Census showed Dallas at first place with an increase of 162,250 residents. Houston came in fourth with 120,544, Austin–Round Rock hit ninth with 65,880, and San Antonio snagged the 10th spot with 53,925 new residents.

Two Noteworthy Texans Take Leave

The year 2007 saw the loss of two famous Texans, former First Lady "Lady Bird" Johnson and syndicated columnist Molly Ivins. Born Claudia Alta Taylor in Karnack, Texas, and an alum of UT, Lady Bird died in Austin at age 94 on July 11, 2007. She was devoted to the beautification of Austin and helped launch the National Wildflower Research Center. On January 31, 2007, liberal newspaper columnist Molly Ivins passed away, also in Austin, at age 62. A native of Texas, Ivins had become a Texas institution of sorts, with her sharp prose directed at conservatives and President Bush, the subject of several of her books. Incidentally, less than five months earlier, Ivins wrote a tribute to former Texas governor Ann Richards, who died in September 2006.

Sizzling San Antonio

From new hotels to a revitalized arts scene, San Antonio is buzzing with new energy and excitement. In the next few years alone, 44 hotels are poised to alter the landscape. The biggest hotel under construction, the Grand Hyatt, opened in spring 2008. Adjoining the Convention Center, the Grand Hyatt offers 79,000-square-feet of business space and 1,003 guest rooms. But the hotel garnering the most gossip is the Hotel Valencia Riverwalk, the city's first boutique hotel. Open since 2003, it's puffed pillows for Hollywood big names like *American Idol*'s Ryan Seacrest, Paula Abdul, and Simon Cowell. The Valencia's bar is the place to see and be seen.

Lights, Camera, Action

Over the past decade, Austin has emerged as the "third coast" of filmmaking. In January 2008 *MovieMaker* magazine named Austin the number-one city to live and make movies in; it's the seventh year in a row for Austin to hit the top spot. Film advocates in the city helped to get a statewide incentive program passed that provides rebates to producers for filming in Texas. Also favorable is the weather and sunshine, a good amount of industry professionals in the area, and easy access to small towns. It's no wonder that film production in Austin has increased ten-fold in the past decade.

Presidential Opening

Texas A&M in College Station has dibs on George Bush Sr.'s presidential mementos, but Southern Methodist University, the current First Lady's alma mater, has gotten the nod from George W. Bush that it will be home to his presidential library, making it the third location in Texas for a presidential library (Lyndon B. Johnson's is in Austin, on the University of Texas campus). SMU's winning bid beat out proposals from several universities—Baylor, Texas A&M, UT, and the University of Dallas, as well as the West Texas Coalition and the city of Arlington. The SMU Board of Trustees approved it in February 2008. The George W. Bush Presidential Center will contain a library, museum, and institute and will focus on the "unique times" of the country during which Bush was president as well as explore his personality.

Victory Park in Dallas

Texas billionaire Ross Perot and his land-developer son, Ross Perot, Jr., masterminded the idea of a creating this new downtown Dallas neighborhood from a former "brownfield" (contaminated area). Named Victory Park, the urban park links Dallas's downtown with Turtle Creek and Uptown Dallas. By the end of 2007 the W hotel, more than a dozen shops, and a handful of restaurants, including the House of Blues, Havana Social Club, and Craft restaurant, had opened. By 2010 the park will also be home to the Dallas Museum of Nature and Science 4-acre complex and Texas's first Mandarin Oriental Hotel, featuring 150 luxury hotel rooms and 90 residential units.

Round Rock Goes Medical

Home to Dell Computers, Round Rock, Texas, just north of Austin, has established itself as a sort of Silicon Valley of Texas. But now its character is about to change, as it also becomes a major medical-education hub, with A&M Medical School set to open by 2010, and Texas State University (out of San Marcos) planning to open a nursing school shortly thereafter.

Austin's Changing Skyline

Real estate in Austin is hot. Hotels, condos, restaurants, and more are being built downtown, with no end in sight to the big development in the works. Among the most notable initiatives is the $250 million Block 21 project, which broke ground in 2007 and will bring to Austin's downtown a W hotel, a children's museum, residential units, and more. Basketball great Earvin "Magic" Johnson is one of the investors.

WHAT'S WHERE

The following numbers refer to chapters.

2 San Antonio. Remember the Alamo? The city's—and state's—famous landmark is here, though it sometimes gets lost amid the charm of the ever-popular River Walk, a shady pedestrian walkway along the San Antonio River that winds through town. Outside of town, Six Flags Fiesta Texas and Sea World make a big splash with families and thrill seekers.

3 Austin. The state capital is home to the sprawling University of Texas campus, energetic 6th Street—where music thumps into the wee hours of the night—and treasures like the Bullock Story of Texas Museum, a repository for exhibits about the Lone Star State's fascinating history.

4 The Hill Country. Dude ranches, lakes, wineries, German-flavored Fredericksburg, and lots of hills comprise Central Texas's Hill Country, west of Austin and north and northwest of San Antonio.

5 Dallas & Fort Worth. Dallas, shopping central and headquarters for many giant corporations, is in the process of transforming its arts scene (constructing the largest urban arts district in the country) and its urban landscape (with

the burgeoning Victory Park development at the edge of Downtown). Fort Worth prides itself in being a rambunctious, Old West town—but you'll also find excellent dining and top-notch cultural institutions.

6 North-Central Texas. With Dallas anchoring the region's northern reaches and Austin its southern swatch, the North-Central Texas region is mostly known as the I–35 corridor. Noteworthy spots along the way include ethnic enclaves like Czech-friendly West and Waco, home to Baylor University.

7 Houston & Galveston. Houston, Texas's largest city (and the fourth-largest in the U.S.), is an international capital of commerce, technology, and, of course, oil. But Houston is also a civic experiment in what can happen when you have no zoning laws, which makes the city quirky beyond belief (in a good way). Just southeast of the city lies Galveston, a resort city with a southern flair.

8 East Texas. The terrain of East Texas resembles Louisiana more than it does Texas. The region has alligators (200,000 of them, in fact) and other swampy features, but it's most known for being the cradle of Texas's booming oil industry and home to several sites related to Texas's struggle for independence.

9 South Texas & the Coast. South Texas is for the birds— literally. Winged creatures arc overhead, and snowbirds (called Winter Texans) flock from colder climes up north. Come Spring Break, college students fly into the area to hit the beaches of South Padre. The Rio Grande Valley boasts a thriving citrus industry, and is one of the gateways into northeastern Mexico.

10 West Texas. To say West Texas is desolate is putting it mildly. You're likely to encounter more tumbleweed than people, especially if you're on a long drive on I-10. But if you get off the Interstate you find civilization, in such towns as El Paso, Midland and Odessa, and San Angelo. Nature's beauty in West Texas is best captured at its number-one attraction: Big Bend.

11 Big Bend National Park. This enormous park is best known for its size (800,000 acres), its remote location (300 mi from El Paso), and the Rio Grande River, which forms its southern border. Visitors can experience the rough beauty of the Chisos Mountains, which form the park's center, or hike through desert, forest, or river valley in a silence broken only by wildlife.

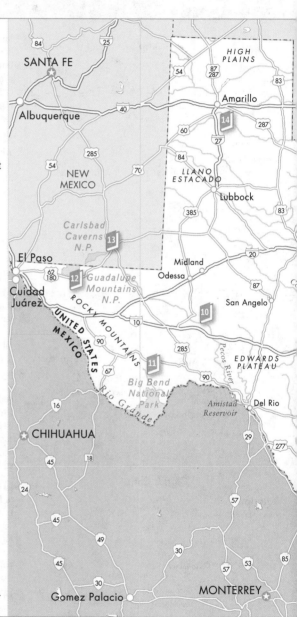

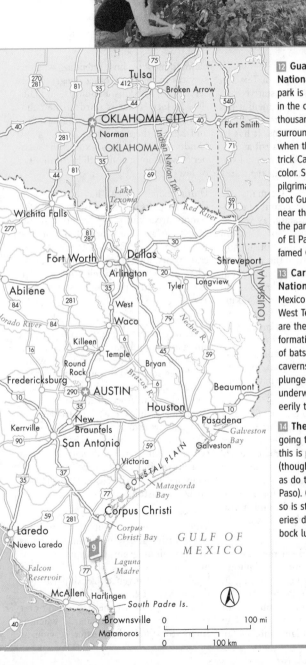

12 Guadalupe Mountains National Park. This rugged park is one of the least-visited in the country, but it draws thousands of visitors from surrounding states every fall, when the hardwoods of McKittrick Canyon burst into flaming color. Serious hikers make the pilgrimage here to scale 8,479-foot Guadalupe Peak. Situated near the New Mexico border, the park is 110 mi northeast of El Paso and 40 mi from the famed Carlsbad Caverns.

13 Carlsbad Caverns National Park. This New Mexico park is just north of West Texas. Its highlights are the bizarre underground formations and the hordes of bats. Visitors reach the caverns via an elevator that plunges 75 stories to an underworld of shadows and eerily twisted rock.

14 The Panhandle. If you're going to see snow in Texas, this is probably where it'll be (though Big Bend sees plenty, as do the mountains of El Paso). Cotton is king here, and so is steak. In the south, wineries draw tourists, and Lubbock lures Buddy Holly fans.

TEXAS TODAY

The People

It's hard to define the people of Texas in terms of demographics. The state has its cowboys but also its businessmen; it has its numerous college students as well as its retirees and Winter Texans. It has its Texas Rangers and border-patrol agents, plus thousands of military personnel stationed at the bases throughout the state.

There are still pockets of Germans and Czech communities, descendants of early-day immigrants to the state, as well as large-scale neighborhoods of Mexican immigrants, both legal and not, in border towns and elsewhere in the state. The people of Texas are as diverse as what you'd find across America. They do tend to share several traits, however: taking immense pride in their state, being passionate about sports and God, and having a friendly and laid-back attitude. And, this is the South; so ladies, smile and say thank you when the gentleman holds the door open for you or tips his hat to you.

Religion

Every town in Texas, big or small, has a good preacher, or two—or three dozen. Some are so good they draw attendees in the tens of thousands to their weekly services (⇨ *Megachurches close-up in the Houston chapter*). Going to church on Sunday is part of the culture for many in this swath of the Bible Belt, and if you didn't go to church on a given Sunday, the joke is that you went to Bedside Baptist.

Texas leads the country in the number of Evangelical Protestants (5 million), and is second, behind Pennsylvania, in the number of Mainline Protestants (1.7 million). It falls third in the number of Catholics, behind California and New York. And while Christian churches lay claim to most of those attending religious services in the state, other congregations serve Jews, Muslims, Buddhists, and Hindus. In fact, Texas is third in the country in number of Buddhist congregations, and fifth in the number of Muslims and Hindu assemblies. It is sixth in the number of Mormons, and tenth in the number of Jews.

Unfortunately, Texas has also seen its share of cults, as the vast terrain with remote areas can make for good hiding places. In 1993 the Branch Davidians' compound near Waco was raided by federal agents, and many lost their lives (⇨ Chapter 6); and in spring 2008 authorities uncovered a polygamist sect in West Texas.

The Economy

Several economic engines keep Texas going: oil, natural gas, and cotton, among them, along with the U.S. military, which has bases scattered throughout the state. Timber still plays a role in East Texas, and Dallas and Austin cater to high-tech companies, while Houston courts Fortune 500 energy firms. Tourism, of course, plays a factor throughout the state, as do education (the state has dozens of colleges and universities) and scientific research, including NASA's Johnson Space Center outside Houston.

The Politics

When it comes to politics, Texas leans conservative and Republican, though as Mexican immigrants continue to pour into the state, many of them becoming legalized and given citizenship to vote, that may change in coming years. Even so, that's not to say the state hasn't ever voted Democrat, particularly when it comes to state office. After serving as

the state treasurer in the 1980s—the first woman in 50 years to hold a state office in Texas—the late Ann Richards, a Democrat, held down the fort in Austin in the early 1990s as the state's second woman governor.

The state has reared such notable politicians as presidents Lyndon B. Johnson and George W. Bush, senator Kay Bailey Hutchinson, and the eccentric businessman briefly turned politician Ross Perot. It also has the unfortunate distinction of being the site of the most memorable presidential assassination, that of JFK, who was killed in Dallas in 1963.

Sports

Football is the state's number-one diversion, and it doesn't matter if it's pro (the Dallas Cowboys), collegiate (UT and A&M are perennial rivals), or high school (West Texas high school football mania provided the inspiration for *Friday Night Lights*). There are always fans ready to cheer the home team to victory.

Texas sports heroes range from baseball greats past and present (Nolan Ryan and Alexander Rodriguez, the latter with the New York Yankees) to football legend Troy Aikman (former quarterback of the Cowboys) and Austinite Lance Armstrong, who spurred a new interest in bicycling and the Tour de France.

Recently the Lone Star State has become basketball crazy, and the Houston Rockets, Dallas Mavericks, and San Antonio Spurs make perennial appearances in the NBA play-offs.

The Texas Sports Hall of Fame in Waco (⇨ Chapter 6) has exhibits on famous connected-to-Texas athletes, from swinging sensation Byron Nelson (golf) to Olympic sweetheart Mary Lou Retton (gymnastics).

The Arts

The arts are thriving in Texas's big cities, and in many of its smaller towns, too. Texas has its share of major cultural institutions, such as Fort Worth's acclaimed Kimball Art Museum and Houston's eclectic Menil Collection, as well as its whimsical, off-beat, and otherwise peculiar art spots like Franco Mondini-Ruiz's Botanica in San Antonio (attached to the new Alameda museum), and Cadillac Ranch, a roadside attraction of ten Cadillacs planted in the ground fins up along I-40 west of Amarillo.

The state also nurtures scores of musicians, with styles as varied as country and rock to blues and zydeco to mariachi music. George Strait, Willie Nelson, ZZ Top, and Bowling for Soup are among the performing artists with ties to Texas.

Austin's Sixth Street is known universally for its rhythmic nature, but don't forget Fort Worth's Billy Bob's, which brings in some of the top country-Western musicians for concerts throughout the year. It's a completely different vibe from Austin's nightlife scene, but that's one thing that makes Texas so special: no two parts are the same, so you have a full gamut of options and diverse experiences.

TOP TEXAS ATTRACTIONS

The Alamo

(A) All Texans know about this site that inspired the battle cry for Texas independence, and John Wayne helped cement this historic mission firmly in the minds of everyone else. The building is small, but significant for its role in the fight against Mexico. All the soldiers who fought to defend it lost their lives here. (⇨ Chapter 2.)

SeaWorld San Antonio

(B) The largest of SeaWorld's marine theme parks, SeaWorld San Antonio is a perennial favorite of families visiting Central Texas. Its newest ride, Journey to Atlantis, looks tame from the ground, but when you're on it you might think differently, as part of the ride spins backward and, for the finale, plunges into the water. The park's highlights are its animals, including the much-beloved Shamu. (⇨ Chapter 2.)

Big Bend National Park

(C) Ride the rapids of the Rio Grande River, trek through classic Old West landscape, and marvel at the moonscape that skirts Boquillas, Mexico, at this 801,163-acre national park in West Texas. It is one of the nation's most geographically diverse parks. Kids love the star-viewing parties and the hot spring in which they can swim. (⇨ Chapter 11.)

Fort Worth Stockyards

(D) This is the Texas you imagined when watching or reading Westerns. Fort Worth's Stockyards National Historic District boasts the Fort Worth Herd (a twice-daily longhorn cattle drive at 11:30 and 4), the Texas Cowboy Hall of Fame, restored 19th century buildings, the Stockyards Museum, the Stockyard Station shopping area, a vintage railroad—and the world's largest honky tonk, Billy Bob's Texas (complete with an

indoor bull-riding ring). Saddle up! (⇨ Chapter 5.)

Schlitterbahn Waterparks

(E) This place has triple the fun, because it has three locations in Texas: Galveston, South Padre, and New Braunfels. The Galveston location has a heated indoor park, for wet fun year-round. The largest of the Texas trio of parks is the 65-acre New Braunfels location. It's been voted the best water park for a decade. Opening in summer 2008, the new thrill-ride attraction Dragon's Revenge consists of creepy caverns, a two-story freefall, special effects, and one angry dragon—everything a pre-teen boy wants. (⇨ Chapters 4, 7, & 9.)

NASA's Space Center Houston

(F) As soon as a shuttle's launched from Florida's Cape Canaveral, Mission Control in Houston takes over. Visitors to this Space Center can take a tram tour through the working NASA area and the old Mission Control station. The on-site museum has lots of hands-on activities related to space. (⇨ Chapter 7.)

South Padre Island

(G) Dolphin-watching, scuba diving, glass-bottom boats doing ecotourism trips, horseback riding on the beach, a fun water park, and of course, sunning and swimming at the beaches—it's all here on South Padre, a favorite with families (except during Spring Break, when college kids take over the island). (⇨ Chapter 9.)

The State Capitol

(H) Texas's majestic State Capitol, in Austin, is taller than the U.S. Capitol and is made of beautiful Texas granite. Tours are available. (⇨ Chapter 3.)

TEXAS'S TOP EXPERIENCES

Stroll the River Walk

More than an attraction, the River Walk is something you experience. Strolling along San Antonio's River Walk, away from the car traffic above, brings serenity and a different perspective on the city. In addition to walking it day or night, you can dine alfresco at one of the dozens of restaurants along the walk, or take a cruise on the river. With the upcoming expansion of the River Walk you'll have even more options and have a way to be connected to almost all of San Antonio's main attractions.

Rope in Some Ranch Life

Visitors looking for a cowboy-type experience have several options, but signing on for a dude ranch is probably the closest they'll get to the real McCoy. For something not as involved, Houston, Dallas, Fort Worth, Amarillo, and other locales feature rodeos with plenty of activities to watch from afar or join in—even kids can get in on the fun.

Spectating Sports

The San Antonio Spurs. The Dallas Cowboys. The Houston Astros. The Texas Rangers. Texas has its top teams in basketball, football, and baseball, so just pick a sport and city and then root, root, root for the home team.

Boogie at Billy Bob's

Forget '70s music. We're talking the boot-scootin' boogie. Practice the Texas two-step or join in some line dances like the Electric Slide at this Fort Worth venue—*the* country-Western dance club in Texas (though Gruene Hall in the Hill Country ranks up there, too). Live music here has included shows by artists like Willie Nelson and George Strait. You can't get any more country than that.

Bird-Watch

The Rio Grande Valley is one of the best places in the state, and the country for that matter, to watch birds as they migrate from the colder climes up north to the south for the winter. Wildlife refuges and parks in the valley provide ideal spots for watching the feathered creatures. So don't forget your binoculars.

Drive the Backroads

Scenic roads meander across the state, perfect for a leisurely afternoon drive, and when it's harvest time, country roads—farm-to-market and ranch (also called ranch-to-market) roads especially—have great fruit stands set up along them, so you can gather in fresh peaches, oranges, grapefruits, and more. In the Hill Country, the Texas Wine Trail helps you appreciate the fruit of the vine.

Roaming Out Yonder

If you're away from the cities, you can experience the wide-open country aspects of Texas: camping, stargazing (try the McDonald Observatory in West Texas), hiking Big Bend or Guadalupe Mountains national parks, or combing the beaches along the coast for shells.

Border Bargaining

Cross the border into Mexico for cheap (and often colorful) shopping. Nuevo Progresso, across from Weslaco in the Rio Grande Valley, is a safe and popular place for U.S. shoppers. Leave your car stateside. Your best bet is to walk across, paying a small fee (bring some pocket change) at the bridge.

BEING A TEXAN 101

Texans have their own history, their own culture, and even their own language. Here's a little primer to help you fit in with the folks of the Great State.

Talk Like a Local

Whether it's the slower, drawn-out speech, the never-ending y'alls, or how they drop off the hard "h" sound when they say things like humble (therefore pronouncing it "umble"), Texans talk differently than the rest of the country. They also fix their verbs quite a bit, as in "I'm fixin' to go the store," "I'm fixin' to drive my pickup truck over there right now." Also, if you're from the Midwest, word to the wise: don't commit the social blunder of calling a carbonated beverage a pop. Everything here is Coke (even if it's a 7Up). Occasionally you'll hear someone say "sodie water."

Eat Meat

It's hard to be a vegetarian in Texas. Not impossible, but challenging, at least if you're a visitor who will be dining out most of the time. (The exception to this is Texas's bigger cities, where dining options cover almost every cuisine type imaginable.) From barbecued brisket to "real" Texas chili (meat but no beans), solid meat options are what tend to fill menus. If you're near the Salt Lick in Austin, you've got to stop and try the barbecue—consider it even if you're vegetarian (we promise not to tell on you).

Drink Dr Pepper or Big Red

Created in Waco within 50-some years of each other, these drinks are the state's alcohol-free beverages of choice. Not too far in the distant past, the live bear mascots of Baylor University used to even guzzle a bottle of Dr Pepper at the home football games. We must warn you that Big Red is an acquired taste.

Wear Your Boots Right

Please, please, please do *not* tuck your jeans into your boots. Unless you're wearing the big rubbery kind to wade through mud or are doing serious ranch work, you should wear your jeans over top (this is the point of boot-cut jeans, after all). For women, it's completely acceptable to wear boots with a skirt. And pair a solid belt with your boots.

Listen to Country Music

You don't have to have half of your set stations tuned to country music in your car or know the lyrics to all (or any) of the songs, but do keep it to yourself if the genre makes you want to run away screaming. Country music in Texas is mainstream, and it's the one type of music you're guaranteed to hear on your radio throughout the state. Prep in advance if you haven't at least heard of Toby Keith, Garth Brooks, and the Dixie Chicks.

Be Friendly

We know you learned the Golden Rule in kindergarten, treat others like you want to be treated, but if for some reason you've forgotten, take a deep breath and remember to smile and be nice, even to the guy who just cut you off on the crazy Houston freeway—in fact, especially to that guy, because in Texas on the road, rude gestures can land you a ticket. By and large, Texans will be friendly back, wishing you a good day and telling you to come back soon. In the smaller towns they may even wave or say hello as they pass you.

QUINTESSENTIAL TEXAS

Barbecue

Texas barbecue will make you forget all about Memphis, Kansas City, and North Carolina. Here barbecue can mean pretty much anything, smoked until it literally disintegrates in your mouth. Most of the time, though, we're talking about brisket. Not that dried-up hunk of meat Grandma used to make—Texas barbecue brisket is moist, tender, and thinly sliced, served over some bread and slathered with sauce. Grab some pickles and sides—baked beans, potato salad, fried okra, jambalaya, broccoli-rice-cheese casserole, corn on the cob, black-eyed peas, green beans, mac 'n' cheese ... maybe even an SOS (side of sausage). Wash it all down with a sweet iced tea or a Shiner Bock, and you'll find culinary nirvana.

Western Heritage

One of the first things you'll notice when you deplane in Texas is that people here are proud of their Western roots. Most of the real cowboys are long gone (though the state is still home to many working ranches), but Texans still dress the part. You're likely to see at least a handful of people wearing cowboy boots and hats in most public places; even some Dallas businessmen sport polished, custom-made boots and pristine Stetsons. The most western of institutions, the rodeo, is alive and well here—Houston's draws almost 2 million over a three-week period each March. Still, if you want to meet Texans who aren't "all hat and no cattle," you'll need to leave the urban areas to visit places where farming and ranching are still a part of the daily rhythm of life.

Living in such a large and bold state, Texans sometimes seem to forget about the rest of the country. They've developed a distinctive culture all their own, which you can delve into by doing as the natives do.

Tejano Culture

Texas's Hispanic heritage goes back to the 16th century, when Spanish conquistadors first visited the region. These explorers were followed by settlers from Mexico, who extended their mission trails throughout the state and brought their religion, customs, and legal system along. They also unknowingly established the beginnings of Tejano (Spanish for "Texan") culture—eventually solidifying this new identity as they fought against Mexico alongside Anglo settlers in the Texas Revolution. Today you can see Tejano influences in the language, architecture, music, and, of course, the food of Texas. And the Census Bureau reports that 35.7% of the state's residents are of Hispanic or Latino origin—a figure that is expected to grow along with the Tejano impact on all Texans' identity.

Football Fervor

In Texas, football is more religion than sport. Every fall, in small towns across the state normal life is put on hold on Friday nights, and businesses shut down so everyone can go watch the high school game. On Saturdays most Texans bleed Longhorn orange or Aggie maroon—but never both. And Sunday afternoons are reserved for watching America's team, the Dallas Cowboys. (Houston's newish team, the Texans, has its own following—but it's clear who's number one in the Lone Star State.) This intense love of the sport has been chronicled in countless books and movies, including *Varsity Blues, North Dallas 40,* and, of course, *Friday Night Lights* (the book, movie, and TV series).

IF YOU LIKE

Outdoor Adventure

There's no shortage of things to do in Texas for those who love spending time outdoors. And this is true not only in regions like the Hill Country and West Texas, but also in the large cities, where hike-and-bike trails and golf courses allow you to get away from the brick and mortar.

- **Big Bend National Park, West Texas.** This mammoth park in Texas's elbow is all about playing outdoors in every way imaginable, from hiking, bicycling, and horseback riding to fishing, bird-watching, and getting out on the water. Avoid this park at the height of summer or you'll feel like you've stepped into a furnace. (⇨ Chapter 11.)

- **Enchanted Rock State Park, between Fredericksburg and Llano.** The "enchanted" pink granite dome, at 425 feet tall, makes the park popular with rock climbers. Others come to hike or simply look at the sky—bird-watching by day, star-gazing by night. (⇨ Chapter 4.)

- **Natural Bridge Caverns, near New Braunfels and San Antonio.** Want to go below the earth's surface to cool off and get a different perspective? Here you travel down 180 feet and then walk through a maze of beautiful rock formations. (⇨ Chapter 2.)

- **Franklin Mountains State Park, El Paso.** Hike, bike, or ride a horse through this park near the New Mexico border. The best parts of a trip here are the visual rewards you get from atop: views of El Paso beneath you. (⇨ Chapter 10.)

Art

The big cities all have traditional sprawling art museums, and little ones, too. Here are a few we like and think you will too.

- **Blanton Museum of Art, Austin.** On the campus of the University of Texas, this is the largest university art museum. It holds works from across the ages, including Renaissance art and contemporary Latin-American art. (⇨ Chapter 3.)

- **Dallas Museum of Art, Dallas.** In its 23,000-piece collection, Big D's premier art museum features everything from European paintings to decorative arts to Asian sculptures. (⇨ Chapter 5.)

- **Houston Museum of Fine Arts, Houston.** World-famous, this collection (housed in a building designed by Ludwig Mies van der Rohe) is both vast and diverse, with sculptures by legends like Matisse and Rodin among its offerings. (⇨ Chapter 7.)

- **Kimbell Art Museum, Fort Worth.** It only holds 350 works of art, but the traveling exhibitions and the exclusivity of its selection are what make the Louis I. Kahn–designed Kimbell one of Cowtown's most suprising (and acclaimed) finds. (⇨ Chapter 5.)

- **McNay Art Museum, San Antonio.** This museum has a homey feel, which makes sense, given that it's housed in a private mansion once owned by artist and oil heiress Marion Koogler McNay. The 24 rooms showcase the talents of Cézanne, Gauguin, and Picasso, among others. (⇨ Chapter 2.)

Family Fun

Families have so much to choose from in the Lone Star State that the choices might be overwhelming: from waterparks, roller coasters, and outdoorsy options to a host of museums that have kids in mind.

- **Schlitterbahn, Galveston, South Padre, and New Braunfels.** The biggest of the three is in New Braunfels, a convenient day trip from San Antonio or Austin, but the Galveston one is great for winter trips, as a heated indoor water park keeps kids wet and happy year-round. (⇨ Chapters 4, 7, & 9.)

- **SeaWorld San Antonio, San Antonio.** The killer whale Shamu is enough of an enticement to get your kids here, but add to that all the rides, large water park, and opportunities to see (and even feed) dolphins and stingrays, and you can't go wrong with a visit to the world's largest marine park. (⇨ Chapter 2.)

- **Six Flags, San Antonio and Arlington.** The thrill-rides chain has two fun parks in Texas, but the San Antonio one maintains its unique personality among Six Flags' many properties due to its Opry-like musical shows that have carried over from its days as simply Fiesta Texas (it's now Six Flags Fiesta Texas). (⇨ Chapter 2 & 5.)

- **The Witte Museum, San Antonio.** Learning is fun at this small science museum with interactive exhibits. The treehouse out back can keep curious young children entertained for hours. (⇨ Chapter 2.)

Antiquing

Antiques shops and malls pop up all over Texas, making the state a great shopping destination for those who love searching through objects with a past.

- **Gladewater, East Texas.** Just a bit west of Longview on U.S. 80 at U.S. 271, this small town is the "Antique Capital of East Texas." The once oil-booming town features more than 200 antiques stores and craft shops. Nearby Longiview also has some antiques stores and general shops. (⇨ Chapter 8.)

- **Gingerbread Antique Mall, Waxahachie.** Furniture, fine antiques, glass works, and collectibles lie in wait at Ellis County's best antiques store. Unlike some shops that close on Mondays, the Gingerbread is open daily. (⇨ Chapter 6.)

- **A Tiskit A Taskit, Hillsboro.** Some people only come to this community off I–35 in North-Central Texas for the big-box outlet malls right off the interstate. But those seeking treasures of another era should make their way to the town's historic square, where antiques stores provide gems like old furniture and household goods. A Tisket A Taskit also serves Blue Bell ice cream, a dish or cone of which is a must for a hot summer day. (⇨ Chapter 6.)

- **New Braunfels, the Hill Country.** Between Austin and San Antonio, this city calls itself the Antique Capital of Texas. (⇨ Chapter 4.)

HISTORY YOU CAN SEE

Most Texans are prone to boast that their state was once a separate nation, but the Texans who achieved that distinction desired annexation to the United States, not nationhood. Here's a recap of how Texas moved from a Spanish colony to become its own nation and then a state.

Spanish Colonial Era

The Lone Star State's name tells part of its story. Texas is a latter-day spelling of the Spanish colonial term Tejas, a translation of the word *taysha*, used by some American Indians from the East Texas Caddo civilization to mean "friend."

The first attempts by the Spanish to Christianize the Indians and colonize the area were tepid at best. Scattered settlements arose in East, South, and Central Texas, but none was populous, wildly prosperous, or able to defend itself from outside hostility. The Apache wiped out dozens of them, crops failed when rain didn't come, hurricanes blew them away, and plagues brought down their populations. And unlike a few spots in equally forlorn northern Mexico, Texas had no important lodes of gold or silver, nothing to inspire feverish immigration.

By the end of the Spanish era, there were few missions left. One that was to play a key role after Mexico achieved independence from Spain was San Antonio de Valero, established by Franciscan priests in 1718 in temporary buildings. The first permanent chapel collapsed in 1744. Work on another—a building later known as the Alamo—began in the 1750s, but it was never completed, and the mission's small Indian population left the area.

What to See: Tour the **San Antonio Missions National Historic Park** (⇨ Chapter 2).

Unrest and Rebellion

The Spanish lost what little control they had over Texas in 1821, when their empire lost Mexico. At the time, Mexico was too involved in central and southern intrigues to turn attention to its sparsely populated northern areas, including Texas. Had it not been for the land hunger of the neighboring United States, the 19th century in Texas might have faded away as unnoticed as it had opened. But in 1819 a gang of American freebooters, known to historians as the Long Expedition, captured the Spanish settlement at Nacogdoches, and declared the independence of Texas. The uprising failed, but it heralded a momentum that ultimately succeeded.

The American and British immigrants who began settling in Texas in 1821 favored Anglo-American jurisprudence, Protestantism, decentralism, and slavery—none of which the Spanish and Mexican governments allowed. Some settlers were content with the Mexican government, and others were opposed to the extension of slavery and converted to Catholicism in order to own land.

The Mexican constitution of 1824 was in tune with the political idealism sweeping the North American continent—a belief that more egalitarian and democratic societies would take root and European corruption and authoritarianism could be discarded. Yet the new Mexican president was soon overthrown. When the charismatic Antonio López de Santa Anna challenged him, Anglo colonists prepared a new state constitution for Texas, which Stephen F. Austin brought to Mexico City. Santa Anna approved it, but Austin was arrested as he traveled back toward Texas and was imprisoned in Mexico City for treasonous

words found in an intercepted letter. While Austin was imprisoned, Texans went ahead with implementing their new state constitution, until Santa Anna declared one-man rule, suspended the 11-year-old Mexican constitution, and made himself the dictator of Mexico.

What to See: A statue of Stephen F. Austin, known as the "Father of Texas," is in the **State Capitol** in Austin (⇨ Chapter 3). Many sites in Texas (and of course the capital city) are named after him.

The Battle of the Alamo

The colony rebelled, and Santa Anna set out from Mexico City to reconquer it. When he arrived in San Antonio in February 1836, he found about 189 Texas revolutionaries holed up in a former Spanish mission complex, San Antonio de Valero, the one now better known as the Alamo.

Santa Anna demanded the mission's surrender. The Texans answered with a cannon shot. Santa Anna ran up the red flag—no quarter, no surrender, no mercy—from atop San Fernando Cathedral and laid siege in what would come to be called the Battle of the Alamo. On the list of defenders were Davy Crockett, James Bowie, and William Barret Travis, who was the lieutenant colonel of the rebels. The revolutionaries fought from the walls and, when these were breached, hand to hand until, as legend has it, all were dead. (There is some evidence that a half-dozen men surrendered and were immediately executed.)

Simultaneously, in Washington-on-the-Brazos, Texas delegates signed their Declaration of Independence and named Sam Houston commander of the Texas army.

What to See: Visit the **Alamo** in downtown San Antonio (⇨ Chapter 2). In East Texas, tour the Washington-on-the-Brazos State Historic Site and visit the Sam Houston Memorial Museum in Huntsville (⇨ Chapter 8).

Republic of Texas

Fearful of Santa Anna's pursuit to wipe out remaining Texas forces, Sam Houston led settlers in a retreat to Louisiana (known as the Runaway Scrape). But they met up with Santa Anna's troops on Vince's Bayou, near present-day Houston, and with the rallying cry "Remember the Alamo" the Texans charged. In 18 minutes, the Mexicans were defeated in what would later be known as the Battle of San Jacinto.

After the victory, Texas became a republic—not because its leaders or people favored the move, but largely because political arrangements in Washington precluded the admission of new slave-holding states. The nine-year history of the Republic of Texas was marked mainly by factional fights and penury, and most of the population was gratified when, in December 1945, Texas was allowed to join the United States. Its first capitol was in Houston.

What to See: Take an excursion from Houston to see the **San Jacinto Monument and Museum of History** (⇨ Chapter 7).

—Excerpted from *Fodor's Compass American Guides: Texas, 3rd Edition*

GREAT ITINERARIES

HILL COUNTRY DRIVING TOUR

The Hill Country is one of Texas's most scenic regions. It spans 23 counties and is filled with small towns, popular lakes, several caves, and historic attractions. The drive can be done in a few days or in a week, depending on how often you stop along the way. For the purpose of this itinerary, we've set it up as a four-day trip, with a full day in Fredericksburg and an afternoon in Austin. We've set it up from San Antonio, but you can jump in anywhere along the route.

Day 1: Cowboys & Art

Leaving from San Antonio, travel about 52 mi northwest to **Bandera**. It's known as the "Cowboy Capital of the World," both a reminder of its Wild West history and a symbol of its present-day Western theme–inspired tourism. The town is surrounded by numerous dude ranches that offer you a chance to take to the saddle for a few days of cowboy fun. Rodeos, country-Western music, and horse racing are also found in the area. If you want to get out and walk a bit, Hill Country State Natural Area is a good place to do it. It has 5,300 acres of hills, creeks, and live oaks.

For lunch, stop in at the Full Moon Café, if you're after healthy fare, or at the O.S.T. Restaurant if you want that artery-busting, but oh-so-good chicken-fried steak.

In the afternoon, head north on Hwy. 173 for approximately 25 mi to **Kerrville**. Attractions in the area include the Y.O. Ranch, one of the most famous in the nation (you can call ahead for a tour; 830/257–4440), and the Museum of Western Art. If you want to stay overnight here, you can try the Y.O. or Gua-

dalupe RV Resort (which has cabins with kitchens as well as campsites). Otherwise, take a brief detour west for 7 mi to **Ingram** to peruse the small cluster of art galleries and shops. (Note that most of the shops are closed on Mondays.) When you're ready to call it a day, drive 32 mi (via Hwy. 16 from Kerrville) to Fredericksburg, the most popular city in the Hill Country (⇨ Chapter 4 for the many lodging options here).

Day 2: German Infusion

Welcome to Texas's enclave of German heritage. **Fredericksburg** is a longtime favorite with shoppers and bed-and-breakfast lovers. Downtown, the National Museum of the Pacific War honors Fredericksburg native Admiral Chester Nimitz, World War II commander-in-chief of the Pacific, and Wildseed Farms is the largest working wildflower farm in the United States.

If hiking rather than shopping is your thing, venture to nearby Enchanted Rock State Natural Area. This park contains the largest stone formation in the West; both easy and challenging climbs are available. In summer, climbers should start early to avoid midday heat. For dinner, try German cuisine at a restaurant on Main Street.

Day 3: LBJ Day

On Day 3, head east on U.S. 290 for about 10 mi to **Stonewall**, the birth and burial place of Lyndon B. Johnson. At the Lyndon B. Johnson State Historical Park, you can catch a guided tour of the LBJ Ranch.

Approximately 10 mi east of Stonewall on U.S. 290 is **Johnson City**, named for LBJ's grandfather's nephew. The future president moved here from Stonewall when he was five years old. The Lyndon

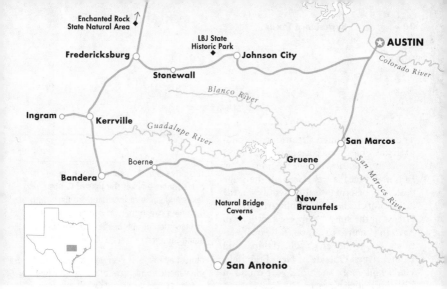

B. Johnson National Historic Park (different from the state one noted above) is here; it is the simply titled Boyhood Home of LBJ. Have lunch at the Silver K Café in Johnson City.

From Johnson City, head east on U.S. 290 for about 40 mi, then north on I–35 into **Austin**. The centerpiece of the city as well as the state government is the State Capitol. Guided tours of the statehouse, which stands taller than the national capitol, are offered daily. If you have time, visit the Governor's Mansion, just south of the capitol. It is filled with historic reminders of the many governors of the Lone Star State. You're taken past the main staircase, through the formal parlor, and finally into the dining room.

But if your time is limited, head just north of the capitol to learn more about LBJ at the University of Texas at Austin, the largest university in the nation. On its campus, the Lyndon Baines Johnson Library and Museum traces the history of Johnson's presidency through exhibits and films. On the eighth floor you can tour a model of the Oval Office as it looked during LBJ's administration. Spend the evening in Austin (⇨ Chapter 3 for the many dining, lodging, and nightlife options in

Austin); if you love live music, be sure to visit Sixth Street while in town.

Day 4: The I–35 Strip

Approximately 40 mi south of Austin at Exit 206 off I–35 is **San Marcos**, a favorite with shoppers from around the state who come to browse its two massive outlet malls. Summer visitors find recreation along the banks of the San Marcos River. It's popular with snorkelers for its clear waters and is home to many fish (including some albino catfish) and various types of plant life.

When you've finished shopping, continue south to **Gruene** (pronounced Green), a former town and now technically a neighborhood in New Braunfels. From its founding in the 1870s, Gruene was a happening place with a swinging dance hall and busy cotton gin. But when the boll weevil arrived in Texas with the Great Depression on its heels, Gruene became a ghost town. Today that former ghost town is alive with small shops and restaurants as well as Texas's oldest dance hall, Gruene Hall—as lively today as it was in the late 1800s.

From Gruene, reach **New Braunfels** by returning to I–35 and continuing south, or by traveling south on Gruene Road.

The self-proclaimed "Antique Capital of Texas" has numerous antiques shops, most in the downtown region. New Braunfels recalls its German heritage with many German festivals and even the name of its waterpark, Schlitterbahn (the largest in the state). Summer visitors will have the chance to canoe, raft, or inner-tube down the city's Guadalupe and Comal rivers. Outside of New Braunfels, you'll find cool conditions year-round in Natural Bridge Caverns.

From New Braunfels, take Hwy. 46 W for about 50 mi back to Bandera, or continue on I–35 back to San Antonio.

TIP

This drive is best in spring, when the bluebonnets blanket the hills of Central Texas and some of the roads are lined with blooming peach trees. If you go in summer instead, stop at one of the peach places along the road.

Almost any time of year you can stop at the wineries, which are primarily bunched around Fredericksburg. Be wary of this tour during heavy rains; many roads have low-water crossings that can be prone to flash flooding.

San Antonio

WORD OF MOUTH

"Many visitors miss King William Historic District, not far from the River Walk. Most of the homes were built in the mid to late 1800's, were beautiful at one time, fell into disrepair, became slum, then were rescued, and are once again simply gorgeous. . . . One of the better breakfast/lunch places in town, Guenther House, is located there, so you could do a drive-by or walk by of the area, and have a terrific lunch at Guenther House the same day. Eat outside on their patio. So pleasant!"

—OO

By Debbie
Harmsen,
Suzanne
Robitaille,
Rogers
Slavens,
and Kevin
Tankersley

WAKE UP IN THE ALAMO City with the scent of huevos rancheros in the air, the sound of mariachis, and the sight of barges winding down the San Antonio River, and you know you're some place special.

San Antonio is quite possibly Texas's most beautiful and atmospheric city, so it's no wonder it's the state's number-one tourist destination. Remember the Alamo? It's here, sitting in a plaza right downtown, so you can easily walk to it from your hotel. But while most visitors check out this famous symbol of Texas liberty when they come to town, the historic mission is by no means the only reason to visit San Antonio.

In fact, the heart of the visitor area is the *Paseo del Rio*—the River Walk—a festive, almost magical place that winds through downtown at 20 feet below street level. Nestled in by tall buildings and cypress trees, and tucked away from the noise of traffic above, the River Walk draws crowds to its high-rise and boutique hotels, specialty shops, and plethora of restaurants with alfresco dining.

Families are drawn to the big theme parks on the northwestern edge of town. San Antonio's Sea World is the largest marine-adventure park in the Sea World chain, and has what every kid wants in a park: animals, roller coasters, waterslides, and swimming pools. Meanwhile, Six Flags Fiesta Texas also boasts a water park and roller coasters, plus many other rides and Branson-like musical shows.

Snuggled firmly in south-central Texas, San Antonio acts as the gateway to the Hill Country—a landscape punctuated with majestic live oaks, myriad lakes, and flush-with-wildflowers hills—as well as the beginning of South Texas, the huge triangular tip of the state that is home to the Rio Grande Valley and South Padre Island, favorite destinations for bird watchers and beach-goers. San Antonio also isn't far from the Mexico–Texas border—between two and three hours to Del Rio to the west and Laredo to the south.

Given the city's close proximity to Mexico and its one-time position as the chief Mexican stronghold in Texas (prior to Texas's independence), it's not surprising that the rich tapestry of San Antonio's heritage has a good deal of Hispanic culture woven into it. Visitors can peruse shops selling Mexican crafts and jewelry, dine on Tex-Mex food, and enjoy Spanish music and mariachi bands at Market Square.

If experiencing San Antonio's multifacted ethnicity—including not only its Latino side but also its German, French, African, and even Japanese influences—is of prime importance to you, then the best time for you to visit may well be during Fiesta each April. An event that began in the late 1800s to pay tribute to the soldiers who died in the Battle of the Alamo and San Jacinto, the 10-day citywide celebration captures the city's many cultures, with music, food, festivals, fairs, parades, a carnival, and more.

PLANNING YOUR TRIP

WHEN TO GO

October and April are the prime months for a comfortable visit to San Antonio, though the spring (when it's not raining) is ideal for seeing the scenery if you're planning to visit the missions or take an excursion into the Hill Country. Also in the spring, a celebratory mood overtakes the town during the annual Fiesta event.

From June through September, intense heat bakes the city, with high humidity to boot. If you come then, you can escape the heat with well air-conditioned inside attractions and at the popular water parks of Sea World and Six Flags Fiesta Texas.

Though not out of the question, winter snows are very rare, as are light ice storms. More expected are the heavy spring rains, which can result in flash flooding in the Hill Country.

GETTING THERE & AROUND

Three interstate highways converge in central San Antonio; I–35, which links San Antonio with Dallas and Austin to the north and Laredo and the Mexican border to the south; I–10, which connects San Antonio to Houston to the east and then veers northwest before heading to El Paso and the West Coast; and I–37, which connects San Antonio to Corpus Christi on the Gulf of Mexico. A number of U.S. highways and Texas state roads also lead into the city, including U.S. 281 to the north and south and U.S. 90 to the east and west. Two other highways loop around the city; I–410 encircles the heart of San Antonio, and Texas Highway 1604 makes a wider circle that encompasses areas beyond the city limits.

In most cases, having a car in San Antonio is extremely helpful. Like most Texas cities, things are quite spread out. That being said, if you're focusing on the Riverwalk and the area immediately surrounding it, you'll probably want to park your car at your hotel and tackle sightseeing on foot (or via the Downtown streetcars, www.viainfo.net/BusService/Streetcar.aspx).

EXPLORING SAN ANTONIO

Much of downtown San Antonio can be explored on foot or by way of the trolley system that runs frequently between points of interest (⇨ *San Antonio Essentials for trolley information*).

Depending on whom you ask, the number of neighborhoods in San Antonio varies. The San Antonio Convention & Visitors Bureau breaks the city into quadrants—Northside, Eastside, Southside, and Westside, with museums in the north, heritage sites on the east and west, and missions in the south.

For the purposes of this guidebook, we've broken San Antonio into five primary neighborhoods that fit where visitors tend to go. In the dining and lodging sections we've given the River Walk its own category due to the multitude of restaurants and hotels around the river's banks.

SAN ANTONIO TOP 5

■ **Peace Like a River Walk:** Meandering through the heart of downtown, the San Antonio River won't elude you. Walk along its cypress-draped serenity for a relaxing stroll, or take a dinner cruise aboard a barge.

■ **On a Mission Trail:** Five missions from the 1700s, including the Alamo, are all within city limits. Follow the signs to find these exquisite buildings with Spanish-colonial architecture.

■ **An Art Attack:** At museums, galleries, and a school devoted to arts education, the arts—and artists—are flourishing in San Antonio. Take in an

exhibition while in town, or watch an artist at work.

■ **Hispanic Culture:** From the new Alameda museum focusing on Latino arts to the shops, restaurants, and entertainment at Market Square, a Mexican sensibility saturates San Antonio.

■ **Family Fun:** Thrill rides, Shamu sightings, serious splashing at the water parks, and a science-themed tree house at the Witte Museum are the reasons kids (and their parents) want to keep coming back to San Antonio.

DOWNTOWN & THE RIVER WALK

Coming from the northeast and heading southwest, I–35 slices through San Antonio, curving around its main downtown area, which is primarily composed of the region south and east of I–35, west of I–37, and north of I–10. The San Antonio River falls along the western part of downtown but makes a little loop into the downtown area around Market and Commerce Streets, producing the ideal conditions for a winding River Walk set a level below the main hubbub of traffic. That's not to say the River Walk is quiet. While the cars and horns are out of sight and earshot, the festive, largely developed River Walk is often bustling with people—both visitors and locals. All of San Antonio comes here to dine, shop, and eat with friends along the river's banks.

Four prime areas downtown are Alamo Plaza, Market Square, La Villita, and HemisFair Park. Alamo Plaza is, of course, where the Alamo is located, but it also serves as a bit of a town square, with many hotels (like the famous Menger Hotel) and tourist traps (such as the wax museum) either off the Plaza or nearby.

The three-block area comprising Market Square (⊠ *West Commerce and Dolorosa streets* ⊕ *www.marketsquaresa.com*) includes the Farmer's Market, a former produce market now filled with crafts, open-air boutiques, and El Mercado, the largest Mexican market in the United States. The history of Market Square dates back to the early 1800s. This was the birthplace of *chili con carne,* the spicy meat and bean mixture that today is generally considered the state dish of Texas. Enjoy the music of roaming mariachis and the delicious foods offered at stalls along the way, and pick up some *pan dulce* (sweet bread) at the famed Mi Tierra Mexican Restaurant and Bakery, open 24 hours a day. The

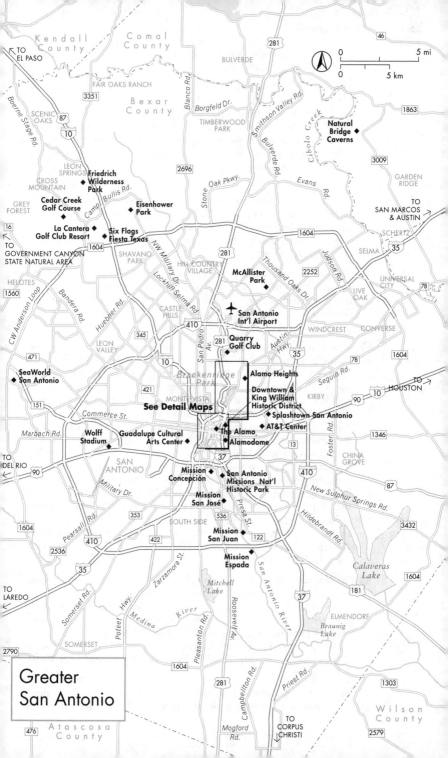

Greater
San Antonio

new Alameda museum and its accompanying *botanica* (a curio shop) is also part of the complex.

Meaning Little Village, La Villita (⊠*S. Alamo St., at the River Walk ⊕www.lavillita.com*), a prime place for shopping *(⇨Shopping)* and entertainment *(⇨Arts & Entertainment)*, was the original settlement in Old San Antonio, with adobe, brick, and stone structures in varying architectural styles. Workshops and boutiques of many of the city's artisans and jewelers are here, as well as a few good restaurants. The historic structures have been well preserved.

The biggest of these areas is HemisFair Park (⊠*S. Alamo St. between Market and Durango Sts.*), a 15-acre green space near the convention center that was the site of the 1968 World's Fair. The park is landscaped with waterfalls and a playground, and features a trio of attractions: the Tower of the Americas, the Institute of Texas Cultures, and the Mexican Cultural Institute.

The River Walk, with its twisting way, is near all of these areas and connects many of the main sites visitors go to downtown. If downtown is San Antonio's heart, the river's many arms are its arteries, bringing everyone to where the action is.

MAIN ATTRACTIONS

🔟 FodorsChoice ★ **Alamo.** At the heart of San Antonio, this one-time Franciscan mission stands as a repository of Texas history, a monument to the 189 Texan volunteers who fought and died here during a 13-day siege in 1836 by Mexican dictator General Antonio López de Santa Anna. The Texans lost, but the defeat inspired a later victory in Texas's bid for independence with the rallying cry "Remember the Alamo" spurring the soldiers on toward success. Today the historic shrine and barracks contain the guns and other paraphernalia used by such military heroes as William Travis, James Bowie, and Davy Crockett, who all died defending the Alamo. You can step inside the small mission and tour on your own, and then listen to a 20-minute history talk (talks occur every 30 minutes during operating hours except at noon, 12:30, and 1). Outside in the peaceful courtyard, a history wall elucidates the story of the Alamo, including its day as a religious mission. ⊠*300 Alamo Plaza, Houston and Crockett, Downtown* ☎*210/225–1391* ⊕*www.thealamo.org* ⊠*Free* ⊗*Mon.–Sat. 9–5:30, Sun. 10–5:30 (it generally stays open until 7 Fri.–Sat. July–Aug.).*

❶ **The Alameda.** The Museo Alameda, in partnership with the Smithsonian Institution (its first formal affiliate outside Washington, D.C.), uses a series of permanent and temporary exhibitions to explore the Latino experience in America. Recent installations include "Nosotras: Portraits of Latinas," and "¡Azúcar! The Life and Music of Celia Cruz." ⊠*101 S. Santa Rosa, Market Square, Downtown* ☎*210/299–4300* ⊕*www.thealameda.org* ⊠*$4* ⊗*Tues.–Sat. 10–6 (until 8 on Wed.), Sun. noon–6.*

⓮ **Institute of Texan Cultures.** Beyond the Tower of the Americas, this interactive museum affiliated with the University of Texas focuses on the

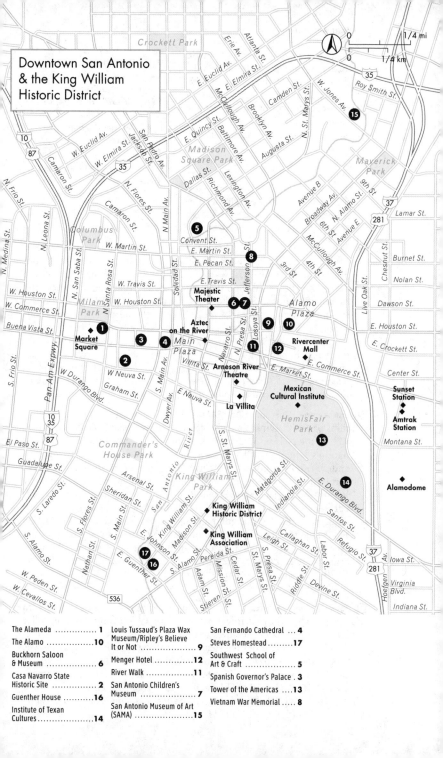

Downtown San Antonio & the King William Historic District

25 ethnic groups who have made Texas what it is today. Walk through a re-created sharecropper's house, or listen to an animated, recorded conversation that might have taken place between a Spanish governor and a Comanche chief in the 1790s. Most days costumed docents mill about the museum, ready to educate visitors on the role of a chuck-wagon cook on a cattle drive or the rigors of frontier life for women. ⊠ *801 S. Bowie St., Downtown* ☎ *210/458–2300* ⊕ *www.texancultures.com* ☑ *$7* ⊙ *Tues.–Sat. 10–5, Sun. noon–5.*

> ### CRUISIN' ON A RIVER
>
> **Rio San Antonio Cruises**
> (☎ *210/244–5700 or 800/417–4139* ⊕ *www.riosanantonio.com* ☑ *$7.75*) provides narrated boat tours and charter dinner cruises. Try to take your trip near twilight, when the sounds and light begin to soften.

⓫ **River Walk.** The *Paseo del Rio* is the city's (and the state's) leading tourist attraction. Built a full story below street level, it comprises about 3 mi of scenic stone pathways lining both banks of the San Antonio River as it flows through downtown, connecting many of the city's tourist attractions. (Soon, however, it will expand to 13 miles, connecting downtown with Brackenridge Park to the north and the missions to south.) In some places the walk is peaceful and quiet; in others it is a mad conglomeration of restaurants, bars, hotels, shops, and strolling mariachi bands, all of which can also be seen from river taxis and charter boats. ⊠ *Access from many points downtown; it starts near the Rivercenter Mall at 849 E. Commerce St.* ☎ *210/227–4262* ⊕ *www.thesanantonioriverwalk.com* ☑ *Free.*

Fodor's Choice
★

⓯ **San Antonio Museum of Art (SAMA).** The museum houses choice collections of pre-Columbian, American Indian, and Spanish colonial art, as well as the Nelson A. Rockefeller Center for Latin American Art—the nation's largest such facility, with more than 2,500 folk-art objects, and an extensive collection of Asian art, with the more than 70 pieces featured in its own wing. Past exhibitions have included works by Impressionists, lacquer over wood and other art by Japanese artist Shibata Zeshin, and lithographs by 20th-century Mexican master David Siquerios. One permanent painting to consider viewing is *Passion Flowers with Three Hummingbirds,* an 1875 piece by Martin Johnson Heade depicting a tropical forest in Brazil; it is located on the third floor in the east tower. ⊠ *200 W. Jones Ave., Downtown* ☎ *210/978–8100* ⊕ *www.samuseum.org* ☑ *$8* ⊙ *Tues. 10–8, Wed.–Sat. 10–5, Sun. noon–6.*

⓭ **Tower of the Americas.** Come here for the views, including dining with a view. The 750-foot tower, which underwent a multi-million dollar renovation in 2006, features the popular Flags Over Texas Observation Deck and the rotating steak-and-seafood restaurant Chart House. Included in the Tower of the Americas admission price is a ticket to the **Skies Over Texas 4D Theater Ride,** a multi-sensory movie experience. ⊠ *600 HemisFair Plaza Way, in HemisFair Park, Downtown* ☎ *210/223–3101* ⊕ *www.toweroftheamericas.com* ☑ *$10.95* ⊙ *Sun.–Thurs. 11–10, Fri.–Sat. 11–11.*

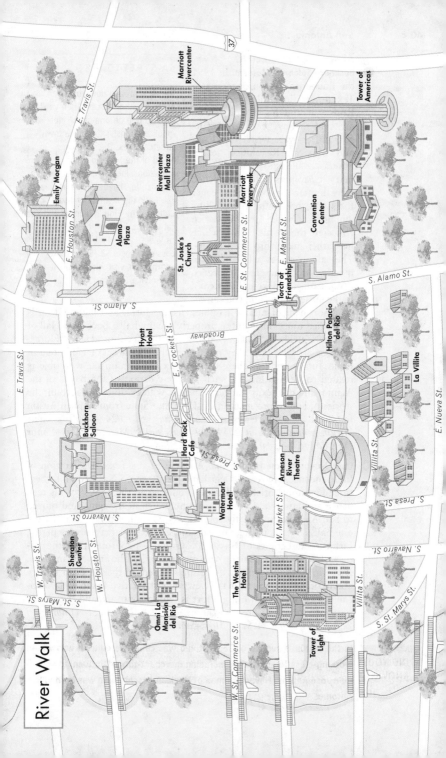

River Walk

ALSO WORTH SEEING

6 Buckhorn Saloon & Museum. In 1881 the Buckhorn Saloon opened as a Texan watering hole, and Teddy Roosevelt and his Rough Riders are said to have been among its patrons, as were writer O. Henry and Mexican Revolution leader Francisco "Pancho" Villa. Its primary customers after it opened were hunters and trappers, eager for a cold brew and to trade furs and horns. Owner Albert Friedrich collected the horns, some which his father made into horn chairs. The saloon serves a full menu of mostly American fare (burgers, BBQ, catfish, chicken, and steak). In the museum portion, you can see an assortment of marine trophies, fishing lures, and mounted birds on guided tours through the property's many halls: Buckhorn Hall of Fins, the Buckhorn Hall of Feathers, and the Buckhorn Hall of Horns. Famous artifacts (and they number in the thousands) include one of Gene Autry's saddles. There's also a wax museum on-site with objects related to Texas's history, such as a re-creation of the Battle of the Alamo; and the Texas Ranger Museum, with exhibits that recount the stories of law enforcement in the Lone Star State from Stephen Austin forward. ⊠*318 E. Houston, Downtown* ☏*210/247–4000* ⊕*www. buckhornmuseum.com* ⊠*$11.99 (museum)* ⊗*Memorial Day–Labor Day, daily 10–6; early Sept.–late May, daily 10–5.*

> **SA STREETCARS**
>
> Traveling around downtown San Antonio without a car? Then you'll want to hop on one of VIA Metropolitan Transit's four downtown streetcar lines. The streetcars hit all of the major downtown attractions, including the Alamo, El Mercado/Market Square, Hemis-Fair Park, the Institute of Texan Cultures, the King William Historical District, Rivercenter Mall, and La Villita. Best of all, a one-day pass only costs $3.75. For more information, visit www.viainfo.net/BusService/Streetcar.aspx.

2 Casa Navarro State Historic Site. A signer of the Texas Declaration of Independence, lawyer and legislator José Antonio Navarro built these three limestone, brick, and adobe buildings in the 1850s for his residence and law office. He had sold his ranch near Seguin and moved to San Antonio to be active on the city council. Open to visitors, the one-half acre site in old San Antonio's Laredito area features period furniture and copies of Navarro's writings—he wrote about the history of Texas from a Tejano's perspective and in the Spanish language. It is San Antonio's only historic site focused on the Mexican history and heritage of Texas from the viewpoint of a native Texan with Mexican ancestry. A fundraising effort is underway to expand the attraction with more interpretive exhibits. ⊠*228 S. Laredo St., Downtown* ☏*210/226–4801* ⊠*$2* ⊗*Tues.–Sun. 9–4.*

DID YOU KNOW?

In the 1900s, a section of San Antonio was called Laredito. It was where working-class Tejanos lived, including merchant-turned–influential statesman José Antonio Navarro, a man of Mexican descent who was born in San Antonio.

CLOSE UP

Juan Seguin: Texican

Juan Seguin was a man of contradictions.

Born into the landed Mexican gentry of San Antonio in 1806, he unaccountably fell in with Stephen F. Austin and the gathering Anglo forces of revolution. Seguin was commissioned a captain in the Texas army and survived the Alamo—he was not among the 189 soldiers, all of whom died, because he had left the battle early as a courier. He reached General Sam Houston in time to help rout Santa Anna at San Jacinto.

After three sessions in the new Republic of Texas's senate, Seguin's rising fortunes abruptly collapsed. The hero of the revolution encountered financial reverses, ethnic tension, and a spreading rumor of Mexican collaborations. As if to confirm the complaint, he fled the Texas he'd helped create and settled in Mexico.

Following the Mexican War, the ex-turncoat was back, re-establishing himself in Texas business and politics. He died in 1890, and is interred at the city east of San Antonio that bears his name.

—Larry Neal

2

❾ **Louis Tussaud's Plaza Wax Museum/Ripley's Believe It or Not!** The Plaza Wax Museum depicts the famous, from Jesus to John Wayne. Many figures are displayed in elaborate sets featuring movie scenes. Alamo visitors will appreciate the "Heroes of the Lone Star" exhibits on the fateful battle. Ripley's displays an assortment of more than 500 oddities ranging from miniatures to freaks of nature. ⊠ *301 Alamo Plaza, Downtown* ☎ *210/224–9299* ⊕ *www.plazawaxmuseum.com* ⊠ *$16.99 for one, $21.99 for two* ☉ *Daily Mon.–Thurs. 10–8, Fri.–Sat. 9–10, Sun. 9–8.*

⓬ **Menger Hotel.** After you visit the Alamo, stop by this adjacent 1859 property. It's San Antonio's most historic lodging, and offers a history book full of "who's who"s who've slept here. Some of its most famous guests include Civil War generals Robert E. Lee and William Sherman, Mount Rushmore sculptor Gutzon Borglum (who had a studio at the hotel), playwright Oscar Wilde, and author William Sydney Porter (O. Henry), who mentioned the hotel in several of his short stories. As legend has it, William Menger built the Victorian hotel to accommodate the many carousers who frequented his brewery, which stood on the same site. Step inside the hotel to see its mahogany bar, a precise replica of the pub in London's House of Lords. Here cattlemen closed deals with a handshake over three fingers of rye, and Teddy Roosevelt supposedly recruited his Rough Riders—hard-living cowboys fresh from the Chisholm Trail. Note that Buckhorn Saloon & Museum also makes the same claim; either someone's been playing too much poker and can't stop bluffing, or Teddy had to go recruiting more than once. (⇨ *Where to Stay for a review of its accommodations.*) ⊠ *204 Alamo Plaza, Downtown* ☎ *210/223–4361* ⊕ *www.mengerhotel.com.*

7 **San Antonio Children's Museum.** Are your kids getting bored with the Alamo? Then head to the San Antonio Children's Museum, where they can provide energy to run the museum's kid-powered elevator, drive a kid-sized front-end loader, and learn about a variety of topics, including bank accounts, skeletons, and flying a plane. ✉ *305 E. Houston St., Downtown* ☎ *210/212–4453* ⊕ *www.sakids.org* ✍ *$4* ⊙ *Mar.–Aug., Mon.–Fri. 9–5, Sat. 9–6, Sun. noon–4; Sept.–Feb., Tues.–Fri. 9–4, Sat. 9–6, Sun. noon–4.*

4 **San Fernando Cathedral.** Still an active parish, San Fernando's was built in 1738 by the city's Canary Island colonists. Later, Mexican general Santa Anna raised a flag of "no quarter" here before he stormed the Alamo in 1836, signifying to the Texans that he would take no prisoners. In 1873, following a fire after the Civil War, the chapel was replaced with the present-day construction. Although a tomb holds the remains of some unknown soldiers, modern historians do not believe these were the bodies of the Alamo defenders because evidence of military uniforms, never worn by the Texans, has turned up among the remains. ✉ *115 Main Plaza, Downtown* ☎ *210/227–1297* ⊕ *www. sfcathedral.org* ✍ *Free* ⊙ *Daily masses starting at 6 AM. Tours available when church isn't in use.*

3 **Spanish Governor's Palace.** The beautiful 18th-century seat of Spanish power in Texas has period furnishings throughout its 10 rooms. Relax on the cobblestone patio and make a wish in the wishing well. ✉ *105 Plaza de Armas, Downtown* ☎ *210/224–0601* ✍ *$2* ⊙ *Mon.–Sat. 9–5, Sun. 10–5.*

5 **Southwest School of Art & Craft.** The school is housed in the former Ursuline Academy, which in 1851 became the first girls' school in the city. The long halls of the once busy dormitory are now filled with photography, jewelry, fibers, paper making, painting, and the like. The school offers adult and youth classes and workshops, and the annual Fiesta Arts Fair is held in April. The Gallery Shop sells hand-crafted items, including silver Southwestern jewelry, hand-painted plates, and wooden Christmas ornaments. Grab a sandwich or salad at the School's Copper Kitchen Café, or some sweets at the Garden Room. ✉ *300 Augusta, Downtown* ☎ *210/224–1848* ⊕ *www.swschool.org* ✍ *Free* ⊙ *Mon.–Sat. 10–5, Sun. 11–4.*

8 **Vietnam War Memorial.** Created by combat artist Austin Deuel, this sculpture in front of Municipal Auditorium represents a Marine holding a wounded soldier looking skyward as he awaits evacuation. ✉ *E. Martin and Jefferson Sts., Downtown.*

KING WILLIAM & MONTE VISTE HISTORIC DISTRICTS

In the late 19th century, leading German merchants settled the 25-block King William Historic District south of downtown. Today the area's Victorian mansions, set in a quiet, leafy neighborhood, are a pleasure to behold. Madison, Guenther, and King William streets are particularly pretty for a stroll or drive. Each December, on the first Saturday, you can tour several of the homes during the King William Home Tour, and during the citywide Fiesta each April the area puts on a fair. For a map of the area and information on district events, contact the **King William Association,** (✉ *1032 S. Alamo St.,* ☎ *210/227–8786* ⊕ *www. kingwilliamassociation.org*).

Northwest of downtown and southwest of Alamo Heights, the Monte Vista Historic District encompasses 100 blocks and features homes from the turn of the 19th century, when San Antonio's "Gilded Age" brought affluent residents to the area. Dozens of architectural styles define the homes; among them are Beaux-Arts, Craftsman, Dutch Colonial, Georgian, Greek Revival, Italianate Renaissance, Mediterranean, Mission, Modern, Neoclassical, Prairie School, Pueblo Revival, Queen Anne, Ranch, Tudor, and Victorian. The entire district is on the National Register of Historic Places. For a map of the area, contact the **Monte Vista Historical Association** (🖃 *Box 12386, San Antonio 78212* ☎ *210/737–8212* ⊕ *www.montevista-sa.org*).

MAIN ATTRACTIONS

16 **Guenther House.** This 1860 home of the family that founded the adjacent Pioneer Flour Mills welcomes self-guided tours. At the latter you'll find a small museum of mill memorabilia, a gift shop, and a cheerful restaurant serving fine German pastries and full breakfasts and lunches. ✉ *205 E. Guenther St., King William Historic District* ☎ *210/227–1061* ⊕ *www.guentherhouse.com* 🎫 *Free* 🕑 *Mon.–Sat. 8–4, Sun. 8–3.*

17 **Steves Homestead.** This 1876 Victorian home is one of the few in the
★ King William Historic District open for touring. It's always been a trendsetter. Not only was its eclectic architecture—a blend of French Second Empire and Italian Villa styles—copied by other well-to-do San Antonians, but the estate was the city's first to have a telephone (1881) and among the first to install electric lights (1894). Completed in 1876, the house, occupied by lumber magnate Edward Steves, also has a slate mansard roof and delicate floral stenciling on the ceilings. Admission includes a guided tour. ✉ *509 King William St., King William Historic District* ☎ *210/225–5924* 🎫 *$6.*

ALAMO HEIGHTS & BRACKENRIDGE PARK

The area north of downtown (but south of the airport) is known as Alamo Heights. This affluent residential neighborhoods contains an abundance of cultural establishments, a top university, and the lush, locally loved (and much used) Brackenridge Park.

MAIN ATTRACTIONS

4 **Brackenridge Park.** The 343-acre green space between U.S. 281 and
Fodor'sChoice Broadway Street (also known as State Spur 368) makes an excellent
★ setting for a picnic or a stroll, and also offers jogging trails, public art, athletic fields, a golf course, concessions, and rides on a carousel and miniature train (⇨ *Sports & the Outdoors for recreational options at the park*). However, the park is much more than just an outdoorsy

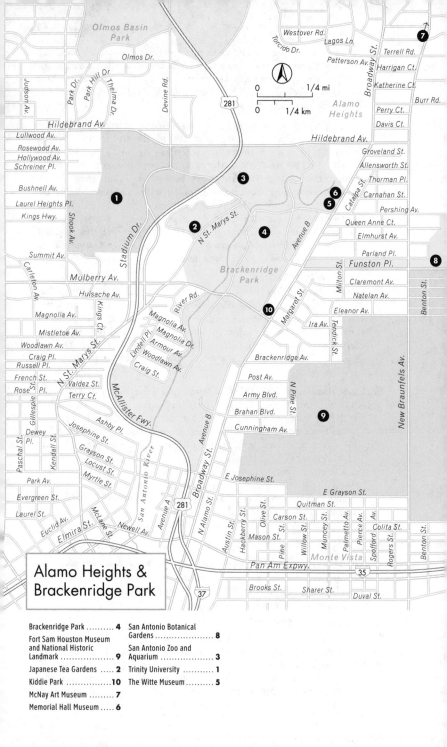

Alamo Heights & Brackenridge Park

retreat. It's home to—or in the vicinity of—many noteworthy attractions: the San Antonio Zoo, the San Antonio Botanical Gardens, the Japanese Tea Gardens, McNay Art Museum, and the Witte Museum *(for more information on these, see their individual listings in this section and also under Also Worth Seeing)*. Families should budget at least half a day here. ⊠*3700 N. Saint Mary's St., Alamo Heights* ☎*210/207-7275* ⛝*Free* ⊙*Daily 5 AM–11 PM.*

⑧ San Antonio Botanical Gardens. Step into 33 acres of formal gardens, wildflower-spangled meadows, native Texas vegetation, and a "touch and smell" garden specially designed for blind people. Among the gardens are older flower varieties, an extensive rose garden, and a Japanese garden. The centerpiece is the Halsell Conservatory, a 90,000-square-foot structure composed of seven tall glass spires. A self-guided tour of the climate-controlled conservatory takes visitors through the plants and flowers found in different environments around the world, from desert to tropics. The conservatory sits partially underground for a cooling effect in the hot Texas summers—a definite draw! ⊠*555 Funston Pl.* ☎*210/207-3250* ⊕*www.sabot.org* ⛝*$7* ⊙*Daily 9–5.*

❸ San Antonio Zoo and Aquarium. Set on 35 acres with more than 3,500 animals of 600 species, the San Antonio Zoo is consistently ranked as one of the best zoos in the country, and with the nation's third-largest animal collection, most in outdoor habitats. The zoo is best known for its excellent collection of African antelopes, as well as other hoofed species. Exhibits include the butterfly house, where about 20 species fly freely about, often coming to rest on visitors; animals from the African plains and the Amazon; critters from the prairies—both dogs and chickens; and cranes from around the world. The Children's Zoo, a $3 million addition, features rides, a nursery, a playground, an education center, and, the highlight, the "Round-the-World Voyage of Discovery" exhibit. ⊠*3903 N. Saint Mary's St.* ☎*210/734-7184* ⊕*www.sazoo-aq. org* ⛝*$9* ⊙*Daily 9–6 (though visitors can remain until 8), Memorial Day–Labor Day; 9–5 (visitors can remain until 6) otherwise.*

Fodor'sChoice ★

❺ The Witte Museum. Teach your kids about science in an adventurous way, with hands-on exhibits and log cabins to explore. The museum covers all things Texan, from the area's dinosaur inhabitants to the white-tailed deer that roam the region today. Children especially love the treehouse out back—some kids (though perhaps not their aunts and grandmas!) also love the exhibits of slithering animals (think snakes and the like). The museum is near the zoo in Brackenridge Park, which lies between Broadway and Highway 281, south of East Hildebrand Avenue and north of I–35. Seniors and kids pay discounted admission. ⊠*3801 Broadway* ☎*210/357-1900* ⊕*www.wittemuseum.org* ⛝*$7* ⊙*Mon. and Wed.–Sat. 10–5, Tues. 10–8, Sun. noon–5.*

�
★

ALSO WORTH SEEING

❾ Fort Sam Houston Museum and National Historic Landmark. This National Historic Landmark, an army base dating back to 1870, has almost 900 historic structures (about nine times as many as Colonial Williamsburg). These include the residence where General John J. Pershing lived in 1917; the Chinese Camp, which was once occupied by Chinese who fled Mexico to escape Pancho Villa; and the home where Lieutenant and Mrs. Dwight Eisenhower lived in 1916. Visitors can stroll past the structures (most are not open to the public). The Fort Sam Houston Museum is filled with exhibits on the site's early days, with items on display ranging from old uniforms and personal papers to firearms and vehicles. ✉ *1210 Stanley Rd., Fort Sam Houston, Alamo Heights* ☎ *210/221–1886* 🎫 *Free* ☉ *Wed.–Sun. 10–4.*

❷ Japanese Tea Gardens. A rock quarry turned lily pond and more, this serene oasis blossoms with lush flowers, climbing vines, tall palms, and a 60-foot-high waterfall. The ponds, with beautiful rock bridges and walkways, are home to hundreds of koi (a type of carp). The vibrant garden celebrated its grand reopening in 2008, after a more than $1.5 million restoration. ✉ *3853 N. Saint Mary's St., in Brackenridge Park, Alamo Heights* ☎ *No phone* 🎫 *Free* ☉ *Daily 8–dusk.*

❿ Kiddie Park. Established in 1925, this is America's original and old-
☙ est children's amusement park. The Herschell-Spillman Carousel's 36 jumping horses have been revolving since it opened in 1925. A Ferris wheel, a small rollercoaster, and many other rides will keep your kids busy for hours. You can get popcorn, pizza, and more at the snack bar. ✉ *3015 Broadway, in Brackenridge Park, Alamo Heights* ☎ *210/824–4351* 🎫 *$1.50 per ride or $9.25 for a day of unlimited rides* ⊕ *www.kiddiepark.com* ☉ *Mon.–Sat. 10–dusk, Sun. 11–dusk.*

❼ McNay Art Museum. In a private mansion with a Moorish-style courtyard, this museum reopened in summer 2008 with a new 45,000-square-foot exhibition center that gives a modernist twist to the landmark home once owned by artist and oil heiress Marion Koogler McNay. Housing a collection of Postimpressionist and modern paintings and sculpture, along with an arts library, the walls of the 24-room house are adorned with works by Gauguin, Cézanne, Matisse, Picasso, and Van Gogh. Twenty-three acres of landscaped gardens surround the museum. ✉ *6000 N. New Braunfels Ave.* ☎ *210/824–5368* ⊕ *www.mcnayart. org* 🎫 *$5 suggested donation* ☉ *Tues., Wed., Fri. 10–4, Thurs. 10–9, Sat. 10–5, Sun. noon–5.*

❻ Memorial Hall Museum. This repository houses history and original lore of Texas pioneers and 19th century trail drivers, with exhibits covering everything from badges to saddlebags. Western art is displayed here as well. ✉ *3805 Broadway, Alamo Heights* ☎ *210/822–9011* 🎫 *$5* ☉ *Mon.–Sat. 11–4, Sun. noon–4.*

❶ Trinity University. Situated to the west of Brackenridge Park, this well-regarded institution of higher education spreads out over 117 acres, with sweeping views of downtown. Walk around the campus and you may see some of the nearly 2,700 enrolled students sitting under the live oak trees or walking to and from class in one of the school's trademark redbrick buildings. If the timing is right, attend a show at the Stieren Theater or Laurie Auditorium. Campus tours are also offered to prospective students and their families. ✉ *One Trinity Place (at McAl-*

lister Freeway/U.S. 281 and Mulberry), Alamo Heights ☏*210/999–7011* ⊕*www.trinity.edu.*

SOUTHSIDE

The main attractions south of downtown are the historic missions. See the Greater San Antonio map at the beginning of the chapter for the locations of these sites.

★ Except for the Alamo, San Antonio's missions constitute **San Antonio Missions National Historical Park** (✉*2202 Roosevelt Ave.* ☏*210/932–1001 visitor center, 210/534–8833 headquarters* ⊕*www.nps.gov/saan* ☑*Free* ⊙*Daily 9–5*). Established along the San Antonio River in the 18th century by Franciscan friars, the missions stand as reminders of Spain's most successful attempt to extend its New World dominion northward from Mexico: the missions had the responsibility of converting the natives (primarily American Indians) to Catholicism. The missions were also centers of work, education, and trade. They represented the greatest concentration of Catholic missions in North America, and were the basis of the founding of San Antonio. Today, the four missions are active parish churches, and each illustrates a different concept of mission life. All are beautiful, in their own ways.

Start your tour at the stunning **Mission San José**, the "Queen of Missions." It's adjacent to the visitor's center, where a National Park Service ranger or docent illuminates the history of the missions. San José's outer wall, American Indian dwellings, granary, water mill, and workshops have been restored. Here you can pick up a driving map of the Mission Trail that connects San José with the other missions. ✉*6701 San Jose Dr.* ☏*210/922–0543* ☑*Free* ⊙*Daily 9–5.*

Mission Concepción, the oldest unrestored stone church in the nation, is known for its colorful frescoes, or wall paintings. The most striking fresco is the "Eye of the God," a face from which rays of light emanate. ✉*807 Mission Rd., at Felisa St.* ☏*210/534–1540* ☑*Free* ⊙*Daily 9–5.*

Mission San Juan, with its Romanesque arches, has a serene chapel. This mission once supplied all its own needs, from cloth to crops, and a trail behind the mission winds along the low river-bottom land and provides a look at the many indigenous plants formerly used by the mission. ✉*9101 Graf Rd.* ☏*210/534–0749* ☑*Free* ⊙*Daily 9–5.*

Mission Espada, the southernmost mission, was named for St. Francis of Assisi, founder of the monastic order of Franciscans. The mission's full name is Mission San Francisco de la Espada. It includes an Arab-inspired aqueduct that was part of the missions' famous *acequia* water management system. ✉*10040 Espada Rd.* ☏*210/627–2021* ☑*Free* ⊙*Daily 9–5.*

NORTH & NORTHWEST

See the Greater San Antonio map at the beginning of the chapter for the locations of these sites.

MAIN ATTRACTIONS

Ⓒ   **Six Flags Fiesta Texas.** Set within 100-foot quarry walls, this amusement Fodor's Choice   park features sectors highlighting Texas's rich diversity, from the state's
★   Mexican and German culture to its rip-roarin' Western past. Eight take-it-to-the-max roller coasters are here, including Superman: Krypton Coaster (the Southwest's largest steel coaster) and the new Goliath, a suspended looping coaster that opened in spring 2008. The more than 40 other rides include a white-water rapids flume and a tower drop. Rounding out the offerings are many excellent family-friendly musical shows (a lasting feature from when the property was owned by Opryland)—Fiesta Texas has won the Golden Ticket award for best theme-park shows in the country for nine straight years. Some of the shows invite audience participation. Concerts with big-name artists are also held periodically throughout the season. ✉ *17000 I–10 W, at jct. of Loop 410, Northwest* ☎ *210/697–5050* ⊕ *www.sixflags.com/fiesta Texas* ☷ *$46.99* ☉ *Mar.–Dec., hours vary.*

Ⓒ   **SeaWorld San Antonio.** Sprawled across 250 acres northwest of the city, Fodor's Choice   this Texas-sized marine-themed amusement park (the world's largest
★   such park) delights animal lovers with its whales, dolphins, sharks, seals, and sea lions, as well as thrilling rides—including the Great White, Texas's first inverted steel coaster; and the Steel Eel, a "hyper-coaster" reaching speeds of 65 mph. Sea World's newest coaster, Journey to Atlantis, has a water component and spins you backward. Amid acres of manicured gardens, the huge park also offers marine shows, trick waterskiing performances, and a water park with swimming pools and waterslides—a guaranteed hit with water-lovin' kids on a hot spring or summer day. Shamu, of course, is the most beloved animal in the park. His performance tank/arena has lots of water—5 million gallons of it, in fact (except when it's being splashed all over audience members who dare to sit too close). ✉ *10500 Sea World Dr., Northwest* ☎ *800/700–7786* ⊕ *www.seaworld.com/sanantonio* ☷ *$50.99* ☉ *Mar.–Dec., hours vary.*

ALSO WORTH SEEING

Ⓒ   **Splashtown.** This 20-acre park north of town has dozens of slides, a kids' activity pool, a giant wave pool, and six sand volleyball courts. ✉ *3600 North IH-35 (I–35 at Exit 160), North* ☎ *210/227–1100* ⊕ *www.splashtownsa.com* ☷ *$24.99* ☉ *June–Aug., Mon.–Thurs. 11– 8, Fri.–Sun. 11–9; Apr., May, and Sept., Sat.–Sun. 11–7.*

SPORTS & THE OUTDOORS

There's plenty for the sports lover in San Antonio. If you like to get outdoors, the city has several fantastic parks and natural areas within its borders, and many others are just beyond the city limits. There are also a number of great golf courses in and around San Antonio.

Six Flags Fiesta Texas

FIESTA BAY BOARDWALK

ROCKVILLE
Rockville High

ROCKVILLE

Spassburg Children's Theater

SPASSBURG

Sangerfest Halle

Lone Star Lil's Amphitheater

CRACKAXLE CANYON

Sundance Theater

Picnic Grove

Zaragoza Theater

Texas State Square

Teatro Fiesta

LOS FESTIVALES

Entrance

WHITE WATER BAY

SeaWorld San Antonio

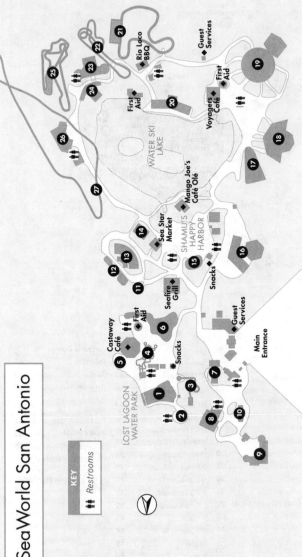

KEY

†† Restrooms

Wave Wash Pool	1
Splash Attack	2
Sky Tubin'	3
Buckaroo Mountain	4
Lil' Gators Lagoon	5
Castaway Cruisin'	6
Clydesdale Hamlet	7
Anheuser Busch	8
Hospitality House	9
Sharks/ The Coral Reef	10
Dolphin Cove	11
Lorikeet Feeding	12
Sea Lion Feeding	13
Sea Lion Stadium	14
Sea Star Theater	14
Shamu Express	15
Beluga Stadium	16
Journey to Atlantis	17
Nautilus Amphitheater	18
Shamu Theater	19
Ski Stadium	20
Rio Loco	21
Great White	22
Boardwalk Games	23
Penguin Plaza	24
Texas Splashdown	25
Penguin Encounter	26
Steel Eel	27

My First Shamu

Whales delight at SeaWorld San Antonio.

I will never forget the first time I saw a killer whale. It was a warm spring afternoon in 1985. The surface of the water was calm, smooth as glass, when suddenly the quiet was shattered by a massive turbulence of churning water, splashing, and then, breaking the surface was this massive black and white animal, as big as a school bus.

Unknowingly, I was holding my breath, watching this sleek torpedo arc over and, as quickly as I felt myself exhale, he slipped back into the depths. The displaced water crashed back and forth, slipping and splashing over the edges of the pool, until only a ripple was left.

Moments later, Shamu hoisted himself up and slid onto the stage, his mouth open as if to smile. A brief whistle from his trainer indicated "good job," and then Shamu raised his tail in a salute. Over time, my reaction has been duplicated by thousands of people when they first encounter Shamu at SeaWorld San Antonio. It is the sheer delight of a moment of discovery that is nearly indescribable, but has kept me coming back every day.

I have seen it written on my son's face the first time he saw a Shamu show. His eyes got so big, I thought his eyebrows would pop off. But what was equally surprising was seeing that same expression on my husband's face at the same encounter. So every time I hear someone say "Oh, SeaWorld is just for kids," I reply, "It certainly is . . . no matter how old you are."

—Fran Stephenson,
director of communications,
SeaWorld San Antonio

If you'd rather watch a game, the San Diego Padre's AA affiliate, the San Antonio Missions, play America's pasttime in "the Wolf" (Nelson Wolff Municipal Stadium), the jewel of the Texas League. The city is also home to an AHL hockey team, the San Antonio Rampage.

The hottest ticket in town, though, is definitely the NBA's World Champion San Antonio Spurs. Tim Duncan, Manu Ginobili, Tony Parker, and Co. put the Spurs into contention for a title every year; the team has won the Larry O'Brien Championship trophy in 1999, 2003, 2005, and 2007.

PARKS & NATURAL PRESERVES

For relaxation and recreation, San Antonio boasts several city parks—Crownridge Canyon, Eisenhower, McAllister, Stone Oak, and Walker Ranch among them. The city's star park, however, is picturesque **Brackenridge Park,** at Broadway and Funston, northeast of downtown in the Alamo Heights neighborhood. In 2006 the comfortably aged park emerged from a five-year, $7.5-million makeover that, among other improvements, transformed roads once used by cars into paved trails for bicyclists and joggers. Additional recreational opportunities at the park include golf *(⇨ Golf, below)*, picnicking (grills are provided), pedal boating, fishing, and, for the little ones, burning off energy on the playground equipment. Another option is simply unwinding with a stroll and feeding the ducks. The San Antonio River runs through the park, as does one main thoroughfare, Red Oak Drive. *(⇨ Exploring San Antonio under the Alamo Heights & Brackenridge Park section for information on the cultural attractions in and near the park.)*

For more information on Brackenridge Park and other parks in San Antonio, visit the San Antonio Parks and Recreation Department's website, www.sanantonio.gov/sapar.

NORTH/NORTHWEST

Friedrich Wilderness Park. On the outskirts of town (about 20 mi from downtown off I–10), this 600-acre hilly haven for rare birds and orchids offers more than 5 mi of hiking trails, including one handicapped-accessible trail (rollerblades and bicycles are not allowed). Bird-watchers from around the world are often spotted here. Some species are seasonal, such as blue jays (fall and winter), eastern meadowlarks (spring), red-winged blackbirds (spring and summer), scissor-tailed flycatchers (spring, summer, and fall), and double-crested cormorants (winter). See turkey vultures, finches, Carolina wrens, doves, northern woodpeckers, northern cardinals, mockingbirds, and more year-round. ⊠ *21395 Milsa St., North/Northwest* ☎ *210/564–6400* ⊕ *www.fofriedrichpark. org* ⊠ *Free* ⊙ *Daily 7:30–sunset.*

Government Canyon State Natural Area. The area is home to numerous varieties of trees and several species of rare birds, such as the golden-cheeked warbler. This 8,600-acre park in Bexar County, just outside San Antonio, opened in 2005. It offers views of surrounding Bexar County and glimpses of San Antonio. Protected Habitat Area trails are open September through February, but other trails are available year-round. The park is for day-use only, and, like any good outdoor area, offers Wi-Fi. ⊠ *12861 Galm Rd., North/Northwest* ☎*210/688–9055* ⊕*www.tpwd.state.tx.us* ⊡*$6* ⊙*Fri.–Mon. 8–6.*

WILDFEST
San Antonio's annual birding and nature festival is held in early May. For more information, visit wildfestsanantonio.com.

PARTICIPANT SPORTS

BIRD-WATCHING

Mitchell Lake. Bird-watchers worldwide come here to see the more than 300 species that visit each year. This 624-acre complex is located on a natural migratory route and serves as a stopping point for thousands of birds annually. ⊠ *10750 Pleaston Rd.* ☎*210/628–1639* ⊕*www.saws. org/environmental/mitchelllake/* ⊡*$2* ⊙*Sat.–Sun. 8–4.*

GOLF

Its enviable position as the southern gateway to the Hill Country makes San Antonio a great destination for golfers. If you have wannabe golf pro youngsters in tow, the **San Antonio Golf Operations Department** (⊠*Box 839966, San Antonio 78283* ☎*210/225–3528*) has set up Saturday clinics year-round for junior golfers (ages 6 to 18).

Brackenridge Golf Course. This historic course was the first inductee of the Texas Golf Hall of Fame. Located in San Antonio's Brackenridge Park, it first opened for play in 1916, and is the oldest municipal course in the city. Brackenridge closed in January 2008 for renovations that will include reworked tee boxes, greens, and fairways, and a return to the original layout of 15 holes; it is scheduled to reopen in late fall 2008 as a 6,185-yard par-71. ⊠*2315 Ave. B* ☎*210/225–3528* ⊕*www.play sanantoniogolf.com.*

Cedar Creek Course. Enjoy scenic views—and isn't that a big part of what golfing is all about?—while perfecting your swing at this 18-hole, par-72, course in the hills. Hazards include waterways and waterfalls. Green fees are $35 Monday through Friday and $41 Saturday and Sunday; price includes cart. ⊠*8250 Vista Colina* ☎*210/695–5050* ⊕*www.playsanantoniogolf.com.*

La Cantera. This course was voted the best in San Antonio by readers of both the *San Antonio Express-News* and the *San Antonio Current.* The resort course offers views of Six Flags Fiesta Texas as well as the Texas Hill Country, while the signature number 4 on the Arnold Palmer course—designed by the legendary golfer—requires a long carry over a waterfall-fed lake at the lip of the green. Greens fees range from $125 to $150. ⊠*16641 La Cantera Pkwy.* ☎*210/558-46453* ⊕*www. lacanteragolfclub.com.*

Quarry Golf Club. The front nine here plays like a links-style course, with no trees and an ever-present breeze to deal with. The back nine, however, is set in a limestone quarry with 100-foot perimeters. Greens fees range from $89 to $109. ✉*444 E. Basse Rd.* ☎*210/824–4500* ⊕*www.quarrygolf.com.*

SPELUNKING

Natural Bridge Caverns. Trek down 180 feet below the earth's surface for a half-mile walk through this beautiful, historic cavern system. Visitors can take the popular North Cavern tour for a look at stalagmites, stalactites, flowstones, chandeliers, and soda straw formations.

The Jaremy Room encompasses two huge underground chambers that use both light and dark to showcase rare formations. ✉*26495 Natural Bridge Cavern Rd.* ☎*210/651–6101* ⊕*www.naturalbridgecaverns. com* 💲*$16.95–$25.95* ⊙*Daily 9–4, 5, 6, or 7, depending on season.*

SPECTATOR SPORTS

BASEBALL

Enjoy a night at the ballpark watching the **San Antonio Missions** (☎*210/675–7275* ⊕*www.samissions.com*), the Double-A affiliate of the San Diego Padres. The Missions play more than 50 home games a year, from April through early September, at **Nelson W. Wolff Stadium** (✉*5757 Highway 90 W, West San Antonio*). Admission is $6.50 to $9.50, and, as with any minor-league baseball team, expect lots of promotions, giveaways, and fun on-field activities during the game.

BASKETBALL

The pride and joy of the Alamo City, the NBA's **San Antonio Spurs** (☎*210/444–5000* ⊕*www.spurs.com*), host games at the **AT&T Center** (✉*One AT&T Center Parkway, Downtown* ☎*210/444–5000* ⊕*www.attcenter.com*) from October through April. Seats are available in every price range; a seat in the rafters can be had for as little as $10—or you can sit courtside for about $900.

Catch great women's hoops action when the Women's National Basketball Association's **San Antonio Silver Stars** ((✉*One AT&T Center Parkway, Downtown* ☎*210/444–5050* ⊕*www.sasilverstars.com*)) play at the AT&T Center from May to September. Tickets for the Silver Stars range from $10 to $200.

FOOTBALL

Alamodome. This 65,000-seat, $186 million sports arena is a busy place. Home of the Valero Alamo Bowl each December, featuring teams from the Big 12 and Big 10 conferences, the site hosts other sporting events as well as concerts, trade shows, and conventions. The Alamodome is the only place in North America with two permanent Olympic-size ice rinks under the same roof. If you're not here during a game, you can still visit during a behind-the-scenes tour, which must be scheduled in advance. ✉*100 Montana St., just east of HemisFair Park, across I–37,*

Downtown ☎*210/207–3652 or 800/884–3663* ⊕*www.alamodome. com* ⊠*Prices vary with events* ⊙*Mon.–Fri. 8–5.*

HOCKEY

If hard-hitting ice hockey is your style, the **San Antonio Rampage** (☎*210/444– 5554* ⊕*www.sarampage.com*) of the American Hockey League play from October through May at the **AT&T Center** (⊠*One AT&T Center Parkway, Downtown* ☎*210/444–5000* ⊕*www.attcenter.com*). Tickets are priced from $8.50 to $39.

ARTS & ENTERTAINMENT

THE ARTS

Guadalupe Cultural Arts Center. Founded in 1980 to preserve and develop Latino arts and culture, the GCAC stages regular dance, music, and theatrical performances. It also displays the art of emerging artists and schedules various classes. Of the center's major annual events, the Tejano Conjunto Music Festival, with over 42 hours of live performances, is in May, and the Cinefestival, five days of Latino film, is in January. ⊠*1300 Guadalupe St., Southside* ☎*210/271–3151* ⊕*www. guadalupeculturalarts.org* ⊠*Free* ⊙*Mon.–Fri. 9–5.*

MUSIC & CONCERTS

Mexican Cultural Institute. Mexican culture is depicted in film, dance, art, and more. ⊠*600 HemisFair Plaza Way* ☎*210/227–0123* ⊕*www. saculturamexico.org* ⊠*Free* ⊙*Weekdays 10–5, weekends 11–5.*

THEATER

Aztec on the River. Closed for construction in 2008, the Aztec's theater doors are scheduled to reopen by 2009. Showing movies and more, the historic theater's crowning glory is its Wurlitzer organ, which was used for its early-day silent films and is still played today. ⊠*201 E. Commerce St., Ste. 300* ☎*210/227–3930, ext. 301 or 877/432–9832 box office* ⊕*www.aztecontheriver.com.*

Majestic Theater. A masterpiece of baroque splendor with Spanish Mission and Mediterranean-style influences, this 1929 movie and vaudeville theater one time showcased such talents as Jack Benny, Bob Hope, and George Burns. Today the fully restored, 2,311-seat theater spotlights current and up-and coming stars while serving as a venue for touring Broadway shows like Miss Saigon, The Color Purple, and Phantom of the Opera. It is also the resident performance space for the San Antonio Symphony Orchestra. ⊠*224 E. Houston St.* ☎*210/226–5700, 210/226–3333 box office* ⊕*www.majesticempire. com* ⊙*Mon.–Fri. 9–5.*

Arneson River Theatre. Erected in 1939, this unique outdoor music and performing-arts venue in the heart of La Villita was designed by River Walk architect Robert Hugman and built by the WPA. Have a seat on the grass-covered steps on the river's edge and watch performers on the small stage. In this open-air format, the river, not a curtain, separates

FESTIVALS & EVENTS

JAN. River Walk Mud Festival and Mud Parade. Parts of the river are drained to clear the bottom of debris, and locals revel in the subsequent parties, parades, and the crowning of a Mud King and Queen. (☎ 210/227–4262 ⊕ www.thesanantonioriverwalk.com.)

FEB. Livestock Exposition and Rodeo Held at the AT&T Center, this event features country, Tejano, and rock music, along with a rodeo and livestock show. ☎ 210/225–5851 ⊕ www.sarodeo.com. **Mardi Gras Parade.** The colorfully festooned floats create a spectacle. If you miss an event, don't worry—there are at least two a month, each with food, music, and lots of entertainment (☎ 210/227–4262 ⊕ www.thesanantonioriverwalk.com.)

MAR. Irish Festival. The San Antonio River is dyed green, and live music, food, arts and crafts, and dances fill the city in honor of St. Patty. ⊕ www.harpandshamrock.org.

Remembering the Alamo Weekend. Educational exhibits about those involved with both sides of the

Battle of the Alamo are on display at 300 Alamo Plaza during this commemorative weekend. ☎ 210/225–1391 ⊕ www.thealamo.org.

APR. Fiesta. The city's top annual event comes to town each spring for 10 days of celebrations throughout the city. Approximately 100 events are held during the festival, which honors the heros of the Alamo and the Battle of San Jacinto. (☎ 210/212–4917 ticket information ⊕ www.fiesta-sa.org.)

JUNE Texas Folklife Festival. During this summertime event more than 40 cultures exhibit their contributions to the development of Texas through music, food, dance, and folktales at the Institute of Texan Cultures in HemisFair Park. ☎ 210/458–2300 ⊕ www.texan cultures.com.

DEC. Fiestas Navidenas. Held in Market Square during the first three weekends of December, this event features childrens choirs, folkloric dance groups, mariachi bands, and a visit by Pancho Claus. ☎ 210/207–8600 ⊕ www.sanantonio.gov.

performers from the audience. Some of San Antonio's top events take place here, including Fiesta Noche del Rio, a summer show presented for more than five decades. ✉ 418 Villita St. ☎ 210/207–8610 ⊕ www. lavillita.com/arneson 💲 Prices vary, with shows starting at $5.

NIGHTLIFE

Around the 3000 block of San Antonio's **North Saint Mary's Street** lie a colorful assortment of bars and restaurants in converted commercial buildings, many with live entertainment.

Sunset Station. Four live-music stages, five dance floors, and three restaurants entertain in a turn-of-the-20th-century Southern Pacific train depot at the heart of downtown San Antonio. There's something for everyone here: the nightly music choices range from country-Western to merengue, and the food runs the gamut from Aldaco's Mexican Cuisine to Ruth's Chris Steak House. The depot is open during the day, but the bands take the stage after dark. Call ahead to see whether any nationally known acts are scheduled. ✉*1174 E. Commerce, Downtown* ☎*210/222–9481* ⊕*www.sunset-station.com* ☜*Varies by performance.*

BARS

DOWNTOWN & THE RIVER WALK

With a great location right on the river, **Dick's Last Resort** (✉*406 Navarro St.* ☎*210/224–0026*) is a nice place to grab a drink in the afternoon—provided you have a thick enough skin to withstand the intentionally surly staff.

Drink (✉*200 Navarro St.* ☎*210/224–1031*) serves tapas and has 85 signature cocktails, 150 wines by the bottle, and 75 wines by the glass.

Durty Nellie's Pub (✉*Hilton Palacio del Rio, 200 S. Alamo St.* ☎*210/222–1400*), where sing-alongs are popular, is a favorite on the River Walk.

Howl at the Moon (✉*111 Crockett St.* ☎*210/212–4770*) is a dueling-piano bar—don't hesitate to sing along!

Iron Cactus Mexican Grill and Margarita Bar (✉*200 Commerce St., near the corner of St. Marys and Crockett* ☎*210/224–9835*) has an extensive selection of tequilas and margaritas; they also·offer tequila flights for the indecisive.

Mad Dogs British Pub (✉*123 Losoya St.* ☎*210/222–0220*) has a wide selection of imported beers; entertainment includes DJs, karaoke, and live acts.

★ Don't miss the **Menger Bar** (✉*204 Alamo Plaza* ☎*210/223–4361 or 800/345–9285* ⊕*www.mengerhotel.com*) at the Menger Hotel, a fun place to go with friends for a drink, or a great place to go to meet the locals. The historic hotel is one of San Antonio's great cultural treasures (⇨ *Where to Stay*).

The San Antonio outpost of New Orleans institution **Pat O'Brien's** (✉*121 Alamo Plaza* ☎*210/220–1076*) serves the bar's wickedly strong hurricane.

At night, **Republic of Texas** (✉*526 River Walk* ☎*210/226–6256*) transforms into a nightclub. Enjoy one of the nightly drink specials, or order the massive 46-ounce margarita.

Fodor'sChoice **Vbar** (✉*150 E. Houston St.* ☎*210/227–9700*), on the River Walk at
★ the Hotel Valencia, is also one of the hottest, hippest places in town—at least this week.

Sip your drink while taking in a bird's-eye view of the city at the Tower of the Americas **Bar 601** (✉*600 Hemisfair Park* ☎*210/223–3101*).

Waxy O'Connor's Irish Pub (✉*234 River Walk* ☎*210/229–9299*) was actually built in County Monaghan, Ireland, and shipped to San Antonio, where it was reassembled.

KING WILLIAM HISTORIC DISTRICT/SOUTHSIDE

★ **Azuca** (✉ *713 S. Alamo St., King William Historic District* ☎ *210/225–5550*) puts a salsa or merengue in your step (on Friday and Saturday nights). When you aren't dancing, you'll be sipping on a Latin or specialty cocktail. A full dinner menu and more than 15 types of mojitos are available.

DANCE HALLS

World-class Jim Cullum's Jazz Band plays superb Dixieland at the **Landing** (✉ *Hyatt Regency, 123 Losoya St., Downtown* ☎ *210/223–7266*).

SHOPPING

With its rich ethnic heritage, this city is a wonderful place to buy Mexican imports, most of them inexpensive and many of high quality. A good number of San Antonio's shopping options are centered on the popular River Walk area that winds through downtown. There you'll find plenty of restaurants and bars that make perfect pit stops as you stroll from one shop to the next.

RIVERWALK/DOWNTOWN

MALLS & SHOPPING CENTERS

El Mercado is the Mexican market building that is part of **Market Square** (✉ *514 W. Commerce St.* ☎ *210/207–8600* ⊕ *www.marketsquaresa. com*). The building contains about 35 shops, including stores selling blankets, Mexican dresses, men's guayabera shirts, and strings of brightly painted papier-mâché vegetables; it's open from 10 to 8 during the summer and 10 to 6 during the winter. The lively **Farmer's Market Plaza,** with more shops and a food court, and the **Produce Row Shops** are other shopping areas in Market Square worth visiting.

LA VILLITA

It's noteworthy for its Latin American importers and demonstrations by its resident glassblower.

The shops and galleries at San Antonio's first residential area, on the southern edge of downtown, **La Villita** (✉ *418 Villita St. just off E. Nueva St., Downtown* ☎ *210/207–8610* ⊕ *www.lavillita.com*), delight shoppers bent on discovering homemade treasures. Some of the shops in this block-long historic arts village along the San Antonio River are in adobe buildings dating from the 1820s. Stores are open daily from 10 to 6, with some staying open later. A few of the stores are noted below.

Peruse paintings (oil, acrylic, and watercolor), pottery, prints, sculpture, and more at **Artistic Endeavors Gallery** (✉ *418 Villita, #2500* ☎ *210/222–2497* ⊕ *www.artend.com*), which specializes in original works by regional artists, many of which turn their artistic eye toward San Antonio's charms. At **Village Weavers** (✉ *418 Villita, #800* ☎ *210/222–0776* ⊕ *www.artend.com* ☉ *Daily 8–8*), the four designers weave together rugs, baskets, blankets, clothes, jewelry, and even toys from a variety of fabrics. **Rivercenter** (✉ *849 E. Commerce St.* ☎ *210/ 225–0000* ⊕ *www.shoprivercenter.com* ⊗ *Mon.–Sat. 10–9, Sun. noon– 6*) is a fairly standard shopping mall right on the river, whose stores include Macy's, Dillard's, and major retail chains.

OUTSIDE SAN ANTONIO

Outlet mall shoppers will delight in the more than 200 stores at **Prime Outlets San Marcos** (✉ *3939 IH-35 S, exit Centerpoint Rd., San Marcos* ☎ *512/396–2200, 800/628–9465* ⊕ *www.primeoutlets.com* ⊗ *Mon.– Sat. 10–9, Sun. 10–7*), located between San Antonio and Austin (about a 45-minute drive from San Antonio). It's the largest outlet mall in the state of Texas—which is definitely saying something.

WHERE TO EAT

THE SCENE

San Antonio is a terrific dining town. It's big enough and has enough demanding conventioneers to support fine dining you'd usually find in much larger cities. But it still has a relaxed small-town feel that makes it easy to eat out almost anywhere without much fuss. You can count on one hand the number of restaurants requiring jackets; the dress codes at most other nice restaurants pretty much stops at "no shorts, please." Reservations and long waits are rare except at a few high-end restaurants and at peak times on the River Walk.

Essentially, San Antonio cuisine is about two things: Mexican-inspired flavors and meat. Mexican, Tex-Mex, Latin, and a variety of other fusion variations crowd this bi-cultural town. You'll find wonderful Mexican breads and pastries, rich sauces with complex flavors heavy with chilies, fresh peppers, even chocolate. Margaritas and local beers, courtesy of the local German immigrant brewing tradition, remedy the occasional chili overdose (though not all Latin food here is spicy—far from it). If your idea of a perfect meal is a steak, ribs, or just a killer hamburger, this is your kind of town. But San Antonio isn't stuck remembering the Alamo at every meal: chef-driven restaurants with a wide range of offerings, including sushi, offer a break from beef and tortillas.

Most restaurants, especially downtown and at the River Walk, are open seven days a week. Outside the downtown tourist area, restaurants generally close at around 10 on weekdays, 11 on weekends. River Walk restaurants and bars stay open later, generally until 2 AM. San Antonio bans smoking in all restaurants except in designated outdoor areas (bars do allow it). Tipping conventions are standard, generally 15% for lunch, 20% for dinner.

WHAT IT COSTS				
¢	$	$$	$$$	$$$$
RESTAURANTS　under $8	$8–$12	$13–$20	$21–$30	over $30

Restaurant prices are per person for a main course at dinner.

ALAMO HEIGHTS

AMERICAN　✕**20nine Restaurant and Wine Bar.** Part of the Alamo Quarry Market
$$–$$$ shopping complex, this upscale spot may make you wonder whether you're going to dinner or a wine tasting. Well, why not have both? The selection of vintages is overwhelming, but the sommelier will help you make the right choices to pair with a small menu of entrées ranging from Stilton-stuffed chicken breast to a NY strip. This is also a great place to wind down from a day at the boutiques with dessert and a glass of port. ⊠*Alamo Quarry Market, 255 E. Basse Rd., Ste. 940, Alamo Heights* ☎*210/798–9463* ⊟*AE, MC, V* ⊙*No lunch weekends.*

AMERICAN　✕**Cappy's Restaurant.** The antidote to big and brash national chains,
$–$$$$ Cappy's caters to a local crowd craving innovative food, classy but
★ cheerful environs, and solid service. You can score great cheap eats like a Kobe burger or splurge for the chef's three-course prix-fixe menu which lets you pick a salad, entrée, and dessert. A simple but exceptional brunch, where eggs are whipped up in unusual ways, is served on Sundays. The main dining room takes advantage of funky brick architecture, tall windows, and an ever-changing gallery of art. The covered outdoor seating is hard to get on a busy night. ⊠*5011 Broadway St., Alamo Heights* ☎*210/828–9669* ⊟*AE, D, DC, MC, V.*

BURGER　✕**Casbeers.** Since 1932, Casbeers has been serving up live music with
¢–$$ their famous enchiladas and mammoth hamburgers. Its down-home approach has made it a local institution, with Kinky Friedman among its many fans. In fact, there's a burger named after him. Come here for the rustic environs, some good music, and a slice of old San Antonio, but don't expect a culinary revelation. Beer and wine flow freely. ⊠*1719 Blanco Rd., Alamo Heights* ☎*210/732–3511* ⊟*AE, MC, V* ⊙*Closed Sun. and Mon.*

BURGER　✕**Cheesy Jane's.** Big burgers, milk shakes and malts, and nostalgic decor
¢–$ dominate this throwback to old-time malt shops. But Jane's is anything but vanilla—literally. Shake and malt flavors include amaretto-espresso, peanut butter and jelly, and peppermint double fudge. The ground chuck burgers come in sizes ranging from ¼- to 1 pound. On the non-meat side there's a good bean burger or triple grilled-cheese sandwich. Adventurous diners should definitely partake of the jalapeño "slivers"—battered and fried slices of onion and peppers. ⊠*4200 Broadway St., Alamo Heights* ☎*210/826–0800* ⊟*AE, MC, V.*

AMERICAN　✕**Earl Abel's.** This hip San Antonio restaurant changed owners in 2007
$–$$$ and moved to a new neighborhood, but the food is still top-notch. The crispy fried catfish is a winner, as is the fried chicken. You can get your fried chicken fix (and other artery-clogging favorites) from the to-go stand in the parking lot, but if you take the time to sit, you can also

Continued on page 64

WHERE SHOULD I DINE IN SAN ANTONIO?

	Neighborhood Vibe	Pros	Cons
Alamo Heights	San Antonio's toniest neighborhood is also where you'll find many of its best restaurants, among residential streets and the occasional upscale strip mall. You'll definitely feel like you're eating where the locals eat (at least the well-heeled ones), but don't expect exotic vistas around every corner—the environs can be quaint but also often nondescript.	Ten minutes from downtown by car; adjacent to the San Antonio Zoo, Brackenridge Park, and other attractions; excellent and varied restaurants; caters to locals, so lacks tourist prices and congestion.	Getting here from downtown requires a car or $15 cab fare each way; the area is not particularly scenic or memorable.
Downtown	Outside the River Walk tourist district, San Antonio's downtown is a mixed bag. Some areas showcase its many historic buildings with cute local restaurants and shops. Others are just plain run-down. Drive or grab a cab if you're going more than four or five blocks from the tourist district.	Many local dining institutions lie just off the beaten path of the River Walk (usually within walking distance) and yet don't draw the usual tourist crowds; possibility to experience something truly Texan.	Some ratty areas not so easy on the eyes and feel unsafe; long distances between some attractions plus busy streets make walking something of a challenge.
North/Northwest	San Antonio's northern neighborhoods have a suburban feel, and popular chain restaurants and stores are in plentiful supply. Though there are many local gems to be found, often tucked away in nondescript shopping centers, strips of familiar restaurants line the major highway frontage roads north of the city.	Many reliable, inexpensive choices; near Fiesta Texas, Sea World, and some great shopping; most restaurants are kid-friendly; ample parking.	Suburban feel; highway driving necessary; packed with locals for lunch and dinner.
River Walk	Finding a variety of local dining options is as easy as taking a stroll along the river, where dozens of restaurants are stacked atop one another. Many have patio dining, for watching the barges go by. National chains join the local spots. Be prepared for large crowds at all of them.	Several top-quality local restaurants; many have patios with views of the boats and passersby strolling along the river.	Tourist and convention crowds can be overwhelming; waits are long at peak times; prices are high.
King William/Monte Vista Historic District	Several of the city's best upscale restaurants are just south of downtown in this National Historic District. Drive or take the trolley to this beautifully preserved neighborhood that seems a world apart from the bustle of downtown.	Peaceful area with tree-canopied streets and restored antebellum homes; top-notch local chefs.	Few lower-priced options; neighborhood feels a little sketchy for late-night dining.

BEST BETS FOR SAN ANTONIO DINING

San Antonio offers just about everything you're looking for in a dining experience, with a wide choice of cuisines ranging from local flavors to French haute cuisine, and a host of atmospheres from casual fun to a luxurious, romantic night out on the town.

Fodor'sChoice ★

Biga on the Banks, $$–$$$$, River Walk

Francesca's at Sunset, $$$$, Northwest

Le Rêve, $$$$, Downtown

Mi Tierra Café and Bakery, $–$$$, Market Square

Silo Elevated Cuisine, $$–$$$$, Northeast

By Price

¢

Casbeers, Alamo Heights

Cheesy Jane's, Alamo Heights

Chris Madrids, North

Magnolia Pancake Haus, North

Rudy's Country Store & Bar-B-Q, Outskirts

Schilo's Deli, Downtown

$

Earl Abel's, Alamo Heights

El Jarro de Arturo, North

Guenther House, King William

Josephine Street Café, North Central

La Fonda on Main, Alamo Heights

Liberty Bar, Alamo Heights

$$

Acenar, River Walk

Azúca Nuevo Latino, King William

Boudro's on the Riverwalk, River Walk

Cappy's Restaurant, Alamo Heights

Mi Tierra Café and Bakery, Market Square

Paloma Blanca, Alamo Heights

Paesanos, River Walk

$$$

Antlers Lodge, Outskirts

Citrus, River Walk

Fig Tree Restaurant, River Walk

Frederick's, Alamo Heights

Las Canarias, River Walk

Little Rhein Steak House, River Walk

$$$$

Biga on the Banks, River Walk

Bohanan's Prime Steaks and Seafood, Downtown

Francesca's at Sunset, Northwest

Le Rêve, Downtown

L'Etoile, Alamo Heights

Silo Elevated Cuisine, Northeast

By Cuisine

AMERICAN

Biga on the Banks, $$–$$$$, River Walk

Cappy's Restaurant, $–$$$$, Alamo Heights

Citrus, $$$–$$$$, River Walk

Earl Abel's, $–$$$, Alamo Heights

Liberty Bar, ¢–$$$, Alamo Heights

Silo Elevated Cuisine, $$–$$$$, Northeast

BARBECUE

Barbecue Station Restaurant, ¢–$, Northeast

County Line Barbecue, $–$$, River Walk

Rudy's Country Store & Bar-B-Q, ¢–$$, Outskirts

BREAKFAST OR BRUNCH

Bawdsey Manor British Tea Room, $–$$$, Outskirts

Crumpets Restaurant & Bakery, $$–$$$$, North Central

Guenther House, ¢–$, King William

Magnolia Pancake Haus, ¢–$, North

CONTINENTAL

Azúca Nuevo Latino, $$–$$$, King William

Fig Tree Restaurant, $$$–$$$$, River Walk

Las Canarias, $$$–$$$$, River Walk

FRENCH

Bistro Vatel, $–$$$, Olmos Park

Frederick's, $$$–$$$$, Alamo Heights

Le Rêve, $$$$, Downtown

L'Etoile, $$$–$$$$, Alamo Heights

HAMBURGERS

Casbeers, ¢–$$, Alamo Heights

Cheesy Jane's, ¢–$, Alamo Heights

Chris Madrids, $, North Central

Timbo's, ¢–$$, Alamo Heights

ITALIAN

Aldo's Ristorante Italiano, $$–$$$$, Northwest

La Focaccia Italian Grill, $–$$$, King William

Paesanos, $–$$$$, River Walk

MEXICAN

El Jarro de Arturo, $–$$$, North

La Fogata, $–$$$, Northwest

La Fonda on Main, $–$$, Alamo Heights

Los Barrios, $–$$, North Central

Paloma Blanca, $$–$$$$, Alamo Heights

Rosario's Café y Cantina, $–$$$, King William

SEAFOOD

Chart House at Tower of the Americas, $$$–$$$$, Downtown

Landry's Seafood House, $$–$$$$, River Walk

Pesca on the River, $–$$$$, River Walk

SOUTHWESTERN

Antlers Lodge, $$$–$$$$, Outskirts

Boudro's on the Riverwalk, $$–$$$$, River Walk

Francesca's at Sunset, $$$$, Northwest

STEAKHOUSE

Bohanan's Prime Steaks and Seafood, $$$$, Downtown

Josephine Street Café, ¢–$$, North Central

Little Rhein Steak House, $$$–$$$$, River Walk

Morton's The Steakhouse, $$$–$$$$, River Walk

Ruth's Chris Steak House, $$$$, Downtown

TEX-MEX

Acenar, $$–$$$, River Walk

La Margarita Mexican Restaurant & Oyster Bar, $$–$$$, Market Square

Mi Tierra Café and Bakery, $–$$$, Market Square

By Experience

CLASSIC SAN ANTONIO

Casbeers, ¢–$$, Alamo Heights

Earl Abel's, $–$$$, Alamo Heights

La Fonda on Main, $–$$, Alamo Heights

Los Barrios, $–$$, North Central

Mi Tierra Café and Bakery, $–$$$, Market Square

Schilo's Deli, $, Downtown

DINING ALFRESCO

Cappy's Restaurant, $–$$$$, Alamo Heights

Fig Tree Restaurant, $$$–$$$$, River Walk

La Fonda on Main, $–$$, Alamo Heights

Las Canarias, $$$–$$$$, River Walk

Mi Tierra Café and Bakery, $–$$$, Market Square

Paesanos, $–$$$$, River Walk

FAMILY FRIENDLY

Cheesy Jane's, ¢–$, Alamo Heights

Chris Madrids, $, North

La Hacienda de los Barrios, $–$$$, Outskirts

Mi Tierra Café and Bakery, $–$$$, Market Square

Rainforest Café, $–$$$, River Walk

Schilo's Deli, $, Downtown

ON THE RIVER WALK

Acenar, $$–$$$, River Walk

Biga on the Banks, $$–$$$$, River Walk

Boudro's on the Riverwalk, $$–$$$$, River Walk

Little Rhein Steak House, $$$–$$$$, River Walk

Paesanos, $–$$$$, River Walk

Pesca on the River, $–$$$$, River Walk

ROMANTIC

Azúca Nuevo Latino, $$–$$$, King William

Biga on the Banks, $$–$$$$, River Walk

Citrus, $$$–$$$$, River Walk

Fig Tree Restaurant, $$$–$$$$, River Walk

Francesca's at Sunset, $$$$, Northwest

Le Rêve, $$$$, Downtown

SINGLES SCENE

20nine Restaurant and Wine Bar, $$–$$$, Alamo Heights

Liberty Bar, ¢–$$$, Alamo Heights

Rosario's Café y Cantina, $–$$$, King William

Silo Elevated Cuisine, $$–$$$$, North

savor a slice of homemade coconut or lemon meringue pie. ⊠*1201 Austin Hwy., Alamo Heights* ☎*210/822–3358* ⌁*Reservations not accepted* ⊟*AE, D, DC, MC, V.*

FRENCH   ✕ **Frederick's.** Chef Perrin marries French and Asian cuisine to create
$$$–$$$$ some fantastic fusion dishes in relaxing yet romantic surroundings. Seafood is a particular standout, especially the truffle-baked sea bass and curry-crusted red snapper—both fine examples of complex flavor and stylish presentation. French staples such as veal tenderloin and rack of lamb have been jazzed up with Asian flourishes. A deep wine cellar offers many choices to complement your meal. ⊠*7701 Broadway St., at West Nottingham, Alamo Heights* ☎*210/828–9050* ⊟*AE, D, DC, MC, V* ⊘*Closed Sun.*

MEXICAN   ✕ **La Fonda on Main.** Open for business in San Antonio since 1932, this
$–$$ family-friendly restaurant in a hacienda-like building is fun and casual,
★   but still upscale. The beautiful dining room opens onto an inviting outdoor patio. The traditional Mexican fare includes such as steak Tampiquena ("Tampico-style": grilled tenderloin strips with a green enchilada and *charro* beans [pinto beans in a slightly spicy sauce]) and a variety of enchiladas. Several Tex-Mex specialties also populate a robust menu. Flan and *tres leches* cake ("three milks" cake—a butter cake soaked in sweetened condensed milk, evaporated milk, and cream) are made daily, and the vibrant bar delivers tasty margaritas. ⊠*2415 N. Main Ave., Alamo Heights* ☎*210/733–0621* ⊟*AE, D, DC, MC, V.*

FRENCH   ✕ **L'Etoile.** Progressive but classic French cuisine, beautifully executed,
$$$–$$$$ makes L'Etoile a local favorite. You might find perfectly grilled lamb chops, lobster theatrically flamed in cognac and presented on a bed of julienned vegetables, or veal *piccata* (sautéed and drizzled with lemon-caper sauce). The menu changes daily. The chocolate Grand Marnier soufflé is incredible; order it with your meal, as it takes 45 minutes to prepare. Great deals include an early-bird special (a 20% discount before 6:30 PM) and a $15 three-course lunch on Tuesdays and Thursdays. ⊠*6106 Broadway St., Alamo Heights* ☎*210/826–4551* ⊟*AE, D, DC, MC, V* ⊘*Closed Sun.*

AMERICAN   ✕ **Liberty Bar.** Built in 1890 and leaning conspicuously on its foundation
¢–$$$ (attributed to a 1921 flood), Liberty Bar is a hip, funky restaurant that's a place to see and be seen. The menu features basic, old-time favorites such as pot roast, peppered steak, and pasta. Dessert may be what they do best: try the chocolate cake or a slice of homemade pie. Guinness is on tap. ⊠*328 E. Josephine St., Alamo Heights* ☎*210/227–1187* ⊟*AE, D, DC, MC, V.*

MEXICAN   ✕ **Paloma Blanca.** A warm, almost clubby atmosphere—especially in the
$$–$$$$ bar, with its fireplace and leather sofas—lets you know to expect more than the typical Mexican fare at this Alamo Heights mainstay. Tempting offerings as varied as grilled snapper, enchiladas *verdes* (covered with green tomatillo salsa), pozole, hand-made flautas, and tacos *al pastor* (marinated pork with pineapple) are sure to please. And don't skip out on dessert—the rich flan and decadent tres leches cake are alone worth the trip to this hacienda-inspired spot. A scrumptious brunch with mimosas is served weekends. ⊠*Cambridge Shopping*

Center, 5800 Broadway St., Alamo Heights ☎*210/822–6151* ▭*AE, D, DC, MC, V.*

MEXICAN ✕**Taco Taco Café.** If you've never had a breakfast taco, this is the place
¢–$ to be initiated. Don't be afraid of the long lines out the door, as the morning crowd moves quickly. However, newbies may pause at the enormous number of possibilities, including *barbacoa* (shredded meat barbecue, Mexican style) and *migas* (eggs scrambled with fried tortilla strips, cheese, and peppers) tacos. Daily specials, a children's menu, and substantial lunch plates round out the taco extravaganza. ✉*145 E. Hildebrand Ave., Alamo Heights* ☎*210/822–9533* ▭*AE, D, DC, MC, V* ⊗*No dinner.*

BURGER ✕**Timbo's.** The owner of legendary San Antonio restaurant Little Hipps
¢–$$ later opened this destination for fabulous burgers, tater tots, and fresh salads. Don't miss the shypoke eggs: toasted bread with two kinds of cheese on top (no eggs in sight). Many tables have their own personal jukeboxes, adding to the modern diner look. ✉*1639 Broadway, at Pearl Pkwy., Alamo Heights* ☎*210/223–1028* ▭*AE, D, DC, MC, V* ⊗*Closed weekends.*

DOWNTOWN

STEAKHOUSE ✕**Bohanan's Prime Steaks and Seafood.** Executive chef and owner Mark
$$$$ Bohanan dishes up only prime-grade, center-cut Aberdeen Angus beef with exclusive selections of ultra-marbled Japanese Akaushi beef. The restaurant also has more than 35 varieties of seafood flown directly to the restaurant from the Gulf of Mexico. Add a selection of single-malt scotches, a cigar bar, a cognac cart, and an expansive wine list, and it's no wonder that the place attracts a power crowd. ✉*219 E. Houston St., Suite 205, Downtown* ☎*210/472–2600* ▭*AE, D, MC, V* ⊗*No lunch weekends.*

STEAKHOUSE ✕**Chart House at Tower of the Americas.** This steak house, opened in 2007,
$$$–$$$$ reigns over the San Antonio skyline, perched at the top of the Tower of the Americas. Its predecessor was primarily popular as a destination for drinks, but Chart House serves up some great steaks and seafood to keep you occupied for an entire night out while enjoying one-of-a-kind views of the city. It's a short stroll and elevator ride from the River Walk and other downtown attractions. ✉*Tower of the Americas, 600 HemisFair Pkwy., Downtown* ☎*210/223–3101* ▭*AE, D, DC, MC, V.*

TEX-MEX ✕**La Margarita Mexican Restaurant & Oyster Bar.** In the heart of Market
$$–$$$ Square, you can eat Mexican fare or oysters or both while surrounded by Spanish tile and light music. Try the fajitas, enchiladas, or puffy tacos, seated inside or on the patio under colorful umbrellas with a great view of the city. Want it all? Go for the Fiesta San Antonio appetizer plate for yourself or to share with friends over a fantastic array of margaritas—it's what the restaurant is named for, and the moniker is justified. There's plenty of live entertainment, and mariachis will serenade your table upon request (and please do tip a couple of dollars). ✉*120 Produce Row, Downtown* ☎*210/227–7140* ▭*AE, D, MC, V.*

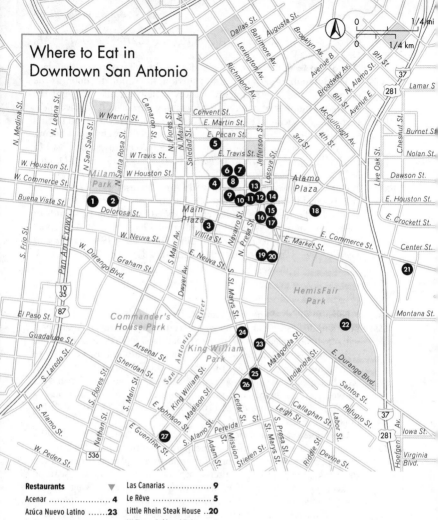

Where to Eat in Downtown San Antonio

2

FRENCH ✕ **Le Rêve.** Largely hailed as one of the finest restaurants in the U.S., the
$$$$ elegant and formal La Rêve serves up romance and fine French food
Fodor'sChoice in equal measure. Chef Andrew Reissman marries the contemporary
★ with the classic in (frequently updated) dishes that feature ingredients
ranging from foie gras to diver sea scallops. The eight-course tasting
menu with matched wines is the best way to enjoy a leisurely dining
experience—be prepared to devote two-plus hours—perfect for special
celebrations. ⊠*Historic Exchange Building, 152 E. Pecan St., Downtown* 🕾*210/212–2221* ⌕*Reservations essential, formal* ▭*AE, D,
DC, MC, V* ⊘*Closed Sun. and Mon.*

TEX-MEX ✕ **Mi Tierra Café and Bakery.** In the heart of Market Square lies one of
$–$$$ San Antonio's most venerable culinary landmarks. Opened in 1941
Fodor'sChoice as a place for early-rising farmers to get breakfast, Mi Tierra is now
★ 24-hour traditional Mexican restaurant, bakery, and bar. Its hallmark
breakfasts are served all day, and the *chilaquiles famosas*—eggs scram-
bled with corn tortilla strips and topped with *ranchero* (mild tomato-
based) sauce and cheese—are alone worth coming back for again and
again. Truly memorable tacos, enchiladas, chalupas, and house special-
ties, all made from fresh ingredients, are served at lunch and dinner.
The giant, carved oak bar serves up aged tequilas, authentic margaritas,
draught beer, and mixed drinks. The bakery has an enormous selection
of *pan dulces* (Mexican pastries) and excellent coffee. ⊠*218 Produce
Row, Market Square* 🕾*210/225–1262* ⌕*Reservations not accepted*
▭*AE, D, DC, MC, V.*

STEAKHOUSE ✕ **Ruth's Chris Steak House.** It's a mainstay in almost every convention
$$$$ town, but you can't go wrong with this upscale purveyor of fillets and
T-bones. The menu's à la carte approach allows you to mix and match
to your heart's content, but be wary of tab creep. Try a cowboy rib eye
for a truly flavorful cut or venture outside the norm for the seared ahi
tuna. ⊠*1170 E. Commerce St., Downtown* 🕾*210/227–8847* ▭*AE,
D, DC, MC, V.*

DELI ✕ **Schilo's Deli.** This venerable downtown institution has been serving up
$ hearty German soul food at breakfast (served daily), lunch, and dinner
since 1917. Fuel up for a walking tour of downtown with thick split-
pea or lentil soup, corned beef, sausage, deli sandwiches, or weekday
lunch specials such as chicken and dumplings or meat loaf. Wash it
down with fantastic homemade root beer and top off your meal with
cheesecake—if you have room. ⊠*424 E. Commerce St., Downtown*
🕾*210/223–6692* ▭*AE, D, DC, MC, V* ⊘*Closed Sun.*

STEAKHOUSE ✕ **The Palm Restaurant.** The San Antonio location of this classic New
$$$–$$$$ York–style steak house maintains the chain's efforts to bring back the
supper clubs of decades gone by. Premium seafood, including jumbo
Nova Scotia lobster, and Italian specialties add plenty of diversity to a
menu populated by prime aged porterhouses and veal rib chops. The
dining room is elegant and stately, putting you in the right frame of
mind to down some serious turf or surf or both. ⊠*233 E. Houston
St., Downtown* 🕾*210/226–7256* ▭*AE, D, DC, MC, V* ⊘*No lunch
weekends.*

KING WILLIAM/MONTE VISTA HISTORIC DISTRICT

CARIBBEAN
$$–$$$
✕**Azúca Nuevo Latino.** If you want something different from San Antonio's usual Mexican or Tex-Mex offerings, venture south to find festive fare hailing from the Caribbean, Spain, and South and Central America. Executive Chef Rene Fernandez mixes up flavors and styles con pasion. Start out with an Amazonian tamale or Bolivian empanada and move onto plantain-crusted salmon and meats basted with *chimichurri*, a tangy basil sauce. A good array of steaks plus a children's menu ensure that everyone leaves happy. There's live salsa music and dancing Friday and Saturday. ⊠*713 South Alamo St., King William* ☎*210/225–5550* ▤*AE, D, DC, MC, V.*

MEXICAN
$–$$$
✕**El Mirador.** Nuevo Mexican and traditional Tex-Mex flavors collide at this family-owned restaurant, a much-loved King William–district mainstay since 1967. Owner Dona Marie's mole enchiladas shine here, with the extra-sweet but smoky sauce designed to be sopped up by homemade corn tortillas. Shrimp and fish play a major role, bringing new life to tacos, nachos, and chiles rellenos. And if you've never had a breakfast taco, this is the place to try one in any of almost a dozen ways. A full bar during dinner and an outdoor dining patio seal the deal on a quintessential San Antonio eating experience. ⊠*722 S. Saint Mary's St., King William* ☎*210/225–9444* ▤*AE, D, MC, V* ⊘*No dinner Sun. and Mon.*

BREAKFAST
¢–$
★
✕**Guenther House.** This popular restaurant in downtown San Antonio is housed in a stately 1860 home built by the founder of Pioneer Flour Mills. Breakfast goodies—fluffy Pioneer Brand biscuits, breakfast tacos (with eggs, beans, and potatoes), waffles, and pastries—are half of the reason to eat here. The other half is the 1920s art-nouveau decor of stained glass, beveled glass, etched glass, and plant motifs that creates the illusion of a fine home's conservatory. ⊠*205 E. Guenther St., King William/Monte Vista* ☎*210/227–1061* ▤*AE, MC, V* ⊘*No dinner.*

ITALIAN
$–$$$
✕**La Focaccia Italian Grill.** A family-owned, classic Italian restaurant, La Focaccia has been luring folks to the King William district for pasta, steaks, and seafood since 1996. House specialties include veal saltimbocca, fresh linguini *pescatora* (with fresh shellfish), and wood-fired pizzas. Match such food with a warm, lush dining room and top-notch service, and you almost forget you're deep in the heart of Texas. ⊠*800 South Alamo St., King William* ☎*210/223–5353* ▤*AE, D, DC, MC, V.*

MEXICAN
$–$$$
✕**Rosario's Café y Cantina.** A fitting gateway to the city's Blue Star Arts District, this vibrant, colorful spot has a contemporary decor enhanced by striking paintings by local artists. The authentic Mexican food includes crowd-pleasing favorites such as super nachos (packed with nearly every topping you could want) and enchiladas to delicacies like tender tips of beef tongue. Many consider their margaritas the best in the city. Live entertainment on weekends kicks the festivities into high gear. ⊠*910 S. Alamo St., King William* ☎*210/223–1806* ▤*AE, D, DC, MC, V.*

NORTH/NORTHWEST

MEXICAN
$–$$

✗**Alamo Café.** A perennial favorite with locals, the Alamo Café is far from the actual Alamo, but you'll still remember it for its fresh tortillas (made while you watch) and no-frills approach to Mexican dishes. This is a good place to try some puffy tacos with grilled chicken or steak, or dive into a mega combination platter of enchiladas, tamales, and chiles rellenos. It's extremely family-friendly, with a kids' menu that serves up near-adult-sized portions. ⊠*14250 US. 281 N., Northwest* ☎*210/495–2233* ▱*AE, D, MC, V.*

ITALIAN
$$–$$$$

✗**Aldo's Ristorante Italiano.** This outpost of northern Italian fare near the Southwest Texas Medical Center and USAA is in a warm and homey century-old house. Fresh, simple fish, chicken, beef, game, and pasta dishes are paired with attentive service. A small patio allows you to dine alfresco, but you may prefer sitting in the bar, which has live piano music in the evenings. ⊠*8539 Fredericksburg Rd., Northwest* ☎*210/696–2536* ▱*AE, D, DC, MC, V* ⊗*No lunch weekends.*

BARBECUE
¢–$

✗**Barbecue Station Restaurant.** When you walk into a true Texas smokehouse, expect to see smoke and taste fire. Though the location is inconspicuous—apart from the long line of hungry patrons—the restaurant meets and exceeds any barbecue hankerings. Mouthwatering, dry-rubbed beef brisket, smoked turkey, pork ribs, and sausages are served up with tangy sauce (on the side), pickles, and slices of white bread. Beer, wine, and creamy sides help soothe the palate. There's a sizable outdoor patio. ⊠*1610 NE Loop 410, Northeast* ☎*210/824-9191* ⚐*Reservations not accepted* ▱*D, MC, V* ⊗*Closed Sun.*

FRENCH
$–$$$

✗**Bistro Vatel.** The bistro is named Vatel, the chef is named Watel, but no matter how you spell it, this up-and-coming spot takes fine French dining to new levels in its elegant dining room. You can go with the reasonable prix-fixe option (lunch is a steal) or mix-and-match entrées such as succulent duck breast or tempura lobster tail with a range of salads and sides. Daily blackboard specials take advantage of the freshest foods and never fail to surprise. ⊠*218 E. Olmos Dr., Northwest* ☎*210/828–3141* ▱*AE, D, DC, MC, V* ⊗*Closed Mon. No lunch weekends.*

BURGER
$

✗**Chris Madrids.** Founded in 1977, this burger and nacho joint goes by the motto "Cook Each Item as if You Were Cooking It for a Friend," and it shows. The six varieties of hamburgers—which locals and tourists alike consider among the best in the world—come in two sizes: regular and Macho. The only other items on the menu are fresh-cut fries, nachos, *chalupas* (open-faced tacos), and a grilled chicken sandwich. Tex-Mex decor adorns the old gas station and cantina, which is a full-service bar with iced-down longnecks and frozen margaritas. It all makes for a fun, family friendly meal out. ⊠*1900 Blanco Rd., North* ☎*210/735–3552* ⚐*Reservations not accepted Fri. and Sat.* ▱*AE, D, DC, MC, V* ⊗*Closed Sun.*

AMERICAN
$$–$$$$

✗**Crumpets Restaurant & Bakery.** The name sounds stuffy, but the dining room is everything but at this European-inspired location far removed from downtown's urban closeness. Views of the forest through large windows and comfortable seating prepare you for a greatest hits approach to continental cuisine, with some unexpected twists such as ostrich fillet. Savory sauces drape chicken, prime rib, and rack of lamb. The on-site bakery serves up fresh breads and pastries. Outdoor dining is plentiful, but beware mosquitoes after dark. ✉ *3920 Harry Wurzbach Rd., North* ☎ *210/821–5454* ☰ *AE, D, DC, MC, V.*

DINER
$–$$

✕ **DeWese's Tip Top Café.** Put the diet on hold if you're coming to this San Antonio institution. And leave white-tablecloth expectations behind, too. Bathrooms are outside, stuffed heads hang on the paneled walls, and the food is definitely home-style. Not much has changed since DeWese's opened in 1938, and that's its great charm. The onion rings and chicken-fried steaks draw a loyal local following. Homemade desserts made fresh every morning, such as banana icebox pie, disappear quickly. ✉ *2814 Fredericksburg Rd., Northwest* ☎ *210/732–0191* ☰ *D, MC, V* ☺ *Closed Sun. and Mon.*

MEXICAN
$–$$$

✕ **El Jarro de Arturo.** For more than 30 years this has been a favorite San Antonio spot for upscale and innovative Mexican cuisine. It's tough to choose between the beautiful, festive dining room and the garden-lush outdoor dining patio. And it's also tough to choose from among the diverse entrées, *antojitos* (appetizers), and desserts. Start out with the *botano* (sampler) platter to get a sample of the flavors, and then consider the house-specialty fajitas or chicken *fundido* (swathed in melted, white Mexican cheese) for the main course. The best value, however, is the extensive lunch buffet served weekdays 11–2. There's a full bar, live music on the weekends, and a kids' menu. ✉ *13421 San Pedro Ave., North* ☎ *210/494–5084* ☰ *AE, D, DC, MC, V.*

SOUTHWESTERN
$$$$
FodorsChoice
★

✕ **Francesca's at Sunset.** As the name would suggest, stunning views of the evening sky are part of the draw at the Westin at La Cantera's showcase restaurant. But chef Ernie Estrada, a San Antonio native, also adds considerable local flare to a Southwestern menu originally crafted by world-renowned restaurateur Mike Miller. Those wanting a truly memorable dining experience can choose from powerful eclectic dishes ranging from fillet of antelope to spicy grilled duck legs to chili-rubbed buffalo rib eye. If you can nab a reservation, it's well worth the trip across town. ✉ *Westin La Cantera Resort, 16641 La Cantera Pkwy., Northwest* ☎ *210/558–6500 Ext. 4803* ⌃ *Reservations essential* ☰ *AE, D, DC, MC, V* ☺ *No lunch.*

STEAKHOUSE
¢–$$

✕ **Josephine Street Café.** This "café" is actually a Texas roadhouse famous for dishing up "steaks & whisky" since 1979. In an early 1900s building on the outskirts of downtown, Josephine's is decidedly casual and friendly. Steaks come in all shapes and sizes, from a tasty chicken-fried variety to a 16-ounce Texas T-bone. Those looking for something different on the menu can opt for choices like Pacific snapper and Cajun chicken breast. The beer on tap and full bar are to be expected—what isn't is the baked-fresh-daily peach cobbler, for a belly-busting finish. ✉ *400 E. Josephine St., North* ☎ *210/224–6169* ☰ *AE, D, DC, MC, V* ☺ *Closed Sun.*

MEXICAN
$–$$$

✕ **La Fogata.** The open and airy spaces of La Fogata's rambling, hacienda-style indoor dining areas plus lush, tropical outdoor patio put you in the mood for some authentic Mexican food. A top-shelf, hand-shaken margarita helps you relax and enjoy an enormous selection of dishes ranging from chicken mole to *calabacita con carne de puerco*

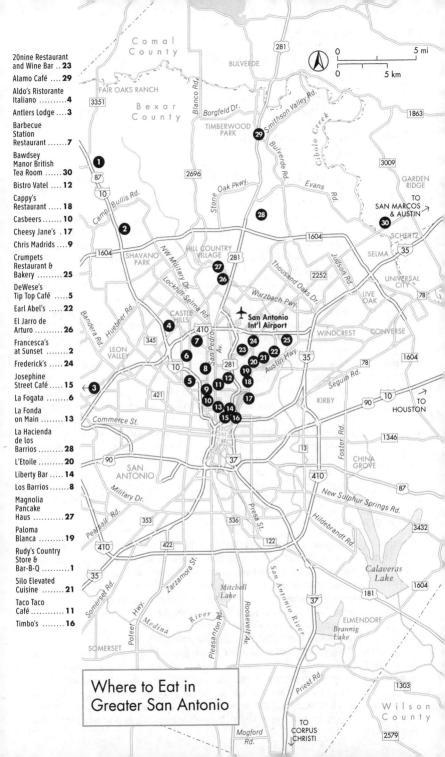

Where to Eat in Greater San Antonio

(a pork stew with fresh squash). The expected Mexican cornucopia of tacos, enchiladas, quesadillas, and everything in between is kicked up a notch with made-on-the-premises tortillas. Live music is common, and mariachis are known to roam, so have a request in mind—besides "La Cucaracha." ⊠*2427 Vance Jackson Rd., Northwest* ☎*210/340–1337* ⊟*AE, D, MC, V.*

MEXICAN ✕**Los Barrios.** Diana Barrios Trevino—a frequent Food Network
$–$$ guest—oversees the kitchen at this family-run restaurant, known for its authentic gourmet Mexican dishes. Eat in a relaxed, casual atmosphere with lots of light. Try the fajitas, tacos, or classic enchiladas. There's a kids' menu and entertainment on the weekend. ⊠*4223 Blanco Rd., North* ☎*210/732–6017* ⊟*AE, D, DC, MC, V.*

AMERICAN ✕**Magnolia Pancake Haus.** Opened in 2000 and already a much-loved
¢–$ breakfast institution, Magnolia prides itself on dishes made from fresh and wholesome ingredients. Fluffy buttermilk pancakes are a mainstay, but for something different, try the jambalaya omelet, smoked-turkey hash, or puffed apple pancakes made with Granny Smith apples, cinnamon, and powdered sugar. Breakfast is served all day, but at lunchtime a diverse selection of salads, soups, burgers, and deli sandwiches rounds out the menu. However, the real reason to come here is for your morning pancake pilgrimage. It's open 7 AM–2 PM daily. ⊠*13444 West Ave., Ste. 300, North* ☎*210/496–0828* ⌘*Reservations not accepted* ⊟*AE, D, DC, MC, V* ☺*No dinner.*

AMERICAN ✕**Silo Elevated Cuisine.** Just a few miles northeast of downtown, Silo has
$$–$$$$ beautiful views of the city from its sleek first-floor bar and second-floor
Fodor'sChoice restaurant. The dining room is modern and modestly glamorous, but
★ not at all pretentious, bringing some of the fun up from the popular bar downstairs. Start out with the chicken-fried oysters or blue-crab spring rolls and move onto the grilled and braised Kurobuta pork shank or seared sea scallops. If you catch a table before 6:30 PM Sunday through Thursday, opt for the prix-fixe three-course dinner: it puts a whole new spin on the typical "early bird" special by allowing you to put together many of the restaurant's specialties for under $30. ⊠*1133 Austin Hwy., Northeast* ☎*210/824–8686* ⊟*AE, D, DC, MC, V.*

RIVER WALK

TEX-MEX ✕**Acenar.** This nouvelle Tex-Mex hot spot sits astride a less-traveled
$$–$$$ section of the San Antonio River Walk. Start out with excellent mar-
★ garitas—many made from exotic ingredients, such as pear cactus—and guacamole made tableside or fresh ceviche. For the main course, move onto fish tacos (grilled or fried) or a host of seasonal fare, all with a fresh, contemporary flare. The outdoor dining area is small, but worth the wait for views of the river. ⊠*146 E. Houston St. (N. Saint Mary's St.), River Walk* ☎*210/222–2362* ⊟*AE, D, MC, V.*

AMERICAN ✕**Biga on the Banks.** Like Texas, enthusiastic chef Bruce Auden's menu
$$–$$$$ is big and eclectic, and the dining atmosphere manages to be both
Fodor'sChoice bigger than life and romantic. Dishes change daily to take advantage
★ of the freshest food available, ranging from seared red grouper grits to 11-spice axis venison chops. Don't skip out on dessert, which may be the best in town: the sticky toffee pudding is a must. This is one

GOD BLESS TEXAS (AND TACO CABANA)

You can't visit the Lone Star State without indulging in some good Tex-Mex. South-of-the-border fare can be found everywhere—from trendy, upscale spots to mobile taco trucks—but only Taco Cabana has managed to deliver fresh Tex-Mex (and adult beverages) at fast-food prices.

The first Taco Cabana opened in 1978; it was essentially a taco stand in the parking lot of a Dairy Queen, serving cheap grub to college students leaving a nearby bar.

Founder Felix Stehling's patio furniture was stolen after the first day of business, and he decided that the best way to deter future theft was to stay open 24 hours. (Many Taco Cabana locations still offer 'round-the-clock service.)

Taco Cabana's food isn't gourmet. That being said, you'll be hard-pressed to find better Tex-Mex value (and this is certainly one of the best fast-food chains in the country). There are a variety of entrées, including Chicken Flame-ante (marinated rotisserie chicken), fajitas served on hot iron skillets (at roughly half the price you'd pay in a sit-down joint), and Tex-Mex breakfast (including great breakfast tacos, served from midnight to mid-morning each day). But TC really makes three things extremely well: flour tortillas (fresh-pressed to order on an awesome machine), salsa (seven freshly made varieties, with varying levels of heat), and queso (delicious hot cheese sauce). For the quintessential Taco Cabana experience, order a stack of tortillas, a bowl of queso, and hit the salsa bar—it's like heaven for $3. Best of all, you can wash down your Taco Cabana with a cold margarita or cerveza, including Texas's own Shiner Bock and, of course, Corona.

Taco Cabana now has more than 140 locations in Texas, Oklahoma, and New Mexico, which means diners can take advantage of warm weather and sit on the patio or in the (weather permitting) open-air dining room.

The original restaurant, at 3310 San Pedro, is still in operation, and there are 35 other Taco Cabana restaurants around San Antonio.

of the best spots for a leisurely dinner on the River Walk, if you can get a reservation. ⊠ *203 S. Saint Mary's St. (W. Market St.), River Walk* ☎ *210/225–0722* ☐ *AE, D, MC, V* ⚑ *Reservations essential* ⊘ *No lunch.*

SOUTHWESTERN   ✕ **Boudro's on the Riverwalk.** A little bit Gulf Coast, a little bit Mexi-

$$–$$$$ can, and a whole lotta Texan, this landmark River Walk establishment

★   caters to almost every taste with exceptional good taste. Fresh fish is the star of the menu, including an unusual seafood platter that matches together a glazed lobster tail, blackened filet du jour, crawfish, chicken-fried oysters, and a shrimp taco. Spicy-charred prime rib gives an extra kick for landlubbers. The main dining room is almost cavelike, and provides several nooks for conversation and romance, but the patio on the river is where you want to be when the weather's fine. ⊠ *421 E. Commerce St., River Walk* ☎ *210/224–8484* ☐ *AE, D, DC, MC, V.*

AMERICAN   ✕**Citrus.** This über-cool restaurant
$$$–$$$$ at the Hotel Valencia (⇨ *Where to Stay*) overlooks the River Walk and serves New American and Spanish-influenced cuisine. Its creative paella and pasta bar (you choose the ingredients) is popular at lunch, while dinner fare ranges from hickory-plank-roasted redfish to honey-orange-glazed duck. Executive chef Jeff Balfour puts on a pretty good show with fresh produce and a diverse repertoire. An extensive wine list and creative cocktails make it a one-stop shop for an evening's enjoyment. ⊠ *150 E. Houston St., River Walk* ☎ *210/230–8412* ☐ *AE, D, DC, MC, V.*

> **DINING WITH KIDS**
>
> It's easy to eat out with kids in San Antonio. Most restaurants have children's menus or an à la carte selections that work well for young diners. An affordable, kid-friendly alternative to fast food is Taco Cabana, a local chain with fast, fresh, and straightforward Mexican food. Some upscale restaurants on the River Walk can be less accommodating during peak times and often lack diaper-changing stations. For older kids, Rainforest Café on the River Walk is a popular (but pricey) option.

BARBECUE   ✕**County Line Barbecue.** Texas is famous for its barbecued ribs, smoked
$–$$ brisket, and related fare, and this contender definitely holds its own among the competition. The barbecue here is dry rubbed with the sauce on the side, and the various combo platters and family-style options let you sample from smoked turkey and sausage, brisket, beef and pork ribs, and more. The atmosphere is rustic–casual, so don't be afraid to put your elbows on the table. ⊠ *111 W. Crockett, Suite 104, River Walk* ☎ *210/229–1941* ☐ *AE, D, DC, MC, V.*

ECLECTIC   ✕**Fig Tree Restaurant.** Exquisite food and impeccable service are main-
$$$–$$$$ stays of this French-inspired restaurant with a cozy interior and an outdoor villa-style terrace overlooking the San Antonio River. Crisp linens drape tables set with fine china and sparkling crystal in elegant yet homey surroundings. Delicate, highly composed dishes such as *tournedos Rossini* (seared beef fillets wrapped around foie gras and truffles), mint-crusted rack of lamb, and prosciutto-wrapped yellowfin tuna are menu standouts. Tableside flamed desserts include bananas Foster and traditional baked Alaska. ⊠ *515 Villita St., River Walk* ☎ *210/224–1976* ☐ *AE, D, DC, MC, V.*

SEAFOOD   ✕**Landry's Seafood House.** In the thick of things right on the San Anto-
$$–$$$$ nio River, this upscale national seafood chain is a pleasurable oasis from the hustle and bustle. Dozens of varieties of fresh fish (reportedly flown in by helicopter each day) prepared in a number of ways include blackened swordfish and Parmesan-crusted sea bass; top steak cuts appease those who prefer turf to surf. The atmosphere is classy yet relaxed; there's a large wine list, a capable bar, and a prompt and knowledgeable waitstaff. ⊠ *517 N. Presa St., River Walk* ☎ *210/229–1010* ⌲ *Reservations not accepted* ☐ *AE, D, DC, MC, V.*

✕**Las Canarias.** In the Omni La Mansion del Rio, this three-level restaurant is known for its sophistication and romance, and has one of the most relaxing and beautiful outdoor dining areas on the San Antonio River. The menu mixes traditional and contemporary Mediterranean fare with Southwest influences. Creative, flavorful dishes of note include blue crab–stuffed swordfish tempura, buffalo carpaccio, and an unusual, delectable array of Spanish tapas. Gentle, live piano or guitar accompanies dinner. There is a stunning dessert tray, a full bar, and on Sundays an à la carte brunch menu. ⊠ *Omni La Mansion del Rio, 112 College St., River Walk* ☎210/518–1063 ⊟*AE, D, DC, MC, V.*

STEAKHOUSE ✕**Little Rhein Steak House.** Housed in a structure built in 1847, this rus-
$$$–$$$$ tic restaurant was originally used as a residence and store by German immigrant Otto Bombach. It's a historically protected site, with antique brass lights, wooden booths, and a smattering of Old West antiques. Specialties include center-cut filet mignon, bone-in prime strip loin, and fresh Norwegian salmon. Terrace dining gives diners views of the San Antonio River, and a full bar reminds you that the spot once served as a saloon. Expect the same dedication to excellence as next-door sister restaurant the Fig Tree (they have the same owner). ⊠ *231 S. Alamo St., River Walk* ☎210/225–2111 ⊟*AE, D, DC, MC, V.*

STEAKHOUSE ✕**Morton's The Steakhouse.** A block from the Alamo and near the River
$$$–$$$$ Walk, this branch of the Morton's chain is appropriately elegant and contemporary. Fabulous steaks, the selection and size of which are truly impressive, range from double-cut fillets to prime rib to Cajun rib eye, and are matched with exquisite wines and service. This is not a spot for vegetarians, who are relegated to side dishes (albeit relatively healthy ones), but non-red-meat options include sesame-encrusted yellow tuna and whole backed Maine lobster. ⊠ *Rivercenter Mall at 300 E. Crockett St., River Walk* ☎210/228–0700 ⊟*AE, D, MC, VC.*

ITALIAN ✕**Paesanos.** This deservedly popular spot at a bend on the San Antonio
$–$$$$ River melds fine Italian dining with a Mediterranean approach. The
★ range of foodie-friendly dishes includes the signature shrimp *paesano*, a delicate and flavorful lightly breaded and baked concoction accented with lemon, butter, and garlic, which you can have as an appetizer or as an entrée. Other standouts include wood-fired pizzas, baked ziti with Italian sausage, cioppino (a seafood stew), and lemon-pepper salmon. Arrive early to nab a primo table on the outdoor patio, right next to the river. ⊠ *111 W. Crockett St., River Walk* ☎210/227–2782 ⚑*Reservations not accepted* ⊟*AE, D, DC, MC, V.*

SEAFOOD ✕**Pesca on the River.** A relatively young addition to the River Walk din-
$–$$$$ ing scene, Pesca is a rising star in San Antonio, thanks to executive chef Scott Cohen's dedication to excellence. This high-energy, but romantic dining room "fishes" for seafood from around the world and matches it with locally grown herbs and produce. Pesca also has an oyster bar, a great wine list, and terrace dining with spectacular views of the river. ⊠ *212 W. Crockett St., River Walk* ☎210/396–5817 ⊟*AE, D, DC, MC, V.*

AMERICAN ✕**Rainforest Café.** Ideal for kids, this fun chain near the Rivercenter Mall
$–$$$ offers up a tropical theme and some decent food. The menu is varied, and dishes range from jambalaya to burgers—pretty basic but solid fare. It's a bit pricey, but well worth ducking out of the hustle-and-bustle to placate your kids even if you have to put up with animatronic jungle antics and overt merchandising. Inventive, colorful cocktails

help you cope. ⊠*110 E. Crockett St., River Walk* ☎*210/277–6300* ⊟*AE, D, DC, MC, V.*

SOUTHWESTERN   ✕ **Zuni Grill.** While its eclectic Southwestern food is nothing special, loft-
$$–$$$$ like Zuni Grill certainly ranks heads above the many tourist traps on the River Walk. The real draws are the views of the river, the spot-on cocktails—including a margarita made with real cactus juice—and a host of great appetizers. If you stay for a meal, you can't go wrong with the scorpion-shrimp-stuffed red chilies or the blue-corn chicken enchiladas. The outdoor patio right on the river is where to roost no matter your dining objective. ⊠*223 Losoya St., River Walk* ☎*210/227–0864* ⊟*AE, D, DC, MC, V.*

ELSEWHERE IN SAN ANTONIO

SOUTHWESTERN   ✕ **Antlers Lodge.** Known for upscale takes on Texan fare—rattlesnake
$$$–$$$$ fritters, quail with chorizo and grits, bison tenderloin—this restaurant in the Hyatt Hill Country Resort also has lighter options like chili-dusted ahi tuna steak. The centerpiece of the elegant dining room is a huge chandelier with more than 500 naturally shed pairs of antlers. The dress code requires collared shirts for men and equally polished "dress resort wear" for women. ⊠*Hyatt Regency Hill Country Resort & Spa, 9800 Hyatt Resort Dr., Outskirts* ☎*210/520-4001* ⊟*AE, D, DC, MC, V.*

CAFÉ   ✕ **Bawdsey Manor British Tea Room.** You may feel like you've stumbled
$–$$$ into stately cottage on the other side of the pond at this restaurant, where British sensibilities abound in decor and menu. For those seeking something a little more genteel than a typical Texas fiesta, Bawdsey complies with high tea—finger sandwiches, scones, the works—and Brit faves like fish-and-chips and meat pies. It's just north of Highway 1604 in Bracken Village. ⊠*18771 FM 2252 (Nacogdoches Rd.), Outskirts* ☎*210/651–7500* ⊟*D, MC, V* ⊘*Closed Sun. No dinner Mon.*

TEX-MEX   ✕ **La Hacienda de los Barrios.** It may feel like you're walking into a centu-
$–$$$ ries-old hacienda at this enormous outpost just outside of the Highway 1604 loop, but the tacos (regular or puffy), nachos, tamales, grilled chicken, and steaks have a slightly modern twist. If you can't decide what to pick from the enormous menu, hedge your bets by going for the enchilada platter—five delectable takes on a Mexican staple. With lots of space and an impressive playground, there's no doubt the place was built with families in mind. It's ideal for large groups and is a sister restaurant to Los Barrios (⇨*above*). ⊠*18747 Redland Rd., Outskirts* ☎*210/497–8000* ⊟*AE, D, DC, MC, V.*

BARBECUE   ✕ **Rudy's Country Store & Bar-B-Q.** What looks like an old gas station
¢–$$ on the outside pumps out some of San Antonio's favorite barbecue.
★   The wait to place your order is worth it once you bite into some tender brisket (the "sause" is on the side) or smoked turkey dry-rubbed with flavor and cooked in wood-fired pits. Everything here—including the ribs, sausages, slaw, and potato salad—is dished up on plastic plates and necessitates lots of napkins. Outdoor picnic-table seating completes the picture. ⊠*24152 W. I–10, Outskirts* ☎*210/698–2141* ⊟*AE, D, DC, MC, V.*

SAN ANTONIO SPECIALTIES

The dish that San Antonio invented is also its best-kept secret: the puffy taco. It starts by cooking a salad-plate-sized disc of corn masa (corn-meal dough) until it becomes chewy and crispy. While it's still warm, it's folded and stuffed with seasoned chicken or beef, shredded lettuce, tomatoes, guacamole, and other fillings. When you're in San Antonio you owe it to yourself to become a tortilla snob. At most Mexican or Tex-Mex restaurants, the meal begins with freshly made tortillas (flour or corn). Locals butter them and eat them as you would a dinner roll. Fresh tortillas bear little resemblance to their grocery-store cousins: they're soft, fluffy and have a buttery taste that you may lie awake nights craving.

Texas-style barbecue generally serves up beef brisket that's been cooked low and slow with dry spices rubbed into the meat. Sauce is served on the side after cooking. It's generally thick and tomato-based with strong flavors (but not particularly hot or spicy). Side dishes include a local style of baked beans that's more smoky than sweet, along with white bread and maybe cole slaw. Prices for barbecue are generally quite reasonable, so even if your budget is limited, you can go big with your barbecue.

WHERE TO STAY

THE SCENE

Many visitors choose to stay downtown to be close to the Alamo, River Walk, museums, and other attractions. Once you're downtown, almost everything is accessible on foot or via river taxi or trolley; a car isn't needed and parking can be expensive. The city has one shuttle service from the airport that serves all downtown hotels ($14 one way, $24 round-trip). It runs from 7 AM to 11 PM right from the airport. Several national chain hotels are concentrated along the River Walk and adjacent to the convention center. The Menger and Crockett hotels lead the list of historic hotels next to the Alamo. In recent years several boutique hotels have opened up, promoting spa weekends and indulgent getaways. Downtown has also seen the opening of some larger, value-oriented and extended-stay chains.

Several full-service resorts within the city limits, most near Sea World and Fiesta Texas amusement park, offer golf, tennis, on-site water parks, children's activities, restaurants, and the services you'd expect from a resort—a good option for families. Most major resorts are a 15- to 20-minute drive from downtown.

Bed-and-breakfasts are concentrated in a few of the national historic districts but still offer a range of mid-range and pricier room options. Virtually all are no-smoking, and only a few accept children younger than 12.

San Antonio is a major convention destination, so it's feast or famine for hotel rooms; peak seasons are generally spring and late fall. At the right time you can get some great deals for top-quality accommodations, but during special events (Fiesta week, the NCAA Final Four tournament, during major conventions) expect to pay top dollar and make reservations months in advance. Because of the city's appeal for business travelers, you can actually find lower rates on weekends at many hotels.

WHAT IT COSTS					
	¢	$	$$	$$$	$$$$
HOTELS	under $50	$50–$100	$101–$150	$151–$200	over $200

Hotel prices are per night for two people in a standard double room in high season, excluding taxes (16.75% for San Antonio) and service charges.

DOWNTOWN

$$$ **Crockett Hotel.** Built in 1909 and listed on the National Register of
★   Historic Places, this hotel (named for frontiersman Davy Crockett) is a relic of turn-of-the-20th-century San Antonio. Location is the big selling point here: you're 10 steps from the Alamo, River Walk, and many sights. The seven-story, light-filled, sandstone-brick atrium lobby with leather club chairs is impressive; some rooms look out onto it. Rooms were thoroughly updated in 2007; they are contemporary and spotless, though a bit bland in the decor department. **Pros:** Great location, new furnishings. **Cons:** Immediate area packed with tourists, bland room decor, views nothing to write home about. ⊠ *320 Bonham St., Downtown* ☎ *210/225–6500 or 800/292–1050* ⊕ *www.crocketthotel.com* ➪ *126 rooms, 12 suites* ☼ *In-room: Ethernet. In-hotel: room service, bar, pool, gym, public Wi-Fi, laundry service, parking (fee), no-smoking rooms* ▤ *AE, D, MC, V* ⑩ *BP.*

$$$$ **Emily Morgan Hotel.** Built in the 1920s and named for the woman who inspired the song "The Yellow Rose of Texas," this boutique hotel sits across from the Alamo on a triangular piece of land. Originally built as a medical school, it's neo-Gothic design stands out from other downtown landmarks. Sleek furnishings and whirlpool tubs in marble bathrooms make it a posh destination steeped in period romance. As in many historic hotels, room size varies greatly, and quarters can be tight. **Pros:** So close to the Alamo, you can see it from some rooms; nice marriage of modern amenities and classic features. **Cons:** Relatively expensive, a bit of a hike to the River Walk. ⊠ *705 E. Houston St., Downtown* ☎ *210/225–5100* ⊕ *www.emilymorganhotel.com* ➪ *154 rooms, 23 suites* ☼ *In-room: Wi-Fi. In-hotel: restaurant, room service, bar, pool, gym, laundry facilities, laundry service, public Internet, public Wi-Fi, parking (fee), some pets allowed, no-smoking rooms* ▤ *AE, D, DC, MC, V.*

$$–$$$ **Fairfield Inn & Suites San Antonio Downtown.** This Fairfield Inn looks like every other, but it's clean and comfortable, with ready access to all of San Antonio's sights. Two blocks from Market Square and a ride on the trolley (which stops in front of the hotel) to the River Walk and Alamo. The free parking is a major plus and a rarity downtown. **Pros:** Refreshingly straightforward, relatively inexpensive, did we mention the free

WHERE SHOULD I STAY IN SAN ANTONIO?

	Neighborhood Vibe	Pros	Cons
Downtown	Staying here, you can walk past one historic building after another within blocks of several attractions. You can also often find some better deals than along the eminently popular River Walk. There's a mix of luxury, boutique, and value hotels to choose from.	Historic hotels, close to all the action but without the noise or bustle (and prices) of the River Walk.	High prices, especially at peak times, packed with tourists, limited and pricey parking.
North/North-west	Family-friendly resorts and reliable national hotel chains cluster along highways with ready access to shopping, restaurants, and attractions north of Loop 410 in a massive sprawl that's technically urban but feels more suburban. Depending on traffic, getting there from downtown could take 15 to 30 minutes.	Easy access to the entire city via highway, many family-friendly amenities, many less expensive lodging options than at the city's center.	Highway driving unavoidable; restaurants are primarily chains; generic, suburban feel.
River Walk	A beautiful, bustling world alongside the San Antonio River. Hotels, from charming boutiques to national chains, overlook the slow currents, towering trees, winding pathways, and arched bridges. But while the River Walk may evoke the romance of Venice, the seemingly endless array of restaurants, shops, and nightclubs also makes it the city's number-one location for fun.	The city's main attractions and restaurants are here, some rooms have balcones overlooking the river.	High premium for convenience and ambience, parking expensive and often inconvenient, many hotels not kid-friendly, late-night noise can be a problem.
King William/Monte Vista Historic District	Inns are tucked amid beautifully restored homes along tree-lined streets in this peaceful National Historic District just a short trolley ride from downtown.	Quiet, quaint, close to downtown (via trolley), easy parking.	B&Bs are the only option, and some lack amenities of conventional hotels.

parking? **Cons:** Cookie-cutter chain hotel with ho-hum decor. ⊠*620 South Santa Rosa, Downtown* ☎*210/229–1000* ⊕*www.marriott.com/ satfi* ↘*73 rooms, 37 suites* ⌂*In-room: refrigerators (some), Ethernet, Wi-Fi. In-hotel: pool, gym, laundry facilities, laundry services, public Internet, public Wi-Fi, parking (no fee), no-smoking rooms* ⊟*AE, D, DC, MC, V* ⋓*CP.*

$$$$ 🏨**The Fairmount.** This historic luxury hotel made the *Guinness Book of World Records* when its 3.2-million-pound brick bulk was moved
Fodor'sChoice
★ six blocks in 1985 to its present location. At the pinnacle of boutique,

BEST BETS FOR SAN ANTONIO LODGING

With more than 330 hotels in the city limits, San Antonio offers the whole gamut of lodging options, from in-town B&Bs and ultra-hip boutiques to full-service resorts and family-friendly venues. The following are our favorites across a variety of styles, locations, and price points. This town aims to please, and we think you'll find there's something for every taste.

Fodor's Choice ★

Brackenridge House, **$$$–$$$$**, King William Historic District

The Fairmount, $$$$, Downtown

Hotel Contessa Suites on the River Walk, **$$$$**, River Walk

Hyatt Regency Hill Country Resort, $$$$, North/Northwest

Ogé House, $$$$, King William Historic District

Watermark Hotel & Spa, $$$$, River Walk

By Price

$$

A Yellow Rose, King William Historic District

Hyatt Place San Antonio/River Walk, River Walk

Riverwalk Vista, River Walk

$$$

Brackenridge House, King William Historic District

Drury Plaza Hotel Riverwalk, River Walk

Grand Hyatt, Downtown

Havana Riverwalk Inn, Downtown

Ogé House, King William Historic District

$$$$

The Fairmount, Downtown

Hotel Contessa Suites on the River Walk, River Walk

Hyatt Regency Hill Country Resort, North/Northwest

Watermark Hotel & Spa, River Walk

By Experience

BEST VALUES

Bonner Garden, **$$–$$$**, Monte Vista Historic District

Drury Plaza Hotel Riverwalk, $$$, River Walk

Fairfield Inn & Suites San Antonio Downtown, $$–$$$, Downtown

Radisson Hill Country Resort & Spa, $$$–$$$$, North/Northwest

FAMILY FRIENDLY

El Tropicano Holiday Inn Riverwalk, $$–$$$, River Walk

Hyatt Regency Hill Country Resort, $$$$, North/Northwest

Marriott Plaza San Antonio, $$$$, Downtown

Radisson Hill Country Resort & Spa, $$$–$$$$, North/Northwest

GREAT VIEWS

Hilton Palacio del Rio, $$$$, River Walk

Menger Hotel, $$$–$$$$, Downtown

Omni La Mansión del Rio, $$$$, River Walk

Riverwalk Vista, $$–$$$, River Walk

Westin La Cantera, $$$$, North/Northwest

HISTORIC

Brackenridge House, $$$–$$$$, King William Historic District

Crockett Hotel, $$$, Downtown

The Fairmount, $$$$, Downtown

Menger Hotel, $$$–$$$$, Downtown

Sheraton Gunter Hotel, $$$–$$$$, Downtown

ROMANTIC

Emily Morgan Hotel, $$$$, Downtown

Hotel Contessa Suites on the River Walk, $$$$, River Walk

Hotel Valencia Riverwalk, $$$$, River Walk

Watermark Hotel & Spa, $$$$, River Walk

2

luxury hotels in San Antonio, it offers premium amenities such as flat-screen TVs, canopy beds, verandas, marble baths, and a courtyard with a fountain. The hotel is full of quirks, with the hotel dog, Luke Tips, manning the concierge desk, and different decor in each room. Across from HemisFair Park, it's fairly close to the River Walk, convention center, and La Villita. **Pros:** Dripping with character and charm. **Cons:** Expensive, and not exactly right in the thick of the River Walk/downtown action. ⊠*401 S. Alamo St., Downtown* ☎*210/224–8800 or 800/996–3426* ⊕*www.fairmountsa.com* ⇪*37 suites* ⚼*In-room: Ethernet, Wi-Fi. In-hotel: restaurant, room service, gym, bar, laundry service, concierge, executive floor, public Internet, public Wi-Fi, parking (fee), some pets allowed, no-smoking rooms* ▤*AE, D, DC, MC, V.*

$$$$ 🏨 **Grand Hyatt.** After much anticipation, the newest of the mega convention hotels opened in spring 2008 and changed the city's skyline. The Grand Hyatt brings San Antonio the biggest array of amenities for business travelers, convention-goers, and family vacationers. Adjacent to the convention center and the River Walk, it's sure to be the hotel of choice for business travelers. But even leisure travelers can enjoy flat-panel TVs and premium beds in every room. And a date with the "fitness concierge" in its premium gym might be just the thing to work off San Antonio's famous puffy tacos. **Pros:** State-of-the-art amenities, brand-new look and feel. **Cons:** At this writing it hasn't opened—so you're the guinea pig. ⊠*600 E. Market St., Downtown* ☎*210/224–1234* ⊕*www.grandsanantonio.hyatt.com* ⇪*940 rooms, 63 suites* ⚼*In-room: safe, kitchen (some), refrigerator (some), Ethernet, Wi-Fi. In hotel: restaurant, room service, bar, pool, gym, spa, laundry service, concierge, executive floor, public Internet, parking (fee), no-smoking rooms* ▤*AE, D, MC, V.*

$$$–$$$$ 🏨 **Havana Riverwalk Inn.** San Antonio's most bohemian boutique hotel ★ occupies a Mediterranean Revival structure built in 1914 and feels as though you've wandered into an exotic British-colonial gentleman's club. You'll find teak and wicker chairs from India, beds fashioned from the grillwork of old buildings, and vintage chairs from French hotels and bistros. Don't miss Club Cohiba, the martini bar in the basement. It's a good 10-minute walk to most River Walk restaurants and bars, which is not all bad if you want to avoid the noise of late-night revelers. A trolley stop serving all downtown attractions is a block away. **Pros:** One of the city's truly unique lodging experiences, decadent and sophisticated, first-rate staff. **Cons:** Must book many months in advance, extremely pricey in peak season, not family friendly. ⊠*1015 Navarro St., Downtown* ☎*210/222–2008 or 888/224–2004* ⊕*www. havanariverwalkinn.com* ⇪*24 rooms, 3 suites* ⚼*In-room: Wi-Fi. In-hotel: restaurant, room service, bar, laundry service, public Internet, public Wi-Fi, parking (fee), no kids under 15, no-smoking rooms* ▤*AE, D, DC, MC, V.*

$$$$ 🏨 **Marriott Plaza San Antonio.** This six-acre resort in the middle of downtown San Antonio has a full health club, jogging and bicycle routes, a heated pool and whirlpool, and lighted tennis courts in a setting of fountains and lush gardens. Most memorable are the Chinese pheasants and peacocks that roam the grounds. It's three blocks from the Alamo

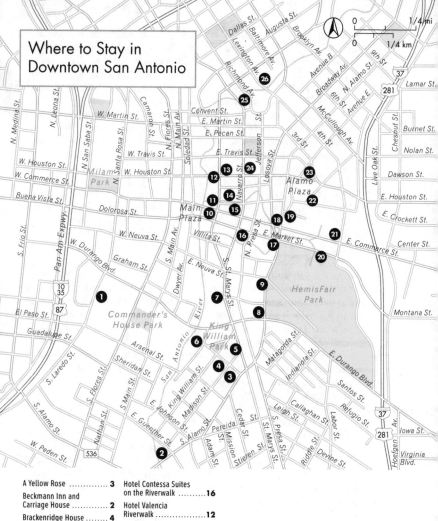

Where to Stay in Downtown San Antonio

and a few steps from the River Walk's myriad attractions. The hotel does a brisk convention and meeting business. Chauffeured transportation to the downtown business district is complimentary on weekdays. The owners allow guests free use of bicycles and there are twice-daily maid service and plush bath robes. **Pros:** Close to River Walk, attentive staff. **Cons:** Not right on River Walk, fees for extras like parking and Internet. ⊠ *555 S. Alamo St., Downtown* ☎ *210/229–1000 or 800/421–1172* ⊕ *www.plazasa.com* ⌨ *246 rooms, 5 suites* ♿ *In-room: Ethernet. In-hotel: restaurant, room service, bar, tennis court, pool, gym, spa, bicycles, laundry service, concierge, executive floor, public Internet, public Wi-Fi, parking (fee), pets allowed, no-smoking rooms* ⊟ *AE, D, DC, MC, V.*

$$$–$$$$ ★ **Menger Hotel.** Since its 1859 opening, the Menger has lodged, among others, Robert E. Lee, Ulysses S. Grant, Theodore Roosevelt, Oscar Wilde, Sarah Bernhardt, Roy Rogers, and Dale Evans. You'll be the envy of many an overheated tourist strolling immediately across the street from the entrance to the Alamo into the cool lobby and up to your room. Balcony rooms overlook the Alamo. Inside, the hotel has a three-story Victorian lobby, sunny dining room, flowered courtyard, and four-poster beds (in the older section). Menger's famous bar, built in 1887, is styled after the House of Lords Pub in London. **Pros:** Close to Alamo, good food. **Cons:** Rooms are more worn than at newer properties. ⊠ *204 Alamo Plaza, Downtown* ☎ *210/223–4361 or 800/345–9285* ⊕ *www.mengerhotel.com* ⌨ *290 rooms, 26 suites* ♿ *In-room: kitchen (some), Ethernet. In-hotel: restaurant, room service, bar, pool, gym, spa, laundry service, concierge, public Internet, public Wi-Fi, parking (fee), no-smoking rooms* ⊟ *AE, D, DC, MC, V.*

$$$–$$$$ **Sheraton Gunter Hotel.** Since 1909 this attractive downtown hotel has been a favorite of cattlemen and business travelers. The marble lobby has a beautiful coffered ceiling supported by massive columns. Rooms have antique reproduction furniture, large desks, and a masculine-contemporary design. The hotel is in a less-developed part of downtown, but is less than a block from the River Walk. It's generally a better value than hotels directly on the river, especially for a historic hotel. **Pros:** Excellent location, doesn't feel like a chain hotel. **Cons:** Many extras and amenities require an additional charge. ⊠ *205 E. Houston St., Downtown* ☎ *210/227–3241 or 800/325–3535* ⊕ *www.gunterhotel.com* ⌨ *322 rooms, 2 suites* ♿ *In-room: DVD, Ethernet, Wi-Fi. In-hotel: restaurant, room service, bar, pool, gym, laundry service, concierge, public Internet, public Wi-Fi, parking (fee), no-smoking rooms* ⊟ *AE, D, MC, V.*

$$$–$$$$ **Wyndham St. Anthony Hotel.** This somewhat formal 1909 historic hotel is decorated with oil paintings, chandeliers, and a handsome central staircase. It is in the center of downtown and near all the major attractions, including the Alamo and River Walk, and is within a short drive of Six Flags, Sea World, the San Antonio Zoo, and area golf courses. Rooms are posh, if overly rococo-esque—with four-poster beds, jacquard linens, and ornate antiques—and the service is what you'd expect in a first-rate establishment. **Pros:** Oozes historic elegance, good-size rooms. **Cons:** Rooms could use an update. ⊠ *300 E. Travis*

St., ☏210/227–4392 or 800/355–5153 ⊕ *www.wyndham.com* ✍308 *rooms, 42 suites* ♿*In-room: Wi-Fi. In-hotel: restaurant, room service, bar, pool, gym, laundry service, concierge, public Internet, public Wi-Fi, parking (fee), no-smoking rooms* ▤*AE, D, DC, MC, V.*

KING WILLIAM HISTORIC DISTRICT

$$–$$$ 🏨 **Beckmann Inn and Carriage House.** This 1886 Victorian with a Greek influence is filled with antiques, Oriental carpets, and floral prints. The two-course breakfast, served on china and crystal, is superb. The inn is convenient to all the River Walk attractions. Only one room has a bathtub; others have a shower only. **Pros:** Romantic and posh; feels like you're stepping back in time, despite being in a big, bustling city. **Cons:** Not many rooms available, difficult to book, lacking full-service amenities. ⊠*222 E. Guenther St., King William Historic District* ☏*210/229–1449 or 800/945–1449* ⊕*www.beckmanninn.com* ✍*5 rooms* ♿*In-room: refrigerator, Wi-Fi. In-hotel: parking (no fee), no kids under 12, no-smoking rooms* ▤*AE, D, DC, MC, V* ⃝*BP.*

$$$–$$$$
Fodor'sChoice
★
   🏨 **Brackenridge House.** The first B&B in the King William Historic District, Brackenridge House has a two-story veranda overlooking a tree-lined street. The three-course breakfast is a highlight, with signature dishes of Texas eggs Benedict (thick Texas toast replaces the English muffin) and pancakes with homemade blueberry sauce. Enjoy the view from front-porch rockers and porch swings as you watch the horse-drawn trolleys go by. Rooms are lushly decorated with turn-of-the-20th-century accoutrements, and the service is top-notch. **Pros:** Reasonably priced for one of San Antonio's most sought-after B&B spots, one of the best breakfasts in town. **Cons:** Rooms are smallish and often difficult to book, especially at peak tourist times. ⊠*230 Madison St., King William Historic District* ☏*210/271–3442 or 800/221–1412* ⊕*www.brackenridgehouse.com* ✍*2 rooms, 4 suites* ♿*In-room: refrigerator, DVD, VCR. In-hotel: pool, hot tub, parking (no fee), no kids under 12, no-smoking rooms* ▤*AE, D, DC, MC, V* ⃝*BP.*

$$$–$$$$ 🏨 **Jackson House.** Built in 1894 and listed in the National Register of Historic Places, this B&B in the historic King William area has elegant Victorian decor. The front porch, parlor, and gardens reflect the period with their antique furnishings and style. All rooms have their own fireplaces, and first-floor rooms have two-person whirlpool tubs; one room has only a shower (no bathtub). The real highlight of the house is the conservatory with stained-glass windows looking out into the garden. The conservatory also houses the heated "swim spa," where guests can unwind. River Walk and downtown are accessible via trolley. **Pros:** Quiet area, free parking, good three-course breakfast. **Cons:** Immediate area is residential and a brisk 10- to 15-minute walk from River Walk area. ⊠*107 Madison St., King William Historic District* ☏*210/225–4045 or 800/221–4045* ⊕*www.nobleinns.com* ✍*6 rooms* ♿*In-room: Wi-Fi. In-hotel: pool, no elevator, parking (no fee), public Wi-Fi, no kids under 13, no-smoking rooms* ▤*AE, D, MC, V* ⃝*BP.*

$$$$
Fodor'sChoice
★
   🏨 **Ogé House.** This gorgeous B&B sits on 1½ acres that back up to a quiet section of the river running through the King William Historic District. From the first steps up the wide staircase to the first-floor

2

veranda, the house captures your imagination about what antebellum life must have been like in South Texas. Each room is individually decorated; yours might have a four-poster carved-wood bed, toile upholstery, and Oriental rugs. Modern conveniences include flat-panel TVs, Wi-Fi, and electric fireplaces (some rooms). One room has a shower only—no tub. The Alhambra Room has less natural light than other rooms. Breakfast, with a menu that changes daily, is served in the dining room or on the veranda. The quiet garden and grounds offer many places to relax—perhaps on a seat in the gazebo or in one of the hammocks. **Pros:** Exquisitely decorated, staff goes beyond the call of duty. **Cons:** Pricey, River Walk area not within easy walking distance. ✉ *209 Washington St., King William Historic District* ☎ *210/223–2353 or 800/242–2770* ⊕ *www.nobleinns.com* ➴ *10 rooms* ⚷ *In-room: refrigerator, dial-up, Wi-Fi. In hotel: laundry service, public Internet, public Wi-Fi, parking (no fee), no kids under 16, no-smoking rooms* ▤ *AE, D, DC, MC, V* ⃝*BP.*

$$ ▦ **A Yellow Rose.** Built in 1878, this B&B is found in the leafy King William Historic District, five blocks from downtown. Traditional English decor with private porches and entrances in all rooms makes it perfect for a quiet weekend for two. Breakfast is delivered to your room, with several menus available. **Pros:** Charming and quaint, reasonably priced. **Cons:** A long-ish walk to the main downtown sights. ✉ *229 Madison St., King William Historic District* ☎ *210/229–9903 or 800/950–9903* ⊕ *www.ayellowrose.com* ➴ *6 rooms* ⚷ *In-room: refrigerators, Wi-Fi. In-hotel: public Wi-Fi, parking (no fee), no kids under 12, no-smoking rooms* ▤ *AE, D, MC, V* ⃝*BP.*

MONTE VISTA HISTORIC DISTRICT

$$–$$$ ▦ **Bonner Garden.** Part of the Monte Vista Historic District (larger but less known than nearby King William), this inn sits amid some of the city's most beautiful homes and best restaurants. Built in 1910 for a Louisiana aristocrat and home to artist Mary Bonner, the 5,000-square-foot, Italianate villa is decorated with Bonner's art and retains many of the details of the original building, such as hand-painted porcelain fireplaces (in three rooms) and tile floors. Suites have luxurious whirlpool baths. The rooftop patio has a panoramic view of downtown San Antonio. **Pros:** Quiet, charming and relaxing, reasonably good value for an in-town B&B. **Cons:** Relatively small rooms, neighborhood a little sketchy at night. ✉ *145 E. Agarita St., Monte Vista Historic District* ☎ *210/733–4222 or 800/396–4222* ⊕ *www.bonnergarden.com* ➴ *4 rooms, 2 suites* ⚷ *In-room: DVD, VCR, Wi-Fi. In-hotel: pool, parking (no fee), no-smoking rooms* ▤ *AE, D, MC, V* ⃝*BP.*

NORTH/NORTHWEST

$$$$
☽
Fodor'sChoice
★

▦ **Hyatt Regency Hill Country Resort.** Step into relaxation at this sophisticated yet homey country resort with lots of shade—a key feature when the mercury soars during a San Antonio summer. On the western edge of the city, it occupies 200 acres of former ranch land, so you feel far removed, even though you're just a few minutes from Sea World, about

15 minutes from Six Flags, and 20 minutes from downtown. Family-friendly touches abound, from the manmade "lazy river," where you can float along with the current in an inner tube to Camp Hyatt's day camp and nightly s'mores at the firepit; older kids can hange out at The Underground, with Internet and games. If you're not interested in the four-acre water park, there are 27 holes of golf, a ¾-mile nature trail, and a spa with a full range of treatments and salon services (and a shop for "retail therapy," quips staff member Jeanne). **Pros:** Great value for an expansive resort, tons of activities to keep the kids busy, great general store on-site. **Cons:** Not within walking distance to the city's main downtown and riverside attractions, fee for Internet use. ⊠ *9800 Hyatt Dr., North/Northwest* ☎ *210/647–1234* ⊕ *www.hillcountry.hyatt.com* ↘ *428 rooms, 72 suites* ⚷ *In-room: safe, refrigerator, Ethernet, Wi-Fi. In-hotel: restaurants, room service, bar, golf course, tennis court, pools, gym, bicycles, children's programs (ages 3–12), laundry facilities, parking (no fee), concierge, public Internet, public Wi-Fi, no-smoking rooms* ▤ *AE, D, DC, MC, V.*

$$$–$$$$ ⊞**Radisson Hill Country Resort & Spa.** A 15-minute drive northwest of downtown you'll find a full-service resort at the base of Texas Hill Country. The hotel is one of the more upscale Radisson properties, with a full golf course, tennis courts, a spa, and even children's programs. The huge, multilevel pool is a favorite with kids. This is the official hotel of Sea World and has package deals available. Free shuttles to and from the park save you from parking fees. **Pros:** Helpful staff, good-size rooms. **Cons:** Driving everywhere (except to SeaWorld) is a necessity. ⊠ *9800 Westover Hills Blvd., North/Northwest* ☎ *210/509–9800* ⊕ *www.radisson.com* ↘ *174 rooms, 53 suites* ⚷ *In-room: refrigerator (some), Ethernet, Wi-Fi. In-room: restaurants, room service, bar, golf course, tennis courts, pool, gym, spa, children's programs (ages 1–18), laundry facilities, laundry service, concierge, public Internet, public Wi-Fi, parking (no fee), no-smoking rooms* ▤ *AE, D, DC, MC, V.*

$$$$ ⊞**Westin La Cantera.** Make a list of the things you'd look for in a luxury, ★   full-service resort, and La Cantera has it. The limestone quarry (*cantera,* in Spanish) on which it's built was a natural foundation for its golf course. It also offers the full compliment of resort services—including a spa, kids' programs, and tennis—and is immediately adjacent to upscale shopping, dining, and movies. On the northern edge of San Antonio, the resort is a short drive to Six Flags and Sea World, 30 minutes to the Alamo and River Walk. Its restaurant, Francesca's at Sunset (⇨ *Where to Eat*), is among the best in the city and has spectacular views of the start of Texas Hill Country. **Pros:** San Antonio's top resort hotel, lush common areas and rooms, virtually every amenity you could ask for. **Cons:** Removed from downtown and the River Walk, expensive. ⊠ *16641 La Cantera Parkway, North/Northwest* ☎ *210/558–6500* ⊕ *www.westinlacantera.com* ↘ *450 rooms, 58 suites* ⚷ *In-room: safe, kitchen (some), Ethernet. In-hotel: restaurant, room service, bar, golf course, tennis courts, pool, gym, spa, children's programs (ages 2–13), laundry facilities, laundry services, concierge, executive floor, public Internet, public Wi-Fi, parking (no fee), no-smoking rooms* ▤ *AE, D, DC, MC, V.*

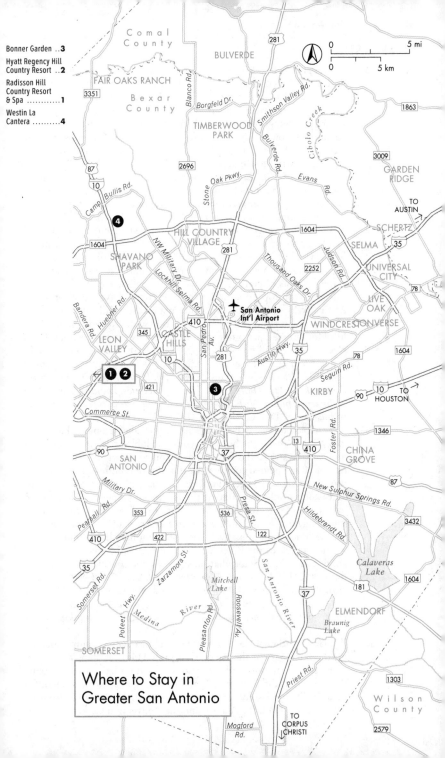

Where to Stay in Greater San Antonio

RIVER WALK

$$$ ⊡ **Drury Inn & Suites San Antonio Riverwalk.** One of the best values among River Walk hotels, the Drury Inn & Suites is in the landmark Petroleum Commerce Building on the riverfront. Ask for a room with a terrace overlooking the river. This isn't a posh or luxurious getaway, but if you're on a budget or want a kid-friendly hotel, you can't beat it. **Pros:** Great value for families and business travelers, premium location for sightseeing, free nightly cocktail reception. **Cons:** Rooms and decor nothing to write home about. ⊠ *201 N. Saint Mary's St., River Walk* ☎ *210/212–5200* ⊕ *www.druryhotels.com* ↜ *90 rooms, 60 suites* △ *In-room: refrigerator, Ethernet, Wi-Fi. In-hotel: pool, gym, laundry facilities, laundry service, public Internet, public Wi-Fi, parking (fee), some pets allowed, no-smoking rooms* ⊟ *AE, D, DC, MC, V* ⊺○⊺ *BP.*

$$$ ⊡ **Drury Plaza Hotel Riverwalk.** In the restored Alamo National Bank
★ building right on the river, the Drury Plaza is giving many of the pricier full-service hotels some competition. It sticks to the formula that makes Drury hotels popular with many budget and leisure travelers: good prices and lots of perks (full breakfast, complimentary cocktail hour). There's a rooftop pool, and riverfront rooms have excellent views. At this writing, a major expansion planned for fall 2008 will bring an indoor pool and two restaurants, one with riverside dining. **Pros:** Ideal for families, just a few steps from the city's top attractions. **Cons:** Needs the planned updates to spruce up decor and amenities. ⊠ *105 S. Saint Mary's St., River Walk* ☎ *210/270–7799* ⊕ *www.druryhotels. com* ↜ *231 rooms, 64 suites* △ *In-room: kitchen (some), refrigerator, Ethernet, Wi-Fi. In hotel: pool, laundry facilities, laundry service, public Internet, public Wi-Fi, parking (fee), some pets allowed, no-smoking rooms* ⊟ *AE, D, DC, MC, V* ⊺○⊺ *BP.*

$$–$$$ ⊡ **El Tropicano Holiday Inn Riverwalk.** If you like "tropical, Latin, and glitzy," then this is the hotel for you. The lobby, restaurant, and common areas capture the feel of an Acapulco resort. A major renovation in 2006 updated common areas and rooms, although the building sometimes shows its age. Kids love the aviary filled with tropical birds, and exotic drinks available at the bar make parents feel like they're one step closer to paradise. Make sure to ask for a riverfront room. The hotel hosts many conferences, so staff are ready to serve a business traveler's needs. In-house Mangos restaurant has alfresco dining along a quiet stretch of the River Walk. **Pros:** Fun and festive, kid-friendly, good value. **Cons:** Somewhat noisy, and some consider the theme too touristy. ⊠ *110 Lexington Ave., River Walk* ☎ *210/223–9461* ⊕ *www. eltropicanohotel.com* ↜ *300 rooms, 8 suites* △ *In-room: Wi-Fi. In-hotel: restaurant, room service, bar, pool, gym, laundry facilities, concierge, public Internet, public Wi-Fi, parking (fee), no-smoking rooms* ⊟ *AE, D, DC, MC, V.*

$$$$ ⊡ **Hilton Palacio del Rio.** A towering complex with a central location on the busy part of the River Walk, this Hilton is steps away from many top restaurants and attractions. Ask for a balcony overlooking the river, and watch the barges and tourists go by. Noise at night can be a problem on some lower floors. It is across the street from the River Center Mall, the Alamo, and the Convention Center. As a large convention hotel, it doesn't have a lot of local flavor, but the service and amenities are top-notch. **Pros:** Great location, facilities to accommodate longer stays. **Cons:** Expensive, even for a nice Hilton, lacks character. ⊠*200 S. Alamo St., River Walk* ☎*210/222–1400* ⊕*www.palaciodelrio.hilton.com* ⮠*473 rooms, 10 suites* ♿*In-room: Wi-Fi. In-hotel: restaurant, room service, bar, pool, gym, parking (fee), laundry facilities, laundry service, concierge, public Internet, public Wi-Fi, no-smoking rooms* ⊟*AE, D, DC, MC, V.*

$$$$ ⊞**Hotel Contessa Suites on the Riverwalk.** This exceptional boutique hotel,
Fodor'sChoice   built in 2005, takes visitors away from the hustle and bustle of the
★   River Walk, and gives them pause to relax in luxury. The decor is contemporary, but warm, with rooms and common areas featuring exposed brick, stone walls, and flora. The service is solid, and not too fussy. Suites are rare among hotels right on the river, and these have some indulgent amenities, such as fireplaces and marble bathrooms. The hotel also has an Aveda spa, as well as a heated outdoor pool (rare in San Antonio) and a hot tub. Definitely a destination for romantic weekends, the hotel also hosts many weddings. **Pros:** A truly sophisticated, unique upscale hotel, top-notch concierge, full-service spa. **Cons:** Reservations hard to obtain. ⊠*306 W. Market St., River Walk* ☎*210/229–9222 or 866/435–0900* ⊕*www.thehotelcontessa.com* ⮠*265 suites* ♿*In-room: safe, Ethernet, Wi-Fi. In hotel: restaurant, room service, bar, pool, gym, spa, laundry service, concierge, public Internet, parking (fee), no-smoking rooms* ⊟*AE, D, MC, V.*

$$$$ ⊞**Hotel Valencia Riverwalk.** One of a crop of new boutique hotels on
★   the river, Hotel Valencia's puffed pillows for Hollywood big names like *American Idol*'s Ryan Seacrest, Paula Abdul, and Simon Cowell. From floor to ceiling, the decor is a modern take on traditional, mixing design elements such as Spanish archways and columns with leather headboards, polished concrete posts, and sleek dark-wood furniture. Rooms have custom-designed beds, imported designer linens, and faux mink throws; all rooms have a big leaning mirror and a flat-screen television. Balcony rooms overlook the lushly landscaped banks of the River Walk. The restaurant, Citrus *(⇨ Where to Eat)*, is highly acclaimed. **Pros:** Hip, posh place to stay; great location on a quiet part of the river; its very popular bar has been rated one of the best places to see and be seen. **Cons:** High demand means difficult to book, especially at peak times; requires a hike to major River Walk attractions. ⊠*150 E. Houston St., River Walk* ☎*210/227–9700, 866/842–0100 reservations* ⊕*www.hotelvalencia.com* ⮠*212 rooms, 1 suite* ♿*In-room: Wi-Fi. In-hotel: restaurant, room service, bar, gym, laundry facilities, laundry services, concierge, public Internet, public Wi-Fi, no-smoking rooms* ⊟*AE, D, DC, MC, V.*

$$–$$$$ ⊞**Hyatt Place San Antonio/Riverwalk.** Many established all-suites and extended-stay hotels provide plenty of space but fall short on style. Hyatt Place, opened in late 2007, challenges the status quo with their customary, luxurious "Grand Bed," and sleek furnishings in every room. Technology lovers enjoy the Wi-Fi throughout, flat-panel TVs, touch-screen room service, automated check-in kiosks, and the "e-room," with free computing and printing. On one of the quiet

sections of the river, the hotel is a short walk from the entertainment district. **Pros:** Brand-new furnishings in 2007, hip and modern feel, tech-friendly. **Cons:** Caters primarily to business travelers, so not great for families. ⊠*601 S. Saint Mary's St., River Walk* ☎*201/227–6854* ⊕*www.hyattplace.com* ⌁*131 rooms* ⌂*In-room: refrigerator, Ethernet, Wi-Fi. In-hotel: restaurant, bar, pool, gym, laundry service, concierge, public Internet, public Wi-Fi, parking (no fee), no-smoking rooms* ⊟*AE, D, DC, MC, V.*

$$$$ **Marriott Rivercenter.** With more than 1,000 rooms, more than 80,000 square feet of meeting space, and a 40,000-square-foot ballroom, this 38-story hotel (attached to sister hotel Marriott Riverwalk) has all the pluses—and minuses—of a very large hotel. You will likely have all the services you could want and you're in the heart of the action, but if you're looking for a secluded getaway, this isn't it. An update of common areas completed in February 2008 modernized the restaurant and two-story lobby. **Pros:** Great location, friendly staff. **Cons:** Pricey parking, outrageous fees for extras like bottled water. ⊠*101 Bowie St., River Walk* ☎*210/223–1000* ⊕*www.marriott.com/satrc* ⌁*916 rooms, 85 suites* ⌂*In-room: refrigerator (some), Ethernet. In-hotel: restaurant, room service, bar, pool, gym, spa, children's programs (ages 2–12), laundry facilities, laundry service, concierge, executive floor, public Internet, public Wi-Fi, parking (fee), some pets allowed, no-smoking rooms* ⊟*AE, D, DC, MC, V.*

$$$$ **Omni La Mansión del Rio.** The hotel was originally built as a school in 1852, and then converted to a hotel for the HemisFair, the 1968 World's Fair. Inside and out it's replete with Spanish tiles, archways, exposed beams, and soft, earthy tones. Many rooms share balconies or verandas looking out on the river—be sure to request a river-view room. Location is a big selling point for this hotel, in a quiet section of the river but still steps away from the entertainment district. **Pros:** Right on River Walk, frequent online discounts on third-party sites. **Cons:** Some complaints about service, undiscounted rooms pricey for quality, lower-level street-facing rooms noisy. ⊠*112 College St., River Walk* ☎*210/518–1000* ⊕*www.lamansion.com* ⌁*307 rooms, 31 suites* ⌂*In-room: dial-up, Ethernet. In-hotel: restaurants, room service, bar, pool, gym, spa, laundry service, concierge, public Internet, public Wi-Fi, some pets allowed, no-smoking rooms* ⊟*AE, D, DC, MC, V.*

$$–$$$ **Riverwalk Vista.** What began as a wholesale grocer's warehouse in the mid-1800s is now one of San Antonio's most noteworthy boutique hotels. The feeling in the hotel is of a converted loft—hardwood floors, exposed-brick walls—with heavy South Texas influences. Many rooms have floor-to-ceiling windows looking out on Alamo Plaza or the River Walk. All rooms have slate-tiled walk-in showers. The location can be noisy, particularly on Saturday nights. The hotel doesn't have its own parking, so guests have to unload and park at a garage down the street (which doesn't offer in-and-out rates). **Pros:** Central location, unique design. **Cons:** No on-site parking, hard-to-spot entry, can be noisy. ⊠*262 Losoya St., River Walk* ☎*210/223–3200* ⊕*www.river walkvista.com* ⌁*17 rooms* ⌂*In-room: safe, Ethernet, Wi-Fi. In-hotel:*

gym, laundry facilities, laundry service, concierge, public Internet, public Wi-Fi, no-smoking rooms ⊟*AE, D, MC, V.*

$$$$
Fodor'sChoice
★

🏨 **Watermark Hotel & Spa.** Luxury accommodations and services are offered at this hotel in the shell of the historic 19th-century L. Frank Saddlery Building with an entrance facing the River Walk. The Watermark has sleek modern rooms and suites ranging in size from 425 to 600 square feet, with 12-foot ceilings and marble whirlpool baths. Plush linens and posh toiletries are similarly luxurious. Rooms have hardwood floors, leather furniture, and wrought-iron canopy beds; some have balconies. A European-style spa offers a hair and nail salon, massages, scrubs, soaks, and other therapies. **Pros:** Everything a five-star hotel professes to be. **Cons:** Pricey, some extra charges for sundries, expensive parking. ⊠*212 West Crockett St., River Walk* ☎*210/396–5800 or 866/605–1212* ⊕*www.watermarkhotel.com* ⇨*97 rooms, 2 suites* ♿*In-room: safe, Ethernet. In-hotel: restaurant, room service, bar, pool, gym, spa, laundry service, concierge, public Wi-Fi, parking (fee), some pets allowed, no-smoking rooms* ⊟*AE, D, DC, MC, V.*

SAN ANTONIO ESSENTIALS

TRANSPORTATION

BY AIR

San Antonio International Airport (SAT) is in northeast San Antonio between Highway 281 and I–410, about 13 miles from the downtown River Walk area. The Pan Am Expressway leads from the airport to the central business district.

VIA Metropolitan Transit *(⇨By Bus, below)*, provides daily bus service between the airport and downtown. SATRANS offers shared-van shuttle service from the airport; the typical fare to a downtown hotel is $9 one-way, $16 round-trip. Taxis provide 24-hour service at a standard metered rate of $1.60 at pick-up plus $0.30 per 0.2 mile. From the airport there is a minimum departure charge of $8.50. A typical airport-to-downtown fare is $15 to $17 plus tip.

Airport Information **San Antonio International Airport** (⊠ *9800 Airport Blvd., San Antonio* ☎ *210/207–3450* ⊕ *www.sanantonio.gov/aviation*).

Shuttle Service Information **SATRANS** (☎ *210/281–9900*).

Taxi Information **Executive Airport and Taxi Service** (☎ *210/824–1037*). **San Antonio Taxis** (☎ *210/444–2222*). **Yellow Checker Cab** (☎ *210/226–4242*).

BY BUS & TROLLEY

Greyhound connects San Antonio with cities in Texas and beyond. The local bus line, Via Metropolitan Transit, serves the city and airport. Local fare is $1 (express $2). A one-day pass is $3.75 and includes service on streetcars, which weave through downtown and come every 10 minutes.

Information **Via Metropolitan Transit** (✉ *1020 San Pedro, San Antonio* ☎ *210/362–2020* ⊕ *www.viainfo.net*). **Greyhound** ((✉ *500 N. Saint Mary's St., San Antonio* ☎ *210/270–5824 or 800/231–2222* ⊕ *www.greyhound.com*)).

BY CAR

Three interstates converge in central San Antonio: I–35 from Dallas and Austin to the north continues south to Laredo, I–10 from Houston to the east continues northwest after passing through San Antonio, and I–37 connects San Antonio to Corpus Christi. Other U.S. routes and Texas highways also lead into the city, including U.S. 281 and U.S. 90. Two highways loop the city: I–410 encircles the heart of San Antonio; Highway 1604 makes a wider circle.

BY TRAIN

Amtrak provides daily passenger service to and from San Antonio. Its Texas Eagle line arrives and departs daily, connecting San Antonio to Austin, Ft. Worth, Dallas, and other cities en route north to Chicago. The Sunset Limited line serves San Antonio three times a week, running east–west across the country between Orlando and Los Angeles.

Train Information **Amtrak** (✉ *224 Hoefgen St., San Antonio* ☎ *210/223–3226 or 800/872–7245* ⊕ *www.amtrak.com*).

CONTACTS & RESOURCES

EMERGENCIES

Dial 911. Each of the following has a 24-hour emergency room.

Hospitals **University Hospital** (✉ *4502 Medical Dr.* ☎ *210/358–4000*). **University Health Center Downtown** (✉ *527 N. Leona* ☎ *210/358–3400*).

VISITOR INFORMATION

Contacts **San Antonio Visitor Convention & Visitors Bureau.** (✉ *203 S. Saint Mary's St., Ste. 200, San Antonio* ☎ *210/207–6700 or 800/447–3372* ⊕ *www. visitsanantonio.com*).

Austin

WORD OF MOUTH

"Pick Austin (over Houston) or get your head checked. Great fun, food, people, sights, music, nightlife. Sooo much fun, you will feel like a teenager . . . But most importantly, enjoy the people there, they are so friendly and willing to tell you whatever you need to know about their town."

—obrienenator

"Austin is very family friendly. We have tons of parks, greenbelts, lakes, rivers, and a small zoo. We also have a great children's museum."

—nma

By Wes
Eichenwald;
Arts &
Nightlife
by Jessica
Norman
Dupuy

THERE'S A MYSTIQUE ABOUT AUSTIN. Even if you've lived for years in this small town turned big city, the reasons why the city functions as it does, and why it seems so different from other U.S. cities, may not be readily apparent.

Austin is an extraordinarily open and welcoming place—a city where you're not only allowed but *expected* to be yourself, in all your quirky glory. The people you encounter are likely to be laissez-faire and may even be newcomers themselves (Austin's population grew 47% during the 1990s, and continues to expand at a healthy pace: 65,800 new residents were added to the Austin–Round Rock metropolitan area from July 2006 to July 2007, according to the U.S. Census Bureau).

It's not pushing it too much to liken Austin to San Francisco: in the middle of a big state and the golden destination where people who are just a bit different and quite self-directed come to realize their fullest selves. Many who would never consider living anywhere else in Texas have relocated here after dreaming the Austin dream. The city ranks high on many national best-places-to-live lists. If it's sometimes hard for Austin to live up to its hype (some of it is self-generated), it's still a place where creativity and maverick thinking are valued.

Such things weren't on the mind of Mirabeau B. Lamar, president-elect of the Texas Republic, when he set out to hunt buffalo in 1838 but returned home with a much greater catch: a home for the new state capital. He fell in love with a tiny settlement called Waterloo, surrounded by rolling hills and fed by cool springs. Within a year the government had arrived, and the town, renamed Austin (after Stephen F. Austin, the "Father of Texas"), was on its way to becoming a city. About a half a century later, in 1883, the University of Texas at Austin was founded.

Fed by the 1970s salad days of the "outlaw country" movement popularized by Willie Nelson, Waylon Jennings, and others, through the growing viewership of *Austin City Limits,* a showcase for bands that began taping for a local PBS station in 1976, Austin's reputation as a music center has grown to the point that the city now bills itself as the Live Music Capital of the World. This is especially true every March, when the city hosts the South by Southwest Conferences and Festivals (widely known as SXSW), which draws people from throughout the world: bands, record-company executives, filmmakers, Internet celebrities, and, of course, legions of fans.

Today Austin is in the midst of reinventing itself yet again. High-tech industries have migrated to the area, making it Texas's answer to Silicon Valley. The city has also become an important filmmaking center. For the moment, Austin retains a few vestiges of a small-town atmosphere—but a quick scan of its fast-growing downtown skyline will tell you that its days as a sleepy college town are long gone.

Despite all the changes that have occurred (and are occurring) in this capital city, Austin is still a town whose roots are planted firmly in the past—a past the city is proud to preserve and show off to visitors.

AUSTIN TOP 5

■ **Great Live Music.** Whether it's country, rock, country-rock, folk, punk, jazz, classical, Celtic, or blue-grass music you're after, Austin's got the musicians and bands to suit your fancy—and the venue could be in an old-time dancehall, grimy hole-in-the-wall, or large, modern performance space. Music festivals happen year-round, with marquee names performing during SXSW in March and the Austin City Limits Music Festival in September, but also local affairs like the Armadillo Christmas Bazaar (December) and the Old Pecan Street Arts Festivals occurring in the spring and fall.

■ **World-class BBQ & Ethnic Food.** Austinites are passionate seekers of, and arguers about, great restaurants and food, not only of the old stand-bys (barbecue joints and authentic Mexican and Tex-Mex eateries), but a wide spectrum of world cuisines, for all tastes and budgets.

■ **City of the Future.** Austin isn't only one of the best cities in the U.S. for free wireless Internet access (practically every hotel lobby has it), it's forward-looking in such areas

as sustainability (green buildings, parkland), revitalizing its downtown through encouraging mixed-use residential and retail space, and promoting free and low-cost public transit. As a result, Austin's downtown is a hip, happening place.

■ **Cowboy Culture.** The Star of Texas Fair & Rodeo in March is a prime opportunity to immerse yourself and your family in a classic rodeo-and-cattle atmosphere, complete with cook-offs, comedy, concerts, and other wholesome entertainment. Your kids will never forget it, and the odds are you won't, either. And if you'd like to bring home some genuine cowboy boots, those are easy to find around here.

■ **The Great Outdoors.** Austinites take full advantage of their city's mostly mild, sunny climate and abundant green space. When they're not working, they're likely running or riding on the hike-and-bike trails along Lady Bird Lake, swimming at Barton Springs or Deep Eddy Pool, golfing at a public course like Lions Municipal, or boating on Lake Travis.

EXPLORING AUSTIN

Austin lies in Central Texas, about 163 mi southeast of the state's true center, Eden. On Austin's western border is the Hill Country, its eastern border the much flatter Blackland Prairie. Dallas is about 190 mi to the north, Houston 160 mi to the east.

The logical place to begin an exploration of the city is downtown, where the pink-granite Texas State Capitol, built in 1888, is the most visible manmade attraction. The Colorado River, which slices through Austin, was once an unpredictable waterway, but it's been tamed into a series of lakes, including two within the city limits. Twenty-two-mile-long Lake Austin, in the western part of the city, flows into Lady Bird Lake (formerly Town Lake), a narrow stretch of water that meanders for 5 mi through the center of downtown.

PLANNING YOUR TRIP

WHEN TO GO

Austin has a humid, subtropical climate, with about 300 days of sunshine. The best times to visit are spring and late fall.

It's no accident that many visitors fall in love with the city when they visit during the SXSW festivals in March—that's when the weather is most pleasant and temperate, and wildflowers cut multicolored swaths on the rolling hills and roadsides.

In summer, when the high is 96° and weeks of daily triple-digit highs are not uncommon, every Austinite able to escape to cooler climes does so. It's usually not before October (average high 81°, average low 60°) that people again start to forego air-conditioned restaurant interiors for outdoor patios. Austin has mild winters, with the average high and low in the coldest month, January, at 60° and 40°, respectively. Snow, while not unheard of, is rare. The wettest month is May, with average precipitation of just over five inches.

If you visit in late September, be prepared for music-crazed fanatics flooding the city for the Austin City Limits Music Festival. Austinites and out-of-towners alike migrate in zombie-like droves toward the bass-pumping, heart-thumping, rhythm jumping beacon of Zilker Park, where the three-day affair takes place.

GETTING THERE

The major entryway into Austin is I-35. Loop 1 (also known as MoPac) joins with I-35 on Austin's northern and southern outskirts, dispersing traffic to the west side of the city. U.S. 183 runs at a slight north–south diagonal through Austin. Although it doesn't serve any major cities, U.S. 183 does serve as a major thoroughfare through town, eventually meandering northward to western Oklahoma and southward toward the gulf. East–west Highway 71 and U.S. 290 connect Austin and Houston.

GETTING AROUND

Although the highways are clearly marked, many of them have been granted other names as they pass through Austin (some joke that every road has at least two names). Keep in mind that U.S. 183 runs parallel to Research Boulevard for one stretch, Anderson Lane at another, and Ed Bluestein Boulevard at yet another, and Highway 71 is also known as Ben White Boulevard. Congress Avenue serves as the major north–south thoroughfare in the downtown area; it is interrupted at the State Capitol, Austin's heart and soul.

The rest of downtown is laid out in a conventional grid of numerical streets. The majority of these are one-way streets: even-numbered streets generally run one way to the west, and odd-numbered streets generally run one way to the east.

With 19 million annual visitors, more than 50,000 university students, and a large commuter population, Austin meets the demand with having more roads per capita than the other major cities in Texas—and it needs all of them. In fact, even with new highways and toll roads added in recent years, Austin's population growth has brought congestion, and it seems that every year rush hour gets longer, running weekdays from 7 to 9:30 AM and 4 to 7 PM, with Friday afternoon's rush starting a bit earlier. Driving can be irksome during rush hours, but Austin is generally navigable and car-friendly.

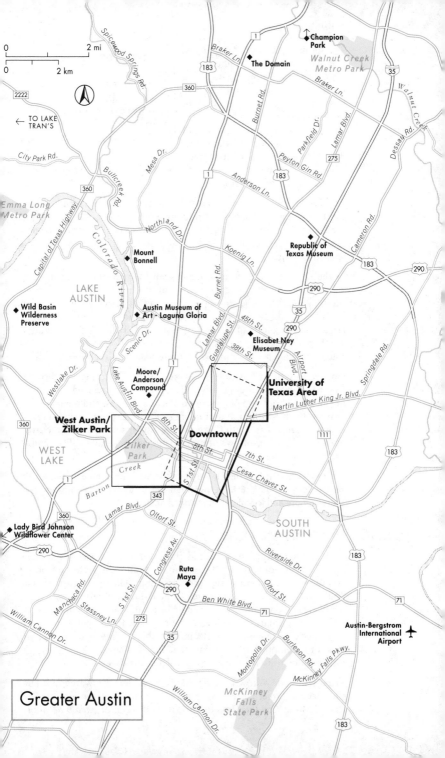

The sprawling University of Texas, one of the largest universities in the United States, flanks the capitol's north end. Among other things, it is home to both the Blanton Museum of Art and the Lyndon Baines Johnson Presidential Library and Museum. UT's northwestern border is flanked by Guadalupe Street,

> **MUSEUM DISCOUNTS**
>
> Many museums have free or reduced admission one day per week (the day varies per museum; research ahead).

which for these blocks is known as The Drag, a fun and funky student-centered commercial strip.

The downtown's Warehouse District and Second Street District, which run from west of Congress to roughly Nueces Street, and north from the lake to 6th Street, are where you'll find some of Austin's liveliest (and newest) restaurants, bistros, and pubs, along with hip boutiques and other shops.

In the late afternoon hours, locals grab their sneakers and head to Zilker Park, just west and a bit south of downtown, for a jog or a leisurely walk. When the sun sets on summer days, everyone's attention turns to the lake's Congress Avenue Bridge, under which the country's largest urban colony of Mexican free-tailed bats hangs out (literally). The bats make their exodus after sunset to feed on insects in the surrounding Hill Country, putting on quite a show in the process.

Finally, no visit to Austin is complete without venturing south of the river to savor the unique creative vibe of South Congress, with its colorful antiques shops and oh-so-cool clubs and eateries, and the laid-back charms down South First and many side streets. (Note that Congress Avenue is known as South Congress—SoCo for short—below the river. North of the river, in downtown Austin, it's generally called simply Congress Avenue.)

■ TIP→ If it's your first time in Austin, your first stop should be the Austin Visitor Center (209 E. 6th St., between Brazos and San Jacinto) for brochures galore and friendly dispensing of advice.

DOWNTOWN & CAPITOL AREA

Downtown Austin is the natural starting point for seeing the city's sights, and is home to many of them, including the state capitol. Its boundaries are generally regarded as being I-35 to the east, Lamar Boulevard to the west, UT to the north, and the river to the south. It's relatively compact and well served by buses and the free 'Dillo trolleys, so if you're primarily interested in touring downtown, you won't need a car. The capitol complex is the most visible landmark, of course, but most of the important museums (save for the Blanton) and many historic buildings are between the capitol and the river.

Areas within downtown are the Market District, the Warehouse District, Second Street District, Congress District, 6th Street, and the Red River District *(see the Downtown Austin & Capitol Area map above for a visual reference to these areas).* Some of these districts are so distinct that we've given them their own neighborhood section within this chapter for categories like shopping, dining, and lodging.

For the sake of soaking up the atmosphere and getting a sense of the city, we highly recommend walking the ten blocks up Congress Avenue between 11th Street and the bridge, in either direction. And at some point, walk down 6th Street between Congress Avenue and I–35.

MAIN ATTRACTIONS

❶ Austin Children's Museum. Kids (and adults) of all ages will get a kick out of this well-designed museum. An open floor plan leads from one diversion to another, including a kid-size "global diner" and rotating exhibits to stimulate growing imaginations. ⊠ *201 Colorado St., Downtown & Capitol Area* ☎ *512/472–2499* ⊕ *www.austinkids.org* ☞ *$5.50* ⊙ *Tues., Thurs.–Sat. 10–5, Wed. 10–8, Sun. noon–5.*

❾ Austin Museum of Art–Downtown. AMOA, as it's known, doesn't have a huge amount of space at either its downtown location or at the gorgeous 1916 Italianate villa of its West Austin Laguna Gloria site, but the exhibitions tend to be well-curated, and interesting—Laguna Gloria is worth visiting for the ambience alone. ⊠ *823 Congress Ave., Downtown & Capitol Area* ☎ *512/495–9224* ⊠ *3809 W. 35th St., West Austin* ☎ *512/458–8191* ⊕ *www.amoa.org.*

❻ Bob Bullock Texas State History Museum. Bob Bullock, Texas's 38th lieutenant governor and a potent political force in his day, lobbied hard to establish a museum of state history in his years of public service. Bullock didn't live to see it happen—he died in 1999—but his dream came true in 2001 with the opening of this 176,000-square-foot museum. Four blocks north of the capitol, the museum hosts exhibitions of archaeological objects, documents, and other materials from regional museums throughout the state and also presents historical and educational programs. Exhibits include everything from the letters of Sam Houston to Indian artifacts. The museum has a 400-seat IMAX. ⊠ *1800 Congress Ave.* ☎ *512/936–8746* ⊕ *www.thestoryoftexas.com* ☞ *Museum $5.50, IMAX $7* ⊙ *Mon.–Sat. 9–6, Sun. noon–6.*

❸ The Bremond Block Historic District. A number of high-style Victorian homes built between 1854 and 1910 fill this area. They were once owned by wealthy Austinites, including several members of the Bremond family of merchants and bankers. Inquire at the Austin Visitor Center about self-guided walking tours. ⊠ *Bounded by 7th and 8th Sts., and Guadalupe and San Antonio Sts., Downtown & Capitol Area.*

❼ Texas State Capitol. Built in 1888 of Texas pink granite, this impressive structure is even taller than the U.S. Capitol (yes, everything *is* bigger in Texas). The building dominates downtown Austin. The surrounding grounds are nearly as striking. Stand in the center of the star on the ground floor under the rotunda and look up, up, up into the dome—it's a Texas rite of passage. Catch one of the free historical tours, offered 8:30–4:30. ⊠ *1100 Congress Ave., Downtown & Capitol Area* ☎ *512/463–0063.*

FodorśChoice ★

FodorśChoice ★

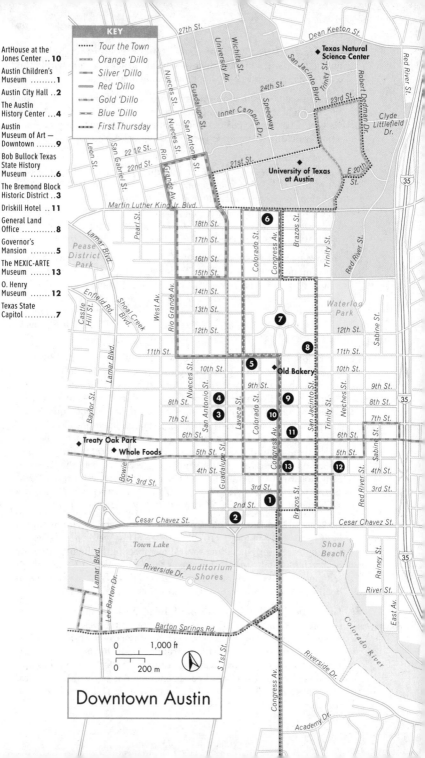

KEY
····· *Tour the Town*
▬▬▬ *Orange 'Dillo*
▬▬▬ *Silver 'Dillo*
▬▬▬ *Red 'Dillo*
▬▬▬ *Gold 'Dillo*
▬▬▬ *Blue 'Dillo*
▬▬▬ *First Thursday*

Downtown Austin

FESTIVALS & EVENTS

MAR. Zilker Park Kite Festival. Austin is also known for enjoying the outdoors. On the first Sunday of March, head down to the soccer fields at Zilker Park for this annual kite event. Be sure to bring a picnic basket, the kids, and even your furry friends for beautiful kite creations and amazing tricks. You can bring a kite or you can just watch the festivities—and if the mood strikes, purchase a kite on-site or attend one of the kite-building workshops. The festival is an ideal way to take in the Austin skyline. ⊠ *2100 Barton Springs Rd.* ☎ *512/448–5483* ⊕ *www.zilkerkitefestival.com* ☒ *Free.*

APR. Texas Hill Country Wine and Food Festival. With the flagship Whole Foods Market on West 6th Street and two locations for the foodie-heaven Central Market, it's clear that Austin is a food-loving town. Each April at this fun-filled festival, celebrity chefs, wine makers, and food lovers alike join together to celebrate fabulous culinary creations and trends, as well as the up-and-coming Texas wine scene. Tickets can be expensive (with some events costing near $150), but the cooking demonstrations, speaker series, and general celebration of food and wine do make for an exciting affair. Buy tickets early; this event sells out quickly. ⊠ *Throughout Austin*

☎ *512/249–6300* ⊕ *www.texas-wineandfood.org* ☒ *Prices vary per event, starting at $35.*

MAY & OCT. Old Pecan Street Art Festival. Austin is no stranger to the arts, and hosts a number of art-driven festivals including this bi-annual event. Few may know that 6th Street was once Pecan Street, but twice a year (in the spring and fall), old Austin roots surface, the street closes during the day and artists set up booths with paintings, jewelry, crafts, and much more for the public to peruse—and hopefully buy. Add to this live musical performances, cold beer, and smoked sausage wraps, and you've got an afternoon of good times. ⊠ *6th Street* ☎ *512/443-6179* ⊕ *www.old-pecanstreetfestival.com* ☒ *Free.*

DEC. First Night Austin. For a family-friendly way to bring in the new year, stroll the plazas and parks of downtown Austin. Each New Year's Eve the city serves as the stage for a variety of artists, street performers, musicians, puppeteers, and dancers. This interactive festival features children-friendly workshops for creating puppets, festive hats, and origami cranes for the final event parade. Admission is free, and parents can feel safe with children in the alcohol-free environment. Throughout Downtown Austin ☎ *512/374–0000* ⊕ *www.firstnightaustin.org* ☒ *Free.*

ALSO WORTH SEEING

🔟 **ArtHouse at the Jones Center.** Set in a squarish building on the northwest corner of 7th Street and Congress Avenue is this center with rotating installations by contemporary Texas artists. It also offers a number of art-related programs. ⊠ *701 Congress Ave., Downtown & Capitol Area* ☎ *512/453–5312* ⊕ *www.arthousetexas.org.*

② **Austin City Hall.** The home of municipal government since November 2004 and the anchor of the Second Street District, City Hall is a strik-

PARKING IN AUSTIN

Both street and garage parking are plentiful in downtown Austin. At this writing, metered parking costs $1 an hour (be warned that many downtown meters have two-hour limits) and is free after 5:30 PM and on weekends. Parking lots and garages will charge anywhere from $5 to $15 a day (prices increase during special events). For visits to the State Capitol, a free, two-hour parking lot is adjacent to the building. Austin's City Hall has a large garage with free parking on Thursdays (the day City Council meets) and on Fridays from 11 AM to 1:15 PM whenever bands perform on City Hall Plaza; the maximum fee otherwise is $10 a day, $5 on weekends. Visitors to City Hall can generally get their parking validated, and many Second Street District retailers can validate tickets for two hours on weekdays, 8 AM to 5 PM. Parking regulations are strictly enforced in Austin, and a ticket will run $15–$35 (fines double if not paid in 21 days), and $250 for parking in a handicapped spot ($300 after 21 days).

ing modern showcase of the New Austin, loaded with energy-saving features like solar panels and decorated with modern art. The angular, four-story limestone-and-concrete building is clad in 66,000 square feet of copper. A 40-foot waterfall flows inside, and bands play on the outdoor plaza during free Friday concerts in spring and fall. Tours are available by appointment. ⊠*301 W. Second St., Downtown & Capitol Area* ⊕*www.ci.austin.tx.us/cityhall*.

④ The Austin History Center. Part of the Austin Public Library system (and next door to the central branch building), this is the central repository of all historical documents relating to Austin and Travis County (of which Austin is a part). Its more than one million items, including more than 700,000 photographic images, form a priceless collection of all things relating to Austin. ⊠*810 Guadalupe St., Downtown & Capitol Area* ☎*512/974–7480* ⊕*www.ci.austin.tx.us/library/ahc*.

⑬ The MEXIC-ARTE Museum. Founded in 1984, this museum is a beguiling, moderate-size museum devoted to traditional and contemporary Mexican and Latino art. The permanent collection includes lithographs, prints, silkscreens, etchings, and traditional ritual masks. If you're in town in time for the museum's popular annual Day of the Dead celebration, you're in for a treat. ⊠*419 Congress Ave., Downtown & Capitol Area* ☎*512/480–9373* ☉*Mon.–Thurs. 10–6, Fri.–Sat. 10–5, Sun noon–5* 🎟*$5*.

NEED A BREAK?

The **Old Bakery and Emporium**—In 1876, Swedish baker Charles Lundberg built this charming, affectionately renovated building near the capitol and operated it as a bakery for the next 60 years. Rescued from demolition by the Austin Heritage Society, the bakery is now a registered historic landmark owned by the city and run by the Parks and Recreation Department. The Old Bakery sells sandwiches and coffee these days, but its real appeal is as an outlet for handmade crafts made by older citizens (50 and over). It makes for a nice stop before or after touring the Capitol. ⊠*1006 Congress Ave., Downtown & Capitol Area* ☎*512/477–5961* ⊙*Mon.–Fri. 9–4 (also Sat. 10–2 Dec. only).*

⑪ Driskill Hotel. If you make time to stroll through one Austin hotel even though you're not staying there, make it the Driskill. A monument to Richardsonian Romanesque style, this delightful—and some say haunted—grande dame is embellished with stone busts of its original owner, cattle baron Jesse Driskill, and his sons. Two-story porches with Romanesque Revival columns surround the arched entrances. Over the years, countless legislators, lobbyists, and social leaders have held court behind its limestone walls, and it seems a few of them never left: according to guests, lights turn on by themselves, pipes bang eerily, elevators without passengers go up and down during the night, and luggage is mysteriously moved. But hotel management is quick to point out that the ghosts seem benign. *(Also see Where to Stay.)* ⊠*604 Brazos St.* ☎*512/474–5911* ⊕*www.driskillhotel.com.*

⑧ General Land Office. The only surviving government building from Austin's first 30 years owes its Gothic style to its German-born and -trained architect, Conrad Stremme. This 2½-story structure of stuccoed stone and brick was opened for business in the spring of 1858 as the first home of the Land Office. Writer O. Henry worked as a draftsman here and used the building as the setting for two of his short stories. In 1989 the legislature approved a $4.5 million renovation project to restore the building to its 1890s appearance. The structure now houses the Capitol Visitors Center and a gift shop, and has space on the second floor for traveling exhibits. ⊠*112 E. 11th St., at Brazos St., Downtown & Capitol Area* ☎*512/305–8400 visitor center* ⊡*Free* ⊙*Mon.–Sat. 9–5, Sun. noon–5.*

⑤ Governor's Mansion. Abner Cook, a leading architect of his day, designed the mansion, one of Austin's most elegant dwellings. The 1865 home has been the home of every Texas governor since the state's fifth, Elisha Marshall Pease. Constructed of bricks made in Austin and wood from nearby forests, the two-story mansion bears the marks of those who have lived here, including Gov. James Hogg, who, to keep his children from speedballing down the banister on their rears, hammered tacks into the railing. The tack holes are still visible. The mansion has many fine furnishings, paintings, and antiques, including Sam Houston's bed and Stephen F. Austin's desk. Unfortunately, in order to visit, you'll have to wait until at least the spring of 2009, when it is expected to reopen after extensive renovations. ⊠*1010 Colorado St., Downtown & Capitol Area* ☎*512/463–5518* ⊕*www.governor.state. tx.us/Mansion.*

⑫ O. Henry Museum. Writer William Sydney Porter, better known as O. Henry, rented this modest cottage from 1893 to 1895. Moved a few blocks from its original location, the home today contains O. Henry memorabilia and period furniture. It has hosted the popular O. Henry Pun-Off World Championships in its backyard every May since 1977; it also sponsors student writing workshops. ⊠*409 E. 5th St., Down-*

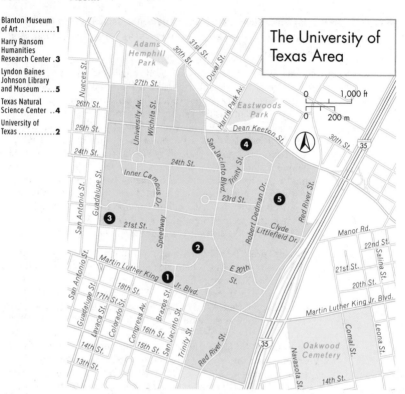

The University of
Texas Area

town & Capitol Area ☎512/472–1903 ⊕www.ci.austin.tx.us/parks/
ohenry.htm ✉Donation suggested ⊗Wed.–Sun. noon–5.

UNIVERSITY OF TEXAS

Envisioning Austin without the University of Texas is well-nigh impossible. The sprawling campus itself is home to both intimate charm (winding pathways past stone university buildings) and spectacle (the landmark UT Tower, the ultra-new Blanton Museum of Art, the LBJ Library and Museum, and of course Memorial Stadium, home of those Longhorns). Parking can be a problem anywhere on or around campus (most parking spaces are reserved for students, faculty, and staff, and the Drag is always crowded when school is in session—and don't even think of driving down there on Longhorn football home game days).

You'll know you're in a college town when you stroll down Guadalupe Street, also known as "the Drag." Guadalupe borders the west side of the UT campus and is lined with trendy boutiques, vintage-clothing shops, and restaurants.

MAIN ATTRACTIONS

2 **University of Texas.** The 350-acre campus breeds Texas Longhorns, as passionate about football (and other sports) as they are about academics (it has one of the country's top research libraries). The university is the largest employer in Austin (even more than the state government), employeeing more than 80,000 people. The number of students here is staggering, too: 39,000 undergraduates and 11,000 at the graduate level. Come to the grounds any time to stroll on your own, visit one of the museums or libraries (the Ransom Center, for example, is the repository for the Watergate papers), or attend a fun annual event like Explore UT, Gone to Texas, and commencement, which includes fireworks. ☎ *512/475–7348* ⊕ *www.utexas.edu.*

1 **Blanton Museum of Art.** Austin's new showcase museum, formerly the Huntington Art Gallery, is the largest university art museum in the United States, and holds one of the country's largest private collections of old master paintings and drawings. Although it's home to a teaching school—this is a center for research and training in conservation studies and visual arts—the Blanton avoids the stifling tendencies of academe, frequently mounting daring special exhibitions. In addition to European holdings rich in Renaissance and baroque works (many by Tiepolo, Poussin, Veronese, Rubens, and Correggio), the museum has a superior sampling of 20th- and early-21st-century American art, with an emphasis on abstract painting. Prints and drawings span the ages, from Albrecht Dürer to Jasper Johns, and the collection of modernist and contemporary Latin-American art is one of the country's largest, encompassing 1,600 works in various mediums. The Blanton's stunning new home, the Mari and James A. Michener Gallery Building, opened its doors in 2006; the adjacent Edgar A. Smith Building will open in fall 2008, adding an auditorium, event spaces, classrooms, a larger museum shop, and a café to the complex. ⊠ *Martin Luther King Jr. Blvd. and Congress St.* ☎ *512/471–7324* ⊕ *www.blantonmuseum. org* 🎟 *$5.*

5 **Lyndon Baines Johnson Library and Museum.** The artifacts and voluminous documents on exhibit here provide some insight into the 36th president's mind and motivations, and though his foibles are downplayed, a clear sense of the man—earthy, conniving, sensitive, and wry—emerges. That he was able to function at all may surprise visitors born during the high-tech era. In an age when the average car is loaded with digital gadgets and 12-year-olds with cell phones are commonplace, Johnson's black Lincoln limousine and clunky, command-central telephone seem quaintly archaic, though they were state-of-the-art during his presidency. If you schedule your visit to the reading room in advance of your arrival, you can listen to recordings of conversations Johnson had using that telephone. The 30-plus hours of tape recordings include ruminations on Vietnam, economic inflation, and a New York City transit strike. Gordon Bunshaft designed the monolithic travertine building that houses the library; like the limo and the phone, it's a bit of a period piece. There are rotating temporary exhibits on the ground floor. Be sure to check out the second floor, where a life-size audio-animatronic

Lady Bird: A Natural Beauty

Nobody didn't love Lady Bird. Born Claudia Alta Taylor in the East Texas town of Karnack, the first lady was 94 when she died at home in Austin in 2007. The nickname that everyone knew came as a toddler when a maid called her "pretty as a lady bird."

Within months of graduating from UT in 1934, she had met and married the boisterous Lyndon Johnson. It was a whirlwind courtship, but there was nothing tornadic about the quintessentially graceful Lady Bird Johnson. She seemed determined to offset LBJ's legendary crudity and relentless ambition with subtlety and good humor.

Some count her the nation's premier environmentalist, and she was the first presidential wife honored by a

The former first lady sits among the wildflowers she loved so much.

Congressional Gold Medal for her work. Lady Bird also was active for six decades in operating the family's broadcasting outlets in Austin.

—Larry Neal

figure of LBJ spins humorous anecdotes; it's a hoot. ✉ *2313 Red River St.* ☎ *512/721–0200* ⊕ *www.lbjlib.utexas.edu* ✆ *Free* ☉ *Daily 9–5.*

❸ **Harry Ransom Humanities Research Center.** Part of the University of Texas, this is one of the world's greatest collectors and exhibitors of important literary papers and other artifacts related to the arts and humanities. Among its fantastic riches are the papers of Norman Mailer, Isaac Bashevis Singer, and Arthur Miller; Woodward and Bernstein's Watergate research materials; over 10,000 film, television, and radio scripts; over 10,000 film posters; one million rare books, including a Gutenberg Bible; and five million photographs. ✉ *21st and Guadalupe Sts., University of Texas* ☎ *512/471–8944* ⊕ *www.hrc.utexas.edu.*

ALSO WORTH SEEING

❹ **Texas Natural Science Center.** French architect Paul Cret's 1936 plans for the Texas Memorial Museum (now the exhibit hall of the Texas Natural Science Center) called for north and south wings to extend from a central building, a tailored limestone box with subtle art deco flourishes. The wings were scuttled because of funding difficulties, leaving only Cret's alabaster midsection. But the chic interior, with brass doors, glass embellishments, and blood-red marble walls, floors, and ceilings, mitigates any sense of abridgement. Among the popular draws at the museum are the dinosaur models (including a 30-foot-long mosasaur and a 40-foot-long pterosaur) and the life-size dioramas, which depict buffalo, roadrunners, cougars, mountain lions, and flying squirrels.

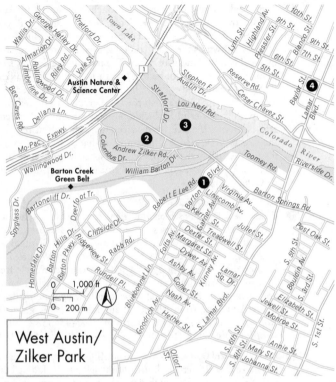

West Austin/
Zilker Park

✉*2400 Trinity St.* ☎*512/471–1604* ⊕*www.utexas.edu/tmm* ✇*Free*
⊙*Mon.–Fri. 9–5, Sat. 10–5, Sun. 1–5.*

WEST AUSTIN/ZILKER PARK

Zilker Park is Austin's regular daily backyard and playground, where
Austinites go to swim, jog, and hang back with a barbecue platter
and a beer. West Austin generally refers to the area just west of Lamar
Boulevard (not to be confused with West Lake, which is the tony area
west of Lake Austin). It's a laid-back, pleasant area with some good
shopping strips and restaurants.

MAIN ATTRACTION

2 **Zilker Park.** Many people and companies have moved to Austin for a
quality of life enhanced by pristine waterways and extensive greenbelts
for hiking, biking, and running. Zilker Park is the city's largest and
connects to **Lady Bird Lake's hike and bike trail.** There's a parking fee
on weekends. (⇨*Sports & the Outdoors for more on Zilker Park and
outdoor offerings in Austin.*) (✉*2100 Barton Springs Rd., West Austin*
☎*512/974–6700* ⊙*Daily 5 AM–10 PM*)

④ Treaty Oak. Many local legends attach themselves to Austin's most
★ famous tree. At least 500 years old, the live oak, on Baylor Street in
the West End between 5th and 6th streets, is the last survivor of a group
of trees known as the Council Oaks, used in ceremonies and meetings
by local Native American tribes. The tree's name derives from a legend
(which may or may not be true) that underneath its branches Stephen
F. Austin negotiated the first boundary agreement between the tribes
and settlers. In 1989 a disturbed individual attempted to poison the
tree with a powerful herbicide; he was later apprehended. Intensive
efforts to save the tree were successful, although nearly two-thirds of
the Treaty Oak died and it is now a shadow of its former self. Still,
it's well worth a visit to pay your respects to this venerable survivor.
⊠ *Treaty Oak Park, on Baylor between 5th and 6th St., Downtown
& Capitol Area.*

ALSO WORTH SEEING

① Umlauf Sculpture Garden and Museum. This pleasant space at the south
end of Zilker Park houses more than 130 works of sculptor Charles
Umlauf in the house where he lived and worked. Umlauf, who taught
at the University of Texas Art Department from 1941 to 1981, created
an incredibly diverse body of work that ranged in style from realistic
to abstract, using such materials as granite, marble, bronze, wood,
and terra-cotta. His subjects were equally wide-ranging, from religious
figures to nudes, from whimsical animals to family groupings. ⊠ *605
Robert E. Lee Rd., West Austin* ☏ *512/445–5582* ⊕ *www.umlauf
sculpture.org* ⊠ *$3.50* ⊙ *Wed.–Fri. 10–4:30, Sat.–Sun. 1–4:30.*

③ Zilker Botanical Gardens. Across from Zilker Park, this botanical garden
has more than 26 acres of horticultural delights, including butterfly trails
and Xeriscape gardens with native plants that thrive in an arid southwestern climate. ⊠ *2220 Barton Springs Rd., West Austin* ☏ *512/477–
8672* ⊕ *www.zilkergarden.org* ⊠ *Free* ⊙ *Daily 7 AM–6 PM.*

NORTH AUSTIN/HYDE PARK

One of Austin's oldest residential neighborhoods, Hyde Park is a calm
area near the University of Texas, filled with charming older houses.
North Austin will be familiar to most visitors via the I–35 corridor,
chockablock with hotels and motels of all sorts, but there's a lot more
to the neighborhood than that one relatively small part. North Austin may seem like one big commercial working-class strip (apart from
myriad medical offices, clinics, and hospitals), but it's also home to the
gourmet supermarket Central Market (Whole Foods' main competitor
in town), many interesting independent upscale shops, and some outstanding ethnic restaurants.

MAIN ATTRACTIONS

★ **Elisabet Ney Museum.** The 19th century lives on at this delightfully eccentric museum, where German Romanticism meets the Texas frontier.
The 70-plus sculptures and busts on display show an artist straining
against convention. The career of Ms. Ney began auspiciously in her
native Germany, where she sculpted eminent figures like the philoso-

pher Arthur Schopenhauer and Germany's "Iron Chancellor" Otto von Bismarck. A nonconformist from birth, Ney eventually tired of social mores on the continent and in 1871 moved to Georgia; two years later, she headed to East Texas. In the early 1890s, Ney, then in her late 50s, designed a house and studio in quiet Hyde Park, calling it Formosa, Portuguese for "beautiful." Over the next several years, Ney would produce some of her most renowned sculptures here, including those of Stephen F. Austin and Sam Houston. Her studio here is set up as she knew it, with sculpting tools, hat, teacup, and other items all in their proper places. The sculptures on view include many Texas heroes. ⊠ *304 E. 44th St., North Austin/Hyde Park* ☎ *512/458–2255* ⊕ *www. ci.austin.tx.us/elisabetney* ⊠ *Free* ⊗ *Wed.–Sat. 10–5, Sun. noon–5.*

☼ **The Republic of Texas Museum.** The Daughters of the Republic of Texas (which also oversees the Alamo in San Antonio), also headquartered in this building, maintains this collection of artifacts from the Republic of Texas era (1836–46), including hands-on exhibits like a scavenger hunt. ⊠ *510 E. Anderson Lane, North Austin/Hyde Park* ☎ *512/339– 1997* ⊕ *www.drt-inc.org/museum.htm* ⊠ *$2* ⊗ *Weekdays 10–4.*

ELSEWHERE IN AUSTIN

★ **Austin Museum of Art–Laguna Gloria.** Set on a lush Lake Austin peninsula, this 1915 Mediterranean-style villa was once home to Clara Driscoll Sevier, who led the fight to save the Alamo from demolition in the early 20th century. In this lovely if relatively diminutive setting, the museum showcases its expanding collection of 20th-century American paintings, sculpture, and photographs, and hosts outside exhibits and family-focused art programs. An art school shares the idyllic setting of this building, which is listed on the National Register of Historic Places. Staffers are extremely helpful and informative. ⊠ *3809 W. 35th St.* ☎ *512/458–8191* ⊕ *www.amoa.org* ⊠ *$3 suggested donation* ⊗ *Daily 11–4 (villa); Mon.–Sat. 9–5, Sun. 11–5 (grounds).*

Moore/Andersson Compound. A rather plebian, nondescript exterior belies the madcap, joyous interior of the former home and office compound of influential postmodern architect and teacher Charles W. Moore (1925–93). Called "a tiny village that wants to be a cathedral" and compared to such architectural treasures as Monticello and Frank Lloyd Wright's Taliesin, the compound of small houses was preserved in the nick of time following Moore's death, thanks to the Charles W. Moore Foundation. The current owners cooperate with the foundation in arranging tours (available by appointment only) and fund-raisers here. ⊠ *2102 Quarry Rd.* ☎ *512/220–7923* ⊠ *$25.*

☼ **Mount Bonnell.** Several miles northwest of Barton Creek Greenbelt stands Mount Bonnell. At 750 feet, the crag offers a sweeping panorama of Austin, the rolling hills to its west, and the Colorado River. You can't get much higher than this in the Austin area, and if the view itself doesn't convince you of that, the 100 steps to the top surely will. (Seriously, though, the short hike shouldn't present a problem to anyone in reasonably good shape.) ✉ *3800 Mount Bonnell Rd., off Scenic Dr.* ☎ *512/974–6700* 💲 *Free* ⊙ *Daily 5 AM–10 PM.*

BEYOND AUSTIN

Champion Park. Kids can dig for stone casts of dinosaur bones (specifically *Mosasuraus Maximus*) buried under sand at a covered children's playscape at this innovative park that opened in October 2007 in Austin's northwest suburbs. Features include a "whale's tail sprayscape" for cooling off overheated kids (and perhaps parents) on warm days, fabricated boulders for climbing, a fishing area, and a picnic pavilion. ✉ *3900 Brushy Creek Rd., Cedar Park* ☎ *512/260-42839.*

SHOPPING

The best way to plumb the depths of any city's character is to go shopping. And once you start browsing in Austin, you'll quickly discover that this city is quite the character.

Sure, Austin has the same chain stores that you'll find anywhere—but the city's true charm dwells in its independently owned establishments. To see the real Austin, browse the funky shops along revitalized South Congress, gaze at the hip downtown storefronts of the up-and-coming 2nd Street District, and stroll among the high-end galleries, antiques, and home-furnishings emporia of the West End. You can trek to legions of book, computer, and music stores, then peruse the handicrafts of local artisans. Along the way, fuel up on organic foods and fresh-roasted coffee.

Out in Northwest Austin and Round Rock, upscale shopping malls are popping up all over the place. The Domain in North Austin, which opened in 2007, is an ambitious project of mixed-use retail, office, and residential space that's extending the affluent downtown vibe practically into the suburbs.

All stores are open daily unless stated otherwise.

UNIVERSITY OF TEXAS

The Drag ((✉ *Guadalupe Street from Martin Luther King Jr. Blvd. to 26th St. and 3 blocks west to Rio Grande between 23rd and 26th streets on western edge of UT campus*)) elicits moans from people upset about its recent semi-invasion by outsiders like Starbucks and Urban Outfitters. But look closely; you'll find plenty of old-timers still around, selling books, imports, vintage clothing, gifts, and pizza by the slice. In truth, it hardly looks gentrified at all.

The crowd here is mostly students, so most shoppers and others you'll encounter are dressed casually or trendy on the hippy side, with a lot of backpacks slug across shoulders. Note that the Drag is not a good place to shop for clothes unless you're into the thrift-store and vintage-clothing look—or of course UT apparel. Books, however, you'll find aplenty.

■ TIP→ Note that parking on the surrounding streets is a chronic pain day or night, anytime school is in session. Within the UT campus, only a very small number of spots are not reserved for students or staff. A good bet for visitors is the San Antonio Parking Garage at 2420 San Antonio Street, one block from Guadalupe; it's a large, multilevel covered facility open weekdays only from 6 AM to 11 PM, with reasonable rates. Another option, this one open 24/7, is the Brazos Garage (at a central location at the south end of campus, at 210 E. MLK Blvd.).

BOOKS

If you want textbooks, you can find them on UT's campus at the University Co-Op (⇨ *UT Wear & Souvenirs, below*), but for general trade books, head to Follett's.

Follett's Intellectual Property. This two-story bookstore, formerly a Tower Records, sells trade books even though it's owned by a large retailer of college and other school textbooks. It's a great bookstore, with CDs, DVDs, a large magazine selection, and even computers. ⊠ *2401 Guadalupe St., University of Texas* ☎ *512/478–0007* ⊕ *www.intellectual propertyaustin.com.*

OPEN-AIR MARKET

★ **Renaissance Market.** This year-round open-air market with roots stretching back to the early '70s is the soul of the Drag. The unreconstructed hippie ambience is at least as much of a draw as the actual merchandise crafted and sold by various local artisans. The wares include jewelry, leatherwork, candles, photographs, paintings, sculpture, textiles, and the inevitable tie-dyed T-shirts. (Note that the market is firmly regulated by the city, and all vendors must be licensed by a commission.) ⊠ *Guadalupe St. at W. 23rd St., University of Texas* ☎ *No phone* ⊕ *www.austinartistsmarket.com.*

UT WEAR & SOUVENIRS

★ **The University Co-Op.** The beating burnt-orange heart of Longhorn Nation is on display at the ultimate showcase of UT sports paraphernalia. You can find burnt-orange-and-Longhorn-logo'd everything at this three-level emporium, from Crocs and dress shirts to bath mats, a full set of luggage, even a $350 pair of Lucchese cowboy boots and a $600 acoustic guitar. An entire room is devoted to children's wear, from the nursery on up. Founded in 1896 and modeled after a similar co-op at Harvard, UT's Co-Op (which offers discounts to faculty, students, and staff) claims to be the largest seller of used textbooks in the country. Even if you have no direct (or indirect) connection to UT, if you're in the neighborhood, do stop in; it's gawk-inducing and unforgettable. ⊠ *2246 Guadalupe St., University of Texas* ☎ *512/476–7211* ⊕ *www. universitycoop.com.*

TOYS & OTHER DIVERSIONS

Toy Joy. This fantastic place is so much the ultimate toy store of your

Fodor's Choice childhood fantasies that it's too good to save for actual children—don't

★ be embarrassed to come in even if you don't have little ones of your own. It's *the* place to get Marie Antoinette, Shakespeare, and Einstein action figures, red rubber duckies with devil horns, puppets of boxing nuns, repros of fave toys you played with as a kid, and floor-to-ceiling diversions for all ages, including science toys, metal robots, stuffed animals, hard-to-find candy, baubles and bangles, and more. On Fridays and Saturdays it's open until midnight. ⊠*2900 Guadalupe St., University of Texas* ☎*512/320–0090* ⊕*www.toyjoy.com.*

DOWNTOWN

Austin's vibrant downtown is home to too many businesses to list them all in this section, but as always, we've culled out the best places for your hard-earned dollars and shopping pleasure. Throngs of Austinites and visitors shop in downtown Austin every day, especially on the main thoroughfares like Lamar Boulevard, a long and diverse commercial strip, and on and near Congress Avenue, a stylish area featuring shops and galleries with high-quality goods. (Note that Congress Avenue south of the river is known as SoCo, or simply "The Avenue" by locals. *See the South Austin section below for shops in that neighborhood.)*

BOOKSTORES

Book People. Texas's largest independent bookstore is a home-grown alternative to the monster chain stores. It began in 1970 as Grok Books, and now stocks best-sellers along with books on topics such as women's studies, personal growth, and alternative home building; there's also a good children's section. Browse magazines; shop for quirky, hard-to-find gifts; and catch readings by local authors as well as literati like Richard Ford, Amy Tan, Jonathan Franzen, and David Sedaris. Former presidents Jimmy Carter and Bill Clinton and celebrities such as Lauren Bacall, David Byrne, and Jane Fonda have also made stops here while on book tours. ⊠*603 N. Lamar Blvd., Downtown & Capitol Area* ☎*512/472–5050* ⊕*www.bookpeople.com.*

GALLERIES

Authenticity Gallery. Colorful glass, ceramic, and metal *objets* and paintings from American and Canadian artists and artisans find a home in Mary Ober's sunny two-story gallery. Wooden items and art cards are also on view. ⊠*910 Congress Ave., Ste. 100, Downtown* ☎*512/478–2787* ⊕*www.authenticitygallery.com.*

OUTDOOR OUTFITTERS

Whole Earth Provision Co. South Congress gets more attention from travel writers, but stores like this huge, sun-filled and fun-filled outdoor/travel outfitters (the local branch of a Texas chain) are why Austinites prize North Lamar as a real-life shopping destination. It carries a lot of the same things you'd find at any REI—backpacks, tents, sleeping bags, running shoes, rugged clothing—but it's much more diverting in several ways: jazz is on the speakers, the front space is filled with kids' toys (and a few adults-only selections), and there's a good variety of books for all ages. The staff is laid-back, but friendly and ever-willing to help. The store also has branches on the UT campus (2410 San Antonio St.) and at the Westgate Mall (4477 South Lamar) in South Austin. ⊠*1014 N. Lamar Blvd., Downtown* ☎*512/476–1414* ⊕*www.wholeearthprovision.com.*

MUSIC

★ **Cheapo Discs.** Hunting for the really elusive CDs and LPs on your want list? If you can't find it at Waterloo, try Cheapo (and vice versa). A slightly more downscale version of Waterloo, Cheapo is a large, no-frills used-CD-and-LP emporium, where Austin goes to unload its unwanted music and look for replacements. The clerks will probably buy your used products, too—but don't expect to make a mint from 'em. The store hosts frequent free daytime live concerts, and it's open until midnight. ⊠*914 N. Lamar Blvd., Downtown* ☎*512/477–4499* ⊕*www.cheapotexas.com.*

FodorsChoice **Waterloo Records & Video.** This large independent shop is an Austin
★ institution that's been an integral part of the local music scene since 1982. Its outstanding selection, customer service, and free in-store concerts (including some pretty impressive names during SXSW week) mean it may be the only Austin record store you'll ever need. ⊠*600A N. Lamar Blvd., Downtown* ☎*512/474–2500* ⊕*www.waterloorecords.com.*

MARKETS

FodorsChoice **Whole Foods Market.** This 80,000-square-foot flagship store for the
★ natural/organic supermarket chain's world headquarters in downtown Austin is both a showcase for the company's philosophy and one of the most entertaining supermarkets you'll ever visit. It's been a major tourist attraction (we kid you not) since it opened in 2005. There are several places inside the massive store to enjoy a casual sit-down lunch, and the options are abundant, whether you're craving sushi, pizza, or seafood (we recommend the Fifth Street Seafood Corner). The store also has one of Austin's largest wine selections and a walk-in beer cooler (to keep those six-packs cold). There's ample free garage parking available. ⊠*525 N. Lamar Blvd., Downtown* ☎*512/476–1206* ⊕*www.wholefoods.com.*

NORTH AUSTIN

It's easy for newcomers to get a bit lost in North Austin, but if you know what you're looking for, you can find some great deals in antiques markets, bookstores, boutiques, and thrift stores.

Kerbey Lane/Jefferson Square (⊠*38th St. from N. Lamar Blvd. to Mopac*) is a seemingly infinite shopping district; it's hard to say where this area along 38th Street begins or ends. At the hub are the specialty shops along Kerbey Lane and in Jefferson Square that sell everything from pasta to dollhouses to fresh-roasted coffee to high-style fashions. Radiating from this center as far east as Central Market and as far west as Mopac are shops dedicated to gardening, architectural artifacts, ergonomic furniture, kids' clothing, plus much, much more. Most shops close on Sundays.

ANTIQUES

Antique Marketplace. More than 50 vendors spread out over nearly 20,000 square feet. Lose yourself in the vintage linens, lunchboxes, posters and postcards, and sparkling rhinestone jewelry scattered among the antique chests of drawers, cabinets, and tables. ⊠ *5350 Burnet Rd., North Austin* ☎ *512/452–1000.*

BOUTIQUES

Envie Boutique. Find elegant to whimsical women's fashions from such designers as Beth Bowley, Lewis Cho, and Rachel Pally, along with PJs, baby clothes, and small gift items at this little wooden-floored stone house near the corner of 49th Street and Burnet Road (across from the Omelettry restaurant). The dresses tend to be pricey, but watch for sales. ⊠ *4901 Woodrow Ave., North Austin* ☎ *512/371–1336* ⊕ *www.envieboutique.com.*

Lotus Boutique. Jennifer Brown, a former costume-and-art person for Austin moviemakers like Robert Rodriguez, opened this cheerful, bright space in the Rosedale neighborhood in 2007. Her hip, discerning sensibility leans to well-made items like Escama Studio purses crocheted from pull-tabs; Virgin, Saints, and Angels belt buckles from San Miguel de Allende, Mexico; jeans from Paris-based purveyor Notify; and other fine clothes, accessories, and scents to delight the eye, nose, and fingertips. ⊠ *4410 Burnet Rd., North Austin* ☎ *512/454–9700.*

MARKETS

♺ **Central Market.** This upscale, foodie-friendly offshoot of the giant Texas-
★ based H-E-B supermarket chain is a few years older than its competitor down Lamar Boulevard, Whole Foods, but no less popular (expect big weekend crowds). It's equally serious about the cheeses, wine, beer, meat, and deli products it purveys, but compared to Whole Foods it seems more like a place real people go to shop (rather than gawk). It's a great spot to grab prepared foods on the run (like the good multi-course brown-bagged Dinners for Two for $14), or join the weekday lunch crowds at the in-house café, where an outdoor patio pleases kids and where various bands play Friday through Sunday evenings. Flag down an on-staff "foodie" (yes, that's the official job title) if you have any questions. The market is in the Central Park Shopping Center, which also houses a number of chic craft galleries, boutiques, and gift shops. There's a newer branch of Central Market in far South Austin's Westgate area. ⊠ *4001 N. Lamar Blvd., North Austin* ☎ *512/206–1000* ⊠ *4477 S. Lamar Blvd., North Austin* ☎ *512/899–4300* ⊕ *www.centralmarket.com.*

THRIFT STORES

Top Drawer Thrift. Run by Project Transitions (an organization providing hospice, housing, and support to HIV/AIDS patients) as a funding source, this large store is fun and funky as all thrift shops should be. Go for posters, vintage costume jewelry, bric-a-brac, even used computer and stereo components. As you'd expect, everything is dirt-cheap. Every fourth Tuesday from 7 to 10 PM, Top Drawer hosts a Moonlight Madness sale with live music and all clothing marked down 50%. ⊠ *4902 Burnet Rd., North Austin* ☎ *512/454–5161* ⊕ *www.top drawerthrift.org.*

NORTHWEST AUSTIN

If at first glance Northwest Austin seems to you like an endless succession of malls and superstores, you're not alone—after all, this is the 'burbs, where family comes first and home improvement right after. But hey, you're reading this page because you want to shop, right? And in a shop-centered land like this, and in a consumer culture like this, you're bound to find some place in this area that strikes your fancy. Read on, intrepid shopper.

MALLS & DEPARTMENT STORES

The Arboretum at Great Hills. No longer considered the premier outdoor mall for well-heeled Austinites, the Arboretum lost some of its luster after the Domain opened. But Pottery Barn, Restoration Hardware, the Cheesecake Factory, Barnes & Noble, and the Sharper Image remain (for now), and the neighboring Renaissance Hotel is still doing booming business. The adjoining 95 acres of tree-studded parkland (for which the center is named) make this a lovely place to while away an hour—or three. Don't miss the life-size marble cow sculptures. ⊠ *10000 Research Blvd., at Great Hills Dr. and Capitol of Texas Highway, Northwest Austin* ☎ *512/338–4437.*

Austin Chinatown Center. This modern, 750,000-square-foot open-air mall is almost completely occupied by Asian businesses (mainly Chinese and Vietnamese), including restaurants, a travel agency, and retail outlets selling clothing, jewelry, and videos. The mall's cornerstone is the 55,000-square-foot MT (My Thanh) Supermarket, which stocks all manner of Asian foods and related items. Dining standouts include First Chinese BBQ and Pho Saigon; though a bit short on atmosphere, both eateries deliver well-prepared, simply presented lunch plates and noodle-based soups at easy-to-digest prices. ⊠ *10901 N. Lamar Blvd.* ⊕ *www.chinatownaustin.com* ☉ *Center is open daily, but some stores close one day a week* ☎ *No phone.*

The Domain. A postmodern vision of an affluent downtown district, the Domain is home to Neiman Marcus, Tiffany & Co., the Apple Store, and other name-brand shops that cater to the platinum-card set. Those on more modest budgets should check out kitchenware emporium Sur La Table, Macy's, and the large, cheerful Borders. Some complain that there's very little Austin-specific about the open-air Domain, but it's a pleasant place to spend a few hours (if only to gawk at the pricey goods in the windows). Domain II, the complex's second shopping area, is slated to open toward the end of 2009, nearly doubling the Domain's space. ⊠ *11410 Century Oaks Terrace, along North MoPac (Loop 1) between Braker La. and Burnet Rd., near the North Austin IBM campus* ☎ *512/795–4230* ⊕ *www.simon.com.*

SECOND STREET DISTRICT

One of Austin's newest neighborhoods, this showcase downtown area around City Hall is tiny—only about two blocks deep by 3½ blocks wide—and still doesn't seem quite real, but it's an admittedly beguiling place to stroll among the boutiques, home-furnishings stores, and bistros among a young, happening, and beautiful downtown crowd. Incidentally, the entire district is managed (and much is owned) by AMLI, a large Chicago-based development firm.

BOUTIQUES

Peyton's Place. This modest-size gem of a boutique on the edge of the district is notable for its affordable prices and friendly staff. Whether you're a hip, young, and swingin' gal in the city or just, well, hip, it's worth checking out its black jeans, little black dresses, red silk thingies, and other accessories and shoes. During the January clearances, some items get discounted by up to 75%. ⊠*215 Lavaca St., Second Street District* ☎*512/477–5224* ⊕*www.peytonsplaceaustin.com.*

SOUTH AUSTIN

South Congress (⊠*S. Congress Ave. from Lady Bird Lake [formerly Town Lake] to Oltorf St.*), or SoCo as locals call it, reflects South Austin's dual passions: bohemian counterculture and recycled style. You'll find truckloads of funky furniture and vintage collectibles, folk art, herbs, natural-fiber clothing, costumes, toys, cowboy boots, and Mexican imports amid a scattering of see-and-be-seen cafés and restored motor courts. The wildly colorful and imaginative storefronts on a few of the blocks (you'll know them when you see them) are natural photo ops. Many stores on this wide boulevard open after 11 AM and stay open late. On the first Thursday of each month about 50 merchants here stay open until 10 PM, and special events create a street-party vibe. SoCo is the poster street for a freewheeling neighborhood that's as much a state of mind as a ZIP code.

IMPORTS

Mi Casa Gallery. Perhaps Austin's premier outlet for quality and unusual Mexican arts and crafts, Mi Casa goes far beyond your usual Mexican-imports souvenir shop. On-site are contemporary paintings and sculpture, painted furniture, religious art, copperware, ceramics, and much more. It's a great place to shop for gifts for folks back home. ⊠*1700 S. Congress Ave., South Austin* ☎*512/707–9797* ⊕*www.micasagallery.com.*

Fodor'sChoice **Tesoros Trading Co.** The buyers for this large, independently owned
★ world-market store comb the planet for colorful and unusual examples of folk art. Chinese gongs, Nepalese jewelry, Vietnamese hand-painted bamboo curtains, Turkish textiles, and lots of Mexican items (including *milagros,* postcards, and rather tacky calendars) are just a few of the goodies stashed away in this delightful place. ⊠*1500 S. Congress Ave., South Austin* ☎*512/479–8377* ⊕*www.tesoros.com* ⊙*Daily, 11-6.*

BOOTS & WESTERN WEAR

Allens Boots. A South Congress landmark for decades, Allens is impossible to miss: just look for the huge red boot above the door. Set amid trendy, touristy SoCo, Allens is anything but. More than a dozen brands of cowboy boots (including Durango, Frye, Justin, Lucchese, Sendra, and Tony Lama) are displayed on rows upon rows of shelves, along with other Western wear. If you're a newcomer to the boot world, study Allens' Web site before your visit for some basics on proper fit. A second store is located north of Austin in Round Rock. ⊠*1522 S. Congress Ave., South Austin* ☎*512/447–1413* ⊠*1051 S. I–35 (just off I–35 to the north at the Round Rock exit), Round Rock* ☎*512/310–7600* ⊕*www.allensboots.com.*

> ## TOWN LAKE BECOMES LADY BIRD LAKE
>
> Lady Bird Lake, a reservoir on the Colorado River, used to be called Town Lake. In July 2007 the Austin City Council voted to rename it in honor of the former first lady who had died earlier that month. The council cited Lady Bird Johnson's tireless efforts to beautify the lake and Austin as reason for the name change.
>
> "Lady Bird Johnson transformed Town Lake from a garbage-strewn eyesore into Austin's scenic and recreational centerpiece," said council member Brewster McCracken. "Town Lake, and life in Austin, wouldn't be the same without her vision."

WEST AUSTIN

The main neighborhood to visit in West Austin is the **West End** (⊠ *W. 6th St. west of N. Lamar Blvd. to W. Lynn St.*) It's a grown-up neighborhood in a town where thrill-seeking college students compose one-tenth of the population. Long-standing merchants sell art, antiques, and collectibles from shops housed in cottages and storefronts built in the 1930s and 1940s. They've been joined by a rash of newcomers, housed in the multistory buildings springing up on street corners once occupied by car dealerships. Good cafés and restaurants added to the mix make the West End one of Austin's most delightful neighborhoods to stroll through for an hour, or an afternoon.

GALLERIES

★ **Artworks.** When you absolutely have to have that $195 Elizabethan-style garnet-topaz-and-crystal letter opener with matching magnifying glass, this is where you can get it. This large, modern space offers contemporary art, custom framing, and art restoration; but it's the large selection of knockout contemporary art glass of the highest quality (including huge pieces of Murano glass) that really sets apart this gallery. Founded in 1985, it also carries exceptional crafts from throughout the world, plus small bronzes and exquisite stemware. ⊠*1214 W. 6th St., West End* ☎*512/472–1550* ⊙ *Closed Sun.* ⊕*www.artworksaustin.com.*

OUTSIDE AUSTIN

Founded in the 1850s and known in Western lore as the site of an infamous 1878 shootout between Texas Rangers and stagecoach/train robber Sam Bass (Bass lost, and is buried here), the prosperous city of Round Rock, 19 mi north of downtown Austin, is today best known as the home base of computer manufacturer Dell Inc. To Austinites, if Round Rock isn't where they work, it's a place to see baseball (at the Dell Diamond, home of the Round Rock Express, ⇨ *See Sports & the Outdoors*) or do some serious shopping.

IKEA. When this well-known, extremely-big-box Swedish home furnishings retailer opened in November 2006, it sent shivers throughout Austin's retail furniture establishment. The 250,000-square-foot outlet is located about 22 mi north of downtown Austin, just off I–35. Set aside at least two hours to wander through the store (you have to follow certain paths to get from one end to the other). IKEA also has a decent and very low-priced café, where you can get one of the best cups of coffee in town for less than a buck. ⊠ *1 IKEA Way, Round Rock* ☎ *512/828–4532* ⊕ *www.ikea.com.*

Round Rock Premium Outlets You should be able to find just about anything you're looking for at this 125-store complex straddling the east side of I–35 northbound. Designer fashions, sportswear, and shoes are particularly strong; also here are leather goods, housewares, children's clothing, and more. ⊠ *4401 N. I–35, Round Rock* ☎ *512/863–6688.*

SPORTS & THE OUTDOORS

With its lakes, abundant greenbelts and parks, and miles of hike-and-bike trails—not to mention year-round mild and mostly sunny weather (searingly hot summers and occasional gully washers aside)—Austin and its surroundings are made for outdoor enthusiasts and weekend athletes of all ages and abilities. Whether you live to run marathons, climb rocks, or just stroll through a wildflower garden, Austin's got you covered.

Although the city lacks major-league pro sports teams, fervor for UT's football team, a perennial collegiate top contender, fills the gap to such an extent that many Austinites avoid driving downtown on UT home game days, when thousands of faithful who "bleed orange" are visibly (and audibly) out and about. The team won the national championship in 2005 (the fourth in Longhorns history, and its first since 1970). UT's baseball team also won the collegiate title that year, its sixth overall since 1949. As for other spectator sports, Austin is home to minor-league basketball, hockey, and arena football teams, and nearby Round Rock hosts the Express Triple-A baseball team.

Just outside of Austin, opportunities for prime fishing, hunting, and lakeside activities are abundant. Outdoor types might consider outfitting themselves for a Central Texas excursion at Cabela's in Buda, a full-service retail store about 15 mi south of Austin en route to San Antonio.

ANNUAL SPORTING EVENTS

Clyde Littlefield Texas Relays. One of the top track and field events in the U.S., the Texas Relays are held in early April at Mike A. Myers Stadium at the University of Texas. The Relays, founded in 1925, attract about 5,000 of the best athletes in Texas (and elsewhere) on the high-school, collegiate, and professional levels. Tickets can be purchased about a month prior to the competition. ☎512/471–3333 ⊕www.texasboxoffice.com for tickets, ⊕www.texassports.com for general information.

Red Eye Regatta. Every January 1st since 1976, the Austin Yacht Club starts the year off with this popular sailboat race on Lake Travis (about a half-hour from downtown Austin). ☎512/266–1336 ⊕www.austin yachtclub.net.

Republic of Texas Biker Rally. Every June, tens of thousands of bikers invade Austin for three days of partying, camping, talking shop, and browsing vendors' wares. Based at the Travis County Expo Center just east of the city, the event includes a huge Friday-evening motorcycle parade from the Expo Center to Congress Avenue with much of Austin looking on, and much partying ensuing (both during and afterward) among bikers and spectators alike on 6th Street. There are also free concerts by local musicians Thursday through Saturday at the Expo Center rally grounds. On its more than 300 acres, the Expo Center provides special lots for RV and tent camping. Other bikers also stay in off-site RV lots and, of course, in hotels. On-site facilities include hot and cold showers, food service, a first-aid station, and a FedEx/UPS drop site. ☎512/252–9768 ⊕www.rotrally.com. .

☽ **Star of Texas Fair & Rodeo.** Did you come to Texas to see some real cowboy stuff? Austin puts on its hat and boots at this very popular perennial affair. The event, held at the Travis County Expo Center, typically runs from the last day of February through the first half of March. It includes an indoor rodeo, a livestock and horse show, various Texas-style cook-offs, and a carnival. Entertainment ranges from name acts like Willie Nelson, George Jones, and Styx to more than 40 local bands. Proceeds go toward scholarships and youth-education programs. ☎512/919–3000 for information, 512/477–6060 for tickets ⊕www.staroftexas.org.

BICYCLING

As you might expect, Lance Armstrong's home base is a great bicycling town. The scenic back roads offer gently rolling hills and tempting diversions—from tucked-away waterfalls to country antiques emporia to barbecue joints. **Loop 360** provides a grueling workout, while the **hike-and-bike trail** around Lady Bird Lake is more leisurely. And the **Lance Armstrong Bikeway,** which at this writing was expected to open in spring 2008, runs east-to-west on a dedicated route through downtown. The path uses a combination of off-street concrete trails, on-street striped bike lanes, and on-street signed bike routes.

Lance Armstrong: His Uphill Battles

Once upon a time, in the world of cycling Lance Armstrong was always near the top, but could never quite get there—especially when it came to the Tour de France, the sport's premier event. And then he got cancer. The rest is history: seven straight yellow jerseys from the Tour, the most ever. Now retired from the cycling world, he barnstorms the planet on behalf of cancer research. The yellow "LIVESTRONG" bands that his founda-tion sold adorn celebrity wrists and started a cottage industry of silicone bracelets. But more than anything, Armstrong used sheer will and his bicycle to give hope to millions of people with cancer. His foundation has raised more than $150 million, which to Armstrong might mean even more than his seven Tour de France victories.

—Lisa Miller

SOUTH AUSTIN

The Veloway. This 3.1-mile paved asphalt loop winding through Slaughter Creek Metropolitan Park is reserved exclusively for bicyclists and rollerbladers. Riders always travel in a one-way clockwise direction. It's off the beaten path in far southwest Austin, not far from the Lady Bird Johnson Wildflower Center. No facilities except for a water fountain that sometimes doesn't work. ⊠*4103 Slaughter La.* ☎*512/974–6700* ⊕*www.veloway.com.*

OUTFITTER

Bicycle Sport Shop (⊠*517 S. Lamar78704* ☎*512/477–3472* ⊠*10947 Research Blvd., Northwest Austin* ☎*512/345–7460* ⊕*www.bicycle sportshop.com*) rents bikes and helmets daily, year-round.

BOATING

⇨*See Zilker Park under Natural Areas & Parks.*

DOWNTOWN/CAPITOL AREA

Capital Cruises. From March through October, this downtown-based company offers nightly bat-watching cruises from an electric paddlewheel boat, along with sightseeing, dinner, and lunch cruises on Lady Bird Lake. Cruise prices vary, but start at $8 for adults. Charters are available. The company also rents canoes, pedal boats, and kayaks beginning at $10 an hour, and Duffy electric launches (seating up to 10) beginning at $45 an hour. ⊠*208 Barton Springs Rd.* ☎*512/480–9264* ⊕*www.capitalcruises.com.*

Lone Star Riverboat. This double-decker paddlewheel riverboat sails every evening for hour-long bat-watching cruises March through October, and every weekend for 1½-hour sightseeing cruises. Tours are $8 or $9. ⊠*Docked on the south shore of Lady Bird Lake between the Hyatt hotel and South First Street Bridge* ☎*512/327–1388* ⊕*www. lonestarriverboat.com.*

BATTY AUSTIN

The world's largest urban bat colony—750,000 Mexican free-tailed bats—hangs out beneath Austin's Congress Avenue Bridge from April through October. Once considered a nuisance, they're now prized as a tourist attraction and municipal symbol. Visitors and locals alike flock downtown to claim a spot before dusk and watch the tiny (and rather smelly) winged critters make their dramatic appearance against the setting sun.

The best viewing spots are from the hike-and-bike trail by the bridge, or from the patio of Shoreline Grill, adjacent to the Four Seasons hotel

(⇨ *Where to Eat*). If you're staying lakeside at the Four Seasons or Radisson hotel (⇨ *Where to Stay*), there are excellent vantage points from some rooms and public spaces, as well as from T.G.I. Friday's at the Radisson. Watching the bats from the lake aboard a paddlewheel cruise ship (⇨ *Boating under Sports & the Outdoors*) is a classy way to go. For a real budget option, there are the pedestrian walkways on both sides of the bridge itself, but arrive early (as much as an hour ahead) in peak season, as it gets crowded; many bring a light folding chair and refreshments and settle in for the duration.

WEST AUSTIN

Daybreak Boat Rentals & Golf Park. On Lake Travis, Daybreak rents pontoons, ski boats, and waverunners, plus a party boat. Hourly prices begin at $55 for pontoons, $75 for ski boats, and $135 for a party boat (including captain). Ask about discounts for longer rentals. ✉ *5171 Hi-Line* ☎ *512/266–2176* ⊕ *www.daybreakboatrentals.com.*

Lakeway Marina. Adjacent to the Lakeway Resort and Spa (⇨ *Where to Stay*), this marina on Lake Travis rents ski boats, pontoon boats, and waverunners. Hourly rates begin at $75 for pontoon boats and waverunners, $80 for ski boats $80; ask about discounts for longer rentals. Also available are fishing guides, beginning at $225 for two people for four hours. The marina is open daily. ✉ *103A Lakeway Dr.* ☎ *512/261–7511* ⊕ *www.lwmarina.biz.*

GOLF

WEST AUSTIN

Barton Creek Resort & Spa. This resort is associated with four private courses, including two of the top-ranked courses in Texas, Fazio Foothills and Fazio Canyons. Unfortunately, you either have to be a member or a hotel guest (⇨ *Where to Stay*) to play here. Greens fees vary widely by season, day of the week, and time of day, but for resort guests the Fazio Canyons and Fazio Foothills courses run from $80 (twilight) to $250 per person, including a forecaddie (but not gratuity). The Crenshaw Cliffside course runs from $60 to $180 (forecaddie not required) and the Palmer Lakeside course from $45 to $155 (forecaddie not required). Various golf packages are also available throughout the year;

check Web site for details. ⊠*8212 Barton Club Dr.* ☎*512/329–4000 or 800/336–6158* ⊕*www.bartoncreek.com/golf.*

A **forecaddie** (also spelled forecaddy) makes suggestions on shots, and help keep the game from delays by running ahead of a golfing foursome to perform such tasks as finding stray balls and raking traps. A forecaddie does not carry any of the players' clubs.

Lions Municipal Golf Course. The likes of Ben Crenshaw, Tom Kite, and Ben Hogan are among those who have played at this affordable 6,001-yard, par-71 public course in West Austin. It was originally built by the Lions Club in 1928 and taken over by the city six years later. It is open daily, dawn to dusk. Greens fees run $7–$20. Cart fees are $22. ⊠*2901 Enfield Rd.* ☎*512/477–6963* ⊕*www.ci.austin.tx.us/parks/ lions.htm.*

NORTHEAST AUSTIN

☺ **Harvey Penick Golf Campus.** Named for a legendary local golf instructor, Harvey Penick opened in 2005 in northeast Austin as a "First Tee" course for the specific purpose of teaching golf to young people (though golfers of all ages and abilities can play). The 112-acre, 9-hole, par-30, PGA Tour–designed course is next door to the East Communities YMCA. Lessons are offered. There's also a driving range and short course. Greens fees are $12 for 9 holes, $18 for 18 holes. Youth pay less. Cart fees are $8.75 for 9 holes, and $13.50 for 18 holes. ⊠*5501 Ed Bluestein Blvd.* ☎*512/926–1100* ☾*Daily, 7–7.*

NATURAL AREAS & PARKS

Austin has more than 200 parks within the city limits. Amenities in the parks range from playgrounds, swimming pools, and skate parks (the city's first was established at Maybel Davis District Park in south Austin) to artwork and historic sites, such as Umlauf Sculpture Garden at Zilker Park and Treaty Oak Square in northwest Austin.

DOWNTOWN

Austin Nature and Science Center. Adjacent to the Zilker Botanical Gardens *(⇨ See Zilker Park below)*, this complex has an 80-acre preserve trail, interactive exhibits in the Discovery Lab that teach about the ecology of the Austin area, and animal exhibits focusing on subjects such as bees and birds of prey. ⊠*301 Nature Center Dr.* ☎*512/327–8180* ⊕*www.ci.austin.tx.us/ansc* ⊡*Suggested donation of $2 per adult and $1 per child* ☾*Mon.–Sat. 9–5, Sun. 12–5.*

NORTH AUSTIN

Mount Bonnell. Rising to a height of 785 feet, Mount Bonnell offers the best views of Austin. Stop by during the day for a glimpse of the sweeping panorama of rolling hills, the Colorado River and the 360 Bridge, and the downtown skyline in the distance. It's an easy climb up from a parking area near the road (more of a diversion than a serious hike); you'll find students, lovers, families, picnickers and just plain old tourists here. ⊠*Mount Bonnell Rd., off E. 35th St.* ☎*817/265–7721 or 800/433–5374* ⊡*Free* ☾*Daily, dawn to dusk.*

WEST AUSTIN/ZILKER PARK

Zilker Park. The former site of temporary Franciscan missions in 1730 and a former American Indian gathering place is now Austin's everyday backyard park. The 351-acre site along the shores of Lady Bird Lake includes Barton Springs Pool (⇨ *See Swimming below*), numerous gardens, a meditation trail, and a Swedish log cabin dating from the 1840s. Canoe rentals are available for the hour or day (⊕ *www. zilkerboats.com*). In March, the park hosts a kite festival (2008 saw the 80th edition). During spring months, concerts are held in the park's Beverly S. Sheffield Zilker Hillside Theater, a natural outdoor

AUSTIN'S BIG 10K

Austin is a runner's kind of town, and space forbids our listing every one of the 5K and 10K races held every year. However, we must mention the Statesman Capitol 10K in late March. Sponsored by the *Austin American-Statesman* newspaper, it's Texas's largest footrace, with as many participants as meters (10,000). ☎ *512/478–4265 (AT&T Austin Marathon) and 512/445–3598 (Capitol 10K)* ⊕ *www.attaustinmarathon.com and* ⊕ *www.cap10k. com.*

amphitheater beneath a grove of century-old pecan trees; in July and August, musicals and plays take over. Umlauf Sculpture Garden & Museum, at the park's southern end, displays 130 or more works by sculptor and former UT art professor Charles Umlauf. Art workshops for both kids and adults are occasionally offered. ✉ *2201 Barton Springs Rd.* ☎ *512/974–6700 (Parks Dept.), 512/477–5335 (theater), 512/445–5582 (museum)* ⊕ *www.ci.austin.tx.us/zilker* 🎟 *Free (main park), parking $3 per vehicle; $3.50 (museum)* ☉ *Daily, dawn to dusk (park); Wed.–Fri. 10–4:30, Sat.–Sun. 1–4:30 (museum).*

WEST LAKE

Barton Creek Greenbelt. This park follows the contour of Barton Creek and the canyon it created west along a 7.9 mi area from Zilker Park to west of Loop 360. It has a trail for hiking and biking, plus swimming holes when the creek is full (very rain-dependent, it's usually in spring and fall). ✉ *Access points: Zilker Park, Loop 360, Twin Falls, and Scottish Woods Trail Falls (near the intersection of MoPac and Loop 360), and Scottish Woods Trail (at the trail's northern border off Loop 360)* ☎ *512/499–6700 or 512/472–1267* 🎟 *Free* ☉ *5 AM–10 PM.*

Wild Basin Wilderness Preserve. Stunning contrasting views of the Hill Country and the Austin skyline make it worth the trip to this area near the 360 Bridge. You can wander along 227 acres of walking trails (there are 10 different ones); guided tours are offered on weekends. The cool folks at Wild Basin offer numerous outdoor-oriented classes, nighttime stargazing sessions, even concerts by well-known touring musicians. ✉ *805 N. Capitol of Texas Hwy.* ☎ *512/327–7622* ⊕ *www.wildbasin. org* 🎟 *$3 suggested donation, $4 guided hikes (weekends and by reservation only)* ☉ *Daily, dawn to dusk (park); daily 9–4 (office), Tues.–Sun. 9–4 (gift shop).*

SOUTH AUSTIN

Lady Bird Johnson Wildflower Center. This 43-acre complex, founded in 1982 by Lady Bird Johnson and actress Helen Hayes, has extensive plantings of native Texas wildflowers that bloom year-round (although spring is an especially attractive time). The grounds include a visitor center, nature trail, observation tower, elaborate stone terraces, and flower-filled meadows. ⊠*4801 LaCrosse Ave.* ☎*512/292–4100* ⊕*www.wildflower.org* ⊴*$7* ☉*Tues.–Sun. 9–5:30.*

OUTSIDE AUSTIN

McKinney Falls State Park. This 744-acre state park is 13 mi southeast of downtown Austin. Per the name, the park has two waterfalls (visitors should exercise extreme caution near the water, as people have drowned here). A 4.5-mi nature trail is used for hiking and biking. Other popular activities in the park are fishing, picnicking, camping, and wildlife-viewing (including bird-watching and sightings of white-tailed deer, raccoons, squirrels, and armadillos). ⊠*5808 McKinney Falls Pkwy., off U.S. 183* ☎*512/243–1643* ⊕*www.tpwd.state.tx.us/ spdest/findadest/parks/mckinney_falls* ⊴*$2* ☉*Daily, dawn to dusk.*

SPELUNKING

☾ **Inner Space Cavern.** This Mesozoic-era karst cavern 24 mi north of Austin was discovered in 1963 and opened to the public three years later. Visitors access the entrance via cable car and can choose from two trails, one that is .75 mi and another that's 1.2 mi. Tours vary in length (and price), from just a little over an hour to nearly four hours. The temperature is a year-round 72°. Kids get discounted admission; the three- to four-hour tour is for ages 13 and older only. On Saturdays, reservations are required and groups can be no larger than four. ■TIP➔ Sometimes there are $1 coupons on the Web site. ⊠*4200 S. I–35, Georgetown* ☎*512/931–2283* ⊕*www.innerspace.com* ⊴*$15–$100 depending on tour* ☉*Mid-May–early Sept., daily 9–6; early Sept.–mid-May, Mon.–Fri. 9–4, Sat.–Sun. 10–5.*

SWIMMING

☾ **Barton Springs Pool.** When those summer days get hotter than a potter's
★ furnace, dip into Zilker Park's 300-yard-long, spring-fed swimming pool, a favorite with locals. The clear springs produce from 12 million to 90 million gallons in any 24-hour period, the water always a rather cool 66° to 70°. ⊠*Zilker Park, 2201 Barton Springs Rd.* ☎*512/476–9044* ⊕*www.ci.austin.tx.us/parks/bartonsprings.htm* ⊴*Free (Nov.–Mar.), $3 rest of year* ☉*Hours vary. Closed 3 weeks in Feb. and Mar. for spring cleaning*

SPECTATOR SPORTS

The Round Rock Express. Next to UT football, Austin's most popular spectator sport may be the Round Rock Express baseball team, a AAA affiliate of the Houston Astros. The Express (owned by a group led by Hall of Fame pitcher Nolan Ryan) began in 2000 as a AA team, and moved up to AAA in 2005. It plays 72 home games from April through September at the Dell Diamond, an extremely pleasant place to pass a few hours, no matter who's winning. The open-air stadium seats about 8,600 with room for more in an outfield grass berm area. No ticket costs more than $12 (as of 2008), and it's hard to find a bad seat in this very fan-friendly (and family-friendly) ballpark. ✉*3400 E. Palm Valley Blvd., Round Rock* ☎*512/255–2255* ⊕*www.roundrock express.com* .

The Austin Ice Bats. This minor-league hockey team plays at the Chaparral Ice Arena (near Pflugerville) from October through March. The team logo is a very cool visual of a shrieking, flying bat wielding a hockey stick; buy a jersey and wow 'em back home. ✉*14200 N. IH–35, Pflugerville* ☎*512/927–7825* ⊕*www.icebats.com.*

The Austin Toros. Formerly the Columbus (Georgia) Riverdragons, the Toros, a team in the NBA's Development League, or "D-League," was rebranded when it moved to Austin in 2005. Affiliated with (and owned by) the San Antonio Spurs, the Toros play home games November through April at the Austin Convention Center. ✉*7800 Shoal Creek Blvd., Ste. 115W, Downtown & Capitol Area* ☎*512/236–8333* ⊕*www.nba.com/dleague/austin.*

The Austin Wranglers. This arena football expansion team began play in 2004, and moved down from the AFL to af2 (the minor leagues) beginning in the 2008 season. The team plays from April to July. Home games are at UT's Frank Erwin Center. ✉*1701 Red River St., University of Texas* ☎*512/339–3939* ⊕*www.austinwranglers.com.*

ARTS & ENTERTAINMENT

By Jessica Norman Dupuy

Even when Austin was a backwater burg, it enjoyed a modicum of culture thanks to the University of Texas. The city's current culture vultures are still indebted to the construction-crazed university for its state-of-the-art concert halls like the Bass, which can accommodate grand symphonic, operatic, and theatrical performances. But in a town as creatively charged as Austin, the venues are virtually limitless, from hillsides in parks to the pavement of the Congress Avenue Bridge and from dark, smoky clubs to Victorian Gothic cathedrals.

Numerous traveling and homegrown bands play nightly in the city's music venues, many of which are clustered around downtown's 6th Street, between Red River Street and Congress Avenue. While not as famous as Bourbon Street in New Orleans, 6th Street has an entertaining mix of comedy clubs, blues bars, electronica, and dance clubs. It's also the site of two "Old Pecan Street" outdoor fairs, held in May and September, with live bands, food vendors, and craftspeople.

College students are a large presence on 6th, but the Warehouse District around 4th Street and the newer 2nd Street District (which runs between San Antonio Street and Congress Avenue for two blocks north of the river) cater to a more mature crowd looking for good food and great drinks. South Congress also has a lively scene, especially on the first Thursday of each month, when vendors set up booths with art, jewelry, and a variety of other creations all along the street. The shops stay open late, and bands perform live along the streets. (Warning: parking during "First Thursdays" is a challenge. Expect to park many blocks back and walk.)

Austin's cultural scene is getting a facelift with the opening of three major arts-related venues. The $14.7-million renovation of the Bass Concert Hall at the University of Texas Performing Arts Center (UT PAC) is set to be completed by late 2008; it will feature a five-story atrium; new seating, flooring, and lighting; better acoustics; and a restaurant. The first phase of the Mexican-American Cultural Center (MACC) on Lady Bird Lake (formerly, and still frequently referred to by locals as, Town Lake) at River Street, opened in September 2007; the MACC will eventually offer 126,000 square feet for exhibits, performances, private events, and classes. And the Joe R. and Teresa Lozano Long Center for the Performing Arts, also on Lady Bird Lake, opened in March 2008 as part of a 54-acre cultural park.

To find out who's playing where, pick up the *Austin Chronicle* (a free alternative weekly) or "XLent," a Thursday supplement to the *Austin American Statesman.* Most of the larger venues in Austin sell tickets through **Front Gate Tickets** (☎512/389–0315 ⊕*www.fronttickets.com*). But **AusTix** (☎512/474–8497 ⊕*www.austix.com*) is a good resource for theater as well as smaller dance and music performances. Meanwhile, **GetTix** (☎866/443–8849 ⊕*www.gettix.net*) is a smaller purveyor of advance tickets in Austin, but sells for popular venues such as La Zona Rosa, Austin Music Hall, and Emo's.

> **DID YOU KNOW?**
>
> The Austin City Limits Festival was inspired by the hit PBS show "Austin City Limits," a homegrown Public Television show that has run for more than 30 years and is known as the longest-running concert music program in the country. Taped in a small studio at KLRU, the Austin PBS affiliate on UT Campus, this acclaimed show hosts a wide range of country, rock, blues, jazz, and folk musicians. Legends Stevie Ray Vaughan, Johnny Cash, and Ray Charles once graced this tiny stage as did Buena Vista Social Club, Tracy Chapman, and Lyle Lovett.

PERFORMING ARTS

THEATER & DANCE

The Long Center for the Performing Arts. The opera scene is alive and well in Austin with the help of this expansive venue along the shores of Lady Bird Lake. With much anticipation from the city of Austin, the Joe R. and Teresa Lozano Long Center opened its doors in the spring of 2008, playing host to a wide variety of performing arts groups. It also serves as the permanent home to: **Austin Symphony Orchestra** (☎512/476–6064 ⊕*www.austinsymphony.org*); **Austin Lyric Opera** (☎512/472–5927

CLOSE UP

Festivals with a Beat

In the self-proclaimed Live Music Capital of the world, it's needless to say the two largest festivals in town are all about music.

SEPTEMBER

Austin City Limits Music Festival. Austinites love any excuse to party outside, especially when music is involved. This unofficial farewell-to-summer shindig takes over Zilker Park for three days in late September. Fans come to hear 130 international, national, and local bands on eight stages. Performers have included the likes of Bob Dylan, Coldplay, Tom Petty, Bjork, the White Stripes, Sheryl Crow, Lucinda Williams, Steve Earle, and the Indigo Girls. ✉ *2100 Barton Springs Rd., West Austin/Zilker Park* ☎ *512/389–0315* ⊕ *www.aclfestival. com* 🎫 *$50–$120.*

MARCH

South by Southwest. The grand-daddy of all music fests arrives in early spring. Usually shortened to SXSW, this event's festivals and conferences combine to form a huge music, film, and interactive extravaganza. In addition to all the fans, SXSW brings a fleet of hundreds of hopeful musicians, producers, and record

Rock, country, folk, hip-hop, jazz, fusion... whatever your preferred music genre, you'll find it in Austin.

label execs to Austin to perform and network. It's such a take-over-the-city event that many Austin families evacuate town to some far-off spring break destination. Hotel rooms are scarce, restaurants and bars are packed, and everything from SXSW VIPs to plain, music-loving plebeians mix and mingle in expectation of finding "the next big thing." ■ TIP→First-time participants should know that it pays to be organized in terms of the bands you want to see since SXSW happens all over town. ✉ *Throughout Austin* ☎ *512/467–7979* ⊕ *www.sxsw.com* 🎫 *$130–$175.*

⊕ *www.austinlyricopera.org*), Austin's premiere opera company putting on three productions a year for the past 20 years; and **Ballet Austin** (☎ *512/476–2163* ⊕ *www.balletaustin.org*). The Long Center for the Performing Arts also houses a wing for community arts education programs. ✉ *701 W. Riverside Dr., South Austin* ☎ *512/482–0800* ⊕ *www.thelongcenter.org.*

Paramount Theatre. A restored downtown vaudeville house and movie palace, this gorgeous 1915 theater presents musicals and plays by touring theater companies and hosts concerts by well-known jazz, folk, and rock artists, along with the occasional stand-up comedian. ✉ *713 Congress Ave., Downtown & the Capitol* ☎ *512/472–5470* ⊕ *www. austintheatre.org.*

Zachary Scott Theatre. Local theater thrives at this center named for an Austin native who was successful in 1930s Hollywood. ✉ *1510 Toomey Rd., South Austin* ☎ *512/476–0541* ⊕ *www.zachscott.com.*

Zilker Theatre Productions. Bring a blanket and picnic basket and enjoy a Broadway-inspired musical under the warm Texas sky. The summer-only shows are pay-as-you-wish admission. ✉ *2201 Barton Springs Rd., West Austin/Zilker Park* ☎ *512/479–9491* ⊕ *www.zilker.org.*

FILM

Alamo Drafthouse. Only in Austin will you find the original concept for this theater experience, where dinner, a movie, and a bucket of beer all happen in one place. At one of the many locations throughout town, moviegoers can order burgers, pizza, and the Drafthouse's famous fried pickles while sitting down to enjoy box-office hits, classics, or indie films. Be warned: you may never want to watch a movie any other way. Open year-round. ✉ *320 E. 6th St.* ☎ *512/476-1320* ⊕ *www.drafthouse.com.*

The Dobie Theatre. When you're searching for the latest in Indie films, the Dobie never fails to accommodate. Located on the artsy UT campus, its small theateers are crammed with students and film fanatics alike for the latest in artistic film. ✉ *2025 Guadalupe St.* ☎ *512/472–FILM(3456)* ⊕ *www.landmarktheatres.com/market/Austin/DobieTheatre.htm.*

Paramount Theatre. During the summer, movie lovers escape the heat at this historic theater for the Summer Classic Film Series, featuring time-honored films from *Gone with the Wind* to *The Wizard of Oz.* ✉ *713 Congress Ave.* ☎ *512/472–5470* ⊕ *www.austintheatre.org.*

MUSIC VENUES

University of Texas Performing Arts Center. There's no end to the types of performances you can catch at this performing arts center that's home to six venues throughout the university campus: Bass Concert Hall, Hogg Memorial Auditorium, Bates Recital Hall, B. Iden Payne Theatre, McCollough Theatre, and Oscar B. Brockett Theatre. **UTPAC** hosts everything from chamber orchestras to alternative rock bands, African dance, and Russian ballet. ✉ *2350 Robert Deadman, University of Texas* ☎ *512/471–7539* ⊕ *www.utpac.org.*

Frank Erwin Center. When music events call for a big arena setting, it's held here, the largest venue in Austin. Also home to the University of Texas's Longhorn ladies' and men's basketball teams, the venue has played host to the likes of Eric Clapton, U2, the Dixie Chicks, and Hannah Montana. ✉ *1701 Red River, University of Texas* ☎ *512/471-7744* ⊕ *www.uterwincenter.com.*

Austin Music Hall. Having recently reopened from a modernizing face-lift in late 2007, the Austin Music Hall offers marquee bands a mid-size venue to avoid arena staging yet still pack in a lively Austin crowd. Some of the first performers to grace the new stage included Van Morrison, Marilyn Manson, and the Cure. ✉*208 Nueces, Downtown & Capitol Area* ☎*512/263–4146* ⊕*www.austinmusichall.com.*

The Backyard. On the western outskirts of town, the Austin Music Hall's sister venue, open from March through October, features an outdoor stage beneath a grove of oak trees. Willie Nelson kicks off the season each year, and a wide variety of performers from Lyle Lovett and David Gray to the String Cheese Incident and Sheryl Crow keeps the crowds coming. Just on the other side of The Backyard, the smaller adjoining venue, **The Glenn** (☎*512/263–4146* ⊕*www.theglennaustin.net*), has soft grass and hillside seating for enjoying more mellow acoustic and singer-songwriter acts. ✉*13101 Hwy. 71 W, West Austin/Zilker Park* ☎*512/263–4146* ⊕*www.thebackyard.net.*

Saxon Pub. If you can get past this pub's low ceilings, sticky beer-stained floors, and dark, small, and crowded room, then you'll find a phenomenal music experience. Bands play every night; usually from the local rock and blues scene. This is a small Austin classic with Shiner Bock on tap and a well-worn pool table that draws regulars from all over the city. ✉*1320 S. Lamar, South Austin* ☎*512/448–2552* ⊕*www. thesaxonpub.com.*

NIGHTLIFE

To say Austin's night scene is dominated by live music is an understatement. In fact, it's hard to fully distinguish bar from club from live-music venue as they tend to all blend together. Bands will play anywhere people will listen, and that's pretty much everywhere. It's one of the reasons the club scene in Austin is fairly small in comparison to music venues and bars. Depending on where you are in town, activity tends to bubble up in two waves: the social and professional, happy hour faction; and the music-loving nightlife crowd. If visiting Austin for a short time, check out some of the classic venues such as Antone's, The Continental Club, and Stubb's.

The swank bar above Lamberts fancy barbecue restaurant also features some amazing jazz and blues performers. And be sure to grab a cold brew at Johnny Cash–inspired Mean-Eyed Cat or a martini at the Hollywood-esque Belmont, and sample the delectable cheese plate with a glass of wine on the patio of the San Jose Hotel.

BARS

WAREHOUSE DISTRICT
With its wide, windswept avenues and unfinished-looking buildings—offering a good contrast to the contained and somewhat urban-yuppie Second Street District—Austin's Warehouse District really is filled with brick-walled converted warehouses (and seemingly endless construction).

It's where Austin wets its whistle at myriad bars, lounges, and slick restaurants, then gets down at a hopping nightclub.

The Ginger Man. For one of Austin's larger selections of beer on tap, brew connoisseurs head to this watering hole, where the long bar serves up more than 70 draft beer varieties and almost double the number of bottled beers from all over the world. ⊠*304 W. Fourth St., Downtown & Capitol Area* ☎*512/473–8801* ⊕*www.austin.gingermanpub.com.*

★ **Saba Blue Water Café.** The blue glowing fountain along the back wall draws the chic thirtysomethings to this Caribbean-island-meets-contemporary-martini-bar like moths to a flame. Stop in for happy hour with specials featuring apple-ginger martinis, lemongrass margaritas, and blue Caraçao Saba coladas, and a flavorful menu of small plates including crunchy plantain-crusted shrimp and creamy spinach con queso. ⊠*208 W. Fourth St., Downtown & Capitol Area* ☎*512/478–7222* ⊕*www.sabacafe.com.*

219 West. The dark and sophisticated lounge here remains cool and mellow in the early evening, when downtown professionals stop in for a post-work drink. But things heat up with a glitzy, albeit fairly young, crowd when the DJ arrives with bass-thumping music later in the night. ⊠*219 W. Fourth St., Downtown & Capitol Area* ☎*512/474–2194* ⊕*www.219west.com.*

★ **SIX Lounge.** Want to take in the see-and-be-seen crowd? Though there are a few hot spots around town, the SIX Lounge certainly provides an attractive glam scene. The warm lighting, exposed brick walls, and hardwood accents give this place a sexy urban-chic appeal, and the rooftop lounge provides amazing views of downtown and the Warehouse District at night. ⊠*117 W. Fourth St., Downtown & Capitol Area* ☎*512/472–6662* ⊕*www.sixlounge.com.*

6TH STREET
Buffalo Billiards. Come here if you're looking for the perfect place to sink an eight ball in the corner pocket. With a floor full of pool tables, the only thing you'll have to worry about is waiting for one to open up. But the foosball and air hockey tables can keep you occupied while you sip a cold brew. ⊠*201 E. 6th St., Downtown & Capitol Area* ☎*512/479–7665* ⊕*www.buffalobilliards.com/austin.*

Shakespeare's Pub. Boasting the pomp of the Warehouse District without the circumstance, is a popular spot for Austin regulars looking for a relaxed spot to catch up with friends. Excellent beer selection and friendly waitstaff are an added bonus. But be ready for a dramatic change in atmosphere after 10 PM—less laid-back local patrons, more rambunctious late-night cruisers. ⊠*314 E. 6th St., Downtown & Capitol Area* ☎*512/472–1666.*

Maggie Mae's. This is one of 6th Street's longest-running bars, which says a lot, considering the turnover is pretty high in this district. Maggie Mae's is touristy and features mainly cover bands; you'll usually find a good crowd and a great beer selection. ⊠*323 E. 6th St., Downtown & Capitol Area* ☎*512/478–1997* ⊕*www.maggiemaesaustin.com.*

WEST 6TH STREET

For a bit of good Irish craic with a local feel, **Mother Egan's** (⊠715 W. 6th St., Downtown & Capitol AreaAustin, ☎512/477–3308 ⊕www. motheregansirishpub.com) fits the bill with Irish and British beers on tap, old-style pub booths, and a classic menu of authentic pub grub. Try the fried Snickers bar—it's a little piece of heaven. This family-owned pub plays host to Tuesday night trivia quizzes and even offers prizes for the sharpest tools in the shed.

Opal Divine's. People love this bar for its laid-back atmosphere, wide-open patios, extensive beer selection, and the crispy chicken-tender basket. The dog-friendly environment makes it a nice place to bring your canine companions and enjoy weekend live music. ⊠700 W. 6th St., Downtown & Capitol Area ☎512/477–3308 ⊕www.opaldivines. com.

J. Black's. The dark-leather couches and chairs arranged in small group-ings throughout the sleek lounge make for an old Vegas "Rat Pack" environment. It's the type of place you'd expect to find Dean Martin curled up with a cigar in the corner. A classy cocktail menu and upscale small plate menu make for a swanky place to intimately share a few drinks with friends. ⊠600 W. 6th St., Downtown & Capitol Area ☎512/477–8550.

AROUND AUSTIN

Fodor'sChoice
★
Hotel San Jose Lounge. It may be the hippest hotel in town, but the San Jose is also home to one of the best wine bars in the city. On nice days, grab a patio seat, order a reasonably-priced bottle of wine and the city-renowned cheese plate—we promise, you won't regret it. ⊠1316 S. Congress Ave., South Austin ☎512/477–3308 ⊕www.sanjosehotel. com.

Brown Bar. When the legislature is in session, this is where the lawmak-ers, Capitol staff, and lobbyists stop in for a quick break. Housed in the historic Brown Building, the small, yet cool environment features a Turkish marble bar that glows a deep amber from lighting beneath it. ⊠201 W. Eighth St., Downtown & Capitol Area ☎512/480–8330 ⊕www.thebrownbar.com.

★ **Driskill Hotel Bar.** The old-fashioned bar at the Driskill is where history is made. Rich carpeting and wood-trimmed walls, cowhide-finished and leather couches, plush green bar chairs, and the spectacular stained-glass dome in the center of the room saw some of President Lyndon B. Johnson and Lady Bird Johnson's first dates as a couple. An excellent wine, beer, and cocktail list make cozying up in this classic Austin spot even more appealing. ⊠604 Brazos St., Downtown & Capitol Area ☎512/474–2214 ⊕www.driskillhotel.com.

Mean-Eyed Cat. Soon to be overshadowed by a towering condo project, this little shack of a bar owes it's name to the Man In Black. It may look more like a lean-to, but this little dive is an Austin cult favor-ite, with worn barn-wood walls covered with tattered Johnny Cash memorabilia, a shabby-chic patio with a random assortment of tables and chairs, and a very impressive beer selection. ⊠*1621 W. 5th St., Downtown & Capitol Area* ☎*512/472–6326* ⊕*www.themeaneyed cat.com.*

Cain & Able's. College students looking for the campus experience need to head to where you're likely to find brothers or sisters from the UT chapter of your fraternity or sorority. Walking distance from most anything on campus, this popular beer joint makes a safe option for non-designated drivers. ⊠*2313 Rio Grande St., University of Texas Area* ☎*512/476–3201.*

Scholz Garten. When not caught up in tailgating parties for the University of Texas Longhorns, sports fans are often living it up in the historic hall here. In continuous operation since 1866, the little beer joint that could is the oldest operating business in Austin, not to mention in the entire state! If you're not a Longhorns fan, Scholz's proximity to the Bob Bullock Texas State History Museum makes for a great stop after taking in some of the state's history. ⊠*1607 San Jacinto, Downtown & Capitol Area* ☎*512/474–1958* ⊕*www.scholzgarten.net.*

Vino Vino. Nestled in the hip Hyde Park neighborhood, Vino Vino serves a not-so-ordinary variety of wines—many of which are by the glass. Everything from Alsatian crémant (sparkling wine) to obscure Argentinian reds graces the perpetually evolving menu. The sleek amber wood floors and bar give a warmth to this wine bar/market. Be sure to try a cheese plate or the flavorful pear, spinach, and goat-cheese salad. ⊠*4119 Guadalupe, North Austin/Hyde Park* ☎*512/465–9282* ⊕*www.vinovinotx.com.*

Ginny's Little Longhorn Saloon. Looking for an authentic Honky Tonk dive experience? Ginny's is an Austin favorite, though from the looks of the rather dull exterior, you may not believe us. We never said it would be glamorous, but the beer is cold and the service is friendly. Local music legend Dale Watson often takes the tiny stage here, and the cast of regulars at this honored saloon is too good to miss. ⊠*5434 Burnet Rd., North Austin/Hyde Park* ☎*512/458–1813* ⊕*www.ginnys littlelonghorn.com.*

Deep Eddy Cabaret. Gone are the smoke-filled rooms of Austin clubs and bars. If you haven't noticed, there's a smoking ban in this town and it couldn't have happened to a nicer place. A favorite dive for the Lady Bird Lake and Deep Eddy locals, there was a time when you could cut the cigarette smoke in this pool hall with a knife. Now it's abuzz most nights of the week with thirty- and fortysomethings looking to escape the downtown hype. ⊠*1607 San Jacinto* ☎*512/474–1958* ⊕*www. scholzgarten.net.*

COMEDY CLUBS

Esther's Follies. There's really one place in downtown Austin known for its rip-roaring comedy shows. Esther's has kept Austin rolling with laughter for more than 25 years. Situated in the heart of the entertaining 6th Street District, it's the perfect place to take in an evening of satire and parody. ✉*525 E. 6th St., Downtown & Capitol Area* ☎*512/320–0553* ⊕*www.esthersfollies.com.*

Cap City Comedy Club. If you find yourself in North Austin, Cap City packs quite a punch with its stand-up comedian series. ✉*8120 Research Blvd., #100, North Austin/Hyde Park* ☎*512/467–2333* ⊕*www.cap citycomedy.com.*

CLUBS & DANCE HALLS

Speakeasy. In keeping with the old 1920s speakeasies, you have to gain entrance to this swanky club through the alley. The main room has that '20s vibe and features nightly live music from jazz, Latin, and big-band genres. This is the place to show off swing and Latin dance moves! For a fantastic view of the city, climb about 60 stairs to the Rooftop bar and catch a glimpse of the ever-growing Austin skyline. ✉*412D Congress Ave., Downtown & Capitol Area (Second Street & Warehouse District)* ☎*512/476–8017* ⊕*www.speakeasyaustin.com.*

The Belmont. The coolest club in this very cool city? We're not absolutely sure, but a prime contender is the Belmont. Inside it feels like the swingin' '60s, Vegas style, with dark green banquettes and gold-on-black accents everywhere. Personable bartenders mix swanky cocktails, Frank and Dean are on the speakers, and Austin's beautiful people hang out on the breezy second-floor patio. During happy hour, appetizers are half-price. Watch out for weekend crowds. ✉*305 W. 6th St., Downtown & Capitol Area* ☎*512/457–0300* ⊕*www.thebelmont austin.com.*

Broken Spoke. Some of the town's most distinctive clubs are removed from the 6th Street scene. If live country music and dancing are your thing, two-step down to this venerable spot, where the old Texas lives (and dances) on. ✉*3201 S. Lamar Blvd., South Austin* ☎*512/442–6189* ⊕*www.brokenspokeaustintx.com.*

Dallas Night Club. For mainstream country-and-western music and dance, this is the place to be. It's a jaunt north from the downtown scene, but you will get some serious two-stepping in here, and even a line dance or two—if that's your kind of thing. ✉*7113 Burnet Rd., North Austin/Hyde Park* ☎*512/452–2801.*

LIVE MUSIC

Antone's. This is a local musical institution that books legendary blues and funk acts. Guiding spirit Clifford Antone, a blues fan's blues fan, passed away in May 2006, but his legacy lives on at the club he founded. ✉*213 W. 5th St., Downtown & the Capitol Area (Second Street & Warehouse District)* ☎*512/320–8424 recording, 512/263–4146 information* ⊕*www.antones.net.*

Fodor's Choice
★ **Cactus Café.** For an intimate live-music experience unmatched by any other venue in Austin, head to this café on the UT campus and get in line for tickets. Texas singer-songwriter legends such as Lyle Lovett, Robert Earle King, Patty Griffin, and Austin-renowned Bob Schneider have graced this tiny stage since the 1970s. It doesn't get much bet-

ter than this. ⊠ *Texas Union, UT Campus, University of Texas Area* ☎ *512/475–6515* ⊕ *www.utexas.edu/txunion/ae/cactus.*

Cedar Street Courtyard. Squeezed between some of the Warehouse District's glam-filled bars, sounds from the open outdoor stage lure a bold and very beautiful crowd with jazzy, big-band, and swing music. Every night is a swinging time at the courtyard—just don't plan on lingering on the sidewalk too long without paying a cover, bands do need to eat, after all. ⊠ *208 W. 4th St., Downtown & the Capitol Area (Second Street & Warehouse District)* ☎ *512/495–9669* ⊕ *www.cedar streetaustin.com.*

Continental Club. Rustic, quirky, and no bigger than your parents' basement, this smoky, no-frills club is one of Austin's signature entertainment spaces. The club hosts a variety of live acts but specializes in country-tinged rock and honky-tonkin'. Try to catch a performance by Heybale, a quintet of local pros that includes Redd Volkaert and Earl Poole Ball. ⊠ *1315 S. Congress Ave., South Austin* ☎ *512/441–2444* ⊕ *www.continentalclub.com/Austin.html.*

★ **Elephant Room.** Jazz fanatics hold court at the basement locale here, where serious jazz plays long into the night all week long. Named one of the top ten jazz venues in the United States by the famed Wynton Marsalis, this longstanding Austin venue is what gives this town its Live Music Capital status. ⊠ *315 Congress Ave., Downtown & Capitol Area* ☎ *512/473–2279.*

Emo's. The thick sea of people swarming the indoor and outdoor stages may seem overwhelming at first, but you'll soon find it's the best way to take in one of Austin's most colorful night scenes. Not interested in fighting the crowd? Take a seat in the slightly less crowded beer garden. Three to four bands of the alternative, hard rock, heavy metal, or punk persuasion play this dark and hard-edged venue every night. Not for the faint at heart. ⊠ *603 Red River, Downtown & Capitol Area* ☎ *512/477–3667* ⊕ *www.emosaustin.com.*

★ **Lamberts.** Barbecue fans will love the fancy spin on traditional Texas cuisine at this 2nd Street District hot spot, but the jazz and blues wailing from the upstairs bar are not to be missed. Strong, Southern-inspired cocktails served at simple heavy wood tables add to the dark and jazzy room, where some of Austin's up-and-coming jazz musicians take the spotlight. ⊠ *401 W. 2nd St., Downtown & Capitol Area (Second Street & Warehouse District)* ☎ *512/494–1500* ⊕ *www.lamberts austin.com.*

Momo's. Although heralded as a prime live music venue, what makes Momo's stand apart from other music facilities is the long and distinguished list of Austin performers who frequent the stage of this 7-year-old venue that has quickly gained legend status. With free parking and a cover charge that goes directly to the band, this is the place to get your fill of Austin tunes. ⊠ *618 W. 6th St., Downtown & Capitol Area* ☎ *512/479–8848* ⊕ *www.momosclub.com.*

Fodor'sChoice **Stubb's.** You know you're in Austin when the smell of smoky barbecue
★ wafts throughout the venue as a top-billed band prepares to take the
outdoor stage. It's not heaven, it's Stubb's, a true Austin live-music
icon. If you're in town long enough and want to revive your spiri-
tual side, take in a session of the Sunday gospel hour where a sizeable buffet brunch awaits along with a soulful performance of gospel
music. ⊠ *801 Red River, Downtown & Capitol Area* ☎ *512/480–8341*
⊕ *www.stubbsaustin.com.*

WHERE TO EAT

Apart from on tourist- and student-heavy 6th Street, Austin's restaurant scene is geared to local tastes and is arguably more diverse than
the celebrated music scene, which is concentrated within a few narrowly defined genres. Though Mexican, Tex-Mex, and barbecue are
the default cuisines, everything from Brazilian to Pacific Rim fusion has
made headway here, and there are strong vegetarian and natural-food
followers. Austinites, in fact, have some of the most adventurous and
educated palates in Texas.

To find the best barbecue, local consensus tends to be that you've got
to head out of town to Lockhart, Luling, or Llano, in the Hill Country.
Nevertheless, there are several fine options within the city limits, the
bulk of them simple places where your meat is sliced and placed uncer-
emoniously on the plate (or even on wax paper), with pickles, onions,
and jalapeño slices, and you eat at picnic tables, using paper towels off
the roll as napkins.

In some places the music and food share nearly equal billing, like
Threadgill's, whose massive chicken-fried steak is as much of a draw
as the well-known blues and rock acts on stage, and Stubb's Bar-B-Q,
which hosts a popular gospel brunch on Sundays and is a major player
on the club scene.

Finer dining has exploded in Austin, and upscale Continental—especially Central European (the area was settled by Germans and Czechs)—
and New American establishments offer traditional fare and inventive
dishes with Southwestern touches. Some of the best restaurants in town
are in well-heeled hotels like the Driskill and the Four Seasons.

Austin is a casual city, and the dress code is almost always "come as
you are"; a few restaurants require a jacket for men. Tips are generally 15% to 20%. Smoking is prohibited in most restaurants and bars
within Travis County, which includes Austin.

DEALS & DISCOUNTS
Around mid-year, many of Austin's best restaurants participate in Restaurant Week, when prix-fixe menus are offered for a low price, with
some of the proceeds earmarked for charity.

DINING WITH KIDS

Austin has plenty of families with young children and plenty of restaurants that work well for them. Burger joint Phil's Icehouse (⊠*5620 Burnet Rd., North Austin*) is a moms' favorite for its kid-friendly menu, play area for ages 3–12, and occasional live music or movies for kids in summer. Luby's is a Texas-based chain with five Austin locations serving affordable Southern food. The staff sees that young children (and their parents) are taken care of and kids eat free with the purchase of an adult meal Wednesday evenings and all day Saturday. Chuy's, Serranos Café & Cantina, and Romano's Macaroni Grill, chains with several Austin locations, are well-attuned to children's needs. Restaurants in this chapter that are especially good for kids are marked with duckies.

WHAT IT COSTS					
	¢	$	$$	$$$	$$$$
RESTAURANTS	under $8	$8–$12	$13–$20	$21–$30	over $30

Restaurant prices are per person for a main course at dinner

DOWNTOWN & CAPITOL AREA

CONTINENTAL
$$–$$$
★

✕**Bess Bistro.** In the restored cellar of a 1918 brick building on the more sedate end of 6th is this casually chic boîte owned by actress Sandra Bullock. (But if you come here to gawk at celebs, you'll likely leave disappointed.) Bess wins out with an eclectic mix of European and Southern American comfort food, including an artful *croque monsieur*: country ham, béchamel, and Gruyère piled atop sourdough toast, served with crisp, thin fries. Other popular entrées include shepherd's pie, grilled wild salmon on toasted herb spaetzle, and porcini-crusted halibut. Bullock designed the interior, which suggests an early-20th-century artists' sanctum, with framed French ads, exposed brick pillars, some half-clad in quilted red leather. The staff is quietly efficient. Sunday brunch is served, and the bistro is open until the small hours. ⊠*500 W. 6th St., Downtown & Capitol Area* ☎*512/477–2377* ♻*Reservations not accepted* ☱*AE, D, MC, V.*

BURGER
¢–$

✕**Casino el Camino.** Slumming on 6th? This two-story club with a pleasant patio out back is the place to chow down. Put in your order at the kitchen window at the back of the bar, then return in 20 minutes for your grilled chicken-breast sandwich (with barbecue sauce, melted cheese, and sautéed peppers and onions), quarter-pound hot dogs, or the best and certainly biggest burgers in town, made from 3/4-pound of Angus beef. If you have an especially daring palate, opt for the Amarillo burger, with roasted Serrano chilies, jalapeño jack cheese, and cilantro mayo. The chicken wings are great, but be forewarned: the "medium" wings would be most other places' "atomic hot," so have plenty of liquid refreshment at hand. ⊠*517 E. 6th St., Downtown & Capitol Area* ☎*512/469–9330* ♻*Reservations not accepted* ☱*MC, V.*

Continued on page 140

WHERE SHOULD I DINE IN AUSTIN?

	Neighborhood Vibe	Pros	Cons
Downtown & Capitol Area	Premier New American and continental restaurants are here, along with wine bars, barbecue joints, and hip, upscale enclaves (especially west of Congress).	Hip and fun bistros, sophisticated nightlife, great upscale dining, something for nearly every taste.	Crowded, expensive, filled with tourists in season.
East Austin	Long a center for Austin's working-class Latinos and African Americans, the area east of I–35 has Italian and Peruvian eateries amid auto-body shops and Mexican restaurants.	Great Mexican restaurants waiting to be discovered—at least, by you; eateries near airport great when you have a plane to catch.	Not the most attractive (or safest) neighborhoods; not the place to dine if you want to experience Austin.
North Austin	It's one of the best neighborhoods for various ethnic cuisines, including Asian and Middle Eastern.	Meet the locals in this low-key, low-pretension area; some good diners and ethnic eateries.	Clogged with traffic most of the time, sprawling, ugly, easy to get lost in.
Northwest Austin	Highways lead to seemingly endless shopping malls, most of them upscale, with fashionable restaurants to match. This is also the land of chain restaurants.	Family-friendly, some of Austin's best shopping, a natural stopping point on your way to Lake Travis.	Don't you have suburbs just like this at home?
Second Street & Warehouse District	A mix of cool-but-friendly bistros lie between the lake and Third Street, and San Antonio and Congress. To the north, the Warehouse District has pubs, clubs, and casual places for post-collegians.	Great pubs and fun clubs, cutting-edge urban diversions, no car required.	Self-conscious hipitude can get a bit precious at times; some of the Warehouse District is a bit grungy.
South Austin	Still largely middle-class, and definitely individualistic, to some residents this area of South Congress (with its exhibitionistic painted facades) and Lamar is the last redoubt of Old Weird Austin. Here you find hippies, quirky stores, and veggie, Mexican, and barbecue restaurants.	Entertaining and unique center of "weird" Austin, great shops and Tex-Mex plates.	If hippies get on your nerves, don't bother.
Zilker Park	Barton Springs Road has several sprawling, ultra-casual barbecue and hamburger joints, where the laid-back Austin lifestyle asserts itself to the fullest.	Great place to go native and surrender to Austin's casual, hip vibe; a morning swim, an afternoon barbecue platter—what else is there?	Parking can be a problem.

BEST BETS FOR AUSTIN DINING

As a foodie center, Austin delights palates daily with the inventions of a new wave of bright young chefs as well as with tried-and-true Mexican and barbecue. Below are some of our favorite restaurants in terms of style, cuisine type, and price points.

Fodor's Choice ★

Castle Hill Café, $$–$$$, Downtown & Capitol Area

Jasper's, $$$–$$$$, North Austin

Lamberts, $$–$$$$, Second Street & Warehouse District

The Salt Lick, ¢–$$, Driftwood

Uchi, $$–$$$$, South Austin

Hudson's On The Bend, $$$–$$$$, West Austin

Driskill Grill, $$$–$$$$, Downtown & Capitol Area

Enoteca Vespaio, $–$$, South Austin

By Price

¢

Casino el Camino, Downtown & Capitol Area

El Mesón Taquería, East Austin

Flip Happy Crepes, Zilker Park

Hut's, Downtown & Capitol Area

$

Asia Cafe, Northwest Austin

Curra's Grill, South Austin

Hoover's, Northwest Austin, University of Texas

Hyde Park Bar and Grill, Hyde Park, South Austin

Iron Works Barbecue, Downtown & Capitol Area

$$

Bess Bistro, Downtown & Capitol Area

Castle Hill Café, Downtown & Capitol Area

European Bistro, Pflugerville

Lamberts, Second Street & Warehouse District

Primizie, East Austin

$$$

Estância Churrascaria, South Austin

Fonda San Miguel, North Austin

The Mansion at Judges' Hill, University of Texas

$$$$

Driskill Grill, Downtown & Capitol Area

Hudson's on the Bend, Lake Travis

Jasper's, North Austin

Shoreline Grill, Downtown & Capitol Area

TRIO at the Four Seasons, Downtown and Capitol Area

By Cuisine

NEW AMERICAN

Castle Hill Café, $$–$$$, Downtown & Capitol Area

Driskill Grill, $$$$, Downtown & Capitol Area

Hudson's on the Bend, $$$$, Lake Travis

Jasper's, $$$–$$$$, North Austin

Lamberts, $$–$$$$, Second Street & Warehouse District

Zoot, $$–$$$$, Downtown & Capitol Area

CONTINENTAL

Jeffrey's, $$–$$$$, Downtown & Capitol Area

Louie's 106, $$–$$$, Downtown & Capitol Area

The Mansion at Judges' Hill, $$–$$$$, University of Texas

Shoreline Grill, $$–$$$$, Downtown & Capitol Area

BARBECUE

Iron Works Barbecue, $–$$, Downtown & Capitol Area

Lamberts, $$–$$$$, Second Street & Warehouse District

Rudy's BBQ, ¢–$, Northwest Austin, Lake Travis, University of Texas, West Lake

The Salt Lick, ¢–$$, Driftwood

MEXICAN & TEX-MEX

Curra's Grill, $–$$, South Austin

El Azteca, ¢–$, East Austin

El Mesón Taquería, ¢, East Austin

Fonda San Miguel, $$–$$$$, North Austin

Juan in a Million, ¢–$, East Austin

Matt's Famous El Rancho, ¢–$$, South Austin

By Experience

KID-FRIENDLY

County Line, $–$$$, West Austin, West Lake

Curra's Grill, $–$$, South Austin

Flip Happy Crepes, ¢–$, Zilker Park

Hoover's, $–$$, Northwest Austin, University of Texas

Hut's, ¢–$, Downtown & Capitol Area

Rudy's BBQ, ¢–$, Northwest Austin, Lake Travis, West Lake

Shady Grove, ¢–$$, Zilker Park

BEST BANG FOR YOUR BUCK

Asia Cafe, ¢–$, Northwest Austin

Casino el Camino, ¢–$, Downtown & Capitol Area

Dog and Duck Pub, ¢–$, Downtown & Capitol Area

Flip Happy Crepes, ¢–$, Zilker Park

Hoover's, $–$$, Northwest Austin, University of Texas

Juan in a Million, ¢–$, East Austin

Magnolia Cafe, ¢–$$, Downtown & Capitol Area, South Austin

DINING ALFRESCO

County Line, $–$$$, West Austin, West Lake

Flip Happy Crepes, ¢–$, Zilker Park

Iron Works Barbecue, $–$$, Downtown & Capitol Area

The Oasis–Lake Travis, $–$$, Lake Travis

The Salt Lick, ¢–$$, Driftwood

Shady Grove, ¢–$$, Zilker Park

YOUNG & HAPPENING

Bess Bistro, $$–$$$, Downtown & Capitol Area

Casino el Camino, ¢–$, Downtown & Capitol Area

Jasper's, $$$–$$$$, North Austin

Lamberts, $$–$$$$, Second Street & Warehouse District

Primizie, $–$$, East Austin

SHORT ON ATMOSPHERE, LONG ON GOOD, CHEAP EATS

Asia Cafe, ¢–$, Northwest Austin

Casino el Camino, ¢–$, Downtown & Capitol Area

Curra's Grill, $–$$, South Austin

Juan in a Million, ¢–$, East Austin

Red Cap Chick, ¢–$$, South Austin

ROMANCE

Driskill Grill, $$$$, Downtown & Capitol Area

Fonda San Miguel, $$–$$$$, North Austin

Hudson's on the Bend, $$$$, Lake Travis

Jasper's, $$$–$$$$, North Austin

Jeffrey's, $$–$$$$, Downtown & Capitol Area

Joe DiMaggio's Italian Chophouse, $$–$$$$, North Austin

The Mansion at Judges' Hill, $$–$$$$, University of Texas

Truluck's, $$$–$$$$, Downtown & Capitol Area, Northwest Austin

NEW
AMERICAN
$$–$$$
Fodor'sChoice
★

✕**Castle Hill Café.** This cheery, upscale downtown hangout rarely disappoints, which is why it's been an Austin mainstay since 1986. Here you'll find great tortilla soup, imaginative salads, and eclectic entrées such as grilled Indian lamb loin with Makhani cream and cauliflower-ginger relish. The menu usually changes every two to four weeks. A wine-and-beer bar was added in 2007. ✉1101 W. 5th St., Downtown & Capitol Area ☎512/476–0728 ═AE, D, MC, V ⊘Closed Sun.

NEW
AMERICAN
$$$$
Fodor'sChoice
★

✕**Driskill Grill.** Dominated by shiny, dark paneling and etched glass, this would-be cattle baron's club inside the Driskill Hotel recalls the palatial restaurants of the 19th century (on a more intimate scale)—until you look at the menu. Executive Chef Josh Watkins takes tasteful liberties with the meat-and-potatoes format by integrating world-cuisine influences. Entrées include hot smoked Bandera quail, pistachio-crusted sea scallops, and pan-roasted duck breast. Nightly piano music adds to the charming ambience. ✉604 Brazos St., Downtown & Capitol Area ☎512/391–7162 ═AE, D, DC, MC, V.

BURGER
¢–$
♻

✕**Hut's.** Locals consistently choose Hut's for the best-burger award in *Austin Chronicle* restaurant polls. Part of the mystique may be the *American Graffiti*–like atmosphere: the joint is a local institution that began in 1939. It's been in its present location since 1969, and old license plates, vintage ads, and UT memorabilia are everywhere. Huge, juicy burgers come in about 25 varieties, and the gigantic onion rings are crunchy and addictive. It's hard not to surrender to the experience. Vegetarians can request substitute patties—this is Austin, after all. ✉807 W. 6th St., Downtown & Capitol Area ☎512/472–0693 ═D, MC, V.

BARBECUE
$–$$
★

✕**Iron Works Barbecue.** From its creekside perch in the shadow of the Austin Convention Center, this spot caters to name-tagged conference attendees, construction workers, and thoroughly starched office workers alike. Dependable house specialties include pepper-crusted smoked pork loin, tender brisket, and Flintstones-size beef ribs (the junior rib plate will satisfy all but the hugest of appetites). Wrought-iron grills, forged here when the building was an ironworks, hang from the rafters. It's a charming and authentic slice of Texas—maybe not the best barbecue joint within city limits, but definitely in the top five. There's also a decent salad bar. ✉100 Red River St., Downtown & Capitol Area ☎512/478–4855 ═AE, DC, MC, V ⊘Closed Sun.

CONTINENTAL
$$–$$$$
★

✕**Jeffrey's.** Executive chef Alma Alcocer holds court at this fine-dining institution in the historic Clarksville area downtown, where the menu of "contemporary Texas cuisine" changes regularly. Expect complex dishes that combine Latin and Southwestern flavors with standbys from more continental traditions. Start with crispy oysters on yucca chips with habanero-honey aioli, then move on to the balsamic duck and shrimp with baby vegetables, apples, and Roquefort cheese for an entrée. The sophisticated wine list is carefully selected. Cozy alcoves, a romantic atmosphere, and consistently attentive service make for a memorable evening. ✉1204 W. Lynn St., Downtown & Capitol Area ☎512/477–5584 ═AE, D, DC, MC, V ⊘No lunch.

NEW
AMERICAN
$$

✕**Parkside.** The bustling array of bars and nightclubs that lines Austin's famed 6th Street welcomes a new upscale restaurant for urban-chic and late-night diners. Parkside's austere, cavernous interior features exposed brick walls and long black cables dangling single lightbulbs above each table. Celebrated Austin chef Shawn Cirkiel has created a menu as simple as the restaurant's decor, but more than delivers on taste with fresh oysters and ceviche-style offerings from the raw bar, as well as bistro entrées including steak and fries, and roasted chicken. Fried oysters with a garlicky aioli make for a great start. The savory grilled lamb served with tangy roasted peppers is perfectly prepared and surprisingly un-gamey. Buttery snapper arrives sashimi-style with piquant lime and chili accents. For dessert, order the homemade doughnuts, which arrive warm and sugar-dusted in a plain paper sack. ⊠ *301 E. 6th St., Downtown & Capitol Area* ☎*512/474–9898* ⊕*www. parkside-austin.com* ⊟*AE, D, MC, V.*

CONTINENTAL
$$–$$$$
★

✕**Shoreline Grill.** Just steps from the Four Seasons hotel, this upscale lakeside restaurant has one of Austin's most intimate terraces (a fine place to watch sunset bat flight). Chef Dan Haverty presents nightly seafood variations that might include seared sea scallops with pistachio–goat cheese polenta, or roasted salmon served with a cashew crust and orange-Dijon butter. Meat lovers enjoy robust Texas platters like chicken-fried venison with mashed potatoes and green-chili gravy, and ancho-cured half rack of lamb with roasted sweet potato and amontillado demi-glace. Inside, floor-to-ceiling windows provide a commanding view of Lady Bird Lake (formerly Town Lake). For a real taste of Texas, try the huge chicken-fried steak (served at lunch only); it's one of the best versions you'll find. ⊠*98 San Jacinto Blvd.,* ☎*512/477–3300* ⊟*AE, D, DC, MC, V* ⊗*No lunch weekends.*

BARBECUE
$–$$

✕**Stubb's Bar-B-Que.** This downtown 6th Street–area institution, which traces its roots to a legendary Lubbock barbecue joint founded in 1968 by the late C.B. "Stubb" Stubblefield, is known as much for music as food. Stubb's hosts an always-crowded Sunday gospel brunch (book ahead), and big-name and lesser-known local and touring acts including Willie Nelson, Johnny Cash, Joan Jett, and the White Stripes have played the outdoor stage. To many local barbecue mavens, the hickory-smoked choices—beef brisket, pork loin, pork ribs, sausage, chicken and turkey breast—are average, but the sides, like spinach with cheese and Serrano peppers, are delicious. Salads, sandwiches, and homemade desserts complete the menu, and there's a full bar. Stubb's also markets a popular line of barbecue sauces and rubs. The venue, an old stone building with wooden floors and tables, suits the fare to a T. ⊠*801 Red River St., Downtown & Capitol Area* ☎*512/480–8341* ⊟*AE, D, MC, V.*

NEW
AMERICAN
$$–$$$$
★

✕**TRIO at the Four Seasons.** Steak, seafood, and wine are the three focal points (thus the name) of this sophisticated, sunwashed oasis. Executive chef Elmar Prambs, a fixture at the Four Seasons since 1987, opened TRIO in 2007. The menus, which change weekly, are planned by inventive chef de cuisine Todd Duplechan, who emphasizes freshness—all the seafood is fresh (some shipped overnight; some brought in that day from the Gulf), including Dover sole from Denmark—and produce and other ingredients sourced locally wherever possible. Prime-quality steaks range from an 8-ounce filet mignon to a 22-ounce bone-in cowboy steak (a rib-eye cut). Diners rave about inventive appetizers

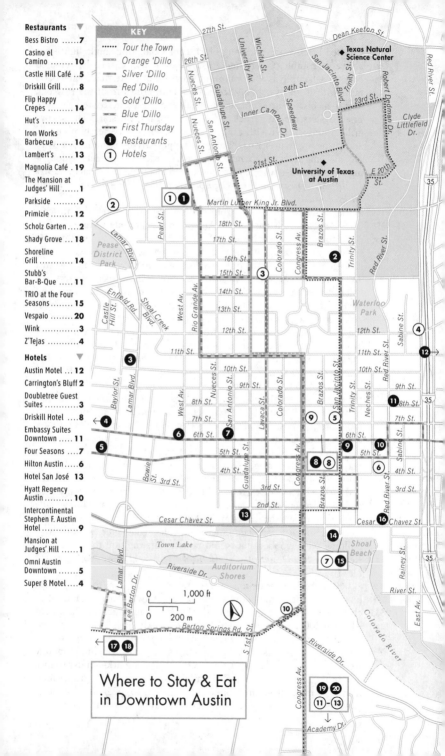

Where to Stay & Eat in Downtown Austin

Restaurants ▼

Bess Bistro **7**
Casino el Camino **10**
Castle Hill Café ..**5**
Driskill Grill **8**
Flip Happy Crepes **14**
Hut's **6**
Iron Works Barbecue **16**
Lambert's **13**
Magnolia Café .**19**
The Mansion at Judges' Hill **1**
Parkside **9**
Primizie **12**
Scholz Garten **2**
Shady Grove **18**
Shoreline Grill **14**
Stubb's Bar-B-Que **11**
TRIO at the Four Seasons **15**
Vespaio **20**
Wink **3**
Z'Tejas **4**

Hotels ▼

Austin Motel ...**12**
Carrington's Bluff **2**
Doubletree Guest Suites **3**
Driskill Hotel **8**
Embassy Suites Downtown **11**
Four Seasons **7**
Hilton Austin.....**6**
Hotel San José **13**
Hyatt Regency Austin **10**
Intercontinental Stephen F. Austin Hotel **9**
Mansion at Judges' Hill **1**
Omni Austin Downtown **5**
Super 8 Motel **4**

KEY

•••••• Tour the Town
Orange 'Dillo
Silver 'Dillo
Red 'Dillo
Gold 'Dillo
Blue 'Dillo
First Thursday
❶ Restaurants
① Hotels

like "bacon and egg" made with pork belly and an egg that's poached, breaded in *panko* (Japanese flaky breadcrumbs), then deep-fried, and squid *a la plancha* (lightly seared). An outstanding wine list is overseen by an in-house sommelier. No detail has been overlooked. Breakfast is served daily. TRIO is worth a visit even if you're staying far from the hotel. ⊠*98 San Jacinto Blvd., Downtown & Capitol Area* ☎*512/685–8300* ⊟*AE, D, MC, V.*

NEW
AMERICAN
$$$
★

✕ **Wink.** Tucked away from Lamar near 12th Street, this petite, sleek restaurant is as dedicated to excellence in service and artful delicious dishes as it is to fresh, quality ingredients from local purveyors. Portions are equally as petite as the contemporary dining room, but somehow you never leave hungry. We suggest putting your trust in chef Eric Poltzer's tasting menu. Each course brings a surprising mix of flavors from bison carpaccio with goat cheese and tomato relish to duck confit with baby yams and wilted greens. The wine list is carefully selected, with an array of varietals from around the world. We were particularly impressed with a rare Alsatian crémant (sparkling wine). ⊠*1014 N. Lamar, Downtown & Capital Area* ☎*512/482–8868* ⊟*AE, D, MC, V* ⊗*No lunch.*

MEXICAN
$-$$$

✕ **Z'Tejas.** This stylish Southwestern fusion outpost started in downtown Austin and currently has 10 locations in Texas and five in other Western states. (In addition to the original, there's another Austin branch at the Arboretum mall.) Z'Tejas is popular for its upscale yet unpretentious vibe and imaginative, attractively presented dishes at fair prices. Try the smoked-chicken chile relleno, a poblano stuffed with chicken, chopped pecans, apricots, jack cheese, and raisins, served with green-chili mole and roasted tomato cream. Appetizers are outstanding, particularly the grilled-shrimp and guacamole tostada bites: herb-and-pumpkin-seed tostada rounds topped with pesto-grilled shrimp, fresh guacamole, and a dash of chipotle. Peak hours can be noisy. ⊠*1110 W. 6th St., Downtown & Capitol Area* ☎*512/478–5355* ⊠*9400-A Arboretum Blvd., Northwest Austin* ☎*512/346–3506* ⊠*10525 W. Parmer La., Northwest Austin* ☎*512/388–7772* ⊟*AE, D, MC, V.*

EAST AUSTIN

MEXICAN
¢–$

✕ **El Azteca.** This old-school family restaurant, now run by the second generation, has been around since 1963 in the heart of bustling, working-class East Austin, and draws local Latinos and downtown workers alike. The decor is a decades-old accretion of Mexican and American kitsch, and great tacky posters featuring half-naked Aztec warriors, swooning women, and volcano goddesses. The servers are no-nonsense, even brusque. You dine at red Naugahyde booths with wood-tone Formica tables with steel-frame chairs, but you're here for expertly rendered Tex-Mex and Mexican platters. The house specialty is *cabrito,* or kid goat, which, at $11.95, is the most expensive dish on the menu, served with guacamole salad, beans *a la charra* (in a smoky broth), and salsa. The cabrito is served in a pile of small chops on the bone; it's lean and just the right side of gamey, and slightly sweet with a hint of baked apple. There's a covered patio with outdoor tables as

well. ⌂2600 E. 7th St., East Austin ☎512/477–4701 ⌂Reservations
not accepted ▭MC, V.

MEXICAN ✕**Juan in a Million.** The not-so-secret weapon of this classic East Aus-
¢–$ tin breakfast spot is its owner and namesake, local legend Juan Meza,
who has run his modest eatery since 1981 and still greets every diner
with a bone-crushing handshake and a smile. Juan's strong community
spirit is catching, but the simple, filling, and reliably good fare will start
your day off right on its own. The Don Juan taco (a massive mound
of eggs, potato, bacon, and cheese) is the true East Austin breakfast of
champions; *machacado con huevo* (shredded dried beef scrambled with
eggs), *migas* (eggs scrambled with torn corn tortillas, onions, chile peppers, cheese, and spices), and huevos rancheros are also above average.
A variety of inexpensive Tex-Mex and Mexican specialties is served
at lunch. ⌂2300 E. Cesar Chavez St., East Austin ☎512/472–3872
⌂Reservations not accepted ▭AE, D, MC, V.

ITALIAN ✕**Primizie.** Opened in mid-2007, this hip-and-modern, foodie-friendly
$–$$ *osteria* (simple Italian-bistro-style restaurant) on a rapidly gentrifying
★ central East Austin block is a magnet for young techies and creative
types. Co-owner Mark Spedale is a native Sicilian, though the menu
hews more toward northern Italian. Salads, pizzas, and entrées are
all fresh and inventive in their simplicity. The pastas and gnocchi are
reliable favorites, and bread and pastries are made in-house. Lunch is
ordered at the counter, at dinner there's table service, and half-price
appetizers are available during happy hour (4–7 weekdays). Try the
bistecca alla griglia, savory grilled marinated sirloin steak with potato,
arugula, garlic, caramelized onion, and melted Gorgonzola butter. A
good selection of Italian, American, and French wines is available by
the glass or bottle, and pastries made in-house. On our last visit, the
only imperfect note was slightly burned espresso. ⌂1000 E. 11th St.,
East Austin ☎512/236–0088 ▭MC, V.

LAKE TRAVIS

NEW ✕**Hudson's on the Bend.** About 20 mi outside downtown in a beauti-
AMERICAN fully restored and landscaped stone ranch house overlooking a bend
$$$$ in the road near Lake Travis, Hudson's has been the place to dine on
Fodor'sChoice wild game in Austin since 1984. Owner/chef Jeff Blank and executive
★ chef Robert Rhoades are kings of imaginative, gutsy cuisine, serving
serve up exotic, seasonal dishes such as pistachio-crusted diamondback rattlesnake cakes with chipotle cream sauce, venison pro-
sciutto–wrapped seared sea scallops topped with sturgeon caviar, wild
boar three ways—scaloppini, sausage, and *taquito* (a thin, rolled and
fried enchilada)—and espresso-, chocolate-, and chili-rubbed smoked
elk backstrap (loin cut) topped with crab. Despite the hefty price tag,
Hudson's is a fun, unpretentious place. There's an extensive wine list,
including half bottles. Six-course tasting menus are available ($140, or
$200 with wine). ⌂3509 Ranch Rd. 620 N., Lake Travis ☎512/266–
1369 ▭AE, D, DC, MC, V ⊘No lunch.

AMERICAN ✕**The Oasis–Lake Travis.** A 2005 fire destroyed most of the wooden out-
$–$$ door deck seating that made the cliffside Oasis–Lake Travis such a
♺ draw, but the Austin institution has been rebuilt and re-emerged with

perhaps even more spirit; some consider the food much improved as well. Scenic views make this a popular spot for sunset dinners—sometimes too popular, as weekend crowds can be overwhelming in nice weather. If you can, try to get one of the tables overlooking Lake Travis (arrive early). The menu includes shrimp, burgers, fajitas, and margaritas. ⊠ *6550 Comanche Trail, Lake Travis* ☎ *512/266–2442* ⊟ *AE, D, MC, V.*

NORTH AUSTIN

3

MEXICAN
$$–$$$$
✕**Fonda San Miguel.** This celebrated villa-style North Loop spot combines sophisticated ambience with a seasonal menu of authentic Mexican classics. Start with quesadillas layered with poblano, chicken, or mushrooms; or go light with ceviche Veracruzano (with chiles, onion, tomato, and spices). Continue with a multilayered dish like the *ancho relleno* San Miguel—a roasted pepper stuffed with chicken, capers, raisins, and olives and topped with cilantro cream—or try the *pollo pibil,* chicken baked in a banana leaf. Shrimp dishes are extraordinary. Yes, most of it is pricey for what you get, but we feel the lovely, romantic atmosphere makes up for it. The extravagant Sunday brunch is the quintessential upscale Austin weekend breakfast. ⊠ *2330 W. North Loop Blvd., North Austin* ☎ *512/459–4121* ⊟ *AE, D, DC, MC, V* ⊙ *No lunch.*

NEW
AMERICAN
$$$–$$$$
Fodor's Choice
★
✕**Jasper's.** Executives and upscale tourists alike are drawn to this handsome, 9,000-square-foot eatery for its "gourmet backyard cuisine"—that's how owner and celebrated chef Kent Rathbun describes his Texas-based chain. This branch is in the chi-chi Domain right across from Joe DiMaggio's. Seafood features prominently in the inventive menu, the star is Allen Brothers dry-aged prime steak, served with a choice of six sauces. Entrées, from a tender grilled flatiron steak with portobello whipped potatoes to a Cajun grilled redfish sandwich, are attractively plated and well conceived. If you want to go upscale on a tight budget, try the pizza-size three-cheese focaccia with caramelized shallots and portobellos for $10. In 2007 the *Austin Chronicle* called Jasper's fried chicken, with its perfectly crispy skin, the best in town (it's served only at lunch on weekends). Servers are attentive, but not overly familiar. Decor is midtown-Manhattan modern. ⊠ *The Domain shopping center, 11506 Century Oaks Terrace, North Austin* ☎ *512/834–4111* ⊟ *AE, DC, MC, V.*

STEAKHOUSE/
ITALIAN
$$–$$$$
✕**Joe DiMaggio's Italian Chophouse.** The designers of this impressive, larger-than-life establishment (the second branch of a nascent chain that began in San Francisco in 2006) have spared no expense to re-create a 1954 lavish, romantic-yet-masculine supper-club, complete with polished floors, plush leather booths, wide marble bar, black-and-white decor with splashes of red, and photos of Joe and Marilyn everywhere (never mind that their marriage only lasted nine months). Fritto misto, pepper-crusted beef carpaccio, and wood-fired mussels appeal as appetizers. Pastas and pizzas—the Pizza Uovo, for example, topped with sopressata sausage and a runny egg (slightly undercooked but otherwise tasty)—get mixed reviews from diners. Steaks are the main event, from an 8 oz. filet mignon to a 24 oz. porterhouse. The house has a

Where to Stay & Eat
in Greater Austin

Restaurants ▼

Asia Café **2**
El Azteca **18**
Enoteca Vespaio **20**
Estância Churrascaria **23**
European Bistro **10**
Fonda San Miguel **12**
Hoover's **17**
Hoover's NW **1**
Hudson's on the Bend **3**
Jasper's **8**
Jeffrey's **16**
Joe DiMaggio's Italian
Chophouse **9**
Juan in a Million **19**
Mandola's Italian Market .. **14**
Matt's Famous El Rancho .. **22**
The Oasis - Lake Travis **4**
Ruby's BBQ **15**
Rudy's BBQ **5, 7, 24**
The Salt Lick **25**
Salt Lick 360 .... **11**
Threadgill's **13**
Uchi **21**
Z'Tejas **6**

Hotels ▼

Barton Creek
Resort & Spa **9**
Crowne Plaza **7**
Doubletree **6**
Habitat Suites Hotel **5**
Hilton Austin Airport **12**
Hilton Garden Inn Austin
Northwest/Arboretum **1**
Hyatt Place **4**
Lakeway Resort and Spa ... **3**
Omni Austin Hotel at
Southpark **10**
Renaissance
Austin Hotel **2**
Woodburn House **8**
Wyndham Garden Hotel -
Austin **11**

3

DOWNTOWN

KEY
❶ Restaurants
① Hotels

good selection of cocktails and sizable appetizers, $5 apiece, at a daily happy hour (3–6 PM). ⊠ *The Domain shopping center, 11410 Century Oaks Terrace, North Austin* ☏ *512/835–5633* ▤ *AE, DC, MC, V.*

ITALIAN ✕ **Mandola's Italian Market.** Mandola's is the closest you'll get to Italy
¢–$ without leaving Austin. Houston restaurateur, winemaker, cooking-
★ show host, and cookbook author Damian Mandola (co-founder of the Carrabba's Italian Grill restaurant chain) opened this throwback "neighborhood grocery store" and the attached café in 2006 in the equally new Triangle apartment complex just north of Central Market. Mandola gets it right with house-made sausage, mozzarella, artisanal breads, cakes, and cookies. They serve up panini, soups, salads, and antipasti, and daily fresh ravioli specials. The pastas, the very decent southern Italian-style pizza, the vegetarian sandwich, and the pignoli cookies are especially good, and the coffees deliver. The staff is friendly and well-trained, and the atmosphere is welcoming. You can also purchase wine from Mandola's winery out in Driftwood, 28 mi southwest. ⊠ *4700 West Guadalupe St., North Austin* ☏ *512/419–9700* ▤ *AE, D, DC, MC, V.*

NORTHWEST AUSTIN

CHINESE ✕ **Asia Cafe.** In the back of the Asia Market food store in a run-down
¢–$ strip mall in far northwest Austin, this unassuming, bare-bones spot gets raves from local foodies as Austin's most authentic Sichuan cuisine. Bypass the standard Chinese options for palate-tingling winners like the Asia Eggplant (in a spicy sauce), Chicken Delight (aka kou shui ji, bone-in, chilled chicken slices in a spicy sauce), and the best Spicy Fish in town. They employ Sichuan peppercorns and fiery red oil liberally, so be prepared. Takeout is available, and a Chinese breakfast is served Saturday mornings. ⊠ *8650 Spicewood Springs Rd., Ste. 115, Northwest Austin* ☏ *512/331–5780* ▤ *MC, V.*

SOUTHERN ✕ **Hoover's.** In recent years local chef Hoover Alexander has created one
$–$$ of Austin's best comfort-food oases, blending mama's home cooking,
☾ diner short-order specials, Tex-Mex favorites, and Cajun influences.
★ The self-styled "Smoke, Fire & Ice House" is known for its large portions, and the chefs aren't shy with the spices, either. The huge, flavorful chicken-fried steak puts most others to shame (even Threadgill's). The moist, flavorful fried chicken, smoked boudin sausage, and jalapeño creamed spinach are additional standouts; extravagant, New Orleans–influenced breakfasts are worth a trip. We've never had room to try the pies, but we hear they're pretty good, too. ⊠ *2002 Manor Rd., University of Texas* ☏ *512/479–5006* ⊠ *13376 Research Blvd., Northwest Austin* ☏ *512/335–0300* ▤ *AE, D, MC, V.*

BARBECUE ✕ **Rudy's BBQ.** Many local barbecue snobs turn up their noses at Rudy's
¢–$ because it's a chain (albeit Texas-based) with hokey decor, but plenty
☾ of Austinites count this as their "go-to" choice for brisket, ribs, or sausage. Takeout is brisk, but many a diner chows down at the vinyl-covered picnic tables. Three kinds of brisket—regular, extra moist, and extra lean—are cooked with a dry spice over wood fired with oak (not mesquite). Go for the extra moist unless you're watching your waist. The peppery "sause" (available bottled) is added at the table. Aside

from brisket, there are pork and baby back ribs, pork loin, prime rib (not worth the extra cost, we think), and even turkey breast. Sides are uniformly good, especially the creamed corn, which has a cult following. ⊠ *11570 Research Blvd., Northwest Austin* ☎ *512/418–9898* ⊠ *2451 Capital of Texas Hwy. S., West Lake* ☎ *512/329–5554* ⊠ *7709 FM 620, Lake Travis* ☎ *512/250–8002* ⚄ *Reservations not accepted* ▭ *MC, V.*

PFLUGERVILLE

EASTERN EUROPEAN
$$–$$$

✕ **European Bistro.** The service here can be scatterbrained (though things have been improving), but occasional lapses are forgiven, since this two-story Central European restaurant in Central Texas is a charmer—an authentic slice of the Old World in downtown Pflugerville, about 15 mi north of Austin. Co-owner Anni Zovek is a true champion of her native Hungarian cuisine, and a delightful hostess. Her sister Piroska whips up some of the most decadent desserts this side of Vienna, and the unusual soups, such as sour cherry, are also worth trying. Main courses of chicken páprikas, pan-fried catfish, and all manner of schnitzels and wursts are reliable comfort food. The restaurant also serves Czech, Russian, Polish, and Armenian specialties. Hungarian, German, and Romanian wines are available, as are Czech and German beers. ⊠ *111 East Main St., Pflugerville* ☎ *512/835–1919* ▭ *AE, D, DC, MC, V* ⊗ *Closed Mon. No lunch Tues.–Thurs.*

SECOND STREET & WAREHOUSE DISTRICT

NEW AMERICAN
$$–$$$$
Fodor'sChoice
★

✕ **Lamberts.** On an up-and-coming block near City Hall, Lamberts draws businessmen, Web types, trenchermen, and foodies for its "fancy barbecue," aka stylish twists on Texas classics. You know this isn't your father's barbecue joint when you hear Belle & Sebastian on the speakers instead of LeAnn Rimes or Merle Haggard. Chimay beer is available *on draft*, and the Frito pie costs $10 and contains goat cheese. Appetizers range from Asian-style crispy wild-boar ribs to broiled Gulf oysters with apple-smoked bacon. Desserts, like lemon chess pie with blueberry sauce, are tangy-sweet and satisfying. They even make a decent cappuccino. Service is competent and cheerful. The restaurant is housed in a historic two-story 1873 brick building; the front room has whitewashed brick, green leatherette '60s banquettes, and a bar serving top single-malt Scotches. The second floor has a bar with a few tables and a stage where bands play the nights away. ⊠ *401 W. 2nd St., Second Street & Warehouse District* ☎ *512/494–1500* ▭ *AE, D, DC, MC, V.*

SOUTH AUSTIN

ITALIAN
$–$$
Fodor'sChoice
★

✕ **Enoteca Vespaio.** Vespaio's kid sister has quickly harnessed the lion's share of popularity on South Congress. Known for its tantalizing antipasti counter filled with delectable charcuterie, pâtés, cheeses, and salads, this more casual café has an authentic trattoria feel complete with brightly colored Italian countryside tablecloths. Sink your fork into a bowl of plump gnocchi bathed in garlicky tomato-arrabiata sauce, or nibble on a slice of classic Margherita pizza studded with garden-fresh basil. Juicy hanger steak and crispy french fries (bistecca con patate fritte) leave you wanting more, but don't fill up on dinner; the dessert case is home to some phenomenal treats—the crème puff is about as close to Paris as you can get. Pastries for breakfast or lunch on the patio are alone worth the visit. ⊠*1610 S. Congress, South Austin* ☎*512/441–7672* ▤*AE, D, MC, V* ⊙*Sunday brunch only 10–3.*

BRAZILIAN
$$$

✕**Estância Churrascaria.** This all-you-can-eat Brazilian steak house owned by Brazilian expats opened in 2007 and quickly became a popular addition to Austin's dining scene. In an attractive limestone building with post-and-beam ceilings, Estância has a prix-fixe menu for lunch and dinner that covers everything except drinks and dessert. Start with the large salad bar, but leave room for the 11 different grilled meats that gaucho-costumed servers carve from skewers tableside. These include *picanha* (rump steak), beef and pork ribs, filet mignon, New Zealand leg of lamb, linguica (seasoned sausage), and chicken. It keeps coming as long as you display the green card on your table. The wine list has some 250 labels. It's a bit out of the way, just off Highway 290 in the Sunset Valley area of South Austin (about 8 mi southwest of downtown), but worth the trip. ⊠*4894 Hwy. 290 W, South Austin* ☎*512/892–1225* ▤*AE, D, MC, V.*

AMERICAN
¢–$$
⊙

✕**Magnolia Cafe.** This locally beloved restaurant serves a full complement of the simple breakfast/brunch foods that Austinites tend to crave at all hours. The typical selection of sandwiches, omelets, salads, and desserts is supplemented by seven enchilada options and hearty hash-brown dishes enhanced with cheese, bacon, and other ingredients. Try the Love Migas (eggs scrambled with crisp tortilla chips and fresh salsa, spiked with garlic-serrano butter and served with black beans) for a savory treat. Breakfast, including stellar plate-filling pancakes—buttermilk, whole wheat, cornmeal, or richly luscious gingerbread—is available 24/7. Service is always friendly. ⊠*2304 Lake Austin Blvd., Downtown & Capitol Area* ☎*512/478–8645* ⊠*1920 South Congress Ave., South Austin* ☎*512/445–0000* ⩋*Reservations not accepted* ▤*AE, DC, MC, V.*

MEXICAN
¢–$$
⊙

✕**Matt's Famous El Rancho.** Opened by the Martinez family in 1952, this South Austin landmark does old-school Tex-Mex extremely well, and you'll hear few complaints from diners. Combination dinners are many and varied, with all the usual standbys: enchiladas, tamales, crispy tacos, and more. Diehards swear by the chiles rellenos and old-fashioned tacos. The expansive dining room can get noisy at peak hours, but the large outdoor patio is pleasant in good weather. Be sure to strike up a conversation with the staff—some employees have worked here for decades. ⊠*2613 S. Lamar Blvd., South Austin* ☎*512/462–9333* ▤*AE, D, DC, MC, V* ⊙*Closed Tues.*

JAPANESE
$$–$$$$
Fodor's Choice
★

✕**Uchi.** You've heard the term "extreme sports"? Uchi is "extreme sushi." Respectful of traditional sushi and sashimi methods—but not limited by them—this standout sushi bar (a consistent critical and popular favorite) starts with super-fresh ingredients. After that, anything goes, including touches of the South or south-of-the-border: yellowtail with ponzu sauce and sliced chilies, tempura-style fried green tomatoes, or seared monkfish cheeks with Vietnamese caramel, Belgian endive, roasted red grapes, and cilantro; unusual salsas enliven most any dish. You can make a tapas-style meal from the cold and hot "tastings" menu. If you sit at the sushi bar you can watch the enthusiastic kitchen staff at work. Attentive, knowledgeable service seals the deal. ⊠ *801 S. Lamar Blvd., South Austin* ☎ *512/916–4808* ⊟ *AE, MC, V* ☉ *Closed Mon.–Wed. No lunch.*

ITALIAN
$$–$$$$
★

✕ **Vespaio.** This buzzing Italian bistro on South Congress consistently attracts Austin's bold and beautiful. Patrons crowd the narrow, warmly-lit bar while waiting for a table in the small, tawny-hued dining room. Noshing on the gratis white-bean puree doused with a shot of basil-infused olive oil makes perusing the menu of delicate handmade pastas, thin wood-fired pizzas, and robust Northern Italian-inspired entrées an even greater treat. Chef specials change daily, including soul-warming risottos of the day—the last bowl we tried included braised veal cheek and earthy wild mushrooms. Smoky grilled prawns wrapped in crispy prosciutto and served with warm suppli (fried risotto balls) never disappoints, nor does the savory veal scallopine wrapped with sage, prosciutto, and wilted spinach. Desserts change daily, but are worth the indulgence. ⊠ *1610 S. Congress, South Austin* ☎ *512/441–6100* ⊟ *AE, D, MC, V* ☉ *No lunch* ⌦ *Reservations not accepted Fri.–Sat.*

UNIVERSITY OF TEXAS

CONTINENTAL
$$–$$$$
★

✕ **The Mansion at Judges' Hill.** One of the most romantic places in town is this intimate, dimly lit dining room in a boutique hotel in a century-old mansion near the UT campus. Chandeliers hang from the ceiling, and portraits of cabaret singers line the walls. The first-course lobster beignets with avocado, roasted tomato, and corn sauce have a crusty exterior and a creamy, delicately-spiced center. The duck confit quesadillas with smoked Gouda, provolone, forest mushrooms, and a tomatillo salsa are subtly complex. Seasonal entrées include petite beef medallions with a trio of sauces that reveal new flavors with each bite, and a 16-ounce rib-eye steak with potato mousseline, lemon-scented broccolini, and a béarnaise sauce. Save room for large, well-conceived desserts like caramelized s'mores with almond ice cream. Glitches in the prompt and considerate service are rare. Breakfast is served daily. ⊠ *1900 Rio Grande St., University of Texas* ☎ *512/495–1857* ⊟ *AE, D, DC, MC, V* ☉ *No lunch Mon.–Sat.*

BARBECUE
¢–$$

✕ **Ruby's BBQ.** On a busy corner of the Drag (UT's commercial strip), this nuevo barbecue joint—which many locals consider among the best in town—has a deep list of menu options not found at old-school pits. The beef is trumpeted as all natural and hormone-free, but perhaps more important, it's tender, tasty, and perfectly juicy. Side dishes are vegetarian-friendly: two kinds of beans (black and BBQ), a couple of slaw options, potato salad, home fries, and collard greens. Also on the menu are garden salads and a few Cajun dishes. There are daily chalkboard specials. ⊠ *512 W. 29th St., University of Texas* ☎ *512/477–1651* ⌦ *Reservations not accepted* ⊟ *MC, V.*

WEST LAKE

BARBECUE ✕**The Salt Lick.** When Texans argue about the relative merits of barbecue
¢–$$ joints, the Salt Lick usually winds up at or near the top of the heap.
Fodor'sChoice Getting here entails a 30-minute drive southwest of Austin, but diners
★ who make the trek are rewarded with finger-licking-good ribs, beef,
chicken, turkey, and sausage slow-cooked over an open pit and accom-
panied by a tangy sauce (unusual for central Texas) and the usual sides.
Slaw is fresh and crisp, not smothered in mayo. If you can manage it,
top your meal off with peach cobbler or pecan pie. The area is dry, alco-
hol-wise, so if you want anything stronger than Dr Pepper, bring it with
you. It's cash-only, but there's an on-site ATM. *Salt Lick 360* (⊠*3801 N.
Capital of Texas Hwy., West Lake* ☎*512/328–4957*), in town, is a fan-
cier offshoot of the original barbecue joint. ⊠*18300 Farm-to-Market
Rd. 1826, Driftwood* ☎*512/894–3117* ☰*No credit cards.*

ZILKER PARK

FRENCH ✕**Flip Happy Crepes.** More than just a restaurant, Flip Happy is the
¢–$ dream-made-real of Andrea Day Boykin and Nessa Higgins, who are
☾ doing their share to "keep Austin weird," serving up French-inspired
★ crepes out of a 1966-vintage silver trailer on a tree-sheltered side street
in South Austin. The crepes are super-moist, salty-spicy, flavorful and
substantial (just one makes a good-size lunch). Chicken, mushrooms,
goat cheese, shredded pork, and smoked salmon are typical ingredients,
and the team also whips up sweet crepes and Saturday breakfast. It's
just a fun place to grab a bite and sit with some of the happiest, in-
the-know diners in town at a motley assortment of mismatched tables
and chairs. Short hours are the main drawback: Flip Happy is gener-
ally open 10–2:30 Wednesday–Friday and 9–3 Saturday, but check the
Web site for changes. Dinner is sometimes served on Saturdays in warm
weather. ⊠*400 Jessie St., Zilker Park* ☎*512/552–9034* ☰*No credit
cards* ⦿*Closed Sun.–Tues. No dinner.*

AMERICAN ✕**Shady Grove.** If any one restaurant defines the laid-back, somewhat
¢–$$ goofy Austin aesthetic, it's probably Shady Grove. On any clear day,
☾ expect the stone patio here to be packed with folks fighting the heat
with schooner-sized frozen margaritas. Visitors to Barton Springs Pool
frequent this state park–theme establishment for its funky vibe, high-
profile music events, and huge servings of simple fare. Burgers and hot
dogs are big movers here, as are the vegetarian "hippie sandwiches"
(roasted eggplant and grilled vegetables) and impossibly large salads.
On summer evenings the patio becomes a dine-in theater, as vintage
movies are projected onto an outdoor screen. ⊠*1624 Barton Springs
Rd., Zilker Park* ☎*512/474–9991* ⚱*Reservations not accepted* ☰*AE,
D, DC, MC, V.*

SOUTHERN ✕**Threadgill's.** Locals take their out-of-town guests to this local legend
$–$$ for "real Texas food." Kenneth Threadgill opened the original loca-
★ tion on North Lamar in 1933 as a gas station that soon evolved into
a honky-tonk that drew local musicians, including a pre-fame Janis
Joplin in the early '60s. Today Threadgill's is a friendly restaurant
with cleaned-up Texas charm, and the main attraction is the massive

chicken-fried steak, followed by homemade cobbler and ice cream. Some other mains may disappoint, though veggie sides are satisfying. Live music happens regularly at both locations. The atmosphere is a bit hokey, but Threadgill's has earned it. At this writing, a third location in Cedar Park is set to open in mid-2008. ⊠*6416 N. Lamar Blvd., North Austin* ☎*512/451–5440* ⊠*301 W. Riverside Dr., Zilker Park* ☎*512/472–9304* ⊟*AE, D, MC, V.*

WHERE TO STAY

Finding a place to stay in Austin isn't hard. Finding a place with personality is harder. Downtown, ample brand-name high-rises offer anonymous luxury, but despite Austin's history and capital status there are only a few stately, historic hotels. The I–35 corridor is a logjam of chain motels ranging from pleasant to horrid, catering largely to travelers with limited expectations. In the tech-centered Northwest, it's hard to drive any distance without passing an all-suites executive lodging.

Fortunately, things are improving. A good number of the hotels we list have benefited from extensive renovations between 2006 and 2008, and Austin is such a competitive market that many managers feel compelled to provide the latest and greatest, whether it's flat-screen TVs, radios with iPod docking stations, or ultra-comfy beds. This being Austin, free, public Wi-Fi is near-ubiquitous.

Downtown, the Driskill and the Intercontinental Stephen F. Austin are two grandes dames that still shine. A couple of old motor courts on South Congress have been rediscovered and refitted, capturing Austin's bohemian charms. In the business district, there are plans to build a 1,000-room Marriott convention-center hotel (to be completed in 2011), ruffling a few local feathers in the process. On the other end of the spectrum are several well-run bed-and-breakfasts in historic homes.

Conventions and university events can pack the city at any time, but you'll especially need to plan ahead during a University of Texas football home game, South by Southwest in March, the Austin City Limits festival in September, or legislative sessions (held in odd-numbered years). At slower times many hotels have deep discounts. Keep in mind that parking at downtown hotels can add over $20 a day to your bill. In general, only hotels near Austin–Bergstrom International Airport have free airport shuttles.

WHAT IT COSTS					
	¢	$	$$	$$$	$$$$
HOTELS	under $50	$50–$100	$101–$150	$151–$200	over $200

Hotel prices are per night for two people in a standard double room in high season, excluding service charges and Austin's 15% hotel tax.

DOWNTOWN & CAPITOL AREA

$$–$$$ 🛉 **Carrington's Bluff.** Pine-covered arbors, a gazebo, and a tree-shaded,
Fodor's Choice gently sloping lawn frame this B&B in a two-story, five-room 1877
★ dairy farm and adjoining 1920 three-room "Writers' Cottage" on a
quiet residential street seven blocks from UT. Phoebe Williams is a
genial hostess who works to accommodate specific needs. The cottage
is filled with well-chosen period antiques; the only anachronisms are
bedside clock radios and cable TVs. **Pros:** One of the most charming and personality-filled historic B&Bs in Austin, close to UT and a
mile from downtown, convenient to bus routes. **Cons:** No pool, spa,
or other luxury-hotel gewgaws; a bit hard to find, especially at night.
✉ *1900 David St., Downtown & Capitol Area* 🕾 *512/479–0638 or
888/290–6090* ⊕ *www.carringtonsbluff.com* ⇆ *8 rooms* ⌂ *In-room:
no phone, Wi-Fi. In-hotel: no elevator, laundry facilities, public Wi-Fi,
parking (no fee), some pets allowed, no-smoking rooms* ⑩| *BP* ⊟ *AE,
D, MC, V.*

$$$–$$$$ 🛉 **Doubletree Guest Suites.** One of the best-managed hotels in the city,
Fodor's Choice the all-suites Doubletree has a staff that anticipates your every need.
★ Business travelers, sports teams, and families frequent the downtown
high-rise. The Capitol—visible from many of the rooms, spectacularly
so from upper-story balconies—is only a few minutes' walk away.
Most of the classically decorated suites have one bedroom and two
TVs; some have two bedrooms, two baths, and three TVs; four are
penthouses. Each has a small kitchen with a full-size refrigerator and
dishwasher. A free shuttle takes you anywhere within a 2-mi radius.
Smoking is only allowed on the third floor. **Pros:** Superbly run, above-
average ambience. **Cons:** Can be crowded, busy area, fee for park-
ing. ✉ *303 W. 15th St., Downtown & Capitol Area* 🕾 *512/478–7000
or 800/222–8733* ⊕ *www.doubletreehotels.com* ⇆ *188 suites* ⌂ *In-
room: kitchen, refrigerator, Wi-Fi. In-hotel: restaurant, room service,
bar, pool, gym, laundry facilities, laundry service, parking (fee), some
pets allowed, no-smoking rooms* ⊟ *AE, D, DC, MC, V.*

$$$$ 🛉 **Driskill Hotel.** Built in 1886 and impeccably restored, the Driskill is a
Fodor's Choice beautiful public space created when people relished mingling in grand
★ settings. The lobby is highlighted by vaulted ceilings, decorative col-
umns, and chandeliers. The entire effect is old-fashioned luxury, and
Texas to the core. Each room is unique: walls are decorated with old
photos, postcards, lace, and bric-a-brac scoured from local antiques
shops. Ceilings are higher in rooms in the historic wing than in the
newer tower wing (which dates merely to 1930) and bathrooms are
old-fashioned and spotless. The Driskill Grill *(⇨ Where to Eat)* and
semi-casual 1886 Café & Bakery are both worth a visit. The elegant
bar, with frequent live piano music, has long attracted Austin's movers
and shakers. The hotel is widely reported to be haunted. **Pros:** Flaw-
less restoration, historic, lots of personality. **Cons:** No pool, immediate
neighborhood is an unattractive city block. ✉ *604 Brazos St., Down-
town & Capitol Area* 🕾 *512/474–5911 or 800/252–9367* ⊕ *www.
driskillhotel.com* ⇆ *176 rooms, 13 suites* ⌂ *In-room: Ethernet, Wi-
Fi. In-hotel: restaurant, room service, bar, gym, parking (no fee)* ⊟ *AE,
D, DC, MC, V.*

WHERE SHOULD I STAY IN AUSTIN?

	Neighborhood Vibe	Pros	Cons
Downtown & Capitol Area	Austin's vibrant downtown is growing into a place with a "real" big-city feel, yet retaining touches of the overgrown village it used to be. Close to most tourist attractions, it's ideal for first-time visitors and many business travelers.	Where the action is, in terms of business and restaurants and clubs; compact and pedestrian-friendly; good public transport.	Rooms tend to be either expensive or seedy, overnight parking pricey, daytime traffic heavy.
Lake Travis	Known for water sports, upmarket resorts, and casual restaurants, parts of the Lake Travis area have an almost Mediterranean look. Leisure travelers, conventioneers, and business groups frequent the hotels.	Luxurious resorts, pretty lake and surrounds, relaxed air, peaceful and untouristy.	Nearly 20 mi from the city; few, if any budget options; a car is a necessity.
Near the Airport	The roads leading to Austin–Bergstrom International Airport pass mainly through drab, working-class commercial and industrial strips of greater or lesser density. Business travelers and flight crews fill most hotels.	Unsurprisingly, convenient to airport; cheap and good Mexican eats nearby.	Properties are about 10 mi from downtown; most hotels uninteresting chains; surrounding areas generic and not pedestrian friendly; a good stretch of Highway 71 is a seedy zone.
North Austin	Hotels and motels line the I–35 corridor for miles on both sides, attracting mainly transient business travelers and some families on weekends. You'll need a car to get around and you should choose your hotel with care, as some areas verge on unsafe.	Easy access to the highway and downtown, some hotels off I–35 are surprisingly characterful and pleasantly quirky.	The I–35 corridor is noisy and traffic-clogged night and day; some areas feel unsafe.
Northwest Austin	Hotels in this sprawling suburban area filled with large upscale malls and superstores are focused on business travelers and families on a budget. There are some worthwhile shops and restaurants, though you'll have to do a bit of research to find them.	Staff well-tuned to needs of business travelers, comparatively good value, tons of malls and big-box stores close by.	Spread-out and generic suburban area; lodgings have little personality; not pedestrian-friendly.
South Austin	Hotels here come in all types and sizes and are relatively close to both downtown and the airport. Some areas are not pedestrian-friendly. The touristy, "fun" areas are nearer to the river.	Excellent business hotels at significant discounts compared to downtown counterparts, South Congress is hotel nirvana if you're looking for artsy and unusual.	Some hotel staff and managers are lax or overly casual; areas below Highway 290 are far from interesting neighborhoods.

BEST BETS FOR AUSTIN LODGING

For all the big hotel chains' efforts at standardization, any lodging's quality still depends largely on the manager and staff at an individual location. Since Austin is a desirable place to live, it draws many of the hospitality industry's best. We've chosen some especially well-run places below.

Fodor's Choice ★

Carrington's Bluff, $$–$$$, Downtown & Capitol Area

Doubletree Guest Suites, $$$–$$$$, Downtown & Capitol Area

Driskill Hotel, $$$$, Downtown & Capitol Area

Four Seasons, $$$$, Downtown & Capitol Area

Hyatt Place, $$$–$$$$, North Austin

Mansion at Judges' Hill, $$$–$$$$, Downtown & Capitol Area

By Price

$

Austin Motel, South Austin

Days Inn University, Downtown & Capitol Area

Howard Johnson Plaza Hotel & Conference Center, North Austin

$$

Carrington's Bluff, Downtown & Capitol Area

Habitat Suites, North Austin

Wyndham Garden Hotel–Austin, South Austin

$$$

Hotel San José, South Austin

Hyatt Place, Northwest Austin

Lakeway Resort and Spa, Lake Travis

Mansion at Judges' Hill, Downtown & Capitol Area

Radisson Hotel & Suites Austin, Downtown & Capitol Area

$$$$

Barton Creek Resort & Spa, West Lake

Doubletree Guest Suites, Downtown & Capitol Area

Driskill Hotel, Downtown & Capitol Area

Four Seasons, Downtown & Capitol Area

By Type

HISTORIC

Carrington's Bluff, $$–$$$, Downtown & Capitol Area

Driskill Hotel, $$$$, Downtown & Capitol Area

InterContinental Stephen F. Austin Hotel, $$$$, Downtown & Capitol Area

Mansion at Judges' Hill, $$$–$$$$, Downtown & Capitol Area

MOST CHARMING

Carrington's Bluff, $$–$$$, Downtown & Capitol Area

Mansion at Judges' Hill, $$$–$$$$, Downtown & Capitol Area

Woodburn House, $$–$$$, Hyde Park

By Experience

FAMILY FRIENDLY

Barton Creek Resort & Spa, $$$$, West Lake

Habitat Suites Hotel, $$–$$$, North Austin

Hawthorn Suites Austin Central, $$–$$$, North Austin

Lakeway Resort and Spa, $$$–$$$$, Lake Travis

Omni Austin Hotel at Southpark, $$–$$$$, South Austin

GREAT VIEWS

Barton Creek Resort & Spa, $$$$, West Lake

Doubletree Guest Suites, $$$–$$$$, Downtown & Capitol Area

Four Seasons, $$$$, Downtown & Capitol Area

Holiday Inn Austin–Town Lake, $$$–$$$$, Downtown & Capitol Area

Lakeway Resort and Spa, $$$–$$$$, Lake Travis

Omni Austin Hotel at Southpark, $$–$$$$, South Austin

$$$–$$$$ **⊞Embassy Suites Downtown.** This central all-suites hotel is across the street from the Lady Bird Lake hiking and biking trail, four blocks from the Convention Center, and 10 blocks from the State Capitol. Rooms look out onto an interior atrium lobby with a 550-gallon aquarium. The standard two-room suites have two televisions, a microwave, and a refrigerator; rates include evening cocktails. In addition to a pool and exercise room, there's a sauna and hot tub. The property is remaining open while it undergoes a complete renovation, expected to be completed in 2009. **Pros:** Attractive, well-run, close to airport. **Cons:** Under renovation until 2009. ⊠ *300 S. Congress Ave., Downtown & Capitol Area* ☎*512/469–9000 or 800/362–2779* ⊕*www.embassysuites. com* ⇆*262 rooms* ⌂*In-room: refrigerator, Wi-Fi. In-hotel: restaurant, room service, bar, pool, gym, laundry facilities, laundry service, parking (no fee)* ⊟*AE, D, DC, MC, V* ⍟*BP.*

$$$$ **⊞Four Seasons.** You get what you pay for in superior service and ame-
Fodor's Choice nities at this elegant hotel on beautifully manicured grounds overlook-
★ ing Lady Bird Lake. Rooms are average size, but stylish. Beds with goose-down pillows and comforters, flat-screen plasma TVs, and iPod docking stations are standard. Some rooms have terraces, and upper-floor units have impressive views. Extras include a lending library of Texas literature and in-room martini bars. The hotel has an attractive outdoor saltwater pool, an indoor pool, and a whirlpool, as well as a modern fitness center and a gorgeous spa, installed during extensive 2007 renovations. There are two business centers. Smoking is relegated to one floor. **Pros:** Beautiful, with resort feel; central downtown location. **Cons:** Expensive, parking among priciest in town. ⊠*98 San Jacinto Blvd., Downtown & Capitol Area* ☎*512/478–4500 or 800/332–3442* ⇆*291 rooms* ⌂*In-room: safe, DVD, Ethernet, Wi-Fi. In-hotel: 2 restaurants, bar, room service, pool, gym, spa, laundry service, concierge, public Wi-Fi, parking (fee), some pets allowed, no-smoking rooms* ⊟*AE, DC, MC, V* ⊕*www.fourseasons.com.*

$$$$ **⊞Hilton Austin.** Austin's largest hotel rises 26 stories over one of downtown's quieter blocks, next to small Brush Park (home to the O. Henry House). But the Hilton is defined by its proximity to the colossal Austin Convention Center, and this is *the* conventioneers' hostelry. It has two proper restaurants, plus a coffee shop and business center, and Austin's second-largest outdoor pool (heated). Standard rooms have two full beds or one king and a leather loveseat; the latter configuration seems roomier. Room safes accommodate a laptop. The entire eighth floor is a 16,000-square-foot health club with a steam room and sauna, and a gym with great views of UT's stadium. **Pros:** Downtown location, easy drive to airport; **Cons:** Huge, rather impersonal. ⊠*500 E. 4th St., Downtown & Capitol Area* ☎*512/482–8000* ⇆*775 rooms, 25 suites* ⌂*In-room: safe, Ethernet, Wi-Fi. In-hotel: 3 restaurants, room service, bar, pool, gym, spa, laundry service, concierge, public Wi-Fi, parking (fee), no-smoking rooms* ⊟*AE, D, DC, MC, V* ⊕*www.hilton.com.*

$$$$ **⊞Hyatt Regency Austin.** On Lady Bird Lake near Auditorium Shores, the
★ hotel has great views of the water and downtown skyline. The huge, skylit lobby, with tons of native stone and a central atrium rising 17 stories, oozes rugged sophistication. Rooms, which were upgraded in

2006, have 32-inch flat-panel TVs and luxe bathrooms. Business meetings and banquets keep the Hyatt hopping year-round. **Pros:** Attractive, luxurious, well-equipped and -staffed for meetings. **Cons:** Some find it too slick and corporate. ⊠*208 Barton Springs Rd., Downtown & Capitol Area* ☎*512/477–1234* ⊕*www.hyatt.com* ➡*448 rooms* ⸫*In-room: Ethernet, Wi-Fi. In-hotel: restaurant, room service, bar, pool, parking (fee)* ☰*AE, D, DC, MC, V.*

$$$$ ★ 🖫**InterContinental Stephen F. Austin Hotel.** This historic 1924 hotel reopened after a 12-year vacancy in 2000 following a top-to-bottom renovation, including restoration of many original architectural features. The location is ideal: one block from 6th Street, four blocks from the Capitol, and next door to the historic Paramount Theater. Rooms are dressed in dark woods, and the decor is sparked with understated nods to Texas, like the Lone Star emblem on the headboards—all in all they are a bit bland apart from the opulent bathrooms with marble vanities. At the end of the day, relax at the terrace bar, whose balcony overlooks Congress Avenue and the Capitol, or at Roaring Fork, a critically praised Western bistro and saloon. **Pros:** Well run, centrally located, historic. **Cons:** Some rooms rather small; pricey valet parking. ⊠*701 Congress Ave,, Downtown & Capitol Area* ☎*512/457–8800 or 800/327–0200* ⊕*www.austin.intercontinental.com* ➡*189 rooms, 16 suites* ⸫*In-room: safe, Ethernet. In-hotel: 2 restaurants, room service, bar, pool, gym, concierge, laundry service, executive floor, parking (fee)* ☰*AE, D, DC, MC, V.*

$$–$$$$ FodorsChoice ★ 🖫**Mansion at Judges' Hill.** History and modern amenities come together in this exquisite boutique hotel near the southern edge of UT's main campus. The Goodall Wooten house, a Texas Historic Landmark completed in 1900, was of fairly simple design until 1910, when the owners remodeled it into a grand Classical Revival mansion. All rooms have high-speed Internet connections, and there's twice-daily maid service. Little touches—his and hers bathrobes, extra pillows, and beautiful bathrooms (in the more expensive wing)—make the difference. There's also an exceptional, fine-dining restaurant, a handsome bar, and occasional cabaret performances in the second-floor banquet hall. **Pros:** Beautifully restored, historic, perfect for romantic getaways, attentive staff. **Cons:** Parking somewhat limited, no pool. ⊠*1900 Rio Grande St., Downtown & Capitol Area* ☎*512/495–1800 or 800/311–1619* ⊕*www.mansionatjudgeshill.com* ➡*48 rooms* ⸫*In-room: Ethernet. In-hotel: restaurant, concierge* ☰*AE, D, DC, MC, V.*

$$$$ 🖫**Omni Austin Downtown.** Your introduction to this bustling, business-oriented hotel is a soaring, granite-and-glass atrium lobby. From atrium-view rooms you can spy on diners and scurrying businesspeople below. Exterior rooms have balconies and city vistas (on upper floors). The decor neither inspires nor offends. At this writing, room renovations are scheduled for completion in May 2008. Most of the suites were once condos and have full kitchens, washers and dryers, and walk-in closets. Some rooms have whirlpool baths, and there's an outdoor swimming pool on the roof. At breakfast, the eggs are cage-free, the bagels are shipped from New York. Service is professional, if on the cool side. **Pros:** Central location, everything for the business

traveler. **Cons:** Can feel impersonal. ✉*700 San Jacinto St., Downtown & Capitol Area* ☎*512/476–3700* ⏧*www.omnihotels.com* ⇶*375 rooms* ⚴ *In-room: Wi-Fi. In-hotel: restaurant, room service, bar, pool, gym, spa, concierge, laundry service, executive floor, parking (fee), no-smoking rooms* ▤*AE, D, DC, MC, V.*

$–$$ 🖵**Super 8 Motel.** For basic, reasonably priced lodging close to downtown, you could do worse than this basic two-story brick motel just off I–35 northbound. There's a clean outdoor pool, and a good view of downtown from the second floor. Be sure to request a room away from highway noise. Rooms have slightly worn carpet and older refrigerators and microwaves, and there are no no-smoking floors (only no-smoking rooms), but for these prices it's hard to complain. An employee cautions to beware of "party people," and ask for a quieter room, especially during UT home games and SXSW. **Pros:** Price, proximity to downtown. **Cons:** Can be noisy, not scenic. ✉*1201 I–35N, Downtown & Capitol Area* ☎*512/472–8331* ⏧*www.super8.com* ⇶*60 rooms, 5 suites* ⚴ *In-room: refrigerator (some), Ethernet. In-hotel: pool, laundry facilities, some pets allowed, no-smoking rooms* ▤*AE, D, DC, MC, V.*

$$ 🖵**Woodburn House.** Built in 1909, Hyde Park's only B&B—listed in the National Register of Historic Places—is a simply and tastefully decorated three-story home with a mix of antiques and newer furniture. Large wraparound porches and mature pecan trees add to the charm. Owners Kristen and Noel De La Rosa can provide a self-guided walking tour of Austin's historic Hyde Park area. The large room in an adjoining detached carriage house has a kitchenette, big-screen TV, and hot tub. Some good restaurants are within walking distance. There's free in-room Wi-Fi, and the entire house is no-smoking. **Pros:** Well-maintained and historic, charming neighborhood, close to public transport, 1 mi from UT and 2 mi from downtown. **Cons:** Only suites have TVs. ✉*4401 Ave. D, Downtown & Capitol District* ☎*512/458–4335 or 888/690–9763* ⏧*www.woodburnhouse.com* ⇶*4 rooms, 2 suites* ⚴ *In-room: Wi-Fi. In-hotel: no elevator, parking (no fee), no kids under 12, no-smoking rooms* ⏨*CP* ▤*AE, MC, V.*

LAKE TRAVIS

$$$–$$$$ 🖵**Lakeway Resort and Spa.** On a finger of land surrounded on three sides by Lake Travis, this sprawling, handsome resort housed in low-rise stone buildings is about 20 mi from downtown. The property has all you'd expect from a large conference center and resort, including a full-service, state-of-the-art spa, built in 2007, and a tiered infinity-edge outdoor pool. Many recreational opportunities are available on the lake and adjacent marina, from sunset cruises to watercraft rentals, and four golf courses are nearby. Rooms (all no-smoking) are tasteful, mocha-hued, and modern, with contemporary art and plush beds. Most rooms have lakeside views and balconies. The upscale Travis Restaurant offers largely steaks and seafood (some diners have noted glaring service glitches). **Pros:** Gorgeous resort hotel in peaceful lakeside location; many high-end amenities. **Cons:** Not convenient to downtown, some may find the ambience stuffy. ✉*101 Lakeway Dr., Lake*

Travis ☎*512/261–6600 or 800/525–3929* ⊕*www.lakeway.dolce.com* ⟿*166 rooms, 2 suites* ⟳*In-room: Wi-Fi, Ethernet (no fee). In-hotel: 2 restaurants, bar, room service, golf courses, tennis court, pools, spa, gym, children's programs (ages 4–12), laundry service, public Internet, public Wi-Fi, airport shuttle, parking (no fee), no-smoking rooms* ▭*AE, D, DC, MC, V.*

NEAR THE AIRPORT

$$$$ 🖩 **Hilton Austin Airport.** On the grounds of the Austin–Bergstrom Inter-
★ national Airport, this circular building was built in the late '60s as a U.S. Air Force base (known as "the donut") and reopened as a hotel in 2001. The atrium is like a Texan starship, with a dome soaring above three balconied floors, and limestone pillars surrounding a central bar area. Rooms overlook the atrium or the large outdoor pool and hot tub with adjacent above-average fitness center. Rooms have well-padded beds, two-cup coffeemakers, and Crabtree & Evelyn toiletries. A touchscreen near the front desk allows you to pay bills, check out, and even print airline boarding passes, and a free shuttle runs to and from airport terminals. Ample meeting space and four ballrooms mean many events and conferences. The hotel is smoke-free. **Pros:** Attractive, well-run, business-oriented, close to airport. **Cons:** Isolated from areas beyond the airport. ⊠*9515 Hotel Dr., Near the Airport* ☎*512/385–6767* ⊕*www.austinairport.hilton.com* ⟿*251 rooms, 11 suites* ⟳*In-room: refrigerator (some), Ethernet. In-hotel: restaurant, room service, bar, pool, gym, laundry facilities, laundry service, concierge, public Wi-Fi, airport shuttle, parking (fee), no-smoking rooms* ▭*AE, D, DC, MC, V.*

NORTH AUSTIN

$–$$$ 🖩 **Crowne Plaza.** A mall and shopping plaza are 2 mi from this seven-
★ story hotel continually bustling with conventions and meetings; downtown is 4–5 mi away. Renovations are ongoing at this writing, slated to be completed in March 2008. Prime rib and similar fare is served in the restaurant, but there are several decent places to eat nearby. Complimentary vans shuttle you within a 3-mi radius. Rooms have plush, comfy beds. One extra is a Sleep Advantage packet with a calming CD, sleep tips, eye mask, ear plugs, and lavender linen spray. **Pros:** Full-service hotel with responsive staff, modern amenities. **Cons:** Large and impersonal, lots of conventions and big groups. ⊠*6121 I–35N, North Austin* ☎*512/323–5466* ⊕*www.crowneplaza.com* ⟿*280 rooms, 13 suites* ⟳*In-room: refrigerator, Ethernet, Wi-Fi. In-hotel: restaurant, room service, bar, pool, laundry facilities, concierge, executive floor, public Internet, public Wi-Fi* ▭*AE, D, DC, MC, V.*

$$–$$$$ 🖩 **Doubletree.** This 1983-vintage hotel turns its back on the rat race of nearby I–35 and transports guests to a surprisingly convincing Spanish colonial world. Huge, arched windows in the lobby open onto a landscaped and terraced courtyard, with pool and hot tub enclosed by six floors of arched walkways. Rooms are spanking clean, spacious, and decorated with plush, high-quality gold-and-cream fabrics, linens, and carpets. Bathrooms are large, with granite sinks. The free local shuttle transports you within a 1-mi radius. **Pros:** Charming, pseudo-grand-hotel atmosphere; close (but not too close) to highway. **Cons:** Few decent restaurants within walking distance; fee for parking, unusual for this area. ⊠*6505 I–35N, North Austin* ☎*512/454–3737* ⊕*www.doubletreehotels.com* ⬐*322 rooms, 28 suites* ♿*In-room: refrigerator (some), Wi-Fi. In-hotel: restaurant, room service, bar, pool, gym, laundry service, parking (fee), no-smoking rooms* ⊟*AE, D, DC, MC, V.*

$$–$$$ ⊞**Habitat Suites Hotel.** Native flowering plants, organic vegetable gardens,
★ and fruit-bearing trees surround this environmentally friendly lodging. A member of the Green Hotels Association, it's won an impressive number of awards for sustainability. The beautifully landscaped pool is sanitized with a salt generator instead of chlorine, the rooms are cleaned with nontoxic products, and the breakfast buffet includes macrobiotic selections. The apartment-like suites are light-filled and roomy, with vaulted ceilings and open kitchens; most have fireplaces. Two-bedroom suites have two stories. Highland Mall, a major shopping center, is just across the road. There's a business center. **Pros:** Eco-conscious, attractive landscaping, peaceful, hospitable staff. **Cons:** Poor-quality furniture, small TVs, can be hard to find. ⊠*500 E. Highland Mall Blvd., North Austin* ☎*512/467–6000 or 800/535–4663* ⊕*www.habitatsuites.com* ⬐*96 suites* ♿*In-room: Wi-Fi. In-hotel: pool, no elevator, laundry facilities, laundry service, parking (no fee), no-smoking rooms* ⊟*AE, D, DC, MC, V* ⦿*CP.*

$$$–$$$$ ⊞**Hyatt Place.** Set back from the roar of I–35, this handsome five-floor
Fodor'sChoice hotel built in 2007 isn't the usual forgettable off-ramp inn. The styl-
★ ish, postmodern lobby has a breakfast/sandwich bar serving Starbucks drinks, bacon and eggs, sandwiches, beer, and wine most of the day. Crisp and contemporary rooms have Asian-influenced touches like a screen separating the lounge area from the bedroom; all have pull-out sofas, kitchenettes, and ergonomic office chairs. The 42-inch flat-screen TVs have input ports for hooking up electronic devices like DVD players, gaming systems, and computers. Several okay restaurants are nearby. There's a business center. **Pros:** Attractive and up-to-date; friendly, young, customer-oriented staffers. **Cons:** Removed from downtown, can be hard to access during rush hour. ⊠*7522 N. I–35, North Austin* ☎*512/323–2121* ⊕*www.hyatt.com* ⬐*120 rooms* ♿*In-room: Ethernet, Wi-Fi. In-hotel: restaurant, bar, pool, gym, laundry service, parking (no fee)* ⊟*AE, D, DC, MC, V.*

NORTHWEST AUSTIN

$$–$$$ ⊞**Hilton Garden Inn Austin NW/Arboretum.** Business travelers and some
★ short-term leisure travelers patronize this five-story hotel in suburban, shopaholic Northwest Austin. Room renovations were completed in early 2008. Set back from the busy highway, the hotel is quiet, and parking is ample. A ground-floor business center provides free Internet and local faxes. There's an indoor pool. Rooms, with contemporary decor, have a mini-refrigerator, microwave, coffeemaker, flat-panel TV, and a bed or beds with Sleep Number mattresses. Large, filling breakfasts (but no other meals) are served in the sunwashed front lobby and

adjacent outdoor patio. Rudy's barbecue joint, a good local chain, is on the opposite side of US 183. **Pros:** Relatively new (2002), well maintained, attentive staff, business center. **Cons:** Few good restaurants in immediate vicinity, far from downtown, not scenic. ✉*11617 Research Blvd., Northwest Austin* 🕾*512/241–1600* ⊕*www.hiltongardeninn. com* ⇆*138 rooms, including 8 deluxe.* ♿*In-room: refrigerator, Wi-Fi. In-hotel: restaurant, pool, gym, laundry facilities, no-smoking rooms* ▭*AE, D, DC, MC, V.*

$$$$ 🏨**Renaissance Austin Hotel.** The enormous, skylit lobby of this hotel—connected to the upscale Arboretum shopping center—is an eccentric mix of Victorian-style street lamps, crystal chandeliers, and giant mobiles. Rooms, on the other hand, are soothingly traditional, and the front doors of most open onto the atrium. Some on upper floors have great views of the surrounding parkland, with the downtown skyline in the distance. You couldn't spend the night any closer to Restoration Hardware, Banana Republic, or any of the mall's other specialty shops. There's also an indoor pool with whirlpool, and the decent-size health club has a good assortment of cycles, treadmills, and free weights. The restaurant overlooks a 95-acre park. All rooms are no-smoking. **Pros:** Luxurious, quiet rooms, nice pool and health club. **Cons:** Removed from downtown, pricey in high season. ✉*9721 Arboretum Blvd., Northwest Austin* 🕾*512/343–2626* ⊕*www.renaissancehotels.com* ⇆*492 rooms, 58 executive rooms, 29 suites* ♿*In-room: Wi-Fi. In-hotel: restaurant, room service, bars, pools, gym, concierge, laundry service, executive floor, public Internet* ▭*AE, D, DC, MC, V.*

SOUTH AUSTIN

$–$$ 🏨**Austin Motel.** What used to be a fading 1938 motor court is now
★   a fun and funky motel. On the hopping South Congress stretch of trendy restaurants, clubs, and shops, this crash pad is a favorite with musicians and artsy folk, who hang by the pool and hot tub, with whimsical concrete statuary for company. Imaginative rooms range from sedate to outrageous and from a diminutive all-white room to palatial pool-view rooms. The '70s-style Flamingo Room is decked out with shag pillows and blue, pink, and turquoise leatherette chairs. The staff aims to please. **Pros:** Fun, hopping neighborhood; friendly staff; hip and artistic. **Cons:** Not for those who prefer their lodgings new and with an excess of amenities. ✉*1220 S. Congress Ave., South Austin* 🕾*512/441–1157* ⊕*www.austinmotel.com* ⇆*39 rooms, 2 suites* ♿*In-room: refrigerator. In-hotel: restaurant, pool, no elevator, laundry facilities, parking (no fee)* ▭*AE, D, DC, MC, V.*

$$$–$$$$ 🏨**Hotel San José.** This quaint-but-hip stand of 1936 bungalows, in the
★   middle of the action on South Congress, was transformed from a derelict motor court into a warren of rooms and suites done up in South Austin chic: a modern, minimalist style adorned with balconies, patios, and tropical vegetation. Rooms have concrete floors, flat-screen TVs, and pine furniture created by a Marfa, Texas, artist. Butterfly chairs abound inside and out. The pool is small (and could be cleaner) but pretty, and there's no on-site restaurant but ever-hip Jo's Coffee Shop is just across the parking lot, and many good eateries are a brief stroll

away. At this writing the owners are building 15 new units, to open in 2008. **Pros:** Epitome of South Austin cool and the antidote to antiseptic motels everywhere. **Cons:** Not for those who don't appreciate Zen-style simplicity. ⊠*1316 S. Congress Ave., South Austin* ☏*512/444–7322* ⊕*www.sanjosehotel.com* ↬*40 rooms* ⌂*In-room: Ethernet. In-hotel: bar, pool, no elevator, laundry service, parking (no fee), no-smoking rooms* ⊟*AE, DC, MC, V.*

$$–$$$$ ▦**Omni Austin Hotel at Southpark.** This elegant 14-story hotel towers near
★ the tangled intersection of I–35 and US 290. It earns high marks for value, but feels removed from the city though it's only about 3 mi from downtown. The regularly renovated property has a resort air, with a semicircular fountain out front; a huge marbled lobby; an outsized indoor-outdoor heated pool; a large exercise room, whirlpool, and sauna; and modest-sized spa. Rooms are decorated with classic restraint, which some might find stuffy or old-fashioned. (For a larger room without breaking the bank, request a corner king.) Upper floors have unobstructed views from the downtown skyline to the airport tower. A city bus stop is within walking distance; a free shuttle makes the 5-mi trip to the airport. **Pros:** Far better value than comparable hotels downtown, customer-oriented staff. **Cons:** Arguably corporate and stuffy, immediate neighborhood is a major highway intersection. ⊠*4140 Governors Row, South Austin* ☏*512/448–2222, 800/THE-OMNI* ↬*306 rooms, 7 suites* ⌂*In-room: refrigerator (some), Ethernet, Wi-Fi. In-hotel: restaurant, bars, room service, pool, gym, concierge, children's programs (ages 2–12), laundry service, airport shuttle, no-smoking rooms* ⊟*AE, D, DC, MC, V* ⊕*www.omnihotels.com.*

$$–$$$ ▦**Wyndham Garden Hotel–Austin.** This five-story hotel 3 mi south of downtown is an impressive sight from the highway, with its stone-and-whitewashed-yellow facade with "lone stars" everywhere. The big-as-Texas motif continues into the contemporary lobby with oversize leather sofas and large portraits of local musicians. Rooms, renovated in 2007, have pale yellow walls, one king or two full beds (in doubles), granite bathroom sinks, and free Wi-Fi. Most guests rave about the friendly, professional staff. An airport shuttle is free, and the screen by the front desk displays arrivals and departures at the international airport. Executive rooms have a leather club chair, 42-inch flat-screen TV, and a separate shower and tub. **Pros:** Good value, exceptionally well-designed, excellent service. **Cons:** You'll need a car. ⊠*3401 I–35S, South Austin* ☏*512/448–2444* ⊕*www.wyndham.com* ↬*190 rooms, 20 suites* ⌂*In-room: refrigerator (some), Wi-Fi. In-hotel: restaurant, room service, bar, pool, gym, laundry facilities, laundry service, airport shuttle, executive floor, parking (no fee), some pets allowed, no-smoking rooms* ⊟*AE, D, DC, MC, V.*

WEST LAKE

$$$$ ▦**Barton Creek Resort & Spa.** Fortune 1000 execs and groups galore
★ flock to this resort on 4,000 acres of prime Hill Country acreage in a tony area west of Austin. Among the many top-resort amenities are four

championship golf courses (two rated among Texas's best), 11 tennis courts, a spa with salon services, and a huge fitness center. Major 2007 and 2008 renovations considerably improved formerly dowdy interiors, but old-money luxury remains the theme. Standard rooms have one king- or two queen-size beds, 1½ baths, a radio with iPod docking station, a 42-inch flat-screen TV, and a well-stocked minibar. Many have panoramic views of the countryside. Downtown is a 15-minute drive outside of rush hour. All rooms are no-smoking. **Pros:** Luxurious, gorgeous views, great golf courses. **Cons:** Expensive, fees for extras like bottled water. ⊠*8212 Barton Club Dr., West Lake* ☎*512/329–4000 or 800/336–6158* ⊕*www.bartoncreek.com* ⌑*285 rooms, 18 suites* ⌂*In-room: safe, Ethernet, Wi-Fi. In-hotel: 3 restaurants, bars, golf courses, tennis courts, pools, gym, spa, children's programs (ages 6 mos–8 yrs), laundry service, concierge, public Wi-Fi, airport shuttle, parking (no fee), no-smoking rooms* ▭*AE, D, MC, V.*

AUSTIN ESSENTIALS

Research prices, get travel advice, and book your trip at fodors.com.

TRANSPORTATION

BY AIR

If you have to be stuck in an airport, it might as well be Austin–Bergstrom International Airport (ABIA), generally regarded as one of the most pleasant airports in the United States. Neither tiny nor overwhelmingly large, it's modern, easy to navigate, and reasonably user-friendly. It even frequently has live music, with area musicians playing concerts on stages at two airport taverns—quite appropriate for the "live music capital." Also, rather than rely on the same chains you'd see in St. Louis, Denver, or Seattle, the concourse's restaurants have a decidedly local slant, with branches of the Salt Lick, Matt's El Rancho, and Waterloo Ice House, to give travelers their first taste (or in some cases, farewell taste) of barbecue and Tex-Mex, Austin style. In addition to the usual souvenir shops and newsstands, Wi-Fi is available (for a fee), and PowerPort stations offer plugs for laptops and chargers, laptop rentals, and printing.

Also, despite its medium-city size, Austin has direct flights to major cities, so you don't necessarily have to fly to or from Austin by first stopping in Houston or DFW. Airlines fly nonstop from ABIA to 37 cities outside Texas, including New York (Delta, JetBlue, Continental), Los Angeles (American, Southwest), Chicago (American, Southwest, United), and Minneapolis/St. Paul (Northwest). Also, if you want to fly from Austin into Mexico, you can fly direct on Aeromexico to Mexico City or on the Mexican budget carrier vivaAerobus to Cancún, Guadalajara, and Monterrey, among other destinations.

Within Texas itself, Southwest Airlines flies to Austin from six cities: Dallas, El Paso, Harlingen, Houston, Lubbock, and Midland/Odessa;

American takes you from Austin to Dallas; and Continental goes to Houston.

The local branch of the national SuperShuttle airport shuttle chain is found at ABIA's ground level (same level as baggage claim). Some cab companies allow for online reservations (although there's no need to reserve a cab to wait for you at the airport; plenty of them should be around). A shared SuperShuttle ride to the airport from a downtown or South Austin hotel will cost $12.75 per person plus tip; add $5 for the Arboretum area. This compares to $20–$25-plus tip for a cab ride between the airport and a downtown-area hotel.

Airport Information **Austin–Bergstrom International Airport** (⊠ *3600 Presidential Blvd., Austin* ☎ *512/530–2242* ⊕ *www.ci.austin.tx.us/austinairport*).

Airport Shuttle **SuperShuttle** (☎ *512/258–3826* ⊕ *www.supershuttle.net*).

Taxis **Austin Cab** (☎ *512/478–2222* ⊕ *www.austincab.com*). **Lone Star Cab Co.** ☎ *512/836–4900* ⊕ *www.lonestarcabaustin.com*). **Yellow Cab** (☎ *512/452–9999* (⊕ *www.yellowcabaustin.com*).

BY BUS

Greyhound's main Austin terminal, which never closes, is in central north Austin near the intersection of FM 2222 and I–35, a block or so from Highland Mall. There are frequent departures to Houston (the trip takes 3 to 3½ hours) and Dallas (averaging 3¾ hours) and many other cities large and small throughout Texas.

Autobuses Americanos, a Mexico-based carrier affiliated with Greyhound, caters largely to a Spanish-speaking market and runs large, late-model coaches between Austin and several Mexican cities from their North Austin base.

Capital Metro, Austin's municipal bus service (full name: Capital Metropolitan Transportation Authority), thoroughly covers the entire Austin metro area, from Leander in the far suburban north to points southwest of the airport. Cap Metro runs frequent service to and from ABIA and four downtown locations. Its Web site is well designed and informative, with comprehensive schedules and maps (the full version of which will probably confuse first-time users with its incredible complexity).

The free 'Dillo (short for armadillo) trolleys run downtown along five routes, from Deep Eddy Pool (just west of MoPac) in the west to Pleasant Valley Road in East Austin, and north–south from the University of Texas to the northern end of South Congress.

Bus & Trolley Information **Autobuses Americanos** (⊠ *1140 Airport Blvd.* ☎ *512/928–9237* ⊕ *www.autobusesamericanos.us*). **Capital Metro** (⊠ *2910 E. 5th Street* ☎ *512/389–7400* ⊕ *www.capmetro.org*). **Greyhound Bus Lines** (⊠ *916 E. Koenig La.* ☎ *512/458–4463* ⊕ *www.greyhound.com*). **'Dillo Trolleys** (⊕ *www.capmetro.org/riding/downtown_trollies.asp* ☎ *512/389–7400*).

BY CAR

Although Greater Austin stretches well beyond these boundaries, most consider the downtown core to be bordered on the west by two highways running in a roughly north–south direction: MoPac (Loop 1) to the west, and I–35 to the east. Other major arteries are Highway 183, which snakes north from the airport (well east of I–35), crossing I–35 and MoPac in north Austin, and continuing to the northwest suburbs; and Loop 360 (Capital of Texas Highway), which runs from the Arboretum area in the northwest, through the upscale West Lake area, crosses MoPac and becomes Highway 71 (aka Ben White Blvd.), running through South Austin to Austin's airport (ABIA).

In addition to the major roads, drivers can choose from a number of local roads to travel relatively smoothly within Austin, notably mighty Lamar Blvd., which runs south from Ben White all the way up to Parmer Lane and I–35 in the far north. Many major roads run in an east–west direction: in general, you'll find a good horizontal artery every five to ten blocks.

If you don't expect to travel outside of downtown, no need to have a car at all. By relying on shoe leather and the extensive public bus-and-trolley system (the free 'Dillo trolleys and the regular Capital Metro bus lines ⊕*www.capmetro.org*) in the central core *(⇨ By Bus)*, you'll avoid getting lost, plus save on unnecessary parking charges at your hotel.

If you need to rent a vehicle, you'll save money by renting it someplace other than the airport.

BY TRAIN

Austin sits at roughly the midpoint of Amtrak's Texas Eagle line, which snakes in a great V from Chicago through Illinois, Missouri, Arkansas, Texas, southern New Mexico, and Arizona before ending up in Los Angeles. Trains depart from Dallas daily at noon, arriving in Austin at 7 PM and then traveling on to San Antonio, with a 10:25 PM arrival time—a nearly 3½-hour journey that by car you could do in half the time.

As is common in much of the U.S., cargo gets priority over people on the rail lines, so keep in mind that your trip may be delayed as you sit in your stopped train watching the many freight trains go by.

Austin's Amtrak station is located conveniently downtown near the intersection of 3rd and Lamar, on the north bank of Lady Bird Lake. Although there are many shops within walking distance, there's little to the station itself other than a ticket counter and waiting room. The ticket office is open Monday through Friday, 7:30 AM to 9:30 PM.

As for local rail travel, although voters narrowly defeated a Light Rail proposal at the ballot box in 2000, a Cap Metro Leander-to-downtown commuter rail service using existing lines is set to begin in the fall of 2008, and Austin's progressive mayor, Will Wynn, is pushing hard for a modern, rapid urban streetcar system. However, most of the powers that be in Texas have focused in recent years solely on building ever larger, longer and more intrusive highways and toll roads.

Information **Amtrak** (⊠ *250 N. Lamar Blvd.* ☎ *512/476–5684* ⊕ *www.amtrak. com*).

CONTACTS & RESOURCES

EMERGENCIES

In an emergency, dial 911. Each of the following medical facilities has an emergency room open 24 hours a day.

Hospitals **University Medical Center at Brackenridge** (⊠ *601 E. 15th St.* ☎ *512/324–7000).* **Dell Children's Medical Center of Central Texas** (⊠ *4900 Mueller Blvd.* ☎ *512/324–0000).* **People's Community Clinic** (⊠ *2909 N. I–35* ☎ *512/478–4939* ⊕ *www.pcclinic.org).* **Seton Medical Center Austin** (⊠ *1201 W. 38th St.* ☎ *512/324–1000).* **Seton Northwest Hospital** ((⊠ *11113 Research Blvd.* ☎ *512/324–6000).* **Seton Southwest Hospital** (⊠ *7900 FM 1826* ☎ *512/324– 9000).* **St. David's Medical Center** (⊠ *919 E. 32nd St.* ☎ *512/476–7111* ⊕ *www. stdavids.com).* **St. David's North Austin Medical Center** (⊠ *12221 N. Mopac Expwy.* ☎ *512/901–1000).* **St. David's South Austin Hospital** (⊠ *901 W. Ben White Blvd.* ☎ *512/447–2211).*

LODGING

Contacts **Austin Hotel & Lodging Association** (⊕ *c/o Denise Garcia, Box 82431* ☎ *512/296–7492* ⊕ *www.austinhotelassn.org*

VISITOR INFORMATION

Contacts **Austin Convention and Visitors Bureau** (⊠ *301 Congress Ave., Ste. 200, Austin* ☎ *866/GO–AUSTIN (462–7846)* ⊕ *www.austintexas.org).* **Austin Visitor Center** (⊠ *209 E. 6th St., Austin* ☎ *866/462–7846* ⊕ *www.austintexas.org/ visitors/center).* **Greater Austin Chamber of Commerce** (⊠ *210 Barton Springs Rd., Ste. 400, Austin* ☎ *512/478–9383* ⊕ *www.austin-chamber.org).*

The Hill Country

WORD OF MOUTH

"Even though Fredericksburg has gotten quite popular, it is still a very quaint and enjoyable town."
—ilovetulips

"Check into Marble Falls. It's a lovely community with beautiful lakes surrounding it."
—Mindibz

By Jessica
Norman
Dupuy

YOU CAN'T GO MANY PLACES in Texas without seeing or hearing the phrase "Texas is a State of Mind." If Texas is indeed a state of mind, the Hill Country is the reason why.

The region is etched with dramatic slopes of rocky terrain, wide-open vistas displaying an endless horizon of blue sky, and roads that go on forever. Countless creeks and old cedar posts wrapped in rusty barbed wire meander through mesquite-filled pastures; in spring, blooming bluebonnets and other wildflowers transform the rough-hewn landscape.

The Hill Country's defining feature is, of course, the hills. (The lovely lakes and rivers are a close second, though.) Geographically, the area comprises the lower region of the Edwards Plateau, which rises from 750 feet to 2,700 feet in some places and is covered primarily by a thin, limestone-based soil that reveals solid, limestone rock just beneath. The calcite-rich limestone formations create perfect environments for the many freshwater springs and extensive caverns that spot the region. The rugged soil has created a perfect environment to sustain grass for cattle, and weeds and tree foliage for sheep and goats, thus making the area a ranching hub and one of the nation's leading Angora goat and mohair-producing regions. The region is also home to the Llano Basin, a stretch of land that lies at the junction of the Llano and Colorado rivers and features outcroppings of granite.

The Hill Country is a retreat for businesspeople from Austin, and even Houston, who trade in their Armani and city sights for Levis and ranch life each weekend at their second homes (and later their retirement homes). It's also been growing in popularity with Winter Texans, who are passing through en route to the Rio Grande Valley at Texas's tip. Tourists make up the third wave of visitors, flying into San Antonio or Austin and driving up for a day or weekend trip. They're drawn by the chance to play in the lakes, travel the Texas Wine Trail, sample fruit at roadside farm stands, and become short-term cowpokes at one of the local dude ranches.

EXPLORING THE HILL COUNTRY

The Hill Country encompasses the region west and southwest of Austin and north of San Antonio. The distance between these two gateway cities is 60 mi. Interstate 35 marks the eastern border, while San Antonio's State Loop 1604 notes the southern limit. The northern border is ambiguous, but generally includes everything south of Lake Buchanan and along Highway 29. The western border is also open to interpretation, but is best followed along U.S. 83 from Junction to Uvalde.

Along the many winding roads of these boundaries are the fabled music towns of Luckenbach and Gruene, the tourist draws of Fredericksburg, Marble Falls, and Boerne, and a few best-kept secrets sprinkled in between: Comfort, Mason, and Wimberley, to name a few.

Fredericksburg is the number-one tourist draw, so we start our coverage there. It's also easily accessed from both Austin and San Antonio.

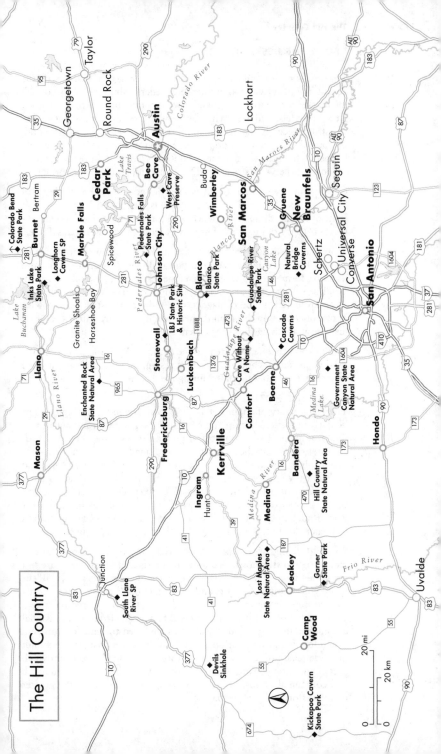

The Hill Country

ABOUT THE RESTAURANTS

The Hill Country is an extension of the great eating opportunities—the amazing Tex-Mex and barbecue—of San Antonio and Austin, with the addition of heavy German influences. Fredericksburg certainly corners the market for relatively authentic German fare, but Boerne, Comfort, New Braunfels, and everywhere in between serve decent schnitzel and wurst. Barbecue bests are spread all over: the Salt Lick in Driftwood, Cooper's in Llano, and Cooper's in Mason (it's not a chain; they just happen to have the same name), and Rudy's Country Store in a number of locations between Austin and San Antonio, and in Leon Springs.

On the Hill Country backroads you're not going to get a whole lot of haute cuisine delivered by celebrity chefs, but you'd be surprised at some of the fine dining experiences you can have here. Two upscale restaurants to try in Fredericksburg are August E's and Rebecca's Table.

Most places are casual in the Hill Country. You may want to don your Sunday best for a few places, but you really don't need to. Boots and jeans are formal enough for the average restaurant, especially for men. You'll see plenty of local women wearing "country-chic" clothing, such as embroidered, tailored blazers, or swishy broomstick skirts—with boots, of course. In the summer heat you'll see many patrons wearing just about anything that keeps them cool.

Don't expect to dine too late into the evenings. With the exception of a few live-music bars and venues, most restaurants and cafés are finished serving by 9 or 10, especially during the week.

ABOUT THE HOTELS

There are plenty of chain hotels speckled throughout the region, particularly in Fredericksburg and Marble Falls, but you're missing out on the local flavor if you don't try or (at least investigate) the many bed-and-breakfasts, guesthouses, ranches, and small resorts in the area—it's the absolute best way to get a feel for the culture. From historic and authentically restored guesthouses such as Palo Alto Creek and Austin Street Retreat in Fredericksburg and The Gamel House in Mason to the plush mini-resort luxury of Escondida Resort in Medina and River Rock Ranch in Comfort, to even retro-country at the Roadrunner Inn in Fredericksburg, there truly is something for everyone here.

Before deciding on the place that's right for you, it's important to make a few distinctions. Bed-and-breakfasts and guesthouses are not the same thing, no matter how close they may be in appearance. B&Bs invite you to join your hosts and sometimes other guests for breakfast each morning. Guesthouses do not. Although you may receive a generous basket of muffins or other breakfast breads from the occasional guesthouse manager, you will more likely need to fend for yourself. When looking at reservation agencies such as the Gästehaus Schmidt in Fredericksburg, or Boerne Reservations, be sure to confirm which accommodation you are choosing. You may like the personalized touch and communal atmosphere of a B&B, or you may prefer the greater privacy afforded by a guesthouse.

PLANNING YOUR TRIP

WHEN TO GO

There really isn't a bad time to visit the Hill Country. Winters are mild, with days averaging 50°. Summers are undeniably the high season, albeit extremely warm in July and August, with temperatures averaging about 85°–90° (but many days above 100°). Sunny, stiflingly hot days keep visitors in constant search of cool activities that usually involve water.

The summer heat doesn't really break until late October (sometimes even later). But once the weather cools, the Hill Country comes alive with food and wine festivals, such as New Braunfels's Wurstfest and Fredericksburg's Oktoberfest, both of which deliver plenty of beer, German sausage, and good times. October is also Texas Wine Month, with many of the Hill Country wineries offering tastings and special events.

Though late winter can be cold and seemingly desolate, the festive holiday season transforms the small towns into Dickens-like portraits of Christmas carolers, building facades with flickering lights, and main-street parades. Fly-fishers usually find fantastic winter action in any of the 100 stocked lakes and rivers for trophy rainbow trout.

By early March, outdoor enthusiasts are ready to head into the wild for cool fresh mornings at a campsite, hiking Enchanted Rock, and cycling the back roads. It's also the season for wildflowers. Brilliant red Indian paintbrushes, yellow brown-eyed Susan's, and the state's famed bluebonnets flourish in fields along the road. It's a sight to behold, and one deeply cherished by Texans statewide.

GETTING THERE & AROUND

The Hill Country is the land of the open road. The best, and really the *only* way to access the Hill Country is by car—or by motorcycle, which is an increasingly popular method.

You can access the region from I–35 or I–10, coming from the north and south or east and west, respectively. The gateway cities are Austin and San Antonio (Austin is technically even part of the Hill Country). These two cites are about 60 mi from each other on I–35. Between these two hubs on the interstate lie New Braunfels, Gruene, and San Marcos. Running north and south through the Hill Country is Highway 281, which intersects with I–10 West and San Antonio, and can be reached from Austin via Highway 71 or Highway 290, the latter traversing the region from east to west.

The most direct, and economical way to reach the Hill Country by air is to come into either San Antonio or Austin, though there is also a small airport at Del Rio (⇨ *West Texas Essentials*). From San Antonio International Airport, take Highway 281 north for about 90 mi to go through Blanco, Johnson City, Marble Falls, and Burnet, or cut across on State Loop 1604 heading west to I–10 West and you'll go through Boerne, Comfort, Kerrville, and can then easily make your way to Bandera and Medina, or Fredericksburg and Mason. From Austin Bergstrom Airport, take Highway 290 west to Highway 281 to get to most of the Hill Country towns.

HILL COUNTRY TOP 5

■ **Fredericksburg:** An afternoon on this favorite town's Main Street will likely net a collection of shopping bags, a hearty German meal, and a few samplings of German beer and Texas wine.

■ **Scenic Drives:** Some of the most spectacular views can be experienced from the seat of a car, or the back of a Harley, if you prefer. Though most of the land along the roadside is private, you will not be hampered from enjoying many a breathtaking vista from the endless roads traversing the region.

■ **Gruene:** It may only be the size of an average city block or two, but this little town packs quite a punch.

Live-music fans must pay homage to the famed Gruene Hall and catch an evening show. Be sure to grab a burger, cold beer, and the sunset on the Guadalupe River at the Gristmill before hitting the hall.

■ **Enchanted Rock State Park:** Who wouldn't be curious about scaling the face of a massive pink rock protruding to an elevation of 1,825 feet? Camping, hiking, and rock climbing are also popular attractions at this legendary state park.

■ **Wine:** Set out on a journey down the Texas Wine Trail and taste for yourself why some wine critics see a robust and full-bodied future for Hill Country wine.

WHAT IT COSTS

	¢	$	$$	$$$	$$$$
RESTAURANTS	under $8	$8–$12	$13–$20	$21–$30	over $30
HOTELS	under $50	$50–$100	$101–$150	$151–$200	over $200
CAMPING	under $10	$10–$17	$18–$35	$36–$50	over $50

Restaurant prices are per person for a main course at dinner. Hotel prices are per night for two people in a standard double room in high season, excluding taxes (8.25%) and service charges. Camping prices are for a standard (no hookups, pit toilets, fire grates, picnic tables) campsite per night.

FREDERICKSBURG AREA

It was once a secret weekend getaway for Texans-in-the-know, but someone in the late 1990s let the cat out of the bag, and Fredericksburg is now a destination hot spot featured in the likes of *Travel & Leisure,* *Gourmet,* and *National Geographic.* Those who love this little slice of Bavarian culture have warmly deemed it the "Aspen" of Texas. Those who wish the best-kept secret in the state had been kept exactly that, echo the sentiments of renowned Texas travel writer Suzy Banks, who once referred to the town as "Touristenburg."

Regardless of which side of the fence you sit on, the truth is that it's hard not to love the town where you can shop a day on Main Street and still not see everything, or spend a day touring the Texas Wine Trail in town and the vicinity, or a morning or afternoon hiking Enchanted Rock, and then unwind at night in one of 300 guesthouses or B&Bs,

after, of course, you've savored a schnitzel or beer stein at a German restaurant. Area attractions include LBJ and Pedernales state park. Among the townships nearby are Stonewall, Luckenbach, and Johnson City.

FREDERICKSBURG

78 mi west of Austin via US Hwy. 290; 70 mi north of San Antonio via I-10 and US Hwy 87.

Fredericksburg is a heavily German-influenced town. The city square is called Marketplatz, there's a "wilkommen" sign hanging from every shop door, and the main B&B booking organization is called Gästehaus Schmidt. It's Oktoberfest year-round in this hot little town, and everyone's invited!

Named for Prince Friedrich of Prussia, Friedrichburg (now Fredericksburg) was established in 1846 by Baron Ottfried Hans von Meusebach (better known as John O. Meusebach in Texas). It was the second main settlement, after New Braunfels, from the Society for the Protection of German Immigrants in Texas, or Adelsverein. This organization of German nobles brokered land in Texas to increase German emigration. Meusebach also managed to broker a peace treaty with the Comanche Indians that prevented raids and helped promote trade in the area (to this day, it is the only American Indian treaty not broken in the state). Cattle and agriculture eventually became the primary sustainable commerce in the city as it grew through the Civil War and moved into the 20th century.

In addition to the town's German roots, something else to keep in mind: Fredericksburg is primarily a weekend destination. Locals enjoy the influx of visitors, but they also say their favorite days are Sundays and Mondays because people pack up and leave, meaning that for a short while it feels like a small town again. If you want that experience, visit during the week, particularly in fall or winter.

WHAT TO SEE

Most of what there is to see is easily located on Main Street and all of the side streets in between Washington Street and Milam Street. It's easily walkable, and parking is easy to find on the side streets, especially when it's not a holiday weekend.

To tour the wineries, hike Enchanted Rock, view Mexican free-tailed bats at the Old Tunnel Wildlife Management area, or pick fresh peaches right off the tree, you'll have to leave the town center, but not more than a few miles.

❸ ★ The National Museum of the Pacific War. Dedicated solely to telling the story of the Pacific battles of World War II, this museum is the only one of its kind in the nation, and is a popular attraction for history buffs and the mildly curious alike. Originally the museum was the Admiral Nimitz Museum, named after Admiral Chester W. Nimitz, who is famed for successfully halting the Japanese advances after the attack

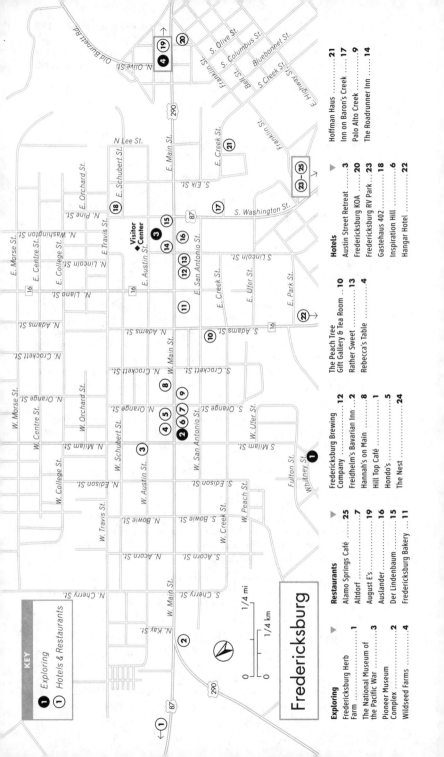

Fredericksburg

KEY

● Exploring
① Hotels & Restaurants

Exploring ▶

Fredericksburg Herb Farm **1**
The National Museum of the Pacific War **3**
Pioneer Museum Complex **2**
Wildseed Farms **4**

Restaurants ▶

Alamo Springs Café **25**
Altdorf **7**
August E's **19**
Auslander **16**
Der Lindenbaum **15**
Fredericksburg Bakery ... **11**
Fredericksburg Brewing Company **12**
Freidhelm's Bavarian Inn .. **2**
Hannah's on Main **8**
Hill Top Café **1**
Hondo's **5**
The Nest **24**
The Peach Tree Gift Gallery & Tea Room .. **10**
Rather Sweet **13**
Rebecca's Table **4**

Hotels

Austin Street Retreat **3**
Fredericksburg KOA **20**
Fredericksburg RV Park **23**
Gastehaus 402 .... **18**
Inspiration Hill **6**
Hangar Hotel **22**
Hoffman Haus **21**
Inn on Baron's Creek **17**
Palo Alto Creek **9**
The Roadrunner Inn **14**

Bluebonnets: the Pride of Texas

Ever since men first explored the prairies of Texas, the bluebonnet has been revered. American Indians wove folktales around this bright bluish-violet flower; early-day Spanish priests planted it thickly around their newly established missions; and the cotton boll and cactus competed fiercely with it for the state flower—the bluebonnet won the title in 1901.

The prized flower pops up across the fields of the Hill Country in March, usually peaking in April. Nearly half a dozen varieties of the bluebonnet, distinctive for flowers resembling pioneers' sunbonnets, bloom throughout the state, even as far west as Big Bend National Park. In fact, from mid-January until late March at least one of the famous flowers carpets the park: the Big Bend (also called Chisos) Bluebonnet has been described as "the most majestic" species, as its deep-blue flower spikes can shoot up to three feet in height. The Big Bend bluebonnets can be found beginning in late winter on the flats of the park as well as along the Camino del Rio (Highway 70), which follows the legendary Rio Grande between Lajitas and Presidio, Texas.

Back in the Hill Country, those out for a springtime Sunday-afternoon drive

Scenic drives bring you close to the Texas bluebonnet (lupinus Texensis).

can see the violet-blue flowers along the road or at several attractions, including Fredericksburg's Wildseed Farms, right off Highway 290 as you enter town from the east, and Austin's Lady Bird Johnson Wildflower Center (4801 La Crosse Ave.). Farther north, in Burnet, the self-proclaimed Bluebonnet Capital of Texas, there's a bluebonnet festival each April.

For information on viewing the bluebonnets, call the Wildflower Center (☎512/292–4100) or the Texas Department of Transportation Hotline (☎800/452–9292) from March to May.

—Marge Peterson

on Pearl Harbor. Today the museum has grown to include the George Bush Gallery, the Plaza of Presidents, Veterans' Walk of Honor, Japanese Garden of Peace, Pacific Combat Zone, and the Center for Pacific War Studies. In its more than 45,000 square feet of exhibit space the museum exhibits both Allied and Japanese airplanes, tanks, and guns among its numerous displays. ⊠*328 E. Main St.* ☎*830/997–4379* ⊕*www.nimitz-museum.org* ⊠*$7* ⊙ *Daily 9–5.*

❷ **Pioneer Museum Complex.** Those looking to dig a little deeper into the history of this area may find a few answers at the Pioneer Museum Complex and its second branch, the **Vereins Kirche Museum** (⊠*Main St. in Market Sq.* ☎*830/997–7832*), a reproduction of an eight-sided church that was Fredericksburg's first public building. Both museums include permanent exhibits with collections of woodworking tools, textile pieces, furniture, paintings, and a number of domestic artifacts from the area. The collection of historic buildings at the Pioneer Museum includes an 1849 pioneer log home and store, an old First Methodist Church, and a smokehouse. Also on the premises stands a typical 19th-century "Sunday house." Sunday houses catered to farmers and their families who traveled long distances to attend church services and had to stay the night. With the advent of the automobile, such accommodations became obsolete. ⊠ *309 W. Main St.* ☎ *830/990–8441* ⊕ *www. pioneermuseum.com* ⊠ *$4 (Pioneer Museum), $1 (Vereins Kirche Museum)* ⊙ *Mon.–Sat. 10–5, Sun. 1–5.*

NEED A BREAK? Known for a number of sweet delicacies, including creamy Danishes and sausage kolaches, **Fredericksburg Bakery** (⊠ *141 E. Main St.* ☎ *830/997–3254* ⊟ *AE, D, MC, V*) whips up affordable flaky German pretzels coated with pecans and a sugary frosting keep customers coming back for more.

❹ **Wildseed Farms.** If you're heading west on Highway 290 to Fredericksburg from Johnson City, you'll inevitably note a large, expansive spread of land flush with vibrant colors. (You may see less of this color in the late fall and winter months, but the expansive fields are still hard to miss.) You're looking at the largest working wildflower farm in the country. Owner John Thomas created Wildseed Farms in 1983 in an effort to share the Hill Country's bounty with all who visited. The farm has more than 200 acres under cultivation and produces 88 varieties of wildflower seeds. You can walk the meadows, step into the live butterfly house, and purchase packets of wildflower seeds. ⊠ *100 Legacy Dr.* ☎ *830/990–1393* ⊕ *www.wildseedfarms.com* ⊙ *Sun.–Thurs. 9:30–5, Fri.–Sat. 9:30–5:30.*

❶ **Fredericksburg Herb Farm.** Just a short jaunt from downtown is a magical little herb farm churning out an endless variety of fresh herbs, serving guests culinary creations inspired by an edible garden, offering blissful relaxation in a cozy B&B and spa, and creating a vast array of heavenly-scented candles, toiletries, cooking oils, and herbal cooking rubs and marinades. One of the gardens is artfully designed in the shape of a star with an old windmill in the center. Each arm of the star represents herbs for specific purposes—medicinal, cosmetic, culinary, crafting, or ornamental. ⊠ *405 Whitney St.* ☎ *830/997–8615* ⊕ *www.herb-farm. com* ⊙ *Mon.–Thurs. 9:30–5:30, Fri.–Sat. 9:30–9, Sun noon–4.*

SPORTS & THE OUTDOORS

Old Tunnel Wildlife Management Area. Hardly worth deeming a state park, this small piece of land (just 16 acres) is managed by the Texas Parks and Wildlife Department. However, it has a particular draw: bats. From April to October this old abandoned railroad tunnel is home to more than three million Mexican free-tailed bats. If you want to view them, arrive at the tunnel just before sunset, when the bats begin emerging in fleets of thousands for their evening hunt. You can view the bats seven nights a week, but may want to opt for an evening Thursday through Sunday, when interesting educational presentations are given on-site. After the bat-viewing, head to the Alamo Springs Café just down the

JUST PEACHY

When driving in and even near Fredericksburg in the summer, you can almost smell the fresh, sweet aroma of peaches all around. The Fredericksburg–Stonewall area is known as the Peach Capital of Texas. More than one-third of the peach production in the state happens in this area. The sandy soils and cool (but not too cold) winter climate merge to create ideal conditions for peach production. The process of pruning the orchards, managing the ripening process, and harvesting is a year-round affair, and one that is well worth the work when peach season comes around. (Depending on the weather, the season can begin as early as the beginning of May and end as late as August.) Some farms will even let you grab a crate and pick your own peaches off the tree.

Here are a few peachy places we recommend:

Fisher & Weiser's Das Peach Haus (⊠ *1406 S. U.S. 87* ☎ *800/880–8526* ⊕ *www.jelly.com*) is also a phenomenal stop for specialty jellies and preserves.

Burg's Corner (⊠ *15194 U.S. 290 E* ☎ *800/694–2772* ⊕ *www.burgscorner.com*).

Hill Country Fruit Council (⊠ *1684 Gelleman La.* ☎ *830/644–2341* ⊕ *www.texaspeaches.com*).

Whitworth Orchards (⊠ *339 Jenschke La.* ☎ *830/997–4796*).

Itz's Fredericksburg Peaches (⊠ *235½ E. Main St.*) is simply a peach stand on the road, but don't miss it!

road *(⇨ Where to Eat)* for one of the best burgers in the Hill Country. ⊠ *102 E. San Antonio, a half-mile east of Fredericksburg, ✛ take Old San Antonio Rd. south for about 10½ mi. The Old Tunnel WMA is on the left at the top of the hill* ☎ *866/978–2287* ⊕ *www.tpwd.state.tx.us* ▢ *Free* ☉ *Daily dawn to dusk*.

NIGHTLIFE

During the week most things seem to close up by about 9 or 10 o'clock. But on the weekend a number of the beer gardens open their stages for live music. Among the best bets for Texas bands playing everything from rockabilly to the blues are **Hondo's** (312 W. Main St., ⇨ *Where to Eat*) and the **Silver Creek Beer Garden and Grill** (310 E. Main St., ⇨ *Where to Eat*), which also hosts an open mike once a week to anyone who wants to belt a tune.

Those looking for a little more sophistication in an evening may enjoy the lounge at **house.wine.** (⊠ *327 E. Main St.* ☎ *830/997–2665*). A home-furnishings store at the front of the building and a high-end wine bar in back, it serves more than 750 bottles from around the world.

SHOPPING

Main Street is deceiving. It has what seems like a simple few blocks of shops and restaurants, but serious shoppers, beware. It's quite possible to spend a whole day here and still not get to everything. Some of the problem, if you can call it that, may be because distractions run high: there's a coffee shop, bakery, or wine-tasting room every few doors

Talking Texan

Texans use the word "y'all" a lot. You'll hear it in pretty much any type of conversation, and you'll likely incorporate it into your vocabulary before heading home. (It really is a useful word, and it sounds so nice—at least when Texans say it.) There are a few other sayings and pronunciations that are unique to the Lone Star State:

"He's all hat and no cattle": Used to describe someone who is all talk and no action.

"This ain't my first rodeo": I wasn't born yesterday.

"You can put your boots in the oven, but that don't make them biscuits": Say what you want, but that doesn't make it true.

"We've howdied, but we ain't shook yet": We've made a brief acquaintance, but have not been formally introduced.

Burnet: "Burn-it"

Pedernales: "Pur-dah-nallis"

Guadalupe: "Gwaa-dah-loop"

Manchaca: "Man-shack"

San Felipe: "San Fill-a-pee"

along the thoroughfare. Shops are open daily unless noted otherwise. Most are open from 10 to 5 Monday through Saturday, and noon to 5 on Sunday.

CLOTHING
Country-chic fashion is defined at the **Haberdashery** (✉ *203 E. Main St.* ☎ *830/990–2462*), where women with a flair for sassy style with unmistakable Western inspiration will find a clothing treasure trove. Also selling clothes, **Root** (✉ *306 E. Main St.* ☎ *830/997–1844*) has a little something for everyone's fashion tastes. Fashion-forward frocks and clothes are found at **Zertz** (✉ *108-2 E. Main St.* ☎ *830/990–8900*).

HOME ACCESSORIES
Homestead and Friends (✉ *230 E. Main St.* ☎ *830/997–5551*) shows impeccable taste in its refined-rustic home styles selection. Tucked away from Main Street, **Jabberwocky** (✉ *105 N. Llano St.* ☎ *830/997–7071*) offers unique gifts, trendy clothes, and a wide array of linens. **Red** (✉ *218 W. Main St.* ☎ *830/990–0700*) is just the place for contemporary furniture and home accents as well as funky gifts and jewelry. A taste of Provence and Tuscany awaits shoppers at **Villa Texas** (✉ *234 W. Main St.* ☎ *830/997–1068*), where the herb of choice is lavender and comes in everything from soaps and lotions. French-inspired home accents also abound here.

WHERE TO EAT
Though you may find a recognizable difference in culinary offerings from one region of Germany to another, German-influenced Texas offers pretty standard fare including a variety of wursts—knackwurst, bratwurst, bockwurst—sauerkraut, warm German potato salad, and of course, schnitzel.

¢–$ ✕ **Alamo Springs Cafe.** You can dig into one of the best burgers in the
★ region here. The more adventuresome eaters order theirs with the
jalepeño-cheese bun—it's really not as spicy as it sounds. If you're here
in peach season, your Alamo Springs experience isn't complete without
a serving of homemade peach crisp. ⊠ *107 Alamo Rd.* ☎ *830/990–
8004* ▤ *AE, D, MC, V.*

$–$$ ✕ **Altdorf.** Although there's usually a long line for lunch here, it's worth
waiting. The food is fantastic, especially the juicy Reuben sandwiches
on toasty pumpernickel. ⊠ *301 W. Main St.* ☎ *830/997–7865* ▤ *AE,
D, MC, V.*

$$$–$$$$ ✕ **August E's.** This polished, contemporary spot is one of the rare places
Fodor'sChoice where you *can't* order schnitzel. Chef-owner Leu Savanh offers a con-
★ stantly evolving seasonal menu. He also adds a subtle hint of his Thai
background to such dishes as the New Zealand lamb with balsamic
honey-glaze, and a cloudlike fillet of Hawaiian escolar pan-seared and
served with a tempura-fried lobster tail, baby bok choy, and mascar-
pone whipped potatoes. August E's is the only place in town for sushi
and sake. ⊠ *203 E. San Antonio* ☎ *830/997–1585* ▤ *AE, D, MC, V.*

$–$$ ✕ **Auslander.** With its authentic German architecture, the Auslander
draws quite a crowd for lunch and dinner. This popular dining attrac-
tion offers more of a Munich Biergarten feel than a fine-dining experience. For more than 20 years it has been one of the town's most
popular beer gardens, and you're bound to find a few things to your
liking—we recommend the Texa-schnitzel, a bold concoction featuring
a hand-breaded pork loin cutlet prepared schnitzel-style, smothered
with Tex-Mex ranchero (tomato-chili) sauce and melted Monterey Jack
cheese. ⊠ *323 E. Main St* ☎ *830/997–7714* ▤ *AE, D, MC, V.*

$$–$$$ ✕ **Der Lindenbaum.** The menu at this family-owned restaurant fea-
tures dishes directly from the Rhineland (bordering the Alsace Lor-
raine region between Germany and France). It has, of course, standard
schnitzel, but the sauerbraten (a Rhineland sweet-and-sour version of
roast beef) and Hühnerfrikassee (chicken fricassee with mushroom
sauce) are among the favorite house specialties. ⊠ *213 E. Main St.*
☎ *830/997–9126* ▤ *AE, D, MC, V.*

$–$$ ✕ **Fredericksburg Brewing Company.** Serving a variety of homemade Ger-
man-style brews from the large copper beer tanks accenting the far
wall, the brewery is a popular nightspot for both locals and visitors.
The German food is all well prepared, but the Texas-sized chicken fried
steak is no slouch either. ⊠ *245 E. Main St.* ☎ *830/997–1646* ▤ *AE,
D, MC, V.*

$$–$$$$ ✕ **Freidhelm's Bavarian Inn.** Driving to the end of town to try this
Haufbraü-Haus-meets-Disneyland restaurant is certainly a trip; in
more ways than one. Schnitzel is available in more ways than you can
count on one hand, and the beer selection is impressive. ⊠ *905 W.
Main St.* ☎ *830/997–6300* ▤ *AE, D, MC, V.*

$$$–$$$$ ✕ **Hannah's on Main.** Friendly service is everything at this fine-dining
Fodor'sChoice establishment. Hannah is the bubbly red-headed daughter of Dean and
★ Kim Brenner, who escaped a fast-paced Dallas life to raise their family
in a more relaxed environment—someone forgot to tell them that serv-
ing breakfast, lunch, and dinner to a increasingly selective dining crowd

is hardly a life of leisure. But they sure make it look easy. Everything on the menu is superbly prepared. New Zealand lamb rubbed with a fresh herb and Dijon mustard crust has rich and bold taste without being too gamey. Seasonal desserts such as the molten butterscotch cake are not to be missed. ⊠ *232 W. Main St* ☏ *830/990–1037* ⊟ *AE, D, MC, V* ⊘ *Closed Sun.–Mon. No dinner Tues.–Thurs.*

$$–$$$ ✕**Hill Top Cafe.** Ten miles north of town, this hilltop dive is in the middle of nowhere. But it's a beautiful trip to nowhere—just ask all the weekend motorcycle cruisers. All menu conventions are thrown out the window. How else would you explain the Athens-meets-New Orleans dishes? On weekends the best bet is to grab a few appetizers, a bottle of wine, and sit back for a little live music. The *kefalotiri saganaki* (a flavorful Greek cheese flambé) and a Cajun-style avocado stuffed with blue crab are fantastic starts. The snapper *pontchartrain* (in a white-wine sauce with mushroom and crab) is a decadent adventure. ⊠ *10661 U.S. Hwy 87* ☏ *830/997–8922* ⊟ *AE, D, MC, V.*

¢–$$ ✕**Hondo's.** Named for John Russell "Hondo" Crouch, self-proclaimed mayor of Luckenbach, this local dive is becoming something of a legend in itself. If the live music and Texas country decor aren't entertaining enough, the menu certainly is. From the "What's David Smokin' Plate" of finger-lickin' fabulous barbecue to the "Supa Chalupa Salad," everything about this place radiates good old-fashioned fun. The half-pound donut burgers, made in the shape of a donut, are excellent, especially the "Blue Ribbon Barbecue Bacon Burger." ⊠ *312 W. Main St.* ☏ *830/997–1633* ⊟ *AE, D, MC, V.*

$$–$$$ ✕**The Nest.** Tucked away in a little historic house off Washington street, The Nest is a nice option for a special occasion. It's probably the best value for fine dining in town. The seasonal menu might include a perfectly prepared Black Angus fillet with a rich bordelaise sauce or plump pan-seared sea scallops served with a citrusy chipotle-lime hollandaise. Enjoy a taste of the Hill Country with a scoop of homemade lavender ice cream. ⊠ *607 S. Washington St.* ☏ *830/990–8383* ⊟ *D, MC, V.*

$ ✕**The Peach Tree Gift Gallery and Tea Room.** The gift shop came first, but since 1984 Cynthia Pedregon has wowed crowds with her homemade soups, sandwiches, and daily quiches. Portions are hearty, but to get a sampling of as much as possible, opt for the Sandwich Sampler, which comes with a quarter sandwich each of tangy chicken salad, fresh tuna salad, perky jalepeño-pimento cheese, and a cup of the soup of the day. Pedregon's cookbooks are prized staples in Hill Country kitchens. ⊠ *210 S. Adams St.* ☏ *830/997–9527* ⊟ *AE, D, MC, V.*

¢–$ ✕**Rather Sweet.** From Main Street, between Llano and Lincoln streets,
★ make your way down a stone path to one of the town's most celebrated treats. This bakery run by chef Rebecca Rather (who runs Rebecca's Table for dinner) serves some of the most decadent baked goods around. Simple oatmeal–chocolate chip cookies taste like heaven, and mammoth chocolate cakes blanketed in buttercream frosting beckon from behind the dessert case. Homemade soups and cold and hot sandwiches are worth a try, too. ⊠ *249 Main St.* ☏ *830/990–0498* ⊟ *AE, D, MC, V* ⊘ *Closed Sun.–Mon. No dinner.*

$$$–$$$$ ✕**Rebecca's Table.** Chef Rebecca Rather's outpost of "fine, farm-fresh cuisine" is giving the Main Street dining scene a run for its money. The dining room balaces rustic and contemporary elements, with exposed limestone walls and dark-stained wood floors and beams. The short menu is driven by what Rather finds daily at Texas-based markets. The thick-cut Niman Ranch pork chop with chunky apple-pear chutney is a happy layering of textures and flavor. Be sure to finish with one of Rather's signature desserts; the sticky toffee pudding is worth every sweet and gooey calorie. The excellent, diverse wine list includes a few Hill Country bottles. ✉*342 W. Main St.* ☎*830/997–5100* ▤*AE, D, V, MC* ⊙*Closed Sun.–Mon. No lunch.*

WHERE TO STAY

Serving Fredericksburg for more than 20 years, the **Gästehaus Schmidt** (✉*231 W. Main St.,* ☎*866/427–8374 or 830/997–5612* ⊕*www.fbg lodging.com*) is the place to consult when seeking the perfect B&B or guesthouse. This booking operation manages more than a third of the 300-plus accommodations in the town, but it's also a great resource to turn to for local travel advice.

$$ ▥**Austin Street Retreat.** One of the most popular downtown guesthouses, the Austin Street Retreat offers five elegantly appointed private suites, each featuring the original Fachwerk log-cabin and limestone architecture used by original Fredericksburg settlers. You're in the heart of the town here, but once you enter the compound you'll likely feel like you're approaching a cabin in the woods. Get directions and reservations through Gästehaus Schmidt *(see above)*. **Pros:** Very authentic in the preservation, beds are large and comfortable, the bathrooms are all spacious and welcoming, with oversized tubs. **Cons:** Two-night minimum can be inconvenient, Victorian accents are tasteful, but may be a little too historic for some. ✉*408 W. Austin St.,* ☎*866/427–8374 or 830/997–5612* ⊕*www.austinstreetretreat.com* ⌑*5 suites* ⌖*In-room: refrigerator, kitchen (some)* ▤*AE, D, MC, V.*

$$ ▥**Gastehaus 402.** Experience Fredericksburg in luxurious style here,
★ where Central Texas–renowned interior designer and owner Jennifer Eggleston has added her personal touch to every detail. This loft-like cottage mixes contemporary country style with a touch of urban flair. A relaxing private patio invites guests to relax and unwind. **Pros:** Decor is fresh, inviting, and comfortable; large pillow-top bed makes it easy for lingering in the mornings; easy walk to Main Street. **Cons:** Somewhat small; not ideal for children due to high-end decor. ✉*402 E. Schubert,* ☎*888/991–6749* ⊕*www.fredericksburg-lodging.com/Gastehaus-402* ⌑*1 room* ⌖*In-room: refrigerator, kitchen, VCR, DVD. In-hotel: no-smoking rooms* ▤*AE, D, MC, V* �*CP.*

$$–$$$ ▥**Hangar Hotel.** This fun (yet not overdone) hotel was built to look like
★ a 1940s airplane hangar. Stepping into the lobby is like entering an old black-and-white movie. The lobby experience extends all the way to the 50 uniform rooms designed meticulously with mahogany accents and club chairs upholstered in bomber jacket leather. At the foot of each of of the plush king-size beds is a neatly folded Army-green wool blanket bearing the Hangar Hotel logo. **Pros:** $10 discounts for mili-

tary and seniors. **Cons:** Not many activity options on-site or nearby, and not an easy location to find. ✉ *155 Airport Rd.,* ☎ *830/997–9990* ⊕ *www.hangarhotel.com* ⤶ *50 rooms* ⚴ *In-room: refrigerator, Wi-Fi. In-hotel: restaurant, bar, public Wi-Fi, no-smoking rooms, free parking* ⊟ *AE, MC, V* �‖ *CP.*

\$\$–\$\$\$\$ ⊞ **Hoffman Haus.** Stepping onto this beautiful property spotted with
★ historic cabins and private courtyards with glowing firepits, you won't believe Main Street is just a stone's throw away. The main lodge is a renovated 1850s barn, with an inviting library and formal dining room on the far part of the building. Rooms are elegantly decorated with individual styles, from rustic Texas to French countryside. A lovely spa is on-site, but the full experience of the Hoffman Haus is in joining one of the terrific cooking classes offered by chef-owner Leslie Washburne (\$65 per person). **Pros:** Close to Main Street yet private and peaceful; excellent, comfortable beds; breakfasts are hot, filling, and delicious— and delivered right to your room. **Cons:** Not ideal for children; difficult to relax if a big event, such as a wedding, is going on in the main lodge. ✉ *608 E. Creek St,* ☎ *830/997–6739* ⊕ *www.hoffmanhaus.com* ⤶ *8 rooms, 4 suites, 1 cabin (sleeps 6)* ⚴ *In-room: kitchen, refrigerator, VCR (some), DVD (some), Wi-Fi, no phone. In-hotel: spa, no elevator, some pets allowed, no smoking* ⊟ *AE, MC, V* �‖ *BP.*

\$\$\$ ⊞ **Inn on Baron's Creek.** Looking for a more traditional hotel atmosphere and want to stay close to town? This locally owned operation fits the bill; it's just a couple of blocks from downtown and offers a feel unique to Fredericksburg. The staff is very friendly and happy to help give tips and advice on the best things to do around town. Four of the suites are extended-stay and include kitchen facilities. **Pros:** Spacious, clean rooms, friendly, helpful staff. **Cons:** Not the quaint experience you'd find in guesthouses or B&Bs; some residual noise when bands play at the nearby Auslander restaurant. ✉ *308 S. Washington St.,* ☎ *866/990–0202 or 830/990–9202* ⊕ *www.innonbaronscreek.com* ⤶ *90 suites* ⚴ *In-room: refrigerator, microwave, DVD (available upon request), Ethernet, Wi-Fi. In Hotel: pool, gym, spa, laundry facilities, public Wi-Fi, no-smoking rooms, parking (no fee)* ⊟ *AE, D, MC, V* �‖ *BP.*

\$\$\$ ⊞ **Inspiration Hill.** If you're looking for a retreat from town with mag-
★ nificent views of the Hill Country, look no further than Inspiration Hill. The home presents a contemporary style with a rustic flair. The designers aimed to bring the Hill Country indoors. You can enjoy the views from the screened porch, which even has a gas fireplace for cold evenings. Each bedroom has plush linens and private bath—the master bath has a river-rock shower and hot tub. The best part is the privacy; you rent the entire home. Pricing is based on the number of bedrooms used, so it's possible for couples to enjoy a quiet getaway by themselves. **Pros:** Beautiful escape for a group of friends or family with lots of privacy, well-equipped kitchen, excellent views. **Cons:** A bit far from downtown. ✉ *1063 Luckenbach-Cain City Rd.,* ☎ *866/427–8374 or 830/997–5612* ⊕ *www.fbglodging.com* ⤶ *3 rooms* ⚴ *In-room: kitchen, refrigerator, DVD, Ethernet. In-hotel: no kids under 12, no smoking, public Wi-Fi* ⊟ *AE, MC, V, D.*

$$$–$$$$ 🏠**Palo Alto Creek.** Just a few miles outside of Fredericksburg and nestled along the shady Palo Alto Creek, this property has the original 1875 buildings built by German immigrant Karl Itz. They've been updated with modern amenities, yet they're perfect for fans of the outdoors. Choose from the main Itz House, which sleeps eight, or opt for the quainter Log Cabin, Barn, or Hideaway cabin, complete with a screened-in porch. Children are not allowed to stay in certain rooms. A breakfast of fresh pastries is delivered to your door each morning. Get directions and reserve through Gästehaus Schmidt *(see above).* **Pros:** A perfect nature escape with glimpses of deer and a view of the creek; each cabin offers utmost privacy; in-room massage therapist option is an added bonus. **Cons:** A bit far from downtown; not ideal for children. ⊠*Palo Alto La.,* ☎*866/427–8374 or 830/997–5612* ⊕*www. paloaltocreekfarm.com* ⬐*4 separate buildings, 6 rooms total* ⚭*In-room: refrigerator, kitchen, VCR (some), DVD (some). In-hotel: No children, no-smoking, parking no fee* ▭*AE, D, MC, V* ⊚*CP.*

$$–$$$ 🏠**The Roadrunner Inn.** Not all B&Bs are stuffed with Victorian decor
★   and period pieces. In fact, Fredericksburg has recently welcomed a few urban-minded accommodations offering a more contemporary environment. The Roadrunner Inn is composed of three little loft-like rooms perched above the Root clothing store on Main Street. Bright, fresh colors and lush green tropical plants create a nouveau-Miami feel. From robin's-egg blue and canary-yellow dishes mounted on the wall to lime-green-and-white accent pillows resting on the 1970s sectional couch, everything screams "we're retro, but we're still Texas-friendly." Kitchens are stocked with juice, milk, tea, coffee, and cereal. Fresh fruit and breakfast pastries are brought to your room each morning. **Pros:** Clean rooms and beautiful bathrooms; proximity to Main Street is hard to beat; complimentary Cheerios a plus. **Cons:** Might be too trendy for some; Main Street–facing rooms get street noise. ⊠*306 E. Main St,* ☎*830/997–1844* ⊕*www.theroadrunnerinn.com* ⬐*3 rooms* ⚭*In-room: kitchen, refrigerator, Ethernet, no phone. In-hotel: no elevator, no smoking* ▭*AE, D, MC, V* ⊚*CP.*

CAMPING

$$–$$$$ ⚠*Fredericksburg KOA.* Though you're a few miles from town, this RV site is happily situated in a beautiful rural area. Both Fredericksburg and Luckenbach are just a few minutes away. Wi-Fi is available, as is a modem dataport. **Pros:** Quiet and spacious camping area, seasonal pool. **Cons:** Need a car to drive to downtown area, not all sites are well shaded. ⊠*5681 U.S. 290 E.* ☎*830/997–4796* ⊕*www.koa. com/where/tx/43153* ⚭*Flush toilets, showers, full hookup, drinking water, dump station, swimming pool, Wi-Fi* ▭*AE, D, MC, V* ⊙*Open year-round.*

$$ ⚠*Fredericksburg RV Park.* Fairly close to downtown, this hospitable RV Park offers nice amenities and friendly service from staff. Laundry and private bath facilities are conveniently on-site. Wi-Fi is available as is cable TV. **Pros:** Close to downtown, clean facilities, nice recreational room. **Cons:** Campsites are close together. ⊠*305 E. Highway St.* ☎*830/990–9582* ⊕*www.fredericksburgtexasrvpark.com* ⬐*100 pull through RV sites* ⚭*Flush toilets, showers, full hookups, drinking* *water, dump station, guest laundry, Wi-Fi ☰AE, D, MC, V ⊙ Open year-round.*

ENCHANTED ROCK STATE NATURAL AREA

16 mi north of Fredericksburg via RR 965.

★ Protruding from the earth in the form of a large pink dome, Enchanted Rock looks like something from another planet. This granite formation rises 1,825 feet—the second-largest in the nation, after Georgia's Stone Mountain—and its bald vastness can be seen from miles away. Today the massive batholith is part of the 624-acre Enchanted Rock State Park and one of the most popular destinations in the Hill Country region. Once considered to have spiritual powers by the Tonkawa tribe, the rock is traversed day in and day out by those curious about its mysterious occurrence. The park is perfect for day hikers, most of whom can't wait to scale the summit. The rock also yields a number of faces to test the skills of technical rock climbers. But even if you're not into rock climbing, the park is a perfect spot for camping, picnicking, and hiking. Arrive early; park officials close the park to protect the resources once parking lots reach capacity. Amenities include restrooms, an interpretive center, and campgrounds *(⇨ Where to Stay).* ✉*16710 RR 965* ☎*325/247–3903* ⊕*www.tpwd.state.tx.us* ⊠*$6.*

WHERE TO STAY

CAMPING

$ ⚠ **Enchanted Rock State Natural Area.** Backpackers can opt for either the closed-in surface tent sites or one of the three primitive camping areas one to two miles from the trails. Either way, your access to good hiking trails and magnificent views of the great granite dome are everywhere you go. **Pros:** Primitive sites are picturesque and private, excellent access to trails from all campsites. **Cons:** Close-in surface sites are close together with little to no privacy, summer camping can be stiflingly hot. ✉*Enchanted Rock State Natural Area* ☎*800/792–1112 or 325/247–3903* ⊕*www.tpwd.state.tx.us* ⇴*60 tent sites* ⚲*Flush toilets (some), dump station, fire pits, picnic tables.* ☰*AE, D, MC, V.*

LUCKENBACH

10 mi from Fredericksburg via Hwy. 290 and RR 1376.

Luckenbach isn't just some fabled Texas town romanticized by classic country singers Willie Nelson and Waylon Jennings. In fact it's hardly a town at all, but more a cul-de-sac at the end of a country road. Luckenbach is an attitude. It's a place to which Texas songwriters and music lovers from Nacogdoches to El Paso dream of traveling to pay homage to Texas music legends. Of course, if you blink while driving south on Ranch Road 1376 from Highway 290 W, you just might miss it. Aside from the general store, post office, rows of picnic tables, and ample parking for the many daily visitors, there's not much else here.

Texas Chili

There's no denying that chili is part of the stick-to-your-ribs heart and soul of Texas cuisine. After all it *is* the official dish of Texas. When the weather turns cool in the fall, crock pots are fired up to make heaping servings of the thick, spicy stew to be enjoyed by the bowl beside the fire—or over a heaping pile of Fritos, garnished with shredded cheddar cheese and diced onions, at high school football games (the legendary Frito Pie). The question is: what defines an authentic bowl of "Texas red?" The simple answer is small chunks of sirloin (or coarsely ground meat) simmered with crushed chilies (or chili powder), garlic, and cumin. From there, myriad additions—possibilities include tomato, onion, venison, and the ever-controversial beans (family feuds have erupted over whether or not to include the protein-packed legume)—can lead to millions of different tasty end results.

Texas chili recipes are such a hot topic that they've spawned competitive cook-offs, a trend that's caught on nationwide. The granddaddy of chili cook-offs is in the tiny West Texas town of Terlingua, where hundreds of established cooks take their best shot at the annual title over a four-day competition each year. (If you look at the distinguished list of winners, you'll find that most of them are Texans.)

Though officially established in 1849 by German immigrants, it wasn't until 1970, when John Russell "Hondo" Crouch purchased the town—with a population of just three at the time—and created what soon became a legendary dance hall, that it became famous. The legend began when Texas singer-songwriter Jerry Jeff Walker recorded his album "Viva Terlingua!" at the dance hall in 1973. Four years later the town was memorialized by Willie Nelson and Waylon Jennings in the famed song "Luckenbach, Texas (Back to the Basics of Love)."

During Crouch's reign as the self-proclaimed town mayor, he coined the famous phrase "Everybody's Somebody in Luckenbach," a motto still heard today.

Whether you're a fan of country music or not, you haven't officially been to Luckenbach without grabbing an ice-cold brew, listening to whoever may be strumming the guitar on stage, and picking up a souvenir bumper sticker for the road.

JOHNSON CITY

30 mi east of Fredericksburg and 30 mi west of Austin on Hwy. 290; 25 mi south of Marble Falls and 60 mi north of San Antonio on Hwy. 281.

Johnson City is often described as a great place to stop on the way to somewhere else. Aside from its proximity to some of the Hill Country's main towns, Johnson City is probably most famous as the home of President Lyndon Baines Johnson—though the president is not the town's namesake.

The town was actually founded in the late 1870s by James Polk Johnson, a second cousin to the former U.S. president. It was established as the county seat for Blanco County, but the town experienced little growth economically. LBJ may have first brought notoriety to the area in the 1930s, when the former president was a junior congressman from Texas. He was the first to lobby for full electric power to the area, and in a 1959 letter wrote, "I think of all the things I have ever done, nothing has ever given me as much satisfaction as bringing power to the Hill Country of Texas."

> **FLASH FLOOD NEWS FLASH!**
>
> Flash flooding is a common phenomenon among the rivers in the Texas Hill Country. If visiting any of the regions' rivers and you notice the water levels beginning to rise, leave immediately. Visitors to state rivers are advised to be aware of weather conditions.

Following his presidency, LBJ offered his family ranch to the United States as a National Historical Park. It is preserved as a peaceful spot about 14 mi west of Johnson City, near Stonewall.

WHAT TO SEE

Lyndon Baines Johnson National Historical Park. History buffs will enjoy wandering through the rooms of LBJ's boyhood home in Johnson City, where every effort has been made to restore the home to its 1920s appearance. ⊠ *100 Ladybird La.* ☎ *830-868-7128* ⊕ *www.nps.gov/lyjo* ⬚ *$6* ⊙ *Daily.*

Lyndon B. Johnson State Park and the LBJ Ranch. It's easy to feel confused, but the state park and the national park are technically separate entities that operate in conjunction with each other. The national park includes Johnson's boyhood home in Johnson City proper, while the state park is confined to the property 14 mi west of town. You're welcome to drive around the state park, but to get the best historical experience it's best to take the 1½-hour bus tour ($6), which departs from the State Park Visitor Center in Stonewall. The bus ride takes you on a guided tour of the ranch, and afterward you can hike the many park trails, fish the Pedernales River, picnic, and even take a dip in the pool during the summer. ⊠ *Hwy. 290 E. at Park Rd. 52, Stonewall* ☎ *830/644–2252* ⊕ *www.tpwd.state.tx.us* ⬚ *Free* ⊙ *Daily.*

WHERE TO EAT

¢–$$ ✕ **Silver K Cafe.** Though you may only be passing through Johnson City, try to do it on an empty stomach and make a stop at the Silver K. The mashed potatoes alone are worth it. The Hill Country photography and Western paintings mixed with the Silver K's diner personality make you feel like you are in someone's home for supper. ⊠ *209 E. Main St.,* ☎ *830/868–2911* ⊟ *AE, D, MC, V.*

NORTH & NORTHWEST OF SAN ANTONIO

BANDERA

52 mi northwest of San Antonio via Hwy. 16, 24 mi west of Boerne via Hwy. 46. 26 mi south of Kerrville via Hwy. 16/173.

Dust off your chaps, loosen your saddle cinch, and stay a while. In Bandera the mythic tales of rodeos, ranches, and the "cowboy way" are all true. Not only will you see beat-up boots, worn Wrangler jeans, and more than a few cowboy hats, you may even catch a glimpse of one of the local ranch hands riding his horse to the general store on Main Street. After all, this isn't considered the "Cowboy Capital of Texas" for nothing. Open rodeos take place twice weekly from Memorial Day through Labor Day, and you can't drive any direction outside of town without passing a dude ranch *(⇨ The Dude Ranch Experience box)*.

This tiny ink spot on the Texas map was originally established in 1853 as a sawmill town based solely on the cypress trees along the Medina River. Throughout much of the late 1800s, both German and Polish settlers made their home here. After the Civil War the town boomed with cattle drives to the Great Western Cattle Trail. But the rugged terrain slowed things down, as railroads couldn't find passages through the hills and most roads weren't even paved until the 1950s.

WHAT TO SEE

Frontier Times Museum. The collection here is truly eclectic. Hand-built in 1933 by Hough LeStourgeon from stones gathered from the region, this popular tourist stop teems with oddities and relics—take for instance the two-headed goat or the mummified cow fetus. ⊠*510 13th St.* ☎*830/796–3864* ⊕*www.frontiertimesmuseum.com* 🖾*$5* ⊗*Mon.–Sat. 10–4:30.*

Hill Country State Natural Area. With more than 5,300 acres of rolling hills, spring-fed creeks, and thick patches of live oaks, this natural park is a slice of backcountry paradise. Adventurers seeking an avenue for primitive camping, mountain biking, backpacking, limited fishing, and even horseback riding will find happiness here. ■ TIP➜ **The park is primitive. You'll need to bring your own water, and you'll need to pack out what you bring in.** ⊠*10600 Bandera Creek Rd.* ☎*830/796–4413* 🖾*$6 ($3 extra for primitive campsite)* ⊗*Feb.–Nov., daily; Dec.–Jan., Fri.–Sun.*

NIGHTLIFE

For such a small town, Bandera certainly offers a lively night scene—at least, if you're into gritty bars, live Texas-style country music, and an occasional turn on the dance floor.

Tucked into a line of stores on Main Street, it may be easy to miss **Arkey Blue's Silver Dollar** (⊠*308 Main St.* ☎*830/796–8826*) during the day. But at night, it turns into a beacon calling all cowboys and bikers to throw back a cold one and forget their sorrows. The truly honky-tonk **11th Street Cowboy Bar** (⊠*307 11th St.* ☎*830/796–4849*), with its outdoor patio and music stage, is crammed with locals. Be ready to

CLOSE UP

The Dude Ranch Experience

Bandera's Cowboy Capital title not only stems from the longstanding cattle ranches in the area, but from all the visitors who pony up the cash for a bit of the cowboy life for themselves, albeit a bit cushier than the real thing in some cases.

The dude ranch experience allows families or individuals (sometimes even a group of women on a girlfriends getaway) to catch a glimpse or what it means to live and work on the open range. Most ranches pride themselves on combining a rustic, outdoorsy, and sometimes primitive environment with today's modern amenities. Depending on the ranch, guests may be able to take daily horseback rides, learn about the area's natural history, watch wranglers barrel race and rope cattle (and sometimes participate), take evening hayrides, and sit around the campfire roasting marshmallows and listening to cowboys sing old trail songs. You don't have to worry about throwing a lasso your first time out, and horseback-riding instruction is available for all levels of experience.

These *City Slickers*-type adventures began with one enterprising couple back in 1920. Ebenezer and Kate Ross of 1901 Buck Ranch decided to open their property on San Julian Creek, just outside Bandera, to guests from Houston who were looking for a change of pace. Before long, other established ranches began opening their gates to those curious about a Western style of living. With the influx of these seasonal wannabe cowhands, Bandera became famous for its resort-like camps, rodeos, cowboy bars, and restaurants to compliment these newly appointed guest ranches. (Before this, small rodeos and live-

Help with the chores on a ranch vacation.

stock shows took place in a lot of the different areas in the Hill Country, but centered primarily around trade through much of the early 1900s, not as much for show as they are today.)

Many of these dude ranches have changed in appearance since the early 1900s. While early ranches were bare-bones, offering room for only a few families, and usually serving not-so-gourmet cuisine, many have added such amenities as rustic cabins or high-end guest accommodations, dining lodges serving old-fashioned Southern dishes with modern twists, cable TV, Wi-Fi, an on-site masseur, and golf courses.

Most ranches operate their guest programs from the early spring to the late fall, providing all-inclusive packages with meals and daily horseback rides included. Prices vary, but average $125 to $150 per person per night.

⇨ *Where to Stay for recommended dude ranches in Bandera.*

—Jessica Norman Dupuy

look the part in some Wranglers and boots, and if you're a woman, be prepared to get pulled onto the dance floor for a little boot scootin'.

WHERE TO EAT

$–$$ ✕**Full Moon Cafe.** Looking for lunch fare other than chicken-fried steak, barbecue, or Tex-Mex? The Full Moon Cafe is for you. A Houston couple took ownership of this pleasant Main Street venue in 2004 with the intent of offering slightly more sophisticated cuisine with a healthy edge. Pasta salad, for example, is spiced up with a zesty lime-cayenne dressing, adding quite a kick to the average rotini mix. Don't leave without a slice of moist pineapple cake. The best dinner menu of the week is offered on Friday. ⊠ *204 Main St.* ☎ *830/460–8434* ⊟ *D, MC, V* ⊘ *No dinner Sat.–Thurs.*

¢–$ ✕**The Grotto.** You have to leave Main Street to find this seemingly suspect hole-in-the-wall with mint-green walls and plywood tables. But don't be fooled, this may be one of the best meals you have in town. The pulled pork sandwich is a mouthwatering concoction of slow-roasted pork shoulder in a hoisin-Shiner Bock (dark Texas ale) marinade. Served on grilled ciabatta with a spicy apple-raspberry chutney, it adds new dimensions to Texas barbecue. ⊠ *907 13th St., at the corner of Sycamore* ☎ *830/796–9555* ⊟ *AE, D, MC, V* ⊘ *No dinner Sun.–Wed. Closed Sun.–Mon.*

¢–$ ✕**O.S.T Restaurant.** This is John Wayne country, and patrons of the O.S.T. (Old Spanish Trail), don't let you forget it. There's a whole wall covered with the Duke's photos and memorabilia. Authentic Tex-Mex and hearty American plates are served, including a Texas-sized chicken-fried steak that flaps over the lip of the plate. ⊠ *305 Main St.* ☎ *830/796–3836* ⊟ *MC, V.*

WHERE TO STAY

DUDE RANCHES

$$ ▦**Dixie Dude Ranch.** One of Bandera's oldest dude ranches, the Dixie ♻ opened its doors to guests in 1937. Cabins and cottages are available for large parties, as are individual rooms in the rustic bunkhouse and main lodge. Though decor is laced with Western kitsch, rooms all include the modern amenities that combat the Texas heat—namely, air-conditioning. Be sure to get the full cowboy experience on the overnight trail ride, with cookouts, swimming, and cowboy serenades. Meals are served family-style in the dining lodge. Rates include two horseback rides per day. **Pros:** Overnight trail-ride package, on-site masseur, excellent for children. **Cons:** Some of the modern amenities are somewhat dated; two-night minimum. ✛ *9 mi southwest of Bandera on FM 1077. The ranch is 7 mi west down 1077 on the right* ✉ *Box 548, 78003* ☎ *830/796–7771 or 800/375–9255* ⊕ *www.dixieduderanch. com* ⇆ *20 rooms* ⚬ *In-room: no TV, Wi-Fi. In-hotel: Public Wi-Fi, pool, no-smoking rooms* ⊟ *AE, D, MC, V* ⎁ *AI.*

$$ ▦**Mayan Ranch.** Each morning here begins with OJ and coffee delivered to your split-timber and riverstone cabin. You can relax the day away or join the ranch crew for two daily horseback rides, swimming, fishing, tubing on the Medina River, and even lessons in the Texas two-step. Rates include two horseback rides per day. Children's programs are offered during summer (June to August). **Pros:** Access to the Medina River, fun and friendly staff. **Cons:** Some rooms not as well maintained as others, activities are set each day, meal-times in the dining room are the only chance to eat. ⊹ *From the courthouse square on Main Street take Pecan Street down to 6th, turn right on 6th, and cross the Medina River* ⊠ *350 Mayan RR, , * ☎ *830/796–3312* ⊕ *www.mayanranch. com* ⇨ *36 rooms, 21 cabins* ⌂ *In-room: no TV, no phone, refrigerator (some). In-hotel: public Wi-Fi, one dining room, bar, tennis court, pool, children's program (ages 3–6), laundry facilities, airport shuttle (fee; from San Antonio only)* ☰ *AE, D, MC, V* ⑩ *AI.*

$$$$ 🏨 **Flying L Guest Ranch.** Though it's been around since 1946, the Flying ☪ L is anything but stuck in the past. Guests can horseback ride, go on hayrides, and enjoy nightly s'mores roasting, as is the case with most dude ranches, but this expansive 772-acre property also has an 18-hole golf course, a water park and lounging pool, and an entire kids' activity program. Accommodations range in size from stand-alone villas with room for 13 to smaller condo-like suites that sleep four to six. All have a gas fireplace and cozy bedding. **Pros:** Well-appointed condos including washer/dryer, variety of activities to choose from. **Cons:** Homesites built up around the golf course take away from the resort feel, thin walls make things audible between condos. ⊠ *566 Flying L Dr.* ⊹ *from Bandera, take Hwy. 173 south; the ranch is approximately 1 mi from town at the intersection of Wharton Dock Rd.* ☎ *800/292– 5134* ⊕ *www.flyingl.com* ⇨ *23 rooms, 36 suites* ⌂ *In-room: cable TV, data ports, kitchen, washer/dryer, refrigerator. In-hotel: 3 dining areas, 2 pools, tennis, golf, concierge, public Wi-Fi* ☰ *AE, D, MC, V* ⑩ *AI.*

MEDINA

14 mi west of Bandera via Hwy. 16.

If you like the remote feel of Bandera, head farther west on Highway 16 to Medina, a quiet treasure along the namesake river. Apple growing became a large part of this tiny town's industry in the late 1980s thanks to pioneer farmer Baxter Adams, who started the town's first apple orchard. Today Medina is known as the Apple Capital of Texas. The bounty can best be tasted in the form of a five-pound pie at **Bit O' Honey Bakery** (⊠ *13611 Hwy. 16 N*). A few shops sell sundry gifts and homemade apple jellies and spreads, and the **Old Timer** gas station at the junction of Ranch Road 337 is a good place for catching local gossip at an old picnic table.

WHERE TO STAY

$$$$ 🏨 **Escondida Resort.** Spanish for "hidden," Escondida is a pristine, luxe Fodor's Choice Mexican-style villa. The small resort and spa is the creation of property host Christy Carnes and Texas television personality Bob Philips.
★ In their stately manor, each guest room is outfitted with elegant hardwood and iron furniture and subtle Mexican tile accents. Some rooms include gas fireplaces. Don't leave without a trip to the spa—you won't be sorry! **Pros:** Beautiful surroundings and private accommodations, on-site chef, library and living rooms in main portion of the villa. **Cons:**

Two-hour drive from either San Antonio or Austin, palatial bathrooms lack large bathtubs. ⊠ *23670 Hwy. 16 N.,* ☎ *888/589-7507* ⊕ *www. escondidaresort.com* ➭ *10 rooms* ♿ *In-room: Refrigerator, safe, DVD, VCR, Ethernet, Wi-Fi, In-hotel: pool, spa, gym, no elevator, public Wi-Fi, some pets allowed, no kids under 21, no-smoking rooms.* ▭ *AE, D, MC, V* ⦿ *AP.*

LOST MAPLES STATE PARK

39 mi west of Bandera via FM 337 and Hwy. 187.

Once you get to Medina, you're slowly slipping farther from civilization and into the Western frontier. But if you can get comfortable with that idea, travel a little farther west towards Vanderpool on Ranch Road 337 and then north on Farm Road 187 to Lost Maples State Park. You'll find yourself on arguably one of the most breathtaking drives in the state.

If you're here during the fall, you'll likely be joined by a few thousand other travelers trying to catch one of the few patches of Texas land where you can actually witness a change in season. At Lost Maples the fall foliage rivals that of the Colorado golden aspens or the magnificent shades of Vermont and New Hampshire maples. ■ TIP➔ **Arrive early; the park only allows 250 cars; note that visitors pack the place during October and November weekends.**

Other times of year you'll have the park almost to yourself. Even in the stark grayness of winter, Lost Maples is lovely. Stroll the Maple Trail amid the towering trees to see rough-hewn limestone canyons, serene creeks, and emerald pools.

⊠ *37221 FM Rd. 187,* ☎ *830/966–3413* ⊕ *www.tpwd.state.tx.us* 🎟 *$5.*

BOERNE

31 mi northwest of San Antonio via I–10.

Just a few years ago Boerne was a quiet little town with a smattering of shops and small-town restaurants. Even though it had easy access to San Antonio (just 30 minutes' drive away), Boerne flew under the radar while Fredericksburg boomed. But in recent years a whole slew of big-city Texans looking for the good life have descended upon Boerne, buying ranches in the hills, or retiring to the many high-end developments that have popped up along Highways 16 and 46. The result is a revitalized downtown district with a number of new restaurants—though still few accommodations—and a passel of new shops along Main Street. Even so, you won't find the shopping hordes here that you might in Fredericksburg.

Now that it's on the map, Boerne has begun attracting a crowd from the San Antonio area looking for a little "Hill Country action." Weekends in December are particularly festive. From the lighting of the town tree to an evening of Charles Dickens–inspired carolers, Boerne knows how to get people in the holiday spirit.

Originally settled in the 1840s by the same group of German "Freethinkers" that set up communities in nearby Comfort and surrounding areas, Boerne (pronounced burr-knee) grew steadily along the banks of Cibolo Creek. The town bears remnants of its German heritage around every corner, including the bilingual German-style streets signs along the *Hauptstrasse* (Main Street).

WHAT TO SEE

Cascade Caverns. Take a half-mile tour past awe-inspiring limestone formations, deep caverns, stalactites, and stalagmites; you may even catch a glimpse of the endangered Cascade Caverns salamander. Watch for the impressive 100-foot waterfall spilling into a black pool at the end of the tour. ⌧*226 Cascade Caverns Rd. (I–10 W, Exit 543)* ☏*830/755-2400* ⊕*www.cascadecaverns.com* ⊗*Daily 10–5* ⌫*$11.*

Ⓒ **Cibolo Nature Center.** Nature lovers will enjoy strolling the trails through this 100-acre park set aside for the conservation of natural grasslands, marshlands, and riverbeds. Educational outdoor workshops and camps are available for kids. ⌧*140 City Park Rd.* ☏*830/249-4616* ⊕*www. cibolo.org* ⌫*Free* ⊗*Daily 8–dusk.*

NEED A BREAK? If you need a quick caffeine fix, hit **The Daily Grind** at the **Boerne Grill** (⌧*143 S. Main St.* ☏*830/249-4677*). It's a relaxed place to read or sip a potent coffee, and the Friday night steak nights at the adjoining Boerne Grill are not to be missed.

OFF THE BEATEN PATH **Guadalupe River State Park.** This park gives some of the best public access to the shady cypress tree–lined Guadalupe River, a great spot for kayaking, swimming, and fishing. In the winter, fly-fishing fanatics have a top opportunity to land rainbow trout stocked here by the state each year. ⌧*3350 Park Rd. 31, Spring Branch* ☏*830/438-2656* ⊕*www. tpwd.state.tx.us* ⊗*Daily 8 AM–10 PM.*

SHOPPING

ANTIQUES & ART

The Iron Pigtail (⌧*470 S. Main St.* ☏*830/249-8877*) has a unique collection of South American art and early Texas pottery and antiques. Find Victorian jewelry and 19th-century furniture at **Simple Treasures** (⌧*195 S. Main* ☏*830/249-5454*).

CLOTHING & ACCESSORIES

Be sure to stop in **Celeste** (⌧*140 S. Main St.* ☏*830/249-9660*) for reasonably priced, stylish outfits. Country meets bohemian on the racks of womens' clothes at **Mon a Me** (⌧*305 S. Main St.* ☏*830/249-2525* ⊗*Closed Sun.*). **Green Bull Jewelry** (⌧*325 S. Main St.* ☏*830/249-7393* ⊗*Closed Sun.*) has hard-to-find jewelry by Jerry Gowen and other one-of-a-kind pieces.

HOME FURNISHINGS

Ordering custom-designed furniture is a pleasurable experience at **Calamity Jane's** (⊠*322 S. Main St.* ☎*830/249–0081*), where owner Shawn Beach meticulously conjures up Texas Hill Country decor. Wander the three small houses and courtyard of **Good & Co.** (⊠*248 S. Main St.* ☎*830/249–6101*) for a variety of rustic home accents such as iron chandeliers. With unique European new and vintage odds and ends, **The Rusty Bucket** (⊠*195 S. Main St.* ☎*830/249–2288* ⊙*Closed Mon.*) is the perfect place to find a housewarming gift.

WHERE TO EAT

¢–$$ ✕**Bear Moon Bakery.** On weekends you may find a line out the door at
★ this town favorite serving up an extensive breakfast buffet with eggs, fruit, and fresh-baked muffins, pastries, and breads. The breakfast crowd arrives early for one of the few inside tables. Most patrons brave the long counter line for cinnamon rolls—bring an appetite, they're as big as a Frisbee! Locals swarm here for lunch as well. ⊠*401 S. Main St.* ☎*830/816–2327* ▭*AE, D, MC, V* ⊙*Closed Mon. No dinner.*

$–$$$$ ✕**The Creek.** Dining alongside Cibolo Creek in this historic house while listening to the rhythmic turn of a water mill is a treat. There's a nice array of steaks, fresh seafood, and wild game. We particularly liked the blue crab fingers lightly sautéed with lemon and wine and the soul-warming rich and hearty beef-potato soup. ⊠*119 Staffel St.* ☎*830/816–2005* ▭*AE, D, MC, V* ⊙*Closed Mon.*

$$–$$$ ✕**Cypress Grille.** People-watching has never been so inviting. From the
★ small bistro tables in the front of the narrow wine bar you can sip a glass of wine and nibble on crisp crab cakes while watching the passersby. The dinner menu also has much to offer. Blackened sea scallops with andouille sausage has a nice Cajun twist. Salads are fairly sizable and not your plain-Jane variety. The Texas Cobb, for example, has spicy grilled shrimp and slices of grapefruit. ⊠*170 S. Main St.* ☎*830/248–1353* ▭*AE, D, MC, V* ⊙*Closed Sun.–Mon.*

$–$$$ ✕**Limestone Grille.** Tucked around the back side of the stately Ye Kendall
★ Inn, the Limestone Grille is one of the most traditional fine restaurants in town. Low lighting and deep greens and earthy tones give the dining room a historical ambience that whispers "This is where Robert E. Lee would have dined." In fact, the Confederate general was a guest at this building's old stagecoach stop. Soups and salads are pretty straightforward with a few exciting surprises, namely the thick and hearty Texas chili served with delicious yucca-root fries. Take your time with the wine list; it's one of the most extensive in the entire region. ⊠*128 W. Blanco* ☎*830/249–2138* ▭*AE, D, MC, V.*

$–$$$ ✕**Po Po Family Restaurant.** You might rub your eyes here; over 21,000 collector plates crowd this country-cooking café. When it first opened in 1929, Prohibition was still in full swing and countless bootleggers would sell moonshine in the parking lot. Now people come for the fried chicken and chicken-fried steak. The fried frogs' legs—yes, frog's legs—are really good, too. Save room for a warm brownie sundae. ⊠*829 FM 289, via the Welfare exit (#533) off I–10 W* ☎*830/537–4194* ▭*AE, D, MC, V.*

WHERE TO STAY

$$ **August House.** Deemed one of the oldest continuously-running B&Bs in Boerne, this charming 1912 white cottage offers two rooms in the main house and a separate Garden House. Each room is decorated with old-fashioned Western and Texan style. Guests are served coffee, juice, and light snacks for their stay and receive breakfast coupons to the Bear Moon Bakery, Boerne's hot spot for fresh-baked pastries. Rooms are spacious and comfortable; the country decor is slightly overwhelming. **Pros:** Located only a couple of blocks from Main Street. **Cons:** Small twin beds in the Cabin Room. ⊠ *109 W. Evergreen St.,* ☎ *830/249–4964* ⊕ *www.augusthousetexas.com* ↙ *3 rooms* ⚲ *In-room: refrigerator. In-hotel: no-smoking rooms* ⊟ *AE, D, MC, V* ⑩ *CP.*

$$$$ **Paniolo Ranch.** You'll have to drive down a winding back road to reach this Hawaiian-named retreat, but once you see the beautiful rolling valley below this hilltop perch you'll be glad you made the trip. The property features four private cottages, each with a suite or two rooms as well as luxurious living spaces. The O'Hana House is the most private and has some of the best views of the ranch; it also has its own hot tub, ideal for star-gazing before bed. **Pros:** Remote property is beautiful, on-site spa. **Cons:** Slightly difficult to find, prices are fairly high in comparison to other Hill Country accommodations. ⊠ *1510 FM 473,* ☎ *866/726–4656* ⊕ *www.panioloranch.com* ↙ *4 cottages* ⚲ *In-room: Ethernet, DVD, kitchen (some), refrigerator. In-hotel: pool, spa, gym, public Wi-Fi, no children* ⊟ *AE, D, MC, V* ⑩ *CP.*

$$–$$$$ ✕ **Ye Kendall Inn.** Built in 1859 as Boerne's stagecoach stop, the inn
★ is now a recognized state and national historic landmark. The main lodge of this nine-acre property features 22-inch-thick hand-cut limestone walls and airy porches giving an authentic Hill Country feel. Beyond the main house is a collection of fully restored cottages—there's even a 19th-century chapel that serves as a lovely bridal suite. Each of the rooms, suites, and cottages is uniquely decorated with vintage pieces as well as modern luxuries. Those interested in the supernatural should inquire about the resident ghosts reputed to haunt some areas of the hotel. **Pros:** Excellent location on river and near Main Street, nice spa and gym. **Cons:** Some rooms are slightly dusty and have an old, musty smell; breakfast is not included with the price of a room, front-desk service isn't overly friendly. ⊠ *128 W. Blanco,* ☎ *800/364–2138 830/249–2138* ⊕ *www.yekendallinn.com* ↙ *36 rooms, suites, or cottages* ⚲ *In-room: Wi-Fi. In-hotel: restaurant, bar, spa, gym, public Wi-Fi, pool, no-smoking rooms* ⊟ *AE, D, MC, V.*

COMFORT

17 mi northwest of Boerne via I–10/U.S. 87.

At first glance, Comfort resembles a lot of quiet Hill Country towns. It has the standard Dairy Queen and a small main street with historic buildings and antiques shops. But Comfort, known as the start of the Texas Hill Country, seems to have a magic effect on the people who visit. You don't find the crowded sidewalks of Fredericksburg, Boerne, and Kerrville. Here time slows to a crawl, and the friendly faces of locals on High Street, the town's main thoroughfare, make you want to pull up a chair and stay a while.

The laid-back mentality mirrors the mindset of those who settled here in 1852 along the banks of the Cypress Creek. Unlike the austere German settlers of Fredericksburg, New Braunfels, and Boerne, Comfort was settled by Ernst Hermann Altgelt and a community of Germans known as the "Freethinkers," who fled political and religious oppression and lived a far less conservative life than did traditional Germans.

The community prospered in this new way of thinking until the outbreak of the Civil War. While most Texans were pledging their oath to the Confederacy, the Freethinkers swore loyalty to the Union army. Fearful of threats from Confederate loyalists, much of the community fled toward the Mexican border for protection. Those who didn't, or didn't make it, met their doom: on August 10, 1862, 36 men were slaughtered in the Battle of Nueces. Today Comfort is home to one of only six flags across the country that fly at half-mast year-round in remembrance of the Union patriots.

4

WHAT TO SEE

Many of the buildings in the center of High Street were constructed in the late 1800s by noted British architect Alfred Giles, and are listed on the National Register of Historic Places. These include the Comfort Common and the remnants of Ingenhuetts General Store, the longest continuously-run operation in Comfort until a fire in 2006 destroyed much of its original structure. Plans to rebuild what many locals consider the heart of the town have not yet been determined.

WHERE TO EAT

$–$$ ✕ **814: A Texas Bistro.** Colorful, quilt-draped walls and a cool ceiling-fanned patio make this a comfortable spot no matter the weather. The menu changes with the season, but you might find an entrée such as a juicy grilled New York strip steak in a balsamic reduction or sautéed rainbow trout. The 814 Burger is a half-pound of grilled bliss. ✉814 High St., ☎830/995–4990 ▤AE, D, MC, V ⊘Closed Mon.–Tues.

¢–$ ✕ **Double D.** Don't be put off by the no-frills atmosphere of this side-of-the-road joint. What it lacks in charm, it more than makes up for with good home cooking. Notable menu options are the hand-battered chicken-fried steak with cream gravy and the thick-cut onion rings. The daily lunch buffets are a great deal at just $7.50. ✉1004 Front St., ☎830/995–2001 ▤AE, D, MC, V.

$–$$$$ ✕ **Welfare Cafe.** A former post office now serves appetites in the middle of nowhere. There are some unusual dishes like mahimahi (a mild, white fish) with tomatillo sauce, but also plenty of German fare. Start with potato pancakes served with apple sauce or sour cream. The schnitzel is fabulous, as is the rouladen—a tenderized beef fillet wrapped around dill pickle, ham, sauerkraut, and Swiss cheese. If it's warm outside, sit beneath the vined trellis and watch the resident goats and donkeys grazing nearby. Live music accompanies your meal on Thursdays and Sundays. Reservations are strongly recommended. ✉223 Waring Welfare Rd., ☎830/537–3700 ▤AE, D, MC, V ⊘Closed Mon.–Tues.

WHERE TO STAY

$–$$$ ⊞ **The Comfort Common.** These B&B guest rooms are tangled in a labyrinth of antiques shops and private cabins; there are even a couple of donkeys in back. British architect Alfred Giles built the Common in 1880 as the Ingenhuett-Faust Hotel. Now it's divided into two areas: the earthy Altgelt room and the more private Victorian Storyville cottage, a block away from the main building and decorated with monochromatic whites. Breakfast is served to you in your room. **Pros:** Beautiful antique decor, perfect location for Christmas in Comfort. **Cons:** Some of the accommodations are spread out, the Storyville is a few blocks from the Inn, heavy tourist traffic through the inn shops on weekends can feel intrusive. ⊠ *717 High St.,* ☎ *830/995–3030* ⊕ *www.comfort common.com* ➽ *3 rooms, 3 suites* ♿ *In-room: kitchen (some), refrigerator, Wi-Fi. In-hotel: no-smoking rooms, no kids under age 12* ⊟ *AE, D, MC, V* ⌯⊙⌯ *BP.*

$–$$$ ⊞ **Meyer Bed and Breakfast.** Originally a stage stop for travelers preparing to cross the Guadalupe River for the Old Spanish Trail, the Meyer is beautifully situated along the banks of Cypress Creek and is also just a few blocks' walk from town shopping. Each room and suite displays a different theme, such as the era of jazz music or an African safari. ■**TIP**➜ Be prepared to book here, and at most other hotels or bed-and-breakfasts more than six months in advance if you're planning to spend Thanksgiving week here (the Saturday after Thanksgiving is "Christmas in Comfort," a huge draw with lots of activities in town. **Pros:** Excellent proximity to shops, riverfront location is serene and inviting. **Cons:** Some of the newer rooms are spacious and clean, but aren't as atmospheric as the rooms in the more historic buildings. ⊠ *845 High St.,* ☎ *888/995–6100 or 830/995–6100* ⊕ *www.meyerbedandbreakfast. com* ➽ *5 rooms, 22 suites* ♿ *In-room: Wi-Fi, refrigerator (some). In-hotel: pool, public Wi-Fi, no-smoking rooms, parking (no fee)* ⊟ *AE, D, MC, V* ⌯⊙⌯ *BP.*

$$$$ ⊞ **Riven Rock Ranch.** It's a bit off the beaten path, but if you can bear with
Fodor's Choice a bend or two in the road, you'll find this Hill Country treasure. Three
★   ranch-style cottages and one late-1800s farmhouse have immaculate Texas-meets-French-countryside interiors, gas fireplaces, and beautiful views of the hills. The ranch also has a large meeting/entertaining hall that accommodates up to 150 people, and an intimate dining room that serves up to 50 guests for special events. Standing in the center of the property, a former water tower has been converted into an observation tower. **Pros:** Immaculate property with beautifully designed accommodations, afternoon refreshments are a nice bonus. **Cons:** Remote location makes visiting area towns a longer journey, fairly expensive compared to other Hill Country accommodations. ⊠ *390 Hermann Sons Rd.,* ☎ *877/726–2490 or 830/995–4045* ⊕ *www.rivenrockranch. com* ➽ *9 rooms* ♿ *In-room: Wi-Fi, DVD, full kitchen. In-hotel: pool, public Wi-Fi, no-smoking rooms* ⊟ *AE, D, MC, V* ⌯⊙⌯ *BP.*

SHOPPING

ANTIQUES & HOME DECOR

Note that several stores close on Mondays. Find classic American selections at **Antiques on High** (⊠ *641 High St.* ☎ *830/995–3662*

⊙ *Closed Mon.*). **Blackbird Antiques** (✉ *724 High St.* ☎ *830/995–2550* ⊙ *Closed Mon.*) offers exquisite folk-art pieces as well as Victorian and copper antiques. Browse the local artwork and artisan designs in **Antiquities, etc & Folk Art Gallery** (✉ *702 High St.* ☎ *830/995–4190* ⊙ *Closed Mon.*), where you'll also find a variety of antique collectibles from jewelry to books. Browse beautiful Mexican and European primitives and hand-made furniture at **Wilson Clements Antiques** (✉ *405 7th St.* ☎ *830/995–2000*). The shops at the **Comfort Common** (✉ *717 High St.* ☎ *830/995–3030*) stock all sorts of home accessories and unique trinkets.

> ### GETTING FOLKSY IN KERRVILLE
>
> The **Kerrville Folk Festival** ((☎ *830/257-7474* ⊕ *www.kerrvillefolkfestival.com*)) is the oldest continuously-running music festival of its kind in the country. It usually begins the Thursday before Memorial Day and runs 24/7 for 18 days straight, with performances by more than 100 singer-songwriters and their bands. Since 1972 the festival has grown to attract more than 30,000 guests. Among those who've graced the stages of this music celebration are Willie Nelson, Lyle Lovett, Mary Chapin Carpenter, and Robert Earl Keen.

KERRVILLE

67 mi northwest of San Antonio via I–10.

Years ago, Kerrville had the small-town appeal that draws thousands to Fredericksburg and Boerne. With the arrival of the railroad in the late 1800s this settlement of primarily shingle-makers became a center for trade and commerce, bringing droves of urban refugees from all walks of life. Happily situated among some of the most dramatic bluffs and valleys in the Hill Country, with the Guadalupe River running through it, the town has some of the more picturesque views in Texas. Now it's one of the biggest little cities in the region. With a population of more than 20,000, Kerrville has become the source for necessities that can't be found in the smaller towns.

WHAT TO SEE

☾ **The Museum of Western Art.** Dedicated to preserving the authenticity of Western American heritage, the museum not only showcases Western art from past and present artists, but also shares the rich history of the cowboys, American Indians, settlers, mountain men, and tradesmen through educational programs. Interactive seminars give youngsters a chance to build their own "home on the range" and see how difficult life was on the open frontier. ✉ *1550 Bandera Hwy.* ☎ *830/896–2553* ⊕ *www.museumofwesternart.org* ▭ *$5* ⊙ *Tues.–Sat. 9–5, Sun. 1–5.*

WHERE TO EAT

$–$$ ✕ **Rails–A Café at the Depot.** Just off the railroad tracks is a cheery historic house with cream timber siding and red trim. Built in 1915, the house once served as a train depot, but was transformed into a fantastic little restaurant offering a variety of homemade soups, salads, and hearty entrées. Daily lunch and dinner specials vary. Look for the spicy grilled-shrimp tostada with creamy chipotle sauce and the grilled venison burger. ⊠*615 E. Schreiner St.* ☎*830/257–3877* ▤*AE, D, MC, V* �*Closed Sun.*

$$–$$$ ✕ **River's Edge–A Tuscan Grille.** Try to get here before sunset, to watch the
★   sky fade from orange to pink and purple over the Guadalupe River. It's
a view you can have from almost any seat at this little Italian locale.
Here every effort is made to create authentic Italian cuisine with a bit
of a Texas flavor. Spark your appetite with a salad of Bibb lettuce, pear,
candied walnuts, and goat cheese. The Bolognese with sweet Italian
sausage is a good standby; another favorite is the beef tips swimming
in a Gorgonzola cream sauce. ⊠*1011 Guadalupe St.* ☎*830/895–1169*
▤*AE, D, MC, V* ☉*Closed Sun.*

¢–$$ ✕ **Mamacita's.** In Kerrville, Mamacita's is as much a tradition as Frito
pie at a high-school football games. Though billed as "authentic" Mex-
ican food, we'd argue that it's more along the lines of standard Tex-
Mex fare, and about as straightforward as you can get. ⊠*215 Junction
Hwy.* ☎*830/895–2441* ▤*AE, D, MC, V.*

WHERE TO STAY

$$–$$$ ▦ **Y.O. Ranch Resort Hotel.** You may be on one of the bustling main
streets of Kerrville, but a stay at the Y.O. Ranch Resort is a little like a
retreat to a star 1950s dude ranch. No, there aren't horses or hayrides,
but the rooms are all decorated in a Western theme, with exposed lime-
stone walls and old-fashioned fixtures and curtains. Almost every room
has a set of mounted deer antlers, just in case you were beginning to
forget you were in Texas. The main lobby flaunts the Lone Star State's
attributes as well: it displays more than 40 full mounts of exotic game
along the high limestone walls and a life-sized sculpture of a cowboy
on a bucking bronco. A special family suite includes a separate room
for kids with bunk beds. **Pros:** Friendly and helpful staff, good for "old-
fashioned" Texas feel, large and affordable rooms. **Cons:** Entire prop-
erty could use some updating and remodeling, room decor is sparse and
drab. ⊠*2033 Sidney Baker,* ☎*830/257–4440* ⊕*www.yoresort.com*
⤴*200 rooms* ⌂*In-room: Wi-Fi. In-hotel: Public Wi-Fi, restaurant,
bar, tennis court, some pets allowed (with deposit), no-smoking rooms*
▤*AE, D, MC, V.*

CAMPING

$$–$$$ ⚠ **Guadalupe RV Resort.** Only a few minutes from downtown, this RV
campsite is really a cream-of-the-crop experience. Along the banks
of the Guadalupe River, this beautifully maintained property offers
shaded, spread-out sites for big-rig pull-thrus and motor-home pull-
ins, each with a concrete patio and picnic table. Fully furnished one-
and two-bedroom cabins are also available to rent with a full kitchen
and bathrooms. There are plenty of distractions, too: a game room
with pool and Ping-Pong tables, three swimming pools, volleyball, bas-
ketball, and the on-site River Rock Saloon. **Pros:** Spacious campsites,
nice landscaping, friendly staff. **Cons:** Not all sites have river views,
need a car to get to town. ⊠*2605 Junction Hwy. 27* ☎*800/582–1916
or 830/367–5676* ⊕*www.guadaluperiverrvresort.com* ⤴ *16 cabins,
202 sites* ⌂*Full hookups, dump station, drinking water, guest laundry,*

showers, picnic tables, general store, play area, pool, electricity, public telephone, Wi-Fi ⊟*AE, D, MC, V* ⊗*Open year-round.*

$ ⚠**Quiet Valley Ranch.** Probably most noted for its stake in hosting the annual Kerrville Folk Festival, Quiet Valley Ranch is an idyllic plot of land 9 mi south of Kerrville. Covering more than 50 acres of rugged Hill Country terrain, half the property is dedicated to the areas used for the festival, while the other half is used for tent and RV camping. The camp itself is fairly primitive compared to some of the other RV parks in town. **Pros:** Perfect location for enjoying the Kerrville Folk Festival, very laid-back and low-maintenance environment. **Cons:** Not as many amenities as RV sites, more suited for primitive camping. ⊠*3876 Medina Hwy.* ☎*830/257-7474* ⊕*www.qvranch.com* ⛺*Full hookups, toilets, fire pits, grills, drinking water.* ⊟*AE, D, MC, V* ⊗*Open year-round.*

INGRAM

Just 7 mi west of Kerrville, along the picturesque Guadalupe River, lies the small town of Ingram, where you can find a thriving art community. There's a turn-off to the south just west of town but it's easy to miss! In 1958 the Hill Country Arts Foundation was established with an emphasis on providing cultural arts to the region. It offers both art classes and theater for professionals and amateurs. An afternoon visiting the studios or the main art gallery displaying rotating exhibits of regional, national, and international artists is a worthwhile experience.

Ingram's many art galleries are in "Old Ingram," the older section of town off Texas Highways 39 and 27. Most galleries are closed on Mondays (some shops will close on Tuesday and Wednesday as well November through January, depending on weather and clientele). A full lineup of plays is produced from the **Point Theater** (⊠*120 Point Theatre Rd.,* ☎*830/367-5121 or 800/459-4223* ⊕*www.hcaf.com*) in both indoor and outdoor venues.

BETWEEN SAN ANTONIO & AUSTIN

GRUENE

38 mi north of San Antonio via I-35.

Gruene is purely Texan. Ask many Central Texans if they've ever two-stepped in this little town and you'll see a nostalgic gleam in their eye. Just north of New Braunfels, Gruene stands as a pristine portrait of Texas history and is revered as a place of Texas legends. After all, the entire town has been added to the National Register of Historic Places, and many of the buildings hold a medallion from the Texas Historical Commission.

Settled in the late 1840s by German farmer Ernst Gruene and his sons, the town gained most of its prosperity from the family's cotton business. Gruene's second son, Henry D. Gruene, built a Victorian-style home that is now the iconic Gruene Mansion Inn. Then in the late 1870s he built the Guadalupe River–powered cotton gin, which now houses the famed Gristmill River Restaurant & Bar, and Guene Hall, a dance hall and saloon that served as *the* social venue for the community before becoming a live music venue in the 1970s.

Though the attack of the boll weevil on cotton crops in the late 1920s and the hostile economic effects of the Depression all but shut down the little town, this Texas star rose again in the 1970s with the restorative support of Pat Molak and Mary Jane Nalley. The two poured their boundless energy into preserving the original turn-of-the-century feel of the town.

ARTS & ENTERTAINMENT

DANCE HALL

★ What really puts Gruene on the Texas map is the legendary **Gruene Hall,** known as the oldest continuously-operating dance hall in the entire state. Many famous musicians owe their success to performances on this fabled stage, including Willie Nelson, Lyle Lovett, George Strait, Garth Brooks, Jerry Lee Lewis, and the Dixie Chicks. A trip to Gruene isn't complete without a turn on the old hardwood floors of Gruene Hall. ⊠ *1281 Gruene Rd.* ☎ *830/606–1281* ⊕ *www.gruenehall.com.*

WHERE TO EAT

¢–$$$ ✕**Gristmill.** Dining at the Gristmill is as mandatory as shuffling your boots along the floors of Gruene Hall when visiting Gruene. On a sunny day, request a seat on the multi-tiered deck that climbs the side of the cliff overlooking the Guadalupe River. Though you can find fabulous soups and salads, there's nothing quite like the Gristburger. The secret to this burger's success is the spicy chili con queso that oozes from the sides. ⊠ *1287 Gruene Rd.* ☎ *830/625–0684* ▤ *AE, D, MC, V.*

¢–$$$ ✕**Gruene River Grill.** Behind the Gruene Mansion Inn, this riverside grill draws quite a crowd. People seem to frequent this locale for the famed rib eye pan-seared in butter and balsamic vinegar, but a cup of the creamy jalepeño corn chowder brimming with fresh crawfish tails makes a notable impact as well. ⊠ *1259 Gruene Rd.* ☎ *830/624–2300* ▤ *AE, D, MC, V.*

WHERE TO STAY

$–$$$ ▦**Gruene Homestead Inn.** Just outside Gruene, and on the way to New Braunfels, it's hard to miss this cluster of historic farm houses scattered along a rolling green. Choose from 21 uniquely decorated suites that reflect a historic late 1800s feel. Each room has its own Texas-themed style, such as the Bluebonnet Room. Included on this expansive eight-acre property is the newly popular **Tavern in the Gruene** ((☎ *830/608–0438* ⊕ *www.taverninthegruene.com*)), a live-music venue hosting a number of up-and-coming Texas artists. **Pros:** Rooms are impeccably clean and well maintained, and remain quiet despite music from the nearby Tavern in the Gruene; friendly and accommodating staff. **Cons:** Close to a new housing development, which takes away from its quaintness; noise from frequent Harley-Davidsons passing on the main road is unavoidable; breakfast is good, yet simple. ✉*832 Gruene Rd.*, ☎*800/238–5534* ⊕*www.gruenehomesteadinn.com* ↪*21 rooms* ♿*In-room: Wi-Fi, Ethernet, refrigerator (some). In-hotel: pool, hot tub, no-smoking rooms* ⊟*AE, D, MC, V* ⦿*BP.*

$$$–$$$$ 🏛**Gruene Mansion Inn.** If you can stay in Gruene for an evening or two, this is the place to do it. The main house is the original home of Henry Gruene, and owners Cecil and Judi Eager have painstakingly worked to restore everything to its original condition. The guest accommodations extend much farther than the main house, including a row of cabins with river views, a renovated corn crib, and a period-designed lodge in the middle of the expansive property. **Pros:** Riverfront rooms have a nice view, close to shopping and restaurants. **Cons:** Big shows at Gruene Hall can be heard in the rooms, not the ideal place for children. ✉*1275 Gruene Rd.*, ☎*830/629–2641* ⊕*www.gruenemansioninn.com* ↪*30 rooms* ♿*In-room: refrigerator, DVD (upon request), Wi-Fi. In-hotel: public Wi-Fi, no-smoking rooms, parking (no fee)* ⊟*MC, V* ⦿*BP.*

SHOPPING

If Gruene Hall is king of the town, the **Gruene General Store** (✉*1610 Hunter Rd.* ☎*830/629–6021*) is its queen. Parts of the building date to the 1850s; the soda fountain is a 1950s time warp. You can find all sorts of unusual Texas gifts, cards, and foods. The store closes by 6 PM on Sunday.

Antiques lovers should duck into the **Gruene Antique Company** (✉*1607 Hunter Rd.* ☎*830/629–7781*), where more than 8,000 square feet of antiques and collectibles await. It's open until 9 PM.

The **Buck Pottery** (✉*1296 Gruene Rd.* ☎*830/629–7975*) building hosts its own workshop, where customers can watch as some of the beautiful earthenware is created by the artists. Unique pieces from a number of local artists keep this family-run shop a main attraction.

Those about to embark on a Hill Country wine tour may want to stop in at the **Grapevine** (✉*1612 Hunter Rd.* ☎*830/606–0093*) to get a sampling of what's ahead on the Hill Country Wine Trail.

NEW BRAUNFELS

6 mi from Gruene; 30 mi north of San Antonio and 45 mi southwest of Austin via I–35.

With a name like New Braunfels, it's a safe bet that Germans had a great deal of influence in this town. And in fact, they did. New Braunfels was the first of the Adelsverein-movement settlements in the 1840s to create secure land in Texas under the German flag. The town was founded by Prince Carl of Solms-Braunfels, the Commissioner General of the Adelsverein. In 1845 Prince Carl led hundreds of sea-lagged German settlers from Galveston to a plot of land north of San Antonio on the banks of the Comal River. The settlement would later be named for his hometown in Germany, Braunfels (pronounced brawn-fells). The settlement endured a shaky beginning with the outbreak of the Mexican-American

War in 1846, wet seasons that produced great floods in the Comal and Guadalupe rivers, and an outbreak of cholera. But by 1850 the town was a thriving community boasting the title of the fourth largest city in Texas.

It lies along the Balcones Fault, where the Hill Country meets rolling prairie land to the east, putting New Braunfels barely inside the realms of the Hill Country region. The fault line produced a string of artesian springs known as Comal Springs that create the Comal River. Stretching a mere 3 mi before flowing into the Gaudalupe River, the Comal is considered the shortest river in the world.

Whereas many Hill Country towns are frequented for the shopping, wine, romantic getaways, or pure beautiful scenery, New Braunfels is considered more of an activity town. People come to tube down the Guadalupe River and splash around at Schlitterbahn WaterPark Resort, or to get a taste (literally) of the annual Wurstfest in late October and early November celebrating the town's German heritage.

WHAT TO SEE

Fodor'sChoice   **Natural Bridge Caverns.** Guides will take you on an incredible journey
★   underground at the largest known cavern in Texas, which has a half-mile of paved trails. View awe-inspiring rock formations that are constantly changing and growing due to the dripping and flowing water. The brave of heart shouldn't miss the flashlight tour of the Jaremy Room, a 120-foot-deep chamber known for its soda straws and delicate formations. If you're claustrophobic, be aware that the underground chambers are connected by fairly narrow passageways. Next to the caverns you can go on a driving safari at the **Natural Bridge Wildlife Ranch** ((⊠*26515 Natural Bridge Caverns Rd.* ☎*830/438–7400* ⊕*www.wildliferanchtexas.com* ✉*$15.50* ⊗*Memorial Day–Labor Day, daily 9–6:30; early Sept.–late May, daily 9–5*)), which is home to white rhinos, antelope, kudus, and dozens of other exotic animals from around the world. ⊠*26495 Natural Bridge Caverns Rd., I–35 Exit 175 (Natural Bridge Caverns Rd./FM 3009)* ☎*210/651–6101* ⊕*www.naturalbridgecaverns.com* ✉*$16.95* ⊗*Daily; call for hours.*

SPORTS & THE OUTDOORS

☾   **Schlitterbahn.** Thousands of sun-beaten travelers seek refuge from the Texas heat each year at this 65-acre waterpark with more than 40 rides and family activities spread over six areas. ⊠*Off I–35, Exit 184 or 190B* ☎*830/625–2351* ⊕*www.schlitterbahn.com* ✉*$36* ⊗*Late Apr.–mid-Sept.; call for hours.*

FISHING & TUBING

The Guadalupe River runs from the western points of Kerr County and stretches down to the Gulf of Mexico through Victoria. The upper river near Kerrville and Boerne is a wide, meandering centerpiece to the Texas Hill Country shaded by pecan and cypress trees. Below Canyon Lake, the Guadalupe River serves as a major recreational spot. Whitewater rafting and kayaking are both popular, but the more relaxed activity of tubing down the river trailing a cooler of beer is the main attraction in summer.

Below the Canyon Dam, the Gaudalupe is also considered one of the top 100 trout streams in the country. The state stocks the river with trout each winter, attracting anglers from miles around. While casting for beautiful rainbow and brown trout, you'll likely get a few hits from the native Guadalupe smallmouth bass (the state fish of Texas), largemouth bass, and Rio Grande perch.

FISHING OUTFITTERS There are many reputable fishing guides in the area. For referrals and to stock up on fishing gear, visit **Gruene Outfitters** (⊠ *1629 Hunter Rd.* ☎ *830/625–4440*).

KAYAKING, RAFTING & TUBING OUTFIITTERS

River outfitters are easily found dotting the banks of the river, where tubes, rafts, and kayaks can be rented for the day. A few to try: **Rockin 'R' River Rides** (⊠ *1405 Gruene Rd.* ☎ *830/629–9999*), **Gruene River Co.** (⊠ *1404 Gruene Rd.* ☎ *830/625–2800*), and **Rio Raft & Resort** (⊠ *14130 River Rd.* ☎ *830/964–3613*).

WHERE TO EAT

$–$$ ✕**Huisache Grille.** Hidden near the train tracks off San Antonio Street, Fodor's Choice the Huisache (pronounced wee-satch) is a must-stop. Consistently ★ delivering fantastic soups, salads, sandwiches, and main dishes, there's a lot to love about this place, and the beautiful historic 1920s building only adds to the experience. For lunch the ham and gouda sandwich with sweet caramelized onions offers a nice adult version of a grilled cheese. Pecan-crusted pork chops soar with a rich bourbon-butter sauce. ⊠ *303 W. San Antonio St.* ☎ *830/620–9001* ☰ *AE, D, MC, V.*

$$–$$$$ ✕**Liberty Bistro.** From the portraits of presidents along the walls to the cleverly named entrées—Freedom Filet, 49th State Wild Salmon Filet, Freedom of the Press Chicken—the patriotic theme is hard to miss at this upscale eatery. The *cabriqueso* is a fantastic starter of melted goat cheese mixed with jalapeño and cilantro pesto and spicy-sweet red piquillo peppers. In an effort to lessen the bistro's carbon footprint, owner Darren Scroggins has created a completely green kitchen free of gas cooking. ⊠ *200 N. Seguin St.* ☎ *830/624–7876* ☰ *AE, D, MC, V* ☻ *Closed Sun.*

WHERE TO STAY

$$$–$$$$ ☷**Lamb's Rest Inn.** Getting a little rest is easy to do at this spot on the Guadalupe River. Expansive wooden decks surround live oaks and hammocks sway in the garden. The spacious rooms have comfortable beds and colorful accents. Warm chocolate-chip cookies tend to present themselves each afternoon. **Pros:** Rooms have an up-to-date look; tiered decks have wonderful river views; excellent staff. **Cons:** Small bathrooms in some rooms, over-the-top decor in some rooms. ⊠ *1385 Edwards Blvd.,* ☎ *830/609–3932* ⊕ *www.lambsrestinn.com* ⇨*4 rooms, 1 2-bedroom suite, 1 2-bedroom cottage* ♿ *In-room: Wi-Fi, refrigerator. In-hotel: Public Wi-Fi, parking, no-smoking rooms* ☰ *AE, D, MC, V* ☽*BP.*

CLOSE UP

Wines of the Hill Country

Newsflash: You don't have to go to Napa or the Saint Ynez valley to sample good wine. Vintners across Texas are abuzz with hearty blends of wine that have started turning heads from wine spectators worldwide. Some of the most talked about wines originate in the Hill Country, straight from the region's arid limestone earth—the same type of soil you'd find in northwest Italy, southern Spain, and Provence.

The best time to come is in the fall, when wine-related festivals are underway. These include the Fredericksburg Food & Wine Fest held at the end of October, the Gruene Music & Wine Fest held in the beginning of October, and the San Antonio New World Wine & Food Festival at the beginning of November. If you come in the spring, you'll be treated to the splash of wildflowers (including the vibrant bluebonnets) along the roads and Austin's Texas Hill Country Wine and Food Festival in mid-March.

The Hill Country has been turning out wines since the 1970s. More than 20 wineries now dot the region and most are open daily year-round, providing tours and tastings (some are free, some are not). This is a great place for a wine-tasting road trip—but remember, those sips add up. Limit your tastes and drink water if you're driving.

At the top of the list is **Alamosa Wine Cellars** (✉ 677 CR 430, ☎ 325/628–3313 ⊕ www.alamosawinecellars.com). About 30 mi north of Llano, Alamosa is where winemaker Jim Johnson makes a superb Viognier, a bold and flavorful Syrah, and the celebrated "El Guapo," a tawny little Tempranillo blend with a horned frog

on the label that has been billed by many connoisseurs as a "revelation."

Happily situated on the sparkling waters of Lake Buchanon, **Fall Creek Vineyards** (✉ 1820 CR 222, ☎ 325/379–5361 ⊕ www.fcv.com) has been a prolific producer of such wines as its refreshing Chenin blanc and the award-winning red blend "Meritus."

The highest concentration of wineries is in the Fredericksburg area, in Fredericksburg as well as the townships of Sisterdale, Comfort, and Stonewall.

Enjoy live music with your wine on Saturdays at the family-run **Torre Di Pietra** (✉ 10915 E. U.S. Hwy. 290, ☎ 830/644–2829 ⊕ www.texashillcountrywine.com). **Sister Creek Vineyards** (✉ 1142 Sisterdale Rd. (RR 1376), ☎ 830/324–6704 ⊕ www.sistercreekvineyards.com) produces Muscat Canelli, an Italian wine, as well as traditional blends. **Comfort Cellars** ((✉ 723 Front St., ☎ 830/995–3274 ⊕ www.comfortcellars.com) reminds you you're in Texas with its hot jalepeño wine, which most use in the kitchen rather than for drinking.

Just east of Fredericksburg, the sprawling estate of **Becker Vineyards** (✉ 464 Becker Farms Rd., ☎ 830/644–2681 ⊕ www.beckervineyards.com) has enchanting fields of lavender and a B&B in addition to the old stone barn where you can taste the fruity Reisling and smooth and rich Cabernet-Syrah blend. **Grape Creek Vineyards** (✉ 97 Vineyard La., ☎ 830/644–2710 ⊕ www.grapecreek.com) also has a B&B attached to the winery (children are not allowed).

Other wineries in the Hill Country:

Enjoy a tasting at Becker Vineyards, near Fredericksburg.

Bell Mountain Vineyards (✉ *463 Bell Mountain Rd.*, ☎ *830/685–3297* ⊕ *www.bellmountainwine.com*).

Driftwood Vineyards (✉ *4001 Elder Hill Rd. (CR 170)*, ☎ *512/858–9667* ⊕ *www.driftwoodvineyards.com*).

Dry Comal Creek (✉ *1741 Herbein Rd.*, ☎ *830/885–4121* ⊕ *www.dry comalcreek.com*).

Flat Creek Estate (✉ *24912 Singleton Bend E.*, ☎ *512/267–6310* ⊕ *www.flatcreekestate.com*).

Sandstone Cellars (✉ *211 San Antonio St.*, ☎ *325/347–9463* ⊕ *www. sandstonecellarswinery.com*).

Off the beaten path—and out of the Hill Country—a couple of wineries in the Panhandle are also worth mentioning. Lubbock's **Llano Estacado Winery** (✉ *3426 E. FM 1585*, ☎ *806/745–2258* ⊕ *www.llanowine. com*), producing fairly consistent wines for the past 30 years, is probably Texas's forerunner in the wine indus-

try. Near Lubbock, **Cap*Rock Winery** (✉ *408 E. Woodrow Rd.*, ☎ *806/863– 2704* ⊕ *www.caprockwinery.com*) has been on the wine scene for some time; recently, however, Cap*Rock's winemaker Kim McPherson has taken the state by storm with his own label, McPherson Cellars, which focuses on Rhone-style wines. His signature Rhone-style Tre Colore has attracted a lot of attention, and his Grenache-Mourverdre and Rosé of Syrah-Grenache blends are successful examples of growing grapes suited to the region. (⇨ *The Panhandle, chapter 14, for more details.*)

Local visitor bureaus and gift shops stock the "Hill Country Wine Trail" (⊕ *www.texaswinetrail.com*) pamphlet with a handy map inside, and the "Texas Wine Country" brochure produced by the Texas Department of Agriculture (*www.gotexanwine.org*) shows a regional view of the different wineries.

—Jessica Norman Dupuy

SAN MARCOS

19 mi northeast of New Braunfels and 30 mi south of Austin via I–35.

San Marcos is the largest town between Austin and San Antonio on I–35. It's home to former President Lyndon B. Johnson's alma mater, Texas State University, the crystal-clear Aquarena Springs that feed the San Marcos River, and the Southwestern Writers Collection at the Alkek Library. For the most part it's a college town, but most visitors to San Marcos buzz right by downtown and hit the state's best outlet-mall shopping at the Prime Outlet and the Tanger Outlet malls.

SHOPPING

For years, Texans anywhere within a 200-mile radius have flocked to the outlets for back-to-school, Christmas, and spring and summer shopping. During these times, patience and dumb luck finding a parking space are virtues. But really, the endless variety of shops at the two adjoining locations draws a steady crowd year-round. For either, take the Centerpoint Road exit off the Interstate. **Prime Outlets San Marcos** (⊠*3939 I–35 S* ☎*512/396–2200, 800/628–9465* ⊕*www. primeoutlets.com*) is the sprawling mall on the north side of Centerpoint Road, and is host to such fashionable shops as Crate & Barrel, J. Crew, Pottery Barn, Giorgio Armani, and Gucci. The better part of a day can be spent strolling through the more than 130 stores. **Tanger Outlets San Marcos** (⊠*4015 I–35 S* ☎*512/396–7446, 800/408–8424* ⊕*www.tangeroutlet.com*), on the southern side of Centerpoint Road, where more than 100 stores, from Old Navy to the Le Creuset kitchen store, await.

WHERE TO EAT

¢–$$ ✕**Root Cellar Café.** If you can spare the time, skip the chain restaurants at the outlet malls and head to San Marcos's town square for lunch at this café and art gallery. The cheerful staff and bright, eclectic art–filled walls make for a very comfortable atmosphere. With choices like the zingy Holy Aioli sandwich of citrus-marinated chicken with cilantro aioli, lunch here beats any fast-food option at the mall. They serve breakfast until 4 PM. ⊠*215 N. LBJ,* ☎*830/392–5158* ▤*AE, D, MC, V* ⊙*No dinner Sun.–Wed.*

WIMBERLEY

14 mi northwest of San Marcos via RR 12.

Wimberley's windy little roads, shady oak and cypress trees, and compact town square give it the feel of an English village. Established in 1848 with only a small trading post to its name, Wimberley's first industries were lumber and shingle making. The Blanco River and Cypress Creek, which run through the city, fueled the Wimberley Mill. But the Great Depression left the town stagnant with the exception of a few working ranches.

The 1980s saw a revitalization in Wimberley as it began to gain notice as a retirement and artists' community. Galleries and shops selling local artists' Hill Country creations, from oils paintings to crafts, are found throughout Wimberley Village Square.

NEED A BREAK? | **Wimberley Pie Company.** Tell anyone in Central Texas that you're heading for Wimberley and the first response you likely may hear: "Be sure to get some pie at the Wimberley Pie Company!" The dimly lit glass case along the front of the shop is filled with fresh, vacuum-sealed pies ready to be picked up and taken to some lucky home, but you can also grab a slice from pies right out of the oven. The traditional cherry pie has a perfect balance of tart and sweet. ⊠ *13619 RR 12, just east of the town square* ☎ *512/847–5588* ⊟ *No credit cards* ⊗ *Closed Mon.–Tues. and major holidays.*

WHERE TO EAT

$$–$$$ ✕**Cedar Grove Steakhouse.** Texas-style elegance radiates through this ★ contemporary steak house. An ambitious and well-executed menu makes this one of the best examples of Hill Country fine dining. The steaks here are excellent, particularly the six-ounce Black Angus fillet wrapped in applewood-smoked bacon. Another favorite is the light, creamy white-chocolate cheesecake with flecks of fresh lavender. ⊠ *9595 RR 12, Ste. 11, at the junction of RR 12 and FM 32* ☎ *512/847–3113* ⊟ *AE, D, MC, V* ⊗ *Closed Mon.*

$–$$ ✕**The Salt Lick.** If you see smoke rising while driving along FM 1826,
Fodor'sChoice don't be alarmed. It's just a barbecue beacon calling you to the perpetu-
★ ally smoking pits, long picnic tables, and dance hall–style compound of The Salt Lick. On weekends, and particularly when the University of Texas Longhorns have a home game, this family-friendly hot spot on the edge of south Austin is tough to get into, but always worth the wait. You'll be joined by locals and travelers from miles around waiting to feast on perfectly smoked brisket, baby back ribs, vinegary German potato salad and cole slaw, and enough soft white bread to sop up a gallon of the secret sauce. Oh, and did we mention the sausage? Get some of that, too. You can order the all-you-can-eat, family-style option and share with friends. Though it may seem impossible to save room for homemade blackberry cobbler with Blue Bell homemade vanilla ice cream on top, we promise it is worth every calorie. If you're driving from the Hill Country back to the Austin airport, this makes a great lunch stop on the way. ⊠ *18001 FM 1826, Driftwood, 5 mi northeast of Wimberley* ☎ *512/858–4959* ⊟ *No credit cards.*

WHERE TO STAY

$$–$$$$ 🛏**Blair House Inn.** There's a lot to experience at this lovely little ★ compound. Unwind with a rejuvenating massage, take a dip in the refreshing pool, or roll up your sleeves for one of the hands-on cooking classes. Even if you just retreat to one of the cowboy-chic rooms, you'll still find an amazing sense of release here. The Laredo Room in the Honeysuckle Cottage is one of the nicest, with its subtle hints of Old Mexico and large limestone fireplace. The romantic San Rafael Cottage is also a great choice for its covered deck and its tin roof that sings a lullaby when the rain blows through. Breakfast alone is nearly worth the price of your stay. **Pros:** Beautiful grounds, comfortable rooms, excellent for a private getaway. **Cons:** Traffic noise from nearby RR 12. ⌧*100 Spoke Hill Rd.,* ☎*877/549–5450* ⊕*www. blairhouseinn.com* ⇆*4 rooms, 7 suites* ⌂*In room: Wi-Fi, DVD, refrigerator. In-hotel: Public Wi-Fi, pool* ▭*AE, D, MC, V* ⦿*BP.*

MARKET DAYS

From April to December, the first Saturday of each month brings a surge of visitors to Wimberley for the famed Market Days at Lions Field on RR 2325. (It's about a quarter of a mile from the junction with RR 12.) Here bargain hunters shop to their heart's content among the 450 booths of arts and crafts, gifts, furniture, and more. Gates open as early as 6 AM and close whenever vendors decide to pack up. You can certainly get excellent deals on items you won't be able to find anywhere else. The question is how to get it all back home!

$$–$$$$ 🖼**Creekhaven Inn.** Though you're only a short walking distance from Wimberley Village Square, the meandering dirt road to the inn makes this feel like a true hideaway. Look for deer in the treeframed meadows nearby. The sprawling main house is shaded by pecan trees and wrapped in a series of wooden decks. Each guest room has a distinct style, with different color schemes and handmade bedspreads. After a good sleep on one of the pillow-top beds, be sure to stroll the grounds along the creek or soak in the hot tub with a glass of wine. **Pros:** Very friendly staff, clean rooms, beautiful grounds and landscaping. **Cons:** Some rooms have less attractive decor, some bathrooms are small or awkwardly laid out. ⌧*400 Mill Race La.,* ☎*800/827–1913 or 512/847–9344* ⊕*www. creekhaveninn.com* ⇆*14 rooms* ▭*AE, D, MC, V* ⦿*BP.*

$$$$
★
🖼**The Inn Above Onion Creek.** Not 10 mi from Wimberley is a little weekend escape set on a 100-acre plot with rolling hills and enchanting vistas. You won't even have to leave the premises to forage for dinner. Instead, a five-course meal is prepared each night and served family-style to you and the other inn guests. (The inn does not serve alcohol, but you're allowed to bring your own wine.) Rooms have romantic fireplaces and views of the fiery Texas sunsets. The new spa is small, but digs in with excellent Swedish and deep-tissue massage therapy. **Pros:** Views of the Hill Country from the west-facing decks are spectacular. **Cons:** Beds aren't as comfortable as the rest of the accommodations, some rooms have much better views than others. ⌧*4444 W. FM 150,* ☎*512/268–1090* ⊕*www.innaboveonioncreek.com* ⇆*7 rooms, 3 suites* ⌂*In-room: DVD (some), VCR (some), Wi-Fi. In-hotel: Kitchen, refrigerator, pool, spa, public Wi-Fi, bicycles* ▭*AE, D, MC, V* ⦿*AP (dinner and breakfast).*

SHOPPING

Upon arriving in Wimberley, it soon becomes clear that the **Wimberley Village Square**—a virtual spider web at the crossroads of RR 12 and a number of small Wimberley streets—is the place for an afternoon of shopping. Duck into the **River House** (⌧*104 Wimberley Sq.* ☎*512/847–7009*) for an inspiring selection of home accessories. The

Old Mill Store (✉*14100 RR 12* ☎*512/847–3068*) has all the knick-knacks of an old-fashioned trading post towards the front, but if you stroll to the back you'll find paintings, sculptures, and hand-made furniture. For that last-minute gift for a friend's new baby or the kids back home, stop in at **Blue Bacon Toys** (✉*14011 RR 12* ☎*512/847–2150*) for an extremely unusual assortment of children's toys. Take a detour to **Wimberley Glassworks** (✉*6469 RR 12*), one of the art community's most impressive contributors, to watch artisans blow and shape beautiful glass creations.

THE HIGHLAND LAKES

4

LAKE TRAVIS & LAKEWAY

Lake Travis, the fifth in the series of Highland Lakes fed by the Colorado River, is a refreshing playscape for the Austin and Lago Vista areas, with dramatic Hill Country slopes. When the sun sets on Lake Travis, some of the most brilliant views are enjoyed from the decks of hillside restaurants, where spectators applaud the visual pyrotechnics.

Along the southwest shores of the lake, the town of Lakeway is home to some of Austin's most celebrated golf courses, tennis centers, and boating operations. The 1970s retirement community Lakeway was little more than a quiet retreat for Austinites. Today, with new renovations to the more than 30-year-old Lakeway Inn, countless upscale residential subdivisions, and the myriad restaurants and shops that have popped up along the southern stretch of RR 620, the area is a thriving extension of the Austin-metro area.

SPORTS & THE OUTDOORS

♻ **Hamilton Pool Nature Preserve.** About 30 mi southwest of Austin off Highway 71 is a small nature preserve that is home to one of the Hill Country's most beautiful natural pools. The continuously flowing Hamilton Creek spills over an enormous limestone outcropping creating a beautiful 50-foot waterfall that gently plunges into the crystal waters of Hamilton Pool. It's particularly crowded on weekends. Parking is limited and controlled by the State, with a nominal fee for entry, so it's best to call ahead to see if spaces are available. ✉*13 mi southwest on Hamilton Pool Rd. from Hwy. 71 W (About 20 miles from Lakeway)* ☎*512/264–2740* ⊕*www.co.travis.tx.us* ☉*Daily 9–6*)

BOATING

For much of the year, even in the cooler months, Lake Travis is alive with boats, waterskis, and wakeboards. Public boat ramps are available in a number of different locations along the shores. Contact the marinas listed to get the nearest location.

To get a little piece of lake action, a few of the reputable boat outfitters include: **Lakeway Marina** (✉*103-A Lakeway Dr.* ☎*512/261–7511* ⊕*www.lwmarina.biz* ☉*Daily 8–5, extended summer hours 8–7*), **Hurst Harbor Marina** (✉*16405 Clara Van Tr.* ☎*512/266–1800*

⊕*www.hhmarina.biz* ⊙*Daily 8–5 [May–Aug. until 7]*)), and **Just For Fun Watercraft Rental** (⊠*5973 Hil-ine Rd.* ☎*512/266–9710* ⊕*www.jff.net* ⊙*Daily.*

GOLF

Lakeway Golf Club. Two of Austin's most honored courses are in Lakeway. Both the Live Oak and Yaupon courses, which are part of the Lakeway Golf Club, have challenging rounds with rolling hills and tree-lined fairways. ⊠*One World of Tennis Sq.* ☎*512/261–7200* ⊕*www.lakewaygolfclub.com* ⊙*Daily. Call for reservations.*

WHERE TO EAT

$$$$
Fodor'sChoice
★

✕**Hudson's on the Bend.** Chase the sun west from Austin to where an unforgettable experience awaits in this refined little ranch house. This is the place for expertly crafted wild-game dishes such as pistachio-crusted rattlesnake cakes or rich pheasant-confit tamales with white chocolate–tomatillo sauce. In celebrated chef Jeff Blank's kitchen, the philosophy is "cooking fearlessly." Although the restaurant can accommodate families, the soft lighting and the conversation-inspiring art cater to an adult crowd. ⊠*3509 RR 620, Austin* ☎*512/266–1369* ⌂*Reservations recommended* ☐*AE, D, DC, MC, V* ⊙*No lunch.*

$–$$　✕**The Oasis.** There are sunsets, and then there are sunsets at the Oasis. Here you can sit on one of the many wooden decks that scale the hillside of this Lake Travis hot spot with a frozen margarita and bid farewell to the day with one of the most spectacular sunsets in the state. The menu offers fairly standard American and Mexican fare, from burgers to enchiladas. Be sure to get there early; you won't be the only one with the bright idea to swing by. ⊠*6550 Comanche Tr.* ☎*512/266–2442* ⌂*Reservations not accepted* ☐*AE, D, MC, V.*

$–$$$　✕**Rocco's Grill.** Pronounced Roh-coh as opposed to Rock-oh, this delightful restaurant owned by the local Piazza family has bright murals depicting family events and traditions in bold caricatures. The menu is primarily American-Italian, with personal touches from family recipes. Try the salmon Allessondra, named for the owner's daughter: a salmon fillet with lump crab meat and a bright lemon–caper butter sauce. The views of the rolling Lakeway Golf Course fairways are stunning ⊠*900 RR 620 S.* ☎*512/263–8204* ☐*AE, D, MC, V.*

¢–$
★

✕**Rosie's Tamale House.** This little nondescript shack proclaiming "Rosie's Food To Go" in big black letters usually has a swarm of locals each morning clamoring for their favorite breakfast tacos. For lunch, you can order takeout and sit at one of the picnic tables outside. But for a sit-down meal, head across the street to the official restaurant in

HIGHLAND LAKES

The Texas Highland Lakes are six lakes in the Hill Country region formed by several dams along the Colorado River. The dams were constructed in the 1930s and '40s to help provide flood control for the river, which used to flood severely. As a result, six lakes were created: Lake Buchanan, Inks Lake, Lake LBJ, Lake Marble Falls, Lake Travis, and Lake Austin. Though built for river control and to help generate hydroelectric power, the lakes now provide main attractions for the neighboring towns of Marble Falls, Horseshoe Bay, Burnet, Lakeway, and Austin.

a big red building where you can order Rosie's signature tamales or enchiladas. Famed Texas singer-songwriter Willie Nelson is a frequent-enough customer to have his very own dish, the Willie's Plate: a crispy beef taco, one cheese enchilada smothered in chili con carne, and a side of guacamole salad. There's no liquor license, so bring your own cooler of beer. ⊠*13436 W. Hwy. 71* ☏*512/263–5245* ▭*No credit cards.*

WHERE TO STAY

$$$–$$$$ ⊡**The Crossings.** This spa and hotel, on a hilltop overlooking Lake Tra-
★ vis, is a luxurious camp for adults. The compound is spread out over several acres, with eco-minded architecture of native limestone and aluminum rooftops. Float in peace at the negative-edge pool; you'll feel like you're hovering over the lake. The guest rooms are contemporary and comfortable, free of distractions from the outside world (read: no television). **Pros:** Beautiful surroundings, spa with excellent massage therapists, healthy food. **Cons:** Difficult to get Internet access in rooms, spotty cell-phone service. ⊠*13500 FM 2769,* ☏*877/944–3003 or 512/258–7243* ⊕*www.thecrossingsaustin.com* ⇄*28 singles, 41 doubles, 25 bunkhouse rooms with twin bed, 1 four-bedroom cottage* ♿ *In room: refrigerator, Ethernet. In-hotel: restaurants, pool, spa, public Wi-Fi, airport shuttle* ▭*D, MC, V* ⍾*BP.*

MARBLE FALLS

48 mi northwest of Austin via Hwy. 71.

Only 45 minutes west of Austin, bustling Marble Falls has become a popular destination for a quick weekend getaway. Three lakes, Marble Falls, LBJ, and Buchanan, are the primary summer attractions here, but a number of other spots in and around town stand out, including the nearby Krause Springs, Quarry Mountain, and the renowned golf courses of Horseshoe Bay Resort.

Though the sides of Highway 281 running through town are littered with your typical retail stores, the town's 19th-century Main Street offers much in the way of gift, home-decor, and apparel shops, as well as excellent restaurants. And if you happen to be in the area around the holidays, Marble Falls is noted for having some of the most amazing Christmas lights along the lake.

Marble Falls is named for the natural falls formed by a shelf of limestone that runs diagonally across the Colorado River that flowed through the area. At the time, the water over the limestone created a bluish appearance that gave the impression of naturally occurring marble, for which the town was later named. However, visitors won't find marble here, and with the formation of the Highland Lakes, the falls are now completely under water and only visible on the rare occasions when the Lower Colorado River Authority lowers the lakes for repairs to the dam and boat docks.

Marble Falls has since gained fame for the amazing granite outcrops resulting from ancient formations in the Llano Basin, the most obvious marker being Granite Mountain, a monolith rising 866 feet above ground and spanning more than 180 acres. In the late 1800s, much of the economic growth of Marble Falls was due to the quarrying of this rock.

WHAT TO SEE

☾ **Longhorn Caverns.** Formed over thousands of years from water cutting and dissolving limestone bedrock, Longhorn Caverns are a fantastic exhibit of Texas natural history. With a history of Comanche tribes seeking refuge in the caves and calcite-crystal beds, the caverns are a perfect destination

> ### GRANITE MOUNTAIN
>
> One of Marble Falls' economic foundations is Granite Mountain. The great granite dome rises 866 feet; its more than 180 acres of exposed granite serve as the largest granite quarry of its kind in the United States. Although visitors are not admitted to the quarry itself, you can get a great view of the mountain from J Street toward 2nd Street.

for families interested in how the limestone caverns in the Hill Country were formed. ■TIP→ **Be sure to wear rubber-soled shoes; it gets slippery down there!** ⊠ *Park Rd. 4, 6 mi west of Hwy. 281* ☎ *877/441–2283 or 830/598–2283* ⊕ *www.longhorncaverns.com* ☉ *Daily dawn to dusk* ☜ *$12.99.*

SPORTS & THE OUTDOORS

☾ **Krause Springs.** If you need a little relief from the Texas heat, a trip here will certainly cool you off. Just a few miles east of Marble Falls in Spicewood, the springs are actually two separate swimming holes on a private ranch opened to the public. From Highway 71, splash through a low-water crossing and up to a hilltop bluff with hypnotic views of rolling grasslands, sprawling oak trees, and an undisturbed horizon. Park your car near the main house and stroll down a flight of outdoor stairs to the spring-fed pools. Be prepared for the biting chill as your toes hit the water. ⊠ *404 Krause Springs* ☎ *830/693–4181* ☉ *9–sundown* ☜ *$10.*

OUTFITTER

☾ **Cypress Valley Canopy Tours** (⊠ *1223 Paleface RR, Spicewood* ☎ *512/264–8880* ⊕ *www.cypressvalleycanopytours.com* ☉ *Mar.–Nov., 9 AM–sundown* ☜ *$65–$125*) zips you through the treetops to experience nature from a bird's eye view. Tucked away in a ravine lined with bald cypress trees, the Canopy Tour leads you along a maze of zip lines and sky bridges. For even more adventure, the Canopy Challenge is an additional course with endurance high ropes obstacles. Bird-watchers may also enjoy the Sunrise Birding Tour, which is guided by a local biologist.

BOATING

Boating Lake Marble Falls and Lake LBJ. In the warmer months, if you want to know where the good time is, you'll have to get out on the water. Most of the recreational activity centers around Lake Marble Falls and Lake LBJ in the spring, summer, and early fall. These two lakes are known for being more family-friendly than Austin's wilder lakes Travis and Austin. **Lake LBJ Yacht Club and Marina** can assist in outfitting you and your crew with the perfect watercraft. ⊠*200 S. Wirtz Dam Rd.* ☎*830/693–9172* ⊕*www.lakelbjmarina.com.*

WHERE TO EAT

¢–$$
★ ✕**The Blue Bonnet Café.** Don't even think about coming to Marble Falls without taking a seat at this small-town diner. There's a sign above the hostess stand that says, "Eat some pie." We suggest you follow these directions. At least 10 different types of pie are made fresh daily. From mountainous meringue to creamy custards, the geniuses behind these sweet concoctions mean business. If you come between 2 and 5, you've made it for "Pie Happy Hour," when you can have a slice of pie and a cup of joe for $3! They also serve everything you'd find at an old-fashioned diner. ⊠*211 Hwy. 281* ☎*830/693–2344* ▤*No credit cards.*

$$–$$$
Fodor'sChoice
★ ✕**Café 909.** You may not be able to see it from Main Street, but we promise it's there. Tucked around the corner, this café with muted exposed brick walls, a long, thin bar, and a cozy New York–sized dining room offers a little bit of urban chic with relaxed Hill Country attitude. Chef-owner Mark Schmidt spikes familiar dishes with bold flavors. Take for instance the seared dayboat scallops with farruto (sort of like risotto), fiery horseradish, and crème fraîche. Be sure to end the meal with the frozen pistachio parfait with burnt honey caramel, which has won national attention. ⊠*909 2nd St.* ☎*830/693–2126* ▤*AE, D, MC, V* ⊗*No lunch. Closed Mon.*

$–$$
✕**Falls Bistro and Wine Cellar.** You may find it odd to see Asian decor in a tapas bar, but the mix of reds and blacks with bamboo plants somehow works. Be sure to bring a friend or two along to share these small plates. Try the scallops wrapped in crispy serrano ham; the roasted corn cream sauce beneath these morsels is not to be missed. The duck tostadas are also a must. The wine list is reasonably priced and offers a good selection of international bottles. ⊠*202 Main St.* ☎*830/265–4580* ▤*AE, D, MC, V* ⊗*Closed Mon.*

$$–$$$$
★ ✕**Patton's On Main.** Chef Patton Robertson has brought haute cuisine to his home town and created quite a buzz at this self-proclaimed "Texas fusion" restaurant. Look for beef tenderloin tacos with tangy guacamole, perfectly grilled salmon with caramelized shallots and a grapefruit and lemon brown-butter sauce. The shrimp and grits, a classic Southern dish, has a vivid spiciness and perfect texture. ⊠*201 Main St.* ☎*830/693–8664* ▤*AE, D, MC, V* ⊗*Closed Sun.*

$–$$$
✕**River City Grille.** On a nice evening, dining on the deck is the thing to do here. The views are amazing, and the food holds up its end of the bargain. The house specialty is a well-seasoned, juicy 12-ounce prime rib. Thankfully, they also serve an 8-ounce portion. The friendly waitstaff expertly coaxes people to order dessert, like warm carrot cake. ⊠*700 1st St.* ☎*830/798–9909* ▤*AE, D, MC, V.*

WHERE TO STAY

$$$
▥**The Moriah.** If you have a large group, and would like a little privacy, we suggest the Moriah, a small collection of three restored historic buildings on a picturesque three-acre property with a private boat dock on Lake Marble Falls, just 8 miles from town. The large wooden porches offer spectacular views of the hills and the expansive backyard,

which includes a full volleyball court, hammocks, and plenty of room to run around. The main timber-frame house has a large main room, a full kitchen, and an upstairs loft with two futons. Two 1850s timber cabins have a master room with comfortable king beds and a bunk-room with two sets of bunk beds. **Pros:** Perfect for a family reunion or a weekend getaway for friends, beautiful decor and amenities, feels like home. **Cons:** Not convenient to town, expensive for smaller groups. ⊠*1741 County Rd. 343,* ☎*650/321–9246* ⊕*www.historiccabins. com* ⌁*5 rooms (sleeps 16 total)* ⚒*hotel: Kitchen, refrigerator, DVD, some pets allowed, no-smoking rooms.* ⊟*MC, V* ☉*Closed Thanksgiving week.*

$$ ⊤**The Wallace Guesthouse.** This stately manor just off Main Street opened in 1907 as the Bredt Hotel, and hosted guests for only 25¢! Today, the guesthouse offers guest suites fully decorated in vintage furniture and elegant fabrics. The rooms are reasonably spacious for a turn-of-the-century building. Each suite is named after one of the Highland Lakes. The staff is exceptionally friendly and happy to help with any questions about what to do in the area. **Pros:** Excellent access to Main Street shopping, friendly and helpful staff. **Cons:** Rooms are somewhat small, antique decor may be a little much for some. ⊠*910 3rd St.,* ☎*830/798–9808* ⊕*www.thewallaceguesthouse.com* ⌁*5 suites* ⚒*In-room: Refrigerator, kitchen. In-hotel: No elevator, parking (no-fee), no-smoking rooms.* ⊟*AE, D, MC, V* ⊙*CP.*

SHOPPING

The best shopping in Marble Falls is on Main Street. Spend an afternoon strolling home-accent and interior shops such as Wisteria and Canyon Trails. The Square at Old Oak Village houses a number of fun shops, including **Zoo La La** (⊠*309 Main St. #6* ☎*830/693—0161*), a food and kitchen gift shop; **It's All About Me** (⊠*309 Main St.* ☎*830/798–9191*), a children's specialty toy store; **Lucky Star** (⊠*309 Main St.* ☎*830/693– 6450*), with trendy apparel; and the place for handmade cards and gifts, **Sakow Cards** (⊠*309 Main St.* ☎*830/798–9191*).

HORSESHOE BAY

5 mi west of Marble Falls via FM 2147.

Adding to Marble Falls' tourist fame is the nearby resort town of Horseshoe Bay. Tucked into an immense cove on Lake LBJ, the resort began in the early 1970s and over the past few decades has added residential subdivisions, lakefront condominiums, a yacht club, and world-class golf courses. In fact Horseshoe Bay is home to some of the most renowned golf courses in the nation.

SPORTS & THE OUTDOORS

GOLF

Horseshoe Bay Resort Golf Courses. With three championship Trent Jones, Sr.–designed courses and a future Jack Nicklaus golf course to open by 2009, the resort is a haven for those who love to spend their days on the green. The Ram Rock course (18 holes, par 71) has been deemed the "Challenger" course, offering some of the toughest fairways in the country. The Apple Rock course (18 holes, par 72) has racked up a number of awards and is known for its amazing scenery as it hugs Lake LBJ. The Slick Rock course (18 holes, par 72) and the Whitewater putting course are also favorite options. ✉ *101 Horseshoe Bay Blvd.* ☎*Slick Rock 830/598–2561, Apple Rock 830/598–6561, Ram Rock 830/598–6561, Whitewater Putting Course 830/598–2591* ⊕*www. hsbresort.com* ☑*$110-$150* ☉*Daily dawn to dusk.*

TENNIS

Whitewater Tennis Center. Tennis fanatics will feel right at home here with 12 professional courts including six red clay courts, four hard courts, and two Pro-Grass courts. The new Andy Roddick Kids' Courts are the first in the United States to feature USTA cutting-edge, shorter, 60-foot courts to give children a training ground for learning the game more quickly. ✉ *101 Horseshoe Bay Blvd.* ☎*830/598–2591* ⊕*www. hsbresort.com* ☑*Free for guests of the resort, $10 for visitors* ☉*Call for reservations.*

YACHT CLUB

Horseshoe Bay Resort Marina ((✉*101 Horseshoe Bay Blvd.* ☎*830/598-2591* ⊕*www.hsbresort.com* ☑*call for pricing* ☉*Call for reservations*)). To get the full experience of a stay at Lake LBJ, be sure to reserve a boat from the marina and cruise the lake for an afternoon. A wide variety of watercraft are available for rent as well as ski and Jet Ski rentals.

WHERE TO STAY

$$$$
★ **Horseshoe Bay Resort Marriott Hotel.** This isn't your typical Marriott experience. The breathtaking views of Lake LBJ spreading its glimmering fingers should be your first clue. Every room overlooks a lush, tropical-meets-Texas landscape. Subdued earth-toned decor keeps the focus on the views. There's enough to keep you busy for days: access to three championship golf courses, a full-service spa, clay and hard-surface tennis courts. Though quiet in location, silence is easily broken if louder guests are returning to their rooms later at night. **Pros:** Excellent activities for kids, top golf and tennis options, comfortable rooms. **Cons:** Caters more to families, staff can be a bit too laid-back. ✉*200 Hi Circle N, Horseshoe Bay,* ☎*830/598–8600* ⊕*www.horse shoebaymarriott.com* ⤺*349 rooms, 64 1-bedroom and 29 2-bedroom condos* ♿*In-room: Wi-Fi, Ethernet, refrigerator, microwave. In-hotel: three pools, lake access, laundry facilities, airport shuttle and limousine service for Austin airport (reservation required, $55), Marriott Kids' Club program, spa, fitness center, pets allowed in condos with deposit* ▭*AE, D, MC, V.*

THE NORTHWEST QUADRANT

BURNET

13 mi north Marble Falls via Hwy. 281.

During most of the year, Burnet is a sleepy little town best known as a stop for people heading south from the Dallas area or east from Llano. Visitors can stop at the town square for a quick stretch, or grab an old-fashioned drive-through burger at **Storm's** ⊠ *700 N. Water St.* ☎ *512/756–7143* ⊟ *AE, D, MC, V* ⊘ *Closed Sun.*

In late March through late April, the town comes alive with visitors from all over Texas who come to celebrate the state flower, the bluebonnet. Named the "Bluebonnet Capital of Texas," Burnet is famous on the Hill Country Wildflower Trail for having some of the best natural crops of bluebonnets anywhere in the state. (The Brenham area comes in a close second.) The second week in April is the Annual Bluebonnet Festival.

WHERE TO STAY

$$–$$$ **Canyon of the Eagles Lodge.** While driving the winding road to this hilltop lodge, it's easy to believe you've taken a wrong turn. But after a few glimpses of sparkling Lake Buchanan, you dead-end right into this state-managed nature preserve and its low-frills guest lodge. This is a great spot for bird-watchers, as you'll have a good shot of seeing the endangered black-capped vereo and golden-cheeked warbler, as well as the glorious bald eagles that nest here from fall to early spring. Most cabins offer spectacular views of the lake and come equipped with comfortable queen beds and full bathrooms. (Plans to update some of the guest accommodations were underway at press time.) Nature-focused children's programs are offered during summer and spring break. **Pros:** Dining lodge has panoramic views, pets are welcome. **Cons:** Accommodations are somewhat primitive, outdoor dangers on trails (bugs, snakes, and poison ivy). ⊠ *16942 RR 2341,* ☎ *800/977–0081* ⊕ *www. canyonoftheeagles.com* ⇆ *62 rooms* ⊜ *In-room: Wi-Fi, no TV, refrigerators (some). In-hotel: pool, public Wi-Fi, children's programs (ages 3–12), some pets allowed* ⊟ *AE, D, MC, V.*

LLANO

36 mi northwest of Marble Falls via Hwy 71.

The greatest attraction to Llano is the drive out there. Whether you're heading north from Fredericksburg on Highway 16 or east from Mason on Highway 29, you'll see some of the most beautiful panoramas of rugged hill country in the region. Perhaps the most inspiring features of the scenery are the dramatic granite outcrops that burst from the landscape in pink, speckled domes.

Much of the town's identity today rests in the ranching, farming, and granite industries. Visitors are often attracted by the relaxed atmosphere and activities along the picturesque Llano River. The town square has a historic feel; it's sprinkled with galleries, antiques and gift shops, and a museum of Hill Country wildlife.

SPORTS & THE OUTDOORS

HUNTING

Though considered a controversial pastime in certain parts of the country, hunting is a favorite hobby among many Texans, and the Llano Basin has the highest density of whitetail deer in the Unites States. As a result, Llano Country is considered by many hunters to be the Deer Hunting Capital of Texas. In the fall, when hunters head to West Texas through Llano, you'll see big pickup trucks towing trailers with deer blinds, feeders, ATVs, and camping gear. In fact, banners are strung across the main streets welcoming hunters to town. There are a number of leases available for hunting deer, quail, dove, and turkey in the Llano area as well as exotic game ranches that attract hunters from across the nation.

Those interested in a lease can check the lease list at the Llano Chamber of Commerce. Hunting licenses and a Hunter's Education certification are required for all in-state and out-of-state hunters. Hunting and fishing licenses are available at most sporting-goods stores, gun shops, and some department stores across the state. See the Texas Parks and Wildlife Department Web site for more details. ⊕ *www.tpwd.state. tx.us/huntwild*

WHERE TO EAT

¢–$ ✕ **Acme Café.** If you want to go where the locals go, head over to the town square for lunch at the Acme. The average fare here is just about anything you'd find at a typical diner. The cheeseburger with a side of steaming, crispy fries is pretty hard to beat, especially when followed by peach pie. ⊠ *109 W. Main* ☎ *325/247–4457* ▤ *AE, D, MC, V* ☉ *Closed Sat.*

$$–$$$ ✕ **The Badu House.** Originally the National Bank of Llano, built in 1891, this stately manor later served as the family home to N.J. Badu, a French immigrant who studied the mineralogy of the Llano Basin. In recent years, the Badu House has been tastefully transformed into a restaurant focusing on local cuisine. If you like wild game, don't miss the grilled Bandera quail. Beneath the skin the meat is tender, and the accompanying chipotle and honey glaze gives the dish a nice kick. The back patio has live music on weekends. ⊠ *601 Bessemer Ave.* ☎ *325/247–1207* ▤ *AE, D, MC, V* ☉ *Closed Sun.–Mon.*

¢ ✕ **Chrissy's Homestyle Bakery.** At this tiny little bakery housed in an old historic building, the enchanting aroma of fresh-baked pies and pastries envelops you the second you walk in the door. The question of what to order immediately overwhelms you as you scour the glass cases showcasing pies, sweet and savory kolaches, and cookies. May we suggest the German-style sweet pretzel and the cream cheese–poppy seed kolache? Of course, the jalapeño, cheese, and sausage kolaches and cinnamon rolls are amazing as well, but you'll have to get there before the hunters, fishers, and early travelers do; they go fast. ⊠ *501 Bessemer Ave.* ☎ *325/247–4564* ▤ *AE, D, MC, V* ☉ *Closed Mon.*

¢–$ ✕ **Cooper's BBQ.** This Texas legend is serious about barbecue, and it expects no less from its clientele. Just look for the smokestacks rising from the tin-roofed portacache and the swarm of Texas-sized pickup trucks lining the parking lot. The menu is literally what's on display in the open pits that greet you at the entrance. Pick your meat from brisket, sausage, smoked turkey, ribs, or whatever else they have on hand for the day and step in line for the typical barbecue sides including cole slaw, potato salad, and plenty of doughy, white bread. Park your tray where you can find a seat at one of the long picnic tables in or outside, but not before grabbing a few pickles, onions, and a bowl of beans from the serve-yourself condiment bar. ⌧ *505 W. Dallas* ☎ *325/247–5713* ▤ *AE, D, MC, V.*

> **NOTABLE NATIVES**
>
> Mason is home to famed novelist Fred Gipson who wrote the classic novel *Old Yeller*. Texans might also recognize historical fiction and non-fiction writer Scott Zesch who wrote the critically acclaimed *The Captured*, which recounts true stories of children abducted by Apache Indians in the Mason area. Zesch is the son of Gene Zesch, a woodcarving artist renowned in the Southwest part of the country for depicting humorous caricature of life on Texas ranches. Original pieces of Zesch's carvings are on display in the Director's Room of the Commercial Bank in Mason .

WHERE TO STAY

$–$$$ ▣ **Railyard Bed and Breakfast.** Don't let the name fool you; you won't be sleeping on the tracks. The Railyard will eventually have a train that will take visitors from Llano to Kingsland for views of the granite outcroups and the rolling hills. This bed-and-breakfast has four separate houses happily situated in close proximity to the rail line, within easy walking distance of restaurants and the town square. Each cottage is uniquely decorated with tasteful antiques and vintage furniture. **Pros:** Within walking distance of shops, charming private cottages. **Cons:** View of the railroad isn't very picturesque; if you aren't an antiques fan, the decor may be a little much. ⌧ *502 Bessemer,* ☎ *325/247–3827* ⏏ *4 cottages (8 bedrooms total)* ⏣ *In-room: DVD, Wi-Fi, kitchen.* ▤ *AE, D, MC, V* ⏱ *CP.*

MASON

35 mi west of Llano via Hwy 29.

You don't just find yourself in Mason; you have to want to get there. Nestled in the rolling hills at the very northwest corner of this region, this pristine town was once a bastion of civilization for hunters on their way to or from various excursions, but today it's one of the Hill Country's best-kept secrets.

Among the many things to see and do around the town, visitors shouldn't miss a trip to Fort Mason. Just up Post Hill, this historic site played a pivotal role in the success of the town by protecting settlers from Indian raids through the late 1870s, and by providing employment opportunities for residents. The fort is also known for producing some of the Civil War's most notable generals, including Albert Sidney Johnston, William J. Hardee, and Robert E. Lee.

SPORTS & THE OUTDOORS

FLY-FISHING

Though the Guadalupe River has received much acclaim for its vast angling opportunities, the Mason County side of the Llano River is little slice of heaven for fly-fishers. It's one of the longest remaining wild rivers without flood control or electric generation in the country. Anglers will delight in the copious amounts of largemouth bass, blue gills, and Guadalupe River smallmouth bass (the state fish of Texas). And if you're lucky, you'll get a hit from the beautiful Rio Grande perch, a dark gray perch dotted with brilliant sapphire spots. Large outcrops of granite protrude from the river depths, creating easily navigable rapids and great deep pools. Some of the river is wadable, but a kayak or canoe is advised.

BLUE-TOPAZ HUNTING

Mason County has the great fortune of being the only place in Texas where you can find blue topaz, the state gem. It is naturally found in many of the granite outcroppings in the area. You can try your hand at panning for the rare blue gem from streambeds and exploring ravines. Two Mason County ranches open their property to the public for topaz hunting, but you have to call in advance to make an appointment. Mike Seaquist of **Garner Seaquist Ranch** (⊠*108 Fort McKavitt* ☎*325/347–5413* ⊕*no Web site* ⊠*$15* ☉*Feb.-Oct.*) will meet you in town and take you to his working ranch for a day of topaz hunting. Be sure to wear comfortable shoes, and bring a shovel. The **Lindsay Ranch** (⊠*460 Lindsay Rd* ☎*325/347–5733* ⊕*no Web site* ⊠*$10* ☉*Feb.–Oct.*) also offers topaz hunting.

BAT WATCHING

One of the largest Mexican free-tailed bat colonies in the world is found in the hills of Mason County. Managed by the Texas Nature Conservancy, **Eckert James River Bat Cave** (☎*325/347–5970* ⊠*$5* ☉*6–9 Thur.–Sun. late May–mid-Oct.* 6), a maternity bat cave, is home to more than 4 million Mexican free-tailed bats. Only females inhabit the cave, inside which they bear and rear their young each spring; they depart from the cave in mid-October. You can watch in the evening and morning as the entrance to the cave swarms with female bats leaving and returning from an evenings hunt to feed their pups. Stand clear of the entrance, unless you don't mind bat guano (droppings) or having thousands of female bats buzz by. The best way to glimpse this phenomenon is from a safe distance a few hundred yards away.

ARTS & ENTERTAINMENT

The **Odeon Theater** ((⊠*122 S Moody St.* ☎*325/347–9010*)), in the town square, is a Texas landmark. In continuous operation since it was built in 1928, the theater serves as both a movie theater and a venue for live shows.

WHERE TO EAT

¢–$ ✕ **The Cat's Meow.** Sandwiched between the Mason Gallery and the Underwood Antique Mall is one of the oldest buildings in Mason. Originally a saloon built in 1879, the Cat's Meow is now a superb little café catering to what owner Cathy Terrell calls the "three S's"— soups, sandwiches, and sweets. Her signature chicken salad bursts with almond slivers and red grapes, while the turkey sandwich with cranberry-apple chutney evokes holiday comfort food. ⊠*106 S. Live Oak* ☎*325/347–5225* ⊙*Lunch only Mon.–Sat.; closed Sun.* ▤*AE, D, MC, V.*

¢–$ ✕ **Santos Taqueria y Cantina.** There's a certain positive energy when you
★   enter this family-run place where you can watch fresh gorditas hand-pressed in the open kitchen and owner Santo Silerio's grandmother stirring up a fresh batch of creamy chili con queso. Be sure to try a squash gordita. A magical thing happens when squash, onions, tomatoes, cilantro, poblano peppers, and a few special ingredients are simmered together and served in a hot pocket with queso blanco and some sautéed chicken. Order the corn gorditas rather than the flour. Though it takes a few extra minutes, the old adage is true: good things come to those who wait. ⊠*205 San Antonio St.* ☎*325/347–6140* ▤*AE, D, MC, V* ⊙*No breakfast; closed·Mon.–Wed.; no dinner Sun.*

¢–$ ✕ **Willow Creek Café.** Seated in the heart of the town square, this cheery café seems to keep a steady flow of business as it serves everything from club sandwiches to hand-battered, chicken-fried steaks. Friday night is fried catfish night—you'll have to fight locals for a table, but the fried crunchy fish is worth it. The cafe opens at 5 AM. ⊠*106 Fort McKavitt St.* ☎*325/347–5365* ▤*AE, D, MC, V.*

WHERE TO STAY

$$ ▥ **Gamel House.** On the town square, the Gamel Guest House is one of the first houses ever built in Mason. Erected in to 1869 by cattle baron John W. Gamel, this guesthouse has a tranquil sitting area off the back porch beneath a shady oak tree The small, two-bed, two-bathroom cabin is well appointed with antiques, including the Gamel family's original dining-room table and claw-foot bathtub. Those who love feeling like they've stepped back in time will feel right at home here. Those who like a little more modernity may feel a bit cramped. $150 per night for the entire house with a two-night minimum. **Pros:** History buffs will love the stories surrounding this property, rooms are comfortable. **Cons:** A little too close to the main roads of town, not ideal for children due to the antique furniture. ⊠*224 San Antonio St.* ☎*325/347–5531* ⊕*www.masontxcoc.com/member/zesch/gamel.htm* ▭*Sleeps 4* ⟐*In-room: Refrigerator, kitchen, dial-up* ▤*AE, MC, V* ℟*CP.*

$$–$$$$ ▥ **Raye Carrington on the Llano River.** If you enjoy fly-fishing or birding, this may be just the ticket. Each suite or cabin on the property feels secluded, while the common areas allow for family-style breakfasts and grilling your dinners by the river. You can also use this as a base for kayaking, mountain biking, and hiking. Guided fishing and casting instruction is available. **Pros:** Rooms are simple and comfortable, perfect place to commune with nature, fly-fishing fans won't want to get off the water. **Cons:** Poor cell-phone reception, dinner options are going

into Mason or grilling for yourself. ✉ *2 mi west on Willow Creek Rd. of U.S. 87 N* ☎866/605–3100 *or* 325/347–3474 ⊕*www.llanoriver. com* ☞*4 cabins (sleep 2–5), 5 rooms (sleep 2–3)* � *In-room: No TV, refrigerator, no phone. In-hotel: public Wi-Fi, no-smoking rooms* ▤*AE, D, MC, V* ⦿*BP.*

THE HILL COUNTRY ESSENTIALS

To research prices, get advice from other travelers, and book travel arrangements, visit www.fodors.com.

TRANSPORTATION

4

BY AIR

Austin Bergstrom International Airport and San Antonio International Airport are served by American, Continental, Delta, Frontier, Northwest, Southwest, United, and US Airways. Hill Country towns begin within 25 to 30 mi of either airport. From Austin's Bergstrom International Airport, follow U.S. 290 west until the terrain changes from flat, to steep and rolling. To get to northern towns such as Marble Falls, Llano, and Burnet, exit U.S. 281 and head north. Fredericksburg, Boerne, Comfort, and Bandera are all farther west from 281, but are easily reached with a little map navigation. New Braunfels, Gruene, and San Marcos are easily accessed from 1–35 between Austin and San Antonio. From San Antonio's International Airport, U.S. 281 North and I–10 West will both take you straight into the heart of the Hill Country.

Information **Austin-Bergstrom International Airport** ((✉ *3600 Presidential Blvd., Austin* ☎*512/530–2242* ⊕*www.ci.austin.tx.us*)). **San Antonio International Airport** ((✉ *9800 Airport Blvd., San Antonio* ☎*210/207–3450* ⊕*www. ci.sat.tx.us*)).

BY CAR

This is the land of the open road. The best—and really—the only way to access the Hill Country is by car (or by motorcycle, which is an increasingly popular method). The towns are small enough that parking is not a problem. And though it's not encouraged, you're probably pretty safe leaving your car unlocked. Locals joke that they can spot an out-of-towner when they hear the "beep" of a car alarm.

You can rent a car from any of the major national chains at Austin Bergstrom International Airport and San Antonio International Airport. ⇨*Car Rental in Texas Essentials for national car-rental agency contact information.*

CONTACTS & RESOURCES

EMERGENCIES

In an emergency dial 911. Each of the following medical facilities has an emergency room open 24/7. A new 120-room hospital, Lake of the Hills, is being built just outside Marble Falls. It is part of the Scott & White healthcare system based out of Temple, Texas, which is known for its top-notch medical facilities. It is expected to open in 2010.

Hospitals **Hill Country Memorial Hospital** (⊠ *1020 S. Hwy. 16, Fredericksburg* ☎ *830/997–4353*). **Sid Peterson Memorial Hospital** (⊠ *710 Water St., Kerrville* ☎ *830/896–4200*). **Seton Marble Falls Healthcare Center** (⊠ *700 U.S. 281, Marble Falls* ☎ *830/693–2600*). **Seton Highland Lakes Hospital** (⊠ *3201 S. Water St., Burnet* ☎ *512/715–3000*).

VISITOR INFORMATION

Bandera Convention & Visitors Bureau (⊠ *126 Hwy. 16 S., Bandera* ☎ *800/364–3833* ⊕ *www.banderacowboycapital.com*). **Boerne Convention & Visitors Bureau** (⊠ *126 Rosewood Ave., Boerne* ☎ *830/249–8000* ⊕ *www.boerne.org*). **Castroville Chamber of Commerce** (⊠ *802 London* ☎ *830/538–3142 or 800/778–6775* ⊕ *www.castroville.com*). **Comfort Convention & Visitors Bureau** (⊠ *630 Hwy. 27, Comfort* ☎ *830/995–3131* ⊕ *www.comfort-texas.com*). **Fredericksburg Convention & Visitors Bureau** (⊠ *302 E. Austin, Fredericksburg* ☎ *830/997–6523* ⊕ *www.fredericksburg-texas.com*). **Johnson City Chamber of Commerce** (⊠ *803 Hwy. 281 S, Johnson City* ☎ *830/868–7684* ⊕ *www.lbjcountry.com*). **Kerrville Convention & Visitors Bureau** (⊠ *2108 Sidney Baker, Kerrville* ☎ *800/221–7958 or 830/792–3535* ⊕ *www.kerrvilletexascvb.com*). **Lake Travis Convention & Visitors Bureau** (⊠ *1415 RR 620 S., Ste. 202, Austin* ☎ *877/263–0073* ⊕ *www.laketravischamber.com*). **Llano Chamber of Commerce** (⊠ *700 Bessemer, Llano* ☎ *325/247–5354* ⊕ *www.llanochamber.org*). **Luckenbach Convention & Visitors Bureau** (⊠ *412 Lueckenbach Town Loop, Fredericksburg* ☎ *830/997–3224* ⊕ *www.luckenbachtexas.com*). **Marble Falls** (⊠ *916 Second St., Marble Falls* ☎ *830/693–2815* ⊕ *www.marblefalls.org*). **Mason County Chamber of Commerce** (⊠ *108 Fort McKavitt, Mason* ☎ *325/347–5758* ⊕ *www.masontxcoc.com*). **New Braunfels Chamber of Commerce** (⊠ *424 S. Castell Ave., New Braunfels* ☎ *800/572–2626* ⊕ *www.nbjumpin.com*). **San Marcos Convention & Visitors Bureau** (⊠ *202 N. C.M. Allen Parkway, San Marcos* ☎ *512/393–5900* ⊕ *www.sanmarcoscharms.com*). **Wimberley Convention & Visitors Bureau** (⊠ *14100 RR 12, Wimberley* ☎ *512/847–2201* ⊕ *www.wimberley.org*).

Dallas &
Fort Worth

WORD OF MOUTH

"The Metroplex has one of the best designed highway systems in America, although congested at times. The weather here is gorgeous. A lot of transplants do complain about the humidity, 'cause it is a stark contrast in comparison with, say New England, for example."

—mireaux7

"Fort Worth is just a short drive west of Dallas, and most foreign visitors really enjoy the history and Old West atmosphere. The Stockyards are very popular! There are daily cattle drives, and lots of truly unique Texas shops, and Billy Bob's honkytonk. You can even stay right in the middle of it all at the historic Stockyards Hotel."

—ChristieP

By Tyra Damm

DALLAS AND FORT WORTH, SEPARATED by 30 mi of suburbs, aren't exactly twin cities—they're more like cousins who squabble more than they get along. Their roots are different, yet intertwined. Dallas has almost always been a center of trade, built on the ideals of capitalism and progress—and great leaps of faith. Fort Worth's prosperity was established when the town became a stop on the Chisholm Trail, and continued when the city became a major railhead. The cattle that were herded through town more than a century ago still define the city, and its nickname, "Cowtown," persists.

In Dallas, image is almost everything. There's a struggle between preservationists and those who prefer to embrace progress—even at the expense of bulldozing pieces of the past. It's hard to imagine the flashy, glitzy Victory Park—Dallas's newest entertainment district—fitting in anywhere in Fort Worth. The city and its people desperately want to be on the cusp of trends rather than following the masses, and they often take themselves very seriously. But Dallas has the results to back up its persona—the city is filled with homegrown success stories, booming businesses, and, increasingly, an evolving emphasis on the arts.

Fort Worth doesn't exactly shun development, but its growth has been slower. The city and its people are more deliberate, mindful of the western legacy forever shaping their identity. That's not to say this is a town of simple country folk—Fort Worth's Cultural District houses world-class art, showcased in architecturally significant buildings.

GETTING ORIENTED

The DFW area has taken advantage of wide-open spaces. People, places, and things are spread out across multiple counties, requiring miles and miles of highways and toll roads. Dallas and Fort Worth are separated by about 30 mi, but during morning and evening rush hour it can take an hour or more to navigate between the two.

Life is sprawled all around the two major cities, with folks commuting from dozens of suburbs to business centers spread all over—Downtown Dallas or Fort Worth, up and down Central Expressway, Las Colinas, the telecom corridor of Richardson, and corporate headquarters in Plano. It's easiest to navigate the roads on weekends or on weekdays between 9 AM and 4 PM, and after 7 PM. There's almost always snarled traffic at certain exchanges—in and out of Downtown Dallas, around Dallas/Fort Worth International Airport, and along Loop 635 (also called the LBJ Freeway).

Many museums are closed Mondays. Some high-end restaurants aren't open Sundays or Mondays. Downtown Dallas often feels like a ghost town on weekends, while Downtown Fort Worth keeps a lively pace seven days a week.

DALLAS-FORT WORTH TOP 5

■ **Incredible Shopping.** Dallas, the city that gave the world Neiman Marcus, continually raises the standards for spending money with style. The Metroplex (Dallas, Fort Worth, and the surrounding suburbs) boasts acres of shopping malls, stores, and boutiques, from high-end to discount.

■ **Top Art Museums.** Fort Worth and Dallas house important collections of art and regularly host major international exhibits.

■ **Stellar Dining.** Sure you'll find Tex-Mex and barbecue here, but you'll also discover fine-dining experiences and multicultural influences.

■ **Year-round Activities.** It's possible to enjoy outdoor activities for about eight months of the year, and there are plenty of festivals, fairs, and parades to entertain every member of your family.

■ **History Lessons.** Not all the area's history revolves around the 1963 Kennedy assassination. History buffs will also find re-creations of frontier life and architecture that reflect power and wealth in the early 20th century.

EXPLORING DALLAS

Many people visit Dallas because of the city's tragic legacy as the assassination site of President John F. Kennedy. Dallas has learned to accept its role in history, offering a museum that pays tribute to JFK's life and legacy and restoring the memorial in his honor. But the city is also learning how to entertain and charm its visitors. Beyond the Schoolbook Depository and the Grassy Knoll, visitors will find an evolving Arts District, flashy Victory Park, a couple of entertainment districts, an improving Downtown, neighborhoods filled with notable architecture and beautiful landscaping, and myriad shopping and dining opportunities.

DOWNTOWN DALLAS

The Downtown area is traditionally defined by the highways that loop 1.3 square mi of disparate districts. Some sections are clean, well lit, and easy for pedestrians to navigate. Others are rough around the edges, blighted by empty storefronts and abandoned buildings, and populated by groups of homeless people. There are gaps between the areas, and blocks that feel forgotten.

This lack of continuity and connectivity is not lost on the people working to promote and improve Downtown Dallas. Millions of private and public dollars are being spent to revitalize the central business district, and three Downtown parks are being developed. Another park project involves building a deck on Woodall Rogers Freeway (the highway that separates the north and west side of Downtown from Uptown) and creating a five-block greenspace that will connect the Arts District to Uptown. As more people take up residence in Downtown apartments and condos, more retailers are moving in, too. Plans call for three San-

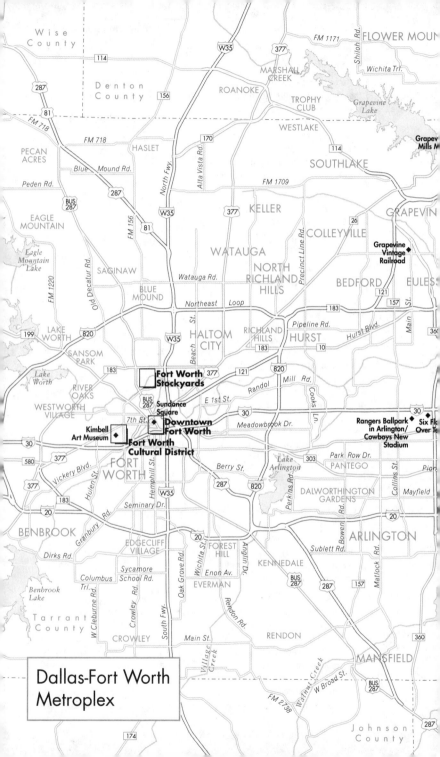

Dallas-Fort Worth
Metroplex

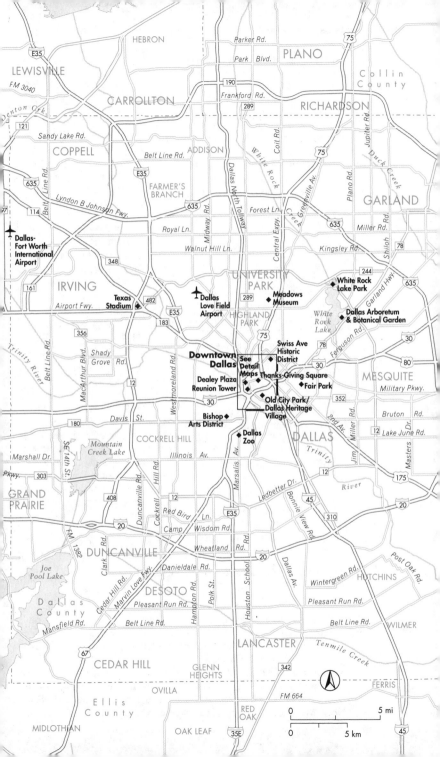

PLANNING YOUR TRIP

WHEN TO GO

The DFW area is reliably hot (and usually humid) in the summer. The forecast during the rest of the year is less reliable, but it's safe to say you rarely need a down parka or snow boots 'round these parts. Early spring can be cold or mild, late spring mild or hot; early fall hot or mild, late fall mild or cold. Winter? Who knows—you may get caught in an ice storm, or you may see children playing outside in shorts and T-shirts.

Spring and fall are great times to visit if you're a fan of festivals. Spring brings Dallas Blooms to the Arboretum; the arts and music festival Wildflower! in suburban Richardson; the Main St. Fort Worth Art Festival; the American Film Institute Festival at Victory Park; Taste Addison; and Main Street Days in Grapevine. Fall offers Grapevine's GrapeFest; the Greek Food Festival at Holy Trinity Greek Orthodox Church, a large Dallas congregation; Addison Oktoberfest; and the biggest attraction of them all, the three-week State Fair of Texas in Dallas.

The Christmas season is also a special time in the area. It never gets North Pole cold, and plenty of folks are eager to celebrate. The Neiman Marcus Adolphus Children's Parade kicks off the season, just about every suburb hosts a tree-lighting or day of festivities, the malls are in high gear, and some neighborhoods spare no expense in decorating homes with blinding light displays.

GETTING THERE & AROUND

There's no trouble getting to the DFW area. The Dallas/Fort Worth International Airport is one of the busiest hubs in the world, hosting 21 national and international airlines. Domestic commercial flights also land at Love Field in Dallas. You can arrive in Fort Worth or Dallas via Amtrak or Greyhound as well. Of course, driving your own car into town is a good option; you'll appreciate having that car even more as you travel from site to site.

Public transit is an evolving industry in the area. You can certainly use the bus system in Fort Worth and the bus and light-rail system in Dallas and some of its suburbs, but the lines are not as ubiquitous or as helpful as in cities such as New York and Chicago. You can get by with public transit in some areas, but it requires determination, research, and patience. To reach some outlying attractions and even some major ones, you'll need access to a car—your own, a taxi, or a rental.

tiago Calatrava bridges to span the nearby Trinity River, now just an empty levee but reimagined as a recreational centerpiece.

MAIN ATTRACTIONS

❶ ★ Sixth Floor Museum at Dealey Plaza. On November 22, 1963, shots rang out on Dealey Plaza, at the west end of Downtown, as the presidential motorcade rounded the corner from Houston Street onto the Elm Street approach to the Triple Underpass. Eventually the Warren Commission concluded that President Kennedy was gunned down by Lee Harvey Oswald, acting alone and firing from the sixth floor of the Texas School Book Depository. The building is now known as the Sixth Floor Museum at Dealey Plaza, where exhibits explore the life and

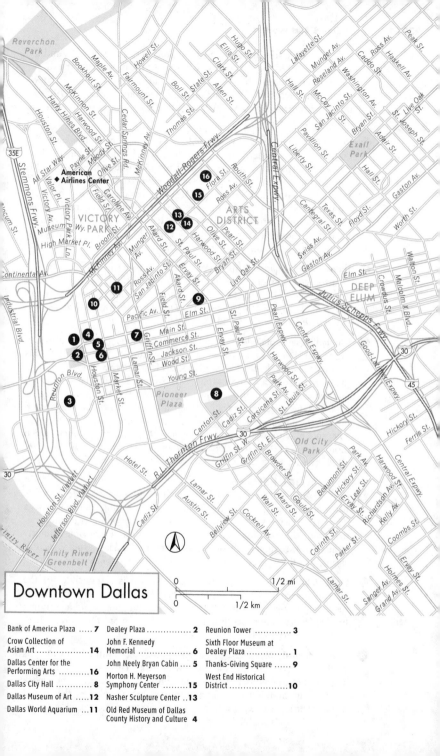

Downtown Dallas

legacy of JFK, offering context of the politics of the early '60s and the importance of Kennedy's Texas visit. One of the most popular exhibits is the re-creation of the sniper's nest at the southeast window, viewable but not accessible. ⊠*411 Elm St., Downtown Dallas* ☎*214/747–6660* ⊕*www.jfk.org* ▱*$13.50, including audio tour* ☉*Mon. noon–6, Tues.–Sun. noon–6.*

❷ **Dealey Plaza.** On the far western edge of Downtown lies Dealey Plaza, designed as the western gateway to the city and completed in 1941 by the Works Progress Administration. The three-acre space is named for George Bannerman Dealey, a newspaper editor and publisher and civic leader. His statue stands in the middle of the park, just across the street from the Old Red Courthouse. The plaza is now forever remembered as the site of Kennedy's assassination. It was designated a National Historic Landmark District in 1993, three decades after the tragedy. ⊠*101 S. Houston St., Downtown Dallas.*

❾ **Thanks-Giving Square.** This small triangular plaza designed by Philip Johnson contains quiet gardens and an interfaith chapel with stained glass by Gabriel Loire. ⊠*1627 Pacific Ave., below Republic Center Tower at Ervay and Bryan Sts., Downtown Dallas* ☎*214/969–1977* ⊕*www.thanksgiving.org* ▱*$2 suggested donation.*

❹ **Old Red Museum of Dallas County History and Culture.** This 1892 Romanesque courthouse, known as "Old Red," contains a museum on Dallas County's history. Each gallery has a short film, interactive exhibits, artifacts, and historical photographs. Discover some of Dallas's claims to fame, such as the invention of the integrated circuit, air conditioning for cars, and the frozen margarita, as well as sports memorabilia. A special draw is the hands-on learning center, where children can dress in period costume, play marbles, and answer history questions on touch-screen monitors. ⊠*100 S. Houston St., Downtown Dallas* ☎*214/745–1100* ⊕*www.oldred.org* ▱*$8* ☉*Mon.–Sat. 9–5, Sun. noon–5.*

ALSO WORTH SEEING

❼ **Bank of America Plaza.** Dallas's tallest building, at 920 feet, is visible for miles at night, thanks to the green argon tubing that outlines its 72 stories. Visitors can access Downtown's maze of underground tunnels from the building's basement. The tunnels, a welcome climate-controlled escape, include dozens of restaurants, delis, drugstores, gift shops, and florists. ⊠*901 Main St., Downtown Dallas.*

❽ **Dallas City Hall.** Renowned architect I. M. Pei is responsible for the striking inverted-pyramid design of City Hall. The modern structure is set on a seven-acre plaza that features reflecting pools and a stunning bronze Henry Moore sculpture. ⊠*1500 Marilla St., Downtown Dallas* ☎*214/670–5111.*

❻ **John F. Kennedy Memorial.** Designed by architect Philip Johnson, this stark, square memorial is a short walk from Dealey Plaza, at Main and Market streets. It was designed to honor the president, not mark the assassination. Some critics and tourists are troubled by the lack of ornamentation or explanation. Johnson, though, delivered a design

CLOSE UP

Bonnie & Clyde: Outlaws of the Old West

Bonnie and Clyde: two crazy kids on a joyride, or ruthless cop-killers who got what they deserved?

The 1930s were hard times for poverty-stricken working people like Bonnie Parker of Rowena and her beau, Clyde Barrow from Ellis County. The soon-to-be celebrity outlaws apparently met by chance in Dallas in 1930. Clyde already boasted a modest criminal record, and Bonnie would begin accumulating one shortly.

In 1932 the "Barrow Gang" killed the first of the nine lawmen it would dispatch. The couple worked their will until May 23, 1934, when they encountered a posse organized by Texas Ranger Frank Hamer. "Clyde Barrow, notorious Texas 'bad man' and murderer, and his cigar-smoking, quick-shooting woman accomplice, Bonnie Parker, were ambushed and shot to death today . . . ." reported *The New York Times.*

With those few strokes of the typewriter, legend was born.

—Larry Neal

that he felt honored the president's legacy and his family's wishes: "Kennedy was such a remarkable man I didn't want to have a statue but sought rather something very humble and spartan . . . It was essential that there would be no sentimentalizing of Kennedy; he would have disapproved anyway!" ⊠*Market St. between Main and Commerce Sts., Downtown Dallas.*

❺ John Neely Bryan Cabin. Bryan is credited as one of the founders of Dallas, and he probably lived in a log cabin that was similar in style to the cabin that sits in Founders Plaza (a recently redesigned pedestrian-friendly space). But this building was not his. This approximate replica was built sometime in the 1920s, and at various times had a home at Fair Park and on the grounds of the Old Red Courthouse. You can't walk in or even peek in—there are closed shutters instead of glass windows. But despite its erratic history and lack of interactivity, the cabin is a beloved Dallas icon. ⊠*At the southwest corner of Market and Elm Sts..*

❸ Reunion Tower. This tower has been an iconic fixture of the Dallas skyline since 1978. The lights on the giant ball at the top of the tower often dance at night. At this writing, access to the tower—which houses a rotating restaurant and lounge—was expected to be closed until late 2008. When it reopens, visitors will be able to ride an elevator up 55 flights to an observation deck that affords views of Dallas and beyond. ⊠*300 Reunion Blvd.* ☎*214/712–7145* ☐*$2* ☉*Sun.–Thurs. 10 AM– 10 PM, Fri.–Sat. 9 AM–11 PM.*

THE ARTS DISTRICT

For the past 25 years Dallas has been growing its Arts District, a 19-block area on the north side of Downtown. The architecture here is stunning (four Pritzker Prize–winning architects contributed to the district), and the collections and performances inside are equally impressive.

MAIN ATTRACTIONS

⑫ **Dallas Museum of Art.** Housed in a series of white limestone galleries built off a central barrel vault, this museum remains one of the city's greatest cultural institutions. The permanent collection covers a lot of territory, from the arts of Africa, Asia, and ancient Greece to a painting collection with works by artists as diverse as esteemed colonial painter John Singleton Copley and contemporary German painter Gerhard Richter (part of a strong and growing contemporary collection). A popular draw at the museum is an installation that re-creates rooms in the Mediterranean villa belonging to Texas swells Wendy and Emery Reves. The Center for Creative Connections, designed for families, allows patrons to interact with art and artists. ⊠*1717 N. Harwood St., Arts District* ☎*214/922–1200* ⊕*www.dallasmuseumofart.org* 🖭*$10.*

⑬ **Nasher Sculpture Center.** The late Raymond and Patsy Nasher—real-estate developers, civic leaders, art lovers, and philanthropists—collected modern and contemporary sculpture for decades, before giving the collection, valued at $400 million, to the city in 1997. The center, which opened in 2003, is an international draw with an extensive representation of great masters—Borofsky, Calder, Dubuffet, Giacometti, Matisse, Miró, Moore, Picasso, and Rodin. The building, which has 10,000 square feet of gallery space, is faced with Italian travertine stone and topped with a glass roof to let in natural light. The 1.42-acre outdoor sculpture garden is landscaped with pools, fountains, pathways, and more than 170 trees. The view of Downtown from the calming green space is spectacular, especially after dusk. ⊠*2001 Flora St., Arts District* ☎*214/242–5100* ⊕*www.nashersculpturecenter.org* 🖭*$10* ☉*Tues., Wed., Fri.–Sun. 11–5, Thurs. 11–9.*

ALSO WORTH SEEING

⑮ **Morton H. Meyerson Symphony Center.** The I. M. Pei–designed space is a place of sweeping dramatic curves, ever-changing vanishing points, and surprising views. Inside is the **Herman W. and Amelia H. Lay Family Organ,** a hand-built, hand-installed Fisk organ with 4,535 pipes. Free tours are offered four days a week (days vary) at 1 PM. Check the Web site, or call the center for current tour information and a list of upcoming performances. ⊠*2301 Flora St., Arts District* ☎*214/670–3600* ⊕*www.meyersonsymphonycenter.com.*

⑭ **Crow Collection of Asian Art.** A pair of 19th-century Chinese guardian lions from the Qing Dynasty is the first clue you've arrived at the Crow Collection (across the street from the Nasher Sculpture Center). The private gallery—a tranquil, intimate space—showcases the remarkable Asian art collection of philanthropists and native Dallasites Trammell and Margaret Crow. The museum also hosts traveling exhibits and displays treasures from China, Japan, India, and Southeast Asia. Don't miss an 18th-century carved sandstone facade from an Indian home. ⊠*2010 Flora St., Arts District* ☎*214/979–6430* ⊕*www.crowcollection.org* 🖭*Free* ☉*Tues., Wed., and Fri.–Sun. 10–5, Thurs. 10–9.*

⓰ **Dallas Center for the Performing Arts.** The Arts District will welcome a number of companies to the fold when this ambitious project opens to the public in late 2009. The multipurpose center will offer performance space for the Dallas Opera, Dallas Theater Center, Dallas Black Dance Theatre, Texas Ballet Theater, and Anita N. Martinez Ballet Folklorico. The complex will consist of an opera house, an indoor theater, and an open-air theater. A 10-acre park is designed to tie the spaces together and attract the public to the site—regardless of performance schedules. ⊠*Flora and Leonard Sts., Arts District* ☏*214/954–9925* ⊕*www. dallasperformingarts.org.*

DEEP ELLUM

This area's happening heyday has past, but Deep Ellum still boasts an energetic nightlife scene. The neighborhood, just east of Downtown Dallas (north of I–30 and east of I–45), is a funky mix of restaurants, clubs, bars, galleries, a few small retail establishments (some not exactly family-friendly), tattoo and piercing parlors, and some housing. As crime rates have increased in Deep Ellum in the past couple of years, some of the nicer restaurants and clubs have closed their doors. ⇨*Arts & Nightlife for entertainment options in Deep Ellum.*

THE WEST END

⓾ The **West End Historic District** (⊠*McKinney and Lamar* ⊕*www.dallaswestend.org*) features brick warehouses built between 1900 and 1930 and brought back to life in 1976. There are plenty of restaurants and clubs here, as well as a few shopping opportunities *(⇨Arts & Nightlife and Shopping sections).* The neighborhood also hosts the annual Taste of Dallas, a food and entertainment festival held each July. If you have transportation, though, consider trying another dining or entertainment neighborhood, as the West End has lost a bit of its luster.

⓫ **Dallas World Aquarium.** The word "aquarium" doesn't fully describe everything to experience at this privately owned Downtown attraction. Sure, there are fish, octopus, anemones, eels, and jellyfish. But there are also penguins in an outdoor exhibit; a rain forest with monkeys, manatees, toucans, crocodiles, turtles, and more, all surrounded by native plants; and an eight-story Mayan exhibit that features a walk-through shark aquarium, flamingos, a jaguar, and an ocelot. The West End DART light-rail station is just a few blocks away. ⊠*1801 N. Griffin St., West End* ☏*214/720–2224* ⊕*www.dwazoo.com* ☎*$16.95* ☺*Daily 10–5.*

VICTORY PARK

The centerpiece of this new entertainment district is American Airlines Center, a 20,000-seat venue that hosts the Dallas Mavericks basketball team, the Dallas Stars hockey team, and big-name concerts and touring acts. Some compare the district to Manhattan's Times Square (albeit on a Dallas scale). That may still be an overstatement, but Victory Park is certainly the flashiest nighttime spot around these parts.

The plaza that leads to American Airlines Center glows with lights from 11 Texas-sized LED screens that project sporting events, movies, and other videos. People gather in the middle of the plaza to sit, eat, drink, and take in the sights or watch a big game or movie. The pedestrian-friendly area is filling with office, residences, hotels, restaurants, galleries, and shops.

EAST DALLAS

East Dallas is the most eclectic section of the city; it's really a conglomeration of proud neighborhoods, each with its own identity. Swiss Avenue is lined with gorgeous mansions. The Hollywood/Santa Monica neighborhood includes Tudor, Craftsman, French eclectic, and Pueblo Revival style homes. In Lakewood you'll find a mix of grand homes and charming cottages, many dating to the 1920s and '30s. Most of East Dallas is pedestrian friendly, and you'll certainly want to get out of your car and walk around to appreciate the neighborhoods' beauty and distinct architectural styles. Sites are spread out, though, so it's ideal to have a car to get from place to place. For locations, see the Dallas & Fort Worth Metroplex map.

MAIN ATTRACTIONS

Dallas Arboretum and Botanical Garden. This lovely attraction is composed of 66 acres of gardens and lawns in White Rock Lake Park. Spend an hour or two here to escape the noise and traffic of the city, walk nature trails, admire sculpture, and recline in soft, manicured grass. The annual Dallas Blooms event, in early spring, boasts spectacular displays of tulips, daffodils, and other blooming bulbs. Fall delivers more than 150,000 autumn flowers as well as great displays of pumpkins and other gourds. ✉ *8525 Garland Rd., East Dallas* 🕾 *214/515–6500* ⊕ *www.dallasarboretum.org* 🎟 *$8, parking $5.*

ALSO WORTH SEEING

Swiss Avenue. This East Dallas strip has the city's best representations of two distinct periods. On lower Swiss Avenue (2900 block), nearer to Downtown, the **Wilson Block Historic District** is an unaltered block of turn-of-the-20th-century frame houses restored as offices for nonprofit groups. Set-back Prairie Style, Italian Renaissance, Tudor, and Colonial Revival mansions are common in the **Swiss Avenue Historic District,** the city's first historic district (designated in 1973). Park anywhere along Swiss Avenue in the 4900–6000 blocks, and walk down the tree-shaded street to admire the grand homes and beautifully landscaped yards. Residents and their household staffs are accustomed to folks stopping to gawk or take photos—but do respect their privacy and stay on the sidewalk.

BISHOP ARTS DISTRICT

Head to this small revitalized neighborhood (part of the Oak Cliff section of Dallas) for unique shopping, eating, and drinking experiences. The crowd is friendly, diverse, and creative. The district is at the corner of West Davis Street and North Bishop Avenue, where a cluster of older buildings houses independently owned restaurants, galleries, and shops filled with antiques, jewelry, vintage clothes, trendy apparel, handmade soap and candles, unusual pet gifts, and locally created art—one even sells more than 200 kinds of soda. On the first Thursday night of each month, the district celebrates with live music, special events, tastings, and longer hours. For locations, see the Dallas & Fort Worth Metroplex map.

ELSEWHERE IN DALLAS

For locations, see the Dallas & Fort Worth Metroplex map.

MAIN ATTRACTIONS

Dallas Zoo. The Fort Worth Zoo is a huge draw in the area, but the Dallas Zoo shouldn't be overlooked. The Wilds of Africa section re-creates the habitats of animals such as African penguins, chimpanzees, saddle-billed storks, and okapi (zebralike cousin to the giraffe). When it's not too hot or too cold, you can ride a monorail (for a fee) through the Africa exhibit to gain a treetop perspective and to learn more about the animals. Zoo North, the older section of the zoo, includes some exhibits that haven't been changed in decades. But other sections are modern and interactive, especially the tiger habitat and the children's zoo. A fabulous aviary allows children to feed birds, some of which will perch on your hand or shoulder. There's also a petting zoo, pony rides, giant fish tank, playground, and stream for jumping and splashing in. The DART red line stops just outside the zoo's entrance. ⊠*650 S. R.L. Thornton Freeway (I–35), South Dallas* ☎*214/943–2771* ⊕*www. dallas-zoo.org* ⊠*$8.75* ☉*Daily 9–4.*

☺ **Fair Park.** In South Dallas, this 277-acre National Historic Landmark
★ has the largest collection of 1930s Art Deco architecture in the United States. It is also home to the State Fair of Texas for three weeks each fall. In the park's **Hall of State** (⊠*3939 Grand Ave.* ☎*214/421–4500* ⊕*www.hallofstate.com* ⊠*Free*), murals tell the story of Texas in heroic terms. The Tower Building (open weekdays, 8:15–5:15) has free brochures that describe the buildings and artwork. A self-guided walking tour takes about 90 minutes. Fair Park also contains six major exhibit spaces (many of which are closed Monday or Tuesday): the **African American Museum** (⊠*3536 Grand Ave.* ☎*214/565–9026* ⊕*www.aamdallas.org* ⊠*Free*); the **Museum of the American Railroad** (⊠*1105 Washington St.* ☎*214/428–0101* ⊕*www.dallasrailway museum.com* ⊠*$5*); the **Dallas Aquarium** (⊠*1462 1st Ave.* ☎*214/670–8443* ⊠*$4*); the **Texas Discovery Gardens** (⊠*3601 Martin Luther King Blvd.* ☎*214/428–7476* ⊕*www.texasdiscovery gardens.org* ⊠*$3*); the **Museum of Nature and Science** (⊠*3535 Grand Ave.* ☎*214/421–3466* ⊕*www.natureandscience.org* ⊠*$8.75*), which spans three buildings and houses one of Dallas's IMAX theaters; and the **Women's Museum** (⊠*3800 Parry Ave.* ☎*214/915–0860* ⊕*www. thewomensmuseum.org* ⊠*$5*). ⊠*1300 Robert B. Cullum Blvd., South Dallas* ☎*214/421–9600* ⊕*www.fairpark.org.*

Meadows Museum. Southern Methodist University is home to one of the world's largest and most significant collections of Spanish art outside Spain. Philanthropist Algur H. Meadows began acquiring the pieces while on business in Spain in the 1950s. He gave his collection to SMU, and the museum continues to acquire pieces today. The collection spans 1,000 years and includes masterpieces by El Greco, Velázquez, Ribera, Murillo, Goya, Miró, and Picasso, grouped chronologically in beautifully lit galleries. The museum also has an admirable sculpture collection and hosts exhibitions of wide-ranging interest. Don't miss the well-edited gift shop. ⌂ *5900 Bishop Blvd.* ☎ *214/768–2516* ⊕ *www. meadowsmuseumdallas.org* ▭ *$8, free after 5 Thurs.* ⊙ *Tues., Wed., Fri., and Sat. 10–5, Thurs. 10–8, Sun. noon–5.*

ALSO WORTH SEEING

Dallas Heritage Village. It may be difficult to imagine Dallas without its shiny skyscrapers, far-flung suburbs, and miles and miles of highway, but Heritage Village at Old City Park allows visitors to experience what life was like in Big D before 1910. The museum, set on 13 acres just south of I–30 and Downtown Dallas, consists of 38 restored buildings, furnished inside and out as they would have been (way) back in the day. You'll also meet a couple of donkeys, a cow, some chickens, and other barnyard animals. Visitors can tour structures such as a log cabin, an antebellum mansion, a schoolhouse, a church, a farmhouse, and a shotgun shack. The re-created Main Street features a sturdy bank (rebuilt on site brick by brick), a print shop, a general store, and a saloon, where you may be able to order an ice-cold root beer, play a game of cards or checkers, and even catch a gunfight that spills into the street. Docents are in period costume and stay in character, describing in detail their daily lives and challenges. ⌂ *1515 S. Harwood* ☎ *214/421–5141* ⊕ *www.oldcitypark.org* ▭ *$7* ⊙ *Tues.–Sat. 10–4, Sun. noon–4.*

EXPLORING FORT WORTH

Many of Fort Worth's major sights are Downtown—the city's financial core, most of its historic buildings, and Sundance Square, a restored turn-of-the-20th-century neighborhood and one of the city's main attractions. The Stockyards and adjacent Western-theme stores, restaurants, and hotels are a few miles north of Downtown, clustered around Main Street and Exchange Avenue. The Cultural District, west of Downtown on Lancaster Avenue, is home to several well-known museums, a coliseum complex, and several parks.

DOWNTOWN FORT WORTH

The centerpiece of Downtown Fort Worth is Sundance Square, but the entire area is worth exploring. The streets, laid on a grid, are easy to navigate, and the size of the central business district is manageable for visitors willing to walk. On the south side are the Fort Worth Water Gardens, a popular destination, especially during the hot summer months. Northeast of the Convention Center is the Intermodal

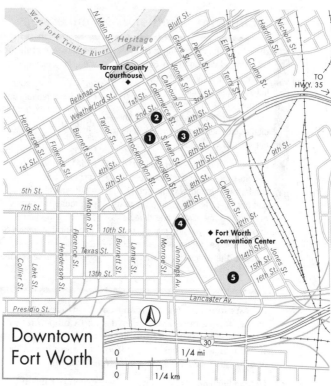

Downtown
Fort Worth

5

Transportation Center, which pieces together rail, bus, and car options. The center of Downtown is crowded with office buildings and hotels that surround the charming Sundance Square. Just east of Sundance Square is Bass Performance Hall, which draws touring musicals and shows and houses four resident companies.

MAIN ATTRACTION

Fodor's Choice
★

① Sundance Square. The billionaire Bass brothers of Fort Worth are to be thanked for what may be the most eye-pleasing juxtaposition of scale: rather than tear down several blocks of brick buildings to accommodate the twin towers of their giant City Center development, they created Sundance Square by restoring the area as a center of tall-windowed restaurants, shops, nightclubs, and offices. Tourists mingle effortlessly with the business crowd during the day, and at night the mood is laidback and down-to-earth—much like the city itself. ⊠*Bounded by Houston, Commerce, 2nd, and 3rd Sts.* ⊕*www.sundancesquare.com.*

ALSO WORTH SEEING

③ Bass Performance Hall. You can't miss the two 48-foot limestone angels on one side of this multipurpose building, which unabashedly fills a city block. The hall opened to great fanfare in 1998 and it continues to draw acclaim for its classic architecture, sight lines, and acoustics.

CLOSE UP

Molly Ivins: The Pen Is Mightier

Liberal newspaper columnist Molly Ivins started writing in the '60s about, as she put it, "militant blacks, angry Indians, radical students, uppity women, and a motley assortment of other misfits and troublemakers." She didn't quit until brutal cancer killed her in 2007.

Ivins found her voice in H.L. Mencken's "comfort-the-afflicted, afflict-the-comfortable" brand of commentary, and her talent for afflicting prompted guffaws in some circles and ridicule in others. Ivins's passion was social justice, and her tool, sharp satire. She called it "the weapon of powerless

people aimed at the powerful," and she used it like a knife.

For a time, Ivins edited the *Texas Observer*, a reliably outraged journal that seemed likelier to be written from Boston than Austin. The California native who grew up in Houston wrote for the *Dallas Times-Herald* until it folded, and was a columnist for the *Fort Worth Star–Telegram* for nearly a decade until she went the syndication route. The prize-winning journalist also wrote a number of books, almost all political in nature. She believed if she could make you laugh or wince, she could make you think.

—Larry Neal

It hosts four resident companies and various touring shows, as well as the Van Cliburn International Piano Competition, held every four years (next in 2009). Free public tours are Saturday mornings at 10:30 if event schedules permit. ⊠*4th and Calhoun Sts., Downtown Fort Worth* ☎*817/212–4325* ⊕*www.basshall.com.*

❹ Flatiron Building. This wedge-shaped structure topped by gargoyles and panthers was built in 1907 as medical offices, patterned after New York's famed building of the same name. There isn't really anything to see inside, but it's worth a stop to look at its exterior. ⊠*1000 Houston St., Downtown Fort Worth* ⊕*www.fortworthflatiron.com.*

❺ ★ **Fort Worth Water Gardens.** This outdoor public sculpture garden contains a dramatic blend of modern sculpture and cascading fountains. Dropping below street level by almost 100 feet, this urban gorge is filled with plants and trees, around which water rushes, spills, swirls, and cascades into a series of pools. It was designed in the 1970s by Philip Johnson and John Burgee and renovated in 2007. ⊠*15th and Commerce Sts., Downtown Fort Worth.*

❷ Sid Richardson Museum. Fort Worth is an appropriate setting for this private collection of art celebrating the American West, with pieces that capture the emotion, movement, and landscape of the frontier. The gallery, which was renovated in 2006, affords space and appropriate lighting for up to 39 pieces at a time. (The late Sid Richardson's collection includes more than 100 paintings.) ⊠*309 Main St., Downtown Fort Worth* ☎*817/332–6554* ⊕*www.sidrichardsonmuseum.org* ▧*Free* ☉*Mon.–Thurs. 9–5, Fri. and Sat. 9–8, Sun. noon–5.*

THE CULTURAL DISTRICT

In one compact location, visitors have access to Georgia O'Keeffe's Rancho Church, New Mexico, Paul Cézanne's Man in a Blue Smock, and Jackson Pollock's Masqued Image. They can watch an IMAX movie and pretend to ride a bucking bronco (and view their wild ride again later online). They can catch a horse show or musical. The Cultural District, roughly bounded by Camp Bowie Boulevard, University Drive, Gendy Street, and Montgomery Street, showcases the best of Fort Worth's culture—Western events and history, fine and performing arts, and continuing education.

MAIN ATTRACTIONS

3 **Amon Carter Museum.** A short walk from the Kimbell, west of Downtown Fort Worth, this museum's collection of American art is centered on Remington and Russell mostly, though in recent decades the curators have incorporated works by many late-20th-century artists. The photographic collection, among the largest in the United States, spans the history of the medium, from 19th-century daguerreotypes to 21st-century digital prints. ⊠ *3501 Camp Bowie Blvd., Cultural District* 🕿 *817/738–1933* ⊕ *www.cartermuseum.org* ✉ *Free* ⊘ *Tue., Wed., Fri., Sat. 10–5; Thu. 10–8; Sun. noon–5.*

8 **Fort Worth Zoo.** The oldest continuous zoo site in Texas, the lush grounds here house more than 5,000 exotic and native animals—including Komodo dragons, koalas, and a rare white tiger—in natural habitat exhibits. The Texas Wild exhibit offers an overview of the wildlife and habitats of the state's different regions. Children love the train, petting zoo, interactive barn, and weather theater. ⊠ *1989 Colonial Pkwy. (south of Cultural District)* 🕿 *817/759–7555* ⊕ *www.fortworthzoo. org* ✉ *$10.50* ⊘ *Mid-Oct.–mid-Feb. daily 10–4; mid-Feb.–late Mar. daily 10–5; late-Mar.–mid-Oct. weekdays 10–5, weekends 10–6.*

5 **Kimbell Art Museum.** Architect Louis Kahn's most famous American building was this museum, composed of six long concrete vaults with skylights running the length of each. Here are top-notch collections of both early-20th-century European art and old masters, including Munch's *Girls on a Bridge* and Goya's *The Matador Pedro Romero,* depicting the great bullfighter who allegedly killed more than 6,000 of the animals without sustaining an injury. The museum also exhibits Greek and Roman antiquities, African and pre-Columbian art, and has one of the largest collections of Asian art in North America. ⊠ *3333 Camp Bowie Blvd., Cultural District* 🕿 *817/332–8451* ⊕ *www. kimbellart.org* ✉ *Permanent collection free; variable admission for special exhibits* ⊘ *Tues.–Thu. 10–5, Fri. noon–8, Sat. 10–5, Sun. noon–5, closed Mon.*

FodorsChoice ★

6 **Modern Art Museum of Fort Worth.** This structure, residing in a gorgeously realized building designed by Japanese architect Tadao Ando and consisting of five glass pavilions built on a shimmering lagoon, sets the right tone for contemplating one of the country's strongest collections of post–World War II painting and sculpture. The 53,000-square-foot exhibition space holds works by icons of modernism and later move-

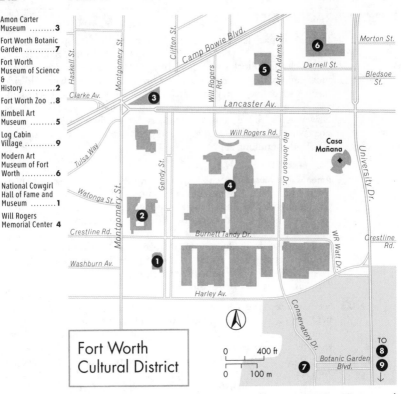

Fort Worth
Cultural District

0   400 ft
0   100 m

ments, from Picasso and Jackson Pollack to Carrie Mae Weems and
Cindy Sherman. If you're lucky, you'll catch works of a future master in the museum's occasional Focus series, which features up-and-
coming contemporary artists. ⊠*3200 Darnell St., Cultural District*
☎*817/738–9215* ⊕*www.themodern.org* ⊠*$10* ⊙*Tues.–Sat. 10–5,
Sun. 11–5.*

❶ National Cowgirl Hall of Fame and Museum. You don't have to be a cowgirl or cowboy to fall in love with this fine museum and its celebration
of pioneering women. The building, just across from the Will Rogers
Memorial Center, shares fascinating Western history through techno-
logically savvy exhibits. The Hall of Fame honors more than 180 pioneering women, including Sacagawea, Mary Ann Goodnight, Georgia
O'Keeffe, Laura Ingalls Wilder, and Sandra Day O'Connor. Each woman's accomplishments are highlighted on easy-to-use touch screens.
Other kiosks allow visitors to listen to female country music stars and
modern-day cowgirls describe life on ranches and the road. Another
area displays flashy rodeo fashions from the past century. Don't miss
the chance to "ride" a bucking bronco and later watch and share the
video online. ⊠*1720 Gendy St., Cultural District* ☎*817/336–4475*
⊕*www.cowgirl.net* ⊠*$8* ⊙*Mon.–Sat. 9–5, Sun. noon–5.*

ALSO WORTH SEEING

❼ Fort Worth Botanic Garden. Among the 23 gardens here are the Lower Rose Garden, whose classical design was inspired by the Villa Lante gardens in Bagnaia, Italy, and the Oval Rose Garden, where many Texas roses grow. The Japanese Garden is beautiful in fall, when the leaves on the maples begin to turn, and in spring, when cherry and other blossoms burst forth. Also on-site is a 10,000-square-foot conservatory. ✉*3220 Botanic Garden Blvd., at University Dr. (south of Cultural District)* ☎*817/871–7686* ⊕*www.fwbg.org* ☑*Free (main grounds), $1 (conservatory), $3.50 (Japanese garden)* ☉*Daily, dawn to dusk (main grounds), hours vary for conservatory and Japanese garden.*

❷ Fort Worth Museum of Science and History. At this writing, this redesigned museum was scheduled to open in fall 2009 with more room for interactive exhibits, a new planetarium, and an improved Omni IMAX theater. Hands-on exhibits will be rotated through the National Cowgirl Hall of Fame and Museum, just across the street from this site, until the new space is ready. ✉*1501 Montgomery St., Cultural District* ☎*817/255–9300* ⊕*www.fwmuseum.org.*

❾ Log Cabin Village. Visitors can roam the grounds and tour log cabins representative of life on the North Texas plains in the 19th century. Staff members and volunteers wear period dress and crush corn, cook on an open fire, help visitors dip candles, and demonstrate the techniques of blacksmiths. Children particularly enjoy ringing the bell outside the schoolhouse and exploring the one-room school's interior. The Seela Cabin allows little ones to try on bonnets, aprons, and workshirts and get to work—sweeping, cooking, and spinning yarn. ✉*2100 Log Cabin Village La. (south of I–30, off University Dr.)* ☎*817/392–5881* ⊕*www. logcabinvillage.org* ☑*$3.50* ☉*Tues.–Fri. 9–4, Sat. and Sun. 1–5.*

❹ Will Rogers Memorial Center. Near Fort Worth's museums, this partially restored coliseum–and–stock pen complex was named after the humorist and Fort Worth booster, who described the city as "where the West begins" (and Dallas as "where the East peters out"). The center boasts an equestrian arena that's used for horse and livestock shows. Will Rogers is host to the Fort Worth Stock Show & Rodeo every January. ✉*3300 W. Lancaster Ave., Cultural District* ☎*817/871–8150* ☉*Daily; hours vary depending on event.*

THE STOCKYARDS

The **Stockyards National Historic District** (✉*131 E. Exchange Ave.*) recalls the prosperity brought to the city in 1902 when two major Chicago meat packers, Armour and Swift, set up plants here to ship meat across the country in refrigerator cars. You can witness a cattle drive here today; cowboys on horses lead a city-owned herd of about a dozen longhorns down East Exchange Avenue every day at 11:30 AM and 4 PM, weather permitting. Between their walks, the cattle can be viewed in their pens behind the **Livestock Exchange Building.**

Information on the Stockyards area is available at the **Stockyards Visitors Center** (✉*130 E. Exchange Ave.* ☎*817/624–4741*).

5

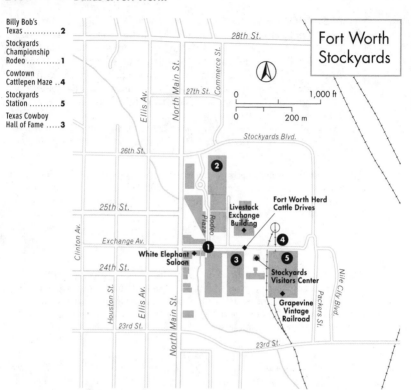

MAIN ATTRACTIONS

② **Billy Bob's Texas.** The renowned honky-tonk has been a cattle barn,
★ airplane factory, and department store. It's now home to live music,
eating, drinking, shopping, playing, and live bull riding. Daytime's
probably the best time to visit if you've got children in tow; nighttime is much rowdier (⇨ *Nightlife*). ⊠*2520 Rodeo Plaza, Stockyards*
☎*817/624–7117 or 817/589–1711* ⊕*www.billybobstexas.com* 📷*$1
until 8* PM; *nighttime varies according to days and events* ☉*Mon.–Sat.
11* AM*–2* AM, *Sun. noon–2* AM.

① **Stockyards Championship Rodeo.** Catch a live rodeo Friday and Saturday
nights to watch competitive bull riding, roping, barrel racing, and more.
The rodeo draws locals, families, tourists, couples on dates—all folks
who want to experience some cowboy culture. ⊠*121 E. Exchange
St., Stockyards* ☎*817/625–1025* ⊕*www.stockyardsrodeo.com* 📷*$15*
☉*Fri.–Sat. 8* PM.

ALSO WORTH SEEING

④ **Cowtown Cattlepen Maze.** Test your navigational skills and patience
in this human maze patterned after Old West cattlepens. For a fee
you can race against the clock or someone else, but it's free to stand
on the observation deck and watch others wander through the
wooden maze. ⊠*145 E. Exchange St., Stockyards* ☎*817/624–6666*

⊕*www.cowtowncattlepenmaze.com* ⊠*$5* ⊙*Weather permitting, Sun.–Thurs. 10–6, Fri. and Sat. 10–10.*

❺ Stockyards Station. Gathered under one roof is a sort of Western-style mall, with restaurants, shops, and benches for resting your boots. If shopping's your game, look for souvenirs, Western wear, specialty foods, jewelry, art, and Western music. If you're hungry, you're bound to find something you'll like among the barbecue, burger, and Mexican food options. ⊠*130 E. Exchange St., Stockyards* ☎*817/625–9715* ⊕*www.stockyardsstation.com* ⊠*Free* ⊙*Daily 10–7.*

❸ Texas Cowboy Hall of Fame. Embrace the rodeo and Western culture at this newer museum. Exhibits share details and gear from members of the hall fame, such as country-and-western singer George Strait, world champion Ty Murray, and rancher and photographer Bob Moorhouse. The museum also houses 60 wagons and carriages and a tribute to legendary bootmaker John Justin. ⊠*128 E. Exchange St., Stockyards* ☎*817/626–7131* ⊕*www.texascowboyhalloffame.com* ⊠*$5* ⊙*Mon.–Thurs. 10–6, Fri. and Sat. 10–7, Sun. 11–5.*

EXPLORING THE GREATER DFW METROPLEX

ARLINGTON

New Cowboys Stadium. The Dallas Cowboys have called Irving home since 1971, but in 2009 they'll move west to their new Arlington home, a state-of-the-art stadium designed to seat about 80,000 (with flexibility for 10,000 more) near Rangers Ballpark. The giant stadium will feature a retractable roof that can open or close in 12 minutes and partially close to resemble the distinctive roof of the team's old Texas Stadium. The roof is supported by two arches that rise 320 feet above the field. Those arches also will hold in place the biggest wall of video screens in NFL history. The stadium will host the 2011 Super Bowl. ☎*972/785–5000* ⊕*www.dallascowboys.com.*

♺ Six Flags Over Texas. In the Metroplex, you can rely on a couple of things here in the summer: It's going to be hot, and if you've got kids, they're going to want to go to Six Flags Over Texas. No wonder. There are more than 50 rides plus musical shows, games of chance, and lots of food. You'll find lots of Warner Bros. and DC Comics tie-ins, such as Looney Tunes USA, where preschoolers can ride attractions sized just for them, and Gotham City, where thrillseekers can speed 70 mph on Mr. Freeze or soar through the air on Batman the Ride. If you're visiting in the summer, be aware that the park will be crowded and you will be hot. But your kids? They probably won't even notice. ⊠*2201 Road to Six Flags* ☎*817/640–8900* ⊕*www.sixflags.com* ⊠*$39.99* ⊙*Varies; call or check Web site for hours.*

Fodor'sChoice **Rangers Ballpark in Arlington.** You can root root root for the Rangers
★ (or a visiting team if you must) in this open-air, fan-friendly ballpark that opened in 1994. The ballpark is styled similar to the new-but-retro

Oriole Park at Camden Yards. It's designed to look old-fashioned, with redbrick and granite facade and a home-run porch in right field, but the amenities are thankfully modern. If you're not in town when the Rangers are, consider a tour of the park through admission to the Legends of the Game Museum, which celebrates America's pastime with famous players' gear, photos, and artifacts. ⊠ *1000 Ballpark Way* ☎ *817/273–5222* ⊕ *www.rangers.mlb.com* ✉ *Legends of the Game Museum, including tour, $12.*

IRVING

About 200,000 residents live in this Dallas suburb, home to the Dallas Cowboys since 1971. The city is about to lose the NFL team to Arlington, though, forcing Irving to consider what to do with all the vacant space that will be created when the Cowboys move out of Texas Stadium. Irving isn't completely defined by football, though. The city claims business district Las Colinas, home to many corporate headquarters and the photogenic Mustangs of Las Colinas, nine giant bronze horses galloping through a fountain. Each spring brings the EDS Byron Nelson Championship golf tournament to the Four Seasons Resort and Club.

GRAPEVINE

Grapevine offers the small-town, friendly feel of Main Street and the over-the-top, flashy shopping and entertainment options at Grapevine Mills Mall and a couple of larger-than-life resort-style hotels. You can also rely on the town north of Dallas/Fort Worth International to throw a great festival—more than a dozen each year, including GrapeFest, which celebrates Texas wines and the city's wine industry.

Grapevine Vintage Railroad. Catch a ride on this line to the Fort Worth Stockyards and back. The railroad uses either a steam engine or a diesel engine on the 90-minute one-way trip. Once in the Stockyards, you have about two hours for exploring—enough time for a quick meal and stroll through the Western sites. Train leaves Grapevine at 1 PM. ⊠ *709 S. Main St.* ☎ *817/410–3123* ⊕ *www.grapevinesteamrailroad. com* ✉ *$20 (round-trip)* ⊙ *Feb.–Mar., Fri.–Sun.; Apr.–Aug., Thurs.–Sun.; Sept.–Dec., Fri.–Sun.*

Historic Downtown Grapevine. Shops and restaurants fill the restored brick buildings in this area that evokes a slower-paced era in Texas. It's easy to spend half a day or more exploring the boutiques, sampling fresh pastries, and catching a performance at the Palace Arts Theatre Center. ⊠ *S. Main St. at E. Texas St.* ⊕ *www.downtowngrapevinetexas.com.*

MESQUITE

Just 12.5 mi east of Dallas, this suburb has been called the Rodeo Capital of Texas. Each year some 300,000 fans pack it in at the **Mesquite Championship Rodeo** over the course of the April-to-September season.

Ross Perot: Big Business, Texas Style

Texas might have more millionaires than steers these days, but billionaire tycoons are still rare enough, and none but H. Ross Perot ever spent a fortune caring for and trying to free Vietnam POWs, sprang employees from Iran's toughest jail, founded a political party, and attracted 19 million votes for president. Perot, who hails from Texarkana but made Dallas his home, captured more of the popular vote in 1992 than any other third-party candidate in history.

He ran again in 1996, but by then the air had gone out of the populist balloon. The campaigns might seem audacious, but it was the rescue of two Electronic Data Systems (EDS) staffers from a Tehran prison that cemented his reputation as a man who moves to his own beat. Perot's money is self-made, generated by the success of his two companies, EDS, which he sold to General Motors, and Perot Systems, now run by Ross Jr.

—Lisa Miller

5

The action inside the arena includes riders atop bucking broncos and bulls, barrel races, steer wrestling, a kiddie calf scramble, mutton busting (for those 4 and younger), and, on the tamer side, pony rides and a petting zoo.

ELSEWHERE IN THE METROPLEX

About 40 minutes north of Downtown Dallas lies one of the city's most enduring landmarks, **Southfork Ranch** (✉ *3700 Hogge Rd., Parker* ☎*972/442–7800* ⊕*www.southforkranch.com* ☎*$9.50*). Built in 1970, the ranch became one of the city's best-known symbols after the TV show *Dallas* premiered in 1978. You can tour the mansion, have lunch at Miss Ellie's Deli, and try to remember who shot J. R. Unless you're a diehard fan of the show or are already in the Plano area, it's probably not worth the drive or expense.

SHOPPING

DALLAS SHOPPING

DOWNTOWN DALLAS

MALLS AND DEPARTMENT STORES

★ The original **Neiman Marcus** (✉*1618 Main St., Downtown Dallas* ☎*214/741–6911*) is a huge Dallas draw and has been since 1907. Skip the elevator and take the escalator to each level to appreciate the whimsical decor and surprising displays of art. Each floor is a distinct experience, all the way up to the sixth floor, where you can dine with ladies (and men) who lunch at Zodiac or get your hair done in the salon. On the way out, stop at the first-floor coffee bar for an affordable treat.

UPTOWN

Young professionals congregate at **West Village** (✉*3699 McKinney Ave., Uptown* 🌐*www.westvil.com*), a mixed-use development with apartments, restaurants, bars, an art-house movie theater, and retailers such as Ralph Lauren, the Paul Frank Store, and Tommy Bahama. Grab a seat outside Starbucks, Taco Diner, or Paciugo for some excellent people-watching.

DID YOU KNOW?

The Dallas–Fort Worth area has more shopping centers per capita than any other city in America. It is home to the original Neiman Marcus as well as Highland Park Village, said to be the oldest shopping center in the country.

NORTH DALLAS

MALLS AND DEPARTMENT STORES

Fodor'sChoice ★ The **Galleria** (✉*13355 Noel Rd., at the Dallas North Tollway, North Dallas* ☎*972/702–7100* 🌐*www.dallasgalleria.com*), with more than 200 retailers and anchor stores Macy's, Nordstrom, and Saks Fifth Avenue, is one of Dallas's best-known malls. Specialty shops include Tiffany & Co., Versace, Lucky Brand Jeans, and Spanish clothier Zara. A soft-structure play area on the third level near Saks (strategically placed near children's specialty shops) is a great place to let little ones (42 inches and shorter) burn off some energy. The bottom level features an ice-skating rink. Just outside the enclosed mall, but still on the Galleria grounds, is the American Girl Boutique and Bistro. Girls and their moms delight in shopping and dining in the cheerfully decorated space dedicated to the American Girl line of dolls and accessories.

NorthPark Center (✉*8687 N. Central Expressway, at Northwest Hwy., Preston Hollow* ☎*214/361–6345* 🌐*www.northparkcenter.com*), developed as the nation's first indoor mall by art collector Ray Nasher, has world-class art on its walls and sculptures in its hallways. Retail outposts include Neiman Marcus, Barneys New York, Bottega Veneta, Oscar de la Renta, Michael Kors, and Salvatore Ferragamo. Elevated features include a gorgeously landscaped greenspace, an indoor duck and turtle pond, and the twice-yearly Fashion at the Park runway shows. December is the best and busiest time to visit—the train exhibit delights children and adults alike, puppets and humans perform throughout the mall, and the building is decked out in tasteful holiday finery.

You'll find well-known high-end retailers like Jimmy Choo, Harry Winston, Tory Burch, St. John, Chanel, and Hermès at **Highland Park Village** (✉*Mockingbird La. at Preston Rd., Highland Park* ☎*214/559–2740* 🌐*www.hpvillage.com*), touted as one of the first planned shopping centers in America.

FORT WORTH SHOPPING

STOCKYARDS

WESTERN WEAR

If you can't leave Cowtown without a cowboy hat or a pair of Justin boots, head to the **Stockyards,** where there are several good Western

Mary Kay Ash: Selling Beauty in a Pink Cadillac

Nothing says Texas like big hair and big makeup, and Mary Kay Ash knew just how to help the women with the big makeup.

The Hot Wells, Texas, native learned how to sell early on, but tired of losing out to men, she went her own way, first as an author and then as a business owner. She turned $5,000 into a business that, by the time of her death in 2001, was selling $2 billion worth of products each year.

Today more than 1.7 million consultants sell Mary Kay products, and a good many of them drive the signature pink Cadillacs that top-sellers earn. The company's headquarters are in Dallas.

Named Texas Woman of the Century in 1999 by the Texas Women's Chamber of Commerce, Ash said her company was guided by the principle, "God first, family second, career third."

—Lisa Miller

wear outlets. **Maverick Fine Western Wear** (⊠ *100 E. Exchange Ave., Stockyards* ☎ *817/626–1129*) has high-end hats, boots, jeans, jewelry, and home decor. **Fincher's White Front** (⊠ *115 E. Exchange Ave., Stockyards* ☎ *817/624–7302*) sells affordable souvenirs as well as practical ranch clothes. The **General Store** (⊠ *101 N. Exchange Ave., Stockyards* ☎ *817/625–4061*) has T-shirts, postcards, Texas-made foods, longhorns to hang on your wall, and pint-size boots. A great place for boots, ready-to-wear or custom-made, is **M. L. Leddy's Boot and Saddlery** (⊠ *2455 N. Main St., Stockyards* ☎ *817/624–3149*).

DFW METROPLEX SHOPPING

GRAPEVINE

MALLS AND DEPARTMENT STORES

Shopaholics shouldn't miss **Grapevine Mills Mall** (⊠ *3000 Grapevine Mills Pkwy., Grapevine* ☎ *972/724–4900* ⊕ *www.grapevinemills. com*), with more than 1.5 million square feet of discount shopping. Families can spend an entire day here, watching movies, playing video games, shopping for bargains, and eating at restaurants like the Rainforest Cafe. If full-price Neiman Marcus isn't in your budget, check out Last Call, the local retailer's discount store. Hello Kitty fans take note: The area's only licensed Sanrio shop is here, too.

SPORTS & THE OUTDOORS

PARKS & RECREATIONAL AREAS

Katy Trail. The scenic 3.5-mi Katy Trail follows the former route of the Missouri-Kansas-Texas Railroad. The tracks were abandoned in the 1980s, and today the area is urban parkland. The trail provides a scenic oasis from nearby development, and there's a sense of community

Nolan Ryan: Throwing Heat

Nolan Ryan never won a Cy Young Award, his win-loss ratio was so-so, and he walked more batters than anybody, but he gets my vote for best pitcher ever. He piled up some better statistics over the years—27-year career, 5,714 strikeouts, seven no-hitters, 3.19 lifetime ERA, eight-time All Star, near-unanimous vote for the Hall of Fame—but it was his attitude that won me over.

I liked Ryan from his first day in an Astros uniform. He worked hard every game, and for most of his nine seasons in Houston he didn't have much to work with.

As an athlete, Ryan was Texas personified, wasn't he? He went out with all guns blazing, every game. He threw so hard and fast it made batters cuss and umpires duck. Even at age 60, he was still throwing 85 mph. And then there was that 1993 incident that Robin Ventura would love to forget. Ventura got hit by a pitch and charged the mound, where Ryan turned him from a White Soxer into a bobby soxer.

In 1988, Ryan got a raw deal from Astros owner John McMullen and headed to the Texas Rangers to finish his playing career. Twenty years later, in February 2008, the Rangers snatched him away from the Astros again. A Dallas Morning News article about his new position hinted at why I'm still a Nolan Ryan fan: "Barely five minutes into his re-introductory news conference Wednesday afternoon, it became clear that new Rangers president Nolan Ryan cared little about the pomp and circumstance of the position, but rather he simply wanted to get down to business."

He still throws hard and fast.

–Lisa Miller

among the active neighbors who bike and walk on the paths. There are a few benches along the trail in case you need to rest; parking is free at the American Airlines Center when events are not taking place ⊠ *Trail endpoints: American Airlines Center (2500 Victory Ave.) to the south; Knox St. and Abbott Ave., west of Central Expressway, to the north.* ☎ *214/303–1180* ⊕ *www.katytraildallas.org.*

White Rock Lake Park. Before Dallas was so big (read: before central air-conditioning), families would flock to White Rock to fish, swim, go boating, and picnic. Swimming's not allowed anymore, but folks still head to the lake to walk, run, bike, fish, go birding, and go boating (small motors are allowed). A 9.3-mi trail loops the lake, offering beautiful views of the water, stately homes, and Downtown Dallas to the southwest. ⊠ *8300 E. Lawther Dr., East Dallas* ⊕ *www.whiterocklake.org.* On the shore of the lake is the **Bath House Cultural Center** (⊠ *521 E. Lawther Dr.* ☎ *214/670–8749*). The restored 1930 building serves as a community center and hosts art exhibits and theater, music, and dance productions, and houses a small lake museum. The annual Run the Rock marathon in December circles the lake. A nearby bicycle shop, **Bike Mart** (⊠ *9040 Garland Rd.* ☎ *214/321–0705*), rents bikes and helmets for $21.75 a day.

SPECTATOR SPORTS

BASEBALL

The **Texas Rangers** (✉ *1000 Ballpark Way, Arlington* ☎ *972/726–4377* ⊕ *texas.rangers.mlb.com*) haven't made it to the World Series yet, but the club does have a rich history of beloved players including Nolan Ryan (now the club's president), Jim Sundberg, Oddibe McDowell, Ferguson Jenkins, Charlie Hough, and Juan Gonzalez. The team plays at the beautiful Rangers Ballpark in Arlington, one of the most pleasant parks in the majors.

BASKETBALL

When the **Dallas Mavericks** (✉ *2500 Victory Ave., Victory Park, Dallas* ☎ *214/222–3687* ⊕ *www.nba.com/mavericks*) are hot, game nights at the American Airlines Center are electric. The Western Conference team, owned by the fiery Mark Cuban, is still chasing its first championship (they came close in 2006, but fell to the Miami Heat in the NBA Finals).

FOOTBALL

It's impossible to exaggerate the passion fans feel for their **Dallas Cowboys** (✉ *2401 E. Airport Freeway, Irving* ☎ *972/438–7676* ⊕ *www.dallascowboys.com*). You can feel the love at Texas Stadium through 2008, and at the new stadium in Arlington beginning in 2009.

HOCKEY

There isn't much naturally occurring ice in Big D, but the city learned to be a hockey town when the **Dallas Stars** (✉ *2500 Victory Ave., Victory Park, Dallas* ☎ *214/222–3687* ⊕ *http://stars.nhl.com*) moved here from Minnesota. Die-hard fans were rewarded with the Stanley Cup in 1999.

SOCCER

FC Dallas (✉ *6000 Main St., Frisco* ☎ *214/222–3687* ⊕ *web.mlsnet.com*) has represented the area in Major League Soccer since 1995 (they were first called the Dallas Burn). Their home field, Pizza Hut Park, seats up to 27,000 fans.

NIGHTLIFE & THE ARTS

Both Dallas and Fort Worth are home to world-class art and nature museums, concert halls, and lively bar and dining scenes.

Much of Dallas bar life swirls around lower and upper Greenville Avenue, north of Downtown. Other hot spots include Uptown, especially along McKinney Avenue, Victory Park, anchored by American Airlines Center, and Deep Ellum, just east of Downtown. Fort Worth's scene is mostly Downtown and in the Stockyards.

The best way to sample the local culture is to check the nightlife and entertainment listings in the local newspapers or alternative weeklies, free at many restaurants and hotels. GuideLive.com, a Dallas Morning News site, offers daily suggestions. It's also wise to talk to a concierge, who can tell you about the best place to catch a late-night meal, movie, or a drink.

DALLAS ARTS

THEATER

The city's highest-profile theater performances are from the **Dallas Theater Center** (☎214/522–8499 ⊕ *www.dallastheatercenter.org*), at the **Kalita Humphreys Theatre** (✉ *3636 Turtle Creek Blvd.*), the only theater designed by Frank Lloyd Wright. The **Majestic Theatre** (✉ *1925 Elm St., Downtown Dallas* ☎214/880–0137 ⊕ *www.liveatthemajestic.com*), a beautifully restored 1920s vaudeville house and movie palace, hosts various performance groups.

MUSIC & CONCERTS

The biggest touring musical acts set up stage at **American Airlines Center** (✉ *2500 Victory Ave., Victory Park* ☎214/222–3687 ⊕ *www.americanairlinescenter.com*), designed by David M. Schwarz. The arena, home to the NBA's Dallas Mavericks and the NHL's Dallas Stars, is the centerpiece of burgeoning Victory Park, an area filled with tony restaurants, clubs, and shops. Tours are available at 10:30 AM Monday, Wednesday, and Friday when there are no scheduled events. The top performing-arts attraction in Dallas is whatever's on at the **Morton H. Meyerson Symphony Center** *(⇨ Arts District in What to See)*, where the **Dallas Symphony Orchestra** (☎214/692–0203 ⊕ *www.dallassymphony.com*) plays. **Superpages.com Center** (✉ *1818 1st Ave., Fair Park* ☎214/421–1111), formerly Smirnoff Music Centre, is the outdoor site of most of the big summer tours. Reserved seats are stadium-style chairs; general admission puts you on the lawn. No outside food or drink is allowed.

DALLAS NIGHTLIFE

BARS

Much of Dallas bar life swirls around lower and upper **Greenville Avenue,** north of Downtown. Locals love the view of Downtown Dallas from the outdoor patio at the Belmont Hotel's **BarBelmont** (✉ *901 Fort Worth Ave., Oak Cliff* ☎214/428–1555 ⊕ *www.belmontdallas.com*).

Ghostbar (✉ *2440 Victory Park Ln., Victory Park* ☎214/720–9909 ☉ *Closed Sun.*) is perched atop the trendy W Hotel in Victory Park. Expect to wait in line Friday and Saturday nights to ride the elevator up 33 flights to the modern, minimalist room that attracts Dallas's most beautiful people for drinking, mingling, dancing, and people-watching. A wall of windows and the outside decks offer spectacular nighttime views of Downtown.

Some say the vibe at **Lee Harvey's** (✉ *1807 Gould St., Cedars* ☎214/428–1555 ⊕ *www.leeharveys.com*) is more Austin than Dallas, and they mean it as a compliment. Regulars love gathering in the yard of this laid-back, unpretentious dive.

Mick's Bar (✉ *2825 Greenville Ave., Lower Greenville* ☎214/827–0039) is a sophisticated place to swill martinis and listen to live music.

Ozona Grill and Bar (✉ *4615 Greenville Ave., Upper Greenville* ☎ *214/265–9105*) has a large, tree-shaded patio where SMU students kick back after class.

Trinity Hall (✉ *5321 E. Mockingbird Ln., Mockingbird Station* ☎ *214/887–3600* ⊕ *www.trinityhall.tv*) draws crowds seeking an authentic Irish experience; there's a good beer selection and live music, and service is exceptional.

CLUBS & DANCE HALLS

Club Dada (✉ *2720 Elm St., Deep Ellum* ☎ *214/742–3400* ⊕ *www.clubdada.com*) hosts eccentric touring and local acts, including the Beatles cover band Hard Night's Day.

For country music and two-stepping, try **Cowboys Red River** (✉ *10310 W. Technology Blvd., Northwest Dallas* ☎ *214/352–1796* ⊕ *www.cowboysdancehall.com*).

Curtain Club and **Liquid Lounge** (✉ *2800 Main St., Deep Ellum* ☎ *214/742–6207* ⊕ *www.curtainclub.com*) are two distinct clubs inside a shared building. Live musical acts, including acoustic, rock, and country, play here Thursday through Sunday.

Gilley's Dallas (✉ *1135 S. Lamar St., South Side* ☎ *214/421–2021* ⊕ *www.gilleysdallas.com*) is a giant honky-tonk with live music (mostly country), a 10,000-square-foot dance floor, and a mechanical bull. It's just south of Downtown.

House of Blues (✉ *2200 N. Lamar St., Victory Park* ☎ *214/978–2583* ⊕ *www.hob.com/dallas*) is an intimate venue that hosts touring musical acts and serves dressed-up Southern-style fare.

Open in some form since 1977, **Poor David's Pub** (✉ *1313 S. Lamar, South Side* ☎ *214/565–1295* ⊕ *www.poordavidspub.com*) is one of Dallas's longest-running live-music venues. It's just south of Downtown.

FORT WORTH ARTS

THEATER

Casa Mañana Theater (✉ *3101 W. Lancaster Ave., Cultural District* ☎ *817/332–2272* ⊕ *www.casamanana.org*), a theater-in-the-round under one of Buckminster Fuller's first geodesic domes, is the site of the performing-arts organization's main-stage productions, as well as its popular Children's Playhouse series.

MUSIC & CONCERTS

Public tours are available of the majestic **Nancy Lee and Perry R. Bass Performance Hall** (✉ *555 Commerce St., at 4th St.* ☎ *817/212–4325* ⊕ *www.basshall.com*), which spans a full city block. Four resident companies call the world-class venue home: the **Fort Worth Symphony Orchestra** (☎ *817/665–6000* ⊕ *www.fwsymphony.org*), **Texas Ballet Theater** (☎ *817/763–0207* ⊕ *www.texasballettheater.org*), **Fort Worth Opera** (☎ *817/731–0833* ⊕ *www.fwopera.org*), and the **Van Cliburn Foundation** (☎ *817/738–6536* ⊕ *www.cliburn.org*). The **Casa Mañana Broadway at the Bass** (☎ *817/332–2272*) series is presented here as well.

FORT WORTH NIGHTLIFE

BARS

★ Cowtown's best Western-style watering hole may be the **White Elephant Saloon** (⊠*106 E. Exchange Ave., Stockyards* ☎*817/624–8273* ⊕*www.whiteelephantsaloon.com*), a legendary Wild West bar with live country music seven nights a week. **8.0** (⊠*111 E. 3rd St., Downtown Fort Worth* ☎*817/336–0880* ⊕*www.eightobar.com*; locals say "eight-oh") is one of the more popular gathering spots in Sundance Square. If the college scene is your scene, try **The Library** (⊠*611 Houston St., Downtown Fort Worth* ☎*817/885–8201* ⊕*www.librarybars. com/fortworth/*), a TCU favorite.

CLUBS & DANCE HALLS

Fodor'sChoice Visiting Fort Worth and not seeing **Billy Bob's Texas** (⊠*2520 Rodeo Plaza,*
★ *Stockyards* ☎*817/624–7117 or 817/589–1711* ⊕*www.billybobstexas. com*) isn't quite as bad as going to Paris and skipping the Eiffel Tower— but it's close. Built in an old cattle-pen building, the world's largest honky-tonk is a vast place—the almost 3 acres of indoor space include several bars, pool tables, a Western store, an arcade, a huge dance floor (in lieu of a disco ball, there's a spinning rhinestone-studded saddle), a stage that draws some of country's top acts, and a bull-riding ring (contests are usually held on Friday and Saturday nights). **City Streets** (⊠*425 Commerce St., Sundance Sq.* ☎*817/335–5400* ⊕*www.citystreetsfort worth.com*), in Sundance Square, rolls four clubs into one, including a karaoke room and a techno hip-hop dance floor.

WHERE TO EAT

Dining in DFW is a beloved hobby, and pockets of great restaurants are spread all over the area. If you'd like to start a lively conversation with locals, ask about their favorite spot for Tex-Mex, barbecue, or pizza. You're unlikely to reach consensus but likely to learn a lot.

In Dallas you'll find plenty of restaurants in the West End Historic District. The area is easy to walk around, but it doesn't claim the best dining options. If you're up for more adventure, walk a bit north of the West End to Victory Park. Or move up McKinney Avenue, through the Uptown neighborhoods. When McKinney hits Knox Street, you've arrived at another restaurant-rich area that spreads east and west. From Knox, head east until the street becomes Henderson Avenue. You'll pass even more restaurants and will eventually dead-end into Greenville Avenue. Head north and you'll be in yet another restaurant-wealthy neighborhood—all within 7 mi. And that's just one sliver of Dallas.

In Fort Worth, restaurants and nightclubs are grouped around Sundance Square (bounded by Houston, Commerce, 2nd, and 3rd streets) and the Stockyards National Historic District, west of the Cultural District.

WHERE SHOULD I DINE IN DALLAS & FORT WORTH?

	Neighborhood Vibe	Pros	Cons
Downtown Dallas	Downtown covers a lot of ground—from the tourist-friendly West End to the underground tunnels that cater to the 9-to-5 crowd. There is no shortage of options, especially during the day.	Wide variety in restaurant styles and prices; many museums, shops, bars, and other attractions within walking distance; emerging sense of community.	Some areas don't feel safe, especially at night; decent inexpensive options difficult to find at night and on weekends.
Victory Park	The newest district in Dallas offers high-end, high-concept entertainment and dining. The crowd tends to be trendy and glitzy.	Multipurpose entertainment district with plenty of nighttime options; area feels secure, even at night.	High-profile restaurants are also expensive; some among the crowd here personify pretension; not family friendly.
Uptown Dallas	Residents, many of them young professional singles, have moved into this area in the past decade, creating demand for high-quality restaurants and nightlife.	Excellent variety of quality restaurants; vibrant nightlife; many sections are pedestrian friendly; quick, free transportation via trolley.	One-way streets and lack of parking can be vexing; party atmosphere doesn't mix well with children.
Downtown Fort Worth	You'll experience the warmth of a small town even while surrounded by business towers and the people who work in them.	Friendly people; palpable sense of pride; easy to navigate by car or foot; plentiful parking (some free).	Area is small, limiting options; panhandlers aren't shy about approaching strangers.
The Stockyards	Tourists flock here for a feel of the Old West and a taste of cowboy culture. There's nothing pretentious for miles around.	Area has activities and options to fill an entire day; fun Western theme; family friendly; laid-back vibe.	Despite the tourists flocking to the area, some restaurants don't put forth their best efforts; cowboy food lacks much innovation.

Dress codes are practically nonexistent—even the Rosewood Mansion on Turtle Creek dropped its jacket-required dress code in 2007. Some restaurants are encouraging longer stays (and higher bills) by offering and promoting more options—come for drinks in the bar, stay for dinner, and linger after in the bar or separate lounge area. Many higher-end restaurants don't serve lunch and are closed on Sunday and/or Monday.

WHAT IT COSTS					
	¢	$	$$	$$$	$$$$
RESTAURANTS	under $8	$8–$12	$13–$20	$21–$30	over $30

Restaurant prices are per person for a main course at dinner.

BEST BETS FOR DALLAS/FORT WORTH DINING

With thousands of restaurants in Big D and Cowtown, how will you decide where to eat in the Metroplex? We've selected some of our favorite restaurants by price, cuisine, and experience in the Best Bets lists below. In the first column, Fodor's Choice designations represent the "best of the best" in every price category. You can also find specific details about each of these restaurants (and many more) in the full reviews listed alphabetically later in this section.

Fodor'sChoice

★

Bijoux, $$$$, Inwood Village

Fearing's, $$$$, Uptown

Lola, $$$–$$$$, Uptown

The Lonesome Dove Western Bistro, $$$–$$$$, Fort Worth Stockyards

Mansion Restaurant, $$$–$$$$, Turtle Creek

Nove Italiano, $$–$$$, Victory Park

By Price

$

AllGood Cafe, Deep Ellum

Angelo's Barbecue, Fort Worth Cultural District

Avila's, Uptown/Medical District

Café Brazil, Deep Ellum

Dream Cafe, Uptown

$$

Bread Winners Cafe and Bakery, Uptown

Gloria's, Lower Greenville

RJ Mexican Cuisine, West End

Zodiac, Downtown Dallas

$$$

Lavendou, Far North Dallas

Saint-Emilion, Fort Worth Cultural District

Tillman's Roadhouse, Bishop Arts

$$$$

French Room, Downtown Dallas

Stephan Pyles, Arts District

Trader Vic's, Mockingbird Station

York Street, Lakewood

By Cuisine

TEX-MEX

Avila's, ¢–$, Uptown/Medical District

Joe T. Garcia's, $, Stockyards

La Calle Doce, $–$$, Oak Cliff

Mia's Tex-Mex Restaurant, $–$$, Uptown

Monica's Aca y Alla, $–$$, Deep Ellum

STEAKHOUSE

Bob's Steak & Chop House, $$$–$$$$, Oak Lawn

Del Frisco's, $$$–$$$$, Far North Dallas

Nick & Sam's, $$$–$$$$, Uptown

Pappas Bros. Steakhouse, $$$$, Northwest Dallas

By Experience

QUAINT & COZY

Lavendou, $$–$$$, Far North Dallas

Lola, $$$–$$$$, Uptown

The Grape, $$–$$$, Lower Greenville

DINING AL FRESCO

Bread Winners Cafe and Bakery, $–$$, Uptown

Gloria's, $–$$, Lower Greenville

Joe T. Garcia's, $, Stockyards

Mansion Restaurant, $$$–$$$$, Turtle Creek

DOWNTOWN DALLAS RESTAURANTS

DOWNTOWN DALLAS

AMERICAN
$$$–$$$$

✕ **Dakota's.** Marble tables, dark wood accents, French doors, and an Italian marble floor create a sleek look in this underground restaurant, accessible by elevator. (If you're driving, you can use the complimentary valet service outside the elevator.) The granite outdoor patio, with lunch and dinner seatings, has a five-tier waterfall. By day you'll join the Downtown business crowd; at night the restaurant takes on a more romantic, candelit feel. The menu relies heavily on dry-aged steaks and seafood. The bone-in 16-ounce fillet is a popular choice. Steaks are à la carte; side dishes include creamed spinach, jumbo onion rings, and baked potatoes. ✉ *600 N. Akard St., Downtown Dallas* ☎ *214/740–4001* ☐ *AE, D, DC, MC, V* ⊘ *Closed Sun. No lunch Sat.–Sun.*

FRENCH
$$$$

✕ **French Room.** Housed in the Beaux-Arts Adolphus Hotel, Dallas's finest old hotel (dating from 1912), this elegant restaurant serves such French-inspired classics as spiced duck breast with seared foie gras in bigarade sauce, venison loin with pineapple confit and cauliflower puree, and soufflés. The highly skilled service staff is gracious and warm. The formal dining room is layered with gorgeous murals and rich textures. The French Room is an excellent choice for an extraordinary occasion. Jeans and tennis shoes are prohibited. ✉ *1321 Commerce St., Downtown Dallas* ☎ *214/742–8200 Jacket required* ☐ *AE, D, DC, MC, V* ⊘ *Closed Sun. and Mon. No lunch.*

NEW
AMERICAN
$$$–$$$$

✕ **Nana.** High atop the Hilton Anatole Hotel, this formal restaurant is a popular choice for a romantic dinner. The nighttime view of Downtown Dallas is breathtaking. The chef plays with the menu based on the freshest products available. Look for elaborate and beautiful creations such as slow-roasted veal with prawns, bananas, and a Thai peanut sauce, or seared venison loin with carrot puree, figs, and pears. Steak lovers will admire the 45-day aged grilled prime rib eye. There's entertainment in the lounge nightly. ✉ *2201 Stemmons Fwy., Downtown Dallas* ☎ *214/761–7470* ☐ *AE, D, DC, MC, V* ⊘ *No lunch.*

CONTINENTAL
$$

✕ **Zodiac.** After shopping at the original Neiman Marcus, head to the store's top floor for lunch at the classic Zodiac, where your meal begins with a cup of hot chicken consommé and a voluminous, eggy popover served with strawberry butter. For a real throwback, order the mandarin orange soufflé, served with chicken salad and fresh fruit. Modern compositions include jerk-spiced snapper salad and seared salmon served with vegetable risotto. Models drift through the dining room, showing off designer outfits (all for sale). The waitstaff unobtrusively anticipates diners' needs and treats everyone as if they're big spenders. ✉ *1618 Main St., Downtown Dallas* ☎ *214/573–5800* ☐ *AE* ⊘ *Closed Sun. No dinner.*

VICTORY PARK

ITALIAN
$$–$$$$
Fodor's Choice
★

✕ **Nove Italiano.** There's no question that Nove is a Las Vegas concept, with its oversized dining room filled with custom furniture, a wall of lights and more than 2,400 bottles of Italian wine, and crystal chandeliers that change colors. It works well in Victory Park, Dallas's giant escape from reality. Nove serves generous portions of creative Italian

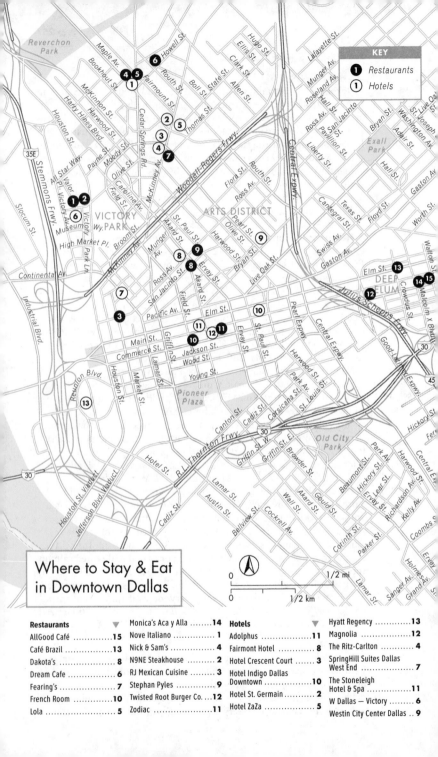

Where to Stay & Eat in Downtown Dallas

fare. Favorites include Nove Spaghetti, prepared in a corner of the dining room on busy nights. The pasta (some strands flavored and colored with squid ink) is surrounded by chunks of lobster, shrimp, calamari, and more. Consider sharing it and an entrée, such as a 20-ounce T-bone steak or fennel-crusted salmon. Knockout starters include Italian-style sashimi and a gorgeous platter of cured meats surrounded by anchovy-stuffed peppers, flatbread, cheese, and spreading sauces. ✉ *3090 Olive St., Victory Park* ☎ *214/720–9903* ▤ *AE, MC, V* ✆ *Closed Sun. and Mon. No lunch.*

STEAK
$$$–$$$$

✕ **N9NE Steakhouse.** With its giant mirrored columns, stark and sleek furnishings, and active bar scene, N9NE feels more like a nightclub than a steak house. At the center of the room a round Champagne and caviar bar is a great perch for people-watching. The kitchen stays busy turning out filets, rib eyes, lobster, a $25 Kobe beef burger, and sides like creamed spinach, potato gnocchi, and onion rings. Other choices include platters of chilled shellfish, tuna tartare, and onion soup. For dessert, try the s'mores: you get a tiny fire, marshmallows and skewers, and graham crackers drizzled with chocolate sauce—the preparation is up to you. ✉ *3090 Olive St., Ste. 110, Victory Park* ☎ *214/720–9901* ▤ *AE, MC, V* ✆ *Closed Sun. No lunch.*

DEEP ELLUM

AMERICAN
¢–$$

✕ **AllGood Cafe.** It doesn't get much more laid back in Dallas than the AllGood Cafe, which doubles as a live-music venue on weekends. Local and Texas music is a big deal here, and tunes take precedence over decor. The kitchen turns out breakfast standards like omelets, giant pancakes, and *migas* (Mexican-style scrambled eggs), until 3 PM. The lunch and dinner menus include just-right chicken-fried steak and the spiciest, most filling version of King Ranch Chicken (a layered, gooey mess of corn tortillas, chicken, peppers, cheese, beans, and more) in town. Giant windows allow a great view of the street life of Deep Ellum, and there's a little room for outdoor seating. ✉ *2934 Main St., Deep Ellum* ☎ *214/742–5362* ▤ *AE, D, MC, V* ✆ *No dinner Sun. and Mon.*

ECLECTIC
¢–$
☾

✕ **Café Brazil.** The eccentric menu here draws eccentric diners all hours of the day. Locals appreciate the bottomless cups of coffee (with several choices at a self-serve bar), extensive omelet and crepe offerings, Tex-Mex inspired entrées, and decadent baked goods. Standouts include crepes stuffed with chicken, spinach, and mushrooms, and French toast covered with fruit, raspberry sauce, and crème anglaise. Breakfast is served all the time, and they're open 24 hours on weekends. ✉ *2815 Elm St., Deep Ellum* ☎ *214/747–2730* ▤ *AE, D, DC, MC, V.*

MEXICAN
$–$$

✕ **Monica's Aca y Alla.** Everyday get-togethers feel like celebrations at this Deep Ellum favorite, which serves great food at inexpensive prices. Try the carne adobo (beef strips with a red salsa), Mexican lasagna, or Greene pasta (named for the owner). You can also find more standard Tex-Mex dishes, such as enchilada combination plates, served with sides of rice and refried beans. A live Latin jazz band plays on weekends. ✉ *2914 Main St., Deep Ellum* ☎ *214/748–7140* ▤ *AE, DC, MC, V* ✆ *No dinner Mon.*

AMERICAN
¢–$

✕ **Twisted Root Burger Co.** The chefs here have culinary school degrees, and they're proud to turn out what some consider to be the best burgers in town. Ingredients are gathered from nearby growers and farmers whenever possible. The menu always includes the basics, half-pound Angus, buffalo, turkey, and veggie burgers. Look for rotating specials, such as a blue cheese and jalapeño burger and a burger topped with green chilies, pepper-jack cheese, and guacamole. Even the ice cream is handmade; it's the base ingredient for adults-only milk shakes spiked with liqueurs. ✉*2615 Commerce St., Deep Ellum* ☎*214/741–7668* ☾*No dinner Sun.–Wed.*

WEST END

MEXICAN
$–$$$

✕ **RJ Mexican Cuisine.** The food here is more Mex than Tex, but you'll still find chips and salsa (red and green) and beans and rice, though both are considerably dressier than usual. Try anything made with corn *masa*, including *gorditas de carne deshebrada* (sturdy pastry pockets stuffed with chunks of stewed beef, tomatoes, and onions) and *tamale de puerco en chile rojo* (two giant pork tamales). The squash-blossom soup is creamy; every spoonful yields fresh vegetables. The burnt-orange dining room is warm and cozy, and the patio is a great place for West End people-watching. ✉*1701 N. Market St., Ste. 102, West End* ☎*214/744–1420* ⊟*AE, D, DC, MC, V.*

ARTS DISTRICT

SOUTHWESTERN
$$$–$$$$

✕ **Stephan Pyles.** Local foodies were thrilled when Southwestern cuisine pioneer Stephan Pyles opened this Arts District restaurant in 2005. Pyles stays true to his roots while layering in global influences, including Spanish, Middle Eastern, and Mediterranean flavors. Crowds flock here for lunch to enjoy poblano-asiago soup, grilled beef tenderloin salad, and the lobster salad club. At dinner, specialties include coriander-cured rack of lamb, bone-in cowboy rib eye, and creative ceviches. Chocolate fans shouldn't pass up the heaven and hell cake. ✉*1807 Ross Ave., Ste. 200, Arts District* ☎*214/580–7000* ᗧ*Reservation essential* ⊟*AE, D, DC, MC, V* ☾*Closed Sun. No lunch Sat.*

GREATER DALLAS RESTAURANTS

UPTOWN

NEW
AMERICAN
$$–$$$$

✕ **Abacus.** This high-profile restaurant fits the "everything's bigger in Texas" image. The interior is as spectacular as it is warm. The menu, which changes frequently, depending on the best seasonal options, melds Southwestern and Asian cuisines, resulting in creations like lobster shooters flavored with red chili and sake. People come back for the sushi. ✉*4511 McKinney Ave., Uptown* ☎*214/559–3111* ᗧ*Reservations essential* ⊟*AE, D, DC, MC, V* ☾*Closed Sun. No lunch.*

TEX-MEX
¢–$$

✕ **Avila's.** This quintessential family-run Tex-Mex joint in an old home dishes up fresh versions of all the tried-and-true favorites, including cheese enchiladas, brisket tacos, and gorditas, and rice and refried beans. It attracts a loyal crowd that relishes the quick, personable service. ✉*4714 Maple Ave., Uptown/Medical District* ☎*214/520–2700* ⊟*AE, D, DC, MC, V* ☾*Closed Sun.*

ECLECTIC
$–$$$

✕**Bread Winners Cafe and Bakery.** The in-house bakery at this café turns out fresh breads and pastries. Regulars love the raspberry–chipotle chicken sandwich for lunch; the buttermilk pan-fried chicken breast is a good choice for dinner. Sunday brunch is popular with the young professionals who live nearby. The large, popular patio offers an excellent view of foot traffic. ⊠*3301 McKinney Ave., Uptown* ☎*214/754–4940* ▤*AE, D, DC, MC, V* ☉*No dinner Mon.*

ECLECTIC
$–$$
☾

✕**Dream Cafe.** The healthy, organic menu at this laid-back restaurant blends Mediterranean-style cuisine with flavors from the American Southwest. Fabulous breakfast options include cloud cakes (ricotta pancakes with fresh strawberries and crème fraîche) and migas (Mexican-style scrambled eggs). If the weather's nice, ask to be seated on the spacious back patio, where you'll likely spot children playing on the restaurant's lawn and fort. ⊠*2800 Routh St., Uptown* ☎*214/954–0486* ▤*AE, D, DC, MC, V.*

NEW
AMERICAN
$$$$
Fodor'sChoice
★

✕**Fearing's.** Dallas celebrity chef Dean Fearing has been winning over new fans with his namesake restaurant in the Ritz-Carlton with three graciously designed rooms: friendly, bustling Dean's Kitchen, the more formal Gallery, and an airy glassed pavilion. Fearing's creations hint at his Southwestern roots, but rely more on his adventurous spirit and relationships with regional and global producers. The maple-marinated buffalo tenderloin is pleasantly sweet, nestled near jalapeño grits and a butternut squash taquito. Every plate reveals a similar layering of flavors, colors, and textures, such as cod atop hijiki rice, stacked with tempura-fried herbs and surrounded by a complex miso-clam broth. For dessert, butterscotch pudding and whipped cream are served next to hot apple fritters and a scoop of praline ice cream. ⊠*2121 McKinney Ave.,* ☎*214/922–4848* ⚄*Reservations essential* ▤*AE, D, DC, MC, V.*

LATIN-
AMERICAN
$–$$$

✕**La Duni Latin Cafe.** Like a culinary tour of Latin America, La Duni's showcases vibrant flavors from Mexico, Central America, and South America, with occasional side trips to Cuba. Citrus-sparked specialty drinks set the mood for roasted chicken napped with a sauce of Champagne and tart oranges or *carne asada*—beef marinated in lime juice and grilled, all accompanied by caramelized plantains, black beans, and rice. Desserts include the *muy rico* (very rich) *cuatro leches* (four milks) cake or chocolate-hazelnut Nutella cake. ⊠*4620 McKinney Ave., Uptown* ☎*214/520–7300* ▤*AE, D, DC, MC, V* ☉*Closed Mon.*

NEW
AMERICAN
$$$–$$$$
Fodor'sChoice
★

✕**Lola.** The tables in this ivy-covered cottage are spread throughout several small rooms decorated with dark wood and rich wall treatments. Look for creations with layered flavors, such as seared foie gras with brioche and caramelized rhubarb, handmade cannelloni stuffed with green pea and ricotta puree, lamb stew with roasted vegetables, and warm chocolate cake served with whipped cream and pistachios. An adjoining tasting room has a 10-course meal, served over two or three hours, for $69. ⊠*2917 Fairmount St., Uptown* ☎*214/855–0700* ▤*AE, D, DC, MC, V* ☉*No lunch. Closed Sun. and Mon.*

TEX-MEX
$–$$

✕**Mia's Tex-Mex Restaurant.** If you're lucky enough to find a parking space in Mia's tiny lot, consider it a sign that you were destined to dine in this colorfully decorated restaurant with legendary status. Diehard

5

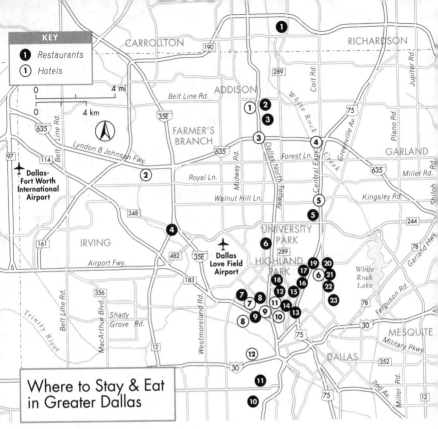

Where to Stay & Eat in Greater Dallas

fans have been scarfing down brisket tacos and cheese enchiladas here for more than two decades. Other favorites include pinto-bean soup, tamales, and beef chile rellenos. There's nothing relaxing about the experience—the walls are filled with a crazy mix of Christmas lights, roosters, piñatas, paper flags, and other treasures, and the waitstaff hustles to keep the crowds moving. ⊠ *4322 Lemmon Ave., Uptown* ☎ *214/526–1020* ⊟ *AE, DC, MC, V* ⊗ *Closed Sun.*

STEAK ✕ **Nick & Sam's.** Expect a cozy and sexy vibe in this Uptown steak
$$$–$$$$ house. A grand piano sits in the dining room, providing background music nightly beginning at 7. Specialties include Chateaubriand for two, served with forest mushrooms, carmelized onion, and foie gras; the center-cut beef is carved tableside. The steak options are plentiful—10-ounce filet mignon, prime bone-in 16-ounce fillet, prime 22-ounce Cowboy cut (a French-cut bone-in rib eye). Lighter appetites can opt for seafood specialties such as sesame-crusted ahi tuna, diver scallops, or tortilla-crusted Atlantic salmon. ⊠ *3008 Maple Ave., Uptown* ☎ *214/871–7444* ⊟ *AE, D, DC, MC, V* ⊗ *No lunch.*

MEDITERRANEAN ✕ **Ziziki's.** The Mediterranean menu here features sophisticated versions
$$–$$$ of Greek classics like spanakopita, dolmades, moussaka, and souvlaki. The lamb salad is a favorite among regulars. The wine list also garners acclaim. Open-air dining is available on the patio. A smaller dining room can be reserved for special events. ⊠ *4514 Travis St., Suite 122, Uptown* ☎ *214/521–2233* ⊟ *AE, MC, V.*

INWOOD VILLAGE

FRENCH **Bijoux.** Dining at Bijoux is a spectacular experience. A stunning chan-
$$$$ delier in the center of the intimate, serene dining room commands
Fodor$Choice attention. More brilliant, though, are the courses created by chef Scott
★ Gottlich, who excels at marrying memorable flavors and textures into artful plates. The menu changes according to season and availability of ingredients, but has included seared prawns with Spanish chorizo, forest mushrooms, and carmelized onions; rabbit wrapped in bacon with fava beans and tomato fondue; and truffled risotto. Most choose the three- or five-course meal from the all-prix-fixe menu; the nine-course tasting menu ($95 per person, $145 with wine pairings) is an extraordinary treat. ⊠ *5450 W. Lovers La., Suite 225, Inwood Village* ☎ *214/350–6100* ⌕ *Reservations essential* ⊟ *AE, DC, MC, V* ⊗ *Closed Sun. No lunch.*

OAK LAWN

STEAK ✕ **Bob's Steak & Chop House.** Women do dine at Bob's, but it's really a
$$$–$$$$ man's world, with its dark-wood paneling, dim lighting, televisions in every dining room, and boisterous conversation. Fans rave about the steak, aged for four weeks and served in manly portions—22-ounce bone-in ribeye, 22-ounce bone-in strip, 28-ounce porterhouse. Rack of lamb is also popular. Entrées are served with a giant glazed carrot and the potato of your choice. Additional sides include creamed corn and creamed spinach. ⊠ *4300 Lemmon Ave., Oak Lawn* ☎ *214/528–9446* ⊟ *AE, D, DC, MC, V* ⊗ *Closed Sun. No lunch.*

5

NORTH DALLAS

SOUTH-
WESTERN
$–$$

✕**Blue Mesa Grill.** Southwestern and Tex-Mex flavors rule at this lively restaurant across a busy street from the fashionable NorthPark Center. Try painted desert soup (a harmonious blend of corn chowder and black-bean soup in one bowl), beef tenderloin tacos, or goat-cheese enchiladas. The bar is a popular spot for professionals most weeknights. There's a children's menu, and brunch is served on Sunday. ⊠*7700 W. Northwest Hwy., North Dallas* ☎*214/378–8686* ▤*AE, D, DC, MC, V.*

STEAK
$$$–$$$$

✕**Del Frisco's.** Regulars have been returning to this Far North Dallas (about 12 mi from Downtown) steak house for almost 20 years. The crowd is primarily button-down corporate during the week and couples and groups out for fun on the weekend. Popular appetizers include baked crab cakes and shrimp cocktail. The real draw is the prime beef, cut off the loin for each order; the filet mignon is another big seller. ⊠*5251 Spring Valley Rd., Far North Dallas* ☎*972/490–9000* ▤*AE, D, DC, MC, V* ☉*No lunch.*

FRENCH
$$–$$$

✕**Lavendou.** Escape the nearby strip malls and traffic and spend some down time in this French-styled bistro in Far North Dallas, where folks come as they are. The dining room is decorated with Provençal blues and yellows and floral prints. Try the cassoulet, roasted chicken or duck, or one of many seafood specialties. Leave room for dessert; the menu is almost as extensive as the entrée choices. ⊠*19009 Preston Rd., No. 200, Far North Dallas* ☎*972/248–1911* ▤*AE, D, DC, MC, V* ☉*Closed Sun. No lunch Sat.*

ITALIAN
$$–$$$$

✕**Mi Piaci.** Plan on a romantic evening at this candlelit restaurant. A moon roof that opens to the sky, huge windows that overlook a patio with a garden and duck pond, and cream-colored archways lend a Tuscan charm to this restaurant. Risottos and homemade pastas are made daily on the premises, and fish and seafood dishes like calamari and Dover sole are delicately prepared with flavorful southern Italian sauces. Osso buco served with saffron risotto is a customer favorite. ⊠*14854 Montfort Dr., North Dallas* ☎*972/934–8424* ▤*AE, D, DC, MC, V* ☉*No lunch Sat.–Sun.*

STEAK
$$$$

✕**Pappas Bros. Steakhouse.** Loyal Pappas fans love the contemporary atmosphere here and the cut and flavor of the dry-aged beef. The dining room is less masculine and better lit than typical steak houses but still feels a bit formal and special. The filet mignon, offered in three weights, is the most popular cut of beef, and au gratin potatoes and creamed spinach are popular side dishes. The wine selection is legendary, as are the cigars offered—60 sizes and brands. ⊠*10477 Lombardy La., Northwest Dallas* ☎*214/366–2000* ⌁*Reservations essential* ▤*AE, D, DC, MC, V* ☉*Closed Sun.*

LOWER GREENVILLE

LATIN-
AMERICAN
$–$$

✕**Gloria's.** The food here is Mexican and Salvadoran, with plentiful servings and intriguing desserts; you must try the chocolate flan. Order the Super Special for an excellent overview of Salvadoran treats; the plate features yuca, plantain, and pupusa. Gloria's also has more varieties of margarita than you might have thought possible. The restaurant's interior reflects its Latin American flavor, and it can get loud at peak times. You can sit outside for air and eccentric people-watching. ✉*3715 Greenville Ave., Lower Greenville* ☎*214/874–0088* ▤*AE, D, DC, MC, V.*

NEW
AMERICAN
$$–$$$

✕**The Grape.** This unpretentious urban bistro is known for the romantic intimacy of the indoor dining areas and the laid-back charm of its sidewalk tables. The menu, which changes every few weeks based on the availability of regional ingredients, begins with Grape's signature creamy mushroom soup. The menu might offer a marinated hanger steak served with fries and a watercress salad, crispy duck breast with a rice pilaf, or baked black cod with smoked ham, clams, and a white-wine garlic broth. Regulars rave about the crispy flatbread and the fried calamari (not on the menu, so be sure to ask). Brunch is served Sunday. ✉*2808 Greenville Ave., Lower Greenville* ☎*214/828–1981* ▤*AE, D, MC, V* ⊘*No lunch.*

AMERICAN
¢–$
☾

✕**Snuffer's.** Burgers and fries are served in huge portions at this SMU student favorite. Don't miss the cheddar fries, a generous serving of fries covered with melted cheddar, jalapeños, chives, and bacon. The kitchen stays open until midnight during the week and until 2 AM Friday and Saturday. ✉*3526 Greenville Ave., Lower Greenville* ☎*214/826–6850* ▤*AE, D, DC, MC, V.*

OAK CLIFF

TEX-MEX
$–$$$

✕**La Calle Doce.** The most mouthwatering *mariscos* (seafood) in Dallas, particularly the fish soup, keeps local customers coming back to this relatively undiscovered restaurant in the little blue house in the Oak Cliff neighborhood of Dallas. The daily lunch specials are a bargain. ✉*415 W. 12th St., Oak Cliff* ☎*214/941–4304* ▤*AE, D, DC, MC, V.*

TURTLE CREEK

NEW
AMERICAN
$$$–$$$$
Fodor's Choice
★

✕**Mansion Restaurant.** Executive chef John Tesar joined Dallas's venerable restaurant in 2006 and led an extensive redesign of the beloved dining room and menu. Simple flavors are layered to produce complex results, such as slow-braised short ribs, poached lobster with risotto, and porcini-crusted filet mignon. Count on dining with DFW's most moneyed folks, who relish the legendary service and exquisite surroundings. The interior design successfully marries contemporary furniture, fixtures, and artwork with the grand, historic feel of the Italian Renaissance–style residence built in 1925. Lunch is less expensive but still fashionable. Views of the landscaped grounds are lovely from the veranda. The outdoor seating is also open at night, lending a more casual feel to one of Dallas's most revered institutions. ✉*2821 Turtle Creek Blvd., Turtle Creek* ☎*214/559–2100* ▤*AE, D, DC, MC, V.*

MEDICAL DISTRICT

BARBECUE
¢–$

✕**Sonny Bryan's Smokehouse.** The original location has been dishing up smoky brisket and fall-off-the-bone pork ribs from the same ramshackle digs since 1958, attracting fans ranging from President George W. Bush to director Steven Spielberg. Locals know to get there early—when Sonny's is out of barbecue, you're out of luck. The restaurant is a good option for folks who are near the medical district. ✉*2202 Inwood Rd., Medical District* ☎*214/357–7120* ▤*AE, D, DC, MC, V* ⊘*Closed Sun. No dinner.*

BISHOP ARTS

AMERICAN
$–$$$

✗**Tillman's Roadhouse.** Don't let the word "roadhouse" fool you—upscale food is served in a quirky, hip Texas setting at Tillman's. Contemporary music plays (sometimes too loudly) while old black-and-white movies are projected on a wall near the bar. Fussy chandeliers hang over sturdy, wood tables; look closely at the animal trophies—they're actually carved from wood. Meals begin with hot roasted peanuts and popcorn coated in truffle oil and black pepper. Be sure to try the moist cornbread, heavy with cheese, peppers, and corn; the thick, gravity-defying burger; and the chocolate birthday cake (even if it's not your special day). ⊠*324 W. 7th St., Bishop Arts* ☎*214/942–0988* ▤*AE, D, MC, V* ⊙*Closed Sun. and Mon.*

MOCKINGBIRD STATION

HAWAIIAN
$$–$$$$

✗**Trader Vic's.** No detail has been overlooked in this Polynesian-style restaurant, lavishly re-opened in 2007 after almost two decades of disrepair. The dining room and bar are exotic hideaways, decked out with intricate wood carvings, thatching, and other symbols of island life. The tropical theme is reflected on the menu, which is heavy on fish (such as Chinese-style steamed Chilean sea bass), Asian specialties (such as wonton soup with prawn and pork dumplings), and fruity drinks with silly names (Potted Parrot, Rum Giggle) served in clever vessels. ⊠*5330 E. Mockingbird La., Mockingbird Station* ☎*214/823–0600* ▤*AE, D, DC, MC, V* ⊙*No lunch.*

LAKEWOOD

NEW
AMERICAN
$$$–$$$$
★

✗**York Street.** Meals begin with a complimentary tot of dry sherry and salted almonds; where you venture from there is up to you, but offerings like Summerfield Farms veal chops, lavender-rubbed quail, and Casco Bay skate throughout the journey will be memorable. The menu changes daily, based on season and availability. The wine list gives poetic descriptions, and sleek pewter chairs and black-and-white photography lend the small dining room an urban feel. ⊠*6047 Lewis St., Lakewood* ☎*214/826–0968* ⌖*Reservations essential* ▤*AE, MC, V* ⊙*Closed Sun. and Mon. No lunch.*

DOWNTOWN FORT WORTH RESTAURANTS

SUNDANCE SQUARE

SOUTH-
WESTERN
$$–$$$$

✗**Reata.** Diners get a modern spin on the Old West at this Fort Worth favorite. The rustic dining room is decorated with saddles, animal trophies, and artistic cacti. Specialties here include stacked enchiladas, tenderloin tacos, and bone-in rib-eye steak. Portions are oversized; an order of the precariously stacked onion rings—thick, tall, and evenly fried—could easily feed four. ⊠*310 Houston St., Sundance Square* ☎*817/336–1009* ▤*AE, D, DC, MC, V.*

FORT WORTH STOCKYARDS RESTAURANTS

STEAK
$$–$$$$

✗**Cattlemen's Fort Worth Steak House.** Steaks are charcoal-grilled at the front of the room, and you can pick out your own cut of meat. Those steaks are the biggest draw, but the menu also includes seafood,

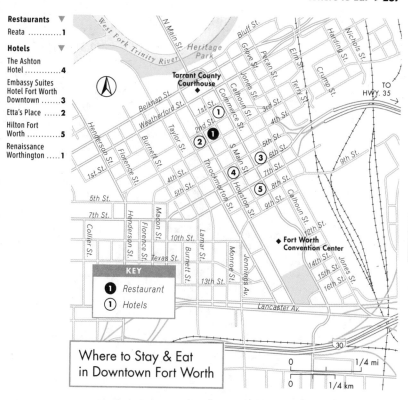

KEY

1 *Restaurant*

① *Hotels*

**Where to Stay & Eat
in Downtown Fort Worth**

0 ————— 1/4 mi

0 ————— 1/4 km

chicken-fried steak, fried chicken, and grilled pork chops. The trusty, basic fare is served in a laid-back, unpretentious setting reminiscent of the 1950s. ✉ *2458 N. Main St., Stockyards* ☎ *817/624–3945* ▤ *AE, D, DC, MC, V.*

TEX-MEX ✕ **Joe T. Garcia's.** This is the ultimate Tex-Mex joint. There's usually a

$ wait for tables, but with seating for more than 1,000 in the maze of din-

★ ing rooms and patio areas, the line moves quickly. Dinner is limited to two choices: an enchilada-and-taco combo plate or fajitas. Lunch offers a more traditional menu, and on weekends there are Mexican breakfast specials, including purported hangover-cure *menudo* (stew made with tripe, hominy, onions, and chili). Folks from all over the area drive to Fort Worth to take out-of-town guests to this lively restaurant about three blocks from the Stockyards—and often hope they'll be seated in one of many relaxing outdoor spots. ✉ *2201 N. Commerce St., Stockyards* ☎ *817/626–4356* ▤ *No credit cards.*

SOUTH- ✕ **The Lonesome Dove Western Bistro.** If you can get to the Stockyards,

WESTERN you shouldn't miss dining at Lonesome Dove, where sophisticated and

$$–$$$$ exotic food is served in a setting of brick walls, rustic hardwoods, and a

FodorsChoice pressed-tin ceiling. Chef Tim Love's creations include kangaroo carpac-

★ cio nachos with avocado relish, chili-rubbed foie-gras brûlée, and grilled

5

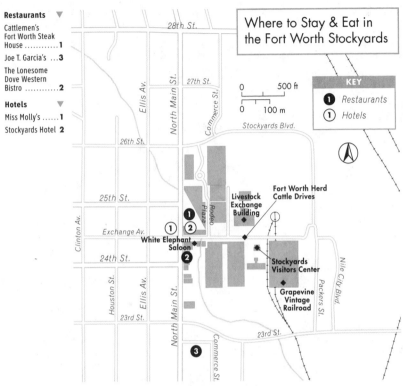

New Zealand red deer chops served with truffle mac and cheese. Less adventurous options include, at lunch, meatloaf with barbecue sauce, chipotle mashed potatoes, and sautéed spinach and a grilled ham-and-cheese sandwich with tomato-basil soup. ⊠*2406 N. Main St., Stockyards* ☎*817/740–8810* ▭*AE, D, MC, V* ☙*Closed Sun. and Mon.*

FORT WORTH CULTURAL DISTRICT RESTAURANTS

FRENCH ✕**Saint-Emilion.** Though it doesn't look like much from the outside,
$$$ this is one of Tarrant County's best restaurants, with a legendary
★ crispy roast duck, lamb, fresh fish, excellent daily specials, and a long wine list. The prix-fixe option ($39.95 for four courses) makes dinner an affordable taste of French country cuisine. The intimate French-inspired dining room holds just 16 tables. ⊠*3617 W. 7th St., Cultural District* ☎*817/737–2781* ▭*AE, D, DC, MC, V* ☙*Closed Sun. and Mon. No lunch.*

BARBECUE ✕**Angelo's Barbecue.** A Fort Worth institution since 1958, Angelo's is
¢–$ famous for succulent smoked ribs, so tender that the meat falls off the bone, and for the stuffed bear that guards the front door. The small parking lot, filled with minivans, European sedans, pickup trucks and motorcycles, reflects the diverse customer base that returns for those ribs, schooners of beer, traditional sides (mustard potato salad, West-

ern-style beans, cole slaw), and other meats, including turkey, sliced or chopped beef, and sausage. Arrive early, as they've been known to run out of ribs well before closing. ✉*2533 White Settlement Rd., Cultural District* ☎*817/332–0357* ✍*Reservations not accepted* ⊟*MC, V* ⊘*Closed Sun.*

GREATER FORT WORTH RESTAURANTS

SOUTHWEST FORT WORTH

MEDITERRANEAN
$$–$$$
✗**Bistro Louise.** People drive 30 mi from Dallas to dine on sautéed foie gras with potato-crusted salmon, tangerine-glazed pork loin, and the like. Wood-beam ceilings and flowered tablecloths add to the charming French setting of this neighborhood favorite. Executive chef and owner Louise Lamensdorf trained in Europe and delights in sharing Spanish, French, and Italian techniques with her devoted customers, who also call on her for catering and cooking classes. ✉*2900 S. Hulen St., Southwest Fort Worth* ☎*817/922–9244* ⊟*AE, D, DC, MC, V* ⊘*No dinner Sun. and Mon.*

WEST SIDE

AMERICAN
$$–$$$
✗**Cafe Aspen.** This cozy eatery is frequented by ladies who lunch and business brokers by day and romantic diners by night. Chicken enchiladas and chicken salad draw rave reviews at lunch. At dinner, look for chicken-fried lobster, beef tenderloin, and rib-eye steak. Dessert pastries are made in-house. ✉*6103 Camp Bowie Blvd., West Side* ☎*817/738–0838* ⊟*AE, D, DC, MC, V* ⊘*Closed Sun. No lunch Sat.*

AMERICAN
$–$$$
✗**Lucile's Stateside Bistro.** There's been a restaurant of some sort in this building since the 1930s; the original pressed-tin ceiling is still in place. The bistro attracts diners from the neighborhood as well as a lot of folks from horse shows and other events at Will Rogers Memorial Center, just 2 mi away. Known for its pasta, wood-roasted entrées, and chicken-fried steak, and weekend prime rib, the restaurant also has seven tables on a patio with umbrellas to ward off the Southwestern sun. Breakfast is available weekends. ✉*4700 Camp Bowie Blvd., West Side* ☎*817/738–4761* ⊟*AE, D, DC, MC, V.*

TEX-MEX
¢–$$
✗**Original Mexican Eats.** President Franklin D. Roosevelt dined here in the mid-1930s, according to lore, after the restaurant had already been open about a decade. One of the restaurant's most popular entrées honors FDR's visit with the Roosevelt special—a cheese enchilada smothered in chili gravy and onions, a tostada, and a crispy taco, a fine sampling of Tex-Mex cuisine. There's nothing fancy about the digs or the food here; both are sturdy, reliable, and continue to draw crowds. ✉*4713 Camp Bowie Blvd., West Side* ☎*817/738–6226* ⊟*AE, MC, V.*

WHERE TO STAY

The Dallas lodging scene has gotten swankier recently with the addition of high profile hotels, including the W, the Ritz-Carlton, and the Hotel Palomar. Still, most of the options are standard chains, the same you'll find across the country, with varying degrees of individuality and charm. There is no paucity of hotel rooms in Dallas, and you can

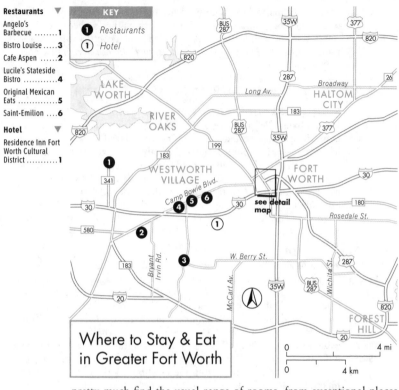

KEY
- **1** Restaurants
- (1) Hotel

Where to Stay & Eat in Greater Fort Worth

pretty much find the usual range of rooms, from exceptional places fit for a king or queen to less impressive quarters to those that barely pass muster. There are few hotels in low price ranges that are worthy of recommendation.

Downtown Fort Worth is where you'll find the city's financial core, most of its historic buildings, and Sundance Square. The Stockyards and adjacent Western-theme stores, restaurants, and hotels are a few miles north of Downtown, clustered around Main Street and Exchange Avenue.

WHAT IT COSTS					
	¢	$	$$	$$$	$$$$
HOTELS	under $50	$50–$100	$101–$150	$151–$200	over $200

Hotel prices are per night for two people in a standard double room in high season, excluding taxes and service charges. Hotel taxes in Dallas and Fort Worth are 15%.

DOWNTOWN DALLAS HOTELS

DOWNTOWN

$$$–$$$$ 🖼**Adolphus.** Beer baron Adolphus Busch created this Beaux-Arts building in Downtown Dallas in 1912, sparing nothing in the way of ornamentation. In the gracious lobby, rich fabrics, dark woods, elaborate floral arrangements, and intimate seating areas belie the hustle of the streets just outside. The romantic European-style rooms, filled with unique floral prints and Queen Anne–style furniture, have modern amenities. A courtesy van takes guests to Downtown and Uptown sites and NorthPark Mall. Book early to stay at the hotel during the annual Neiman Marcus Adolphus Children's Parade, which marches in front of hotel the first Saturday in December. **Pros:** Smooth service, unique furnishings, sense of history. **Cons:** Most attractions and shopping experiences require transportation. ✉*1321 Commerce St., Downtown Dallas* ☎*214/742–8200 or 800/221–9083* ⊕*www.hotel-adolphus.com* ⇆*422 rooms* ♿*In-room: kitchen (some), refrigerator, DVD, Wi-Fi. In-hotel: 3 restaurants, room service, bar, gym, laundry service, concierge, public Internet, parking (fee), no-smoking rooms* ▤*AE, D, DC, MC, V.*

$$$–$$$$ 🖼**Fairmont Hotel.** This 24-story hotel is in the middle of Downtown Dallas, at the heart of the city's arts district and near Uptown hot spots. The massive lobby has polished columns, elaborate chandeliers, and grand tapestries. The hotel was renovated in 2007, with rooms transformed with new floor coverings, beds and linens, and high-definition flat-screen televisions. Three floors have been reinvented as an exclusive boutique hotel within the hotel. Be sure to join the chain's loyalty program to avoid paying for Internet access. **Pros:** Proximity to attractions, refurbished interior. **Cons:** Lacks a sense of fun or whimsy. ✉*1717 N. Akard St., Downtown Dallas* ☎*214/720–2020* ⇆*545 rooms* ♿*In-room: safe, refrigerator, Wi-Fi. In-hotel: restaurant, room service, bar, pool, gym, laundry facilities, laundry service, concierge, executive floor, public Wi-Fi, parking (fee), some pets allowed, no-smoking rooms* ▤*AE, D, DC, MC, V.*

$–$$$$ 🖼**Hotel Indigo Dallas Downtown.** Conrad Hilton built this hotel in 1925; today the InterContinental property is a National Historic Landmark. The hotel is on the eastern edge of Downtown, next to the Universities Center at Dallas and within walking distance of the original Neiman Marcus and the Majestic Theatre. Common areas and guest rooms reflect the Indigo chain's emphasis on refreshment, with cheerful colors and beach accents. Complimentary transportation is provided within a 3-mi radius, an area that includes Music Hall at Fair Park. **Pros:** Good value for Downtown lodging; cheerful, accommodating staff. **Cons:** Surrounding neighborhood is somewhat sketchy, nearby dining options are limited. ✉*1933 Main St., Downtown Dallas* ☎*214/741–7700* ⊕*www.hotelindigo.com* ⇆*170 rooms* ♿*In-room: refrigerator (some), Wi-Fi. In-hotel: restaurant, room service, bar, gym, laundry service, concierge, public Wi-Fi, parking (fee), some pets allowed, no-smoking rooms* ▤*AE, D, DC, MC, V.*

$$$$ 🖼**Hyatt Regency.** The 50-story Reunion Tower, a Dallas skyline icon, is adjacent to this 18-story hotel, which is popular with business and

WHERE SHOULD I STAY IN DALLAS & FORT WORTH?

	Neighborhood Vibe	Pros	Cons
Downtown Dallas	If you have business in the vicinity, or want to sample the evolving nightlife scene, Downtown Dallas is a good bet with plenty of options ranging from hip and trendy to staid and serious.	Within walking distance of light-rail stops and many major attractions; close to convention facilities.	Not especially family-friendly; some areas don't feel safe after dark.
Uptown Dallas	Uptown's residents tend to be young and style conscious, enjoying countless bars and restaurants. The hotels in the area follow the same trend.	In the middle of a vibrant dining and nightlife scene; some unique and luxurious lodging options that don't feel cookie-cutter.	Pricey neighborhood; removed from many major attractions.
Downtown Fort Worth	There is no shortage of options in Downtown Fort Worth. The closer you stay to Sundance Square, the closer you'll be to revelry and the associated night-time noise.	Easy access to Sundance Square, dining, nightlife, and a few museums; pedestrian-friendly business district.	The Cultural District and Stockyards are too far away to walk; Downtown is vibrant but there's not enough to do here for days on end.
The Stockyards	You may feel as if you've stepped back in time when you stay in the Stockyards. You'll have plenty of tourist-friendly options and dining opportunities within walking distance.	Surrounded by Western-style attractions and nightlife scene; pedestrian-friendly area.	If you want to see the city's world-class art, you'll need transportation; noise at night may disturb light sleepers.
North Dallas	North Dallas is spread out, and so are the hotels. Most properties are near business districts or shopping areas, and most are not in pedestrian-friendly areas.	Some rooms are cheaper compared with Downtown and Uptown options; close to shopping and businesses.	Generic areas and properties; far removed from most major attractions; most neighborhoods are not conducive for walking.

convention travelers. (The tower is closed for renovations in 2008.) A permanent collection of photographs inside the hotel marks the city's history in the 1950s, '60s, and '70s. Since this is a chain, rooms are less personalized, but they are fitted with quality furnishing and linens. The hotel connects to Union Station, a hub with access to three train lines: Amtrak, Trinity Railway Express, and DART light-rail. **Pros:** Access to transportation, walking distance to Dallas Convention Center, kiosks for self-serve check-in and check-out. **Cons:** Nearby train noise, generic rooms, lack of personalized service. ⊠ *300 Reunion Blvd., Downtown Dallas* 📞 *214/651–1234* ⊕ *dallasregency.hyatt.com* 🛏 *1,122 rooms* ⚐ *In-room: Wi-Fi. In-hotel: 3 restaurants, room service, bar, pool,* *gym, laundry facilities, laundry service, concierge, executive floor, public Internet, public Wi-Fi, airport shuttle (fee), parking (fee), no-smoking rooms ⊟AE, D, DC, MC, V.*

$$-$$$$ ⊡**Magnolia.** When it opened in 1922, the 29-story Magnolia building was the tallest structure south of Washington, D.C. Today it is best known as the home of the red-neon Pegasus sign, installed atop the structure in 1934. (The current sign is a replica.) The building opened as a hotel in 1999, with tailored, oversized rooms that have an urban loft feel; the 129 suites have full kitchens. **Pros:** Relatively new property in Downtown, ideal for guests who want to try nearby clubs and restaurants, free nightly reception. **Cons:** Weekend nights can be noisy, most nearby shops and restaurants cater to weekday crowds and are closed weekends. ⊠*1401 Commerce St., Downtown Dallas* ☎*214/915–6500 or 888/915–1110* ⊕*www.magnoliahotels.com* ⟿*330 rooms* ⸝*In-room: kitchen (some), refrigerators (some), Ethernet, Wi-Fi. In-hotel: restaurant, room service, bar, gym, laundry facilities, laundry service, concierge, public Internet, airport shuttle, parking (fee), no-smoking rooms* ⊟*AE, D, MC, V* ⊌⦿*CP.*

$$$-$$$$ ⊡**Westin City Center Dallas.** This hotel's Downtown location offers business and leisure travelers plenty of options nearby or via the DART light-rail, which stops just outside. The 16-story hotel is part of the Plaza of the Americas complex, which has shops and restaurants that cater to the 9-to-5 crowd as well as an ice-skating rink. Rooms were renovated in 2006 and include the Westin-branded luxury linens. The lobby was updated in 2004 with earth tones and contemporary lines. **Pros:** Access to public transportation, quality bedding. **Cons:** Most restaurants and shops in connecting building are closed weekends, convoluted self-parking system. ⊠*650 N. Pearl St., Downtown Dallas* ☎*214/979–9000* ⊕*www.westin.com* ⟿*407 rooms* ⸝*In-room: safe, refrigerator, Ethernet, Wi-Fi. In-hotel: restaurant, room service, bar, gym, laundry service, concierge, executive floor, public Wi-Fi, parking (fee), some pets allowed, no-smoking rooms* ⊟*AE, D, DC, MC, V.*

THE WEST END

$$-$$$ ⊡**SpringHill Suites Dallas West End.** This all-suites property in one of the better lit and cleaner sections of Downtown is a pleasant option. There's nothing extraordinary about the standard rooms, but the location allows easy access to Victory Park and the Arts District as well as many of the Downtown office towers. Weekday guests are typically business travelers; weekends bring visitors interested in shows at the House of Blues or American Airlines Center. Walking to the convention center will take about 15 minutes—an unpleasant quarter of an hour during the heat of summer. **Pros:** Ideal location for Downtown, good value. **Cons:** Street noise may disturb some guests, inconsistent service from staff. ⊠*1907 N. Lamar St., West End* ☎*214/999–0500 or 888/287–9400* ⊕*www.marriott.com* ⟿*149 suites* ⸝*In-room: kitchen, refrigerator, Ethernet, Wi-Fi. In-hotel: room service, pool, gym, laundry facilities, laundry service, public Wi-Fi, parking (fee), no-smoking rooms* ⊟*AE, D, DC, MC, V* ⦿*CP.*

BEST BETS FOR DALLAS/FORT WORTH LODGING

Chain hotels, with the same linens, layouts, services, and design found in cities across the United States, dominate the Dallas/Fort Worth market. A few of those chain properties are superior, though, and some hotels offer first-class service, amenities, and special Texas charm. Here, we help you choose the very best place to lay your head.

Fodor's Choice ★

Adolphus, $$$–$$$$, Downtown Dallas

The Ashton, $$$$, Downtown Fort Worth

Four Seasons Resort and Club, $$$$, Irving

Rosewood Mansion on Turtle Creek, $$$–$$$$, Turtle Creek

The Ritz-Carlton, $$$$, Uptown

W Dallas–Victory, $$$$, Victory Park

By Price

$

Fairfield Inn Dallas Market Center, Medical District

Hotel Indigo, Downtown Dallas

$$

Belmont Hotel, North Oak Cliff

Embassy Suites–Dallas Love Field, Love Field

Magnolia, Downtown Dallas

$$$

Adolphus, Downtown Dallas

Ashton Hotel, Downtown Fort Worth

$$$$

Four Seasons Resort and Club, Irving

Rosewood Mansion on Turtle Creek, Turtle Creek

The Ritz-Carlton, Uptown

W Dallas–Victory, Victory Park

By Type

BOUTIQUE HOTEL

Hotel Palomar, $$$–$$$$, Mockingbird Station

Hotel St. Germain, $$$$, Uptown

Hotel ZaZa, $$$$, Uptown

Rosewood Mansion on Turtle Creek, $$$–$$$$, Turtle Creek

RESORT

Four Seasons Resort and Club, $$$$, Irving

Gaylord Texan Resort and Convention Center, $$$$, Grapevine

Great Wolf Lodge, $$$$, Grapevine

By Experience

FAMILY FRIENDLY

Four Seasons Resort and Club, $$$$, Irving

Great Wolf Lodge, $$$$, Grapevine

Omni Dallas Hotel at Park West, $–$$$, Far Northwest Dallas

GREAT VIEWS

Hilton Anatole, $$–$$$$, Northwest Dallas

The Ritz-Carlton, $$$$, Uptown

W Dallas–Victory, $$$$, Victory Park

HISTORIC

Adolphus, $$$–$$$$, Downtown Dallas

Hilton Fort Worth, $$–$$$$, Downtown Fort Worth

Stockyards Hotel, $$$–$$$$, Stockyards

Warwick Melrose Hotel, $$–$$$$, Uptown

VICTORY PARK

$$$$ **W Dallas–Victory.** The first hotel in Dallas's burgeoning Victory Park
Fodor'sChoice makes a dramatic statement, altering the Uptown skyline with a
★ 33-story tower topped with glowing blue light. The crowd here is
trend-conscious and pampered, and the decor is comfortable and minimalist—eggplant-colored walls, neutral bed linens, low-profile furniture. Look for some whimsical nods to the chain's first Texas setting,
including a curtain of cowboys, horses, and cows in the lobby. The W is
just steps from the American Airlines Center—home to the NBA's Dallas Mavericks and the NHL's Dallas Stars—and minutes from Downtown. **Pros:** Gracious service, proximity to American Airlines Center,
hip scene. **Cons:** Awkward room design that allows no privacy between
shower and bedroom, may be too trendy for conservative or traditional
travelers. ⊠*2440 Victory Park La., Victory Park* ☎*214/397–4100*
⊕*www.whotels.com* ⥾*252 rooms* ⌁*In-room: safe, DVD, Wi-Fi. In-
hotel: restaurant, room service, bars, pool, gym, spa, laundry service,
concierge, public Wi-Fi, airport shuttle (fee), parking (fee), some pets
allowed, no-smoking rooms* ▤*AE, D, DC, MC, V.*

GREATER DALLAS HOTELS

UPTOWN DALLAS

$$$$ ⊡ **Hotel Crescent Court.** The centerpiece of the Crescent Complex (which
includes office buildings, shops, and galleries), this hotel is on the edge
of Dallas's central business district and Uptown art scene. Each room
has French doors, a vanity, and down-feather love seat. Suites are
either one- or two-story, and may have spiral staircases and hardwood
floors. The rooms were renovated in 2007, taking on a contemporary
feel with neutral tones and receiving new luxury linens. **Pros:** Ideal
for the traveler who wants to feel pampered, near vibrant Uptown
scene. **Cons:** Expensive, some complain of pretentious or aloof service. ⊠*400 Crescent Ct., Uptown* ☎*214/871–3200 or 800/654–6541*
⊕*www.crescentcourt.com* ⥾*220 rooms* ⌁*In-room: safe, refrigerator
(some), DVD, VCR (upon request), Ethernet. In-hotel: 5 restaurants,
room service, bars, pool, gym, spa, laundry service, concierge, public
Internet, parking (fee), some pets allowed, no-smoking rooms* ▤*AE,
D, DC, MC, V.*

$$$$ ⊡ **Hotel St. Germain.** Built as a private residence in 1906, this tiny
★ boutique inn with white-glove service is one of the most romantic in
the city. The beautiful rooms are filled with antiques and collectibles;
each has a working fireplace. Three suites have Jacuzzi tubs. The dining room (closed Sunday and Monday) is known for its $85 prix-fixe
seven-course dinner. Guests can relax in a New Orleans–style courtyard. Vibrant Uptown, with dozens of dining and shopping options, is
within walking distance. **Pros:** Ideal for romantic getaway, proximity
to Uptown, personal service. **Cons:** Expensive, no children allowed.
⊠*2516 Maple Ave., Uptown* ☎*214/871–2516* ⊕*www.hotelstger-
main.com* ⥾*7 suites* ⌁*In-room: refrigerator, DVD, VCR, Wi-Fi. In-
hotel: restaurant, room service, no elevator, laundry service, concierge,*

public Wi-Fi, parking (no fee), some pets allowed, no children under 18, no-smoking rooms ⊟*AE, MC, V.*

$$$$ 🏨 **Hotel ZaZa.** The ceilings are high, the linens Italian, the pillows poufy, and the pampering nonstop. This Uptown boutique hotel is a luxurious oasis known for its 25 suites, each decorated around a theme: the Texas suite is accented with Austin stone, cowhide, and horns; the Metropolitan is sleek and chic; the East Indies displays exotic carved woods; and the Shag-a-delic takes you right back to the 1960s with beanbag chairs, beads, and shag carpet. **Pros:** Unique decor, near active dining and nightlife scene. **Cons:** Not comfortable for families, trendy scene may not appeal to traditional travelers. ⊠*2332 Leonard St., Uptown* ☎*214/468–8399 or 800/597–8399* ⊕*www.hotelzaza.com/dallas* 📮*152 rooms* ⚬*In-room: safe, Wi-Fi. In-hotel: 2 restaurants, room service, bars, pool, gym, spa, laundry service, executive floor, public Wi-Fi, parking (fee), some pets allowed, no-smoking rooms* ⊟*AE, D, DC, MC, V.*

$$$$
Fodor'sChoice
★
🏨 **The Ritz-Carlton.** Uptown was the logical choice for Dallas's latest luxury hotel, surrounded by high-dollar high-rise condos and other elite lodging options, dozens of fine restaurants, and upscale shopping. The hotel opened in mid-2007 and has sleek yet comfortable furnishings and awesome views of Downtown. Guest rooms include flat-panel HDTVs, high-end linens, and Bulgari bath products. The Ritz-Carlton recruited Dallas celebrity chef Dean Fearing to open his namesake restaurant at the hotel; the restaurant and its bar is a popular draw for Dallas's young, trendy, and moneyed. **Pros:** Proximity to Uptown entertainment, gracious service, luxurious accommodations. **Cons:** Too far from Downtown attractions to walk comfortably, expensive rates. ⊠*2121 McKinney Ave., Uptown* ☎*214/922–0200 or 800/542–8680* ⊕*www.ritzcarlton.com* 📮*218 rooms* ⚬*In-room: safe, DVD, Ethérnet, Wi-Fi. In-hotel: restaurant, room service, bar, pool, gym, spa, laundry service, concierge, executive floor, public Wi-Fi, parking (fee), some pets allowed, no-smoking rooms* ⊟*AE, D, DC, MC, V.*

$$$$ 🏨 **The Stoneleigh Hotel & Spa.** The re-imagined Stoneleigh Hotel & Spa, on fashionable Maple Avenue in the Uptown area of Dallas, embraces its 1920s roots with old-style Hollywood glamour. The legendary hotel reopened in March after a complete renovation, revealing modernized Art Deco details throughout the dramatic lobby, cozy bar, and generously sized rooms. The hotel's location at the edge of Uptown makes it an excellent choice for visitors who want to be close to restaurants, art galleries, and nightlife while escaping late-night noise and revelry. Guests seeking solace can also retreat to the luxury spa and chef David Bull's modern Italian restaurant, Bolla. **Pros:** Luxurious rooms and furnishings, sense of history combined with modern amenities. **Cons:** Transportation required to reach most major Dallas attractions. ⊠*2927 Maple Ave., Uptown* ☎*214/871–7111 or 800/921–8498* ⊕*http://stoneleighhotel. com* 📮*170 rooms* ⚬*In-room: safe, Wi-Fi. In-hotel: restaurant, room service, bar, gym, spa, laundry service, concierge, public Wi-Fi, parking (fee), no-smoking rooms* ⊟*AE, D, DC, MC, V.*

$$–$$$$ 🏨 **Warwick Melrose Hotel, Dallas.** Nestled near an active dining and nightlife neighborhood, this historic building houses a luxury hotel that emphasizes personal service and a residential experience. The spacious rooms have marble baths, dark-wood furniture, and deep rich colors; the 20 suites have four-poster beds. A courtesy SUV shuttles guests within a 3-mi radius of the hotel. The nearby nightlife scene is popular with gays and lesbians. **Pros:** Attentive service, unique architecture and furnishings. **Cons:** Transportation required to get most anywhere. ✉ *3015 Oak Lawn Ave., Uptown* ☎ *214/521–5151 or 800/521–7172* ⊕ *www.warwickmelrosedallas.com* ⬚ *184 rooms* ⬚ *In-room: safe, Ethernet, Wi-Fi. In-hotel: restaurant, room service, bar, gym, laundry service, concierge, public Internet, public Wi-Fi, parking (fee), some pets allowed, no-smoking rooms* ☰ *AE, D, DC, MC, V.*

NORTH DALLAS

$$–$$$$ ▦**Hilton Anatole.** Politicians, including George W. Bush and Colin Powell, have made this huge glass-and-chrome complex their home away from home. The rooms are standard, but the Anatole has seven bars, a nightclub, and a piano bar to keep you entertained. The public spaces feature a massive collection of fine Asian arts and antiques. The massive property tries to offer on-site everything a traveler needs—especially a business traveler. You'll need a car or hired transportation to take you to the nearby American Airlines Center, the hospital district, or Downtown. **Pros:** Multiple dining and activity options on-site, unique art, ample meeting space. **Cons:** Proximity to attractions still requires transportation, lack of intimate service. ✉ *2201 Stemmons Fwy., Northwest Dallas* ☎ *214/748–1200* ⊕ *www.wyndham.com* ⬚ *1,609 rooms* ⬚ *In-room: safe, Ethernet. In-hotel: 5 restaurants, room service, bars, tennis courts, pools, gym, spa, laundry service, concierge, executive floor, public Internet, public Wi-Fi, parking (fee), no-smoking rooms* ☰ *AE, D, MC, V.*

$–$$$$ ▦**Omni Dallas Hotel at Park West.** This hotel's spacious, modern rooms—renovated in 2006—have flat-screen TVs, quality bed linens, and are decorated with contemporary neutral tones. The landscaped grounds include a 12½-acre lake surrounded by a 10-km trail. The pool area is beautiful; poolside lunch service during the summer is a necessary extravagance. **Pros:** Family-friendly grounds, resort feel. **Cons:** If you want to do anything off-site, you must have transportation. ✉ *1590 L.B.J. Fwy., Far Northwest Dallas* ☎ *972/869–4300* ⬚ *337 rooms* ⬚ *In-room: Wi-Fi. In-hotel: restaurant, room service, bars, pool, gym, spa, laundry service, concierge, executive floor, public Wi-Fi, parking (no fee), some pets allowed, no-smoking rooms* ☰ *AE, D, DC, MC, V* ⊕ *www.omnihotels.com.*

$$$–$$$$ ▦**Renaissance Dallas Hotel.** A breathtaking chandelier graces the lobby of this Marriott property that attracts business folks during the week and leisure travelers and wedding parties on weekends. The curved building is a distinct landmark on I–35; it sort of resembles a giant tube of lipstick. The entire hotel was renovated in 2007. Ask for a room with a Downtown view. **Pros:** Renovated public spaces and guest rooms, heated outdoor pool. **Cons:** Area isn't pedestrian-friendly, you'll need transportation to reach anything off-site. ✉ *2222 Stemmons Fwy., Northwest Dallas* ☎ *214/631–2222* ⊕ *www.renaissance-hotels.com/dalbr* ⬚ *518 rooms* ⬚ *In-room: safe, refrigerator, VCR,*

Ethernet. In-hotel: 2 restaurants, room service, bar, pool, gym, laundry facilities, laundry service, concierge, executive floor, public Wi-Fi, parking (fee and no fee), some pets allowed, no-smoking rooms ▤AE, D, DC, MC, V.

$$–$$$$ ▥ **Westin Galleria Hotel.** This 20-story hotel has direct access to the sleek Galleria mall, which has an ice-skating rink, upscale dining, and more than 200 shops. The property was renovated in 2007 and early 2008, giving the guest rooms a contemporary look more in line with the mall. Rooms are light, with blond wood and white linens atop Westin's Heavenly Bed. The hotel sits at the busy intersection of the Dallas North Tollway and the LBJ Freeway. **Pros:** Access to shopping mall, central North Dallas location, ideal for families with children. **Cons:** If you want to leave the mall or its surrounding shopping centers, you'll need transportation. ⊠*13340 Dallas Pkwy., North Dallas* ☎*972/934–9494* ⊕*www.westin.com* ☞*432 rooms* ⌂*In-room: safe, Ethernet, Wi-Fi. In-hotel: 2 restaurants, room service, bar, pool, gym, children's programs (ages 3–12), laundry service, concierge, executive floor, public Wi-Fi, parking (fee and no fee), no smoking rooms ▤AE, D, DC, MC, V.*

$$–$$$$ ▥ **Westin Park Central.** This hotel, popular with business travelers, frequently hosts conferences. Guests can request a Westin Workout room with in-room equipment, including treadmills, stationary bicycles, and medicine balls. In-room spa services are also available. **Pros:** Caters to business travelers, access to the Telecom corridor, good value on weekends. **Cons:** Area isn't friendly for pedestrians, fee for Internet access. ⊠*12720 Merit Dr., North Dallas* ☎*972/385–3000* ⊕*www.westin.com* ☞*536 rooms* ⌂*In-room: safe, Ethernet, Wi-Fi. In-hotel: 2 restaurants, room service, bars, pool, gym, children's programs (ages 3–12), laundry service, concierge, executive floor, public Wi-Fi, parking (fee and no fee), some pets allowed, no-smoking rooms ▤AE, D, DC, MC, V.*

NORTH OAK CLIFF

$$–$$$ ▥ **Belmont Hotel.** Musicians, artists, and European travelers frequent the Belmont, a recently restored (2005) motel that first opened in 1946. The hotel embraces its history rather than glossing over it, with original tile in the bathrooms, smaller rooms that accommodate just one queen bed, and mid-century inspired furniture. Some rooms have screened-in porches; others face a peaceful garden landscaped with native plants. The buildings are on a cliff, and have stunning views of Downtown Dallas, especially at night. The hotel bar attracts a laid-back, artistic crowd, and the restaurant has become a neighborhood favorite. **Pros:** Unique Dallas experience, sense of history, enthusiastic service. **Cons:** Smaller rooms, surrounding neighborhood is transitional, few nearby retail options. ⊠*901 Fort Worth Ave., North Oak Cliff* ☎*214/393–2300 or 866/870–8010* ⊕*www.belmontdallas.com* ☞*68 rooms* ⌂*In-room: refrigerator (some), Ethernet. In-hotel: restaurant, room service, bars, pool, gym, no elevator, laundry service, public Wi-Fi, parking (no fee), some pets allowed, no-smoking rooms ▤AE, D, DC, MC, V.*

MEDICAL DISTRICT

$–$$ ⬚Fairfield Inn Dallas Market Center. You won't find many frills, but you should find a comfortable room and pleasant service. The hotel was renovated in 2005 and shares amenities with the connected Courtyard by Marriott at Market Center. Families enjoy the indoor pool. **Pros:** Good value, quick drive to Downtown. **Cons:** Some security and crime concerns in nearby neighborhood, noise from nearby highway. ⊠*2110 Market Center Blvd., Medical District* ☎*214/760–8800* ⊕*www.marriotthotels.com* ⤷*116 rooms* ⊘*In-room: Wi-Fi. In-hotel: room service, nighttime room service, laundry facilities, public Wi-Fi, parking (no fee), no-smoking rooms* ⊟*AE, D, DC, MC, V* ⦿|*CP.*

ADDISON

$$–$$$$ ⬚Hotel InterContinental. This North Dallas hotel, which was renovated in 2007, is about 2 mi from the Galleria and about 5 mi from the Shops at Willow Bend. Nearby Belt Line Road offers plenty of dining and nightlife options. Rooms have rich wood tones and subtle Texas accents. Some common areas still reflect the original glitzy chrome and marble accents of its '80s heyday. ⊠*15201 Dallas Pkwy., Addison* ☎*972/386–6000 or 800/386–1592* ⊕*www.interconti.com* ⤷*528 rooms* ⊘*In-room: Ethernet. In-hotel: restaurant, bar, tennis court, pool, gym, parking (no fee)* ⊟*AE, D, DC, MC, V.*

MOCKINGBIRD STATION

$$$$ Hotel Palomar. Once you step inside this hotel, you'll forget that you've just exited the busy, crowded Central Expressway. Lush green plants, subdued earth tones, and a fountain create a sense of calm. Rooms, decorated in white, cream, brown, and yellow, are equally relaxing, with Italian Frette bed linens, L'Occitane bath products—even a goldfish in a fishbowl upon request. The infinity-edge outdoor pool and adjacent Exhale spa round out the soothing experience. The location is convenient to the DART light-rail stop at Mockingbird Station, Southern Methodist University, Downtown Dallas, and Love Field airport. **Pros:** Relaxing getaway, beautiful common spaces, proximity to restaurants, movie theater, and SMU. **Cons:** Not a good option for children, service can be aloof. ⊠*5300 E. Mockingbird La., Mockingbird Station* ☎*214/520–7969* ⊕*www.hotelpalomar-dallas.com* ⤷*198 rooms* ⊘*In-room: safe, DVD, Wi-Fi. In-hotel: 2 restaurants, bars, pool, gym, spa, children's program (ages 3–12), laundry service, concierge, public Wi-Fi, parking (fee), some pets allowed, no-smoking rooms* ⊟*AE, D, DC, MC, V.*

TURTLE CREEK

$$$$ ⬚Rosewood Mansion on Turtle Creek. Opulent rooms are appointed with
★   fine linens, antiques, and original artwork, lending a unique residential feel to the hotel. Guests have complimentary use of the property's Lexus vehicles, and a house car can also ferry you to nearby destinations. Celebrities feel comfortable here, tucked away from the larger hotel districts. The service is legendary, as is the hotel restaurant *(⇨Mansion Restaurant, in Where to Eat)*. The bar is a popular gathering place for locals, guests, and celebrities. **Pros:** Attentive service, seclusion, luxurious accommodations.**Cons:** Expensive, transportation required for sightseeing and shopping. ⊠*2821 Turtle Creek Blvd., Turtle Creek*

☎214/559–2100 ⊕*www.mansiononturtlecreek.com* ⇦*143 rooms* △*In-room: safe, DVD, VCR, Ethernet. In-hotel: restaurant, room service, bar, pool, gym, laundry service, concierge, public Wi-Fi, parking (fee), some pets allowed, no-smoking rooms* ☰*AE, D, DC, MC, V.*

DOWNTOWN FORT WORTH HOTELS

$$$$ **The Ashton Hotel.** This small boutique hotel and its eponymous gour-
Fodor'sChoice   met restaurant occupy two renovated early-20th-century Downtown
★   buildings. Luxe Italian Frette linens and plush duvets dress the beds;
coffee is delivered to each room every morning, and cookies are left
during turn-down service. The Ashton is only one block from Sundance
Square entertainment and restaurants, two blocks from the stunning
Bass Performance Hall, and seven minutes' drive from Fort Worth's
Museum District. **Pros:** Unique experience in ideal location, more luxurious setting than nearby competitors, suitable for couples seeking
a romantic getaway. **Cons:** Not ideal for families. ⊠*610 Main St.,
Downtown Fort Worth* ☎*817/333–0322 or 866/327–4866* ⊕*www.
theashtonhotel.com* ☰*AE, D, DC, MC, V* ⇦*39 rooms* △*In-room:
safe, refrigerator, ethernet, Wi-Fi. In-hotel: restaurant, room service,
bar, gym, laundry service, concierge, public Wi-Fi, parking (fee), some
pets allowed, no-smoking rooms.*

$$$–$$$$ **Embassy Suites Hotel Fort Worth Downtown.** Bass Performance Hall
is across the street from this all-suites hotel opened in 2007. Guests
can easily walk to the Convention Center, Fort Worth Water Gardens,
and the shops and restaurants in Sundance Square. The hotel hosts
a two-hour guest reception each evening. All rooms include 32-inch
plasma HDTVs, refrigerators, and microwave ovens. **Pros:** Clean, mod-
ern common spaces and rooms, proximity to Downtown attractions,
accommodating for families. **Cons:** Cultural District and Stockyards
attractions too far to reach without transportation. ⊠*600 N. Com-
merce, Downtown Fort Worth* ☎*817/332–6900* ⊕*www.embassys-
uites.com* ⇦*156 suites* △*In-room: safe, refrigerator, Ethernet, Wi-Fi.
In-hotel: restaurant, room service, bar, pool, gym, laundry facilities,
laundry service, concierge, executive floor, public Wi-Fi, parking (fee),
no-smoking rooms* ☰*AE, D, MC, V* ⊚*BP.*

$$–$$$$ **Etta's Place.** This three-story B&B is named for Etta Place, the girlfriend of the Sundance Kid. It originally served as living quarters for
traveling artists who performed at Caravan of Dreams (now Reata
restaurant) at Sundance Square (which is just around the corner) during the 1980s. A handsome music room has a baby grand Steinway.
Smoking is not permitted. Some rooms have refrigerators. The hon-
eymoon suite has a Jacuzzi tub for two. **Pros:** Personal service, quiet
lodging in the middle of Downtown. **Cons:** Few big-hotel amenities,
front desk staffed just until 8 PM. ⊠*200 W. 3rd St., Downtown Fort
Worth* ☎*817/654–0267* ⊕*www.ettas-place.com* ⇦*10 rooms* △*In-
room: kitchen (some), refrigerator (some) DVD, VCR, Ethernet. In-
hotel: laundry facilities, laundry service, public Internet, parking (fee),
some pets allowed, no kids under 10, no-smoking rooms* ☰*AE, D,
DC, MC, V* ⊚*BP.*

$$–$$$$ 🏨**Hilton Fort Worth.** President John F. Kennedy and first lady Jacqueline Kennedy spent their last night together in this hotel, a national historic landmark. The property, which was renovated in 2006, is popular with business travelers; it's located near the Convention Center and Sundance Square. You'll be among families and tourists on weekends. **Pros:** Proximity to dining and nightlife, sense of history. **Cons:** Building's layout feels cramped, interior lacks unique style. ⊠ *815 Main St., Downtown Fort Worth* ☎*817/870–2100* ⊕*www.fortworth.hilton. com* ⟿*294 rooms* ⌂*In-room: Ethernet, Wi-Fi. In-hotel: 2 restaurants, room service, bars, gym, laundry service, concierge, executive floor, public Wi-Fi, parking (fee), no-smoking rooms* ⊟*AE, D, DC, MC, V.*

$$$$ 🏨**Renaissance Worthington.** This 12-story, white-concrete structure
★   stretches along two city blocks in the middle of Downtown Fort Worth near Sundance Square. The hotel has emerged from about three years of complete renovation. The Texas-sized lobby is outfitted in elegant reds and blues and establishes the upscale, slightly Western atmosphere found throughout the property. Rooms are outfitted with luxury linens, and many have excellent views of Downtown Fort Worth, just steps outside the massive entry. **Pros:** Excellent location, attentive service, quality furnishings. **Cons:** Expensive parking, lacks a sense of intimacy. ⊠*200 Main St., Sundance Square* ☎*817/870–1000 or 800/468–3571* ⊕*www.renaissancehotels.com* ⟿*504 rooms* ⌂*In-room: refrigerator (some), DVD (some), VCR (some), Ethernet. In-hotel: 2 restaurants, room service, bars, tennis courts, pool, gym, laundry facilities, laundry service, concierge, executive floor, public Wi-Fi, parking (fee), some pets allowed, no-smoking rooms* ⊟*AE, D, DC, MC, V.*

FORT WORTH STOCKYARDS HOTELS

$–$$$ 🏨**Miss Molly's.** Once a prim little inn, then a raucous bordello, this place above the Star Café has been reincarnated as a unique B&B. Each room is different, but all are furnished with Old West antiques. Only one has a private bath; guests in other rooms share three bathrooms. Folks say Miss Molly's is haunted by friendly ghosts, which scares some guests away and attracts others. While there is no policy excluding children as guests, families with children under 10 are discouraged from staying here. **Pros:** In the middle of the action at the Fort Worth Stockyards, half-price rates during the week. **Cons:** Credit cards not accepted, potential paranormal encounters, not good for families. ⊠*109½ W. Exchange Ave., Stockyards* ☎*817/626–1522* ⊕*www. missmollyshotel.com* ⟿*8 rooms, 1 with bath* ⌂*In-room: no phone, no TV (some), Wi-Fi. In-hotel: no elevator, public Wi-Fi, parking (no fee).* ⊟*No credit cards* ⦶*CP (weekends only).*

$$$–$$$$ 🏨**Stockyards Hotel.** A storybook place that's seen more than its share of cowboys, rustlers, gangsters, and oil barons, this hotel has been used in many a movie. If you're visiting the Stockyards, take a moment to walk through the 1907 hotel's richly appointed lobby (even if you're not a guest), sit a spell on comfy leather sofas and upholstered chairs, and watch folks walk down Exchange Avenue. There are four styles of rooms to choose from: Victorian, Native American, Mountain Man, and Western. In the Booger Red Saloon, the bar stools are saddles. **Pros:** In the heart of the Stockyards action, sense of history, personal service. **Cons:** Lacks some big-hotel amenities, street noise from Stockyards revelers. ⊠*109 E. Exchange Ave., Stockyards* ☏*817/625–6427 or 800/423–8471* ⊕*www.stockyardshotel.com* ⊰*52 rooms* ⌂*In-room: Wi-Fi. In-hotel: restaurant, bar, laundry service, public Wi-Fi, parking (fee), some pets allowed, no-smoking rooms* ▤*AE, D, DC, MC, V.*

FORT WORTH CULTURAL DISTRICT HOTELS

$$–$$$$ **Residence Inn Fort Worth Cultural District.** You can drive from this clean all-suites hotel to Fort Worth's Cultural District in about three minutes; complimentary transportation delivers guests to the Cultural District and Downtown. The hotel, which opened in 2005, draws praise for its spacious rooms and friendly customer service. Rates are adjusted for longer stays. An outdoor sports court, near the heated outdoor pool, offers space for basketball. **Pros:** Friendly staff, comfortable space for large parties. **Cons:** Generic room decor, surrounding area isn't ideal for pedestrians. ⊠*2500 Museum Way, Cultural District* ☏*817/885–8250* ⊕*www.marriott.com* ⊰*150 suites* ⌂*In-room: kitchen, refrigerator, Ethernet. In-hotel: gym, pool, laundry facilities, laundry service, public Wi-Fi, parking (no fee), some pets allowed, no-smoking rooms* ▤*AE, D, DC, MC, V* ⋈*BP.*

DFW METROPLEX HOTELS

$$$$
Fodor'sChoice
★
Four Seasons Resort and Club. Looking like a Frank Lloyd Wright–designed country club, this hotel is quite possibly the city's best. Rooms have balconies that overlook the Tournament Players Course, site of the Professional Golfers' Association's EDS Byron Nelson Championship. All guest rooms were renovated in 2007 and 2008, with the luxurious resort-style rooms taking on warm earth tones. Guests have access to the private golf course as well as racquetball, squash, and tennis courts and a 5,500-square-foot pool. **Pros:** Luxurious resort, personalized service, secluded grounds, reasonable weekend rates. **Cons:** Expensive weekday rates, removed from major Dallas-Fort Worth attractions. ⊠*4150 N. MacArthur Blvd., Irving* ☏*972/717–0700 or 800/332–3442* ⊕*www.fourseasons.com/dallas* ⊰*441 rooms* ⌂*In-room: safe, DVD, Ethernet, Wi-Fi. In-hotel: 2 restaurants, room service, bars, golf courses, tennis courts, pools, gym, spa, children's programs (ages 6 months–13), laundry service, concierge, public Wi-Fi, parking (fee), some pets allowed, no-smoking rooms* ▤*AE, D, DC, MC, V.*

$$$$
☼
Gaylord Texan Resort and Convention Center on Lake Grapevine. Even inside this massive hotel you feel like you're outside (minus the Texas weather). Glass rooftops allow natural light to fill the climate-controlled space, filled with indoor gardens (4.5 acres worth), bodies of water, and region-specific architecture. The atmosphere is festive, especially on weekends, when guests and gawkers stroll through the common areas, shop, dine, and enjoy various live entertainment options. Dallas/Fort Worth International Airport is about 5 mi south of the com-

plex. **Pros:** All-inclusive means plenty of dining, drinking, and entertainment options, ground floor offers condensed overview of Texas. **Cons:** Staff can be overwhelmed by massive crowds, which happens often at this convention-friendly property, removed from most Dallas-Fort Worth attractions, dining options are expensive. ⊠*1501 Gaylord Trail, Grapevine* ☎*817/778–1000 or 866/782–7897* ⊕*www.gaylordhotels.com/gaylordtexan* ⇆*1,511 rooms* &*In-room: safe, refrigerator, Ethernet, dial-up, Wi-Fi. In-hotel: 5 restaurants, room service, bars, pools, gym, spa, bicycles, laundry facilities, laundry service, concierge, public Internet, public Wi-Fi, airport shuttle, parking (fee), no-smoking rooms* ▤*AE, D, DC, MC, V.*

$$$$ 🏨**Great Wolf Lodge.** Once you check in, you may have trouble convincing anyone to leave before check-out. The resort-style hotel, opened in late 2007, caters to families with a giant indoor and outdoor water park that is available only to hotel guests. The grounds also include game rooms, a full-service spa for adults, and an ice-cream themed spa for children. The rooms are decorated like an old-fashioned lodge; more expensive rooms have more features for children, including bunk beds and flat-screen TVs in separate sleeping areas. **Pros:** Plenty of attractions and entertainment for families, climate-controlled recreation options for cold of winter and heat of summer. **Cons:** Not ideal for couples looking for a quiet getaway, dining options aren't sophisticated. ⊠*100 Great Wolf Dr., Grapevine* ☎*817/488–6510 or 800/693-9653* ⊕*www.greatwolflodge.com* ⇆*402 rooms* &*In-hotel: safe, refrigerator, Wi-Fi. In-room: 2 restaurants, bar, gym, spas, laundry facilities, laundry service, concierge, public Wi-Fi, parking (no fee), no-smoking rooms* ▤*AE, D, DC, MC, V.*

DALLAS & FORT WORTH ESSENTIALS

To research prices, get advice from other travelers, and book travel arrangements, visit www.fodors.com.

TRANSPORTATION

BY AIR

DFW International, situated centrally between the two cities, offers about 1,900 flights daily. The airport is huge, and its five terminals are connected by a high-speed train. It's imperative when you depart from the airport that you know from which terminal you're leaving—you don't want to show up at Terminal B and then discover your airline leaves from Terminal E. Drivers can access the airport from the north or south via Highway 183 to the south and Highway 121 to the north.

Most traffic in and out of the much smaller Dallas Love Field is with Southwest Airlines. There are no international flights to and from Love Field, which is just 6 mi north of Downtown Dallas. The airport sits about halfway between I–35 to the west and the Dallas North Tollway to the east.

Airport Information **Dallas/Fort Worth International Airport** (✉ *3200 E. Airfield Drive, DFW Airport* ☏ *972/574–8888* ⊕ *www.dfwairport.com*). **Dallas Love Field** (✉ *8008 Cedar Springs Rd., Dallas* ☏ *214/670–6073* ⊕ *www.dallas-lovefield.com*).

Ground Transportation **Super Shuttle** (☏ *972/615–2410* ⊕ *www.supershuttle. com*). **Go Yellow Checker Shuttle** (☏ *214/841–1900* ⊕ *www.yellowcheckershuttle. com*). **Yellow Cab** (☏ *214/426–6262 or 817/426–6262* ⊕ *www.dallasyellowcab. com*). **Cowboy Cab Company** (✉ *1306 Wall St., Dallas* ☏ *214/428–0202 or 817/428–0202* ⊕ *www.cowboycab.com*).

BY BUS

It's possible to get to Dallas, Fort Worth, or suburbs including Carrollton, Garland, Irving, Lewisville, and Richardson via Greyhound. The bus company's major area stops are the Intermodal Transporation Center in Fort Worth and the station in the middle of Downtown Dallas at 205 S. Lamar St.

Once in either major city, local bus transportation is possible to most major destinations. Tarrant County's option is The T, which provides service in Fort Worth and suburban Richland Hills. From Downtown, passengers can take Route 7 to the Cultural District, the Fort Worth Zoo, and Texas Christian University. Route 15 heads north to the Stockyards and back.

Dallas visitors can ride a DART bus between major Dallas neighborhoods and the suburbs that are part of the DART system (Addison, Carrollton, Cockrell Hill, Dallas, Farmers Branch, Garland, Glenn Heights, Highland Park, Irving, Richardson, Rowlett, Plano, and University Park).

Both The T and DART require fares. If you have more than one trip planned, a day pass is an economical choice, and it allows for use of the TRE, the train that connects Dallas and Fort Worth, and the DART light rail.

If you're exploring Dallas's Uptown area, a fun, free option is the McKinney Avenue Transit Authority's trolley system. Trolleys travel from the edge of the Arts District up to West Village—about 4 mi total.

Information **Greyhound** (✉ *1001 Jones St., Fort Worth* ☏ *817/429–3089* ⊕ *www. greyhound.com*). **Greyhound** (✉ *205 S. Lamar St., Dallas* ☏ *214/849–6831* ⊕ *www. greyhound.com*). **Dallas Area Rapid Transit System** (✉ *1401 Pacific Ave., Dallas* ☏ *214/979–1111* ⊕ *www.dart.org*). **The T** (✉ *1600 E. Lancaster Ave., Fort Worth* ☏ *817/215–8600* ⊕ *www.the-t.com*). **McKinney Avenue Transit Authority** (✉ *3153 Oak Grove Ave., Dallas* ☏ *214/855–0006* ⊕ *www.mata.org*).

BY CAR

In general, the DFW area is not pedestrian-friendly. Sure, there are pockets where walking is possible and even enjoyable—including parts of Downtown Dallas, most of Downtown Fort Worth, quaint main streets of many suburbs, and White Rock Lake. But to get from one of these neighborhoods to another you need wheels. If your sites are spread out, having your own car is the easiest option (as opposed to using a cab or relying on public transportation).

Traffic is reliably awful on most highways and tollways during morning and evening rush hours and sporadically on weekends, depending on construction and event schedules. If you can, avoid driving on highways from 7 AM to 9 AM and again from 4 PM to 6:30 PM. If you must venture out during those hours, be sure to allow plenty of time to reach your destination—and pack a good attitude.

BY LIGHT RAIL

Dallas Area Rapid Transit (called DART by locals) operates a 45-mi light-rail system in Dallas and some surrounding suburbs. The lines, open since 1996, extend as far north as Plano in Collin County, east to Garland, and south to South and West Dallas. There are two lines—the red and the blue, which overlap in the middle of Dallas and diverge at points north and south. Cars are crowded during morning and late afternoon rush hours, filled with commuters who appreciate being removed from the crowded highways.

If you're staying Downtown, it's possible to use the train system to reach attractions such as the Dallas Zoo to the south and NorthPark Center to the north. If the train doesn't take you to your final destination, you may be able to use DART's bus or the Trinity Railway Express, which heads west toward Dallas/Fort Worth International Airport (accessible via shuttle) and Downtown Fort Worth. DART's Web site is a good resource for schedules and stops, or you can call the customer information center for trip planning. Downtown stops include Pearl, St. Paul, Akard, West End, Union Station, and Convention Center.

An all-day pass allows unlimited rides on the rail and the DART bus system; a premium all-day pass ($5) is for travel in all surrounding areas including The T in Fort Worth, although the local pass ($3) excludes travel into Tarrant County. Single-ride tickets are cheaper. All tickets can be purchased at kiosks at light-rail platforms. Passengers do not have to present a ticket to board, but DART employees do walk through the cars to check for purchased fares.

The young system is expanding. A green line to areas including Victory Park, Deep Ellum, and Fair Park is scheduled to open in fall 2009. Other districts and suburbs are scheduled for access through 2013.

Information **Dallas Area Rapid Transit System** (⊠ *1401 Pacific Ave., Dallas* ☎ *214/979-1111* ⊕ *www.dart.org*).

BY TRAIN

Amtrak's Texas Eagle stops in Fort Worth and Dallas every day as part of the line from Chicago to San Antonio. The route continues to Los Angeles three days a week. A separate route, the Heartland Flyer, provides daily service between Fort Worth and Oklahoma City.

The Trinity Railway Express is a commuter train that runs west to east and back again, connecting Fort Worth, Dallas/Fort Worth International Airport, and Dallas. It is operated jointly by The T in Fort Worth and Dallas Area Rapid Transit. A premium pass from either system will allow transportation on the TRE.

Information **Union Station** (✉ *400 S. Houston St., Dallas* ☎ *214/653–1101*). **Fort Worth Intermodal Transportation Center** (✉ *1001 Jones St., Fort Worth* ☎ *817/332–2931*). **Trinity Railway Express** (✉ *4801 Rock Island Rd., Irving* ☎ *817/215–8600 or 214/979–1111* ⊕ *www.trinityrailwayexpress.org*).

CONTACTS & RESOURCES

EMERGENCIES

In an emergency, dial 911. Each of the following facilities has an emergency room open 24/7.

Hospitals **Baylor University Medical Center at Dallas** (✉ *3500 Gaston Ave., East Dallas, Dallas* ☎ *214/820–0111* ⊕ *www.baylorhealth.com*). **Methodist Dallas Medical Center** (✉ *1441 N. Beckley Ave., Oak Cliff, Dallas* ☎ *214/947–8181* ⊕ *www.methodisthealthsystem.org*). **Parkland Health & Hospital System** (✉ *5201 Harry Hines Blvd., Medical District, Dallas* ☎ *214/590–8000* ⊕ *www.parklandhospital.com*). **Presbyterian Hospital of Dallas** (✉ *8200 Walnut Hill La., North Dallas, Dallas* ☎ *214/345–6789* ⊕ *www.texashealth.org*). **Baylor All Saints Medical Center of Fort Worth** (✉ *1400 Eighth Ave., Fort Worth* ☎ *817/926–2544* ⊕ *www.baylorhealth.com*). **Cook Children's Medical Center** (✉ *801 Seventh Ave., Fort Worth* ☎ *682/885–4000* ⊕ *www.cookchildrens.org*). **Harris Methodist Fort Worth Hospital** (✉ *1301 Pennsylvania Ave., Fort Worth* ☎ *817/250–2000* ⊕ *www.texashealth.org*). **Arlington Memorial Hospital** (✉ *800 W. Randol Mill Rd., Arlington* ☎ *817/548–6100* ⊕ *www.texashealth.org*).

VISITOR INFORMATION

Dallas Convention and Visitors Bureau (✉ *325 N. St. Paul St., Dallas* ☎ *214/571–1000* ⊕ *www.dallascvb.com*). **Fort Worth Convention & Visitors Bureau** (✉ *415 Throckmorton St., Fort Worth* ☎ *817/336–8791* ⊕ *www.fortworth.com*). **Arlington Convention & Visitors Bureau** (✉ *1905 E. Randol Mill Rd., Arlington* ☎ *800/433–5374* ⊕ *www.arlington.org*).

North-Central Texas

THE I-35 CORRIDOR

WORD OF MOUTH

"Waxahachie is full of historic Victorian homes. The first weekend in June is the Gingerbread Trail, when about six of them are open for tours. The entire downtown area is full of cute shops and is perfect for strolling and shopping. Many Saturday mornings there is a farmer's market, too."

—ChristieP

"If you want shopping, stop at the Hillsboro Outlet Mall—but leave yourselves several hours to shop! Also, last time I checked, there were several little antique malls around the square in the actual little town of Hillsboro . . ."

—Missypie

By Kevin
Tankersley
& Debbie
Harmsen

NORTH-CENTRAL TEXAS—OTHER THAN THE DALLAS–FORT Worth metroplex—isn't usually thought of as a destination in and of itself. However, many find themselves going through this area because they're heading elsewhere in the state via Interstate 35. In Texas, I–35 stretches from the Oklahoma-Texas border down to Laredo at the Texas-Mexico border, passing through Dallas, Austin, and San Antonio—all the state's biggest cities except Houston.

We've created this chapter to help you see what interesting things are lined up along the northern two-thirds of the I–35 corridor, should you decide to mosey off the highway for little look-see. We reckon you'll be surprised at some of the things to do along the way. Did you know, for example, that Waco is home to the Dr Pepper Museum and Texas Rangers Hall of Fame? Or that there's a Munster Mansion (based on the TV show) in Waxahachie?

The trick is that you have to get *off* the highway to really see the sights. In this chapter, we've tried to keep you close to this state throughway, with towns and sites that don't venture too far off the beaten path, but we've also included a few places that warrant a somewhat longer excursion. So don't rush by too quickly. Slow up on the gas and pull over to poke around at great shops and intriguing museums.

EXPLORING NORTH-CENTRAL TEXAS

ABOUT THE RESTAURANTS

As it does in many places throughout Texas, barbecue reigns here. Steak is also popular, as are fried chicken, Texas-style chili (no beans), and Tex-Mex. Along I–35, or a little ways off it, you're sure to see the regional chains Whataburger (made-to-order burgers with 100% beef and five-inch buns), Taco Cabana (sort of an upscale Taco Bell where you can get margaritas, handmade tortillas, and homemade salsa for not much more than pocket change), and the Black-eyed Pea (think Applebee's with down-home cookin'). In the tiny town of West, the Czech community still influences cuisine, with kolaches for sale at a gas station/deli/bakery combo right off the freeway.

ABOUT THE HOTELS

The lodging here tends to be basic, with major chains, including the popular La Quinta inns, and an assortment of bed-and-breakfasts (if you want to stay in a Victorian house, try Waxahachie or Granbury). There are many options right off I–35, and most have swimming pools to keep the kids happy.

WHAT IT COSTS					
	¢	$	$$	$$$	$$$$
RESTAURANTS	under $8	$8–$12	$13–$20	$21–$30	over $30
HOTELS	under $50	$50–$100	$101–$150	$151–$200	over $200
CAMPING	under $10	$10–$17	$18–$35	$36–$50	over $50

Restaurant prices are per person for a main course at dinner. Hotel prices are per night for two people in a standard double room in high season, excluding taxes and service charges. Lodging taxes vary between 6% and 15%. Camping prices are for a standard (no hookups, pit toilets, fire grates, picnic tables) campsite per night.

NORTH OF DALLAS–FORT WORTH

North of the sprawling Dallas–Fort Worth metroplex lie dozens and dozens of towns that are just the opposite: small, compact communities. They are a mix of personalities. Some have the cowboy feel, some are cozy Victorian. Others thrive on their outdoorsy offerings, while others boast of their outlets. Still others hug the DFW boundaries with an air of urban sophistication on a smaller scale. Some of these destinations make good day trips from Dallas, especially if you want to while away some time with activities like hiking, shopping, and water sports.

THE DENISON & SHERMAN AREA

Sherman is 64 mi north of Dallas via Hwy. 75; Denison is 12 mi farther north.

Nestled up against the Oklahoma border, Denison, population 20,000, is small-town America with an artsy edge. Downtown, pedestrians stroll a main street lined with antiques shops, boutiques, art galleries, even artists' studios. An old-fashioned movie palace brings in crowds for musicals, concerts, and variety-type shows. In nearby Sherman, top draws are antiques stores and the Victorian homes of Heritage Row (the prize jewel being the 1896 C. S. Roberts House).

WHAT TO SEE

C. S. Roberts House. Part of the local preservation league's Annual Tour of Homes each April, this Victorian beauty with balconies, gingerbread trim, and a wraparound porch is open for tours each Sunday afternoon. View period furniture inside, and the gazebo and gardens out back. ⊠*915 S. Crockett Dr., Sherman* ☎*903/893–4067* 🖃*$5* ⊗*Sun. 1–4.*

★ **Eisenhower Birthplace State Historical Park.** Tour the home where Ike was born in 1890 and then view exhibits on this five-star general and Republican president at the park visitor center. Dwight D. Eisenhower moved away from Denison at age 2, to Abilene, Kansas, where his presidential library and museum are. ⊠*609 S. Lamar Ave., Denison* ☎*903/465–8908* ⊕*www.eisenhowerbirthplace.org* 🖃*$3* ⊗*Tues.– Fri. 10–4, Sat. 9–5, Sun. 1–5.*

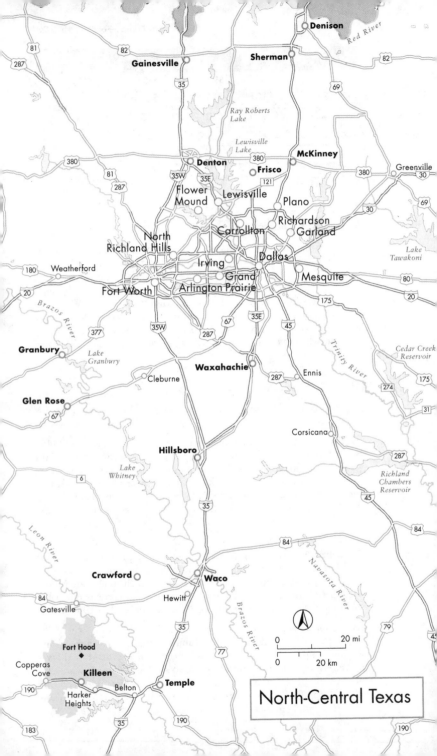

North-Central Texas

PLANNING YOUR TRIP

GETTING THERE & AROUND

I–35 is the quickest, most direct route between northern and south-central Texas. More scenic routes through the area include heading from Dallas–Fort Worth to Austin via Highway 377 or 67 along with 281 going south to Burnet or Marble Falls before cutting southeast across the Hill Country. These non-interstate drives take travelers through charming communities like Grandbury and the scenic Hill Country.

WHEN TO GO

The weather in North-Central Texas depends on where you are along the I–35 corridor. The climate for the upper one-third of the route mirrors that of Dallas–Fort Worth, with hot summers and mild winters—even with occasional snowfalls, but the mercury continues to climb the farther south you go. By the time you've reached San Antonio, you'll notice an upward change of several degrees compared to Dallas.

OFF THE BEATEN PATH

Famous Texas politician Sam Rayburn, who was elected at age 24 to the state congress, grew up in Bonham, 30 mi east of Sherman. He became Speaker of the House four years later, and by age 30 was representing his district in Washington. He continued to serve until his late 70s. Just outside of Bonham is the **Sam Rayburn House Museum** (⊠ *Off Hwy. 56, 1½ mi from Bonham* ☎ *903/583–5558* ☞ *Free* ⊙ *Tues.–Fri. 8–5, weekends 1–5*), the two-story, 12-room home Rayburn used as a Texas refuge from the Washington political world. Tours are given on the hour. In Bonham proper is the **Sam Rayburn Library and Museum** (⊠ *800 W. Sam Rayburn Dr. (Hwy. 56)* ☎ *903/583–2455* ☞ *Free* ⊙ *Mon.–Fri. 10–5, Sat. 1–5, Sun. 2–5*), with Rayburn's library and his speaker's rostrum as well as photographs, political cartoons, and other mementos of his life of public service.

SPORTS & THE OUTDOORS

Eisenhower State Park. Hike, bike, fish, swim, camp, and view wildlife at this 423-acre park near Lake Texoma, the region's premier lake for water sports. ⊠ *50 Park Rd. 20, Denison* ☎ *903/465–1956* ⊕ *www.tpwd.state.tx.us* ☞ *$3* ⊙ *Daily, dawn to dusk (park), 8–5 (office).*

Hagerman National Wildlife Refuge. Migrating birds, such as snow and Canadian geese, as well as a few varieties of ducks come each winter to nest in this 11,320-acre waterfowl refuge along Lake Texoma. In summer snowy egrets and sandpipers are among the residents, and in spring pelicans delight visitors. Vultures, blue herons, flycatchers, and owls call Hagerman home year-round. Alltogether, more than 300 types of birds live here for one season or more. Each second Saturday of the month, free nature tours are offered, and on Tuesday and Thursday mornings visitors can sign up for free birding tours. ⊠ *On FM 1417, 6 mi off Hwy. 75 (4 mi east of Sadler and 15 mi west of Sherman)* ☎ *903/786–2826* ⊕ *www.fws.gov/southwest/refuges* ☞ *Free* ⊙ *Daily, dawn to dusk (park) 8–5 (office).*

Lake Texoma. Just 4 mi from Denison, this huge lake is a weekend destination for outdoorsy DFW Metroplexers. It offers every kind of water sport imaginable—fishing, swimming, waterskiing, boating, you name it—plus there's plenty nearby: parks, refuges, campgrounds, even golf courses. In the fall, keep an eye out for bald eagles. ⊠ *U.S. 82 to U.S. 377 or U.S. 69* ☎ *580/564–2334* ⊕ *www.laketexomaonline.com* 🎫 *Free* ⊙ *Daily.*

GAINESVILLE

72 mi north of Dallas on I–35.

You can't miss the outlets as you breeze by Gainesville on the Interstate. And if you venture away from I–35, you can see the 19th-century structures of Gainesville's historic downtown. Brick is the material of choice, used for paving the streets and for constructing the Victorian homes. Historic structures include more than two dozen homes, a handful of churches, and an 1884 firehouse.

SHOPPING

Gainesville Factory Shops. Find discounts on clothing, home accessories, toys, books, jewelry, and more at the two-dozen outlets at this right-off-the-interstate complex. On certain holidays there are additional discounts at sidewalk sales, and every Tuesday seniors are treated to special rates at select stores. An RV park is on the premises (the overnight fee is $15), as is a playground in case your little ones need to run off some energy from sitting in the car too long. ⊠ *4321 N. I–35, Exit 501* ☎ *888/545–7220* ⊙ *Mon.–Sat. 10–8, Sun. 11–6.*

SOUTHWEST OF DALLAS–FORT WORTH

GRANBURY

40 mi southwest of Fort Worth on U.S. 377.

Granbury (pronounced Gran-berry) is a growing community that is situated around Lake Granbury and its more than 100 mi of shoreline. Like many small towns in Texas, life revolves around the square, looking in many ways like it did in the 1800s.

WHAT TO SEE

Hood County Jail and Museum. Have you been around the block? That is, the original cell block and hanging tower at the Hood County Jail, which operated from 1885 to 1978. After you tour the old jail, view jail memorabilia and exhibits. ⊠ *208 N. Crockett St.* ☎ *817/279–0083* ⊙ *Mar.–Oct., Sat.–Sun, 1–4* 🎫 *$2.*

**OFF THE
BEATEN
PATH**

The Windmill Farm. About 5 mi outside of Granbury, in Tolar, you can walk or drive through a 26-acre display of more than 40 restored windmills. ⊠ *6625 Colony Rd.* ☎ *254/835–4168* ⊙ *Daily, dawn to dusk* 🎫 *Free, but donations accepted.*

CLOSE UP

Sam Rayburn: A Quarter Century in Politics

"If you want to get along, go along."

That's the advice freshmen congressmen still get, and it's famously attributed to Texas political giant Sam Rayburn.

Mr. Speaker to most and Mr. Sam to the few, Rayburn's name is still legend in Bonham and Washington. He was the only speaker of the Texas House and the U.S. House, too, and one of the Texas Democrats who ruled America during the mid-20th century. Allies included the likes of John Nance Gar-

ner and Lyndon Johnson—Texans who got things done.

Rayburn's reign was colored by the threats of the Depression, global war, and communism, and the nation's response was sometimes sealed over whiskey and cards in his nightly "board of education" in the Capitol.

A Tennessean, Rayburn arrived in Texas at age 5, married once and briefly, and died in his sleep at 79.

—Larry Neal

ARTS & ENTERTAINMENT

Granbury Opera House. Dramas and musicals are performed throughout the year in this 1886 theater. ⊠*116 S. Houston* ☎*817/573–9191* ⊕*www.granburyoperahouse.net* ⊙*Mid-Apr.–Dec.*

Granbury Riverboat. Come for entertainment and food on a lunch, dinner, or murder-mystery cruise aboard this 96-foot, 200-passenger boat on Lake Granbury. A gospel music and brunch cruise sets sail on Sunday mornings. ⊠*2323 S. Morgan* ☎*817/279–8687* ⊕*www.granbury riverboat.com* ⊙*Thurs.–Sun.* ⛴*Prices vary.*

☾ **The Brazos Drive-In.** Yes, these fun throwbacks to an earlier era still exist! The Brazos is one of only a handful of drive-in movie theaters still operating in Texas. Double features—most of which are family-friendly—are shown beginning at dusk each Friday and Saturday. ⊠*1800 W. Pearl St.* ☎*817/573–1311* ⛴*$12 per person or $18 a car, up to six people ($4 for each additional person if more than six in a vehicle)* ⊙*Fri.–Sat. (weather permitting).*

WHERE TO EAT

¢–$$$ **Stringfellow's.** For lunch, the menu is classic American, with such standbys as burgers, sandwiches, soups, salads, and daily lunch specials. Beef tops the evening menu, which also features some seafood dishes in the $18–$29 range. Dine on the patio when weather permits. ⊠*101 E. Pearl St.* ☎*800/354–1670 or 817/573–6262* ⊙*Closed Mon.–Wed.* ⊟*AE, D, DC, MC, V.*

¢–$$ **Niester's Restaurant and Deli.** This little German place has received rave
★ reviews in the *Fort Worth Star-Telegram* and is a favorite of locals as well, with its sausage, steaks, and signature Wiener schnitzel. Pick up meat to go at the deli for your own grilling back home. It's also open daily for breakfast. ⊠*4426 E. U.S. 377* ☎*817/573–0211* ⊙*No dinner Sun.–Wed.* ⊟*AE, D, MC, V.*

6

GLEN ROSE: DINOSAURS, FOSSILS & LIVE ANIMALS, OH MY!

20 mi south of Granbury via Hwy. 144.

If your kids are way into dinosaurs, there are a few stops in or near Glen Rose you may want to add to your itinerary. While in the vicinity, check out Fossil Rim Wildlife Center, featuring animals from the African savanna as well as some native-to-Texas species.

WHAT TO SEE

☾ **Creation Evidence Museum.** Could dinosaurs and humans have roamed the earth side by side? After doing extensive research in the limestone along the area's Paluxy River, the Creative Evidence Museum's founder, Dr. Carl Baugh, answers with a resounding yes. His displays of human and dinosaur footprints—since the museum opened in 1984, he and his teams have found scores of examples—along with other fossils, including dinosaur bones, are the main exhibits here. If you time it right, you can get in on one of the periodic public digs (not for young children) or first Saturday lectures. ⊠ *3102 FM 205* ☎ *254/897–3200* ⊕ *www. creationevidence.org* ☾ *Tues.–Sat. 10–4* 🎟 *$2.*

☾ **Dinosaur Valley State Park.** If your kids like seeing bear footprints in the forest, they'll flip for dinosaur tracks left from ancient times. Some of the world's best footprints of these gigantic lizards are embedded in the limestone, sand, and mud of this state park's riverbed. ⊠ *4 mi west of Glen Rose on Park Rd. 59* ☎ *254/897–4588* ⊕ *www.tpwd.state.tx.us* ☾ *Daily 8–10* 🎟 *$5.*

Dinosaur World. With parks also in Kentucky and Florida, the chain of lifesize dinos constructed of fiberglass and concrete entered the Lone Star State in 2008, with a grand opening of this Glen Rose attraction in early March. Kids can go on fossil digs, learn about raptors through exhibits, buy educational products at the gift shop, and walk through a forested area, where the 150 dinosaurs pop out along the way. ⊠ *1058 Park Rd. 59 (near Dinosaur Valley State Park), Glen Rose* ☎ *254/898– 1526* ⊕ *www.dinoworld.net* ☾ *Daily 9–6* 🎟 *$12.75.*

☾ **Fossil Rim Wildlife Center.** Zebras in Texas? Giraffes, bison, cheetahs,
★ ostriches, and antelopes, too. Oh, and don't forget the rhinoceroses. Just an hour or so from Fort Worth, and a few miles from Glen Rose, an 1,800-acre conservation park and educational center provides visitors with a glimpse into safari life in Africa. Both native and non-native species reside in the park, with a total of more than 1,000 animals. Visitors can drive leisurely through the site, visit the children's zoo and gift store, pull over for a picnic, trek along the ½-mile walking trail, and, maybe the best part: feed the animals. Guided tours are also available. ⊠ *2155 CR 2008, Glen Rose* ☎ *254/897–2960* ⊕ *www.fossilrim. org* ☾ *Nov.–Feb., daily 8:30–3:30; Mar., daily 8:30–4:30; Apr.–Oct., daily 8:30–5:30 (closing time indicates when last car is admitted; park closes two hours later)* 🎟 *$15.95–$22.95; tour fees and bag of animal feed additional.*

**OFF THE
BEATEN
PATH**

Dr Pepper & Old Doc's Soda Shop. In the small community of Dublin, the oldest Dr Pepper bottling plant still operates, and is in fact the only one still using the original formula (with pure cane sugar rather than corn sweeteners). You can tour the facilities (the bottling happens on Wednesdays only) and peruse Old Doc's Soda Shop, where you can buy Dr Pepper paraphernalia and order a fountain drink. Tour times vary, so call ahead. Nearby attractions include a rodeo museum. ⊠*105 E. Elm St., Dublin* ☎*888/398–1024* ⊕*www.dublindrpepper. com* 🎫*$2.50* ۞*Closed Mon.*

SOUTH OF DALLAS–FORT WORTH

WAXAHACHIE

31 mi south of Dallas on I–35E.

Waxahachie is a small town just brimming with history, its early days of wealth and prestige from cotton perhaps lost but not forgotten. It bills itself as "picture perfect," reflecting the numerous movies and TV shows that have been shot in and around the city. From the sculpted faces on the facade of the historic Ellis County Courthouse to the ghost stories involving a historic hotel and a popular restaurant, there are many tales to be heard from this captivating locale.

WHAT TO SEE

Ellis County Courthouse. As you stroll around the historic Ellis County Courthouse, notice the series of faces sculpted into the porch capitals. When the building was being constructed in the late 1890s, as the story goes, the German artist, a fellow named Harry Herley, fell in love with local girl Mabel Frame and began sculpting her face for inclusion on the building. When his love was not returned, the depictions of her face became progressively more grotesque and deformed. Did it actually happen? Who knows, but it makes for a good tale nonetheless. What is true, however, is that the courthouse is a gorgeous example of Richardson Romanesque architecture. ⊠*101 W. Main St.* ☎*972/825–5000* ⊕*www.co.ellis.tx.us* 🎫*Free* ۞*Mon.–Fri. 8–5.*

Munster Mansion. Does the address 1313 Mockingbird ring a bell? That's the address on the front gate of Herman and Lily Munster's house in the 1960s TV series "The Munsters," and it's also on the front gate of the Munster Mansion, a private home that's an exact replica of the Munsters' estate. It's only open for tours around Halloween each year, but visitors are welcome to take pictures through the front gate— though that can be tricky, as the mansion is located on a treacherous corner of a busy street. ⊠*3636 F.M. 813* ☎*No phone* ⊕*www.munster mansion.com* ۞*Select times in Oct. only.*

SHOPPING

Shop for fruits and vegetables at the **Downtown Farmers' Market** (⊠*Historic Town Square*) each Saturday from May to October.

Voted the best antiques store in Ellis County for 14 consecutive years, **Gingerbread Antique Mall** (⊠*310 South College St.* ☎*972/937–0968* ☽*Mon.–Fri., 10–5, Sat. 10–5:30, Sun.1–5:30*) specializes in Victorian furniture, antiques and collectibles, and fine glass, with no reproductions or craft items to be found.

For collections of self-taught and anonymous art, visit **Webb Gallery** (⊠*209 W. Franklin* ☎*972/938–8085* ☽*By appointment and Sat.– Sun. 1–5*). On display among an assortment of bizarre items gathered on the owner's trips crisscrossing the country are carnival banners, tramp art (art created by itinerant artists who passed through the area), and memory jugs—ceramic jugs (and sometimes bottles) that have had everyday objects like keys, shells, and jewelry placed on the outside using glue, putty, and cement.

NEED A BREAK?

Besides being a good, homey place to stop for lunch—or slice of pie—the **Dove's Nest** (⊠*105 W. Jefferson St.* ☎*972/938–3683* ⊕*www.thedovesnest restaurant.com* ☽*Mon.–Sat. 10–5*), on Waxahachie's town square, is also a dandy antiques and country-style gift shop.

ARTS & ENTERTAINMENT

FESTIVALS & EVENTS

Each June you can follow the **Gingerbread Trail** (Ellis Country Museum, ☎*972/937–0681*) through Waxahachie, visiting several historic homes in town, in a variety of architectural styles from Queen Anne and Victorian to Gothic Revival and Gingerbread. On Wyatt Street, view the shotgun dwellings from the early 20th century.

On the fourth Saturday in October, **Bob Phillips's Texas Country Reporter Festival** (⊠*On the downtown square* ☎*972/938–9827* ⊕*www.texas countryreporter.com* ✉*Free*) features colorful artists and musicians— all of whom have been on Phillips's long-running TV show—sharing their talents, plus Phillips telling tales of what he's discovered as he's traipsed through the state looking for offbeat stories.

The biggest names in country music descend on the area each May for **Country Thunder U.S.A.** (⊠*315 Griffith Rd., Ennis* ☎*262/279–6960* ⊕*www.countrythunder.com* ✉*$20 per day; up to $500 for a VIP three-day pass covering parking, food, alcohol-free drinks, and more*), a three-day camping and music fest. Past performers have included George Strait, Reba McEntire, Big and Rich, and Gretchen Wilson.

For six weekends in April and May, the **Scarborough Renaissance Festival** (⊠*2511 FM 66* ☎*972/938–3247* ⊕*www.scarboroughrenfest.com* ✉*$20*) transports visitors back to a time of swordplay, with comedy, music, and more than 200 quaint shops of unique finds rounding out the affair.

WHERE TO EAT

$–$$ ✕**Catfish Plantation.** As many folks come to this place for the haunting spirits as for the catfish, which is pretty darn good. Ghost hunters and others swear they can sense the presence of three beings, Caroline, Elizabeth, and Will, and stories abound about their activities—flying

The Movie Capital of Texas

Waxahachie touts itself as the Movie Capital of Texas as well as the Hollywood of Texas, and these assertions may very well may be true.

The area's movie industry started in 1967 when some scenes for *Bonnie and Clyde*, written by Waxahachie native Robert Benton, were shot here. Benton returned to the area in 1983 to film the Oscar-winning *Places in the Heart*, which he wrote and directed, and which starred such notable cast members as Sally Field, Ed Harris, Danny Glover, and John Malkovich.

More than 30 movies, several made-for-TV films, and a couple of television series have been filmed in or near Waxahachie, including other Oscar champs like *Tender Mercies* and *The Trip to Bountiful*, as well as such films as *Pure Country*, David Byrne's *True Stories*, and *Walking Tall 2* and *3*. The crew that was here the longest was for the seven years that the "Walker: Texas Ranger" TV series—with actor-turned-political-backer Chuck Norris—filmed here, from 1993 to 2000.

It's no wonder that Waxahachie, known as Gingerbread City because of all is historic structures in that style, calls itself "picture perfect."

—Kevin Tankersley

6

glasses, unexplained cold spots, slamming doors, and even many a claim that Elizabeth has followed customers home. In addition to seafood, the menu boasts fried chicken, chicken-fried steak, and other Southern favorites, including sides and starters like Cajun hushpuppies and sweet-potato fries—even on the children's menu you'll find black-eyed peas. Kids 10 and younger eat free on Sunday (ask for details). ⊠*814 Water St.,* ☎*972/937–9468* ⊙ *Closed Mon.–Tues. No lunch Wed.–Fri.* ⊟*AE, MC, V.*

¢–$$ ✕ **1879 Chisholm Grill.** This warm restaurant in the Hatch's historic downtown was voted by readers of the local newspaper as having the best steak in town—the "Roxanne Ribeye" is particularly popular. The chicken-fried steak is bountiful, and chicken, seafood, burgers, pasta, and soup and salads round out an all-American menu. The restaurant is housed in a historic building the owner's grandparents visited for ice cream on their first date in 1930. ⊠*111 S. College St.,* ☎*972/937–7261* ⊙ *Closed Mon. Also serves breakfast Sat. and Sun.* ⊟*AE, D, MC, V.*

WHERE TO STAY

$$$–$$$$ ▦ **Chaska House.** Owners Linda and Louis Brown raised their family here before opening as a B&B in 1993. It closed in 2004 for restoration and renovation, but opened a year later as a quiet, luxurious old house with modern amenities, including flat-screen TVs in all guest rooms. Guests run the gamut from baby boomers to newlyweds to couples celebrating multi-decade anniversaries. Rooms are named after famous folks: Teddy Roosevelt, Scott Fitzgerald, Margaret Mitchell, William Shakespeare, and Mark Twain. **Pros:** Six blocks from downtown; full Southern breakfast. **Cons:** Occasionally, a passing train can be noisy. ⊠*716 W. Main St.,* ☎*972/937–3390* ⊕*www.chaskabb.com*

☝7 *rooms* ☝*In-room: no phone, refrigerator (some), DVD, Wi-Fi. In-hotel: public Wi-Fi, parking (no fee), no kids in main house, no elevator, no-smoking rooms* ⍟|*BP* ⊟*AE, MC, V.*

$–$$　⍟**Rogers Hotel.** Guests, employees, and professional ghost hunters have reported three spirits in the historic Rogers Hotel, including one who plays the piano and Sara, a little girl who drowned in the bath there years ago. Folks say they've seen Sara in both the kitchen and the bar. Live bands belting out Texas country and blues bring in the younger crowd on Friday and Saturday nights, though most guests are in the 40-and-up age group. Plans for live comedy, interactive theater, and ballroom dancing are in the works. **Pros:** Within walking distance of town shops and restaurants, owners are on-site most of the time, and excellent on-site restaurants overseen by executive chef Josh Hopkins, who trained under Dallas celebrity chef Stephan Pyles. **Cons:** The nearly 100-year-old building of concrete walls sometimes makes for spotty cell-phone reception; the small parking lot sometimes means guests park on downtown streets, which can be a challenge during the day. ⊠*100 N. College,* ☎*972/938–3688* ⊕*www.rogershotel.com* ☝*27 rooms* ☝*In-room: refrigerator (some), Wi-Fi. In-hotel: 2 restaurants, room service, bar, laundry service, concierge, public Wi-Fi, parking (no fee), no-smoking rooms* ⊟*AE, D, MC, V.*

EN ROUTE　Truck drivers have known about **Willie's Place at Carl's Corner** for awhile, but with the 2008 re-opening of a much expanded Willie's Place—and that would be Willie as in Willie Nelson—the once-little spot on the road about 7 mi north of Hillsboro has gotten much bigger, both in its physical size and in its scope of clientele. The glorified truck stop—the 10-foot-tall frogs atop the gas pumps should help you see it from the road—has a 24/7 restaurant with, "crazy" we know, menu options named after Willie's songs; a 750-seat venue for live concerts; a saloon; a store with Willie gear as well as necessities; the XM Radio booth from which "Willie's Place" broadcasts; and a host of amenities for truck drivers. The truck stop is known for its "green" status as being the first to sell "BioWillie" biodiesel fuel. ⊠*On FM 2959 (Exit 374) off I–35E.*

HILLSBORO

62 mi south of Dallas and 56 mi south of Fort Worth, just past where I–35W and I–35E merge into I–35.

Many stop at Hillsboro to shop, and it's little wonder: the sprawl of outlet malls is what you see from the interstate. But those who've thought of this old town built on railroad and cotton wealth in terms of only retail purchases are in for a pleasant surprise if they head a few blocks west of the freeway to Hillsboro's downtown area, where historic structures include the gorgeous Hill County Courthouse, which underwent a $12 million renovation in the early 1990s; the MKT Depot, a restored railroad station that now houses the town's visitor center; and the High Renaissance-style library.

WHAT TO SEE

Texas Musicians Museum. From gospel and R&B to Tejano and honky-tonk, the sounds of Texas are celebrated at this collection of exhibits on the state's musical heritage. Rotating exhibits include entries from Ernest Tubb and the Dixie Chicks. Beaumont native J. P. Richardson—better known as the Big Bopper, whose biggest hit was "Chantilly Lace"—died in a plane crash, along with music greats Buddy Holly and Ritchie Valens in 1959. One of the museum's attractions—at least at the time of this writing—is the casket in which Richardson was first buried. The city of Beaumont unearthed the casket in 2007 to relocate Richardson's remains and to perform an autopsy on the body to confirm or rule out conspiracy theories about foul play aboard the plane. (The coroner confirmed that no gun shot wounds were inflicted.) Richardson was reburied in a new container, as required by state law. The casket is on loan from Richardson's family, which is trying to sell the piece of music history, so it might not be in Hillsboro forever. ☒*212 N. Waco St.* ☎*254/580–9780* ⊕*www.texasmusiciansmuseum.com* ☉*Wed.–Thurs. 10–6, Fri.–Sat. noon–9.*

SHOPPING

Shoppers can get big discounts at the more than 70 name-brand outlets—such as Bass Outlet, Children's Place, Gap, Lane Bryant, Liz Claiborne, Nike, Nine West, Polo, and Vitamin World—clustered around I–35 at the **Outlets at Hillsboro** (☒*104 N. I–35, Exit 368A* ☎*254/582–9205* ⊕*www.outletsathillsboro.com* ☉*Mon.–Sat. 10–8, Sun. 10–6*). AAA members can pick up a VIP card for additional discounts. For antiques shops, head west from the outlets into downtown Hillsboro. Shops are around the historic square, though antiques are primarily on Elm and Franklin streets. In addition to antiques and whatnots, **A Tiskit A Taskit** (☒*71 N. Waco St.* ☎*254/582–3807* ☉*Mon.–Sat. 10–5*), on the square, serves sandwiches and Texas's own Blue Bell ice cream. If you've got a group—make that a large, hungry group—try the Big Scoop Special: a banana split made with a dozen scoops of ice cream.

WHERE TO EAT?

Frenkie's. This downtown Hillsboro establishment is known for generous portions of Italian cuisine. Hot and cold subs, pizza, pasta, chicken, seafood, and veal entrées also highlight the extensive menu. ☒*57 W. Franklin St.* ☎*254/582–1230* ▤*AE, D, DC, MC, V.*

NEED A BREAK?

If you think it's only a Shell station, you are sorely mistaken. After you fill up your car, refuel your own engine with a fruit-filled kolache or one of the many other menu items at the **Czech Stop & Little Czech Bakery** (☒*Exit 353, off I–35 in West, Texas* ☎*254/826–5316 (bakery), 254/826–4161 (deli)* ⊕*http://czechstop.net*). The tiny town of West once attracted a large number of Czechoslovakian immigrants. Many of their traditions have been passed down through the generations, causing the town to be named the "Czech Heritage Capital of Texas." Each Labor Day weekend the town's big Westfest celebration brings out kolaches, polka music, and Old World costumes.

WACO

96 mi south of Dallas, 102 mi north of Austin.

Sitting smack dab between Austin and Dallas, Waco sometimes gets a bad rap for being a biggish small town with a bit of a collegiate feel but not much else to recommend it. Part of this reputation comes from the concrete view you get from I–35, which winds through the eastern part of town. Away from the highway—especially near Lake Waco but also in large Cameron Park along the Brazos River—Waco has a greener side to offer, with plenty of gems tucked into it.

The city boasts the world's largest Baptist university, 18 museums, 35 parks, a 7,000-acre lake with 60 mi of shoreline, and a downtown on the verge of revitalization—not to mention the many new restaurants that have emerged over the past dozen of so years, which have livened up the city's main drag, Valley Mills Drive.

The focus of the downtown area has for years been the 474-foot Suspension Bridge. Built in 1870 by engineers who later designed the Brooklyn Bridge, this Waco landmark was at the time the longest single-span suspension bridge west of the Mississippi River. At the bridge's western base is Indian Spring Park, where the community gathers for numerous open-air concerts and a massive Fourth of July celebration.

If you find yourself amid a backpack-toting crowd and a sea of Greek letters, you may be on the campus of Baylor University, the oldest college in Texas. The school colors—green and gold—are proudly displayed at various establishments across town, along with the school mascot and slogan, "Sic 'em Bears."

WHAT TO SEE

② ★ **Armstrong-Browning Library.** Housing the world's largest collection of books, letters, and manuscripts of Victorian poets Robert and Elizabeth Barrett Browning, this gem on the Baylor University campus is world-renowned. The facility also contains a substantial collection of primary and secondary materials relating to the Victorian era. It's a working research library but is open for tours (guided tours are available depending on docent availability). It's on the eastern edge of campus. ✉ *710 Speight Ave.* ☎ *254/710–3566* ⊕ *www.browninglibrary. org* ⤷ *Free* ⊗ *Mon.–Fri. 9–5, Sat. 9–noon.*

③ **Mayborn Museum.** Sixteen themed discovery rooms encourage hands-on learning for visitors of all ages. Rooms are devoted to vertebrates and invertebrates, communication, health, American Indians, optics and sound, water and bubbles, energy, simple machines, and other subjects. **The Gov. Bill and Vara Daniel Historic Village,** a 15-building complex adjacent to the Mayborn, gives visitors a view of Texas life from the early 20th century. ✉ *1300 S. University Parks Dr.* ☎ *254/710–1110* ⊕ *www.maybornmuseum.com* ⤷ *$6* ⊗ *Mon.–Wed., Fri., Sat. 10–5, Thurs. 10–8, Sun. 1–5.*

④ **Texas Sports Hall of Fame.** Paying homage to many legendary Texas sports figures, this museum also has areas devoted to tennis, high-

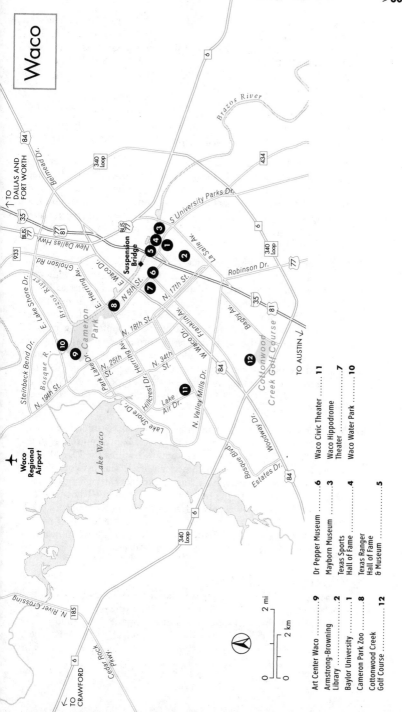

Waco

TO DALLAS AND FORT WORTH

Brazos River

Belmead Dr.

New Dallas Hwy

Gholson Rd

S University Parks Dr.

La Salle Av.

Robinson Dr.

Brazos River Av.

Suspension Bridge

E Waco Dr.

N 5th St.

N. 17th St.

E. Herring Av.

Cameron Park

N. 18th St.

N. 25th St.

N. 34th St.

Herring Av.

Franklin Av.

W Waco Dr.

Bagby Av.

Cottonwood Creek Golf Course

TO AUSTIN ↓

Lake Air Dr.

N. Valley Mills Dr.

Woodway Dr.

Estates Dr.

Bosque Blvd.

Lake Shore Dr.

Park Lake Dr.

N. 25th St.

Lake Hillcrest Dr.

N. 19th St.

N. Bosque R.

Brazos River

E. Lake Shore Dr.

Steinbeck Bend Dr.

Waco Regional Airport

Lake Waco

TO CRAWFORD

Cedar Rock Pkwy.

N. River Crossing

0   2 mi

0   2 km

Art Center Waco **9**

Armstrong-Browning
Library **2**

Baylor University **1**

Cameron Park Zoo **8**

Cottonwood Creek
Golf Course **12**

Dr Pepper Museum **6**

Mayborn Museum **3**

Texas Sports
Hall of Fame **4**

Texas Ranger
Hall of Fame
& Museum **5**

Waco Civic Theater **11**

Waco Hippodrome
Theater **7**

Waco Water Park **10**

school basketball, and high school football. Interactivity abounds as guests can watch clips of important Texas sports moments in the Tom Landry Theater, compare hand and shoe sizes to larger-than-life NBA players, and sing along to college fight songs. ⊠*1108 S. University Parks Dr.* ☎*254/756–1633 or 800/567–9561* ⊕*www.tshof.org* 🖾*$6* ⊗*Mon.–Sat. 9–5, Sun. noon–5.*

Petty officer Doris Miller, who helped defend the USS *West Virginia* during the attack on Pearl Harbor, was born in Waco. Cuba Gooding Jr. played the role of Miller in the 2001 film *Pearl Harbor*.

❺ **Texas Ranger Hall of Fame and Museum.** This is the official museum and hall of fame of the Texas Rangers, the state's storied law-enforcement agency. Exhibits focus on the history of and equipment used by the Rangers throughout the years. Shotguns belonging to Bonnie and Clyde are here as well. ⊠*100 Texas Ranger Trail (I–35 at University Parks exit)* ☎*254/750–8631* ⊕*www.texasranger.org/halloffame/HOF.htm* 🖾*$6* ⊗*Mon.–Sun. 9–4:30.*

❻ **Dr Pepper Museum.** While working at the Old Corner Drug Store in

Fodor'sChoice Waco, pharmacist Dr. Charles Alderton was experimenting with some
★ chemicals and accidentally invented the soft drink he later called Dr Pepper. The drugstore is gone, but the original bottling plant remains open as a museum. Interesting exhibits and films offer a look at some early promotional materials as well as the manufacturing process. Much of the second floor is devoted to promotional materials tracing its history. After a look through the museum, most travelers make their last stop the re-creation of the Old Corner Drug Store fountain for an ice-cream soda or (what else?) a Dr Pepper. ⊠*300 S. 5th St.* ☎*254/757–1025* ⊕*www.drpeppermuseum.com* 🖾*$6* ⊗*Mon.–Sat. 10–4:15, Sun. noon–4:15.*

❼ **Baylor University.** The oldest institution of higher learning in the state
★ of Texas, Baylor University is also the oldest Baptist university in the world. The 450-acre, tree-covered campus features the Bear Habitat, where Baylor's two live North American black bear mascots live; the Martin Museum of Art, which rotates exhibits throughout the year; and a new memorial to the Immortal 10, a group of Baylor students who died when their bus collided with a train in Round Rock while en route to a basketball game in Austin in 1927. ⊠*Off I–35 at University Parks Dr. E. (Exit 335-B)* ☎*254/710–2407* ⊕*www.baylor.edu* 🖾*Free* ⊗*Daily, Building hours vary; call ahead for prospective student tours.*

SPORTS & THE OUTDOORS

Cameron Park. Offering hiking and mountain-bike paths, a disc golf course, and wildflowers for the nature lover, the 416-acre Cameron Park is formed by bluffs and gullies forged by the Brazos and Bosque rivers. Easy-access boat ramps are in place for kayakers and canoers. ⊠*The main park entrance is at University-Parks Drive at MLK, about 2 mi west of I–35* ☎*254/750–8080* 🖾*Free* ⊗*6 a.m.–midnight.*

❽ Cameron Park Zoo. Adjacent to the Brazos River and nestled into 416-acre Cameron Park (where mountain-biking trails are bountiful), this award-winning 52-acre zoo displays creatures in their natural habitats. It features a state-of-the-art herpetarium (think snake house), lemur island, tortoises, birds, and lions in lush surroundings. ✉ *1701 N. 4th St.* ☎ *254/750–8400* ⊕ *www.cameronparkzoo.com* 🎟 *$7* ⊙ *Mon.– Sat. 9–5, Sun. 11–5.*

Lake Waco. A dozen parks surround the 7,000-acre Lake Waco. It is operated by the U.S. Army Corps of Engineers and boasts picnic areas, boat ramps, camping, and hike-and-bike trails. ⊹ *From I–35, take Exit 330 west toward Meridian. The twin bridges will pass directly over the lake.* ☎ *254/756–5359* ⊕ *www.swf-wc.usace.army.mil/waco* 🎟 *$4 per vehicle* ⊙ *Most parks are open daily,* 6 AM–10 PM.

❿ Waco Water Park. Featuring two pools, a 22-foot slide, and water depths for all ages, this fun water park sits at the intersection of the Bosque and Brazos rivers in Waco Riverbend Park. ✉ *900 Lake Shore Dr.* ☎ *254/750–7900* 🎟 *$6* ⊙ *Mon.–Fri. noon–7, Sat. 10–7, Sun. 1–7.*

GOLFING

⓬ Cottonwood Creek Golf Course. This 7,140-yard, par-72 public course ★ that winds through rolling plains was voted the 13th-best municipal course in Texas. ✉ *5201 Bagby Ave.* ☎ *254/745–6009* 🎟 *Greens fees $17–$26, carts $10–$14* ⊙ *Daily, 7–dark.*

SHOPPING

At **Laverty's** (✉ *600 N. 18th St.* ☎ *254/754–3238* ⊙ *Tues.–Sat. 10–6*), find all manner of antiques, collectible furniture, books, linens, hardware, and more. **The Shops at River Square Center and Spice Home Furnishings** (✉ *213 Mary St.* ☎ *254/757–0921* ⊙ *Mon.–Sat. 10–7, Sun. noon–5*) feature more than 30 vendors of new and vintage furniture, unique clothes and home accessories, gifts, toys, and collectibles. **Tehuacana Creek Vineyards** (✉ *6826 E. Hwy. 6* ☎ *254/875–2375* ⊙ *Fri. noon–5, Sat. 11–6, Mon.–Thurs. by appointment*) produces and sells blush, red, white, glogg, and port wines on the banks of the Tehuacana ("To-walk-in-a-creek") River just east of Waco, and also hosts tours and tastings.

ARTS & ENTERTAINMENT

THE ARTS

❾ Located on the McLennan Community College campus, **Art Center Waco** (✉ *1300 College Dr.* ☎ *254/752–4371* ⊕ *www.artcenterwaco.org* 🎟 *$2 donation suggested* ⊙ *Tues.–Sat. 10–5, Sun. 1–5*) hosts major exhibits in its main gallery and smaller showings in other rooms, as well as weekend classes and demonstrations. A 35-piece sculpture garden is open all hours.

❼ The **Waco Hippodrome Theatre** (✉ *724 Austin Ave.* ☎ *254/752–7745*) hosts national touring productions in a 1914 building in the heart of downtown.

⓫ The **Waco Civic Theatre** (✉ *1517 Lake Air Dr.* ☎ *254/776–1591*) produces several plays a year that feature local talent. The **Bosque River
Stage** (✉ *1400 College Dr.* ☎ *254/299–8200*), set on the banks of the
Bosque River bordering the McLennan Community College campus,
hosts numerous concerts each year.

NIGHTLIFE

Locals will steer you toward **Treff's Bar** (✉ *520 Austin Ave.* ☎ *254/759–
1209*), especially on Thursday nights, when the "piano man" (no, not
Billy Joel, but a local pianist) makes an appearance. Visit **Wild West**
(✉ *115 Mary Ave.* ☎ *254/759–1081*), also in downtown, for your boot-
scootin' fix. Just down the street, **Cricket's Grill and Draft House** (✉ *221
Mary Ave.* ☎ *254/754–4677*) features more than 100 on-tap beers.
Want a more subdued atmosphere? Try **The Grape** (✉ *2006 N. Valley
Mills Dr.* ☎ *254/772–1866*) for wine, sandwiches, and appetizers. Or
mingle at the **Dancing Bear Pub** (✉ *1117 Speight Ave.* ☎ *254/753–0025*),
which has a good selection of domestic and imported beers, as well as
hearty fare like pizza, nachos, and burritos.

WHERE TO EAT

$$$–$$$$ ✕ **Green Room Grille.** Beef and seafood dominate a menu that changes
monthly at this upscale restaurant in a renovated building downtown.
Offerings have included Angus tenderloin stuffed with wild mush-
rooms, salmon with horseradish crust, and ahi tuna with cantaloupe
salsa. The tomato, basil, and mozzarella salad is not to be missed, nor
is the chocolate pot de crème for dessert. The Green Room boasts one
of the best wine lists in town. ✉ *725 Austin Ave.* ☎ *254/756–7666*
☾ *Closed Sun.–Mon.* ⊟ *AE, D, MC, V.*

$–$$ ✕ **El Siete Mares.** A favorite of the White House press corps when they're
at President Bush's ranch in nearby Crawford, this Veracruz-style Mex-
ican seafood joint is "where fresh, vivid cooking impresses even the
most jaded out-of-towners," *Texas Monthly* wrote. The combination
de mariscos features sautéed oysters, shrimp, octopus, crab, crawfish,
squid, frogs' legs, and mussels, while the *pescado entero* is a whole
red snapper, fried. More traditional dishes like tacos and fajitas are
also available. Each day brings new lunch specials. ✉ *1915 Dutton
Ave.* ☎ *254/714–1297* ⊕ *www.elsietemares.net* ☾ *Closed Sun.–Mon.*
⊟ *AE, D, MC, V.*

¢–$$ ✕ **Baris.** This casual, friendly diner quickly became a favorite of locals
when it opened a dozen years ago. Pizza, available as whole pies or
by the slice, is the best in town. Also outstandng are the chicken pasta
dishes—*cacciatore* (with onions, mushrooms, and tomatoes), *cachovie*
(with artichoke hearts), *aristocrat* (with eggplant and mozzarella in a
white-wine cream sauce and *diavolo* (with basic, garlic and onions).
From the basic spaghetti and meatballs and fettuccine to the sand-
wiches, everything's good here. There's no beer or wine, but feel free to
bring your own. ✉ *904 N. Valley Mills Dr.* ☎ *254/772–2900* ☾ *Closed
Mon.* ⊟ *MC, V.*

¢–$$ ✕ **Georges.** Chicken-fried steak, burgers, and the Big O (a frosty two-
Fodor'sChoice handed-size mug of beer) top the menu at this family-friendly Waco
★ landmark that has been around since the 1930s. Popular with college

CLOSE UP
The Branch Davidian Standoff

Though technically not in the city limits and closer to the town of Bellmead than Waco, the Branch Davidian compound and Waco will forever be linked due to the indelible images broadcast worldwide of the raid by the Bureau of Alcohol, Tobacco and Firearms on February 28, 1993.

Four AFT agents and four Davidians died in a firefight that early Sunday morning, the beginning of a 51-day standoff that ended in a fiery conclusion on April 19, after agents released tear gas into the building and several fires broke out and spread quickly. Seventy-six Branch Davidians died that day, including their cult leader, David Koresh, a controversial figure who the *Waco Tribune-Herald* had begun publishing a series about the day the standoff began. Autopsies showed that many who perished had died not

from the gas or fire but from single gunshot wounds to the head.

Today, there's very little left of the original complex. A neglected swimming pool and an underground bunker are pretty much all that remain. Near the entrance to the land stands a collection of stone markers with names engraved to memorialize those who died there. On the site of the original building stands a modest chapel where religious services are held each Saturday morning—if not for the history of the place, it could easily pass for any small church on a wind-swept prairie in Central Texas.

The compound is at 1785 Double E Ranch Rd. From Waco, take I–35 north to the Loop 340 exit and head west. Turn left onto FM 2941 and then left onto Double E Ranch Rd. The compound is on the left.

students—especially on Thursday, Friday, and Saturday nights—as well as an all-age cross section of Waco, Georges is packed on Baylor football game days and busy most other times, though it's usually easy to get a table for a hearty, reasonably priced breakfast. For the youngsters, there's a kids' menu. ⊠*1925 Speight Ave.* ☎*254/753–1421* ⊕*www. georgesrestaurant.com* ⊙*Closed Sun.* ⊟*AE, D, MC, V.*

¢–$ ✕**Kitok.** It's a Korean restaurant, and yet Kitok's been mentioned in *The*
★ *New York Times* as home of one of the best burgers in Texas. The Liplocker (double cheeseburger) and Oriental fries (a battered, deep-fried nest of thinly sliced vegetables) comprise what is arguably the best meal for the money in Waco. Korean cuisine fills out the remainder of the menu. Chicken and beef bulgogi receive rave reviews, as does the kimchee, a side dish of spicy, fermented (in a good way) cabbage. ⊠*1815 N. 18th St.* ☎*254/754–1801* ⊙*Closed Mon.* ⊟*MC, V.*

WHERE TO STAY

$$–$$$ 🏨**Waco Hilton.** Waco's premier full-service hotel, the Hilton underwent a $19 million renovation that was to be completed in May 2008. The only things that remain the same are the hotel's doors (from guestroom doors to closet doors). Everything else has been redone—even the main entrance has shifted, from University Parks Drive to Third Street and Franklin Avenue, allowing more space for drop-offs. It's a favorite of business travelers (it's connected to the Waco Convention Center) and guests connected with nearby Baylor University. Some of

the spacious, luxurious rooms overlook Indian Spring Park and the historic Suspension Bridge just across the street. **Pros:** Several restaurants, shops, and attractions within walking distance; rooms are quiet. **Cons:** Probably the most expensive property in town; some weekends (Baylor homecoming and graduation, for example) are booked months in advance. ⊠*113 S. University Parks Dr.,* ☎*254/754–8484* ⊕*www. hilton.com* ⇋*194 rooms* ⌂*In-room: refrigerator (some), ethernet, Wi-Fi. In-hotel: restaurant, bar, room service, pool, gym, laundry service, concierge (for "executive level" floor), public Internet, public Wi-Fi, airport shuttle, parking (no fee), some pets allowed, no-smoking rooms* ⊟*AE, D, MC, V.*

$–$$
⟳ 🏠**Judge Baylor House.** Less than two blocks from Baylor University's campus, and just a short drive from downtown, this five-room B&B truly fits the "grandmotherly elegant" description given by owner Bruce Dyer, who lives with his wife Dorothy in an on-site cottage. Visiting faculty and other Baylor-related folk are often guests here, but families (including children, often a rarity among B&Bs) will feel right at home as well. Wonderful breakfasts include Dorothy's signature homemade granola atop blueberry yogurt. **Pros:** No guest room has adjoining walls with another guest room; about a 5-minute drive to the downtown business district and the Waco Convention Center. **Cons:** Very rarely, there are noise concerns from an apartment complex behind the inn; there's no pharmacy nearby. ⊠*908 Speight St.,* ☎*254/756–0273 or 800/522–9567* ⊕*www.judgebaylorhouse.com* ⇋*5 rooms* ⌂*In-room: Wi-Fi* ⏐⃝*BP* ⊟*MC, V, D, AE.*

OFF THE BEATEN PATH

For years, about the only thing the tiny town of Crawford was known for was its public school system, consistently ranked as one of the best in the state. That changed however in 1999, when a 1,600-acre piece of prairie land was purchased by George W. Bush. Almost overnight, Crawford began drawing tourists from all points on the political map. Some locals were chagrined about being in the national spotlight; others took advantage of the attention and opened souvenir shops.

The initial furor has quieted, and tourists aren't as frequent anymore, but for those who venture 21 mi southwest of Waco, don't expect a hearty Texas welcome at the gates of Bush's ranch. Signs along Prairie Chapel Road, where the ranch is located, make it clear: "No Stopping, No Standing, No Parking." (Considering the amount of security that's in the area, it's probably not a good idea to defy the signs and stop for a photo op.)

Travelers will be welcome with open arms, however, at the two dining spots in downtown Crawford. The **Coffee Station** (⊠*6659 Lone Star Parkway* ☎*254/486–2561*) is known for its steak fingers and Texas toothpicks—fried jalapeño peppers and onions—as well as its burgers. And **The General Store** (⊠*6756 Lone Star Pkwy.* ☎*254/486–2636*) is known by locals as "The Fina," whether that brand of gasoline is still sold there or not. It's recommended for the burgers as well.

NORTH-CENTRAL TEXAS ESSENTIALS

Research prices, get travel advice, and book your trip at fodors.com.

BY AIR

Outside the Dallas–Fort Worth Metroplex, the primary airports in North-Central Texas are Waco and Killeen–Fort Hood. Both are small, with a handful of flights departing to Dallas or Houston via American and Continental affiliates; from Killeen, there are also flights to Atlanta and Wendover, Nevada, on Delta and Xtra Airways, respectively.

Airport Information **Killeen-Fort Hood Regional Airport** (⊠ *8101 S. Clear Creek Rd.* ☎ *254/501–6100*). **Waco Regional Airport** (⊠ *300 Austin Ave.* ☎ *254/750-5600 or 866/FLY-WACO (359–9226)* ⊕ *www.waco-texas.com/airport*).

BY BUS

Greyhound (☎ *800/231–2222* ⊕ *www.greyhound.com*) serves most large towns in the region, with connections to Dallas, Fort Worth, and Austin. Driving is usually a much faster way to reach destinations.

BY TRAIN

Amtrak (☎ *800/872–7245* ⊕ *www.amtrakcalifornia.com*) runs the Texas Eagle through this area, going from San Antonio to Dallas, with stops in San Marcos, Austin, Taylor, Temple, McGregor, Cleburne, Fort Worth, and Dallas before moving onto the East Texas cities of Longview, Marshall, and Texarkana, and into Shreveport.

CONTACTS & RESOURCES

EMERGENCIES

In an emergency, dial 911. Temple is home to world-class medical facilities, including Scott & White, one of the country's top hospitals. Each of the following facilities has an emergency room open 24/7.

Hospitals **Hillcrest Baptist Medical Center** (⊠ *3000 Herring Ave., Waco* ☎ *254/202–2000* ⊕ *www.hillcrest.net*). **Scott & White Hospital** (⊠ *2401 S. 31st St., Temple* ☎ *254/724–2111* ⊕ *www.sw.org*).

VISITOR INFORMATION

Denison Area Chamber of Commerce and Visitor Center (⊠ *313 W. Woodard St., Denison* ☎ *903/465–1551* ⊕ *www.denisontexas.us*). **Gainesville Area Chamber of Commerce** (⊠ *101 S. Culberson, Gainesville* ☎ *940/665–2831 or 940/668–4500* ⊕ *www.gainesville.tx.us*). **Granbury Convention & Visitors Bureau** (⊠ *116 W. Bridge St., Granbury* ☎ *800/950–2212 or 817/573–5548* ⊕ *www.granburytx.com*). **Hillsboro Area Chamber of Commerce** (⊠ *115 N. Covington, Hillsboro* ☎ *254/582–2481* ⊕ *www.hillsborochamber.org*). **Waco Convention and Visitor's Bureau** (⊠ *100 Washington Ave., Waco* ☎ *254/750–5810 or 800/321–9226* ⊕ *www.wacocvb.com*). **Waxahachie Chamber of commerce** (⊠ *102 YMCA Dr., Waxahachie* ☎ *972/937–2390* ⊕ *www.waxahachiechamber.com*).

Houston & Galveston

WORD OF MOUTH

"I love the Rothko chapel. The few works that are there were done toward the end of his life and you can really feel the contemplation. That whole area is great. Less than a block away from Rothko is the Cy Twombly museum, the Menil, and the Byzantine chapel. All are free and there is a nice little park there that I love to hang out at. I even bring a small easel and bring my painting stuff out there sometimes to play while my honey reads on a beautiful day."

—maria_so

By Tim
Moloney

SPRAWLING, BRASH, FRIENDLY, AND PROSPEROUS, Houston is arguably Texas's most cosmopolitan city. The forceful, wildcatter temperament that transformed what was once a swamp near the junction of the Buffalo and White Oak bayous into the nation's fourth-largest city also made it a world energy center and pushed exploration into outer space—indeed, the first words spoken from the moon broadcast its name throughout the universe: "Houston, Tranquility Base here. The Eagle has landed."

This same wild spirit (and a lack of zoning laws) explains much about the unrestricted growth that resulted in the city's patchwork layout: It's not unusual to find a luxury apartment complex next to a muffler repair shop, or a palm reader's storefront adjacent to a church. In the past few years a migration has begun back to the city's historic core, and new residential buildings and loft conversions are popping up all over downtown and midtown, with new restaurants, shops, and services following. Four-to-a-lot town houses are replacing quaint bungalows in older neighborhoods like Montrose and the Heights, and though some charm has been lost, the city's center has been recharged.

Houston is an international business hub and the energy capital of the United States; only New York City is home to more Fortune 500 headquarters. The massive Texas Medical Center, with 46 member institutions, is the largest in the world, drawing patients (and doctors) from many countries. Top-notch museums, galleries, performance halls, and resident opera, ballet, and symphony companies affirm the city's commitment to creativity and expression, and its many ethnic restaurants add to the global flavor. Houston's millions of trees, including majestic old oaks, soften and beautify the flat and often unremarkable landscape, which is too often punctuated by tawdry billboards, generic strip centers, and other visual blight (especially along its freeways).

Historic Galveston, 50 mi south of Houston, is itself experiencing somewhat of a beachside boom, from its historic Strand District to new communities all along the waterfront.

GETTING ORIENTED

Viewed from above, Houston resembles a dartboard: a series of concentric rings (highways) spreading out from the bull's eye, downtown. Since the city spreads—OK, sprawls—far and wide, encompassing an area of more than 600 square mi, your best game plan is to rent a car, get a map, and prepare for some exciting freeway driving.

The main thing to remember is that most locations can be characterized as being "In the Loop" or "Outside the Loop," the Loop being I–610, the highway that encircles the inner part of the city. (Not to be confused with "the Beltway," a larger loop highway that rings Houston near George Bush Intercontinental Airport.) Radiating out from the city's center are I–10, heading east to Louisiana and west to San Antonio; U.S. 59, heading northeast to Longview or southwest to Victoria; and I–45, heading southeast to Galveston or north to Dallas.

HOUSTON

Houston can be divided neatly into three major areas. The city's very modern downtown (which includes the theater district) inspired one architecture critic to declare Houston "America's future." A few miles south of downtown are some of the Southwest's leading museums, along with Rice University and the internationally renowned Texas Medical Center. Finally, 15 minutes west of downtown is the Uptown/ Galleria area, a thriving shopping and business center.

EXPLORING DOWNTOWN HOUSTON

Only a few years ago, downtown Houston's skyscraper-lined canyons were a ghost town at night, save for the occasional underground club or white-table restaurant. Then, at the turn of the millennium, downtown experienced a Renaissance—the place was suddenly booming, filled with bars, nightclubs, restaurants, hotels, limousines, Rolexes, silicone—it was an honest-to-goodness "scene." For whatever reason, the boom stalled, and today downtown is reinventing itself again, this time with national retailers like American Apparel, House of Blues, and Lucky Strike Bowling Lanes, and new residential high-rises. The party crowd has moved on, but a real community has taken root.

Getting around downtown Houston on foot is easy: the city is laid out in a grid system, so it's hard to get lost. Right below your feet, there's a whole other city in Houston's Tunnel System, which links 77 downtown buildings via 7 mi of passageways replete with restaurants, stores, barbers, doctors' offices, banks, and more. The air-conditioned tunnels are a great way to get around during the unbearable heat of summer.

MAIN ATTRACTIONS

1 Discovery Green. Houston's newest park opened in April 2008, across from the George R. Brown Convention Center. The 12-acre greenspace features Wi-Fi access, a lake, a model-boat pond, an amphitheater, and **The Grove** (⊠*1611 Lamar St.* ☎*713/337–7321* ⊕*www.thegrove houston.com*), serving steaks, seafood, and acclaimed burgers. ⊠*Bordered by Av. de las Americas, McKinney St., La Branch St., and Lamar St., Downtown* ☎*713/400–7336* ⊕*www.discoverygreen.com.*

3 JPMorgan Chase Tower. Get a quick overview of Houston by taking in the entire urban panorama from the 60th-floor observation deck of Texas's tallest building (weekdays 8–5). Architect I. M. Pei designed this 75-story structure, built in 1981. ⊠*600 Travis St., Downtown* ☎*713/223–0441* ⊕*www.chasetower.com* ⊠*Free.*

2 Minute Maid Park. The Houston Astros play in this modern-but-retro baseball stadium, which has a retractable roof and a monster a/c system to defy Houston's frequently changing weather. Upper-deck seats on the first base side have great views of the downtown skyline—even when the roof is closed, due to a very cool retractable glass wall. The stadium incorporates Houston's 1911 Union Station (designed by Warren and Wetmore of New York's Grand Central Station fame), which houses the ball club offices, retail stores, and eateries. Heavy

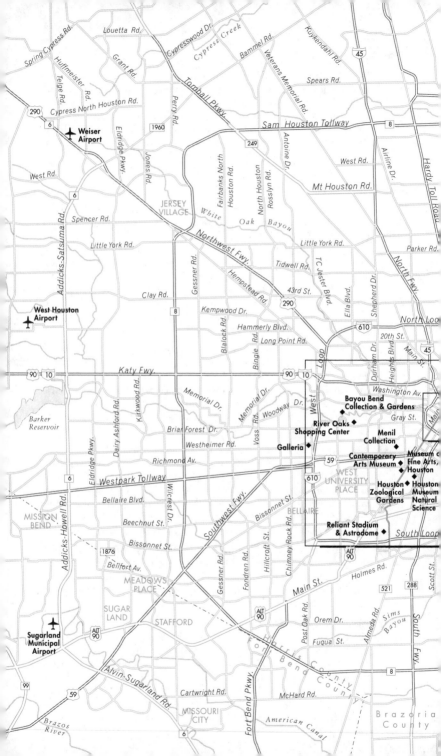

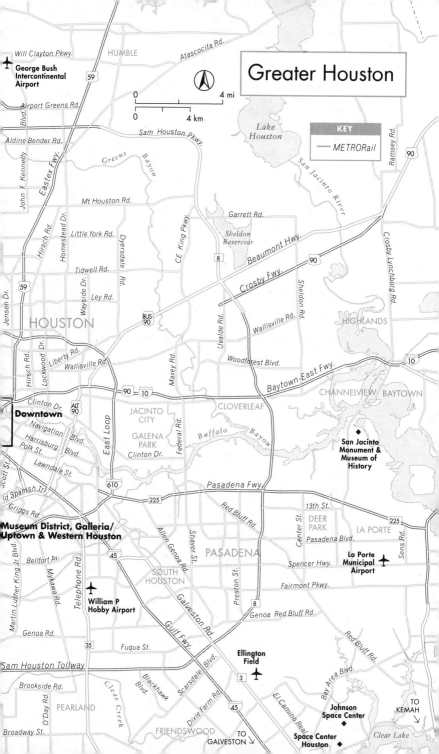

HOUSTON & GALVESTON TOP 5

■ **World-class Art.** Houston is home to eclectic institutions like the Menil Collection, the Rothko Chapel, and world-famous Museum of Fine Arts, as well as off-the-wall places like the Art Car Museum and the kitschy Orange Show.

■ **Sports Lovers' Paradise.** Root for any number of home teams. Major League Baseball's Astros, the National Basketball Association's Rockets, the National Football League's Texans, the American Hockey League's Aeros, the WNBA's Comets, and Major League Soccer's Dynamo are all here.

■ **Black-belt Shopping.** Houston's famed Galleria—with a Neiman Marcus, Saks Fifth Avenue, Cartier,

Chanel, YSL, Louis Vuitton, and an indoor-skating rink—draws affluent shoppers from all over the world.

■ **Affordable International Dining.** Houston's best-kept secret is that it's one of America's best dining cities. Korean barbecue? Check. Texas Barbecue? Check. You'll find pretty much every cuisine imaginable in the Bayou City, without pretense and at a great price.

■ **Parks & Trees.** Skyscrapers loom in the distance, yet the natural beauty along Allen Parkway reminds you that Houston was built along a wild bayou. Green spaces flourish in all corners of the city. The two crown jewels are Memorial Park and Hermann Park.

hitters can rent out Union Station's rooftop, which has views into the stadium from above. ⊠ *501 Crawford St., at Prairie St., Downtown* ☎ *713/259–8000* ⊕ *www.astros.mlb.com* ⊠ *$9 (tours).*

ALSO WORTH SEEING

❺ **City Hall.** Northwest of Tranquility Park, this 1939 modernist structure of Texas limestone was designed by Joseph Finger, Houston's premier architect of the time. There's a visitor center on the ground floor. ⊠ *901 Bagby St., Downtown* ☎ *713/437–5200, Ext. 311.*

❽ **George R. Brown Convention Center.** This massive convention center on the east side of downtown, one of the 10 largest in the nation, is named for Houston entrepreneur, civic leader, and philanthropist George R. Brown. Adjacent to the hotel are the new Discovery Green park and the newish Hilton Americas-Houston, which is connected to the convention center via several skywalks. With 1,800,000 square feet, the center hosts the nation's largest quilt show, as well international technology conferences like ITEC. ⊠ *1001 Av. de las Americas, Downtown* ☎ *713/853–8000.*

❹ **Sam Houston Park.** Houston's first and oldest municipal park contains nine historic structures and a museum gallery. The Kellum-Noble House is Houston's oldest standing brick structure still on its original foundation. If you're visiting around the holidays, try to catch the annual Candlelight Tour in the Park, when costumed actors give tours of the park's homes. ⊠ *1100 Bagby St., Downtown* ☎ *713/655–1912* ⊕ *www.heritagesociety.org* ⊠ *Free; $6 to tour historic structures.*

PLANNING YOUR TRIP

WHEN TO GO

From October through early May, Houston's weather is ridiculously pleasant (barring the rare late-season hurricane). Once summer rolls around, though, four long months of extremely high temperatures (and humidity) bake the city, and Houstonians jump at any opportunity to get out of town. Air-conditioning here is arctic-grade and widespread; almost every indoor space you visit will have a controlled climate (even the underground tunnels downtown). Festivals are timed to occur during Houston's more livable months (namely, the spring).

GETTING THERE & AROUND

All major airlines fly into either Houston George Bush Intercontinental Airport on the city's north side or the smaller Hobby Airport on the southeast side. Continental Airlines dominates Intercontinental, and Southwest rules Hobby. Hobby is much more convenient to downtown.

Houstonians love their cars—which may explain why public transportation here is sorely lacking compared to other large U.S. cities. Things are slowly improving, though. In 2004 METRO, Houston's transit authority, opened the city's first light-rail line, which runs along Main St. from UH-Downtown to Reliant Park, home of the NFL Texans. Initially viewed as a novelty, ridership for the train has really taken off, and several new routes are already on the drawing board and/or approved. Many of Houston's top attractions are on the current light-rail line, and METRO's bus system provides access to other parts of the city. Amtrak also has a station in Houston, right behind the Main Post Office on Franklin St.

For the foreseeable future, the best way to see Houston is by car with a good map (or a GPS unit). Parking spots are generally plentiful and free; the only places you'll pay to park are in the Medical Center and downtown.

High Occupancy Vehicle (HOV) lanes, tollways, and crosstown connectors have reduced traffic congestion, but all of Houston's highways can be extremely crowded during rush hours. Driving isn't too treacherous during non-rush hours, but give yourself plenty of time—the trip from downtown to George Bush Intercontinental Airport can take 25 minutes—or more than an hour, depending on traffic.

7

❼ **The Toyota Center.** The National Basketball Association's Houston Rockets, the WNBA's Comets, and the American Hockey League's Houston Aeros play in this downtown arena. Concerts and other events are also held here. ⊠*1510 Polk St., Downtown* ☎*713/758–3200* ⊕*www.houstontoyotacenter.com.*

❻ **Tranquility Park.** This cool oasis of fountains and walkways was built to commemorate the first landing on the moon by the *Apollo 11* mission. The terrain of mounds and depressions throughout the two-block park evokes the cratered surface of the moon, and the fountain's stainless steel cylinders are designed to resemble rocket boosters. ⊠*Bordered by Walker, Smith, Rusk, and Bagby Sts., Downtown.*

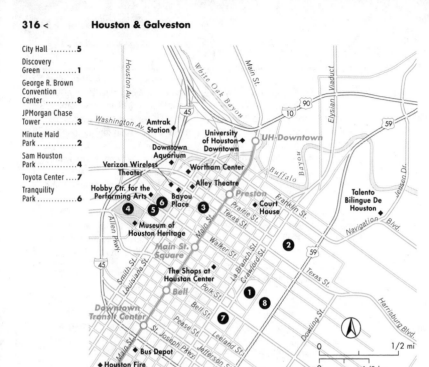

EXPLORING THE MUSEUM DISTRICT, RICE UNIVERSITY & THE TEXAS MEDICAL CENTER

As you head south on Main Street from downtown Houston, the urban landscape begins to fade, and things slow down a bit. Dense blocks and seas of concrete give way to tree-lined boulevards after you pass under Southwest Freeway (U.S. 59), signaling that you're entering the Museum District. A bit farther down the street you'll pass lush Hermann Park and the live oak–filled campus of Rice University—if you like to picnic, you're going to want to visit this part of town. Past the park and university, the urban jungle returns as the skyscraping towers of the Texas Medical Center, one of Houston's "other" downtowns, poke above the majestic trees.

MAIN ATTRACTIONS

③ Byzantine Fresco Chapel Museum. Frescoes from a 13th-century votive chapel have been preserved in this jewel in the Menil complex, located one block from the Rothko Chapel. The dome and apse were rescued from thieves and restored under a unique arrangement with the Greek Orthodox Church and the Republic of Cyprus. ⊠ *4011 Yupon St., Museum District* ☎ *713/521–3990* ⊕ *www.menil.org/byzantine.html* ⊠ *Free* ⊗ *Fri.–Sun. 10–6.*

9 Hermann Park. There's plenty to see and do on this 545-acre oak-shaded urban oasis. Kids love riding the miniature train (just $2.25 a pop) that winds through the trees and taking a pedal boat out on eight-acre McGovern Lake. Duffers can tackle a challenging 18-hole course, and horticulturalists may swoon over the Japanese Garden and the Houston Garden Center, surrounded by 2,500 rose bushes. The park also contains the Houston Zoo, The Museum of Natural Science, and the Miller Outdoor Theater (with a hill that's fun to run—or roll—down). ⊠*Main St. and Hermann Dr.* ⊕*www.hermannpark.org.*

> ## FLOWERS 24/7
>
> Got a date? On your way to visit a friend at the hospital? Or perhaps for some reason you need fresh tulips at 3 AM? The 24-hour **Fannin Flower District** (⊠*The stretch of Fannin Street between U.S. 59 and the Museum District*) is filled with shops offering super-cheap flowers, plants, and arrangements any time, night or day. While you're there, you can stock up on garish knickknacks like teddy bears, bonsai trees, giant topiary monkeys, and helium balloons, plus greeting cards.

7 Houston Museum of Natural Science. You've got to hand it to this Houston museum for expanding the definition of traditional science programming with recent blockbuster shows on jeweler Fulco Verdura, life in Imperial Rome, and Diana: A Celebration, which detailed the life and work of the Princess of Wales. The museum's permanent exhibits are a little more traditional and include Wiess Energy Hall, the dazzling Smith Gem Vault, and the Farish Hall of Texas Wildlife. Also housed within the museum are the **Burke Baker Planetarium,** the **Wortham IMAX Theatre,** and the **Cockrell Butterfly Center,** where you can commune with 1,500 live butterflies. If you plan to see everything, buy the combination ticket. ⊠*1 Hermann Circle Dr., Museum District* ☎*713/639–4600* ⊕*www.hmns.org* ☞*$9 entry, plus additional charges for each venue* ⊙*June–Aug., Mon., Wed.–Sat. 9–6, Tues. 9–8, Sun. 11–6; Sept.–May, Mon., Wed.–Sat. 9–5, Tues. 9–8, Sun. 11–5.*

11 Houston Zoological Gardens. This small but pleasant zoo is home to 4,500 animals, housed in carefully designed ecosystems along shaded trails. Be sure to visit the boardwalks and treehouses of the Wortham World of Primates. If you need a break from the heat, take a spin on the climate-controlled Wildlife Carousel near the Children's Zoo. ■**TIP→ The zoo is free on certain holidays: Memorial Day, July 4th, Labor Day, the Friday after Thanksgiving, and Martin Luther King Jr. Day.** ⊠*1513 N. MacGregor St., Museum District* ☎*713/533–6500* ⊕*www.houstonzoo.org* ☞*$10* ⊙*Daily 9–6 (and open until 7 during Daylight Savings Time).*

1 Menil Collection. This is one of the city's premier cultural treasures. Italian architect Renzo Piano designed the spacious building, with its airy galleries. John and Dominique de Menil collected the eclectic art, which ranges from tribal African sculptures to Andy Warhol's paintings of Campbell's soup cans. A separate gallery across the street houses the paintings of American artist Cy Twombly; Richmond Hall, a few blocks away, houses one of only two permanent Dan Flavin installations

Fodor's Choice
★

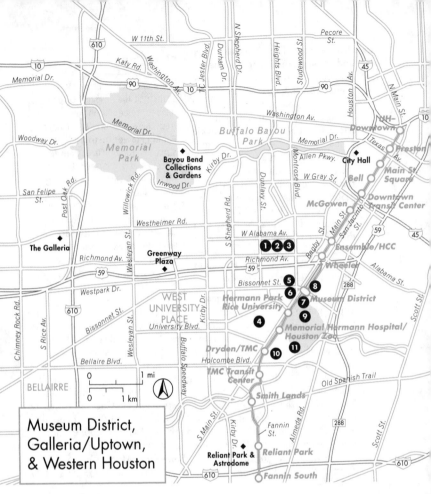

Museum District, Galleria/Uptown, & Western Houston

in America. ✉*1515 Sul Ross St., Museum District* ☎*713/525–9400* ⊕*www.menil.org* ⊠*Free* ☉*Wed.–Sun. 11–7.*

❻ Museum of Fine Arts, Houston. Remarkable for the completeness of its ★ enormous collection, the MFAH is housed in a complicated series of wings and galleries, many designed by Ludwig Mies van der Rohe. When the Audrey Jones Beck Building, the work of famed Spanish architect Rafael Maneo, opened in 2000 it doubled the museum's size. Renaissance and 18th-century art is particularly well represented, and there's a fine selection of Impressionist and post-Impressionist works. You'll also find an ample survey of Asian, Pre-Columbian, Oceanic, and African art, and an impressive collection of modernist paintings, prints, and sculpture. Across the street, the **Lillie and Hugh Roy Cullen Sculpture Garden** (⊠*Free*) displays 19th- and 20th-century sculptures by Rodin, Matisse, Giacometti, and Stella in an outdoor space designed by Isamu Noguchi. ✉*1001 Bissonnet St., north of Rice University, between Montrose Blvd. and Main St., Museum District* ☎*713/639–7300* ⊕*www.mfah.org* ⊠*$7, free Thurs.* ☉*Tues. and Wed. 10–5, Thurs. 10–9, Fri. and Sat. 10–7, Sun. 12:15–7.*

❹ Rice University. Across the street from Hermann Park is top-ranked Rice ★ University, where 3,000 undergraduates from all over the country (and the world) live in an Oxford-inspired Residential College System. The campus is filled with live oaks, Mediterranean-style architecture, and some extremely hefty squirrels. It's a quiet place to escape from the city, and there are many wonderful places to picnic. Rice also houses the James A. Baker III Institute for Public Policy, named for George H. W. Bush's secretary of state. The Rice Owls play football at Rice Stadium, where in 1962 President John F. Kennedy gave his famous "Moon Speech," in which he reaffirmed his earlier call to Congress and the nation that the United States would put a man on the moon in that decade. The 3-mi-long gravel path rings the campus; it's a popular place to walk or jog; massive trees shade most of the route. ✉*6100 Main St., Museum District* ☎*713/348–0000* ⊕*www.rice.edu.*

❷ Rothko Chapel. Adjacent to the lawns surrounding the Menil complex, this moody octagonal sanctuary designed by Philip Johnson houses 14 Mark Rothko paintings. Outside the ecumenical chapel is Barnett Newman's sculpture *Broken Obelisk*, symbolizing the life and death of Martin Luther King, Jr. ✉*1409 Sul Ross St., Museum District* ☎*713/524–9839* ⊕*www.rothkochapel.org* ⊠*Free* ☉*Daily 10–6.*

❿ Texas Medical Center. The world's largest medical center is just a few blocks south of the Museum District. As you drive down Main Street, the soaring glass towers and sprawling campuses of the 1,000-acre complex begin to take shape. About 5.5 million patients are treated in the center each year, and its 46 member institutions include two medical schools, 13 renowned hospitals, 4 nursing schools, and schools of dentistry, public health, and pharmacy. ✉*2450 Holcombe Blvd., Museum District* ☎*713/791–6161* ⊕*www.tmc.edu.*

MISSION: PUT A MAN ON THE MOON

"We meet at a college noted for knowledge, in a city noted for progress, in a state noted for strength, and we stand in need of all three, for we meet in an hour of change and challenge, in a decade of hope and fear, in an age of both knowledge and ignorance. The greater our knowledge increases, the greater our ignorance unfolds.

". . . this city of Houston, this state of Texas, this country of the United States was not built by those who waited and rested and wished to look behind them. This country was conquered by those who moved forward—and so will space.

". . . why, some say, the moon? Why choose this as our goal? And they may well ask why climb the highest mountain? Why, 35 years ago, fly the Atlantic? Why does Rice play Texas?

". . . We choose to go to the moon. We choose to go to the moon in this decade and do the other things, not because they are easy, but because they are hard, because that goal will serve to organize and measure the best of our energies and skills, because that challenge is one that we are willing to accept, one we are unwilling to postpone, and one which we intend to win. . . ."

—*John F. Kennedy, excerpted from his September 12, 1962, speech at Rice University*

ALSO WORTH SEEING

⑤ Contemporary Arts Museum. Housed in an aluminum-sheathed trapezoid, this non-collecting institution hosts traveling avant-garde art shows. Once recent exhibition was "Design Life Now: National Design Triennial," showcasing the experimental projects, emerging ideas, major buildings, and new media that were at the center of contemporary culture from 2003–06; firms represented in the show included Apple and Nike. The museum also throws "Steel Lounge," an evening get-together of music, drinks, and mingling masses, on the final Friday of every month. ⊠*5216 Montrose Blvd., Museum District* ☎*713/284–8250* ⊕*www.camh.org* ☜*Free* ☉*Tues., Wed., Fri., and Sat. 10–5, Thurs. 10–9, Sun. noon–5.*

⑧ Holocaust Museum Houston. This memorial and education center to those who died and survived the "Final Solution" is housed in a stark, cylindrical edifice. Devastating and uplifting, the main exhibit, "Bearing Witness: A Community Remembers," can be viewed individually or by tour. The newest addition to the permanent exhibit is a 1942 German Holocaust–era railcar, the type that was used to carry millions of innocent victims to their deaths. ⊠*5401 Caroline St., Museum District* ☎*713/942–8000* ⊕*www.hmh.org* ☜*Free* ☉*Mon.–Fri. 9–5, Sat.–Sun. noon–5.*

EXPLORING THE GALLERIA & UPTOWN

In the nearly 40 years since Gerald Hines opened the Galleria, Houston's trophy retail property, at the corner of Westheimer and Post Oak, its department stores, designer boutiques, restaurants, hotels, health club, indoor ice-skating rink, and office towers have attracted millions upon millions of visitors. Calling this place a mall is a bit like calling Notre Dame de Paris a church.

The Galleria also spurred the development of an entirely new neighborhood: Uptown Houston. The area's attractions include the soaring Philip Johnson–designed Williams Tower (occasionally referred to by its former name, Transco Tower) and the Waterwall, as well as buildings designed by I. M. Pei and Cesar Pelli. Developer Giorgio Borlenghi's Uptown Park is a charming, European-style shopping and dining village filled with local and national specialty retailers. It's just north of the Galleria, and adjacent to his distinctive high-rise residential towers and outrageously luxurious new hotel, the Granduca. The nearby Tanglewood neighborhood rivals River Oaks and Memorial for spectacular mansions and magnificent trees, and is home to many of Houston's Old Guard—including President George H. W. and Barbara Bush.

The Galleria (⇨ *Shopping*) is the main attraction, but if the weather is nice, take some time to drive around the mansions and dine at Houston's nicest restaurant, Café Annie (⇨ *Where to Eat*).

EXPLORING MONTROSE

Although having a car in Houston is pretty much a necessity, that doesn't mean the city is devoid of walkable neighborhoods. Most strollable parts of town are located inside the Inner Loop—including quirky-cool Montrose. Established in 1911 as a planned community and streetcar suburb, Montrose is just a few miles west of downtown, essentially where Montrose Boulevard crosses Westheimer Road. Things don't feel so suburban here anymore, and today Montrose teems with cafés, gay bars, resale stores, art galleries, boutiques, tattoo parlors, and pawn shops. And although its hipness is gradually being worn away by new town houses replacing old bungalows, there's still enough raffish charm and bohemian flavor to entertain any visitor. Nightlife and shopping are the main draws here (⇨ *Nightlife and Shopping sections*).

EXPLORING THE HEIGHTS

The heart of the historic Houston Heights neighborhood—Montrose's only true competitor for king of weird and artsy—is up on 19th Street, a few miles northwest of downtown. Heights residents have fierce pride in their homes and their neighborhood; preservation efforts are strong, and family-friendly festivals and events are plentiful. Take a walk or jog along Heights Boulevard to see 19th-century Houston in all its splendor. If you're not in the Heights to see its gloriously strange Art Car Museum—featuring rolling masterpieces in all media—you're probably here for the nightlife or shopping (⇨ *Nightlife and Shopping sections*).

CLOSE UP

Mega-Spirited Texas

If you see motorcycles flying overhead while you're in Texas, forget the state fair or rodeo, you just might be in church. As surely as Texas history is seen in its missions like the Alamo, a slice of the state's current culture can be seen in its Battlestar Galactica–like churches. Beyond their sociological significance, the sheer "wow" factor alone (generated by their immense size and offerings) makes Texas's megachurches tourist-worthy sites. In fact, many of them even cater to tourists, with building tours, special events, and book signings.

Inspirational author Max Lucado pastors one of San Antonio's mega-churches.

Texas has more than 182 megachurches (those with a weekly attendance greater than 2,000)—many more per capita than California, which has about the same number of big churches but twice as many residents. Statisticians say that Texas ranks first in the nation in the number of evangelical Protestants and third in number of Catholics.

Houston features the truly stupendous Lakewood Church, the largest church in the country with a Sunday attendance of 45,000, spread out over three services. Its Texas-sized slogan is "Dreaming Big," and its leaders, Joel and Victoria Osteen, have plunked the church into the sports arena formerly occupied by the Houston Rockets. With a Texas-twanged smile Joel welcomes people to "our big living room." His most recent book *Become a Better You*, released in October 2007, was at the time of this writing expected to sell more than 5 million copies. Visitors can take self-guided tours of the church, or stop in for music concerts, seminars, conferences, and classes held throughout the week.

Houston has lots of other "biggest of the big" religious sites to visit. Rev.

Kirbyjon Caldwell, who presided over George W. Bush's presidential inaugurations, also presides over the largest Methodist church in the country: Kingdom Builders Center. Mega-synagogue Beth Yeshurun is the largest Conservative Jewish congregation in the country (with more than 4,000 attendees), and in 2008 Catholics—not to be outdone—built a mega-European style Co-Cathedral of the Sacred Heart with 32 million pounds of concrete and one-half million pounds of steel. Even Rick Warren has an outpost in Houston; at Fellowship of The Woodlands, Pastor Shook's services are known for dramatic sermon illustrations like motorcycles leaping over his head when he discussed having faith.

If you're single and looking, then be sure to visit Second Baptist Church, which claims it hosts the largest adult singles gatherings at any church in the country—7,313 to be exact. And every March the largest Cowboy Church in the world forms on Sundays at the world's largest rodeo, the Houston Livestock Show and Rodeo.

Not to be religiously out-bigged by Houston, Dallas proclaims itself as the newest buckle of the Bible belt.

Basketball fans may recognize Lakewood Church. Until 2003 it was the Summit/Compaq Center, where the Houston Rockets played.

The city is a sort of Disneyland of big churches. You can attend various churches' weekday power lunches, use their mega-sports centers to play ball, or attend conferences that attract more than half a million attendees. On 140 acres (and growing rapidly), Dallas-area's Prestonwood Baptist gathers 28,000 every Sunday to listen to Dr. Jack Graham and the 650-member choir, the largest in Texas. If you like the Texas Rangers, Dallas Cowboys, or other Texas sports teams, then Prestonwood's PowerLunches on Tuesdays are the place to hear the athletes talk.

T.D. Jakes's The Potter's House sponsors the biggest conferences, including, in 2008, a men's conference featuring excursions, concerts, and seminars in one of Texas's grand cowboy-styled resorts. Author of the mega-hit book *Woman, Thou Art Loosed*, Jakes held a four-day Megafest in 2004 that had more than half a million attendees. On Sundays 30,000 congregants pack his church, along with a Grammy-winning choir. Bishop Jakes has twice been featured on the cover of *Time* magazine as "America's Best Preacher" and one of this nation's "25 most influential evangelicals."

But if you want to visit the mega-author of Texas churches who has written more books than any pastor in the U.S., then you must go to San Antonio to Max Lucado's Oak Hills Church. After 14 refusals, Lucado finally found a publisher and then batted out more than 100 books and counting (with more than 55 million in print). He preaches—simply and directly—three times a month at his very tourist-friendly megachurch of 5,300 weekly attendees.

—Tony Carnes

Tour Houston By METRORail

Board METRORail at **UH-Downtown** (One Main Street), housed in the "M&M" Building, which is listed on the National Register of Historic Places. The University moved here in 1974 and quickly built up the neighborhood campus. As you travel over the bayou, look to your left and you'll see **Allen's Landing** (1001 Commerce St.). It was here in 1836 that brothers August C. Allen and John K. Allen stepped ashore and founded the Bayou City.

Exit at the **Main Street Square** stop (Main St. between Walker & Dennis) for downtown's pedestrian-only central plaza, with dramatic water fountains and landscaping, plus easy access to shopping. The flagship **Macy's** (formerly Foley's, at 1110 Main St.) spans an entire city block and is 10 stories tall. A block south at 1212 Main is **The Tipping Point**, home of limited-edition sneakers. They have great books, too.

Back on the train! The next action-packed stop is **Ensemble Theater/Houston Community College.** Exit here, and in addition to the theater and the school you'll find a midtown block of Main Street filled with stores and entertainment options. Hungry? Stop in at the hippie-dippy **Tacos-A-Go-Go** (3704 Main St.) for cheap, homemade, and delicious Tex-Mex (breakfast is served all day). Next door is the comic, toy, and vinyl emporium (and art gallery) **Sig's Lagoon**, open late for interesting shopping. Also on

this block are nightlife spots like the **Continental Club, The Big Top,** and **The Mink,** as well as Latin-inspired **Julia's Bistro.**

At the **Wheeler** rail stop, it's just a short walk to **Lawndale Art Center,** in the former Barker Brothers Studio at 4912 Main St. (originally designed in 1931 by noted Houston architect Joseph Finger, who also designed City Hall). Lawndale exhibits contemporary works in all mediums; see what's new at ⊕ www.lawndaleartcenter.org.

Minutes later, you're at the **Museum District** stop on San Jacinto between Ewing and Binz. No matter which way you turn, you'll be at a major museum within minutes. You're also steps away from the **Hotel ZaZa** (formerly The Warwick), Houston's newest, splashiest, and showiest hotel, where everything is over the top—including many of the guests.

The **Hermann Park/Rice University** stop brings you to Houston's leading university and its leafy 300-acre campus, as well as the city's "Central Park." Sail through the skyscraper canyons of the **Texas Medical Center**—the largest in the world—and before long you'll find yourself at the **Reliant Park** stop, where the massive retractable-roof **Reliant Stadium** is home to the rodeo and the NFL's Houston Texans. It replaced the nearby, now-empty **Astrodome.**

—Tim Moloney

MAIN ATTRACTION

Art Car Museum. If you can't visit Houston during the annual Art Car Parade (though do try to if you can), the next best thing is a visit to this funky museum, where you can see several of the over-the-top autos plus cutting-edge temporary exhibits (of the non-car kind). ⊠ *140 Heights Blvd., Heights* ☎ *713/861–5526* ⊕ *www.artcarmuseum.com* ⊠ *Free* ☉ *Wed.–Sun. 11–6.*

EXPLORING RIVER OAKS

Houston's moneyed set has long called the tony River Oaks neighborhood home. As you stroll (or drive) down River Oaks Boulevard, you'll be able to see just how they live; be sure to turn left or right on Inwood to check out some the gorgeous mansions clustered around River Oaks Country Club. The area is a must-see during the holidays, when fantastic light displays go up. This leafy enclave, just minutes from downtown, is bordered by Montrose on the east and Uptown on the west.

When you're done gawking, head to the neighborhood's top spot, **River Oaks Shopping Center** (⊠ *S. Shepherd Dr. at West Gray* ⊕ *www. riveroaksshoppingcenter.com*), Houston's first, to grab a coffee or some lunch, catch a movie, or pick up a new outfit.

MAIN ATTRACTION

Bayou Bend Collection and Gardens. This estate houses the MFAH's decorative arts collections and lets you step back in time to witness the elegant lifestyle of the first half of the 20th century. Noted Houston philanthropist and collector Ima Hogg donated the 28-room mansion, complete with period pieces dating back to the 1600s, to the Museum of Fine Arts. Be sure to take the time to wander through the beautifully manicured gardens—you'll feel as if you're strolling the grounds of a French château. The woodland trails are especially wonderful, like something out of a fairy tale. Guided and self-guided tours of the mansion must be scheduled in advance (no reservations are necessary in order to tour the gardens). ⊠ *1 Westcott St., River Oaks* ☎ *713/639–7750* ⊕ *www.mfah.org/bayoubend* 🖃 *$10 (home), $3 (gardens); ask about guided tours* ☉ *Tues.–Sat. 10–5, Sun. 1–5).*

EXPLORING ELSEWHERE IN HOUSTON

MAIN ATTRACTION

☾ **Space Center Houston.** Remember Apollo 13's "Houston, we have a
Fodor'sChoice problem?" This is the "Houston" that Jim Lovell and his crew were
★ talking to—and the home of the Mission Control that NASA astronauts communicate with today when they're in space. Visitors to the center can learn about the history and science of space exploration at the **Living in Space** exhibit, which simulates what life is like aboard the space station—and how even "simple" tasks like showering and eating get complicated in zero-gravity. In the **Kids Space Place,** children can ride on a lunar rover and try out tasks in an *Apollo* command module. Want to know exactly how it feels to be launched into space? Then check out the Blast Off Theater, where you'll experience the rocket boosters and billowing exhaust of liftoff. You'll then dock at the International Space Station to get started on your mission. The adjacent **Johnson Space Center** tour includes a visit to (the real) Mission Control and laboratories that simulate weightlessness and other space-related concepts. You can also see a real Saturn V, the launch vehicle for the Apollo moon missions, in **Rocket Park.** Be sure to allow several hours for your visit. ⊠ *1601 NASA Parkway, off I–45, 25 mi south of downtown, Houston* ☎ *281/244–2100* ⊕ *www.spacecenter. org* 🖃 *$18.95* ☉ *Mon.–Fri. 10–5, Sat.–Sun. 10–6.*

THE ORANGE SHOW CENTER FOR VISIONARY ART

The Orange Show Center for Visionary Art's two installations—celebrating the work of individuals with extraordinary imaginations—are definitely two of Houston's strangest (and coolest) attractions. The **Orange Show monument**, located near the University of Houston at 2401 Munger St., is a handmade architectural spectacle constructed by late postman Jefferson Davis McKissack from 1956 to 1979. The outdoor 3,000-square-foot installation, which celebrates the artist's favorite fruit, includes a wishing well, a pond, a stage, a museum and a gift shop; McKissack built it with concrete, brick, found objects, wagon wheels, and statues. The Orange Show Center's other sight is the **Beer Can House** at 222 Malone St., near Memorial Park. Recently refurbished from top to bottom, the house—completely covered and decorated with aluminum beer-can "siding," and garlands of cut beer cans hanging from the roof edges—represents the meticulous beer chugging and recycling work of the late John Milkovisch. More than 50,000 cans were used! ✉ *2402 Munger St.* ☎ *713/926-6368* ⊕ *www.orange-show.org* 🎟 *$1* ⊙ *Office and library daily 9–5:30; Orange Show late Mar.–Memorial Day, Sat. and Sun. noon–5; Memorial Day–mid-Aug. Wed.–Fri 9–1, Sat. and Sun. noon–1; Labor Day–Mid Dec., Sat. and Sun. noon–5; Beer Can House Sat. and Sun noon–5.*

ALSO WORTH SEEING

★ **Kemah Boardwalk.** OK, we'll cut to the chase—the Kemah Boardwalk is a commercial, touristy development run by Landry's Restaurants (the folks who brought you Joe's Crab Shack and Saltgrass Steakhouse)—but most people love it. Just off I–45 between Houston and Galveston, this cluster of moderately priced restaurants, amusement-park rides, game arcades, and inns is set on a bustling ship channel. It's a family-oriented destination where you can catch a Gulf breeze, eat seafood, shop, or just watch the ships sail by. Kids can get up close to some of nature's most misunderstood creatures at Stingray Reef—they can even feed them. A 96-foot-tall wooden coaster called the Boardwalk Bullet was recently added to the mix. It reaches speeds of 51 mph—only five feet from the water's edge. Don't eat first! ✉ *215 Kipp Ave. (off 2nd St.), Kemah* ☎ *877/285–3624* ⊕ *www.kemahboardwalk.com.*

San Jacinto Monument & Museum of History. Alfred Finn, a Houston architect, designed this 570-foot-tall monument, which rises over the site (in nearby La Porte) where Sam Houston triumphed over General Antonio López de Santa Anna in the final battle of the Texas Revolution of 1836. The cenotaph, built between 1936 and 1939, is made of concrete and 100-million-year-old Cordova shellstone quarried north of Austin. At its top rests a nine-point, 35-foot-tall star weighing 220 tons. The park also includes the San Jacinto Museum of History; The Jesse H. Jones Theater for Texas Studies, which shows a movie about the battle called Texas Forever!; the Battleship Texas; and the Albert and Ethel Herzstein Library, covering Texas history. ✉ *One Monument Circle, La Porte* ☎ *281/479–2421* ⊕ *www.sanjacinto-museum.org* 🎟 *$1 park entrance fee; $4 observation deck; $4.50 Texas Forever!*

movie; $5 museum special exhibits; $5 library ⊙ Park, observation deck, museum daily 9–6; battleship daily 10–5; theater daily 10–6; library by appointment.

SPORTS & THE OUTDOORS

OUTDOOR RECREATION

Memorial Park (✉ *6501 Memorial Dr.* ☎ *713/845–1000* ⊕ *www.houston tx.gov/parks/memorialpark.html*) is located near the intersection of I–10 and the West Loop (I–610). One of the city's nicest parks, Memorial has facilities for tennis, hiking, biking, picnicking, and mountain biking, as well as one of the city's premier golf courses. The park's 2.93 mi **Seymour Lieberman Exercise Trail** (also referred to as the Memorial Park Loop), a gravel and packed-earth trail, is where Houston's fit go to run—and see and be seen.

Buffalo Bayou/Eleanor Tinsley Park (☎ *713/845–1000* ⊕ *www.houstontx. gov/parks/ourparks.html*) is a scenic, hilly swatch of parkland running along the bayou; it connects downtown to River Oaks. Running and walking trails run through the park, and it's a great place to escape the rush of the city without actually leaving town. To see some unusual urban wildlife, head to the park's **Waugh Bridge Bat Observation Deck,** at the corner of Waugh Dr. and Allen Parkway, where thousands of Mexican free-tailed bats depart at each night at dusk to hunt for insects.

SPECTATOR SPORTS

The **Houston Astros** (☎ *800/278–7672* ⊕ *www.astros.mlb.com*) play downtown at Minute Maid Park, a retractable roof stadium that began life as Enron Field. The **Houston Rockets** (☎ *713/627–3865* ⊕ *www. nba.com/rockets*), Houston's NBA franchise, play their home games at Toyota Center downtown, just a few blocks from Minute Maid Park and the George R. Brown Convention Center. The American Hockey League's **Houston Aeros** (☎ *713/974–7825* ⊕ *www.aeros.com*) share the Toyota Center with the Rockets. The Aeros are the primary developmental affiliate of the NHL's Minnesota Wild. Major League Soccer's **Houston Dynamo** (☎ *713/276–7500* ⊕ *http://web.mlsnet.com*) were MLS Cup champs in 2006 *and* 2007. The team plays at the University of Houston's Robertson Stadium, just south of downtown on I–45.

SHOPPING

If you can only hit one shopping destination in Houston, make it the Galleria. More than a mall, the Galleria is an experience—more than 24 million people visit each year. Stop by even if you aren't a shopaholic it's quite the scene.

Rodeo Time!

For two solid weeks in March, Houston returns to its Wild West roots. It begins with the trail rides . . . suddenly, the highways and byways leading into the nation's fourth-largest city are filled with cowboys and cowgirls of all ages, races, and sizes, all galloping toward the annual Houston Livestock Show and Rodeo. The huge event at Reliant Park (the complex that houses the Astrodome) brings the entire city together with big-time entertainment (all the biggest country stars, plus crowd-pleasers like Hannah Montana, Fergie, John Legend, and Beyoncé, to name a few recent performers), plus livestock auctions, a chili cook-off, carnival rides, and rodeo competitions. The calf scramble and chuck-wagon races are always fun to watch, and all events benefit a scholarship fund that doles out millions of dollars in support each year.

A cowboy ropes a calf at the Houston Livestock Show and Rodeo.

Unlike the trail riders, you don't have to ride your horse to get there: off-site parking and shuttles operate from all over the city, or you can take the convenient METROrail. Be warned, though: this is one time of the year when you'll have to book a hotel room way in advance.

If you have time to visit *two* of Houston's shopping hot spots, then you have some choices to make. Want a laid-back, alfresco afternoon of retail therapy? Then venture over to the Rice Village. In the mood for something a bit edgier? Then head to the Heights. Are you a hardcore outlet shopper? Then you might want to hop on I–10 and make a trip out to Katy Mills.

GALLERIA/UPTOWN

Houston's premier shopping area is the Galleria/Uptown area, which is barely outside the loop, literally on the other side of 610 at Westheimer Road, just 15 minutes from downtown. The business, office towers, and shopping complexes here have made the neighborhood one of the most important business districts in the city. Many of Houston's best restaurants are here, and the River Oaks neighborhood, with its multi-million-dollar mansions and garden parkways, is nearby.

Fodor's Choice ★ **Galleria.** Not to be confused with the neighborhood, this is the actual Galleria, the region's anchor shopping complex. It's famous for high-quality stores like Neiman Marcus, Cartier, Yves Saint Laurent, Chanel, and Saks Fifth Avenue. But don't be scared off by all these big-ticket names—also here are establishments like Urban Outfitters, Macy's, Banana Republic, and the man-friendly Fox Sports Grill. Kids (and adults) will enjoy the year-round indoor ice rink; during the holidays you can skate around the giant Christmas tree. ⊠ *Westheimer Rd. at Post Oak Blvd.* ☎713/966–3500 ⊕ *www.galleriahouston.com.*

Uptown Park. This charming European-style outdoor shopping center gladly accepts plastic (and you'll need plenty of it) at its cafés, upscale restaurants, designer-clothing boutiques, fine jewelry shops and day spas. ⊠ *Uptown Park Blvd., at Post Oak Blvd.* ☎713/850–1400 ⊕ *www.uptownparkhouston.com.*

Highland Village. Chic national retailers like Anthropologie, Williams-Sonoma, and Crate & Barrel grace this elegant 50-year-old shopping plaza, where you also find scene-y restaurants Smith & Wollensky and RA Sushi (⇨ *Where to Eat*). ⊠ *4055 Westheimer Road* ☎713/850–3100 ⊕ *www.shophighlandvillage.com.*

MUSEUM DISTRICT

The Museum District is—no surprise here—known for art galleries. This area is also popular with college students, due to Rice's proximity.

★ **Rice University Village.** Just west of Rice University, this pedestrian-friendly shopping district is a pleasant, laid-back place to stroll, with an eclectic mix of restaurants, bars, boutiques, and galleries. This is where you'll find a jam-packed five-and-ten store around the corner from yet another Urban Outfitters, plus mainstream national retailers like The Gap, Express, and of course, Starbucks (there are two here). College students abound (you'll bump into quite a few Rice Owls at Two Rows Restaurant and Brewery and Jason's Deli). ⊠ *Bordered by Kirby Drive, Greenbriar, Bissonnet, and University Boulevard* ⊕ *www.ricevillageonline.com.*

ART GALLERIES

4411 Montrose Blvd. A one-stop culture shop, this arts complex features the top-tier Barbara Davis, Joan Wich, Wade Wilson, and Anya Tish galleries, as well as the smart Peel Gallery Shop and the intimate and tasty T'art Café. ⊠ *4411 Montrose Blvd.* ☎713/533–9263.

Colquitt Street. This "Gallery Row" includes a series of important dealers housed in a striking, Arquitectonica-designed postmodern building. ⊠ *Colquitt Street halfway between Montrose and Greenway Plaza.*

THE HEIGHTS

For antiques, vintage clothing, and folk art, try the stores on 19th Street in the Heights, a re-gentrified neighborhood north of I–10 (between Heights Boulevard and Shepherd Drive). The mix varies from junk stores like Sand Dollar to the extremely high-end Wind Water Gallery, which specializes in Asian art and antiques. Also in the Heights, but along 11th Street, are G Gallery, Redbud Gallery, and the Apama Mackey Gallery.

Chippendale Eastlake. You never know what you'll find at this local favorite. A few years ago we spotted this Heights establishment selling Hollywood actress Gene Tierney's massive oil portrait that once hung in her Houston home. ⊠ *250 W. 19th St.* ☎713/869–8633.

Kay Bailey Hutchison: From Pom-Poms to Politics

To critics, she was all big hair and bigger ambition, but U.S. Sen. Kay Bailey Hutchison's friends—and they topped 4 million in her last election—always delivered more than 60 percent of the vote in three Senate races.

The state's first woman senator is a Galveston girl with roots deep enough to include a signer of the Texas Declaration of Independence. She lived a storybook life of easy social status leavened by hard-won achievement:

the University of Texas cheerleader earned a law degree well before women were deemed suitable for lawyering, and then made a mark at Houston's KPRC–TV. She wed Dallas lawyer Ray Hutchison, a Texas GOP force in his own right, but it was Kay who hit it big in politics, serving in Austin before making the leap to Washington in 1993.

—Larry Neal

DOWNTOWN

If you're exploring or staying downtown, you're not out of luck shopping-wise. The landmark Foley's building at 1110 Main Street is now a **Macy's** (⊠*1110 Main St.* ☎*713/407–7033* ⊕*www.macys.com*) and features everything you'd expect in a full-line department store. A few blocks away, **The Park Shops** (⊠*1200 McKinney St.* ☎*713/650–0815* ⊕*www.shopsathc.com*) are a collection of downtown stores; many are junky, but there are a few good ones—plus a completely re-done food court. Scheduled to open in late 2008 is **Houston Pavilions** (☎*713/654-7110* ⊕*www.houstonpavilions.com*), a massive four-block shopping, entertainment, and office complex spanning Main St. to Caroline St. between Dallas and Polk. Already signed on to the project are House of Blues, Lucky Strike Bowling Lanes, McCormick and Schmick's, Marble Slab (ice cream, similar to Cold Stone Creamery), and more.

Additional shopping options lie under the surface within **Houston's tunnel system** (⊠*Accessed via most large buildings downtown*). Just about every service—food courts, dry cleaners, barbers, post offices, specialty shops, florists, even doctors (but no supermarket)—can be found here. The tunnels are open during normal business hours Monday through Friday.

WEST HOUSTON

Trader's Village Flea Market and RV Park. Discover everything from treasure to junk at this 60-acre sprawl of merchants and peddlers. It's only open on Saturday and Sunday, and there's a cost ($2) to search the bounty. ⊠*7979 Eldridge Rd., West Houston* ☎*281/890–5500* ⊕*www.tradersvillage.com*.

FAMILY PICKS

Kemah. If you visit Houston with kids, chances are you're going to end up at this Landry's development just outside the city. There's a small amusement park, a hotel, and, of course, lots of Landry's seafood restaurants. Sure, it's pretty commercial . . . but so's Disney World. And your little ones will have a blast. *For more information, see listing, above.*

Houston Children's Museum. Located in the Museum District, just a short stroll from Hermann Park, the Children's Museum of Houston offers fun, hands-on exhibits and activities for children of all ages. Your kids can work in a TV station, shop in a supermarket, enter an inventors' competition, and much more. At this writing, the museum is in the middle of a large capital campaign to fund its physical expansion and additional programming—so by the time you get here, it may be bigger and better than ever! ⊠ *1500 Binz St., Museum District* ☎ *713/522–1138* ⊕ *www. cmhouston.org* ☞ *$5* ⊘ *Tues., Wed., Fri., Sat. 9–5, Thurs. 9–8, Sun. noon–5; closed Mon.*

Downtown Aquarium. Well, it's another Landry's property with a themed restaurant . . . but, like Kemah, this one's a lot of fun for the kids. There's a giant Ferris wheel, arcade games, and rides, plus an enormous aquarium with exhibits that include a Louisiana swamp, a 17th century shipwreck, a tropical rain forest, a shark voyage, and an exhibit featuring white tigers. ⊠ *410 Bagby St., at Memorial Dr., Downtown* ☎ *713/223–3474* ⊕ *www. aquariumrestaurants.com* ☞ *$9.25; additional charges for rides* ⊘ *Sun.–Thurs. 10–10, Fri.–Sat. 10–11.*

Hermann Park. Houston's version of Central Park is bursting with attractions and activities, including a zoo, paddle boats, a science museum, a miniature train, and countless places to run around or have picnics. *For more information, see listing, above.*

Houston Arboretum and Nature Center. This park, adjacent to Memorial Park, has more than five miles of winding nature trails and 150 acres of woodlands; it's beautifully landscaped and filled with local native plants. Kids love the Discovery Room, with a 25-foot learning tree and pondering pond; challenge them to spot the turtles and crawfish in the water. Classes are also available for both adults and children. ⊠ *4501 Woodway Dr.* ☎ *713/681–8433* ⊕ *www.houstonarboretum.org* ☞ *Free; donations appreciated* ⊘ *Daily dawn to dusk.*

7

OUTSIDE HOUSTON: THE OUTLET MALLS

There are regional outlet centers in LaMarque (southeast of Houston, toward Galveston) and Conroe (northeast of Houston, toward Dallas), the Greater Houston area's main outlet mall is in Katy, about one-half hour west of Houston on I–10.

Katy Mills. Built in the round, this gigantic shopping center features Neiman Marcus Last Call, Off 5th Saks Fifth Avenue, Bass Pro Shops Outdoor World, Kenneth Cole Outlet Store, Cole Haan, the J. Crew Factory Store, and hundreds of other well-known stores. Need a break from shopping? Take in a movie at the AMC Theatres or enjoy a

HOUSTON'S BEST FESTIVALS

MAR. & OCT. Bayou City Art Festival. Held in the spring in Memorial Park and again downtown in the fall, this festival began life as the Art Colony Association's Westheimer Art Festivals. The festival changed it's name when it became more grown up (and, some lament, cleaned up and classed up), and today the Bayou City Art Festival is one of the country's top juried fine-art festivals. ⊕ *www.bayoucityartfestival.com*

APR. Houston Children's Festival. Held downtown in Sam Houston- and Tranquility parks, this all-day event includes food, drinks, and rides—with all proceeds benefiting Child Advocates. Disney Channel guest stars, popular cartoon characters, and a $5,000 scholarship treasure hunt are just some of the highlights. ⊕ *www. houstonchildrensfestival.com*

APR. Houston International Festival. This late-April extravaganza hosts 1,500 musicians from around the world, with countless vendors selling exotic wares and tasty fare over a 20 city-block area. It's a city favorite. The festival always kicks off with the beloved Art Car Parade—stake out your spot along Allen Parkway for this bizarre rolling spectacle. ⊕ *www.ifest.org*

APR. Worldfest Houston International Film Festival. As the third-largest film festival in the U.S., Worldfest honors and promotes cinematic talent on an international scale. It runs more than 50 feature films (the best of more than 4,500 entries) in categories that include student films and documentaries. Each year the festival honors a different country. ⊕ *www.worldfest.org*

tropical-themed meal at the kitschy Rainforest Café. ✉ *5000 Katy Mills Circle, Katy* ☎ *281/644–5000* ⊕ *www.katymills.com.*

NIGHTLIFE & THE ARTS

Houston's nightlife scene seems to be constantly on the move. Right now most of the action is centered in Midtown—between the Pierce Elevated and West Alabama on the north and south, respectively, and stretching from San Jacinto St. on the East to Brazos on the West. Healthy outposts can also be found downtown, in Montrose, and along Washington Avenue (streching from downtown to Memorial Park). There are popular places in the Uptown/Galleria area, too, but you'll find more international tourists and an older crowd than hard-partying twenty- and thirtysomethings.

The great thing about Midtown is that once you park you're within walking distance of all the area's hottest new places, as well as some old standbys. If you don't like crowds, loud drunks, or young people in general, this might not be the best place for you.

Houston's performing-arts scene is located downtown, and the city is one of the few in the United States with four resident performance companies (symphony, ballet, opera, and theater). Shows are staged at Jones Hall, the Alley Theatre, and the Wortham Theater Center.

CLOSE UP

Howard Hughes: From Houston to Hollywood

Test Pilot. Moviemaker. Engineer. Philanthropist. Addict. Recluse.

He had so many interests that the above barely describe Howard Robard Hughes. By 19, the Houstonian had lost his parents and inherited most of their money. His life's work—entertainment and aviation—sprang from their cash and his daring.

In Hollywood Hughes was a ladies' man, and the list of his love interests—Ava Gardner, Katharine Hepburn, and Bette Davis among them—is longer than his movie credits. Even so, a few of the films he produced were nominated for Academy Awards. The director, Lewis Milestone, of Hughes's

1927 *Two Arabian Knights,* a silent picture, took home an Oscar for Best Director of a Comedy Picture.

Hughes lasting success was as an aviation pioneer. His genius in this arena built a fortune and earned him a number of awards, including a Congressional Gold Medal that President Truman had to mail to Hughes when he declined to pick it up.

Hughes's end was no less Hollywood-esque than his life. Crippled by drugs and an obsessive-compulsive disorder, he hid from the world until his death in 1976.

—Lisa Miller

For complete listings of current events, check out the *Houston Chronicle, Houston Press,* and *Where* magazine.

THE ARTS

DOWNTOWN/THEATER DISTRICT

It should come as no surprise that New York has the largest number of theater seats in a concentrated downtown area. But guess who's number two? Houston. The major buildings of the theater district (⊕*www.houstontheaterdistrict.org*) are downtown near Tranquility Park.

Alley Theatre. Houston's resident professional theater company, set in a fortress-like low-lying structure, won a special Tony Award for outstanding achievement by a regional theater in 1996. ⊠*615 Texas Ave.* ☎*713/228–8421 or 800/259–2553* ⊕*www.alleytheatre.org.*

Gus S. Wortham Theater Center. The Houston Grand Opera and the Houston Ballet perform in this center's two side-by-side venues, the Roy and Lillie Cullen Theater and the Alice and George Brown Theater. ⊠*500 Texas Ave.* ☎*713/237–1439 or 800/828–2787* ⊕*www.worthamcenter.org.*

Hobby Center for the Performing Arts. This Robert A. M. Stern–designed center's two opulent theaters, Zilkha Hall and Sarofim Hall, host Broadway Across America and Theater Under the Stars productions. ⊠*800 Bagby St.* ☎*713/315–2400* ⊕*www.thehobbycenter.org.*

Jesse H. Jones Hall for the Performing Arts. This hall, home to the Houston Symphony Orchestra and the Society for the Performing Arts, appears almost encased by a second, colonnaded building. Its teak auditorium is more attractive than the exterior. ⊠*615 Louisiana St.* ☎*713/227–1910 or 800/828–2787.*

MIDTOWN

Ensemble Theater. The largest professional African-American theater company in the Southwest stages gripping performances on its own stage in Midtown. ✉*3535 Main St., Midtown* ☎*713/520–0055* ⊕*www.ensemblehouston.com.*

NIGHTLIFE

DOWNTOWN/THEATER DISTRICT

★ **Bayou Place** (✉*500 Texas Ave., Downtown*), Houston's largest entertainment complex, is a 130,000-square-foot, two-story center of evening activity, with restaurants, clubs, a movie theater, and a live music venue. Bayou Place's **Angelika Film Center** (☎*713/225–5232* ⊕*www. angelikafilmcenter.com*), a spin-off of the famous NYC cinema, screens independent, and foreign films. If you're downtown, head to the hip supper club **Sambuca** (✉*909 Texas Ave., Downtown* ☎*713/224–5299* ⊕*www.sambucarestaurant.com*). Housed in the historic Rice Hotel, it's open for weekday jazz and weekend dance music, and a full menu is available. Knocking one back at **Warren's Inn** (✉*307 Travis St., Downtown* ☎*713/247–9207*) is like traveling back in time. A shrine to bars past, this Market Square institution has dark wood and kitschy dated decor everywhere, and the tables are cramped—but the drinks are strong, and everyone's having a good time.

MIDTOWN

Continental Club (✉*3700 Main St., Midtown* ☎*713/529–9899* ⊕*www. continentalclub.com/Houston.html*), a sister of the legendary Austin original (which has been open since the 1950s), this Houston branch brings more loud, live music to an even bigger dance floor. The classic dive bar **Leon's Lounge** (✉*1006 McGowen St., Midtown* ☎*713/659–3052*) is allegedly Houston's oldest drinking establishment. There are cheap drinks, a random juke box, and table-top shuffleboard. Some of the patrons, like the bar itself, are a little rough around the edges. It's indie rockers vs. dance partiers at **The Mink** (✉*3718 Main St., Midtown* ☎*713/522–9985* ⊕*www.themink.org*), a two-building venue that celebrates classic vinyl, electronic dance music, disaffected emo youth, and the oddness in all of us. Looking for the young and beautiful crowd? Then head out to **Red Door** (✉*2416 Brazos St., Midtown* ☎*713/526–8181* ⊕*www.reddoorhouston.com*). You'll know you found it when you see the unremarkable grey building with the, uh, red door. Upstairs you'll experience one of Houston's better patios, with a terrific view of downtown. Sophisticated wines meet an environment of polished industrial decay at **13 Celsius** (✉*3000 Caroline St., Midtown* ☎*713/529–VINO* ⊕*www.13celsius.com*), a wine bar and retail shop set in a former dry cleaners. This is the only wine bar in town that keeps its vino in a temperature-controlled cellar, set at, you guessed it, 13 Celsius. Take a break from the "see and be seen" scene at **The Tipsy Clover** (✉*2416 Brazos St., Midtown* ☎*713/524–0782*), an attitude-free neighborhood bar where you can either lounge on the couch by the fireplace or participate in classic bar games like pool and darts. Lots of beers to choose from.

CLOSE UP

Houston's Fair Play

Fancy some feast food, a little sword-play, and maybe a nice, friendly joust? Then you might try traveling back five centuries at the Texas Renaissance Festival, conducted each year 50 mi outside of Houston. Each year more than 300,000 people attend the enormously popular festival, staged during eight weekends in October and November. Some go for the pleasure of tearing into a turkey leg, hefting a tankard of ale, and taking in fully costumed jousts conducted each weekend day. Others like the live performances—like glass blowing, minstrel music, and juggling.

Knights joust at the Texas Renaissance Festival.

The festival has grown from its humble beginnings in 1974 to inhabiting a permanent, 53-acre theme park. During each of the eight weekends it engulfs the park (and each weekend has a theme, like "Roman Bacchanal" or "Highland Fling"), 300 vendors set up shop, and 14 performance stages boast live entertainment—as well as two wedding chapels. Even among the brightly costumed performers, musicians, and attendees, though, food takes center stage.

The food. Oh, the food. The aforementioned turkey legs—a popular Texas fair food—are ubiquitous, but there are plenty of other tasty dishes served on sticks. There is steak-on-a-stick, chicken on a stick, sausage on a stick

. . . and there is also more "normal" food like ice cream and popcorn. Visitors can purchase tickets to the King's Feast ($95), where roasted and savory dishes are served according to the weekend's theme. There is also a King's Wine Tasting ($50), where eight different wines are served up with cheese and fruit.

■TIP➜**Bring plenty of gold (and a little silver for the entertainers).** There are price breaks for the little ones—$10 for children 5–12 and free for kids 4 and younger.

Texas Renaissance Festival. ⊠ *On FM 1744, between Plantersville and Magnolia, Texas, 50 mi NW of Houston, Plantersville* ☎ *800/458-3435* ⊕ *www.texrenfest.com* ⌸ *$21* ⊙ *9 AM to dusk Fri.–Sun., Oct. 6–Nov. 25.*

—Jennifer Edwards

THE HEIGHTS

Who says a wine bar has to be all high-falutin? That's certainly not the case at **The Corkscrew** (⊠ *1919 Washington Ave., Heights* ☎ *713/864-9463* ⊕ *www.houstoncorkscrew.com*), a friendly wine bar/shop that features more than 250 wines in a rotating stock—*all* of them available by the glass. Brought to you by the same people who own the hyper-trendy Red Door in Midtown, the **The Drake** (⊠ *1802 Washington Ave., Heights* ☎ *713/526-3616*) is the latest bar–club addition to the booming Washington Avenue scene. With high ceilings and low lighting, this is where former Midtown nightlife decathletes settle into their 30s.

WHERE TO EAT

THE SCENE

In the U.S.'s fourth-largest city, the average resident eats out four times per week. There are thousands of choices—from Pan-Asian to Italian, barbecue to nouvelle Southwestern, and burgers to bistros to Bolivian and beyond. You can even find fusion cuisines like Chinese and hamburgers. And of course, Tex-Mex rules. It can all be a bit overwhelming, but it's a nice problem to have: dining in Houston spoils you completely. From downtown's white-tablecloth business spots to the burgeoning Washington Corridor scene to quirky Montrose to the eclectic Heights to booming Midtown and into the strip-mall world of the suburbs, there are excellent eating establishments at all price levels.

WHAT IT COSTS				
¢	$	$$	$$$	$$$$
RESTAURANTS under $8	$8–$12	$13–$20	$21–$30	over $30

Restaurant prices are per person for a main course at dinner.

DOWNTOWN

NEW AMERICAN
$$$–$$$$

✕**Bistro Lancaster.** Breakfast—make that power breakfast—and lunch are popular with the business set at this small, classy restaurant in the Lancaster Hotel downtown, but dinner is the ticket, especially for the pre-theater crowd. Chef Jamie Zelko offers a changing seasonal menu based on fresh local ingredients. Try the crab cakes and bread pudding. Brunch is available on weekends. The adjacent Bistro Bar has a terrific wine list and a cozy, intimate setting. ⊠*701 Texas Ave., Downtown* ☎*713/228–9500* ⚘*Reservations essential* ▭*AE, D, MC, V.*

CREOLE/ CAJUN
$$$–$$$$

✕**Brennan's.** A cousin of New Orleans's Commander's Palace, Brennan's puts a Texas spin on Creole cuisine. This is one of the few restaurants in Houston where people still dress up. Not that it's in any way formal: the landmark building's interiors are as charming as the hospitality is Southern-gracious. Chef Randy Evans's specialties, like turtle soup with sherry and pecan-crusted fish, repeatedly impress. Brunch in the peaceful courtyard is a memorable experience. For an extra-special night, book the Kitchen Table, a private dining room that seats 10 and offers a ringside view of all the cooking action. ⊠*3300 Smith St., Downtown* ☎*713/522–9711* ⚘*Reservations essential* ▭*AE, D, DC, MC, V.*

ITALIAN
$$–$$$$

✕**Damian's Cucina Italiana.** "Timeless" is the word for this sophisticated, authentic Tuscan restaurant located where downtown becomes midtown. It's been a business luncheon favorite for more than 20 years, and at night couples and families come to enjoy the cozy, old-world interior; extensive menu offerings; comprehensive wine list; and leisurely pace. The menu is huge; if you're having trouble deciding, try the deftly grilled veal chops or the ravioli *del giorno* (of the day). Chef Napoleon Palacios creates weekly specials, too, so there's always something new

WHERE SHOULD I DINE IN HOUSTON?

	Neighborhood Vibe	Pros	Cons
Downtown	After a bit of a lull in the early 2000s, when light-rail construction immobilized Main St., downtown Houston is booming with new restaurants both above and below ground. (Downtown's tunnel system is loaded with restaurants.) During weekdays, white-collar workers crowd these spots in Houston's business center; on weekends, you might have them pretty much to yourself.	Walkable neighborhood, many fine hotel restaurants, alfresco dining.	Can feel deserted at night, parking can be hard to find, and wildly expensive if you use valet.
Montrose	The bohemian vibe is alive and well in funky Montrose, which is home to some of the city's best and most interesting restaurants as well as tattoo and piercing parlors. Dining choices range from hyper-expensive to laughably cheap, and include virtually every cuisine imaginable.	Lots of choices, great people-watching, convenient center-city location.	Transvestite prostitutes, panhandlers, and street kids are part of the offbeat fabric of Montrose, even during the daytime.
The Heights	Montrose's rival in the diversity department is the historic Houston Heights, developed as one of the city's first suburbs, even though it's just a few miles from downtown. Long known as a diner's no-man's-land, the Heights now has several fine restaurants, in addition to hole-in-the-wall treasures on charming 19th Street. Parts of the Heights are still "dry," and some restaurants are BYOB. Call ahead to make sure.	Historic surroundings, walkable and safe neighborhood, family friendly.	Somewhat dead after dark, restaurants cannot serve alcohol in some spots.
Uptown/ Galleria	An international crowd and lots of shoppers gather in the restaurants of the Uptown/Galleria area. High-end chains like Kona Grill, Del Frisco's Steakhouse, and Morton's compete with local favorites like Arcodoro, Uptown Sushi, and Café Annie.	Reliable high-end chains, great business-lunch choices.	Traffic and congestion a frequent problem, strip centers have little character.
West End/ Memorial Park	Trendy restaurants catering to young professionals, fun singles, and urban couples line up along rapidly gentrifying Washington Avenue. Many cheap and delicious taquerias remain, too.	Bustling new restaurants, interesting cuisines.	Parking can be a hassle if you don't like valet; fratty, young atmosphere prevalent.

7

to try. ✉ *3011 Smith St., Downtown* ☎ *713/522–0439* ▭ *AE, D, DC, MC, V* ☺ *Closed Sun. No lunch Sat.*

AMERICAN ✕ **Dharma Cafe.** On rapidly gentrifying Houston Avenue—in a historic
$$ industrial building that's beginning to be surrounded by new town
Fodor'sChoice houses—cool, laid-back Dharma Cafe continues to put forth an inno-
★ vative menu and presentation unlike anything else found in the city.

BEST BETS FOR HOUSTON DINING

Maybe it *is* a good thing that Houston's so spread out; that way, you can find fine restaurants at all different price points all over town. Houston is one of America's great eating cities, for budget travelers and businesspeople alike. Here are some of the best of the best in terms of style, price, and cuisine.

Fodor's Choice ★

Cafe Annie, $$$–$$$$,Uptown/Galleria

Dharma Cafe, $$, Downtown

Max's Wine Dive, $$–$$$, West Side/ Memorial Park

Strip House, $$$–$$$$, Downtown

t'afia, $$–$$$$, Midtown

By Price

$

Chuy's, River Oaks

Dolce Vita, Montrose

Goode Company Texas Bar-B-Q, Rice Village (West University)

Pronto Cucinino, Montrose

$$

Daily Review Cafe, Montrose

Dharma Cafe, Downtown

Max's Wine Dive, West Side/Memorial Park

Shade, The Heights

$$$

benjy's, Rice Village

Catalan, West Side/ Memorial Park

Ibiza, Midtown

La Griglia, River Oaks

t'afia, Midtown

$$$$

Cafe Annie, Uptown/Galleria

Strip House, Downtown

Tony's, Midtown

By Cuisine

NEW AMERICAN

benjy's, $$–$$$, Rice Village

Daily Review Cafe, $$–$$$, Montrose

Ouisie's Table, $$–$$$, River Oaks

Shade, $$–$$$, The Heights

SEAFOOD

Pesce, $$$–$$$$, River Oaks

Reef, $$$, Midtown

Tony Mandola's Gulf Coast Kitchen, $$–$$$, River Oaks

STEAKHOUSE

Pappas Bros. Steakhouse, $$$–$$$$, Uptown/Galleria

Strip House, $$$–$$$$, Downtown

Taste of Texas, $$$–$$$$, West Side/ Memorial Park

TEX-MEX

Chuy's, $, River Oaks

El Tiempo, $$, West Side/Memorial Park

Ninfa's, $–$$, Downtown

By Experience

ARTSY

Baba Yega, $–$$, Montrose

Dharma Cafe, $$, Downtown

t'afia, $$–$$$$, Midtown

BUSINESS-LUNCH CROWD

Bistro Lancaster, $$$–$$$$, Downtown

Damian's Cucina Italiana, $$$–$$$$, Downtown

La Griglia, $$–$$$, River Oaks

Tony's, $$$–$$$$, Midtown

DINING ALFRESCO

Arcodoro, $$$–$$$$, Uptown/Galleria

Baba Yega, $–$$, Montrose

Daily Review Cafe, $$–$$$, Montrose

Dolce Vita, $–$$, Montrose

Ouisie's Table, $$–$$$, River Oaks

SOCIAL SCENE

Armandos, $$–$$$, River Oaks

Cafe Annie, $$$–$$$$, Uptown/Galleria

Tony's, $$$–$$$$, Midtown

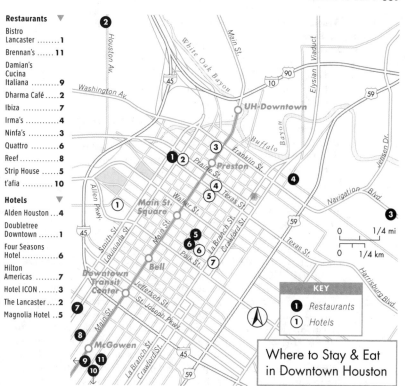

**Where to Stay & Eat
in Downtown Houston**

You just never know what chefs Susan and John will find in their pantry and cooler that morning to whip up for lunch and dinner. Maybe it will be Blueberry Chicken Breast, chicken breast filled with blueberries, almonds, and ricotta and drizzled in a blueberry-brandy glaze. Or it could be a spinach salad topped with barbecued oysters and hot bacon dressing. Don't miss the ever-changing selection of desserts, including homemade cinnamon gelato. The Sunday all-you-can-eat buffet brunch, which includes a mimosa, is an amazing value at $15. ⊠*1718 Houston Ave., Downtown* ☎*713/222–6996* ⊟*AE, D, DC, MC, V* ⊗*Closed Mon.*

MEXICAN ✕**Irma's.** Irma and her family dish out home-style Mexican specialties
$–$$ to a wait-in-line breakfast and lunch crowd (weekdays only) of lawyers, judges, cube-dwellers, and sports fans. The surroundings may be homey, but this place is not cheap—still, the food has made Irma's a local landmark. There's no menu: your server will tell you what is available. Opt for the chicken-and-spinach enchiladas with green chili sauce, and wash it all down with the famous lemonade. Irma opens on weekends when the Astros are in town—and stays open until 6 PM during the week on home-game days. ⊠*22 N. Chenevert St., Downtown* ☎*713/222–0767* ⊟*AE, DC, MC, V* ⊗*Closed weekends, no dinner.*

TEX-MEX
$–$$
★
✗**Ninfa's.** The original—and still the best—of the chain, Ninfas on Navigation holds a special place in the hearts of generations of Houstonians. Always busy, and filled with everyone from politicians to young families to the gay mafia to savvy tourists, this East End landmark serves up warm, fresh tortillas made on-site, killer margaritas in all their forms, and a trademark green salsa made with avocados and tomatillos. Don't miss the Tacos a la Ninfa or the "chilpanzingas"—corn empanadas stuffed with smoked ham, cheese, and chilies, and topped with *queso fresco* (mild, crumbly white cheese). The Ninfa's shuttle runs to downtown sporting venues; call ahead for information. ✉*2704 Navigation Blvd., East End* ☎*713/228–1175* ▭*AE, DC, MC, V.*

> **DINING WITH KIDS**
>
> Family-centered restaurants abound in the Bayou City. Beyond the Chuck E. Cheeses and fast-food joints there are lots of local establishments, like Lupe Tortillas, that have kids' menus and playgrounds—and margaritas for harried parents. West University, River Oaks, and the Heights—neighborhoods where families are teeming with children—are good bets for kid-friendly dining.

ITALIAN
$$$–$$$$
✗**Quattro.** Though the Four Seasons Hotel is sort of fussy and dated, its in-house restaurant is a sleek, lively set of smartly designed dining rooms with inspiring food. Quattro—its name representing the four "faces" of the restaurant—breakfast, lunch, dinner, and the antipasto bar—focuses on popular American-Italian dining that's fresh, simple and seasonal. The wine list includes 25 wines by the glass, 250 bottle selections, and a private cellar selection of reserve and boutique wines. It's frequented by lots of political types, pampered travelers, birthday boys and girls, and theater-goers. From maitre d' to server, attention to your enjoyment is given unobtrusively and plentifully. ✉*1300 Lamar St., Downtown* ☎*713/652–6250* ▭*AE, D, DC, MC, V.*

STEAK
$$$–$$$$
Fodor's Choice
★
✗**Strip House.** Naughty vintage pinups fill the walls of this sexy downtown steak house, where the menu is chock-a-block with old-school prime cuts of beef charred to perfection. Don't miss the black-truffle creamed spinach or the goose-fat potatoes. Yes, it's expensive, but it's worth it. Wine recommendations are easy to come by and always a good match. This is the place for that big date, an important business dinner, or just a great night out on the town. Four private dining rooms can accommodate eight to 100 guests for lunch or dinner. Strip House is within walking distance of the Toyota Center, the George R. Brown Convention Center, The Four Seasons, and the Hilton Americas. ✉*1200 McKinney St., Downtown* ☎*713/659–6000* ▭*AE, D, DC, MC, V.*

MIDTOWN

SPANISH
$$$
✗**Ibiza.** Gutsy, sometimes playful cuisine prepared by Chef Charles Clark is served in a bustling Midtown dining room as seductive as its namesake island off the coast of Spain. Generous portions of seasonal dishes intermingle with delectable Spanish tapas and hearty entrées

such as braised lamb shank with mint oil. Oenophiles appreciate Ibiza's ever-changing wine list of rare tastes at fair prices. Don't miss the outdoor patio on pretty days or the homemade sangria chock-full of fresh fruit. Insider tip: cotton candy is available as a lunch dessert; just ask! An adjacent lounge, Ibiza Lounge Next Door, opened in 2007 and packs in a young, good-looking, and chic crowd in a cozy dark room with lots of low seating. ⊠ *2450 Louisiana St., Ste. 300, Midtown* ☏ *713/524–0004* ⊟ *AE, D, DC, MC, V* ⊗ *Closed Mon.*

SEAFOOD
$$$

✕ **Reef.** Chef Bryan Caswell, late of Bank at the Hotel Icon, re-emerges at Midtown's bustling Reef, a loud, showy seafood house packed to the gills with movers and shakers and their friends. Although the food is often a mixed bag, when it's good, it's great. Shrimp wrapped with bacon and stuffed with avocado; crispy-skin Gulf Coast snapper; and the jumbo crab cake served with taqueria-style pickled vegetables are good choices. Fish not regularly seen on conventional menus, from amberjack to wahoo, make a splash here as well. For a seafood joint, Reef has a mean "naked" rib eye, served with brown-butter gnocchi. Check out the glass-enclosed wine wall, filled to the ceiling with remarkably well-priced, unusual selections. ⊠ *2600 Travis St., Midtown* ☏ *713/526–8282* ⊟ *AE, D, DC, MC, V* ⊗ *Closed Sun.*

MEDITERRANEAN
$$–$$$$
Fodor'sChoice
★

✕ **t'afia.** Sleek and open t'afia's coastal Mediterranean cuisine blasted with local ingredients is a consistently great dining choice in the Midtown/Montrose area. Chef Monica Pope, a local food celebrity, changes the menu daily, depending on what treasures she finds fresh in the greater Houston area. It could be spicy crab and peanut soup with okra one day, and Texas quail with braised cabbage the next. A full range of interesting sides—including decadent macaroni and cheese infused with black truffle oil—completes the picture. Getting inspired? Buy your own local ingredients at the Midtown Farmers Market, held in the restaurant's parking lot every Saturday from 8 AM to noon, rain or shine. ⊠ *3701 Travis St., Midtown* ☏ *713/524–6922* ⊗ *Closed Sun. and Mon.* ⊟ *AE, D, DC, MC, V.*

CONTINENTAL
$$$–$$$$
★

✕ **Tony's.** This adult playground is the place where deals get done, life celebrations are marked, and people keep an eagle eye out for the next boldfaced type (as in boldface type in the social columns) to walk through the water-wall-surrounded front doors. Oh right, the Euro-Italian food is excellent, too, and the über-elegant surroundings, complete with contemporary artworks by Jesus Moroles, Robert Rauschenberg, and Donald Sultan, are sensory overload. Tony Vallone and his trained staff take excellent care of each and every customer. Watch for him and wife Donna moving around the room at lunch and dinner, personally greeting diners. Call ahead to order the towering molten white-chocolate soufflé, a local favorite. The cellar holds more than 1,000 labels, and is particularly strong in wines of France, Italy, and California. Lunch is a prix-fixe steal. ⊠ *3755 Richmond Ave., Greenway Plaza* ☏ *713/622–6778* ⊟ *AE, D, DC, MC, V* ⊗ *No lunch Sat. Closed Sun.*

MONTROSE

VEGETERIAN
$–$$

✗ **Baba Yega Restaurant.** An excellent choice for vegetarian cuisine, this eclectic bungalow in the Montrose neighborhood serves an avocado-and-mushroom-topped veggie burger plate that has been popular since 1975. Named after a Slavic witch, Baba Yega offers an award-winning weekend brunch, and full bar as well. Enjoy people-watching out front under the shade of a century-old oak tree, or dine on the covered patio before a waterfall and herb garden. ✉*2607 Grant St., Montrose* ☎*713/522–0042* ⚐*Reservations not accepted* ▭*AE, D, DC, MC, V.*

NEW
AMERICAN
$$–$$$

✗ **Daily Review Cafe.** This casual eatery housed in a former printing plant proves that comfort food and urbanity can coexist. The menu's appeal is as broad as the crowd is diverse—from buzz-cut hip young things to Downtown suits. Ladies who lunch often lunch here, too. Families are prevalent during weekend brunch. Entrées are imaginative twists on traditional favorites, such as the chicken potpie perked up with shaved fennel and carrots in cream sauce. Go early to avoid a wait. There is open-air dining on a covered patio, or you can sit in the garden when the weather's nice. ✉*3412 W. Lamar St., Montrose* ☎*713/520–9217* ▭*AE, D, DC, MC, V* ☺*No dinner Mon.*

ITALIAN
$–$$
★

✗ **Dolce Vita.** For fresh gourmet pizzas and interesting starters, head directly to buzzing Dolce Vita on lower Westheimer's restaurant row. Extremely casual, with gracious dining areas scattered throughout a restored older house, the restaurant has unexpected appetizers like marinated mussels tossed with capers, parsley, and potatoes, and calamari with mint, orange, and olives. Smoky Neapolitan pies are baked in the 800-degree wood-fired oven and include the crowd-pleasing *margarita,* with tomato, basil, and buffalo mozzarella and the *salsiccia e friarelli,* with sausage, rapini, and pecorino. Sit outside in good weather and bad—the patio's covered. ✉*500 Westheimer Rd., Montrose* ☎*713/520–8222* ▭*AE, D, DC, MC, V* ☺*Closed Mon. No lunch.*

ITALIAN
$$–$$$

✗ **La Strada.** This large, trendy restaurant is primarily known for its loud, boozy Sunday brunch featuring Houston's young glitterati in all their drinking, dancing, and dining glory. The interior is brightened by large windows, yet subdued with dark-wood tables and chairs. Contemporary paintings are scattered about. While no one really comes for the food, it's actually very good. Try the spinach dip or the Black Angus beef fillet. Michael's Favorite—chicken scaloppine with tomatoes and capers—is a favorite for a reason. Don't miss the chocolate mousse pie for dessert. There's late-night dining until 3 AM Friday and Saturday. ✉*322 Westheimer Rd., Montrose* ☎*713/523–1014* ▭*AE, D, DC, MC, V.*

THAI
$–$$
★

✗ **Nidda Thai.** Don't let the strip-center location or the dreary brown-and-grey interior fool you: this may be the best Thai restaurant in Houston. From the moment you walk in, you're greeted warmly and served attentively. Menu standouts include pad Thai in all its rich peanuty goodness, along with a top-of-its-class chicken satay served with a zesty cucumber relish. Warning: if the server asks you if you'd like your dish "Thai hot," you might as well bring along a fire extinguisher. The wine list is kind of disappointing, but you're here for the food. ✉*1226 Westheimer Rd., Montrose* ☎*713/522–8895* ▭*AE, D, DC, MC, V.*

ITALIAN ✗**Nino's.** This granddaddy of Houston restaurants was one of the first
$$–$$$ to bring fine, reasonably priced Italian cooking to the city. Nino's appetizers and entrées can go head to head with those at trendier and tonier places in town. Owner Vincent Mandola continually updates the menu but retains the classics that put him on the map. Start with antipasto *misto* (mixed) of marinated and roasted vegetables, then enjoy wood-fired rotisserie lemon-garlic chicken with mashed potatoes for inspired comfort food. ⊠*2817 W. Dallas St., Montrose* ☎*713/522–5120* 🖃*AE, DC, MC, V* ⊙*Closed Sun. No lunch Sat.*

ITALIAN ✗**Pronto Cucinino.** Houston's first family of restaurateurs, the Mando-
$ las, have put their stamp on this casual eatery (they also own Nino's, ⇨*above*) that offers classic Italian dishes in a warm, vibrant atmosphere. The affordable offerings include a fantastic spinach salad with pancetta, chopped eggs, and goat cheese, plus the house specialty: wood-roasted lemon-garlic chicken, served with garlic mashed potatoes and Italian-style green beans. There's also a great selection of pasta dishes, and a decent wine list. Sit outside when the weather's nice, or order ahead to-go—they'll bring it right out to your car. ⊠*1401 Montrose Blvd., Montrose* ☎*713/528–8646* 🖃*AE, D, DC, MC, V.*

MUSEUM DISTRICT/RICE VILLAGE

NEW ✗**benjy's in the village.** The self-designated "modern American cuisine"
AMERICAN continues to evolve, but the cool factor and the quality remain the same
$$–$$$ at this Rice Village mainstay. Owners Benjy and Erica Levit deliver sat-
★ isfying lunch, brunch, and dinner offerings, including warm pistachio-crusted goat-cheese cakes, seared sashimi-tuna pizza, and a standout grilled beef fillet with roasted-garlic mashed potatoes. If you're in the mood to stay late or arrive early, you can head upstairs to the lounge for beautiful people, generous-sized cocktails, and mid-century glam. ⊠*2424 Dunstan Rd., Rice Village* ☎*713/522–7602* 🖃*AE, D, DC, MC, V.*

BARBECUE ✗**Goode Company Texas Bar-B-Q.** Down-home Texas barbecue is pre-
¢–$ pared ranch-style—mesquite-smoked and served with tasty red sauce.
★ Patrons young and old line up on the sidewalk to eat at picnic tables on the covered patio. A standard order is the chopped-beef brisket sandwich on jalapeño-cheese bread. Don't skip the celebrated pecan pie for dessert. Goode Company Hamburgers and Taqueria across the street serves—no surprise here—hamburgers and tacos, as well as great weekend breakfasts. And for some honky-tonk atmosphere, shuffleboard, dominoes, pool, and lots of cold beer, check out Goode's Armadillo Palace next door. You can't miss the place: it's the building with the giant stainless-steel armadillo standing guard out front. ⊠*5109 Kirby Dr., West University* ☎*713/522–2530* 🖃*AE, D, DC, MC, V.*

FRENCH ✗**La Colombe d'Or.** If you're looking for modern cuisine from the French
$$$$ Riviera with a Texas twist, La Colombe d'Or is the place. Dripping with luxe touches, this restaurant occupies the first floor of a turn-of-the-20th-century mansion whose upper floors have been converted into a small luxury hotel by longtime owner Steve Zimmerman. Forget about budgets and calories, and succumb to classic preparations of

7

lobster, lamb, prime cuts of beef, and vegetables. Expect the elaborate desserts to be—what else?—rich. ⊠*3410 Montrose Blvd., Museum District* ☎*713/524–7999* ⌒*Reservations essential* ⊟*AE, D, DC, MC, V* ⊙*No lunch weekends.*

RIVER OAKS

$$–$$$ ✕ **Armandos.** Don't look for the sign—there isn't one at this clubby,
★ see-and-be-seen River Oaks sorta-Tex-Mex favorite. Re-opened in its third incarnation in March 2007, Armando Palacios's eponymous eatery—fashioned after 1920s Mexico City—is consistently packed with friends and regulars who love the clean, simple signature fajitas, *queso flameado* (a cheese dip made with chorizo and served with flour tortillas), and fresh lime-juice margaritas. "It's like our version of New York's Waverly Inn," says the owner. The bar is always hopping, and not with the young and the restless, either. Reserve the private room in the back for your next air-kissing celebration. ⊠*2630 Westheimer Rd., at Kirby Dr., River Oaks* ☎*713/520–1738* ⊟*AE, D, DC, MC, V* ⊙*No lunch.*

ITALIAN ✕ **Carrabba's.** After all these years, the original location of Carrabba's
$$–$$$ remains the busy and quintessential Inner Loop destination for reliable, Americanized Italian cooking. This location is not part of the national chain: here the founding families retain control and you can tell the difference. From steaming vessels of robust pasta dishes (heavy on the garlic) to crusty pizzas and hefty grilled meats, the kitchen fires on all cylinders to keep the customers happy. Service is fast and ultra-chummy, and servers will even sing an Italian song for your birthday if you so desire. ⊠*3115 Kirby Dr., River Oaks* ☎*713/522–3131* ⊟*AE, D, DC, MC, V.*

TEX-MEX ✕ **Chuy's.** Part wacky Tex-Mex restaurant, part shrine to Elvis, dogs,
$ and hubcaps, and part kitschy gift shop, Chuy's is a true Texas original.
★ Always busy and always fun, this is the place to go for large, many-flavored margaritas and original dishes like the Elvis Green Chile Fried Chicken, which is coated in potato chips. The Chuychanga—a fried flour tortilla filled with chicken, cheese, cilantro, and green chilies, and best when ordered with Deluxe Tomatillo Sauce—is bigger than most people's forearms and is life-alteringly good. Be sure to request complimentary creamy jalapeño dip to accompany your chips and salsa (trust us on this one). At happy hour, poor college kids and high-rolling energy traders dig into complimentary nachos served out of the trunk of a classic Cadillac. ⊠*2706 Westheimer Rd., River Oaks* ☎*713/524–1700* ⊟*AE, D, DC, MC, V.*

ITALIAN ✕ **La Griglia.** You know you've come to a dining hot spot when you're
$$–$$$ greeted by the cement handprints of local notables outside the front
★ doors of the ebullient La Griglia. Even after all these years (it opened in 1991), no other Houston restaurant can match its buzzy social energy. Dramatic decor, an open kitchen, imaginative and dependable food, and fair prices make this River Oaks favorite a touchstone among those in the know (and in the gossip columns). This place fills by 7 PM, so arrive early or prepare to enjoy the scenery for a while. Try the sea-

food cheesecake, maybe the richest appetizer in town and worth every calorie or smooth, silky shrimp bisque. Soft-shell crabs and fillet of red snapper are excellent entrées. La Griglia has open-air dining on a covered side patio. ⊠ *2002 W. Gray St., River Oaks* ☏ *713/526–4700* ▤ *AE, D, DC, MC, V* ⊗ *No lunch weekends.*

NEW ✕ **Ouisie's Table.** At Elouise "Ouisie" Adams Jones's casually elegant,
AMERICAN ersatz preppy restaurant, American cuisine is prepared with eclectic,
$$–$$$ Southern accents. Dine in the main room, or request a table on adjoining Lucy's Porch for a view of the herb plantings snipped daily by the kitchen staff. Fine dinner choices include a brace of roasted quail with apple-smoked bacon, and a shrimp curry with lemon-ginger rice. There's a fabulous weekend brunch and an afternoon "little bites" menu. ⊠ *3939 San Felipe Rd., River Oaks* ☏ *713/528–2264* ▤ *AE, D, DC, MC, V.*

SEAFOOD ✕ **Pesce.** For a glamorous (and noisy) scene in River Oaks, head for
$$$–$$$$ this lavish seafood emporium. Look around and dive in: a stunning aquarium fills one corner, and the ceiling undulates like waves. The kitchen, led by chef Mark Holley, prepares catches from all over the world, from Gulf Coast shellfish to Dover sole. You can feast on global flavors: Mediterranean, Thai, Spanish, Vietnamese, French, and Louisiana Creole. And although Pesce is now part of the Landry's restaurant group, you don't feel as though you've settled for a boring chain. ⊠ *3029 Kirby Dr., River Oaks* ☏ *713/522–4858* ⌖ *Reservations essential* ▤ *AE, D, DC, MC, V* ⊗ *Closed Sun.*

SEAFOOD ✕ **Tony Mandola's Gulf Coast Kitchen.** It's a strange fact of Houston life
$$–$$$ that many of the city's finest restaurants are found in strip shopping centers, albeit the more glamorous ones. Tony Mandola's, in the art deco–themed River Oaks Shopping Center, is an upscale restaurant that proves, with loads of tastebud-pleasing menu choices, that the concept of a Texas-, Italian-, and (some) Mexican-influenced seafood restaurant is here to stay. Off-the-menu items, such as Calamari a la Mama, lightly battered with lemon-butter sauce, may make you see stars. You'll see everyone you know at this neighborhood joint, if everyone you know is rich, famous, and well connected. There's open-air dining and a kids' menu. ⊠ *1962 W. Gray St., River Oaks* ☏ *713/528–3474* ▤ *AE, D, MC, V* ⊗ *No lunch Sun.*

THE HEIGHTS

NEW ✕ **Shade.** Amid the home-grown antiques, oddities, and furnishings
AMERICAN stores of the still-wacky main street of the Heights, Shade is a slice
$$–$$$ of cool sophistication and attentive, hospitable service. The seasonal
★ menu—creative, fresh, and very well priced—includes local favorites like the massive bacon, lettuce, and fried-green-tomato sandwich; and an unbeatable butternut squash risotto with pan-seared scallops. On the vegetable plate are chicken-fried asparagus, possibly the most perfect veggie comfort food ever invented. Because this part of the Heights is dry, you'll have to join the Shade Club if you want to drink, but membership is free, so drink up! Brunch is served on weekends. ⊠ *250 W. 19th St., Heights* ☏ *713/863–7500* ▤ *AE, D, DC, MC, V.*

UPTOWN/GALLERIA

LATIN
AMERICAN
$$–$$$

✕ **Américas.** A colorful mosaic-tiled, multistoried room delivers outstanding New World cuisine that includes roasted pork filet mignon with grilled shrimp and lump crabmeat and the crowd-favorite Encamisado, a chicken breast crusted with plantains and Chontaleno cheese over black-bean sauce. The executive lunch, available weekdays, is just $15.95 and includes a signature entrée and dessert, plus your choice of soup or salad. At this writing the entire shopping center and the blocks around the restaurant are slated to become a megacomplex called Boulevard Place (estimated completion is 2010), but the developer assures us that Américas will continue on. There's a kids' menu. ✉ *1800 S. Post Oak Blvd., Uptown/Galleria* ☎ *713/961–1492* ▭ *AE, D, DC, MC, V* ✆ *Closed Sun. No lunch Sat.*

ITALIAN
$$$–$$$$
★

✕ **Arcodoro.** With executive chefs hailing from Sardinia, Italy—whose cookbook, *Sweet Myrtle and Bitter Honey*, was published in 2007—Arcodoro is the place to go for authentic Sardinian cuisine. The various pasta dishes, such as artichoke-filled ravioli and *gnochetti* (teardrop pasta) with wild-boar *ragu* (stew), are very popular, as are the chicken dishes and osso buco, and the rib-eye steak is succulent. Alfresco dining is available year-round, but only truly enjoyable in the cooler months and when you're sitting far enough away from the parking lot to be out of exhaust range. Check out the online store for authentic Sardinian products. ✉ *5000 Westheimer Rd., Uptown/Galleria* ☎ *713/621–6888* ▭ *AE, D, DC, MC, V.*

NEW
AMERICAN
$$$–$$$$
Fodor'sChoice
★

✕ **Cafe Annie.** Chef–owner Robert Del Grande, one of the founders of Southwestern cuisine, serves the best of his innovative, fiery cooking at this acclaimed restaurant. Start any meal with the layered Gulf-crabmeat tostada, then move to the wood-grilled beef fillet with poblano-and-walnut pesto, or salmon with warm garlic and ginger-mint butter. For a more festive atmosphere, plant yourself (if you can find room) at the restaurant's Bar Annie, with its own fun, tasty menu that includes a towering crab tostada and arguably the city's best cheeseburger. The bar has a table-hopping social scene and bartenders who really know how to make a drink. ✉ *1728 Post Oak Blvd., Uptown/Galleria* ☎ *713/840–1111* ◭ *Reservations essential* ▭ *AE, D, DC, MC, V.*

STEAK
$$$–$$$$

✕ **Pappas Bros. Steakhouse.** The operative word at this popular steakhouse is "prime": prime beef, a prime setting, and a clientele primed for coddling, conversation, and cholesterol. The Steakhouse, poshest of the Pappas restaurant dynasty, gains a clubby look from dark wood, cushy booths, and phones at the tables. Thumbs-up to a beefsteak-tomato-and-Roquefort salad (big enough to share) and to the fork-tender New York strip steak with peppercorn sauce. Creamy mashed potatoes and giant fried onion rings provide delicious accompaniments to fillets. Expect a wait, even with reservations. ✉ *5839 Westheimer Rd., Uptown/Galleria* ☎ *713/780–7352* ◭ *Reservations essential* ▭ *AE, D, DC, MC, V* ✆ *Closed Sun. No lunch.*

AMERICAN
$$–$$$

✕ **Post Oak Grill.** Since 1989 this Houston standby has dished up reliable meals of salads, pastas, seafood, and chops for smartly dressed businesspeople and the monied Tanglewood and Memorial crowds. Wait a minute . . . is that George and Barbara Bush over there? It just might be.

The patrons come in for escargots Bourguignonnes with Provençal herb sauce, as well as barbecue chicken quesadillas with roasted-corn-and-black-bean salsa. The handily adjacent Oak Club serves up live music Tuesday through Saturday nights. ⊠*1415 S. Post Oak La., Uptown/Galleria* ☎713/993–9966 ▤*AE, D, DC, MC, V* ⊘*Closed Sun.*

JAPANESE
$$–$$$

✕**Uptown Sushi.** Sure it's trendy, and maybe more stylish than substantive, but if you're looking for the decadent sushi experience, it's hard to beat the pricey and delicious Uptown Sushi. With its ethereal, white-on-white and Lucite-and-low-light decor, this Galleria-area hot spot offers fresh, interesting takes on sushi and sashimi. The Seven-and-a-Half Roll (tuna, salmon, yellowtail, masago, and avocado, all tempura fried) is not to be missed, nor is the Ribeye Roll (slices of beef wrapped around avocados and sweet Japanese yams). Try to snag a mezzanine-level table so you can see all the glamour go down. While waiting for said table, cool your designer heels at the raucous, pick-up-line-laden bar, with great, expensive wines and strong mixed drinks. ⊠*1131-14 Uptown Park Blvd., Uptown/Galleria* ☎713/871–1200 ▤*AE, D, MC, V.*

WEST SIDE/MEMORIAL PARK

SPANISH
$$$
★

✕**Catalan Food & Wine.** From the people who brought Houston Ibiza Restaurant and Lounge comes Catalan Food and Wine Bar, a smashing Spanish tapas emporium with consistently outstanding service, innovative food, and reasonably priced wines. Tables are cozily jam-packed together, and a cheerful hum reigns over a high-ceilinged, chandeliered dining room. Outstanding small plates include foie-gras bonbons with watermelon jelly, crispy pork belly, and spicy gulf shrimp. On the big-plates side are seared tuna over foraged mushrooms, roasted lamb porterhouse, and fillet of beef a la plancha (grilled). Save room for desserts like the white-chocolate and dried-cherry bread pudding with vanilla ice cream. Be sure to make reservations—this place is always packed. ⊠*5555 Washington Ave., West Side/Memorial Park* ☎713/426–4260 ▤*AE, D, DC, MC, V* ⊘*Closed Mon.*

TEX-MEX
$–$$

✕**El Tiempo.** Wildly popular and wildly good, El Tiempo on Washington (there are other locations on Richmond and Montrose) is the go-to Mexican restaurant for socialites, families, singles (check out the swinging bar scene), and serious eaters. The place gets raves for its margaritas, fajitas, guacamole, green sauce, and the whopping, table-filling mixed grill, with beef and chicken fajitas, jumbo shrimp, quail, baby-back ribs, *carnitas* (spicy roasted pork), and jalapeño sausage. You're likely to leave happy, bloated, and smelling like Mexican food. It's open for breakfast on weekends. ⊠*5602 Washington Ave., West Side/Memorial Park* ☎713/681–3645 ▤*AE, D, DC, MC, V.*

MEXICAN
$$–$$$

✕**Las Alamedas.** You could forget you're in the city at the grand hacienda of Las Alamedas, which overlooks a peaceful wooded ravine in Memorial. The menu is upscale Mexican (not Tex-Mex!) cuisine, and the kitchen is sometimes uneven, but generally very good. Two splendid entrées are *tacos de cochinita pibil* (chunks of pork simmered in achiote sauce) and *huachinango à la azteca* (red snapper stuffed with corn mushrooms in poblano sauce). A 60-foot Champagne Brunch, with

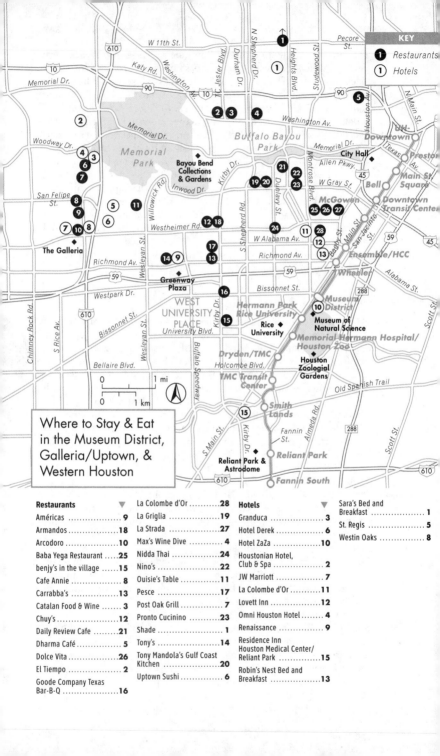

KEY

- ❶ *Restaurants*
- ① *Hotels*

Where to Stay & Eat
in the Museum District,
Galleria/Uptown, &
Western Houston

an ever-changing selection of delicacies, commences at 11 AM every Sunday. There's a kids' menu. ⊠ *8615 Katy Fwy., West Side/Memorial Park* ☎ *713/461–1503* ⊟ *AE, D, DC, MC, V* ⊘ *No lunch Sat.*

AMERICAN
$$–$$$
Fodor's Choice
★

✕ **Max's Wine Dive.** Come to this loud, silicone-and-Rolex-filled place with a big appetite and a taste for a great selection of Texas and world-wide wines. This local favorite packs in young movers and shakers every night with upscale comfort food, including Lobster Thermadelphia—a twist on a Philly cheesesteak, with lobster, tequila, lime, and jalapeño cheddar cheese on a baguette, and the Texas Haute Dog, an all-beef hot dog with pickled jalapeño, Texas venison chili, cotija cheese, and crispy fried onion rings. Portions are huge! Pair them up with an awesome selection of wines, many available by the glass, but much better priced as bottles. It's open until 2 AM Thursday, Friday, and Saturday ⊠ *4720 Washington Ave., West Side/Memorial Park* ☎ *713/880–8737* ⊟ *AE, D, DC, MC, V* ⊘ *Closed Mon.*

STEAK
$$$–$$$$

✕ **Taste of Texas.** With Texana to the max, this expansive place is as much about pride as prime beef. The entry looks like a sprawling ranch house and the lobby, complete with rockers, invites long evenings spent on the front porch. So relax, as you and your fellow carnivores will likely wait a while for your table. Famous for its steaks, the kitchen also whips up chicken, lobster, and grilled shrimp. Taste of Texas also has an online store selling steaks, gourmet gift boxes with steaks and grilling supplies, and restaurant-themed merchandise. ⊠ *10505 Katy Fwy., West Side/Memorial Park* ☎ *713/932–6901* ⚐ *Reservations not accepted* ⊟ *AE, D, DC, MC, V* ⊘ *No lunch weekends.*

7

WHERE TO STAY

THE SCENE

Like most big cities, Houston has a wide variety of hospitality options. Downtown, you'll find many national business-class hotels (Doubletree, Hilton, Hyatt, Four Seasons) geared for traveling workers and conventioneers, plus some pretty fabulous independent properties. Most are connected to the underground tunnel system and/or skybridges, so it's easy to get around in climate-controlled comfort (you can access the tunnel system via most large buildings downtown). The majority of Houston's other hotels are in the Uptown/Galleria area, with shopping and entertainment attractions. If hitting Neiman Marcus and Saks Fifth Avenue is your thing, this is the place for you. This also seems to be where the international set nests, especially vacationing Mexicans and South Americans.

At certain times of the year, like during the Houston Livestock Show and Rodeo in March and during large trade shows and conventions like technology-centered OTC and ITEC, both in May, Houston's hotel rooms fill up quickly, so call ahead to see what's going on that month. When the city hosted the Super Bowl in 2004, every hotel room in Houston was taken and residents began renting out their houses.

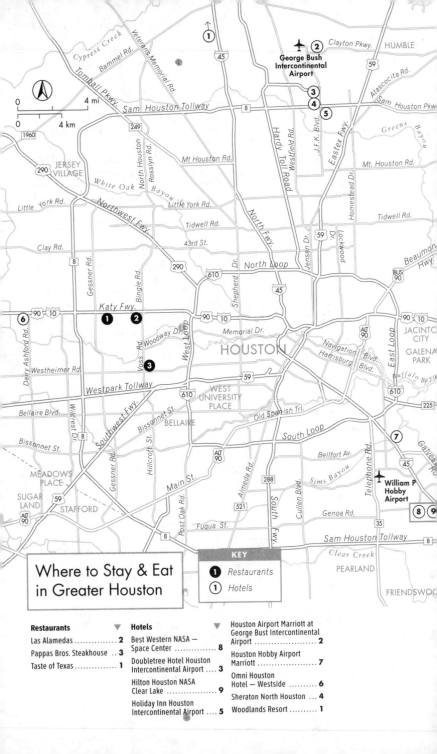

Where to Stay & Eat in Greater Houston

Restaurants ▼

Las Alamedas **2**

Pappas Bros. Steakhouse .. **3**

Taste of Texas **1**

Hotels ▼

Best Western NASA — Space Center **8**

Doubletree Hotel Houston Intercontinental Airport **3**

Hilton Houston NASA Clear Lake **9**

Holiday Inn Houston Intercontinental Airport **5**

Houston Airport Marriott at George Bust Intercontinental Airport **2**

Houston Hobby Airport Marriott **7**

Omni Houston Hotel — Westside **6**

Sheraton North Houston ... **4**

Woodlands Resort **1**

WHAT IT COSTS					
	¢	$	$$	$$$	$$$$
HOTELS	under $50	$50–$100	$101–$150	$151–$200	over $200

Hotel prices are per night for two people in a standard double room in high sea-son, excluding taxes and service charges. Hotel taxes in Houston are 17%.

DOWNTOWN

$$$$ 🏨**Alden Houston.** This small luxury boutique hotel (formerly the Sam
Fodor'sChoice Houston Hotel) is decidedly modern and well located near bustling
★ Main Street and the ballpark. The guest rooms are stylish, with fine lin-ens, granite bathrooms, high-tech workstations, and suites with plasma TVs. The hotel's restaurant, 17, is just as modern and attracts a hip international crowd of epicures hungry for contemporary American food. Don't miss it. **Pros:** Interesting modern decor, great bath products. **Cons:** Somewhat lonely block, expensive parking. ⊠*1117 Prairie St., Downtown* 🕾*832/200–8800 or 877/348–8800* ⊕*www.aldenhotels. com* ↻*97 rooms* ⚭*In-room: DVD, Ethernet, Wi-Fi. In-hotel: Restau-rant, room service, bar, gym, concierge, laundry service, public Wi-Fi, parking (fee), some pets allowed* ⊟*AE, D, DC, MC, V.*

$$$$ 🏨**Doubletree Downtown.** This full-service business hotel is right in the middle of downtown and within walking distance of the Theater Dis-trict, Bayou Place, Minute Maid Park, and the George R. Brown Con-vention Center. Sky bridges connect the hotel to the Allen Center office complex, as well as to Texaco Heritage Plaza. It's also connected to the downtown underground tunnel system. Guest rooms have views of the Sam Houston Park and Memorial Park greenbelt, the Downtown skyline, or the Allen Center Courtyard. **Pros:** Great location, excellent customer service, oversized rooms. **Cons:** Expensive valet-only parking. ⊠*400 Dallas St., Downtown* 🕾*713/759–0202* ⊕*www.doubletree. com* ↻*350 rooms* ⚭*In-room: Ethernet. In-hotel: restaurant, room service, bar, gym, concierge, laundry service, parking (fee)* ⊟*AE, D, DC, MC, V.*

$$$$ 🏨**Four Seasons Hotel.** Even after a renovation last year, this landmark
★ downtown hotel is a bit dated, but services and amenities are top-notch and it has a great location close to the convention center, Downtown businesses, and major sports facilities, including Minute Maid Park (home of the Astros) and Toyota Center (home of the NBA Rockets and the AHL Aeros). The hotel's restaurant, Quattro, which serves Italian-accented cuisine, is a glamorous outpost for business-lunchers and nighttime event-goers. The lobby bar is always a lively scene. The fitness center and completely renovated pool area are awesome. **Pros:** Great location, excellent service, great restaurant and happening bar. **Cons:** '80s decor, expensive valet parking. ⊠*1300 Lamar St., Down-town,* 🕾*713/650–1300 or 800/332–3442* ⊕*www.fourseasons.com* ↻*404 rooms* ⚭*In-room: refrigerator, Ethernet, dial-up. In-hotel: res-taurant, room service, pool, gym, laundry service, concierge, executive floor, public Internet, airport shuttle, parking (fee), some pets allowed, no-smoking rooms* ⊟*AE, D, DC, MC, V.*

WHERE SHOULD I STAY IN HOUSTON?

	Neighborhood Vibe	Pros	Cons
Downtown	These days, the corporate canyons of downtown Houston are booming with new restaurants, shops, and hotels, as well as bars, nightclubs, and live entertainment venues. Downtown is the headquarters of Houston's performing-arts scene, and of many Fortune 500 companies—thus hotels here are most popular with, and geared toward, business travelers.	Lots to do and see, close to performing-arts and sports facilities, walkable neighborhood.	Can feel deserted at night, not enough cabs, parking can be expensive.
Museum District	There's really only one hotel to stay at in Houston's Museum District, but it's so over-the-top, so ridiculously done up, you don't want to miss it: the Hotel ZaZa, which debuted in 2007 to much fanfare. The surrounding leafy neighborhood is home to Hermann Park and the much-heralded Museum of Fine Arts, and just a short stroll from Rice University and the Texas Medical Center.	Quiet, leafy neighborhood, close to the city's best cultural attractions, proximity to Texas Medical Center.	Nothing really to do at night, not many hotel options.
Intercontinental Airport	There's nothing glamorous about this neighborhood; its appeal is that it's near the airport and has a variety of lodging options, from motels through high-end properties. It's also close to many golf courses, and some corporate headquarters. But if you want to see the city sights, this isn't the place to stay.	Location close to airport, reliable chain hotels.	Dull surroundings, no fine dining, far from any interesting attractions.

$$$–$$$$ ⚑ **Hilton Americas.** Finally, Houston has a great convention-center hotel right in the heart of downtown's sporting venues. Massive, ornate, and luxurious, this is the largest hotel in Houston, with 1,203 rooms. Almost a city within a city, the Hilton Americas has three restaurants and lounges, a gigantic fitness center, and a rooftop bar/grill that's not cheesy at all. The views from its 24th-floor location are pretty amazing, especially at night when the downtown skyline comes alive. **Pros:** Connected to George R. Brown Convention Center, outstanding services and amenities, multilingual staff. **Cons:** No self-parking, valet can take what seems to be forever. ⊠ *1600 Lamar St., Downtown* ☎ *713/739–8000* ⊕ *www.hilton.com* ⊷ *1,164 rooms, 39 suites* △ *In-room: Ethernet, Wi-Fi. In-hotel: restaurants, room service, bars, pool, gym, laundry service, concierge, airport shuttle, parking (fee)* ⊟ *AE, D, DC, MC, V.*

$$$$ Hotel ICON. Easily Downtown's most glamorous hotel, Hotel ICON
Fodor'sChoice combines historic architecture with shabby Chinoiserie, contemporary
★ finishes, overstuffed furniture, and attentive service. Rooms have large
flat-screen TVs, Molton Brown bath products, and marble bathrooms.
Right on Main Street, the former Union National Bank building also
houses BANK restaurant, the ICON Bar, and the Balance Day Spa. The
top-floor multilevel suites are almost unbelievably grand and gorgeous.
Pros: Great location, excellent service, outstanding amenities. **Cons:**
Super-expensive parking ($25 for the night), sometimes loud crowds
on street. ⊠*220 Main St., Downtown* ☎*713/224-4266* ⊕*www.hotel
icon.com* ↝*135 rooms, 9 suites* ⚿*In-room: Ethernet, Wi-Fi, safe,
laundry service, room service. In-hotel: restaurant, gym, spa, parking
(fee)* ⊟*AE, D, DC, MC, V.*

$$$$ The Lancaster. In the heart of the Theater District, this small luxury
hotel has the feel of a European manor house. The Chippendale furniture, plaid upholstered chairs, oil landscapes and portraits, and brass
cachepots contrast with the steel-and-glass surroundings. Power break-
fasters crowd Bistro Lancaster, and the hotel's wine bar is both highly
rated and highly popular. **Pros:** Historic setting, central location, complimentary town-car service. **Cons:** Expensive overnight parking ($27).
⊠*701 Texas Ave., Downtown* ☎*713/228–9500* ⊕*www.thelancaster.
com* ↝*93 rooms* ⚿*In-room: refrigerator, VCR, Wi-Fi. In-hotel: restaurant, room service, bar, gym, parking (fee)* ⊟*AE, D, DC, MC, V.*

$$$–$$$$ Magnolia Hotel Houston. Formerly the *Houston Post-Dispatch* news-
paper building and the original corporate headquarters for Shell Oil
Company, the chic Magnolia takes a historic property in a modern,
well-designed direction. Guests enjoy a complimentary nightly cock-
tail reception, as well as a milk-and-cookies buffet right before bed-
time. The rooftop pool offers great downtown views. Bedding and
linens are amazing, some of the best we've experienced. **Pros:** Great
central location and outstanding customer service. **Cons:** No self-park-
ing, immediate blocks offer few dining and nightlife options. ⊠*1100
Texas Ave., Downtown* ☎*713/221–0011 or 888/915–1110* ⊕*www.
magnolia hotelhouston.com* ↝*255 rooms, 59 suites* ⚿*In-room: Wi-
Fi. In-hotel: restaurant, room service, bar, pool, gym, laundry service,
concierge, airport shuttle, parking (no fee)* ⊟*AE, D, DC, MC, V.*

HOBBY AIRPORT

$$$–$$$$ Houston Hobby Airport Marriott. Only 1 mi from Hobby Airport, this
10-story atrium hotel is completely no-smoking and has one of the larg-
est conference facilities in South Houston. It also has a concierge level
with private lounge. Complimentary transportation is available to the
Almeda Mall and a golf course, both 3 mi away. **Pros:** Well equipped
for business travelers and meetings, 32-inch plasma-screen TVs in each
room. **Cons:** Depressing neighborhood, far from city's main attractions,
dining, and shopping. ⊠*9100 Gulf Fwy., Hobby Airport* ☎*713/943–
7979* ⊕*www.marriott.com* ↝*287 rooms* ⚿*In-room: Wi-Fi. In-hotel:
restaurant, bar, pool, gym, laundry service, concierge, public Wi-Fi,
airport shuttle, no-smoking rooms* ⊟*AE, D, DC, MC, V.*

BEST BETS FOR HOUSTON LODGING

Downtown or the Galleria, which are close to business centers and halfway between the airports, may seem like the only places to stay, but other neighborhoods—the Heights, Montrose, and the Museum District—are quiet, walkable, and full of cultural and dining surprises. The choices here are some of our favorites by price, hotel type, and atmosphere or style.

Fodor's Choice ★

Alden Houston, $$$$, Downtown

Granduca, $$$$, Uptown/Galleria

Hotel ICON, $$$$, Downtown

Hotel ZaZa, $$$$, Museum District

St. Regis, $$$$, River Oaks

By Price

$$

Lovett Inn, Montrose

Robin's Nest Bed and Breakfast, Museum District

Sara's Bed and Breakfast, The Heights

$$$

Hilton Americas, Downtown

Magnolia Hotel Houston, Downtown

Residence Inn Houston Medical Center/ Reliant Park, Museum District (Medical Center)

$$$$

Four Seasons, Downtown

Hotel Derek, Uptown/Galleria

The Houstonian Hotel, Club & Spa, Uptown/Galleria

By Type

B&B

Lovett Inn, $$, Montrose

Robin's Nest Bed and Breakfast, $$–$$$, Museum District

Sara's Bed and Breakfast, $$–$$$, The Heights

BOUTIQUE HOTEL

Hotel ICON, $$$$, Downtown

La Colombe d'Or, $$$$, Museum District

The Lancaster, $$$$, Downtown

RESORT

Houstonian Hotel, Club & Spa, $$$$, Uptown/Galleria

Omni Houston Hotel, $$$$, Uptown/Galleria

Woodlands Resort, $$$$, The Woodlands (North Houston)

By Experience

CELEBRITY MAGNETS

Hotel ZaZa, $$$$, Museum District

La Colombe d'Or, $$$$, Museum District

St. Regis, $$$$, River Oaks

GREAT VIEWS

Four Seasons Hotel, $$$$, Downtown

Hotel ZaZa, $$$$, Museum District

Renaissance, $$$$, Midtown

HIGH COOL FACTOR

Alden Houston, $$$$, Downtown

Hotel Derek, $$$$, Uptown/Galleria

Hotel ICON, $$$$, Downtown

NEAR UNIVERSITIES

Hotel ZaZa, $$$$, Museum District

La Colombe d'Or, $$$$, Museum District

Residence Inn Houston Medical Center/ Reliant Park, $$$$, Museum District (Medical Center)

INTERCONTINENTAL AIRPORT

$$$$ [icon] **Doubletree Hotel Houston Intercontinental Airport.** In a leafy, wooded complex known as the World Houston Business Development, this hotel is 1 mi from Houston's Bush Intercontinental Airport. Rooms are decorated in a sophisticated, modern style of cool blues and greys, with oversized work areas designed with business travelers in mind. **Pros:** Pretty setting, lots of amenities for the price, near the airport. **Cons:** Far from Houston's best dining, shopping, and attractions. ✉15747 J.F.K. *Blvd., Intercontinental Airport* ☎281/848-4000 ⊕www.doubletree. com ➥313 rooms ♿In-room: Wi-Fi. In-hotel: restaurant, room service, bar, pool, gym, laundry service, airport shuttle, parking (no fee) ▤AE, D, DC, MC, V.

$$ [icon] **Holiday Inn Houston Intercontinental Airport.** Two miles south of the airport and 18 mi from downtown, this Holiday Inn is convenient to Redstone Golf Club, home of the Shell Houston Open. Rooms (renovated in 2002) are pretty much what you'd expect from a Holiday Inn—nothing too luxurious but well equipped for both business and leisure travelers. **Pros:** Excellent health and fitness center, fun sports facilities for basketball, tennis, and horseshoes. **Cons:** Far from good shopping and dining and the city's leading attractions. ✉15222 J.F.K. *Blvd., Intercontinental Airport* ☎281/449–2311 ⊕www.holiday-inn. com ➥415 rooms ♿In-room: Ethernet. In-hotel: restaurant, room service, bar, tennis court, pool, gym, laundry facilities, public Wi-Fi, airport shuttle, parking (no fee) ▤AE, D, DC, MC, V.

$$$$ [icon] **Houston Airport Marriott at George Bush Intercontinental Airport.** This no-smoking hotel is on the grounds of Bush Intercontinental Airport and has complimentary underground train service to the airport. A rooftop restaurant provides great views of all the arriving and departing flights, and downtown's skyline in the distance. All rooms feature luxurious bedding and linens, including down pillows if you like. **Pros:** Convenient aiport location, reliable upscale chain hotel. **Cons:** Far from the city's attractions. ✉18700 J.F.K. Blvd., Intercontinental Airport ☎281/443–2310 ⊕www.marriott.com ➥565 rooms ♿In-room: refrigerator, Ethernet. In-hotel: 2 restaurants, bar, pool, gym, public Wi-Fi, airport shuttle, parking (no fee), no-smoking rooms ▤AE, D, DC, MC, V.

$$$$ [icon] **Sheraton North Houston.** Just a mile from the airport, the Sheraton is a full-service resort hotel perfect for business travelers or golf enthusiasts: six of the city's leading courses, including Tour 18 and the Redstone Golf Club (home of the Shell Houston Open) are just minutes away. Rooms have contemporary furnishings, with sitting and work areas so you can really spread out. **Pros:** Close to airport, indoor pool, spacious rooms. **Cons:** Far from downtown Houston, not a walkable neighborhood, lack of fine dining/shopping in immediate area. ✉15700 J.F.K. *Blvd., Intercontinental Airport* ☎281/442–5100 ⊕www.sheraton. com/northhouston ➥420 rooms ♿In-room: refrigerator (some), Ethernet. In-hotel: restaurant, room service, bars, gym, concierge, airport shuttle, parking (no fee) ▤AE, D, DC, MC, V.

7

MIDTOWN

$$$$ **Renaissance.** At first glance, this tower in an office complex may seem all business, but it's attached to a Starbucks and the underground Greenway Plaza shops, which include the Landmark Greenway Cinema. The rooms, at the top of the tower, are spacious, with floor-to-ceiling windows offering great city views, and some rooms with walk-in closets. There's a lovely outdoor pool area, with lush vegetation shielding guests from street traffic; the pool has lanes are marked for lap swimming. The Galleria mall is nearby. **Pros:** Great central location between downtown and the Galleria mall, reliable upscale property. **Cons:** Confusing entryway off freeway access road, not a walkable neighborhood. ⊠ *6 Greenway Plaza E, Greenway Plaza* ☎ *713/629–1200* ⊕ *www.marriott.com* ⇆ *389 rooms* △ *In-room: refrigerator (some), Ethernet. In-hotel: restaurant, room service, bar, pool, gym, parking (fee).* ▤ *AE, D, DC, MC, V.*

MONTROSE

$–$$ **Lovett Inn.** Once the residence of Houston mayor and Federal Court Judge Joseph C. Hutcheson, this historic home is in the heart of the Montrose area is also convenient to leading museums. It's a great location for avid walkers and joggers, as the neighborhood is filled with restaurants, bars, galleries, and shops. Most rooms overlook the inn's finely landscaped grounds and pool. **Pros:** Quaint, historic property, interesting neighborhood. **Cons:** No restaurant. ⊠ *501 Lovett Blvd., Montrose* ☎ *713/522–5224 or 800/779–5224* ⊕ *www.lovettinn.com* ⇆ *9 rooms, 3 suites* △ *In-room: refrigerator (some), Wi-Fi. In-hotel: no elevator, pool, spa, parking (no fee), no-smoking rooms* ▤ *AE, D, DC, MC, V* ⦿ *CP.*

MUSEUM DISTRICT/TEXAS MEDICAL CENTER

$$$$ **Hotel ZaZa.** Opened in 2007 with flashy, over-the-top celebrations, **Fodor's Choice** the party at the ZaZa hasn't ended yet. Think taxidermy, chandeliers, ★ prints on prints on prints, video walls, a pool area that rivals Vegas casinos, and lots of lacquer. It can come across as trying too hard, but there's nothing else like it in the city. Eight themed guest suites ("The Magnificent Seven") pay homage to the international jet set, rock stars, and Texas cowboys. The Monarch Restaurant and Lounge has some of the best food in town, but the bar clientele is not always as sophisticated as the diners. The hotel's location at the foot of Hermann Park means all rooms have gorgeous views. **Pros:** Fun atmosphere, beautiful location, great pool scene. **Cons:** Loud, sort of isolated from the city's after-dark activities, expensive parking. ⊠ *5701 Main St., Museum District* ☎ *713/526–1991* ⊕ *www.hotelzaza.com* ⇆ *300 rooms* △ *In-room: refrigerator, Ethernet, Wi-Fi. In-hotel: restaurant, pool, gym, spa, parking (fee)* ▤ *AE, D, DC, MC, V.*

$$$$ **La Colombe d'Or.** This exclusive, European-style hotel, originally the W. W. Fondren mansion, has lost some exterior charm due to the addition of a banquet facility, but the rooms, lounge, and restaurant nevertheless draw the rich and famous (and discreet). Genuine antiques, usually of dark wood with luxe brocade, do much to complete the Montrose hotel's old-world charm. The tiny but warm bar and a small library are both perfect spots for a cozy drink. **Pros:** Luxurious decor and great location near museums and universities. **Cons:** Rooms can be ridiculously expensive. ⊠*3410 Montrose Blvd., Museum District* ☎*713/524–7999* ⊕*www.lacolombedor.com* ⌐*6 suites* ⟁*In-room: kitchen. In-hotel: restaurant, room service, bar, no elevator, parking (fee)* ☰*AE, D, DC, MC, V.*

$$$–$$$$ **Residence Inn Houston Medical Center/Reliant Park.** Ideal for people on longer stays, this no-smoking, all-suites property is close to the Medical Center and 1½ mi from the Reliant Park complex, where the Houston Texans play. All suites have fully equipped kitchens. **Pros:** Spacious, well-equipped suites, complimentary shuttle to Texas Medical Center. **Cons:** Neighborhood is kind of boring and not a destination in itself. ⊠*7710 S. Main St., near Reliant Park, Medical Center* ☎*713/660–7993* ⊕*www.marriott.com/houas* ⌐*287 suites* ⟁*In-room: kitchen, Wi-Fi. In-hotel: bar, pool, public Wi-Fi, parking (no fee), no-smoking rooms* ☰*AE, D, DC, MC, V* ⊙*CP.*

$$–$$$ **Robin's Nest Bed and Breakfast.** This group of three historic houses is 1½ mi south of downtown Houston. Most of the artwork and the furnishings come from the various foreign countries that owner Robin Smith visited during her work with the U.S. Foreign Service. Antiques and hardwood floors decorate the rooms. Smoking is not permitted. All rooms have private baths, and three apartments are available for long-term stays. **Pros:** Owner/manager on site and helpful, great neighborhood, interesting decor. **Cons:** No restaurant or pool. ⊠*4104 Greeley St., Museum District* ☎*713/528–5821* ⊕*www.therobin.com* ⌐*9 rooms* ⟁*In-room: Wi-Fi. In hotel: no elevator, parking (no fee), some pets allowed, no-smoking rooms* ☰*AE, D, MC, V* ⊙*BP.*

NEAR NASA SPACE CENTER

$ **Best Western NASA–Space Center.** Near NASA and the Johnson Space Center, the Kemah Boardwalk, Baybrook Mall, and Clear Lake Area marinas, this basic, reliable property is a good value in the Clear Lake area. Plus, there's a complimentary breakfast buffet. Rooms have microwaves and coffeemakers. **Pros:** Proximity to water activities, low price. **Cons:** Far from downtown Houston, cookie-cutter design and decor. ⊠*889 W. Bay Area Blvd., Webster* ☎*281/338–6000* ⊕*www.bestwestern. com* ⌐*80 rooms* ⟁*In-room: refrigerator, Ethernet, Wi-Fi. In-hotel: pool, public Internet, parking (no fee)* ☰*AE, D, DC, MC, V* ⊙*CP.*

$$$–$$$$ **Hilton Houston NASA Clear Lake.** On the shores of Clear Lake, Hilton Houston NASA Clear Lake is a suburban resort hotel with a number of water sports—including jet skiing and waterskiing—and easy access to NASA/Johnson Space Center and Space Center Houston, which are just across the street. **Pros:** Right on the water; close to NASA, Galveston, and Kemah. **Cons:** Far from Houston's cultural, sports, fine-dining, and shopping attractions. ⊠*3000 NASA Pkwy., Nassau Bay* ☎*281/333–9300* ⊕*www.hilton.com* ⌐*243 rooms* ⟁*In-room: Ethernet. In-hotel:*

restaurant, bar, pool, gym, public Wi-Fi, laundry service, room service, concierge, parking (no fee) ☰*AE, D, DC, MC, V* ❍❘*CP.*

THE HEIGHTS

$–$$$ **Sara's Bed and Breakfast.** This Queen Anne mansion, complete with wraparound porch and rocking chairs, is in the historic Heights neighborhood and 4 mi from Downtown. Each room has its own theme and is decked out with antiques and floral-patterned linens. Smoking is not permitted. **Pros:** Charming neighborhood with jogging trail across the street. **Cons:** No restaurant or pool. ✉*941 Heights Blvd., Heights* ☎*713/868–1130 or 800/593–1130* ⊕*www.saras.com* ⟿*12 rooms and suites* ⚘*In-room: DVD, Wi-Fi. In-hotel: no elevator, no-smoking rooms, parking (no fee)* ☰*AE, D, DC, MC, V* ❍❘*CP.*

THE WOODLANDS

$$$$ **Woodlands Resort.** Just 30 minutes from downtown Houston (on a good day), this lakefront lodge is set on acres of manicured lawns, creating a quiet and lovely retreat with all the amenities anyone could ask for. There are 21 tennis courts, more than 140 miles of hiking/biking trails, and a luxurious spa. Minutes away are the Woodlands Mall and Market Street, with 400 upscale retailers and restaurants. **Pros:** Well-kept grounds, good for families, close to airport. **Cons:** Not close to Houston at all, not geared toward the single traveler. ✉*2301 N. Millbend St., the Woodlands* ☎*281/367–1100, 800/433–2624 toll-free outside TX, 800/533–3052 toll-free in TX* ⊕*http://woodlandsresort. com* ⟿*440 rooms* ⚘*In-room: Ethernet, Wi-Fi. In-hotel: 3 restaurants, room service, bars, golf courses, tennis courts, pools, gym, bicycles, airport shuttle, parking (no fee)* ☰*AE, D, DC, MC, V.*

UPTOWN/GALLERIA

$$$$ **Granduca.** Developer Giorgio Borlenghi (Uptown Park, Four Leaf
Fodor's Choice   Towers, Four Oaks Place) doesn't do things on the cheap. Witness his
★   latest effort: this magnificent European-style residential palace that's big with the international crowd opened in 2007. The super-luxurious all-suites property is just steps away from the Uptown Park shopping and dining village. A multilingual staff anticipates your every need. Suites come as big as 2,100 square feet. **Pros:** Near fine dining and shopping, superior service, luxurious decor. **Cons:** Views of shopping center and freeway can be pretty dull. ✉*1080 Uptown Park Blvd., Uptown/Galleria* ☎*713/418–1000* ⊕*www.granducahouston.com* ⟿*126 suites* ⚘*In-room: kitchen, Ethernet, Wi-Fi. In hotel: restaurant, room service, pool, gym, laundry service, concierge, public Wi-Fi, parking (no fee)* ☰*AE, D, DC, MC, V* ❍❘*CP.*

$$$$ **Hotel Derek.** While service and general atmosphere seem to be slipping lately, the Hotel Derek is still a good value for its location and sophistication. Modern furnishings grace the glossy-floored lobby and the 314 sleek, contemporary rooms. It's a favorite of both business and leisure travelers looking for an alternative to a traditional chain hotel. The scene-y Bistro Moderne restaurant and bar closed in late 2007; new concepts are on the drawing board at this writing. **Pros:** Interesting decor, complimentary shuttle around town, great pool area. **Cons:** Congested location, expensive valet parking. ⊠2525 W. Loop S, Uptown/Galleria ☎713/961–3000 ⊕www.hotelderek.com ➬314 rooms ♿In-room: safe, Ethernet. In-hotel: restaurant, pool, gym, laundry service, concierge, public Wi-Fi, parking (fee), some pets allowed.

$$$$ ⊡**Houstonian Hotel, Club & Spa.** Spread over 18 acres in a wooded area ★ near Memorial Park, the quiet, lodge-like Houstonian has luxurious rooms and sports facilities galore—golf (off-site), tennis, a climbing wall, and indoor racket games, plus one of the nation's largest fitness centers, weighing in at 125,000 square feet. **Pros:** Beautiful natural setting, excellent service, fantastic fitness facilities. **Cons:** Relatively isolated location, nothing to really walk to in the neighborhood. ⊠111 N. Post Oak La., Uptown/Galleria ☎713/680–2626 or 800/231–2759 ⊕www.houstonian.com ➬288 rooms ♿In-room: Ethernet, Wi-Fi. In-hotel: 3 restaurants, room service, bar, tennis court, pools, gym, children's programs (ages 3–16), parking (fee) ☰AE, D, DC, MC, V.

$$$$ ⊡**JW Marriott.** Directly across from the Galleria mall, this completely no-smoking hotel is a shopper's haven. Business travelers enjoy easy access to Fortune 500 companies headquartered in the I-610/Uptown corridor. Rooms have opulent granite bathrooms and the finest bedding and fabrics. You can play basketball and racquetball on-site. **Pros:** Excellent location, easy to walk to shopping and dining. **Cons:** Traffic/ congestion. ⊠5150 Westheimer Rd., Uptown/Galleria ☎713/961– 1500 or 800/228–9290 ⊕www.marriott.com ➬487 rooms, 28 suites ♿In-room: safe, refrigerator, Ethernet. In-hotel: restaurant, pool, gym, public Wi-Fi, parking (fee), no-smoking rooms ☰AE, D, DC, MC, V.

$$$$ ⊡**Omni Houston Hotel.** This upscale resort-style high-rise has a dramatic ★ modern lobby and an especially large pool, as well as fountains and sculpture. Guest rooms have sitting areas, marble vanities and bathrooms, dark-wood furniture, and floor-to-ceiling windows. The Black Swan bar is packed with May to December romances of all varieties, and is consistently popular with the young social set. **Pros:** Top-notch services and beautiful surroundings. **Cons:** Right off congested Woodway Drive, traffic often frustrating. ⊠4 Riverway, Uptown/Galleria ☎713/871–8181 or 800/843–6664 ⊕www.omnihotels.com ➬378 rooms and suites ♿In-room: Wi-Fi. In-hotel: restaurant, room service, bar, tennis court, pools, gym, laundry service, concierge, airport shuttle, parking (fee and no fee) ☰AE, D, DC, MC, V.

$$$$ ⊡**St. Regis.** Well-heeled travelers enjoy the hotel's plush accommodations Fodors Choice and thorough service (including butlers on some floors), and local swells ★ arrive for afternoon tea. Rooms are luxuriously furnished, with individually selected artwork, plus Pratesi linens, fully stocked minibars, terrycloth robes, and marble bathrooms. Floor-to-ceiling windows let you gaze on the magical downtown skyline or lush Memorial Park. In River Oaks, the St. Regis is convenient to Downtown and the Galleria area. The pool area is elegant and relaxing, and there's a spa on site to melt your cares away. In addition to a restaurant, the hotel has a tea lounge and a bar serving light fare. **Pros:** Ultra-luxurious service, fast valet, knowledgeable concierge. **Cons:** Not geared toward the young and fun, not much to walk

to in the neighborhood. ☒ *1919 Briar Oaks La., Uptown/River Oaks* ☎ *713/840–7600 or 877/787–3447* ⊕ *www.stregis.com/houston* 🛏 *232 rooms* ♿ *In room: safe, Ethernet. In-hotel: restaurant, room service, bar, pool, gym, spa, parking (fee)* ▤ *AE, D, DC, MC, V* †○┤*CP.*

$$$$ 🏨**Westin Oaks.** Rooms and suites at this 18-story hotel are oversized and elegantly decorated in cream and white. The hotel (and its near-identical sister property, The Westin Galleria) is within the Galleria shopping and office complex in Uptown Houston, so Neiman Marcus and 350 other stores and restaurants are just a short stroll away. There is an outdoor jogging track. **Pros:** Connected to Galleria, reliable upscale chain. **Cons:** Traffic is bad, some public rooms in need of refurbishing. ☒ *5011 Westheimer, Uptown/Galleria* ☎ *713/960–8100* ⊕ *www.westin.com* 🛏 *395 rooms, 11 suites* ♿ *In-room: Ethernet. In-hotel: 2 restaurants, room service, bar, pool, laundry service, parking (fee)* ▤ *AE, D, DC, MC, V.*

WEST SIDE/MEMORIAL PARK

$$$$ 🏨**Omni Houston Hotel–Westside.** With a peaceful water garden in its atrium lobby and grounds with a 2-acre lake, being at the Omni is not like being in the city at all. The hotel is convenient to the Energy Corridor, is within 3 mi of the Memorial City and Town & Country malls, and 16 mi from downtown. Rooms are clean, current, and comfortable, and the fitness facility is well equipped. **Pros:** Near business centers, reliable upscale property. **Cons:** Not convenient to downtown or Houston's best cultural and dining spots, service can be hit or miss. ☒ *13210 Katy Fwy., West Side* ☎ *281/558–8338* ⊕ *www.omnihotels.com* 🛏 *400 rooms* ♿ *In-room: Wi-Fi. In-hotel: restaurant, room service, pools, gym, laundry service, concierge, airport shuttle, parking (fee and no fee)* ▤ *AE, D, DC, MC, V.*

GALVESTON

A thin strip of an island in the Gulf of Mexico, Galveston is big sister Houston's beach playground—a year-round coastal destination just 50 mi away. Many of the first public buildings in Texas, including a post office, bank, and hotel, were built here, but most were destroyed in the Great Storm of 1900. Those that endured have been well preserved, and the Victorian character of the Strand shopping district and the neighborhood surrounding Broadway is still evident. On the Galveston Bay side of the island (northeast), quaint shops and cafés in old buildings are near the Seaport Museum, harbor-front eateries, and the cruise-ship terminal. On the Gulf of Mexico side (southwest), resorts and restaurants line coastal Seawall Boulevard. The 17-foot-high seawall abuts a long ribbon of sand and provides a place for rollerblading, bicycling, and going on the occasional surrey ride.

Galveston is a port of embarkation for cruises on western Caribbean itineraries; some Panama Canal cruises leave from here as well. It's an especially popular port of embarkation for people in the Southeast who don't wish to fly to their cruise. Carnival, Royal Caribbean, Celebrity, and Princess have made Galveston their home port.

EXPLORING GALVESTON

① **Broadway.** The late 1800s were the heyday of Galveston's port (before Houston's was dug out). Victorian splendor is evident in the meticulously restored homes of this historic district, some of which are now museums. If you're in town the first two weekends of May, don't miss the **Galveston Historic Homes Tour.** In addition to visiting the neighborhood's museums, you can walk through privately owned homes dating from the 1800s. For more information about area house museums or the tour, contact the Heritage Visitors Center. **Moody Mansion** (⊠*2618 Broadway* ☎*409/762–7668*), the residence of generations of one of Texas's most powerful families, was completed in 1895. Tour its interiors of exotic woods and gilded trim filled with family heirlooms and personal effects. **Ashton Villa** (⊠*2328 Broadway* ☎*409/762–3933*), a formal Italianate villa, was built in 1859 of brick. Look for the curtains that shielded the more modest Victorian guests from the naked cupids painted on one wall. ⊠*2328 Broadway* ☎*409/765–7834* ⊕*www. galvestonhistory.org* ✑ *Visitor center free, museums $6 each, tour $20* ⊙ *Mon.–Sat. 10–4, Sun. noon–4.*

② **Moody Gardens** is a multifaceted entertainment and educational complex inside pastel-colored glass pyramids. Attractions include the 13-story **Aquarium Pyramid,** showcasing marine life from four oceans in tanks and touch pools; **Rainforest Pyramid,** a 40,000-square-foot tropical habitat for exotic flora and fauna; **Discovery Pyramid,** a joint venture with NASA featuring more than 40 interactive exhibits; and two **IMAX theaters,** one of which has a space adventure ride. Outside, **Palm Beach** has white-sand beach, landscaped grounds, man-made lagoons, a kid-size waterslide and games, and beach chairs. ⊠*1 Hope Blvd.* ☎*409/741–8484 or 800/582–4673* ⊕*www.moodygardens.com* ✑*$8.95–$15.95 per venue, $44.95 day pass or $49.94 two-day pass* ⊙*Memorial Day–Labor Day, daily 10–9; Labor Day–Memorial Day, weekdays 10–6, weekends 10–8.*

⑤ **Pier 21 Theater.** At this theater on the Strand, watch the Great Storm of 1900 come back to life in a multimedia presentation that includes video clips of archival drawings, still photos, and narrated accounts from survivors' diaries. Also playing is a film about the exploits of pirate Jean Lafitte, who used the island as a base. ⊠*Pier 21, Harborside Dr. and 21st St.* ☎*409/763–8808* ⊕*www.galveston.com/pier21theatre* ✑*Great Storm $5, Pirate Island $4* ⊙*Sun.–Thurs. 11–6, Fri. and Sat. 11–8.*

③ **The Strand.** This shopping area is defined by the architecture of its 19th- and early-20th-century buildings, many of which survived the storm of 1900 and are on the National Register of Historic Places. When Galveston was still a powerful port city—before the Houston Ship Channel was dug, diverting most boat traffic inland—this stretch, formerly the site of stores, offices, and warehouses, was known as the Wall Street of the South. As you stroll up the Strand, you'll pass dozens of shops and cafés. ⊠*Between Strand and Postoffice St., 25th and 19th Sts.*

④ **Texas Seaport Museum.** Aboard the restored 1877 tall ship *Elissa,* detailed interpretive signs provide information about the shipping trade in the

A Texas-Size Storm

On October 8, 1900, Galveston was slammed by a Category 4 hurricane. Winds reached 120 mph, destroying most of the city's buildings, and storm surges engulfed the island.

When it was all over, about 6,000 of Galveston's 40,000 residents had died (along with 4,000–6,000 people on the mainland), making this the deadliest natural disaster in U.S. history.

After the storm (which is still referred to as "The Hurricane"), Galveston built the Seawall, which rises 17 feet above the mean low tide for protection. It may not be much to look at, but it has been effective—waves have topped the Seawall during bad storms, but the barrier has prevented the city from experiencing the full brunt from the storm surges that have hit since its construction.

1800s, including the routes and cargoes this ship carried into Galveston. Inside the museum building is a replica of the historic wharf and information about the ethnic groups that immigrated through this U.S. point of entry after 1837. ⊠*Pier 21* ☎*409/763–1877* ⊕*www. tsm-elissa.org* ✉*$8* ⊙*Daily 10–5.*

SPORTS & THE OUTDOORS

BEACHES

The **Seawall** (⊠*Seawall Blvd. from 61st St. to 25th St.*) on the Gulf-side waterfront attracts runners, cyclists, and rollerbladers. Just below it is a long, free beach near many big hotels and resorts. **Stewart Beach Park** (⊠*6th St. and Seawall Blvd.* ☎*409/765–5023* ✉*$5 per vehicle*) has a bathhouse, amusement park, bumper boats, miniature-golf course, and a water coaster in addition to saltwater and sand. It's open weekdays 9 to 5, weekends 8 to 6 from March through May; weekdays 8 to 6 and weekends 8 to 7 from June through September; and weekends 9 to 5 during the first two weekends of October. **Galveston Island State Park** (⊠*3 Mile Rd., 10 mi (16 km) southwest on Seawall Blvd.* ☎*409/737–1222* ✉*$3*), on the western, unpopulated end of the island, is a 2,000-acre natural beach habitat ideal for birding, walking, and renewing your spirit. It's open daily from 8 AM to 10 PM.

WATER PARKS

Schlitterbahn. The entire family will have a fun time at this new water park, located on the bay side of the island. Schlitterbahn features speed slides, lazy river rides, uphill water coasters, a wave pool (with surfing), and water playgrounds for the little ones. There's even a heated indoor water park for chilly winter months. During summer, less expensive afternoon-only rates are in effect, and ticket prices drop in the off-season. ⊠*2026 Lockheed St.* ☎*409/770–9283* ⊕*www.schlitterbahn.com* ✉*$35.99* ⊙*Daily 10–8.*

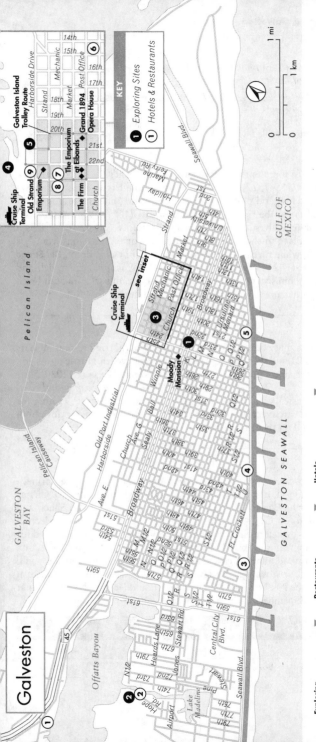

Galveston

KEY

- **1** Exploring Sites
- **①** Hotels & Restaurants

0   1 mi

0   1 km

GALVESTON BAY

Pelican Island

GULF OF MEXICO

GALVESTON SEAWALL

Cruise Ship Terminal

see inset

Moody Mansion ♦

Inset:

Cruise Ship Terminal · Old Strand Emporium

Galveston Island Trolley Route · Harborside Drive

Grand 1894 Opera House

Eibands ♦ · The Emporium

The Firm · Emporium

Strand · Market · Mechanic · Post Office · Church

Exploring ►

Broadway	1
Moody Gardens	2
The Strand	3
Texas Seaport Museum	4
Pier 21 Theater	5

Restaurants ►

Clary's	1
Fisherman's Wharf	9
Gaido's	4
Merchant Prince	8
Mosquito Café	6

Hotels ►

Hotel Galvez	5
Moody Gardens Hotel	2
San Luis Resort	3
Tremont House	7

7

SHOPPING

The **Strand** (⊠ *Bounded by Strand and Postoffice Street (running east–west) and 25th and 19th streets (running north–south))* is the best place to shop in Galveston. Old storefronts are filled with gift shops, antiques stores, and one-of-a-kind boutiques. More than 50 antiques

dealers are represented at **The Emporium at Eibands** (⊠ *2201 Postoffice St.* ☎ *409/515–1517*), an upscale showroom filled with custom upholstery, bedding and draperies, antique furniture, and interesting architectural finds. **The Firm** (⊠ *2218 Postoffice St.* ☎ *409/762–8300*) was the first retail business along quaint Postoffice Street. Today it is a favorite place to shop for trendy, unique women's fashions from Los Angeles, while reveling in the boutique's shabby-chic decor. **Old Strand Emporium** (⊠ *2112 Strand* ☎ *409/515–0715*) is a charming deli and grocery reminiscent of an old-fashioned ice-cream parlor and sandwich shop, with candy bins, packaged nuts, and more.

NIGHTLIFE

For a relaxing evening, choose any of the harborside restaurant-bars on piers 21 and 22 to sip a glass of wine or a frozen Hurricane as you watch the boats go by. The **Grand 1894 Opera House** (⊠ *2020 Postoffice St.* ☎ *409/765–1894 or 800/821–1894* ⊕ *www.thegrand.com*) stages musicals and hosts concerts year-round. It's worth visiting for the ornate architecture alone. Sarah Bernhardt and Anna Pavlova both performed on this storied stage.

WHERE TO EAT

As in most coastal cities, Galveston's dining scene is focused primarily on seafood, much of it caught fresh in the Gulf of Mexico. Chains abound (the Landry's empire—which includes Joe's Crab Shack and the Rainforest Café—was born here), but there's also a great selection of family-owned restaurants that, in some cases, have been around for generations. In the Strand Historic District you'll find cafés, bars, and neighborhood joints as casual as they come. Along the Seawall, you'll find the tourist traps and a few fine establishments (though none can be described as "formal"). Gentlemen should leave jackets and ties at home—remember, you're at the beach!

WHAT IT COSTS					
	¢	$	$$	$$$	$$$$
RESTAURANTS	under $8	$8–$12	$13–$20	$21–$30	over $30

Restaurant prices are per person for a main course at dinner.

SEAFOOD
$$$–$$$$

✕**Clary's.** Out-of-the-way Clary's is a favorite with locals and visitors thanks to the picturesque view, zesty Cajun-style seafood, and great service. The Bloody Marys are outstanding and pair well with the seasonal gumbo and broiled flounder. ⊠*8509 Teichman Rd.* ☎*409/740–0771* ⊟*AE, D, DC, MC, V.*

SEAFOOD
$$–$$$

✕**Fisherman's Wharf.** Even though Landry's has taken over this harborside institution, locals keep coming here for the reliably fresh seafood and reasonable prices. Dine indoors or watch the boat traffic (and waiting cruise ships) from the patio. Start with a cold combo, like boiled shrimp and grilled rare tuna. For entrées, the fried fish, shrimp, and oysters are hard to beat. ⊠*Pier 22, Harborside Dr. and 22nd St.* ☎*409/765–5708* ⊟*AE, D, DC, MC, V.*

SEAFOOD
$$–$$$

✕**Gaido's.** A Galveston landmark for almost 100 years, Gaido's offers the freshest, highest quality seafood, all prepared with family recipes. They still peel shrimp, shuck oysters, and filet fish the same way they've been doing it for four generations. Try the famous oyster platter, but get there early, since they don't take reservations. Similar fare can be found next door at their sister restaurant, Casey's. ⊠*3900 Seawall Blvd.* ☎*409/762–9625* ⊟*AE, D, DC, MC, V.*

CONTINENTAL
$$–$$$

✕**Merchant Prince.** Hotel restaurants usually aren't very good, but that's not the case here. Housed inside the historic Tremont House, the Merchant Prince is an upscale, tasty alternative to the island's proliferating chains. The restaurant features continental fare and a great selection of seafood; it's open for breakfast, lunch, and dinner. ⊠*2300 Ship's Mechanic Row* ☎*409/763–0300* ⊟*AE, D, DC, MC, V.*

AMERICAN
$$–$$$

✕**Mosquito Café.** This chichi eatery in Galveston's historic East End serves fresh, contemporary food—including some vegetarian dishes—in a hip, high-ceilinged dining room and on an outdoor patio. Wake up to a fluffy egg frittata or a homemade scone topped with whipped cream, or try a large gourmet salad for lunch. The grilled snapper with Parmesan grits is a hit in the evening. ⊠*628 14th St.* ☎*409/763–1010* ⊟*AE, D, DC, MC, V* ⊗*No dinner Sun.–Wed.*

WHERE TO STAY

The majority of Galveston hotels are geared toward families. The usual chains are here, but you can also find retro-chic Atomic Age beachfront motels and grand historic resorts, most just steps from the water.

WHAT IT COSTS				
¢	$	$$	$$$	$$$$
HOTELS	under $50	$50–$100	$101–$150	$151–$200	over $200
CAMPING	under $10	$10–$17	$18–$35	$36–$50	over $50

Hotel prices are per night for two people in a standard double room in high season, excluding taxes and service charges.

$$–$$$$

🏨 **San Luis Resort, Spa and Conference Center.** A long marble staircase alongside a slender fountain with sculpted dolphins welcomes you to the beachfront elegance of this resort. The upper-floor facade isn't much to look at, but don't let that fool you; inside, the colors of cool, cream marble and taupe stone in the lobby are echoed in the guest rooms. The sculptural lines of pink granite on the headboards and armchairs say "Italian villa." All rooms have balconies facing the Gulf, and prices rise with the floor height. New Club Ten guestrooms on the 10th floor offer upgraded linens, down comforters, iPod docking stations, and huge plasma TVs. Back on ground level, step into the meandering (and heated) grotto pool with a rock waterfall set amid coconut palms and bougainvillea; then have a Balinese massage (or a wildflower compress) at the Spa San Luis. The resort offers free parking for the duration of a cruise as well as transportation to the cruise terminal. **Pros:** Great Gulf views, nice pool area. **Cons:** Public parking (non-valet) is not convenient. ⊠*5222 Seawall Blvd.,* ☎*409/744–1500 or 800/445–0090* 🖷*409/744–8452* ⊕*www.sanluisresort.com* ⇲*244 rooms* ⚘*In-room: dial-up. In-hotel: restaurant, room service, bars, tennis courts, pools, gym, spa, children's programs (ages 4–12), laundry service, executive floor, public Internet, parking (free), no-smoking rooms* ▤*AE, D, DC, MC, V.*

$$$–$$$$ 🏨**Hotel Galvez.** This renovated six-story Spanish colonial hotel, built in 1911, was once called "Queen of the Gulf." Teddy Roosevelt and Howard Hughes are just two of the many well-known guests who have stayed here. Traditional dark wood and plush upholstery pieces furnish both the public and private areas. A pool, swim-up bar, and outdoor grill have been added to the tropical garden facing the sea. **Pros:** Directly on beach, incredible pool area, beautiful grounds. **Cons:** Rooms can be small (especially the bathrooms) ⊠*2024 Seawall Blvd.,* ☎*409/765–7721* 🖷*409/765–5780* ⊕*www.wyndham.com* ⇲*231 rooms* ⚘*In-hotel: Wi-Fi. In-hotel: Restaurant, pool, gym, laundry service, public Internet, no-smoking rooms* ▤*AE, DC, MC, V.*

$$–$$$ 🏨**Moody Gardens Hotel, Spa & Convention Center.** Look for the glass pyramids once you cross the bridge into Galveston, and you'll find the Moody Gardens Hotel, Spa & Convention Center. Talk about family fun—this sprawling 242-acre property features a living rain forest, an aquarium with penguins and sharks, and an IMAX theater all on-site. Moody Gardens even has its own white-sand beaches and blue lagoons. The hotel has a swim-up bar, childcare services, and a shuttle to the Strand District. **Pros:** Family-friendly, lots to do. **Cons:** Far from the main Seawall Blvd. beaches. ⊠*Seven Hope Blvd.,* ☎*409/741–8484* 🖷*409/765–5780* ⊕*www.moodygardenshotel.com* ⇲*428 rooms* ⚘*In-room: Wi-Fi. In-hotel: spa, public Wi-Fi, pool, no-smoking rooms* ▤*AE, DC, MC, V.*

$$–$$$$ 🏨**Tremont House.** A four-story atrium lobby, with ironwork balconies and full-size palm trees, showcases an 1872 hand-carved rosewood bar in what was once a busy dry-goods warehouse. This actually is a historic place: Republic of Texas president Sam Houston presented his last speech at this hotel, both Confederate and Union soldiers bunked here, and Great Storm victims took refuge under this roof. Rooms have high ceilings and 11-foot windows. Period reproduction furniture and Victorian-pattern wallpapers add to the authenticity. It's the closest full-service lodging to the port, just a short walk from shopping on the Strand—and it's also a completely no-smoking environment. **Pros:** Beautiful, historic environment, great location. **Cons:** Not a fun scene for young single travelers. ✉*2300 Ship's Mechanic Row,* ☎*409/763–0300* 🖶*409/763–1539* 🌐*www.wyndham.com* 🛏*119 rooms* ⚕*In-room: dial-up, Ethernet. In-hotel: restaurant, room service, bar, laundry service, public Internet, parking (fee), no-smoking rooms* 🟰*AE, D, DC, MC, V.*

HOUSTON & GALVESTON ESSENTIALS

Research prices, get travel advice, and book your trip at fodors.com.

TRANSPORTATION

BY AIR

Houston has two major airports: Hobby Airport, 9 mi (15 km) southeast of downtown, and George Bush Intercontinental, 15 mi (24 km) northeast of the city. All the major rental companies have a presence at these airports, so for convenience's sake, it's best to rent them there. However, car-rental offices can be found all over the area, so if you you're in Galveston and decide to take a day trip to Houston, or vice versa, you can easily rent a car from an outpost near your hotel.

Airport Information **Houston Intercontinental Airport** (✉ *2800 North Terminal Rd., Houston* ☎ *281/230–3100* 🌐 *www.fly2houston.com*). **William P. Hobby Airport** (✉ *7800 Airport Blvd., Houston* ☎ *713/640–3000* 🌐 *www.fly2houston.com*).

Ground Transportation **Galveston Limousine Service** (☎ *800/640–4826* 🌐 *www.galvestonlimousineservice.com*). **Yellow Cab of Galveston** (☎ *409/763–3333*). **Super Shuttle** (☎ *800/258–3826*). **United Cab (Houston taxis)** (☎ *713/699–0000*).

BY BUS

METRO buses serve most of Houston; its Web site features route maps, schedules, and a useful Trip Planner tool. Be aware that Houston is a vast city, so traveling long distances by bus may take quite a long time. Until METROrail's new lines open, your best bet is to travel by car (unless you're sticking to downtown, the Museum District, or other areas currently served by METRO's light-rail line). Galveston is accessible from any region of Texas via the state's extensive intercity bus network. Kerrville Bus Company provides daily bus service between Houston's Greyhound Terminal and Galveston Island. Contact Greyhound Lines for further information.

The City of Galveston's public transportation system is Island Transit. Service covers 27 square mi and all buses are ADA compliant. Island Transit also operates a trolley system, serving Seawall Boulevard, 25th Street, downtown, and the Strand District.

Information **Island Transit** (☎ *409/797–3900* 🌐 *www.islandtransit.com*)). **Greyhound Lines** (☎ *800/229–9424* 🌐 *www.greyhound.com*). **METRO** (☎ *713/635–4000* 🌐 *www.ridemetro.org*).

BY CAR

In case you haven't noticed yet, Houston is huge. Driving across the sprawling city can take over an hour, so be aware how far your destination is before setting out. To travel between Houston and Galveston, jump on I-45, the Gulf Freeway, which links the two cities. It's a pretty uneventful ride, especially during non-rush hours, but can get very congested on summer weekends. From Intercontinental Airport, the ride will be about two hours. From downtown Houston to Galveston, the trip's about an hour. Plan extra time into your schedule, since you never know what can happen on Texas freeways.

> ### DICKENS ON THE STRAND
>
> For one weekend in December each year, Galveston's The Strand National Historic Landmark District transforms into a 19th-century British town. The fun includes street musicians, costumed vendors, performances, parades—and snow. For more information, visit ⊕ www.galvestonhistory.org

BY TRAIN & LIGHT RAIL

Houston is a stop along Amtrak's Sunset Limited route, which runs between Louisiana and California. Houston's train station, originally built as the Southern Pacific railroad station in 1905, is located at 902 Washington Ave., behind the Main Post Office.

A few years ago Houston's light-rail system—METRORail—made its debut along Main Street, traveling from UH-Downtown to Reliant Park, home of the NFL Texans, and passing through the Museum District, Hermann Park, and the Texas Medical Center along the way. Several new routes are planned, and the system will reach more parts of the city in the coming years.

Information **Amtrak** (☎ 713/224–1577 ⊕ www.amtrak.com). **METRORail** (☎ 713/635–4000 ⊕ www.ridemetro.org).

CONTACTS & RESOURCES

EMERGENCIES

In an emergency, dial 911. Each of the following medical facilities has an emergency room open 24 hours a day.

Hospitals **Ben Taub General Hospital** (⊠ 1504 Taub Loop, Houston ☎ 713/873–2000). **Memorial Hermann—Texas Medical Center** (⊠ 6411 Fannin, Houston ☎ 713/704–4000). **St. Luke's Episcopal Hospital** (⊠ 6720 Bertner St., Houston ☎ 832/355–4750).

VISITOR INFORMATION

Contacts **Galveston Chamber of Commerce** (☎ 409/763–5326 ⊕ www. galvestonchamber.com). **Greater Houston Convention and Visitors Bureau** (☎ 713/437–5200 ⊕ www.visithoustontexas.org).

East Texas

WORD OF MOUTH

"Jefferson is a cute little town that has a lot of history behind it."

—ChristieP.

By Michael
Ream

EAST TEXAS TAKES LIFE SLOWER than the more urbanized parts of the state. To be sure, all the traditional Texas touchstones are here: cattle grazing on the prairie, pickup trucks rolling down dirt roads, the smell of barbecue smoking in roadside shacks, and a fanatical devotion to high-school football. The region played a role in the rise of Texas oil, starting with the Spindletop Well near Beaumont, which began gushing in 1901. Other oil discoveries followed, including the legendary East Texas Oil Field near Kilgore, which by the 1930s had made Texas the leading producer of "black gold."

East Texas also has a landscape distinct from the rest of Texas. At one time it was covered with large swaths of forests, which contributed to the region's Piney Woods nickname. Some roads still snake through thick stands of trees across the area's sweeping plains. Swampy areas centered around the Big Thicket National Preserve remind visitors they're not far from Louisiana.

EAST TEXAS TOP 5

■ **Sam Houston Memorial Museum:** Pay tribute to a Texas hero at this Huntsville gem.

■ **Caldwell Zoo:** Tyler may be small-town USA, but its zoo has creatures from around the world.

■ **Big Thicket Nat'l Preserve:** Explore natural habitats, including swamp, forest, and desert.

■ **Jefferson:** It's easy to imagine the town's glory days, when it was a leading deepwater port that connected Texas with the world.

■ **Stone Fort Museum:** Immerse yourself in the story of Texas's sociological evolution at this Nacogdoches top spot.

EXPLORING EAST TEXAS

With a largely flat terrain—though hilly in some areas—East Texas is fairly easy to explore, although distances between towns and attractions can be long. U.S. 59 cuts north-south through the heart of East Texas and will take a visitor through some of the region's most interesting places. Starting north of Marshall at Jefferson, it winds south to Nacogdoches and Diboll, skirts the Davy Crockett National Forest, and runs just northwest of Big Thicket National Preserve. From here, visitors can head west to Huntsville, just over an hour north of downtown Houston. The coastal area, centered on Beaumont and Port Arthur, is about an hour and a half east of Houston on Interstate 10.

ABOUT THE RESTAURANTS

East Texas has a bit of a Southern, near-the-bayou flavor. So while Texas mainstays like barbecue and chili populate the menus at the region's main-street cafés, so do chicken-fried steak and fried catfish—and even fried alligator tail on occasion. Most restaurants serve standard American and Southern fare, heavy on grilled meats and simple side dishes like potatoes and steamed vegetables. There's also ample Mexican and Tex-Mex cuisine: nearly every sizable town has at least one restaurant serving south-of-the-border staples. Dress tends to be casual, even at the fancier restaurants in the larger towns.

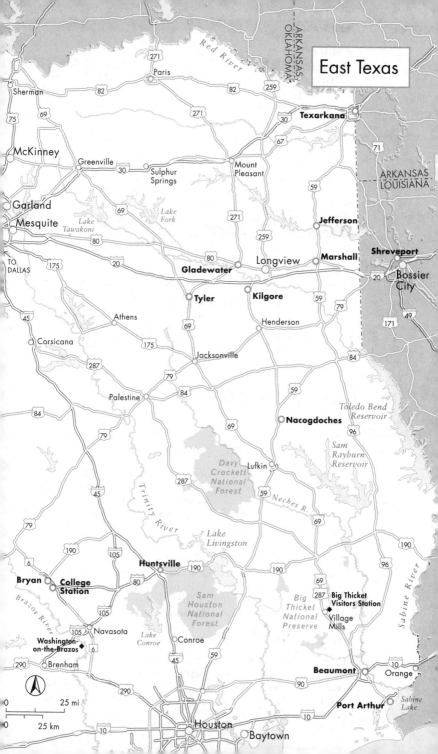

ABOUT THE HOTELS

Throughout East Texas, lodging tends toward chain motels, with the occasional bed-and-breakfast. Older, historic towns like Nacogdoches and Jefferson often offer B&Bs in historic homes; you may even find yourself in a Victorian mansion that was once part of a plantation.

ABOUT THE CAMPGROUNDS

Camping areas tend to be several miles or more from major towns. Campsites are available at a handful of state parks, including Huntsville and Tyler state parks, which have RV hookups, as well as at national forests (Davy Crockett, Sabine, and Sam Houston national forests all have developed campsites, including some with RV hookups, while Angelina National Forest has tent-only sites.

WHAT IT COSTS					
	¢	$	$$	$$$	$$$$
RESTAURANTS	under $8	$8–$12	$13–$20	$21–$30	over $30
HOTELS	under $50	$50–$100	$101–$150	$151–$200	over $200
CAMP-GROUNDS	under $10	$10–$17	$18–$35	$36–$49	over $50

Restaurant prices are per person for a main course at dinner. Hotel prices are per night for two people in a standard double room in high season, excluding taxes and service charges. The lodging tax rate is 13% in the major towns, including Huntsville, Jefferson, Nacogdoches, and Tyler. Camping prices are for a standard (no hookups, pit toilets, fire grates, picnic tables) campsite per night.

TEXARKANA & SHREVEPORT

TEXARKANA

About 175 mi northeast of Dallas via I–30.

With two separate cities divided by the Texas–Arkansas border and sharing the same downtown, Texarkana's location has long been its main attraction. Both H. Ross Perot and Scott Joplin hailed from the Texas side of the border. (Those looking to pay tribute to the famous ragtime musician can view the Scott Joplin mural on Main Street.)

WHAT TO SEE

There's not a lot to see here, although you do have the chance to stand inside a building with your feet in two states—State Line Avenue runs beneath the middle of the combination post office and federal courthouse, which is built out of both Texas granite and Arkansas limestone. The surrounding downtown sidewalks and storefronts are largely abandoned, as is the grand but faded Union Station, a tangible reminder of the city's long history as an important railroad center.

Museum of Regional History. Texarkana's railroad history is on display here. The downtown museum also has exhibits on the Caddo Indians and Texarkana's struggle with racial desegregation during the Civil Rights era. ⊠ *219 N. State Line Ave.* ☎ *903/793–4831* 🖾 *$5* ⊘ *Tues.– Sat. 10–4.*

PLANNING YOUR TRIP

WHEN TO GO

Like much of the state, East Texas experiences hot summers. July and August temperatures easily hit 90°, and 100° is not abnormal. Humidity also gets uncomfortably high. The coastal area around Beaumont/Port Arthur is within the hurricane belt, and in fact suffered damage from Hurricane Rita in 2005. Hurricane season for the Gulf Coast area lasts from June through November (to track developments, consult ⊕*www. nhc.noaa.gov*).

Considered by many to have the best fall foliage in the state, East Texas offers stands of cottonwood, elm, oak, and maple, providing a full palette of leaf colors. The colorful display is complemented by the carpet of needles from the ubiquitous pine trees. The fall foliage season generally runs from late October through Thanksgiving, peaking in late November.

Spring foliage in East Texas is also magnificent. Nacogdoches is a good starting point, with its 20-mile plus Azalea Trail, showcased from mid- to late March, as well as the largest Azalea Garden in Texas on the campus of Stephen F. Austin State University. Dogwood blooms annually in March (a popular spot to see them is the Alabama Creek Wildlife Management Area in the Davy Crockett National Forest).

GETTING THERE & AROUND

Driving is by far the easiest way to get around. Being largely rural, East Texas has few public transit options. The train stops in Texarkana, Marshall, Longview, Beaumont, and of course nearby Houston, and Greyhound travels to most towns. East Texas is also far from major cities—Houston is over two hours from Nacogdoches, and Dallas is at least a few hours to the west of most parts of East Texas.

8

SHREVEPORT, LOUISIANA

About 70 mi from Texarkana via U.S. 71.

An industrial city reborn as a gambling hot spot, Shreveport stretches out from the banks of the Red River, and feels less like Louisiana and more like the easternmost town in Texas: the rolling plains surrounding the city are dotted with herds of cattle and old oil wells, and the town still has the raw and busy feel of the days when derricks drilled for black gold and locally-grown cotton was shipped out to the world. The city has retained wealth from those hectic days, reflected in several tony residential neighborhoods.

Downtown's waterfront features the Red River District, a cluster of restaurants and nightclubs located just off the Texas Street Bridge. Crossing the bridge to Bossier City brings visitors to Louisiana Boardwalk, a large outdoor shopping mall with numerous restaurants and sweeping views of the river. Nearby are the neon-encrusted towers of numerous casino hotels that have turned gritty Bossier City, home of Barksdale Air Force Base, into a small-scale Las Vegas.

WHAT TO SEE

2 **Sci-Port Discovery Center.**, This fun, three-in-one place in downtown Shreveport has 92,000 square feet of hands-on exhibits, a planetarium, and an IMAX. Kids ages 3–12 get $3 off admission. ⊠ *820 Clyde Fant Pkwy.* ☎ *318/424–3466* ⊕ *www.sciport.org* ⊠ *$12 (IMAX additional)* ⊙ *Mon.-Fri. 10–5, Sat. 10–6, Sun.1–6.*

1 **Louisiana Boardwalk.** Just across the Red River from Shreveport more than 50 outlet stores await shoppers. Stores include Banana Republic, Bass Pros Shops Outdoor World (complete with a live alligator exhibit), Eddie Bauer, Guess?, Lane Bryant, Nine West, Samsonite, and Vitamin World. The entertainment district also houses several restaurants (many with riverfront dining), a cineplex, a carousel, and nightlife venues. A trolley runs between the boardwalk and the parking garage. ⊠ *390 Plaza Loop (Exit 19B off I–20), Bossier City* ☎ *318/752–1455* ⊕ *www.louisianaboardwalk.com* ⊠ *Free* ⊙ *Mon.–Thurs. 10–9, Fri.–Sat. 10–10, Sun. noon–7 (hours are for shops only).*

3 **Municipal Auditorium.** This hulking brick structure, completed in 1929, may be in a rundown area just outside downtown, but it has a special claim to fame. In 1954 a 19-year-old entertainer named Elvis Presley burst onto the national scene when he performed on the popular "Louisiana Hayride" radio show. The program broadcast for more than a decade from the auditorium, hosting numerous pop and country music stars, including Hank Williams, Sr., and Johnny Cash. The stage still hosts musical shows, and a small museum is inside. Tours of the building last about 30 minutes. ✉ *705 Elvis Presley Ave. (off Milam St.)* ☎ *318/220–9434* ⊕ *www.stageofstars.com* ✉ *Donation requested (tours)* ⊙ *Wed.–Sat. 11–4, Sun. 1–4 (tours).*

❹ **R.W. Norton Art Gallery.** Located in a leafy residential neighborhood, this museum's extensive galleries feature American and European artists, with a focus on 19th-century American art. The collection includes a large number of works by Frederic Remington and Charles Russell. ✉ *4747 Creswell Ave.* ☎ *318/865–4201* ⊕ *www.rwnaf.org* ✉ *Free* ⊙ *Tues.–Fri. 10–5, Sat.–Sun. 1–5.*

> ## SCOTT JOPLIN: KING OF RAGTIME
>
> Born near Marshall in 1867 or 1868, Scott Joplin spent his childhood years in Texarkana, where he learned to played the banjo and the piano. Later he composed music, including many "rags" for the pre-jazz genre ragtime and an opera that earned him a Pulitzer Prize Special Award posthumously. In Texarkana, an exhibit at the Museum of Regional History recalls Joplin's life and works, and a Joplin mural is painted on the side of a building at 311 Main St.

JEFFERSON–MARSHALL AREA

Jefferson provides a good gateway to East Texas, especially if traveling between Dallas and Shreveport on I–20. Highway 59 runs south from Jefferson and crosses the interstate at Marshall.

8

JEFFERSON

About 60 mi south of Texarkana on U.S. 59, and 50 mi northwest of Shreveport on I–20 and U.S. 59.

Jefferson is a charming small town with a unique claim to history: from the 1840s to the 1870s it was Texas's northernmost deep-water port. Steamboats crowded the waterfront, loading up the vast Texas cotton harvest and unloading consumer goods to be sent via railroad into America's rapidly settling frontier. A boomtown atmosphere prevailed, with numerous hotels, saloons, and a generally raffish air.

The good times ended as quickly as they began, with the coming of the railroad and the decline of East Texas river shipping, and today Jefferson's streets are much quieter. Port facilities are long gone, and the waterfront now lies stagnant, with only a lone boat ramp left. Still, the town has rebounded, preserving and renovating historic downtown buildings—including the Excelsior Hotel (⇨ *Where to Stay*), the Ruth Lester Memorial & Jefferson Playhouse (a former synagogue) at the corner of Market and Henderson streets, and the Carnegie Library on West Lafayette.

WHAT TO SEE

House of the Seasons. Built in 1872, at the tail end of Jefferson's glory days as a busy river port, this is one of the more interesting buildings in town. Its most striking feature is an interior dome that telescopes into a stained glass-lined cupola. The house was the residence of Ben Epperson, a prominent Texas politician beginning in the 1840s. Today the house serves as a bed-and-breakfast inn, with four suites named after famous Texans, including George W. and Laura Bush, who spent a night in 1996, and Lady Bird Johnson, who attended Jefferson High School and visited the house twice. Tours are by appointment only, beginning at 11 AM. ⊠*409 South Alley St.* ☎*903/665–8000* ⊕*www.house oftheseasons.com* ✑*$7.50* ⊙*Tours by appointment only Mon.–Sat.*

TOUR TO TAKE

The **Historic Jefferson Foundation** (⊕ *www.historicjefferson foundation.com*) sponsors a candlelight tour for two weekends in late November/early December. Visitors can admire antebellum architecture, period furniture, and a wealth of antiques in local historic homes, including Scarlett O'Hardy's, a Greek Revival house at 408 Taylor St. that re-creates the style of the Old South in its architecture and decor (next door is a museum with *Gone With the Wind* memorabilia). Holiday home tour tickets ($15 for adults, $2 for children), can be purchased at the chamber office at 118 N. Vale St.

☼ **Atalanta.** The private rail car of tycoon Jay Gould, built in 1888, is now stationed permanently on Jefferson's main street. The interior recalls a luxurious era of rail travel, with stained-glass windows, Persian rugs, and mahogany and brass fittings. The car has four state rooms, a lounge, kitchen, dining room, and butler's pantry. It is open for guided tours only. ■TIP➔It's best to arrange a tour before arriving in Jefferson. ⊠*211 W. Austin St.* ☎*903/665-2513* ✑*$2.50* ⊙*Daily 10–12 and 2–4 by appointment only.*

SPORTS & THE OUTDOORS

Jefferson is the gateway to nearby Caddo Lake, formed by a giant log-jam on the Red River, which also turned Jefferson into a bustling port. Boat tours are available from several private companies; information is available at the chamber of commerce.

ANTIQUES ## SHOPPING

Der Baskit Kase Village (⊠*215 N. Polk St.* ☎*903/665–7996* ⊙*Tue.– Sun. 10–5*) features restored musical instruments and a selection of books, along with antique glassware and jewelry. **Gold Leaf Antique Mall** (⊠*207 N. Polk St.* ☎*903/665–2882* ⊙*Daily 10–5, Mar.–Dec.; Thur.–Tues. 10–5, Jan.–Feb.*) specializes in furniture, glassware, and a wide selection of odds and ends. With an old-fashioned soda fountain and shelves groaning under an endless assortment of toys, sweets, and knickknacks, **Jefferson General Store** (⊠*113 E. Austin St.* ☎*903/665– 8481* ⊙*Sun.–Thur. 9–6, Fri.–Sat. 9 AM–10 PM*) is a trip back in time.

WHERE TO EAT & STAY

$$–$$$$ ✕**Stillwater Inn.** Fresh ingredients and eclectic decor are the rule at this converted house, where rocking chairs grace the front porch and beaded table lamps sit atop white linen tablecloths in a series of intimate, crystal-chandeliered dining rooms. Diners can choose from a wide selection of fresh seafood, including jumbo shrimp scampi, pecan-encrusted trout, and grilled salmon with balsamic vinaigrette. New York strip steak with a divine bordelaise sauce, accompanied by hand-cut bistro fries and grilled breast of duck are also good choices, and deserts are worth waiting for. The flan is wonderfully accented with Grand Marnier, and the velvety smooth *tartufo al limoncello* (a half-scoop of lemon liqueur–flavored gelato swathed in lemon meringue), topped with fresh raspberries, has just the right touch of both tartness and sweetness. Extensive wine list. ⊠*203 E. Broadway St.* ☎*903/665–8415* ⊟*AE, D, DC, MC, V* ⊘*Closed Sun.–Mon. No lunch.*

$–$$ 🏨**Excelsior House Hotel.** Every room has its own unique style at this historic two-story hotel in the heart of Jefferson's old downtown. Built in the 1850s and restored in the early 1960s, the hotel has several rooms named after famous guests, including Presidents Ulysses S. Grant and Rutherford B. Hayes. Several rooms overlook a small brick courtyard, capped by a fountain that hosts turtles and goldfish. The hotel's breakfast room is accented with marble columns, chandeliers, Persian rugs and lace curtains. **Pros:** Very comfortable beds, excellent location for strolling the streets of the historic downtown. **Cons:** Some rooms are on the small side, with little space for sitting; restaurant serves only breakfast, with a set menu. ⊠*211 West Austin St.,* ☎*903/665–2513 or 800/490–7270* ⊕*www.theexcelsiorhouse.com* ⇥*15 rooms* ♿*In room: refrigerator (some). In hotel: Public Wi-Fi. No elevator. No-smoking rooms* ⊟*AE, D, MC, V* ⏀*BP.*

MARSHALL

15 mi south of Jefferson on U.S. 59

More than perhaps any other town in East Texas, Marshall was a creation of the railroad. Strategically situated between Dallas and Shreveport, the town was an ideal base in the late 1800s for the Texas & Pacific Railway, which for nearly a century had many of its maintenance and repair operations in Marshall for trains heading west into the vast frontier. At its heyday nearly 3,000 people—roughly one-third the town's population at the time—worked for the "T & P." Trains still rumble along the tracks north of downtown, but the massive complex of machine shops that once hummed with the clanking of steam engines is long gone.

WHAT TO SEE

Texas & Pacific Depot. The importance of trains in Marshall may be significantly diminished, but the town's stately redbrick station remains. It contains a museum dedicated to Marshall's railroading glory days. You can peer inside an old Union Pacific caboose parked on the lawn outside the station, or take a look over the tracks that once bustled with

CLOSE UP

East Texas Flora & Fauna

Thick stands of pine trees are the most obvious natural feature in East Texas, but lush growths of flowers and other colorful plants flourish in the region's hidden corners. Notable concentrations of roses and azaleas can be found in Tyler and Nacogdoches, respectively. A seemingly endless number of plants and wildlife thrive in Big Thicket National Preserve, where a unique confluence of habitats has created a foundation for 85 species of trees, 60 shrubs, and nearly 1,000 other flowering plants, such as ferns, orchids, and four types of insect-eating plants.

East Texas's reptile residents include the American alligator.

The swampy features of Big Thicket also make it a haven for reptiles, with numerous frogs, toads, salamanders, and snakes, plus less-seen alligators. Many animals found here are nocturnal, including coyotes and armadillos. The preserve is also a prime spot for bird-watching and part of the Great

Texas Coastal Birding Trail. Nearly 186 kinds of birds, from songbirds to the bald eagle, make their home in or migrate through Big Thicket.

Swamplike conditions in other places, such as Caddo Lake, near Jefferson, also produce a wealth of wildlife, ranging from egrets, woodpeckers, and herons to alligators and turtles.

---

freight cars being coupled and switched for departure across Texas and the southern United States. ⊠*800 N. Washington St.* ☎*903/938–9495* ⊕*www.marshalldepot.org* ⌷*$2* ⊙*Tues.–Sat 10–4.*

EN ROUTE

About 30 mi west of Marshall on I-20, and then 5 mi south on U.S. 259 lies **Kilgore.** The epitome of a Texas oil boomtown, Kilgore gushed "black gold" for years. In 1930 oil began to flow from the legendary East Texas Oil Field, which became the largest in the lower 48 states. For 10 wild years derricks crowded Kilgore's streets, and wildcatters drilled wherever they thought they might strike it rich—including a hole drilled through the floor of a local bank. More than five billion barrels of oil have been pumped from the plains in and around town. A thick stand of derricks still looms over Kilgore's dusty downtown, but they're purely ornamental—oil began to dry up in the 1960s.

A massive, 72-foot-high replica derrick stands outside Kilgore's **East Texas Oil Museum** (⊠*Hwy. 259 at Ross St.* ☎*903/983–8295* ⊕*www. easttexasoilmuseum.com* ⌷*$6, $3 ages 3–11* ⊙*Tues.–Sat. 9–4, Sun. 2–5*). The museum contains numerous exhibits on the oil industry, including a simulated "Elevator ride to the center of the Earth" that explains the geological phenomena that lead to big oil strikes.

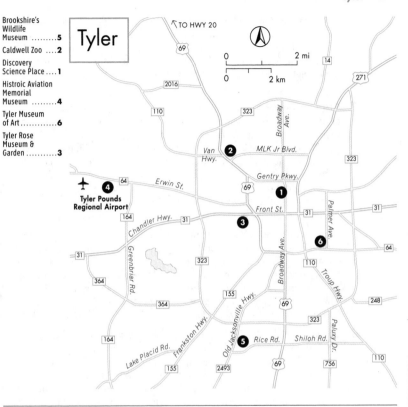

TYLER

15 mi west of Kilgore on I–20, then 10 mi southwest on U.S. 271.

The commercial and cultural center for East Texas, Tyler has seen a population boom in recent years. Retirees and second-home owners are moving into town, prompting new housing to sprout up in former cotton fields and alongside the nearly century-old mansions built by the cotton and oil barons who once called the town home. Sculpted hedges and winding streets in Tyler's historic neighborhoods provide a respite from the unending prairie that dominates the surrounding landscape.

The local economy has shifted from the boom-and-bust heyday of the Texas oil industry to that of a regional banking and medical center, with three major hospitals in town. Tyler is a regional cultural center as well, with a symphony, ballet, and an art museum.

The town has also been known for harboring quite a few green thumbs—or pink thumbs, as they say in Tyler, since the gardeners have been particularly passionate about roses. At one point, some 80 percent of all roses sold in the United States were grown here. Though local rose growing has since declined, many out-of-state growers send roses to Tyler for cutting and packing before they are shipped to destinations worldwide. Rose sheds can be seen along the smaller roads leading in and out of town, along with the occasional field of rose bushes and a 14-acre municipal rose garden, the nation's largest. Each October the town celebrates its rosy past with the Texas Rose Festival.

WHAT TO SEE

❸ Tyler Rose Garden & Museum. An impressive collection of rose bushes—more than 38,000—is spread over 14 acres, with nearly 500 different varieties of roses on display. An accompanying museum relates Tyler's long history of rose growing and also has extensive exhibits on Tyler's annual rose festival, including gowns worn by the Rose Queen, who is chosen every year to preside over the festival events. ⊠*420 Rose Park Dr.* ☎*903/597–3130* ⊕*www.tylerrosemuseum.com* ☞*$3.50 (museum), free (garden)* ☉*Mon.–Fri. 9–4:30 (except closed on Mon. Nov.–Feb.), Sat. 10–4:30, Sun. 1:30–4:30.*

❺ Brookshire's World of Wildlife Museum & Country Store. This museum features a large collection of stuffed and mounted wild animals collected on hunting trips, mainly in Africa, by the longtime owners of the Brookshire Grocery Company. The collection includes bears, zebras, and numerous reptiles. Also on-site is a 1920s country store. ⊠*1600 S.W. Loop 323, at Old Jacksonville Hwy.* ☎*903/534–2169* ⊕*www. brookshiresmuseum.com* ☞*Free* ☉*Mar.–Sept. 9–5, Oct.–Feb. 10–4.*

❷ Caldwell Zoo. Lush, verdant foliage lines the pathways of this well-stocked zoo, which holds close to 2,000 animals. Highlights include a rare white tiger, a showcase of animals native to Texas, a replica African savanna, and a "wild bird walkabout" that offers visitors the opportunity to feed cockatiels and parakeets while balancing the birds on a stick. An open-air café overlooks the environmentally life-like enclosures for the zoo's elephants, giraffes, and zebras. Those 55 and older are admitted free to the zoo. ⊠*2203 Martin Luther King, Jr. Blvd.* ☎*903/593–0121* ⊕*www.caldwellzoo.org* ☞*$8.50* ☉*Mar.–Labor Day 9–5, after Labor Day–Feb. 9–4.*

❶ Discovery Science Place. This hands-on museum has exhibits designed for children ages pre-kindergarten to 6th grade. Activities include looking for fossils in a cave, experiencing an earthquake, and exploring a large-scale explorer's ship. There's also an aerospace exhibit and a replica volcano. In a separate room, "HomeTown, USA" features a simulated Main Street with a hospital, dairy farm, and bank. ⊠*308 N. Broadway Ave.* ☎*903/533–8011* ⊕*www.discoveryscienceplace.org* ☞*$5* ☉*Mon.–Sat. 9–5, Sun. 1–5.*

❹ Historic Aviation Memorial Museum. Housed in an old airport terminal on the grounds of the Tyler airport, this museum extensively documents Tyler's long-running relationship with aviation, which includes the airport's use as a training center during World War II. View a collection of military uniforms and other exhibits focused on both civilian and military aviation, taking into account air power in all wars of the 20th century. ⊠*150 Airport Dr.* ☎*903/526–1945 or 903/526–1939* ⊕*www.tylerhamm.org* ☞*$5* ☉*Wed.–Sat. 10–5, Sun. 1–5.*

6 Tyler Museum of Art. Both internationally known artists as well as those from Texas are featured at this museum in a high-ceilinged, award-winning building on Tyler Junior College's campus. The largest art museum east of Dallas, it has close to 900 works, including paintings, photographs, and sculptures by such reputed artists as James Brooks, Alexander Calder, and Fairfield Porter. ⊠*1300 S. Mahon St.* ☎*903/595–1001* ⊕*www.tyler museum.org* ☜*$3.50* ☉*Tues.–Sat. 10–5, Sun. 1–5.*

WHERE TO STAY

$$ 🏠**Roseland Plantation.** Eight miles from downtown Tyler, along a road lined with the area's famous rose nurseries, this former cotton plantation once served as a stopping point for stagecoaches running between Dallas and Shreveport. Rooms do not have televisions, however there is a television in the house library. Breakfast and afternoon tea are served in a large dining room stuffed with antiques. **Pros:** Very relaxing, with lots of space for sitting and reading. **Cons:** Remote location not close to attractions in town. ⊠*2601 Hwy. 64, Ben Wheeler* ☎*903/849–5553* ⊕*www.roselandplantation.com* ☜*5 rooms* ⌂*In-room: refrigerator (some), microwave (some), no TV. In-hotel: No-smoking rooms* ▤*AE,D,MC,V* ❘◎❘*BP.*

> ## TOP FESTIVALS IN EAST TEXAS
>
> ■ **Texas Blueberry Festival:** Live music and blueberry farm tours celebrate the blueberry harvest. *Mid-June, Nacogdoches.*
>
> ■ **Texas Rose Festival:** Numerous events, including a parade and rose show, are part of this multiday affair. *Mid-Oct., Tyler.*
>
> ■ **Fire Ant Festival:** The pesky critters have been honored for more than 20 years. A parade with costumed "fire ants" is the highlight. If you so desire, you might even be able to find a bowl of chili with the fire ant as one of the ingredients! *Mid-Oct., Marshall.*

NACOGDOCHES

About 80 mi southeast of Tyler via U.S. 69 and Hwy. 21.

The historic heart of East Texas, Nacogdoches was the cradle for the idea of Texas's being its own nation. Three unsuccessful campaigns for Texas independence originated here, and the town played a significant role in Texas's ultimate victory and establishment as a republic. Today the flags of the earlier rebellions fly alongside the Spanish, Mexican, and Lone Star flags outside city hall. Just across the downtown square on Main Street is Nacogdoches's visitor information center—stop in if you're looking to do a self-guided walking tour of downtown, as brochures are available. The center also has information on an architectural tour featuring buildings designed by Diedrich Rulfs, whose vision defined numerous structures throughout Nacogdoches. Down the street from the visitor center is a statue of Antonio Gil Y'Barbo, the Spanish settler who established the town in 1779.

Nachogdoches is also home to Stephen F. Austin State University, which includes the largest azalea garden in the state of Texas.

WHAT TO SEE

Sterne-Hoya House. This modest wood-frame house is rich in history. Adolphus Sterne, a German immigrant who became a prominent merchant and catalyst for Texas independence, lived here from about 1830 until his death in 1852. Sam Houston and Davy Crockett each spent a night, and troops encamped here on their way to the Alamo. The house has been restored to its original design and contains period objects from when the Sterne family lived here. The outlying gardens feature a wide selection of native trees, including crepe myrtle, dogwood, and Texas sugarberry. ⊠ *211 S. Lanana St.* ☎ *936/560–5426* ⊡ *Free* ⊙ *Tues.–Sat.10–4.*

★ **Stone Fort Museum.** This rough-hewn structure on the Stephen F. Austin State University campus showcases local history, with exhibits that chronicle Nacogdoches's evolution from a French trading post and Spanish mission to a staging point for rebels fighting for Texas independence. The building is a replica of the home that Gil Y'Barbo built after founding the town of Nacogdoches. The abode later served as a focal point for the rebellions that swept through the area. ⊠ *Griffith and Clarke boulevards* ☎ *936/468–2408* ⊕ *www.sfasu.edu/stonefort* ⊡ *Free* ⊙ *Tues.–Sat. 9–5, Sun. 1–5.*

NEED A BREAK? ✕ **Olde Towne General Store**—Wedged into a narrow storefront across the street from the visitor center is this converted general store that offers cheap and filling soups and sandwiches; a wide selection of breads is on hand. Your sweet tooth is not forgotten either: a glass pastry case offers cookies and other dessert items. It's closed on Sundays. ⊠ *205 E. Main St.* ☎ *936/560-3210* ⊟ *AE,V* ⊙ *Mon.-Fri. 9-4, Sat. 10-2.*

SPORTS & THE OUTDOORS

Lake Nacogdoches, located about 10 mi west of town, offers swimming, boating, and fishing. Maps and guides are available at the town visitor center. Within the surrounding area are three national forests: Davy Crockett, Angelina, and Sabine. They're worthwhile destinations for outdoor activities such as boating, camping, fishing, and hiking.

WHERE TO STAY

$-$$ **Haden Edwards Inn.** This 1891 house, owned over the years by some of Nacogdoches's more prominent residents, sprawls across a lot complemented with fountains and flowering plants. Rooms are handsomely appointed, with 12-foot ceilings, hardwood floors, and fireplaces in some rooms. All rooms have private baths. The inn is just down the street from Nacogdoches' historic Sterne-Hoya House and Oak Grove Cemetery. **Pros:** Large front porch provides a perfect spot for an al fresco breakfast. **Cons:** Two-night minimum stay required on weekends. ⊠ *106 N. Lanana St.,* ☎ *936/622–6051* ⊕ *www.haden edwardsinn.com* ⏎ *4 rooms* ⟲ *In-room: Wi-Fi, DVD, no phone* ⊟ *AE,D,MC,V* ⏉ *BP.*

**EN
ROUTE**

A blink-and-you'll-miss-it kind of place, **Diboll** sits astride U.S. 59 as it swells with traffic speeding south to Houston. This archetypal timber town's history is tightly intertwined with the Temple family, who, beginning in the late 1890s established a sawmill that grew into a large, diversified wood products company. The Temples provided opportunities for timber employees to purchase their own homes, helped to integrate the local schools, and built a library, civic center, and recreational facilities. These and other aspects of the town's history are preserved at **The History Center** just off the highway. Photos and exhibits give a detailed picture of timber workers' lives at work, home, and play. Constructed almost entirely out of local woods, the building has a steam locomotive and train cars sitting outside the front door. ⊠ *102 N. Temple St.* ☎ *936/829–3543* ⊕ *www.TheHistoryCenterOnline.com* ☜ *Free* ☉ *Mon–Fri. 8–5, Sat. 9–1.*

BRYAN–COLLEGE STATION

135 mi southwest of Nacogdoches via Hwy. 7, Hwy. 21, and U.S. 190; 92 mi southeast Waco via Hwy. 6.

Welcome to Aggieland! As you drive into Bryan–College Station, you'll notice a marked increase in the number of maroon shirts, hats, signs— even cars—bearing the ATM logo (with the hat of the T stretching over the A and M). This is the home of Texas A&M University, the second largest institution of higher learning in the state (second only to A&M's number-one rival, UT Austin), and one of the ten largest schools in the country. As with many university towns, life here pretty much revolves around the school—especially on football weekends. College Station's main drags are University Drive (FM 60), Texas Avenue, and George Bush Drive, all of which border the campus. Historic downtown Bryan is less commercial and has a slower pace.

8

COLLEGE STATION

WHAT TO SEE

★ **George Bush Presidential Library and Museum.** On display here are items representing the life and times of the 41st U.S. president, George H. W. Bush. Highlights of the museum include a huge piece of the Berlin Wall and the "Seat of Power," where visitors can take a seat in an exact replica of Bush's presidential desk. ⊠ *1000 George Bush Dr. West, Texas A&M University campus* ☎ *979/691–4000, 979/691–4091 TTY* ⊕ *http://bushlibrary.tamu.edu* ☜ *$7; $10 with audio tour* ☉ *Mon.– Sat. 9:30–5, Sun. noon–5.*

Texas A&M University. Everything is bigger in Texas, including the universities. A&M has one of the nation's largest student bodies. (The A&M stands for "agricultural and mechanical," and students are known as Aggies.) The massive campus (5,200 acres!) is bound by Texas Avenue, George Bush Drive, FM 2818 (Harvey Mitchell Parkway), and University Drive. It's one of only a handful of institutions that are land-, sea-, and space-grant institutions. While A&M has an excellent academic

CLOSE UP

Washington-on-the-Brazos: Birthplace of Texas

Most Texans know about the Lone Star State's two most famous shrines to liberty: the Alamo, where a band of Texas soldiers were besieged and massacred by Mexican General Antonio Lopez de Santa Anna's troops, and San Jacinto, the battlefield where Sam Houston and his troops defeated Santa Anna's army and won Texas independence. Both of these historic sites overshadow the tiny town of Washington-on-the-Brazos, where the Texas Declaration of Independence from Mexico was signed in 1836, and the actual Republic of Texas was born.

Several sites are part of the **Washington-on-the-Brazos State Historic Site** (✉ *12300 Park Rd. 12, Washington* ☎ *936/878-2214* ⊕ *www.tpwd.state.tx.us* ✉ *Free, but attractions cost extra* ⊙ *Daily 8–sundown*).

Like the American patriots, the Texas delegates met in a building called **Independence Hall** (✉ *$4* ⊙ *Daily; tours at 10, 11, 1, and 2*). It bore no resemblance to its Philadelphia counterpart—this was an unfinished one-room wood building without windows. Today visitors can tour a replica that

sits on the foundation of the original building, and imagine what it was like on the bitterly cold March day when 59 men gathered here to found the Lone Star Republic (at the same time Santa Anna was preparing his final assault on the Alamo in San Antonio).

The **Star of the Republic Museum** (☎ *936/878-2461* ⊕ *www.star museum.org* ✉ *$4* ⊙ *Daily 10–5*) gives an excellent overview of Texas history (particularly helpful if you haven't been able to get to Austin's Bob Bullock Texas State History Museum). For a real peek into the past, stop at the **Barrington Living History Farm** (✉ *$4* ⊙ *Mon.–Sat. 10–5, Sun. 11–5*), a re-created 19th-century farm. Visitors can tour Republic of Texas president Anson Jones's actual home, Barrington, as well as a replica log kitchen, chicken coop, smokehouse, livestock barn, and slave quarters. Interpreters in period dress are on hand to answer questions while they go about the daily chores necessary to raise crops and livestock and run the farm.

—Mike Nalepa

reputation, football is really what makes this place tick. When you drive onto campus, it's impossible to miss Kyle Field, the Aggies' pigskin cathedral. A&M's rivalry with the UT Longhorns is legendary, and the highlight of each season is the schools' Thanksgiving showdown. Traditions—like the Aggie ring, the Corps of Cadets, Reveille, and the 12th Man—are important here, and Aggies have a fierce pride in their alma matter. To learn more about the school, its student body, and its history, take a campus tour (tours depart from the Applet Aggieland Visitor Center, near Houston Street and Joe Routt Boulevard). Gig 'em Aggies! ✉ *Texas A&M University,* ☎ *979-845-3211 campus operator, 979/845-5851 visitor center* ⊕ *www.tamu.edu* ⊙ *Daily (campus), Mon.–Fri 8–5, Sat. 10–4, Sun. 1–4 (visitor center).*

NEED A BREAK?

Freebirds World Burrito—Mexican food with barbecue sauce? Lady Liberty riding a motorcycle? Sculptures made of aluminum foil? A burrito called the Super Monster? Trust us, it all works here. If you're near A&M and you're hungry, go to one of the three Freebirds College Station locations. Now. ✉ *319 University Dr.* ☎ *979/846-9298* ✉ *2050 Texas Ave.* ☎ *979/695-0151* ✉ *700 Earl Rudder Freeway* ☎ *979/260-9086* ⊕ *www.freebirds.com.*

BRYAN

WHAT TO SEE

Historic Downtown Bryan. Outside of the university, College Station can feel like strip-mall city. For a change of pace, head to sister city Bryan's historic downtown, which is filled with unique shops, restaurants, and hotels. ✉ *About 5 mi north of College Station via South College Avenue or Texas Avenue* ⊕ *www.downtownbryan.com.*

★ **Messina Hof.** East Texas is probably one of the last places you'd expect to find an award-winning winery, but the Lone Star State is full of surprises. Messina Hof consistently produces some of the best wines in the state. Visitors can tour the property and participate in wine tastings, as well as sample wines by the glass (along with tapas) at the wine bar, dine at the on-site Vintage House restaurant, and stay at the Villa, the winery's B&B. Messina Hof also offers sunset seminars and cooking classes. ✉ *4545 Old Reliance Rd., Bryan* ☎ *979/778-9463* ⊕ *www. messinahof.com* ✉ *Tour $5* ⊙ *Mon.–Sat. 10–7, Sun. 11–4.*

OFF THE BEATEN PATH

Blue Bell Creameries—Ice-cream connoisseurs visiting East Texas, take note: you're going to want to set aside a few hours to stop at the little creamery in Brenham. This is where Blue Bell ice cream—which might as well be the Lone Star State's official dessert—is made. Visitors can tour the production facilities and watch as raw ingredients are turned into finished, packaged ice cream (the ice-cream sandwich machine is especially mesmerizing). At the end of your journey, you'll get to sample the plant's finished products. You really can't go wrong picking a flavor, but if you've never had Blue Bell ice cream before, go for the Homemade Vanilla, the vanilla ice cream against which all others should be judged. ✉ *1101 S. Blue Bell Rd., Brenham* ☎ *800/327-8135* ⊕ *www.bluebell.com* ✉ *$3* ⊙ *Mar.–Sept., weekdays 10–4, last tour at 2:30; Oct.–Feb., call for times.*

8

HUNTSVILLE

About 60 mi east of Bryan/College Station on Hwy. 30; about 70 mi north of Houston on I-45.

Huntsville is proud of Sam Houston—more so than the metropolis just over an hour to the south that bears his name! A 67-foot-tall statue of Houston looms over Interstate 45 south of the town center, and Houston's home has been preserved just across the street from Sam Houston State University. Houston kept a home in town while serving in the U.S. Senate and retired to Huntsville after a distinguished career as a soldier and statesman. He died in Huntsville in 1863, and is buried in Oakwood Cemetery, a few blocks north of the downtown square. The Lone Star and American flags flutter above his grave, which includes a

CLOSE UP

Sam Houston: Controversial, Celebrated Texan

Known for his wit, occasional unruly behavior—he allegedly beat one of his accusers with a cane—and service in politics, Houston is one of the most controversially celebrated characters in Texas's history.

A native of Virginia, for which he served in Congress in the 1820s and '30s, Sam Houston loved his adopted state of Texas with a passion, and fought in the military for its freedom from Mexico, leading the Texas forces at the Battle of San Jacinto, the decisive victory that secured the state's independence. Prestige followed, and in 1836 he became the first president of the Republic of Texas. Once Texas joined the rest of the country in 1845, Houston represented the Lone Star State in the U.S. Congress as a senator.

In 1859 Houston traded his D.C. digs for the Governor's Mansion in Austin, and while in office attempted to run for U.S. president on the Union Party ticket, but lost out to John Bell. He served as Texas governor for only a year and three months before he was ousted from office after refusing to pledge allegiance to the state when it chose to secede from the Union on the brink of the Civil War. He declared, "I love Texas too well to bring civil strife and bloodshed upon her."

Retiring to Huntsville, he died of pneumonia before the war ended. He is buried at Oakwood Cemetery in north Huntsville.

granite monument displaying Houston on horseback in command of the Texas Army.

Huntsville's other claim to fame is its prisons. It is home to the headquarters of the Texas Department of Criminal Justice, which maintains seven prisons in the Huntsville area, holding nearly 14,000 inmates and employing nearly 7,000 area residents. One prison, known as "The Walls," is located just a short drive from the downtown square—guards peer down from towers at passing cars—and next door is an arena that formerly hosted prison rodeos.

WHAT TO SEE

★ **Sam Houston Memorial Museum.** This domed and colonnaded structure, located on a portion of Sam Houston's farm, documents in detail the statesman's remarkable career as leader of the fight for Texas independence and both president of the Republic of Texas and governor of Texas after it joined the union. The museum also focuses on Houston's lesser-known early life as a frontiersman and governor of Tennessee—he's the only American to have served as governor of two states. Houston's modest homes, as well as his law office and other original and replica structures, are located on the grounds outside the museum. ⊠ *19th St. and Sam Houston Ave.* ☎ *936/294–1832* ⊕ *www.samhouston. memorial.museum* ☑ *Free* ⊙ *Tues.–Sat. 9–4:30, Sun. noon–4:30.*

Texas Prison Museum. Get behind bars at one of the more unusual museums in Texas. Here visitors can don prison stripes and step into an actual cell. Outside stands a replica guard tower, while inside, a replica death chamber holds a retired electric chair. Museum displays give

The Famous Inmates of Huntsville

As a state with one of the largest prison populations in the United States—it contends with California for most inmates held by a state prison system—Texas has held some of America's more (in)famous inmates, in particular, those whose accomplishments and notoriety in some cases outshone the offenses that landed them behind bars. A few of the notable inmates:

"Candy Barr": Juanita Phillips, a native of Edna, Texas, gained fame in the 1950s as "Candy Barr," a marquee stripper at Dallas's Colony Club. Busted on drug charges in 1957, she served over three years at the Goree Unit in Huntsville, where she sang in the prison rodeo. She was also an acquaintance of Jack Ruby, whom she knew from her days as a Dallas stripper, and who visited her days before President Kennedy was assassinated. She was pardoned in 1967 and spent most of her later years in Edna. She died in 2005.

David Crosby: A hugely recognizable name in pop music due to his role in the successful acts the Byrds and Crosby, Stills & Nash, David Crosby for years battled drug problems that eventually caught up with him in Texas. Numerous drug-possession and illegal-weapons charges led to a prison sentence, which he began serving in 1986 at the Wynne Unit near Huntsville. While incarcerated, Crosby worked in the prison's mattress factory, as well as with the prison rodeo band. Crosby spent five months locked up, during which time he finally kicked his drug addiction. He was later inducted into the Rock and Roll Hall of Fame, as a founding member of the Byrds and Crosby, Stills & Nash.

John Wesley Hardin: This notorious Texas gunfighter was convicted of murder in 1878 and sentenced to 25 years in the Huntsville State Penitentiary. After numerous unsuccessful escape attempts, Hardin settled into prison life and was pardoned after serving 15½ years. He later became a lawyer, but returned to his old ways; he was shot to death in 1895.

Bob Hayes: A standout player for the Dallas Cowboys in the 1960s and '70s and an international track champion, Bob Hayes pled guilty to a narcotics charge in 1979, and served 10 months behind bars near Huntsville. As a Cowboys wide receiver, "Bullet" Bob ran with such speed that opposing teams developed a defense that allowed more than one player to cover him, leading to the zone defense that is a mainstay of the game today. Hayes won a Super Bowl ring with the Cowboys and won two gold medals at the 1964 Olympics, with a world record–tying performance in the 100-meter dash, and an incredible, come-from-behind sprint in the 400-meter relay that earned him the nickname "The World's Fastest Human."

Karla Faye Tucker: The first woman put to death in Texas since the Civil War, Karla Faye Tucker was executed in Huntsville on February 3, 1998, at the age of 38. A longtime drug abuser who ran with a violent crowd, she was sentenced to death for her role in a double murder in which she and a male companion killed two people with a pickax. She became a born-again Christian while in prison, and later was the subject of songs by the Indigo Girls and Mark Knopfler.

—Michael Ream

Babe Didrikson Zaharias: All-American Athlete

Babe Didrikson Zaharias was a competitor right down to the sewing prize she won at the 1931 State Fair of Texas. But the Port Arthur native is better known for athletics, conquering every sport she tried. She was an All-American in basketball, earned her nickname by swatting home runs just like Babe Ruth, and medaled in track and field in the 1932 Olympics, establishing a world record (in the 80-meter hurdles) in the process.

Golf was her game, though. In 1950 she completed the women's Grand Slam, reached 10 wins faster than any woman ever, and ultimately won every golf title available.

She developed cancer just three years later, but in 1954, one month after surgery, won her 10th major championship, the U.S. Women's Open. No wonder she's known for her athletic talents, and not her sewing.

—Lisa Miller

details on prison life and capital punishment in Texas, as well as the Texas prison rodeo, which ran for many years in Huntsville until 1986. Also on exhibit are crafts produced by prisoners and captured inmate contraband. ■TIP➜**Admission is free for those younger than 6, but we recommend that kids under 12 skip this museum.** ⊠*491 Hwy. 75 N. (Exit 118 off I–45)* ☎*936/295–2155* ⊕*www.txprisonmuseum.org* ⊠*$4* ⊗*Mon.–Sat. 10–5, Sun. noon–5.*

BEAUMONT & PORT ARTHUR

About 125 mi southeast of Hunstville via U.S. 190 and U.S. 69.

An industrial duo of cities located just inland from the Gulf of Mexico on the deepwater Neches River, Beaumont and Port Arthur have been key to the Texas oil industry since the Spindletop Well began gushing nearby in 1901. Today numerous oil refineries dot the area, which is also an important center of shipbuilding and papermaking. The region is also a gateway to the Big Thicket National Preserve.

■TIP➜**Some local sites were damaged by Hurricane Rita in 2005 and had to close temporarily—call before visiting.**

WHAT TO SEE

☼ **Fire Museum of Texas.** Inside the Beaumont Fire Department Headquarters are displays of antique engines and firefighting equipment, including uniforms and alarm systems. Some exhibits feature hands-on activities. ⊠*400 Walnut St., Beaumont* ☎*409/880-3927* ⊕*www. firemuseumoftexas.org* ⊠*Free* ⊗*Mon.–Fri., 8–4:30.*

Museum of the Gulf Coast. Numerous artifacts related to multiple facets of the region's history are on display, including a large mural highlighting significant historical events, the original light from the nearby Sabine Point Lighthouse, and a replica of the Porsche once owned by Port Arthur native Janis Joplin. ⊠*700 Procter St., Port Arthur* ☎*409/982–*

7000 ⊕*www.museumofthegulfcoast.org* 🖼*$3.50 adults, $3 over age 62, $1.50 ages 6-18, $.50 under age 6* ⊙*Mon.–Sat. 9–5, Sun. 1–5.*

Spindletop–Gladys City Boomtown Museum. Structured as a re-created oil town, this museum recalls Spindletop's past glory days with "black gold." Visitors can see an old saloon, general store, blacksmith shop, and more. ⊠*Hwy. 69 at University Dr., Beaumont* ☎*409/835–0823* ⊕*www.spindletop.org* 🖼*$3* ⊙*Tue.–Sat. 10–5, Sun. 1–5.*

🕃 **Texas Energy Museum.** In Beaumont's museum district, this high-tech place has robots depicting the Texas oil industry's long, colorful history. Displays note the local connection, including the famous Spindletop Well that led to Texas's becoming the unchallenged leader in oil production. Children receive free or discounted admission. ⊠*600 Main St., Beaumont* ☎*409/833–5100* ⊕*www.texasenergymuseum. org* 🖼*$2* ⊙*Tue.–Sat. 9–5, Sun. 1–5.*

OFF THE BEATEN PATH

A cornucopia of flora and fauna flourish in the nearly 100,000 acres of woodland, savanna, and swamp at **Big Thicket National Preserve.** A confluence of geological habitats created a landscape where arid plains bump up against boggy glens, and Eastern bluebirds soar over coyotes. Snakes, bobcats, and salamanders also reside here. The preserve and surrounding wilderness once covered nearly 3.5 million acres, but was sharply reduced in size by human settlement, oil exploration, lumbering, and agriculture. It was declared a national preserve in 1974. Today 12 separate "units" offer nature exploration on hiking trails or via canoe down creeks and bayous. The units stretch from the Neches River near Jasper to just north of Beaumont. The **Big Thicket National Preserve Visitor Center** (☎*409/951–6725* ⊙*Daily 9–5*) is located about 8 mi north of the town of Kountze at the intersection of U.S. 69 and 287. Some trails may be closed in the late fall due to hunting season. ■TIP➔This is the wilderness, so bring insect repellent to ward off bees, wasps, and mosquitoes. Keep an eye out for snakes as well.

8

EAST TEXAS ESSENTIALS

Research prices, get travel advice, and book your trip at fodors.com.

TRANSPORTATION

BY AIR

Dallas/Fort Worth International Airport and George Bush Intercontinental Airport are both within a two- to four-hour drive of most East Texas attractions. Additionally, Tyler has regular service from Dallas or Houston, as does Southeast Texas Regional Airport, near Beaumont. Shreveport has service to cities including Dallas and Houston.

Information **Tyler Pounds Regional Airport** (⊠ *700 Skyway Blvd., 6 mi west of downtown off Highway 64, Tyler* ☎*916/874-0700*). **Southeast Texas Regional Airport** (⊠*4875 Parker Dr., Beaumont* ☎*409/722-0251*). **Shreveport Regional Airport** (⊠*5103 Hollywood Ave., Shreveport* ☎*318/673-5370*).

Janis Joplin: Rockin' the Blues

Port Arthur may not have thought much of daughter Janis Joplin while she lived, but thousands sang *Me and Bobby McGee* when a memorial bust was unveiled there 18 years after she died of so much booze, so much heroin, and so little self-esteem.

A child of the '60s, Joplin's meteoric career crashed to earth in 1970 at age 27. She didn't accept too many rules—or laws, either—and the rebellious teenager became an outrageous artist who sought acceptance in an explosion of talent and fame.

Success with the band Big Brother and the Holding Co. opened a road that led through Woodstock, Ed Sullivan, and Europe. "Imagine a white girl singing blues like that!" said somebody early on. *McGee* was recorded days before Janis died, and became her biggest success.

—Larry Neal

BY BUS

Greyhound (☎ *800/231–2222* ⊕ *www.greyhound.com*) serves most large towns in the region, with connections to Dallas, Houston, and Shreveport. Driving is often a much faster way to reach destinations. Most towns in the region have no mass transit available, but in Tyler, **Tyler Transit** (☎ *903/533-8057*) runs buses Monday through Saturday.

BY CAR

Traveling by car is by far the most convenient way to see East Texas. The region is bounded on the west by I–45, which runs from Dallas to Houston, passing through Huntsville along the way. Several highways branch off to run through the heart of East Texas: Hwy. 7 runs east to Nacogdoches, while U.S. 79 hooks northeast, eventually hooking up with I–20. Tyler, Longview, Marshall, and Jefferson all lie either on or a short distance from I–20, as it runs from Dallas to Shreveport, and Texarkana is on I–30, which also runs out of Dallas.

BY TRAIN

Amtrak (☎ *800/872–7245* ⊕ *www.amtrak.com*) operates the Texas Eagle, which stops in Texarkana, Marshall, and Longview. The Sunset Limited, skirting the southern edge of East Texas as it runs between New Orleans, Houston, and San Antonio, stops in Beaumont.

CONTACTS & RESOURCES

Camping & Outdoor Activities Texas Parks & Wildlife Department (✉ *4200 Smith School Rd., Austin* ☎ *800/792-1112* ⊕ *www.tpwd.state.tx.us*) provides information on state park campsites as well as state regulations on boating, fishing, and hunting. **National Forests & Grasslands in Texas** (✉ *415 S. First St., Ste. 110, Lufkin* ☎ *936/639-8501* ⊕ *www.fs.fed.us/r8/texas*) gives information on campsites within national forests and details on activities to do in the forests.

Fall Foliage Autumn Trails Association (✉ *201 W. Broadway St., Winnsboro* ☎ *903/342-1958* ⊕ *www.tpwd.state.tx.us*) can help you plan your fall foliage–

themed trip to East Texas. **Fall Foliage Report** (⊕ *www.easttexasguide.com/fall foliage/foliage.html*) provides regular updates on color changes in East Texas.

EMERGENCIES

In an emergency, dial 911. Each of the following medical facilities has an emergency room open 24 hours a day.

Hospitals **Mother Frances Hospital–Tyler** (✉ *800 E. Dawson St., Tyler* ☎ *903/593–8441*). **East Texas Medical Center Tyler** (✉ *1000 S. Beckham Ave., Tyler* ☎ *903/597–0351*). **Good Shepherd Medical Center–Marshall** (✉ *811 S. Washington Ave., Marshall* ☎ *903/927–6000*). **Nacogdoches Medical Center** (✉ *4920 N.E. Stallings Dr., Nacogdoches* ☎ *936/569–9481*). **Nacogdoches Memorial Hospital** (✉ *1204 N. Mound St., Nacogdoches* ☎ *936/564–4611*). **Huntsville Memorial Hospital** (✉ *110 Memorial Hospital Dr., Huntsville* ☎ *936/291–3411*).

VISITOR INFORMATION

Contacts **Beaumont Convention & Visitors Bureau** (✉ *505 Willow St., Beaumont* ☎ *409/880–3749 or 800/392–4401* ⊕ *www.beaumontcvb.com*). **Bryan-College Station Convention & Visitors Bureau** (✉ *715 University Dr. E, College Station* ☎ *979/260–9898 or 800/777–8292* ⊕ *www.visitaggieland.com*). **Huntsville Convention & Visitors Bureau** (✉ *1327 11th St., Huntsville* ☎ *936/295–8113 or 800/289–0389* ⊕ *www.huntsvilletexas.com*). **Jefferson/Marion County Chamber of Commerce** (✉ *118 N. Vale St., Jefferson* ☎ *903/665–2672* ⊕ *www. jefferson-texas.com*). **Marshall Chamber of Commerce** (✉ *213 W. Austin St.,* ☎ *903/935–7868* ⊕ *www.marshalltxchamber.com*). **Nacogdoches Convention & Visitors Bureau** (✉ *200 E. Main St., Nacogdoches* ☎ *936/564–7351 or 888/653–3788* ⊕ *www.visitnacogdoches.org*). **Port Arthur Convention & Visitors Bureau** (✉ *3401 Cultural Center Drive, Port Arthur* ☎ *409/985–7822 or 800/235–7822* ⊕ *www.portarthurtexas.com*). **Shreveport-Bossier City Convention & Tourist Bureau** (✉ *629 Spring St., Shreveport* ☎ *318/222–9391 or 800/551–8682* ⊕ *www. shreveport-bossier.org*). **Texarkana Chamber of Commerce** (✉ *819 State Line Ave., Texarkana* ☎ *903/792–7191* ⊕ *www.texarkana.org*). **Tyler Convention & Visitors Bureau** (✉ *315 N. Broadway Ave., Tyler* ☎ *903/592–1661 or 800/235–5712* ⊕ *www.visittyler.com*). **Winnsboro Area Chamber of Commerce** (✉ *101 N. Main St., Winnsboro* ☎ *903/342–3666*).

8

South Texas & the Coast

WORD OF MOUTH

"Progreso is a good little border town . . . lots of small shops and restaurants. The best part about it is that it is just a small walk across the bridge to the main street where all the vendors are. You don't have to take a cab anywhere. The only warning I have is to avoid it during spring break. Many college kids that come to South Texas to party on South Padre Island fly into McAllen and make a pit stop at Progreso to buy liquor on the way to SPI."

—MtnSoccer

By Stewart
Coever

THIS CORNER OF TEXAS IS too often ignored by the state and the nation because it lacks the sprawling metropolises that anchor other areas of the state. But South Texas historically has been an important region in shaping and coloring the entire nation, and it continues to be involved in political and cultural issues at the forefront of the American political psyche. Down here at some of the southernmost points in the United States, the issues of immigration and the integration of the multiplying populations of Mexicans are more than ideas.

Fun is part of everyday life in South Texas, too. Mile after mile of beaches beckon families to play in the gentle surf. Locals make time to hunt, fish, golf, windsurf, and bird-watch. This is not a land of 80-hour work weeks and bumper-to-bumper traffic, but of cold Mexican beer and warm sunsets.

All the unique combinations—Texas and Mexican, cowboys and surfers, agriculture and big business, palms and mesquite, English and Spanish, rapid development and staunch conservationism—make for a fascinating landscape. That all the food and fun can be had at some of the cheapest prices in the country means you can afford to see it all.

EXPLORING SOUTH TEXAS

The majority of the main cities of South Texas are along the shore of the Gulf of Mexico or along the Rio Grande and the border with Mexico. In between are the endless scrublands of some of the largest privately owned ranches in the world. Corpus Christi is seen as a gateway city to Padre Island National Seashore (which includes South Padre) and the Rio Grande Valley. Situated elegantly on Corpus Christi Bay, it has long been the class act of South Texas. McAllen is catching up in terms of the finer things, and could surpass Corpus in the future.

ABOUT THE RESTAURANTS
South Texas is not a place for trendy gourmet cuisine. A few high-end restaurants experimenting with interesting combinations and the newest food fads can be found dotting Corpus Christi and McAllen, but nowhere else. That doesn't mean the food here is bad, just cheap, informal, and reliable. Family-owned Mexican restaurants dominate the scene in all corners of the region. Good seafood and barbecue establishments also are found in proliferation.

ABOUT THE HOTELS
Because of the region's relatively recent growth spurt, the majority of hotels that hustled in to fill the need are of the national chain variety. Each major town in South Texas typically has one historic or grand hotel and one or two notable bed-and-breakfasts, if you're looking for a more original experience.

ABOUT THE CAMPGROUNDS
South Texas has become literally the home away from home for thousands of Winter Texans fleeing the cold and snow of the upper Midwest and Canada. Their preference for RV travel has created a number of terrific RV parks with fantastic locations and amenities.

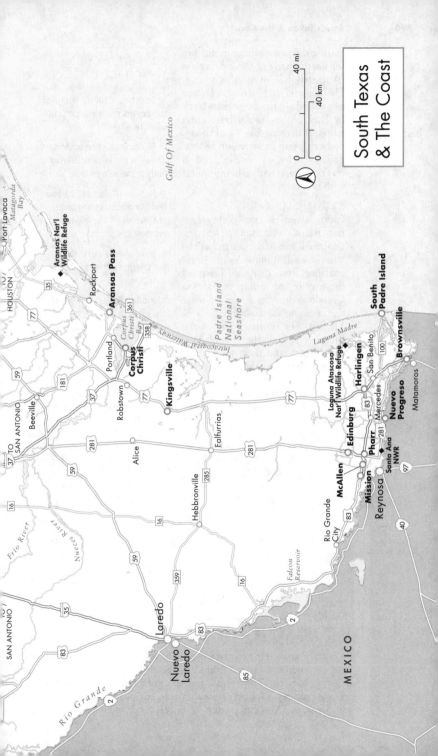

South Texas
& The Coast

40 mi

40 km

Gulf Of Mexico

TO HOUSTON

Port Lavaca
Matagorda
Bay

Aransas Nat'l
Wildlife Refuge

Rockport

Aransas Pass

Portland

Corpus
Christi
Bay

Corpus Christi

Padre Island
National
Seashore

Intracoastal Waterway

Robstown

Kingsville

Laguna Madre

Laguna Atascosa
Nat'l Wildlife Refuge

Harlingen

San Benito

**South
Padre Island**

Brownsville

Matamoros

TO SAN ANTONIO

Beeville

Edinburg

McAllen

Pharr

Mercedes

**Nuevo
Progreso**

Mission

Santa Ana
NWR

Reynosa

Alice

Falfurrias

Hebbronville

Rio Grande
City

Falcon
Reservoir

Frio River

Nueces River

SAN ANTONIO

Laredo

Nuevo
Laredo

MEXICO

Rio Grande

During the worst winter months in the north, many of these parks are completely full for months on end. The summer is much slower and less crowded after these snowbirds fly back home. As for traditional tent-and-sleeping-bag camping, you can camp in state and federal parks, forests, on beaches, and in places teeming with fish or popular with birds.

ABOUT THE BEACHES

Padre Island, a long skinny barrier island with sandy weather and persistent winds, stretches the more than 100 mi of South Texas coastline from Corpus Christi all the way to the mouth of the Rio Grande. It protects the region from the ravaging waves of the Gulf of Mexico. The northern end of the island is part of the city of Corpus Christi, and there are public, drive-on beaches that are convenient if you like hauling a ton of beach accoutrements and staying all day. The southern end makes up South Padre Island, one of the nation's most popular beach towns. Some of the beaches on this end are more protected and do not allow cars to drive on them. In between are miles and miles of protected shoreline and pristine beaches that belong to the National Park Service. Many South Texas beaches charge a few dollars per vehicle.

SOUTH TEXAS & THE COAST TOP 5

- **Beaches:** Cool off at one of the dozens of affordable South Texas beaches.

- **Birds:** Grab some binoculars and view the incredible array of birds at the refuges here.

- **Mexican Cuisine:** Sink your teeth into outstanding tacos, enchiladas, fajitas, and more for insanely low prices.

- **Border Proximity:** Cross the bridge to Progreso for fun shopping.

- **Hidden Gems:** Venture off the highways to discover beautiful views and local establishments.

WHAT IT COSTS				
	¢	$	$$	$$$	$$$$
RESTAURANTS	under $8	$8–$12	$13–$20	$21–$30	over $30
HOTELS	under $50	$50–$100	$101–$150	$151–$200	over $200
CAMPING	under $10	$10–$17	$18–$35	$36–$49	over $50

Restaurant prices are per person for a main course at dinner. Hotel prices are per night for two people in a standard double room in high season, excluding taxes of 13 to 15 percent and service charges. Camping prices are for a standard (no hookups, pit toilets, fire grates, picnic tables) site.

CORPUS CHRISTI & THE COASTAL BEND

Centered around the city of Corpus Christi, the Coastal Bend refers to the communities in and around the horn of Texas's steep turn south toward Mexico. The region is the nexus of a unique blend of disparate Texas cultures. Like all of South Texas, the population is a Hispanic majority, and Mexican culture, language, food, and music have a heavy

PLANNING YOUR TRIP

GETTING THERE & AROUND

South Texas is definitely an area visitors should explore by car. The region is too spread out for bikes and too remote for point-to-point flying. There can be long stretches of highway with no gas stations, so it is prudent for the unfamiliar visitor to fill up the tank when an opportunity presents itself.

All the major cities in the region have airports served by at least one major carrier. Continental Airlines serves Brownsville, Harlingen, McAllen, and Corpus Christi. Southwest Airlines also serves McAllen and Corpus Christi. American Airlines also serves McAllen and Corpus Christi.

WHEN TO GO

Winter Texans take up residence here during the late fall and winter because the lows rarely dip under 50 degrees and the highs can be near 75. Spring Break is a big attraction on the shore. March through May the weather fluctuates between 65 at night and 85 during the day. Summer and early fall can be unbearably hot, though the gulf breezes keep the heat from being as stifling as in inland cities along I–35.

The region is more crowded in the winter and spring, but the crowds rarely become a problem outside of the rowdy (and raunchy) Spring Break students at South Padre.

influence. The Gulf of Mexico, with its sandy shores and gusting winds, gives it a breezy beach-town feel that lasts year-round. The enormous King Ranch to the immediate southwest adds a rugged cowboy element to the pot. The result is an eclectic region full of spice and grit, with a palpable appreciation for life's simpler pleasures.

CORPUS CHRISTI

220 mi southwest of Houston via U.S. 59 and U.S. 77; 143 mi south of San Antonio via I–37.

As beach communities around the United States become more and more expensive, Corpus Christi remains an affordable destination for sun and fun. True to Texas, this city has a lot of personality. During a weekend here, a visitor will hear English and Spanish spoken in the same incomprehensible sentence, will eat some combination of Mexican food, barbecue, and seafood in obscene quantities, will see someone wearing flip-flops to a fancy restaurant, and will wonder aloud, "Does the wind always blow this hard?"

WHAT TO SEE

Most attractions are in the northern downtown area, with the exception of the beaches and, of course, Padre Island National Seashore across the bay. Note that Hwy. 358 turns into South Padre Island Drive (S.P.I.D.) to the south.

❸ **Art Museum of South Texas.** The museum's focus is on works of the Americas, specifically Texas and Mexico. Not to be missed is Dale Chihuly's magnificent blue glass chandelier. Stop in the café for a snack and views of the bay and the huge tankers lumbering into the ship channel.

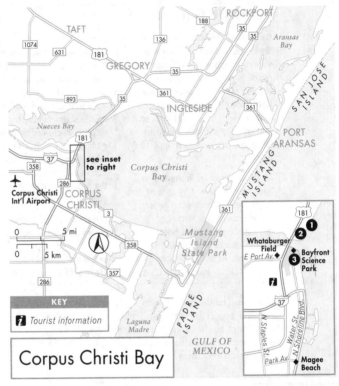

Corpus Christi Bay

Designed by world-renowned architect Philip Johnson, the building is just across the Harbor Bridge from the Texas State Aquarium. ✉*1902 Shoreline Blvd.* ☎*361/825–3500* ⊕*www.artmuseumofsouthtexas.org* ✉*$6 (free on Thursdays)* ☉*Tues.–Sat. 10–5, Sun. 1–5.*

❷ Texas State Aquarium. Conveniently located a short walk from the USS *Lexington*, this aquarium is more than just a cool refuge from the blazing Texas sun. The dolphin training show is the main attraction, but also enjoyable is watching the playful river otters and petting the stingrays and sharks in the touch pool. ✉*2710 N. Shoreline Blvd.* ☎*361/881–1200* ⊕*www.texasstateaquarium.org* ✉*$14.95* ☉*Daily 9–5.*

❶ The USS Lexington Museum. The first thing that catches your eye as you arrive in downtown Corpus Christi is the massive aircraft carrier floating in the bay. The USS *Lexington* Museum is a monument to the longest-serving carrier in the history of naval combat. Go below deck to marvel at the amazingly tight quarters and narrow passageways; however, spend most of your time up on the flight deck. Here you can walk among fighter planes, see where a kamikaze struck, and take in beautiful views of the city and Corpus Christi Beach. ✉*2914 N. Shoreline Blvd.* ☎*361/888–4873* ⊕*www.usslexington.com* ✉*$11.95* ☉*Daily 9–5.*

SPORTS & THE OUTDOORS

Padre Island National Seashore. Bird-watching, fishing, camping, beach combing, stargazing, campfire programs, ranger walks, and more await at the national park on the northern part of Padre Island National Seashore *(⇨ South Padre Island later in this chapter for activities in the more developed area a few hours to the south).* Youngsters can participate in the junior ranger program, and young and old alike can watch the periodic sea-turtle releases and learn about space during star parties. Park entrance is 13 mi south of Corpus Christi, off Hwy. 358 and the JFK Causeway. ⊠*Malaquite Visitor Center, 20402 Park Rd. 22, Corpus Christi* ☎*361/949–8068* ⊕*www.nps.gov/pais* ⊗*Daily* ☞*$10 for a 7-day pass.*

BEACHES

Magee Beach (⊠*N. Shoreline Blvd. at Park St.*) is directly in front of downtown, next to the marina. **Corpus Christi Beach and North Beach** (⊠*Off Surfside Blvd., north of the Harbor Bridge*) make up the sandy shoreline that runs away from the USS *Lexington*. Because they are on the calm bay waters, locals hardly consider these beaches at all. For locals, "going to the beach" means driving the 15 minutes out to Padre Island, where the beaches face the Gulf of Mexico. The drive-on beaches between **JP Luby Park and Bob Hall Pier** (⊹*Take S.P.I.D to Padre Island and turn left at signs for JP Luby Park*) are popular with rowdy spring breakers and families alike. Pets and small bonfires are allowed; glass is not.

BASEBALL

When the **Corpus Christi Hooks** (⊠*734 E. Port Ave.* ☎*361/561–4665* ⊕*www.cchooks.com*) baseball team began play in 2005 at the pristine Whataburger Field, the Double-A Texas League franchise became an instant sensation. Partially owned by Texas legend Nolan Ryan and affiliated with the Houston Astros, the Hooks frequently play to capacity crowds. The ballpark experience is what keeps 'em coming back. There isn't a bad seat in the stadium or on the grassy berm. Friendly mascots roam the confines. Fans enjoy a Whataburger and a cold beverage while up-and-comers hustle to make their dreams come true.

FISHING

★ The Laguna Madre, the body of water that separates Padre Island from the coast of Texas, is widely recognized as one of the finest shallow-water fishing destinations anywhere. Running the entire length of the Padre Island National Seashore, the Laguna Madre offers strong fishing opportunities both near Corpus Christi and by South Padre Island. The area in the middle is protected park lands. The water is on average about three feet deep and provides a great venue to hook redfish, speckled trout, and other local species. For information on fishing licenses and specific laws and limits, contact the **Texas Parks and Wildlife Department** (☎*800/792–1112* ⊕*www.tpwd.state.tx.us*).

WIND SPORTS

Fodor'sChoice ★ Corpus Christi is one of the nation's best locations for all manner of wind sports. The U.S. Open Windsurfing Regatta has been held here for 20 years and running. One of the newest additions to the sport is kiteboarding, where a rider has a board under his feet and a wind-harnessing "kite" pulling him at sometimes insane speeds over the water and often into the air. Corpus is hailed by kiteboarding practitioners as one of the best spots in the world for the sport. **Oleander Point at Cole Park** (⊠ *Ocean Dr. and Oleander Ave.*) is said to be the best launching site, but any Corpus Christi beach will do if the winds are right. Visit ⊕ *www.corpuschristiwindsurfing.com* for a list of launching sites.

WHERE TO EAT

$$–$$$ ✕ **The Yardarm.** Food lovers pack into this cozy bayside restaurant for the fresh seafood, the ample wine list, and the beautiful water view. Regulars return for the ever-changing menu of specials, depending on what's fresh and how the chef wants to lovingly prepare it. The small menu contains consistent gems like the snapper topped with a crabmeat stuffing and steamed *en papillote* (in a paper bag) to tender nirvana. The oysters Rockefeller and homemade crème brûlée delight as well. ⊠ *4310 Ocean Dr.* ☏ *361/855–8157* 🖃 *AE, D, MC, V* ⊗ *No lunch. Closed Sun.–Mon. Closed mid-Dec.–Jan.*

$–$$ ✕ **La Playa Mexican Restaurant and Cantina.** Corpus Christi is filled with taquerias serving cheap and often delicious Mexican standards. La Playa is bursting with raucous groups every night because it offers something more. The house specialty is the deep-fried avocado stuffed with cheese and your choice of chicken, beef, or shrimp. *El Yucateco* is a mixture of seafood smothered in rich chili con queso and pico de gallo and stuffed into a tender eggplant. The plates are huge, the margaritas are cold, and the prices are very reasonable. ⊠ *4201 South Padre Island Dr. (S.P.I.D.)* ☏ *361/853–4282* 🖃 *AE, D, MC, V.*

¢–$ ✕ **Snoopy's Pier.** The entirety of Corpus Christi's beach culture is embodied in this rustic delight and its come-as-you-are attitude. There's nothing fancy on the menu, mostly fried and fresh seafood with a couple of rice dishes for good measure. Keep it simple: order the fish-and-chips, grab a cold bottle of beer, find a table outside on the deck, and mostly just try to keep your napkins from blowing away while the sun shines, the pelicans perch, and the seagulls hover. ⊠ *13313 South Padre Island Dr. (S.P.I.D.)* ⊕ *Below you as you descend on to Padre Island* ☏ *361/949–8815* 🖃 *No credit cards.*

WHERE TO STAY

$$$–$$$$ 📺 **V Boutique Hotel.** A hip new addition to downtown Corpus Christi, the V offers exquisitely designed rooms with leather and suede furniture, 35-inch plasma TVs, and the distinct sense that your natural energy is in harmony. The best feature of all may be ordering room service from Vietnam ($$$, 866/724–0855), the Vietnamese restaurant of impeccable quality on the first floor. There's also a surprisingly good gym for a boutique hotel. **Pros:** The only lodging in Corpus with this combination of modern style and luxury. **Cons:** Its eight rooms fill up quickly; lacks the amenities and facilities of larger hotels. ⊠ *701 N. Water St.,* ☏ *361/883–9200* ⊕ *www.vhotelcc.com* ⇨ *8 rooms* ⚒ *In-*

What a State, Whataburger

Whataburger by the Bay in Corpus Christi is the company's flagship restaurant.

Texas is a huge state, with vastly different regions and climates and cultures, but the one thing you will find everywhere in Texas is Whataburger. Founded in 1950 and easily recognized by its bright-orange "flying W" logo, this family-owned fast-food chain grew from one tiny burger stand in Corpus Christi into a state icon with more than 650 locations and legions of devoted customers. The menu is full of Texas tastes that require condiments like jalapeños, picante sauce, and white-cream gravy. The signature Whataburger is big, fresh, and normally served Texas-style with mustard, although they will make it any of the 36,864 possible ways you might want it.

Whataburger's iconic status also grew out of the unique A-frame shape of its restaurants in the 1960s and the bold orange and white stripes painted down both sides. In Corpus Christi you can still eat at one of the original A-frame designs at the 3220 Gollihar Rd. location. Or you can visit the flagship of modern Whataburgers, the Whataburger by the Bay at 121 N. Shoreline Boulevard. This is the company's largest restaurant, with more than 6,000 square feet, a second-story deck overlooking the bay, and a life-size statue of founder Harmon Dobson. How fanatical is the state about Whataburger? In 2001 the Texas legislature declared it a Texas treasure.

room: *refrigerator, Wi-Fi. In-hotel: restaurant, bar, gym, laundry facilities, concierge, parking (no fee)* ⊟*AE, MC, V* ⦿*CP.*

$$–$$$ ⛺**Omni Bayfront Hotel.** This well-appointed hotel is perfectly located on Shoreline Boulevard downtown, just minutes from many attractions and nightlife options. Business folks and vacationing families alike fill the Omni year-round because of its free airport shuttle, spotless rooms, and professional staff. Kids love the indoor-outdoor pool and hot tub. On the top floor is the terrific, upscale steak house Republic of Texas ($$$–$$$$, 361/886–3515), with panoramic views of the city and bay. **Pros:** Waterfront/downtown location puts you at the heart of the action. Fabulous views. **Cons:** Service can be surprisingly inconsistent for a nice hotel chain. ⊠*707 N. Shoreline Blvd.,* ☎*361/887–1600* ⟿*445 rooms* ⚷*In-room: safe (some), Wi-Fi. In-hotel: 2 restaurants,* *room service, 2 bars, pool, gym, spa, laundry service, concierge, airport shuttle, parking (no fee), some pets allowed, no-smoking rooms* ⊟*AE, D, DC, MC, V.*

$–$$$ 🏠**George Blucher House.** Perennially hailed as the best B&B in the city and one of the finest in the state, this century-old Victorian home offers a unique and elegant experience in each of its six rooms. Innkeeper Tracey Smith tends to every detail of the house and her guests with total devotion. Her three-course gourmet breakfasts are not to be slept through. **Pros:** Breakfast is often amazing, and the house is gorgeous. **Con:** Some of the beds too small for an adult couple. ⊠*211 N. Carrizo St., 78401* ☎*361/884-4884* ⊕*www.georgeblucherhouse.com* ⬱*6 rooms* ⬧*In-room: DVD (some), VCR, Wi-Fi. In-hotel: no elevator, no kids under 12, no-smoking rooms* ⊟*MC, V* ⫶○⫶*BP.*

CAMPING

$$–$$$ 🏕**Colonia del Rey RV Park.** This RV park is head and shoulders above other area parks because of its immaculate, palm tree–dotted facilities and friendly, helpful staff. A second home to droves of Winter Texans, Colonia del Rey feels like a welcoming community more than a gathering of transients. There are potluck dinners and happy hours, a newsletter, and all kinds of group activities. Lots are rented daily, weekly, or monthly, and there are spaces that can fit very large rigs. It is always full from December through February. Call ahead. **Pros:** Great community feel. Spotless restrooms. **Cons:** Not within walking distance of beaches or attractions. ⊠*1717 Waldron Rd.,* ☎*361/937-2435* ⬱*210 sites* ⬧*Flush toilets, full hook-ups, cable, drinking water, guest laundry, showers, grills (some), picnic tables (some), electricity, public telephone, play area, swimming (pool)* ⊟*D, MC, V.*

OUTSIDE CORPUS CHRISTI

Although Corpus Christi combines the cattle-ranching and beach-going cultures of the Coastal Bend region, to experience either of these facets to the utmost you can take a day trip or, even better, stay the night in one of these little Texas towns. Every South Texan knows them well, but many visitors make the mistake of driving right by.

KINGSVILLE

44 mi southwest of downtown Corpus Christi via U.S. 77

Fodor'sChoice ★ A straight shot southwest and less than an hour's drive from Corpus Christi is Kingsville, the town center of the **King Ranch** (⊠*Santa Gertrudis and Hwy. 141* ☎*361/592–8055*), one of the largest ranches in the world today. At 825,000 acres, the legendary ranch is larger than the state of Rhode Island, and its fences could stretch the distance from Kingsville, Texas, to Boston, Massachusetts. Much of the working ranch is off-limits to the public, but from the visitor center you can take part in historic and nature tours ranging from an hour-and-a-half to four hours long. In town, the **King Ranch Museum** (⊠*405 N. 6th St.* ☎*361/595–1881*) will pique your interest with its endearing historical photos and antique cars and guns. For luxurious, hand-crafted leather goods and souvenirs, visit the **King Ranch Saddle Shop** (⊠*201 E. Kle-*

berg Ave. ☎800/282–5464) and watch the saddle maker work the leather, making real saddles for real cowboys who often walk right in the door—spurs and all—to check on the progress.

OFF THE BEATEN PATH

King's Inn. If you are going to be in Kingsville, it is worth it to drive 15 minutes more south to have lunch or dinner at this well-known restaurant. The King's Inn is close to absolutely nothing, but somehow on a Saturday afternoon the huge, unassuming dining room will be teeming with people from who-knows-where. There are no menus. You order the fresh seafood by the pound and it's served family style, grilled or fried. Must-haves are the avocado salad and the giant fried shrimp. Entrées range from $20 to $25. Call ahead for a table. ⌧*Loyola Beach on Hwy. 1 in Riviera (pronounced ree-Verra by locals)* ✛ *Take U.S. 77 south from Kingsville and go left at FM 628; keep going until you hit the water* ☎361/297–5265 ☰*AE, D, MC, V.*

PORT ARANSAS

39 mi northeast of downtown Corpus Christi via S.P.I.D. and Hwy. 361

Although Corpus Christi is a city with nearby beaches, **Port Aransas** (or "Port A" as everyone here calls it) is a real beach town, located about a 45-minute drive around the bay from downtown Corpus. You can drive on the beaches in Port A, but wooden posts keep the cars 50 pleasant feet from the gulf water. The town has cute restaurants, swimsuit-'n'-souvenir shops, and places to rent little buggy carts to cruise the beaches and streets. At the very north end of Port A is the **Fisherman's Wharf** (⌧*900 N. Tarpon*), where you will find a host of charter boats for fishing trips, sunset cruises, nature trips to see whooping cranes and dolphins, and a ferry to take you to nearby "St. Jo" island. Its primitive beaches that make for excellent seashell gathering.

WHERE TO STAY

CAMPING **Goose Island State Park.** The park has a great combination of facilities (like water and electricity, restrooms and showers) and natural beauty, sitting right on the waterfront of Aransas Bay. The largest live oak tree in Texas resides in the park, considered to be more than 1,000 years old. Popular activities are birding, hiking, and fishing. ⌧*202 S. Palmetto St., Rockport* ☎361/729–2858

RIO GRANDE VALLEY

This border region that runs along the final miles of the mighty Rio Grande River takes Mexican influence on Texas culture to a whole different level. With a more than 90-percent Hispanic population in many areas, the culture of the Valley might best be described as Mexican with a touch of Texan influence. In many of the cities and towns your average service worker may speak Spanish to you first, regardless of your skin color. Throngs of people pass daily from one country to other. White-and-green border-patrol vehicles are ubiquitous. Meanwhile, tens of thousands of silver-haired retirees visit every winter, swelling the population and the economy with their vast neighborhoods of

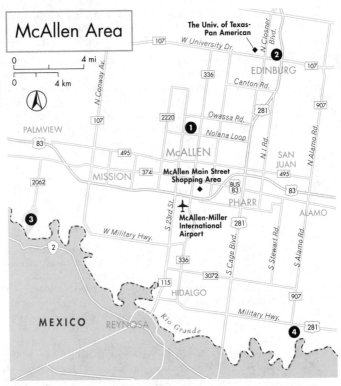

recreational vehicles. Quietly protected from all the hubbub are pristine wildlife refuges, state parks, and birding centers of international renown. This truly is a unique corner of the American landscape.

MCALLEN & VICINITY

240 mi south of San Antonio via I–37 and U.S. 281; 160 mi southwest of Corpus Christi via U.S. 77 and U.S. 281.

Any consideration of McAllen must include the surrounding towns of Edinburg to the north, Mission to the west, and Pharr to the east. This area is undergoing such rapid growth that these places are quickly becoming suburbs to the larger McAllen. Much of the expansion is due to the city's leadership in the new business arenas of the post-NAFTA world. McAllen, as a result, has the most options for the finer elements of shopping and dining of any city in the Valley.

WHAT TO SEE

1 **International Museum of Science and Art.** IMAS is a gem of a small museum, with traveling exhibits and a permanent collection with everything from Mexican folk art to works by Pablo Picasso. Families love the learning areas where kids can perform experiments and create art. Outside are sculptures and a huge playground that is fun, safe, and educational. ⊠*1900 Nolana Ave., McAllen* ☎*956/682–0123* ⊕*www.imasonline. org* ☜*$5* ⊙*Tues.–Sat. 9–5, Sun. 1–5.*

❷ **Museum of South Texas History.** Did you know that multiple future presidents of the United States led troops into battle in the Valley? Did you know the Nazis tried to get the Mexicans to go to war with the U.S. to distract us from conflicts in Europe? To understand the mix of culture and conflict that has shaped the Rio Grande Valley, make this your first stop. The Edinburg museum attempts to explain the area's formative elements, from the dinosaurs to the Republic of Texas to World War II; it achieves its goal with surprising elegance and simplicity. Fully interactive, the beautiful exhibits have accompanying sounds and voices that bring the objects and scenes to life. ⊠*12 E. McIntyre, Edinburg* ☎*956/383–6911* ⊕*www.mosthistory.org* ☜*$5.50* ⊙*Tues.–Sat. 10–5, Sun. 1–5.*

SPORTS & THE OUTDOORS

❸ **Bentsen-Rio Grande Valley State Park.** Located just southwest of Mission, this park is an exceptional bird-watching location. The 750-acre subtropical park backs up to the Rio Grande and features miles of trails and a two-story observation tower. The facilities are in great shape, and the park allows bicycling (on specific trails), primitive camping, and fishing. Find maps, bird checklists, and all sorts of information on the Rio Grande Valley's birding opportunities at the park's **World Birding Center** (⊕*www.worldbirdingcenter.org*). ⊠*2800 S. Bentsen Palm Dr., Mission* ☎*956/585–1107* ☜*$3.*

❹ **Santa Ana National Wildlife Refuge.** Considered by many birders to be ★ the gem of the area's parks, Santa Ana features everything from cactuses to palms, small *resacas* (an ox-bow lake formed from an old river bed) to the mighty Rio Grande, and hundreds of animal species not often found in parks across the country. On rare occasions hikers might spy ocelots, jaguarondis, coyotes, and bobcats. The park is just a few minutes south of Pharr, near the border. No camping is allowed. ⊕*On FM 907, 7 mi south of Alamo, about ¼ mi east of U.S. 281* ☎*956/784–7500* ☜*$3 per vehicle.*

SHOPPING

Although many Americans are aware that the Valley is a great place to cross into Mexico for all kinds of cheap goods, many are surprised to see how many Mexicans think the same thing about crossing into the United States. For a taste of Mexican shopping on this side of the border, head to the **downtown shopping district** centered on Main Street in downtown McAllen. A quick survey of license plates finds more Mexican cars than American. The signs are almost all in Spanish, with most stores advertising *Mayoreo y Menudeo*—wholesale and retail. All kinds of goods are on display: fabrics, perfume, clothes, shoes, jewelry, and formal wear. It's a fun walk even if you don't buy anything.

WHERE TO EAT

$$–$$$ ✕**Republic of the Rio Grande Restaurant & Cantina.** A popular choice with locals, this restaurant merits the crowds that pack into its parking lot. The menu is a sumptuous mix of Mexican seafood dishes, wood-fired brick-oven pizzas, and Angus beef cuts. If it's not too hot out for soup, the poblano chicken chowder is a creamy delight that will have you cleaning the bowl. The bacon-wrapped quail shish-kebabs and seafood enchiladas are also outstanding. Don't miss the historic photos of Pancho Villa and other banditos hanging in the bar. ⊠*1411 S. 10th St., McAllen* ☎*956/994–8385* ▭*AE, D, MC, V.*

$–$$ ✕**Poncho's Restaurant.** This offbeat little place was recently rated by
★ *Texas Monthly* magazine as having one of the tacos Texans have to eat before they die. The windowless blue building makes it look like a dance club from the outside, but the inside is pure little Mexico in decor and cuisine. The servers flutter about in traditional Mexican cotton dresses while a *vieja* works tirelessly making fresh tortillas and chips in view of the diners. The chicken tacos live up to the hype. ⊠*808 N. Cage, Pharr,* ☎*956/782–9991* ▭*AE, D, DC, MC, V.*

WHERE TO STAY

$$–$$$ ▥**The Renaissance Casa de Palmas Hotel.** When tourists dream of staying
★ in lovely Spanish architecture near the border of Texas and Mexico, the Casa de Palmas is what they envision. Two lush patios greet guests before they enter into the luxurious lobby. The hotel, built originally in 1918, is a square surrounding a cozy, palm tree–lined courtyard and pool. Be sure to ask for one of the 53 rooms that have balconies overlooking the courtyard. The slight price difference is well worth it. Popular with business travelers, this hotel is usually much cheaper on the weekends. **Pros:** Arguably the most beautiful and the most historic hotel in South Texas. **Cons:** Interiors are a little outdated (a major renovation is expected). ⊠*101 N. Main St.,* ☎*956/631–1101* ⊕*www.casadepalmas.com* ⇆*165 rooms* ⌂*In-room: refrigerator (some), Wi-Fi. In-hotel: restaurant, room service, bar, pool, gym, laundry service, concierge, public Wi-Fi, airport shuttle, parking (no fee), no-smoking rooms* ▭*AE, D, MC, V.*

**EN
ROUTE**   With only 80 mi separating McAllen's western edge from South Padre Island's shores to the east—and with a potpourri of funky and historic places in between—the Valley is a great place to explore by car. As you drive east from McAllen, one area to check out is the neighboring cities of Weslaco and Mercedes. The big draw in Mercedes is the **Rio Grande Valley Premium Outlets** (⊕*Off U.S. 83 about 20 mi east of McAllen in Mercedes* ☎*956/565–3900* ⊙*Mon.–Sat. 10–9, Sun. 11–7*), with 140 stores like Banana Republic, Ann Taylor, Coach, and Sony.

When you get done shopping, drive the short distance to the cute little downtown of Weslaco. It's an increasingly rare treat to explore a main street that was not manufactured recently by real-estate conglomerates. For a fantastic Italian meal, dine at **Milano's** (*$$–$$$*) (⊠*2900 W. Pike Blvd., Weslaco* ☎*956/968–3677* ▭*AE, D, MC, V*).

HARLINGEN

35 mi east of McAllen via U.S. 83.

Compared to the other cities of the Rio Grande Valley, Harlingen has little to offer visitors beyond its airport and central location at the intersection of U.S. 77 and 83. But for these two reasons, the city is often a jumping-off point for touring the Valley.

If you fly into Harlingen, on the way out of the airport drive by the **Iwo Jima Monument** (⊠ *320 Iwo Jima Blvd.*), a half-block east of the terminal. The 100-foot statue is the original working model for the famous bronze memorial in Arlington, Virginia.

FUN FESTIVAL — **Every November, Harlingen hosts the area's biggest and best birding festival. For 15 years the Rio Grande Valley Birding Festival (⊠ 311 E. Tyler St. ☎ 956/423–5440 or 800/531–7346 ⊕ www.rgvbirdfest.com ⊠ Price varies) has drawn crowds because of its reputation for having terrific guided field trips and a host of birding products available in the Birders Bizarre. Also part of the extravaganza are seminars, kids' activities, and the joy of meeting others with an enthusiasm for birds.**

BROWNSVILLE

25 mi east of Harlingen via U.S. 83 and 77.

Brownsville takes great pride in being one of the most historic cities in Texas, as great battles of the Mexican-American War and the Civil War were fought here. As Texas's southernmost city, Brownsville is at the forefront of developing regional and national news with the proposed border fence cutting through its backyards, parks, and even potentially dividing its university grounds. Through all the dramatic chapters of its history, Brownsville has remained a family-oriented community with a relaxed pace and a friendly populace.

WHAT TO SEE

❶ Gladys Porter Zoo. This spectacular zoo is noted as one of the nation's 10 best small zoos. It has every animal adults and kids love to see, just in a small, well-designed layout. A family of 10 gorillas is so entertaining and fascinating that you may just want to sit on one of the benches and watch for a while. But don't miss out on the kangaroos, tigers, lions, giraffes, orangutans, and exotic birds. The animals here appear healthy and active, the zoo is clean, and the staff offers a walking tour most days, usually in the morning. ⊠ *500 Ringgold St.* ☎ *956/546–2177* ⊕ *www.gpz.org* ⊠ *$9* ⊙ *Daily 9–5.*

Fodor's Choice ★

❷ Brownsville Children's Museum. For those traveling the Valley with young children (under 9), a welcome refuge from the heat and sun is this museum for tots, and the adjacent **Costumes of the Americas Museum.** At the children's museum, kids can play on interactive exhibits with local flavor, like a shrimp boat and a lighthouse. There is a big playground outside. Under the same roof, the costumes museum displays more than 400 indigenous costumes from all over the Americas and

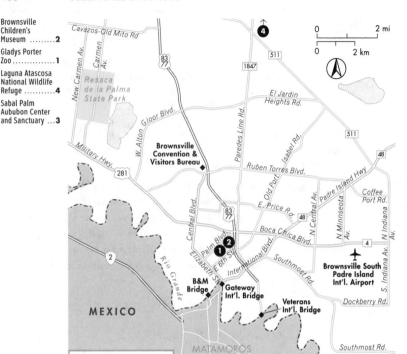

Brownsville

is free with paid admission to the children's museum. It is especially delightful for little girls. ⊠ *501 Ringgold St. (in Dean Porter Park)* ☎*956/548–9300* 🖃*$5* ⊘*Tues.–Sat. 9–5, Sun. noon–4.*

SPORTS & OUTDOORS

❹ Laguna Atascosa National Wildlife Refuge. At 90,000 acres, this is the larg-
Fodor'sChoice est of all the parks in the Valley. It attracts more than 400 species of
★ birds, more than any park in the country. What's amazing is that some of the most prized birds can be seen within a short walk of the visitor center. Out in the wilds of the park are also all kinds of waterfowl and shore birds, alligators, javelina, and the rare ocelot. With so much to explore, you could spend a whole weekend just in this park. ⊕ *17 mi east of Rio Hondo* ☎*956/748–3607* 🖃*$3.*

❸ Sabal Palm Audobon Center and Sanctuary. A beautiful ecosystem of stands
★ of Sabal palms once lined the Rio Grande. After all of the work by set-tlers to tame the area and create reliable agriculture, only tiny pockets of Sabal palms survive, now protected in this sanctuary. Because of its abundant flora and its location in the bird-happy Valley, the site draws amazing numbers of bird species. The prehistoric feel of the thick groves of palms provides a rare look at a fascinating natural habi-tat and is not to be missed. ⊕ *Off FM 1419, southeast of Brownsville* ☎*956/541–8034* 🖃*$5* ⊘*Daily 7–5.*

NIGHTLIFE

According to locals, there isn't much nightlife accessible and safe for outsiders in Brownsville. One of the few exceptions is **Shenanigans Irish Pub & Grill** (⊠ *2451 Pablo Kisel Blvd., behind Chili's* ☎ *956/986–2337*). This lively pub is covered in surprisingly elegant custom woodwork, features high-definition, flat-screen televisions for watching sports, and has 25 beers on tap. Crowded to standing room only on Thursday, Friday, and Saturday nights, Shenanigans usually has live music starting at 10 PM. The sizable menu of delicious pub food includes standard burgers and fries plus Irish specialties like shepherd's pie.

WHERE TO EAT

$$–$$$ ✕**Chuck E. Cheese's.** After a warm day at the zoo, a great place to take the family is to this pizza and playland restaurant. Rest your feet, cool off in the air-conditioning, while the kids entertain themselves with the rides and games. Just try not to stare directly at the singing robotic animals. You can get a large pizza, drinks, and some tokens for around $27. ⊠ *2800 N. Expressway* ☎ *956/541–2245* ▤ *AE, D, MC, V.*

$$ ✕**Tre Fratelli.** If you're looking for something a little nicer and more romantic than the ubiquitous Mexican fare, try this Italian eatery. The decor is simple and elegant, the wine list is long, and the menu is full of well-executed Mediterranean favorites—the calamari is irresistible. ⊠ *3001 Pablo Kisel Blvd.* ☎ *956/574–9888* ▤ *AE, D, MC, V.*

¢–$ ✕**Emilia's Restaurant.** This cheap Mexican eatery is one of hundreds of cheap Mexican eateries in the area, and every local has his or her favorites. This typical dive has little decor and less-than-elegant lighting, but the stomach-stuffing portions of classic Mexican dishes, like the gooey enchiladas, will explain the attraction. This is a tidy sample of how the majority of locals eat, and it's open for breakfast as well. ⊠ *605 W. Elizabeth* ☎ *956/504–9899* ▤ *AE, D, DC, MC, V.*

WHERE TO STAY

$$–$$$ ▤**Inn at Chachalaca Bend.** Visited once by former President Jimmy Carter, this luxury inn is truly "one of the best-kept secret travel destinations" in Texas, as it bills itself. Tucked away near the tiny town of Los Fresnos, it sits on 40 acres of gorgeous prairies and native brush land. Although it is off the beaten path, the inn is minutes from Laguna Atascosa, South Padre Island, and the heart of Brownsville. **Pros:** Amazing nature outside and terrific service inside. **Cons:** No restaurants or attractions are very close to this remote location. ⊠ *20 Chachalaca Bend Dr.,* ☎ *956/233–1180* ⊕ *www.chachalaca.com* ⇨ *7 rooms* ⌂ *In-hotel: no-smoking rooms, no elevator.* ▤ *AE, D, DC, MC, V* ⧉ *BP.*

BORDER TOWNS

Matamoros is directly across from Brownsville; Nuevo Progreso is 7 mi south of Weslaco on FM 1015.

MATAMOROS

Unfortunately, Matamoros is the perfect example of a once-fun border town that has now become complicated. Brownsville residents used to love to cross into this neighboring town, but police corruption and

CLOSE UP

Birding in South Texas

The World Birding Center at Bentsen-Rio Grande Valley State Park

It is hard to overstate the powerful relationship between South Texas and birding. South Texas gives birders the most amazing array of bird species that can be found in the U.S. and Canada. To put the number in perspective, there have been more than 900 bird species spotted in the entire country, and the tiny lower Rio Grande Valley alone boasts more than 500 species. There are tropical birds at the northernmost tip of their range along with local birds that are unique to particular areas of the Valley. The result is that South Texas benefits greatly as birders flock to the area and put millions and millions of tourist dollars into the local economies.

The science behind the phenomenon has to do with migratory patterns and South Texas's location at the intersection of four disparate climate zones: desert to the west, tropics to the south, the gulf to the east, and plains to the north. The temperate climate means that every season of the year offers birding opportunities.

I interviewed park ranger Mike Carlo from the Santa Ana Wildlife Refuge, asking him about how each season shapes up with the birds.

Spring Migration. For birding fanatics, this is prime time, says Carlo. The resident birds are here, the migratory birds are passing through, and others still are coming to the region to breed. The highest number of species typically can be found from mid-April to early May.

Summer Heat. This is the slowest time of year for the wildlife refuges and parks. The weather is often unbearably hot and mosquitoes are out in full force. But, Carlo says, the peaceful solitude of the parks and the pleasant early mornings can yield great birding experiences. Call ahead; many parks have shorter hours due to less demand.

Fall Unpredictability. The weather and the timing of the migrations are hard to predict during the fall season. The huge population of birds that will stay in the Valley for the winter starts coming, but it can be hard to say how many birds will be arriving during a given week. Hit the right weekend and you can find perfect weather and hordes of species. Migrating hawks and vultures are usually the reliable ones to see. Also, note that the last few days of September and early October can bring thousands of raptors to Bentsen State Park and Santa Ana National Wildlife Refuge.

Winter Crowds. This is the most crowded time of year for birding. Thousands of Winter Texans flock to the region to avoid the frigid weather of Canada and northern states. Ranger Carlo says this is a wonderfully social time at the parks, where newer birders can learn a lot from the numerous veterans as they swap stories and species counts.

Year-Round. Among the hundreds of species, there are four superstar birds that attract great enthusiasm in the region and can be seen reliably for much of the year: the exotic green jay, with its stunning combination of blue, green, and yellow feathers; the Altamira oriole's radiant orange body and head; the yellow-breasted songbird great kiskadee; and the chachalaca, a clumsy bird named for the raucous noise it makes.

BIRDING TIPS

Here are some of Ranger Carlo's tips to having the best experience:

■ Bring binoculars, a field guide, water, insect repellant, and sunscreen, and dress in layers—a cool South Texas morning can quickly turn into a stifling afternoon! If you forgot any of these items, check with the visitor center. Staff there might let you borrow or rent them for a small fee.

■ Take advantage of park personnel. Staff and volunteers are enthusiastic and can quickly point you to the best things happening at a park. Call ahead to see if any exciting species have visited recently.

■ Plan your day. Mornings and evenings have the most comfortable temperatures of the day and the most birds.

■ Try staying in your car—it can act as a terrific bird blind. While some birds scatter from approaching humans, they may not be as disturbed by a parked or slow-moving vehicle. The air-conditioning helps you to stay comfortable, too.

■ Use your ears as much as your eyes. Walking quietly and listening is a great way to locate nearby birds.

■ Be patient!

—Stewart Coerver

9

The long list of birds you might spot in South Texas includes the green jay.

10 ESSENTIAL BORDER-CROSSING TIPS

1. Talk to locals before you cross. Safety issues, traffic delays, hot spots, and just the general level of appeal can change in Mexican cities overnight. Just a few years ago Nuevo Laredo was a great place to cross, but now there is serious crime and most Americans don't dare to cross there. Residents of Texas's border towns have the pulse of what's going on, so seek their advice.

2. Remove your valuables. Don't advertise to thieves or corrupt policemen that you have money. Leave your expensive jewelry and excess cash safely stowed in the U.S.

3. Park your car in the U.S. Why risk having your car stolen or damaged? There is always affordable (around $2/day) parking in lots close to the bridges. Walking is faster, easier, and often more fun.

4. Bring a passport. Americans cannot fly into Mexico without a passport. That regulation soon goes into effect for land crossing as well, so we strongly advise that you bring your passport with you. If you don't have a passport, contact the U.S. State Department (⇨ *Texas Essentials in the back of the book*) to find out what you will need before you come to South Texas.

5. Bring no weapons with you. Weapons of any kind—even switchblade knives—are taken very seriously at the border.

6. Don't change money. The shops and restaurants at the border will accept American dollars readily.

7. Bring pocket change. The walking bridges require very small tolls, like 30¢ to 60¢ each way.

8. Declare everything you bring back to the U.S. Americans are allowed to bring across hundreds of dollars' worth of merchandise from Mexico, but they must declare it at the border. There are limits on items such as alcohol, tobacco, and agricultural goods, so know the rules.

9. Be prepared to pay taxes on the cheap alcohol and cigarettes. The Texas Alcohol Beverage Commission will tax liquor and cigarettes brought back, usually only around a dollar fee, but much steeper for cartons of cigarettes and any large quantities of alcohol. Check the signs on the U.S. side as soon as you cross.

10. Grab a town map. Many places in Mexico are not safe for unaware tourists wandering off the beaten path. Bring or pick up a town map with the tourist spots highlighted, and stay close to the crowds.

drug cartel activities had grown so rampant by early 2008 that the Mexican government brought in the military to calm the crisis. The sight of green-clad soldiers carrying machine guns has been disconcerting to local Mexicans and tourists alike. Most Brownsville residents advise tourists to avoid Matamoros altogether or to go only during the day, and only as far as **Garcia's** (⊠ *Av. Obregon #82* ☎ *011–52–868/813–1566*), a large *curios* store and a touristy but clean and delicious Mexican restaurant that is 100 yards from the border.

Nuevo Progreso, Mexico

Bridge to U.S.

Mexico Customs

Coahuilla

Old Town Restaurant

Arturo's

Rio Grande

Sonora

Tamaulipas

Calle Victoria

Av. Benito Juarez

Tampico

Rio Bravo

Jiminez

San Luis Potosi

Nuevo Leon

Riverena

Mante 6

Laredo

Reynosa

Chihuahua

Baja California

Free Parking

Market

Revolucion

Durango

Miguel Aleman

0   1/4 mi

0   1/4 km

NUEVO PROGRESO

Into the void created by all the problems of the other border cities has stepped the little town of Nuevo Progreso (often simply called Progreso, though technically Progreso is the U.S. town, and Nuevo Progreso is the Mexican one). It lies south of Weslaco, Texas, but is not directly across from any Texas counterpart. Most visitors park in convenient lots for $2 and walk across the bridge for a 25¢ toll.

■TIP➔**Pick up a map at the visitor information stand near the customs office after you cross into Progreso.**

As soon as visitors cross the border, they know why Texans flock to the shops in Progreso. The scene is exactly as Hollywood might have drawn it up. The dusty streets are highlighted by a variety of brightly colored buildings that line a long stretch of Avenida Benito Juarez, the main street that bustles all day with shoppers and Mexican hawkers of all ages and selling styles. Dentists and pharmacies occupy many of the storefronts: Winter Texans living the cheap life in South Texas like to cross for affordable procedures and highly discounted drugs.

Shoppers cruise the sidewalks with a cold beer in hand while Mexican children offer shoe shines and wind chimes, young men sell pirated DVDs, women stand at the front of their salons offering haircuts and the infamous hair braiding, while the older men sell everything in between: piñatas, jewelry, *chimineas* (small Mexican stand-alone chimneys that people put on their porches with little fires in them, or just as decoration), glassware, *lucha libre* (Mexican wrestling) masks—anything you can imagine. "Great rates! Cheap price," they all say as you pass by.

All of Progreso boils down to one big blur of touristy shopping mania. The vast majority of visitors never step off Avenida Benito Juarez, and the crush of shops and stalls makes it hard to distinguish one area from another. This thriving market is aimed squarely at American and Canadian tourists and their desire for cheap prescription medication, affordable dental services, and discounted alcohol and tobacco. Everything that pops up in between is to entice the *gringos* to spend more of their money on souvenirs, hand-crafted housewares, and oddities. Everyone seems to find that one item that they just can't leave without. Most shops on Juarez Avenue close at 6.

■TIP➔Make this a day trip only. Residents of Progreso we spoke with were pretty adamant that there's nothing for gringos off the main drag.

WHERE TO EAT

While shopping is fun here, the other can't-miss activity in Progreso is eating at one of the safe and tourist-friendly restaurants. **Arturo's** (⊠ *Av. Benito Juarez, Block 2 E.* ☎*011–52–899/93–0127*) is conveniently located in a large stand-alone building in the middle of the action. The Mexican food and steaks are outstanding, the bow tie–clad service is excellent, and the staff, for the most part, can converse in English. People rave about Arturo's *cabrito*, a regional specialty for those interested in tasting roasted young goat. Another great spot, which is immediately to your left as you step off the bridge, is **Old Town Restaurant** (⊠ *Av. Benito Juarez, No. 231.* ☎*011–52–899/93–0127*). It offers great Mexican food at affordable prices ($5–$6 a plate), and the waiters are friendly and speak English. Start with the *queso fundido* (cheese dip) and then try one of the taco enchilada plates or *chiles rellenos*. End with a slice of *pastel de tres leches* or flan. ■TIP➔You can start your shopping on the right side and end your trip with a Mexican dinner here.

■TIP➔If you need to bring your car across, the best plan is to park in Arturo's lot, get your ticket stamped when you eat inside, and then tip the parking attendant a few bucks to keep an eye on your vehicle while you shop.

SOUTH PADRE ISLAND & PORT ISABEL

75 mi east of McAllen via U.S. 83 and Hwy. 100; 28 mi northeast of Brownsville via the Brownsville–Port Isabel Hwy.; 292 mi south of San Antonio via I-37 and U.S. 77.

This vacation area really has two completely separate identities. For much of the year it is a quiet set of beaches with a few thousand residents. Texan tourists visit their rental homes or the resort hotels and enjoy the serene beaches and the many outdoor activities. Then for a few weeks each year Spring Break descends upon the area, injecting a monetary boon but also a youthful, reckless energy bent on partying, partying, and more partying. The prices for most things skyrocket during March. Debauchery reigns supreme. And then, just as suddenly, the storm lifts and the town quickly returns to its windswept calm, nothing but bright sunshine and crashing waves.

The big attractions here are obviously the sand, sun, and surf, but if you want a better understanding of the history and culture of the area—or if ugly weather has you looking for different activities—head across the causeway to Port Isabel.

WHAT TO SEE

Museums of Port Isabel. For one entry fee you can see three different historic sites. The **Point Isabel Lighthouse** has been a local landmark since 1852 and is the only publicly accessible lighthouse on the Texas coast. The **Port Isabel Historical Museum** will illuminate the area's rich past, while the Treasures of the Gulf Museum highlights the riches found in three Spanish shipwrecks in nearby waters. ⊠ *317 E. Railroad Ave.* ☎ *956/943–7802* ⊕ *www.portisabelmuseums.com* 🖃 *$7* ⊙ *Tues.–Sat. 10–4.*

☺ **Schlitterbahn Beach Waterpark.** Are you and the kids growing weary of the saltwater in your eyes and the sand in your swimsuit? This popular park with two other Texas locations as well (Galveston and New Braunfels) offers chlorinated water relief. Highlights are a huge sand castle–themed play area and America's largest surfing machine. Schlitterbahn also has a swim-up bar and a restaurant. (You can bring your own cooler, but no glass or alcohol.) ⊠ *33261 Park Rd.* ☎ *956/772–7873* ⊕ *www.schlitterbahn.com* 🖃 *$35* ⊙ *Closed Oct.–Mar.*

SPORTS & THE OUTDOORS

Nearly any type of beach vacation activity is available on South Padre Island: surfing, parasailing, snorkeling, scuba diving, horseback riding on the beach, kiteboarding, and windsurfing. You can even take sand-castle lessons from experts. For more vendor information, call the **South Padre Island Visitors Center** (☎ *800/767–2373*).

BEACHES

The beaches on the gulf side offer what most visitors are looking for: breezy winds, breaking surf, and pristine sand. The "bay side" on the Laguna Madre is mostly muddy, shallow, and calm. **Isla Blanca Park** (☎ *956/671–5494* 🖃 *$4 per vehicle*) sits on the southernmost tip of the island and offers clean beaches and a number of nearby activities.

FISHING

If you want to go wade fishing, head away from the breaking waves of the gulf. Instead, go to the calm Laguna Madre waters on the bay side. They're teeming with redfish, speckled trout, and other sought-after species. For deep-water fishing, there are a bevy of options on and around the island. **The Sea Ranch Marina** (⊠ *1 Padre Blvd.* ☎ *956/761–7777*), on the southern end of the island, is home to many independent fishing charter companies. Operating off the pier at the South Padre

South Padre Island

South Padre Island Convention Center

Andy Bowie County Park

Nature Trail/ Birding Boardwalk

White Sands

Hacienda

Kings Court

Sunset

Palmetto

Morningside

Padre Blvd

Gulf Blvd

GULF OF MEXICO

Constellation

Venus

Oleander

Laguna Dr

Bahama

Laguna Madre

Red Snapper

Gulf Blvd

Marlin

Corral

Sunny Isles

Padre Blvd

South Padre Island Visitors Center

Queen Isabella Causeway

100

TO PORT ISABEL

Schlitterbahn Beach Waterpark

Isla Blanca County Park

0   1/2 mi

0   1/2 km

Island KOA RV Park, **Osprey Fishing Trips** (⊠*1 Padre Blvd.* ☎*956/761–6655* ⊕*ospreyfishingtrips.com*) has two boats operating deep-sea fishing charters and a third for bay fishing trips. On the west side of the island, **Jim's Pier** (⊠*209 Whiting St.* ☎*956/761-2865*) operates deep-sea and bay fishing trips, and has a bait and tackle shop, a gas station, and a boat-launching facility if you have your own boat. Just across the causeway from South Padre Island, in Port Isabel, **Dolphin Docks** (⊕*Queen Isabella Blvd. and S. Garcia St.* ☎*956/943-3185*), boasts the area's largest deep-sea fishing boat, and has been in business for more than 30 years. For a complete list of the dozens of experienced local fishing guides, ask at the South Padre Island Visitors Center just north of the causeway entrance.

BOAT TRIPS

If you want to get out on the water just for the relaxing scenery, the same marina areas listed above under Fishing offer other pleasure cruises: dolphin-watches, sunset cruises, marine ecology tours, and seasonal Friday night fireworks cruises (late May through Labor Day). Ask locals and shop around to find the best guides and rates.

ECOTOURISM

Second in popularity to the dolphins cavorting around the island, the endangered sea turtles often nest in sites up and down South Padre Island. **Sea Turtle, Inc.** (⊠*6671 Padre Blvd.* ☎*956/761–4511* ☞*$3 donation*) leads the conservation charge and offers daily morning feedings and educational presentations for visitors. ■TIP→**If you happen to be on the island during the summer, you can also call them to find out whether there are any imminent hatchings in the area. You might get to watch these adorable baby turtles make a run for the water.**

WHERE TO EAT

★ ✕**Sea Ranch.** This is one of the pricier restaurants on the island, and
$$–$$$ the seafood here is worth it. The view of the returning boats late in the day also draws people for a drink on the outdoor deck. The restaurant prides itself on the freshness of its fish, especially the house specialty, red snapper. This is not a place to wear your bathing suit or shorts. ⊠*1 Padre Blvd.* ☎*956/761–1314* ▤*AE, D, DC, MC, V* ⊘*No lunch.*

$ ✕**Dirty Al's Bait Stand and Seafood Kitchen.** Dirty Al's serves fresh seafood but in a noticeably informal—and sometimes rowdy—environment. This place gets packed with pilgrims who have heard about its delicious fried shrimp and reasonable prices. The people-watching is often fantastic. ⊠*1 Padre Blvd., next to Sea Ranch* ☎*956/761–4901* ☜*No reservations* ▤*MC, V.*

$ ✕**Manuel's.** Once tourists have satisfied their urge to taste the fruits of
Fodor's Choice the sea at island establishments, they discover that many of the best
★ alternative places to eat are located in Port Isabel. One place visitors and locals alike go nuts for is this tiny taco joint near the lighthouse. The tacos are bigger than your head and filled copiously with whatever you want. Those in the know say the humongous breakfast tacos are the real gem. This place often has a wait, so get there early. ⊠*313*

9

Maxan St., Port Isabel ☎*956/943–1655* ⚄*No reservations* ▭*No credit cards.*

WHERE TO STAY

$$–$$$ 🏨**Sheraton South Padre Island.** This is the place on the island that has
★ it all: clean, pretty rooms, balconies with beautiful views of the beach,
and the biggest pool on the island (with a swim-up bar, too). The beach
is directly out the back door, and the friendly, professional staff can
help you arrange popular activities. Every fall this hotel hosts the Sand
Castle Days festival on its beach. **Pros:** Well-appointed rooms with balconies over-looking the beach. **Cons:** Huge condominium tower being
constructed directly next to hotel. In-hotel food can be overpriced.
⊠*310 Padre Blvd.* ☎*956/761–6551* ⇄*251 rooms* ⚅*In-room: safe
(some), kitchen (some), refrigerator (some), Wi-Fi. In-hotel: 2 restaurants, room service, 2 bars, pool, gym, beachfront, children's programs
in summer (ages 5–12), no-smoking rooms* ▭*AE, D, MC, V.*

$–$$$ 🏨**Casa de Siesta Bed & Breakfast.** This Southwestern-style inn was
founded in 2000 and has a dozen rooms. The peaceful courtyards have
lush plant life and trickling fountains. All rooms face the courtyard and
are decorated with saltillo tile floors and regional antiques. Guests say
the "upscale continental" breakfast is good but not the main attraction.
Pros: Decorated with personality. Spacious rooms. **Cons:** Breakfast is
basically continental and not very memorable. ⊠*4610 Padre Blvd.*
☎*956/761–5656* ⊕*www.casadesiesta.com* ⇄*12 rooms* ⚅*In-room:
refrigerator. In-hotel: pool, no children under 12, some pets allowed,
no-smoking rooms* ▭*AE, D, MC, V* ℃*CP.*

$–$$$ 🏨**Holiday Inn Express.** One of the newest hotels on the island, the Holi-
day Inn Express has the advantage of not having been through decades
of Spring Break punishment. This has left the rooms clean and the
lobby feeling sunny and cheerful. Because it isn't directly on the beach,
the rate is cheaper, but the sandy gulf shores are still only a short walk
away. **Pros:** Very clean and pet-friendly. **Cons:** No direct beach access.
⊠*6502 Padre Blvd.* ☎*956/761–8884* ⊕*www.southpadreexpress.com*
⇄*104 rooms* ⚅*In-room: refrigerator, Ethernet (some). In-hotel: pool,
gym, executive floor, no-smoking rooms* ▭*AE, D, MC, V* ℃*CP.*

CAMPING

$$$–$$$$ ⛺**South Padre Island KOA RV Park.** It is hard to imagine an RV park on
★ better real estate than this one. Surrounded by water on three sides, the
site is conveniently located among all the bustling restaurants, marinas,
and beaches of the southern end of South Padre Island. The park is
clean, the community generally fun and friendly, and there are uncom-
mon facilities like a fishing pier, boat launch, seafood restaurant, and
fitness center. **Pros:** You might catch sight of a dolphin right out your
window. **Cons:** No tent camping. ⊠*1 Padre Blvd.* ☎*956/761–5665*
⊕*www.southpadrekoa.com* ⇄*200 sites (5 with water and electric)*
⚅*Flush toilets, full hookups, dump station, cable (some), drinking
water, guest laundry, showers, electricity, swimming (pool and bay),
play area, Wi-Fi* ▭*AE, D, MC, V.*

SOUTH TEXAS & THE COAST ESSENTIALS

To research prices, get advice from other travelers, and book travel arrangements, visit www.fodors.com.

TRANSPORTATION

BY AIR

No matter where you plan on spending your time in South Texas, an airport will be relatively nearby. For travelers to South Padre Island, Brownsville and Harlingen airports are battling for your business. Brownsville has the closer airport, but Harlingen's is served by more airlines. Fly into Harlingen on Southwest through Austin, Houston, and San Antonio; on Continental through Houston; and on American through Dallas. Sun Country also runs non-stop flights from Minneapolis to Harlingen from November to April. Brownsville has daily flights year-round to and from Houston on Continental. McAllen's airport has daily flights through Houston on Continental, and through Dallas on American. Flights into Corpus Christi come directly only through Houston (on Continental and Southwest), and Dallas (on American).

Contacts **Brownsville South Padre International Airport** (⊠ *700 S. Minnesota Ave.* ☎ *956/542–4373* ⊕ *www.flybrownsville.com*). **Corpus Christi International Airport** (⊠ *1000 International Blvd.* ☎ *361/289–0171* ⊕ *www.corpuschristiairport. com*). **McAllen International Airport** (⊠ *2500 S. Bicentennial Blvd.* ☎ *956/682– 9101* ⊕ *www.mcallenairport.com*). **Valley International Airport** (⊠ *3002 Heritage Way, Harlingen* ☎ *956/430–8600* ⊕ *www.flythevalley.com*).

BY BUS

Greyhound (☎ *800/231–2222* ⊕ *www.greyhound.com*) and its area subsidiary, **Valley Transit** (☎ *956/423–4710* ⊕ *www.valleytransitcompany. com*), both offer bus service in locations across South Texas.

CONTACTS & RESOURCES

EMERGENCIES

In an emergency, dial 911 (for emergencies in Mexico, you typically dial 066; in some areas it's 060). Each of the following facilities has an emergency room open 24/7.

Hospitals **Christus Spohn Hospital–Memorial** (⊠ *2606 Hospital Blvd., Corpus Christi* ☎ *361/902–4000*). **Rio Grande Regional Hospital** (⊠ *101 E. Ridge Rd., McAllen* ☎ *956/632–6000*). **Valley Baptist Medical Center–Brownsville** (⊠ *1040 W. Jefferson St., Brownsville* ☎ *956/698–5400*).

VISITOR INFORMATION

REGIONAL CONTACTS The **Rio Grande Valley Chamber of Commerce** (⊡ *Box 1499, Weslaco* ☎ *956/968–3141* ⊕ *www.valleychamber.com*). **Valley Texas Travel Center** (⊠ *2021 W. Harrison (U.S. 77 and U.S. 83), Harlingen* ☎ *956/428–4477*) has free maps and brochures.

LOCAL
CONTACTS **Brownsville Information Center** (⊠ *650 Ruben M. Torres Blvd., Brownsville* ☎ *956/541–8455* ⊕ *www.brownsville.org*). **Corpus Christi Visitors Center** (⊠ *Downtown Branch, 1823 N. Chapparal St., Corpus Christi* ☎ *800/766–2322* ⊠ *The Island Branch, 14252 S.P.I.D., Corpus Christi* ☎ *361/949–8743* ⊕ *www.corpuschristicvb.com*). **Harlingen Area Chamber of Commerce** (⊠ *311 E. Tyler St., Harlingen* ☎ *956/423–5440 or 800/531–7346* ⊕ *http://www.visitharlingentx.com*). **McAllen Chamber of Commerce** (⊠ *1200 Ash Ave., McAllen* ☎ *956/682–2871* ⊕ *www.mcallen.org*). **Padre Island National Seashore** (⊠ *Malaquite Visitor Center, 20402 Park Rd. 22, Corpus Christi* ☎ *361/949–8068* ⊕ *www.nps.gov/pais*). **South Padre Island Convention and Visitors Bureau** (⊠ *7355 Padre Blvd., South Padre Island* ☎ *800/767–2373* ⊕ *www.sopadre.com*).

West Texas

WORD OF MOUTH

"Lots of stuff worth seeing in West Texas, but it's an area that you either love or you hate."

—TheWeasal

10

By Jennifer
Edwards

AS SOON AS VISITORS SET their soles on the dry-as-the-Sahara soil of West Texas, they'll realize they've entered a completely different world. Remote from urban population centers, isolated within the northern plains of the Chihuahua Desert, West Texas lives by its own rules, not unlike Australia's Outback. It's a land of flat and rugged beauty and twisted vegetation like the kind that might float on the bottom of the sea.

And, in fact, once upon a time it did. In its ancient past, a majority of the territory now known as West Texas lay on the bottom of the Permian Sea. Now that the seas have drained (leaving behind vast reserves of crude oil), visitors can partake of a vista so limitless it seems to be viewed from an aerial vantage point. Few trees reach farther than three feet above the surface, allowing one a limitless view. What has managed to survive in the desert, however, is as intricate as sea life. Cacti rise like coral, and ground squirrels, horned lizards, and serpents wiggle like eels among the mesquite bushes populating the landscape—the same mesquite that bequeaths its poignant, smoky taste to everything from fajitas to barbecue chips.

West Texas is a land of severe beauty, with clutches of exquisiteness and quiet civilization—a rural, traditional culture that has an equal mix of Old West and Old Mexico. Cowboy hats are worn here not for fashion, but for duty: "cowboy" and "cowhand" are occupational titles of many folk, as is "oilman." Working cowboys roam the plains and make fires at night, and there are still cattle drives to the south.

> ## WEST TEXAS TOP 5
>
> ■ **Jumping Jackrabbits:** West Texas wildlife runs the gamut, from prairie dogs to roadrunners.
>
> ■ **Bumpy El Paso:** View the striking Franklin Mountains.
>
> ■ **Tex-Mex Culture:** Neither entirely Mexican nor entirely Texan, it's a mishmash of both.
>
> ■ **Remember the Alamo:** To see the set where John Wayne ignited an interest in Western movies, head to Alamo Village in Brackettville.
>
> ■ **Park It:** Three national parks (⇨ Chapters 11–13), especially Big Bend, are the region's gems.

EXPLORING WEST TEXAS

While some consider "West Texas" to begin just outside of Fort Worth, locals say it begins a lot farther west than the outskirts of the DFW Metroplex. Some West Texans say that it begins at Abilene (⇨ *The Panhandle, chapter 14*), while some government agencies have decided it begins at tiny Mason County, population 3,900. Most Texans, however, claim Mason for Central Texas (⇨ *The Hill Country, chapter 4*).

For the purposes of this guide, we'll consider West Texas as beginning 300 mi west of Fort Worth at Midland and stretching another 300 mi west to El Paso, right on the cusp of the Mexico, Texas, and New Mexico borders.

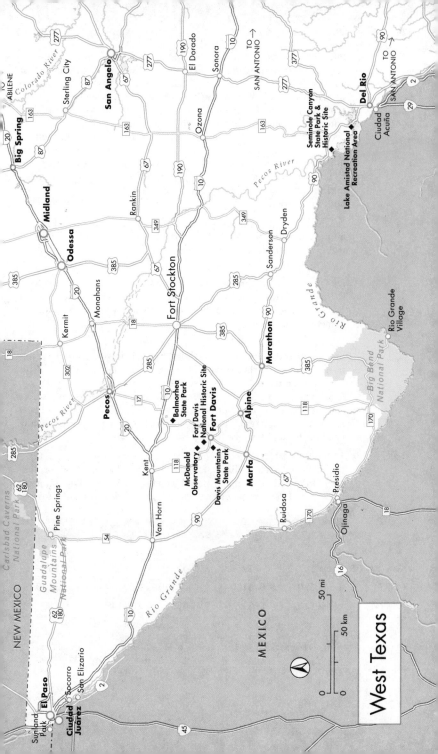

Interstates 10 and 20, along with highways 87, 277, and 90, are the main roads traversing the region. Traveling from Midland and Odessa west on I–20 takes visitors to the small town of Monahans, home to Monahans Sand Hills State Park, where pallid sands spill across thousands of acres and visitors sled down dunes as tall as 70 feet; then onto Pecos, home to what may well be the nation's oldest rodeo. From Pecos, travelers can slip south on Highway 17 to the unique culture mix that defines Marfa, and then south on Highway 118 to Alpine in the Fort Davis mountains. In both towns, urban east coast culture blends with ingrained ranching traditions and campers often lodge in both cities on their way to Big Bend National Park and the Rio Grande, both to the south.

Meanwhile, I–10 takes visitors up to the region's largest city, El Paso, home to the Fort Bliss Military Reservation. Other towns in the region include San Angelo and Del Rio.

ABOUT THE RESTAURANTS

Due to a mix of geographic isolation and Hispanic heritage, the food is a redolent, sumptuous mix of north Mexican cooking and Southern home cooking, giving area dishes a very rich, heavy and spicy character. Sometimes the menus are in Spanish.

Tex-Mex, Mexican, and Southern cooking are what this region does best. In general, steer away from East Asian; stick with items like country-fried steaks, barbecue, and Mexican dishes like burritos, *asado* (a tangy dish, often pork, cooked in oil and ground-up chiles), *chiles rellenos* (raw green chiles that are stuffed with meat, cheeses, and spices and then baked; can be hot or mild), and *barbacoa* (slow-cooked beef seasoned with tangy marinade). (Note that some barbacoa is actually from the head of the cow [called *barbacoa de cabeza*].)

ABOUT THE HOTELS

Major chains, such as Hilton, Holiday Inn, Days Inn, and Comfort Inn, are represented in the major population centers such as Odessa, Midland, and El Paso. It may be difficult to find lodging in smaller towns.

WHAT IT COSTS					
	¢	$	$$	$$$	$$$$
RESTAURANTS	under $8	$8–$12	$13–$20	$21–$30	over $30
HOTELS	under $50	$50–$100	$101–$150	$151–$200	over $200
CAMPING	under $10	$10–$17	$18–$35	$36–$49	over $50

Restaurant prices are per person for a main course at dinner. Hotel prices are per night for two people in a standard double room in high season, excluding taxes and service charges. Lodging tax rate is 6 percent statewide with an additional county tax, which varies by county. Camping prices are for a standard (no hook-ups, pit toilets, fire grates, picnic tables) campsite per night.

PLANNING YOUR TRIP

WHEN TO GO

Though the temperatures can reach 100° in the summer, nights are beautifully cool, combed by winds from the north. (It's easy to tell which direction they blow, too; just look for the piles of tumbleweed driven into the fences by the breeze. They're hard to miss; some get as big as a baby elephant.) Snows carpet the area a few times each winter. Those who live here might tell you there's nothing so disconcerting—or beautiful—as snow on the many cacti in the plains of the northern Chihuahua Desert.

Visitors are bound to find something going on each month—from rodeos to art festivals to Cinco de Mayo and Diez y Seis De Septiembre (Mexican Independence Day) celebrations. However, since temperatures in this scrubby, desert land can soar into the three digits during the summer, it's often best to catch what this land has to offer during the more temperate months between January and June or in early fall.

GETTING THERE & AROUND

Most of West Texas is easy to access via the region's small airports in El Paso and Midland, as well as via the airports in the neighboring Panhandle cities of Abilene and Lubbock.

Though Greyhound does offer service between major cities, it's not an ideal way to get around, because you really need a car once you're in a West Texas town. Train options are scarce, with just Abilene and El Paso stops along Amtrak's route.

CROSSING THE BORDER

Border crossing has become more complicated. Americans crossing back over the border must now show passports along with secondary identification. In West Texas the best places to cross are El Paso to Juárez, Mexico; Del Rio to Ciudad Acuña; and Presidio to Ojinaga.

EL PASO & JUÁREZ

EL PASO

About 306 mi west of Midland via I–20 and I–10.

Fabled El Paso, just barely in Texas and in fact on Mountain Time (rather than Central), was at one time part of the New Mexico Territory. It is still an important crossing point for those entering from or departing for Mexico. One glance at a map will show why this city along the Rio Grande has become the transportation and business hub for southern New Mexico and West Texas, as well as a destination for outdoor adventurers and history buffs. Most residents speak English and at least some Spanish, and the mix of American Indian, Spanish, and American cultures is evident in the city's art and music, architecture, and cuisine.

Many of El Paso's downtown gems, such as the historically protected Plaza Hotel (one of Conrad Hilton's first hotels), unfortunately today stand empty. Hotels during the 1950s were often full, sometimes with Hollywood stars and the wealthy heading for a cheap and easy divorce

WEST TEXAS FESTIVALS & EVENTS

JAN. Sandhills Stock Show and Rodeo. Each January, organizers stage a full rodeo, complete with roping, steer wrestling, barrel racing, and exhibits of top livestock, including goats, horses, and cattle. The events feature a Christian youth night with radio entertainment, and a rodeo dance, open to all. ✉ *Ector County Coliseum, Odessa* ☎ *432/366–3951* ⊕ *www.sandhillsstockshowandrodeo.com.*

MAY Cinco De Mayo. The country's got it all wrong. The festival day known as Cinco De Mayo isn't Mexican Independence Day, as some believe, but rather a celebration of the Battle of Puebla. The fracas took place on May 5, 1862, and became an important moral victory when the smaller and less-well-equipped Mexican Army defeated a large French force near Puebla. Throughout West Texas, energetic celebrations commemorating the historic date shut down streets and liven up crowds with mariachi and tejano music and often traditional dancing.

JUNE West of the Pecos Rodeo. Arguably the oldest rodeo within the States, it features everything a true rodeo should—steer and calf roping, bronc and bull riding, barrel racing, and even a "wild mare" competition. ✉ *Buck Jackson Arena, Pecos* ☎ *800/558–2855* ⊕ *www.pecosrodeo.com.*

AUG. Rock the Desert. Tens of thousands fly in from all over the country to listen to two days of music performed by some of the top names in Christian rock and praise music, such as Jars of Clay, Rebecca St. James, and Chris Tomlin. Vendors are on hand with a variety of fare, and camping is available off-site. ✉ *Rock the Desert Encampment, 2000 N. FM 1788, Odessa* ☎ *432/697–4548.*

SEPT. AMIGO AIRSHO. The Amigo Airsho, one of two major air shows in West Texas, is a rollicking event filled with historical displays, a car show featuring everything from classic cars to Monster Trucks, and of course, spectacular aerial displays. For the youngsters, the Kidsho features rides, games, prizes, and sometimes rock climbing. ✉ *Fort Bliss, Biggs Army Airfield, El Paso* ☎ *915/562–6446* ⊕ *www.amigoairsho.org.*

SEPT. Diez y Seis de Septiembre. On Sept. 16, 1810, influential priest Father Miguel Hidalgo y Costilla launched the Mexican War of Independence against Spain after reading his Grito de Dolores ("Cry of Dolores") in the city of the same name. Each year in September, cities party like it's Cinco de Mayo all over again, with special fiestas, live music, festive foods, Ballet Folklórico, and mariachi bands.

in Ciudad Juárez (often called just Juárez), across the river. Adding to the town's bravado back then were live alligators in the plaza pond. (A sculpture of writhing alligators has replaced the real reptiles, which ended their residency in the 1960s.)

Sixteenth-century Spanish explorer Don Juan de Oñate dubbed the entire Rio Grande Valley Paso del Rio del Norte ("the pass through the river of the north")—from which El Paso derives its name. Oñate was so grateful that the expedition of about 500 ragged colonists had

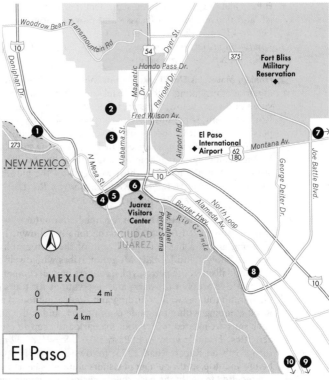

reached the Rio Grande that he ordered his people to don their best clothes for a feast of thanksgiving on April 30, 1598—a celebration that preceded the arrival of the pilgrims in Massachusetts by nearly a quarter century.

WHAT TO SEE

6 Chamizal National Memorial. In 1964 nearly a century of dispute between Texas and Mexico, caused by the shifting banks of the Rio Grande, came to an end. Both the United States and Mexico founded memorials within their borders to commemorate this event. Texas created a 55-acre park, on formerly Mexican land, with a visitor center, three galleries, drama festivals, and long walking paths. Across the border, easily accessed by the Bridge of the Americas, is the Mexican counterpart, the 800-acre Parque Chamizal. ⊠*800 S. San Marcial* ☎*915/532–7232* ⊕*www.nps.gov/cham* ⊠*Free* ☉*Daily 5 AM–10 PM.*

1 El Paso Desert Botanical Gardens. Located in Keystone Heritage Park, these gardens juxtapose the exotic—an Asian-style koi pond and little waterfall—with native cacti and other succulents set against the backdrop of the northern Chihuahua Desert. There's even a natural wetlands area. ⊠*4200 Doniphan Rd.* ☎*915/584–0563* ⊕*www.elpasobotanicalgardens.org* ⊠*$2* ☉*Sept.–May, Sat. and Sun. noon–3; June–Aug., Sat. and Sun. 8–11AM.*

④ El Paso Museum of Art. The museum features a striking array of Spanish and native art, from Picasso and Goya to Southwest artists Tom Lea and Henrietta Wyeth. ⊠*1 Arts Festival Plaza* ☎*915/532–1707* ⊕*www.elpasoartmuseum.com* 🎫*Free* ⊘*Tues., Wed., 9–5, Thurs. 9–9, Fri., Sat. 9–5, Sun. noon–5.*

② Franklin Mountains State Park. Within the park's 37 square mi are hiking, mountain-biking, and horseback-riding trails, all offering amazing views of the city below. Plans are in the works for 100 mi more of trails. Rock climbing is permitted. This is a good place to get up close and personal with native species like foxes and kestrels and bluebirds, as well as plants found nowhere else in Texas, like the stout barrel cactus. Limited camping is available for tents; there are five RV sites. Tours are offered on the first and third weekends of the month; call ahead to reserve a space. ⊠*1331 McKelligon Canyon Rd.* ☎*915/566–6441* 🎫*$4, additional for camping* ⊘*Daily 8–5.*
★

⑦ Hueco Tanks Historic Site. This park, named after natural, water-holding stone basins called *huecos,* is internationally renowned for its rock climbing and is a big draw for lovers of the pictographs left by the Apache, Kiowa, and Jornada Mogollon tribes who dwelt here. Due to past vandalism of the petroglyphs, rangers now accompany visitors to the sensitive areas of the park, and reservations for tours (such as the pictograph tour, as well as birding and bouldering tours) are required. Rock climbing without a guide is an option, and so is camping, since park staff are located throughout the park and keep an eye on visitors' activities . From downtown El Paso, take U.S. 62/180 32 mi northeast, turn north on Ranch Road 2775; follow signs. ■TIP➔**Call two days before your trip, as the number of visitors allowed is limited. Reservations are required to get in the park, unless visitors are among the first ten at the door when the park opens at 8** AM. ⊠*6900 Hueco Tanks Rd., No. 1, El Paso* ☎*915/857–1135 or 800/792–1112, option 3* 🎫*$4 per person, per day; camping $12–$16* ⊘*Oct.–Apr., daily 8–6; May–Sept., Mon.–Thurs. 8–6, Fri.–Sun. 7–7. Tours times for the more protected areas vary* 🔒*Reservations required.*

⑤ Magoffin Home State Historical Park. This 19-room Territorial-style adobe home near downtown El Paso was erected in 1875 by early El Paso pioneer Joseph Magoffin, and occupied by the Magoffin family for 110 years. The city of El Paso grew out of Magoffinsville, a town started by this prominent and powerful family that vastly influenced the area by encouraging trade, organizing area merchants, establishing perhaps the first alfalfa crop in the region, and later leasing buildings for the incipient Fort Bliss. ⊠*1120 Magoffin St., follow signs off I–10; westbound traffic takes Cotton St. exit; eastbound traffic takes Downtown exit to Kansas St.* ☎*915/533–5147* 🎫*$3* ⊘*Tues.–Sun. 9–5.*

⑧ Mission Ysleta. Around 1681, Spanish refugees from the Pueblo Revolt in and around Santa Fe established this *ysleta* (small island) mission. Like other old missions in the area, Ysleta is still an active church. Guided tours of the mission are available from downtown El Paso via Sun Metro Buses and the El Paso-Juárez Trolley Co. Nearby, the Tigua

Fodor'sChoice
★

Indian Reservation sells Tigua pottery, jewelry, and art. ⊠*Old Pueblo Rd. at Zaragosa and Alameda, take Zaragosa exit off I–10, east of El Paso* ☎*915/859–9848* ✆*Free* ⊘*Mon.–Sat. 9–5; Sun. openings vary with church schedule.*

❾ **Presidio Chapel San Elizario.** This 1789 Spanish fortress provided set-
★ tlers protection from raiding Comanches and Apaches. It was near this site that the expedition of Spanish explorer Don Juan de Oñate stopped to conduct a thanksgiving celebration in 1598. It's located in the San Elizario Historical District, 17 mi southeast of downtown El Paso. Tours are conducted on-site by friendly volunteers but feature only the museum, and not the church. The **El Paso Mission Trail Association** (☎*915/534–0677*) offers more extensive tours. ■TIP➔ **Call ahead if you're planning to visit the church. The father might be able to leave it open a bit later than 11.** ⊠*1556 San Elizario Rd., San Elizario* ☎*915/851–1682* ✆*Free* ⊘*Tues.–Sat. 10–2, Sun. 10–noon (visitor center and museum); Mon.–Fri. 10–11 (church).*

❿ **San Elizario County Jail.** Thought to have been built as a private residence in the early 1800s, this adobe building at some point became El Paso County's first courthouse and jail, and, according to Pat Garrett's book *Authentic Life of Billy the Kid,* was the only jail the Kid broke *into,* which he did in order to free his friend Melquiades Segura. ⊠*On Main Street (100 yards west of the chapel), San Elizario* ☎*915/851–1682 San Elizario Genealogy and Historical Society* ✆*Free guided tours of jail and plaza beginning at the Los Portales building* ⊘*Tues.–Sun. 10–2, and after hrs by special arrangement.*

❽ **Wyler Aerial Tramway.** Touted as the only public-accessible tram in
☺ Texas, this tramway totes visitors up 5,632-foot Ranger Peak, which
★ provides a striking view of three states, two nations, and 7,000 square mi. ⊠*1700 McKinley Ave.* ☎*915/566–6622* ✆*$7* ⊘*Sun.–Mon. and Thurs. noon–6, Fri.–Sat. noon–8.*

SPORTS & THE OUTDOORS

El Paso has a landscape rife with hiking trails through desert flatlands and up mountain peaks, while southeastern New Mexico, not far away, offers isolated streams and rivers—the Gila River, for example, is a popular waterway for white-water rafting.

There's a flood of fishing and boating opportunities just outside El Paso and just inside New Mexico, including Bonito Lake (Ruidoso, N.M.) and Caballo Lake (Truth or Consequences, N.M.), where skiers ski, boaters boat, and swimmers swim. There are fishing areas along the Pecos and Gila rivers. Within El Paso, anglers cast their lines into the lake at Ascarate Park. Catfish bite in Plain View and Hideaway lakes, private water bodies in El Paso County that charge a pittance to fish.

FISHING

Ascarate Park (⊠*6900 Delta Ave.* ☎*915/772–5605* ✆*$1 per vehicle Fri.–Sun. Free otherwise* ⊘*Daily 6 AM–11 PM*) has almost 70 picnic shelters with grills, two children's playgrounds, and a golf course, and offers activities such as boating and fishing on a 48-acre lake.

ARTS & ENTERTAINMENT

El Paso Opera. A dress-up, professional opera, this company presents classic operas by Verdi, Puccini, and other masters, and welcomes guests ages 7 and up. ⊠ *Abraham Chavez Theatre, 1 Civic Center Plaza* ☎ *915/581–5534* ⊕ *www.epopera.com.*

Speaking Rock Entertainment Center. You never know what's playing, but a good guess is mariachi music. A bar and restaurant are on-site, and smoking is allowed. ⊠ *Tigua Indian Reservation, 122 Old Pueblo Rd.* ☎ *915/860–7777.*

WHERE TO EAT

$$$–$$$$
★
✕ **Café Central.** The old saw "evolve or perish" has served this restaurant well. In 1918 Café Central opened in Juárez and served alcohol (and tasty food) to the Prohibition-weary masses from the United States. Once Prohibition ended, the café moved north across the border, changed hands, and became part of the local scene. Today, bold decoration, an airy courtyard, and innovative Southwestern–Asian food combine to make this urbane eatery a popular destination for the city's hip crowds. The menu changes seasonally, according to the availability of ingredients. Although you can enjoy a gourmet experience for about fifteen bucks by ordering a soup and a salad, it's worth the splurge to explore other menu options. Lunch is a bit less expensive than dinner, yet equally tantalizing. ⊠ *Texas Tower, 109 N. Oregon St.* ☎ *915/545–2233* ⌂ *Reservations required* ⊟ *AE, D, DC, MC, V* ⊘ *Closed Sun.*

$$–$$$$
⟳
Fodor'sChoice
★
✕ **Cattleman's Steakhouse.** Twenty miles east of El Paso, this is pretty much in the middle of nowhere, but it's worth the trip, as much for the quirky theme rooms as for the terrific steaks. Consistently voted a local favorite, the succulent steaks are so tender they almost melt in your mouth. The mesquite-smoked barbecue and seafood on the menu are as tempting as the steaks—note that strict vegetarians won't find a happy meal here. A children's zoo, playground, lake walk, hayrides (on Sunday), and a movie set are among the numerous nonculinary diversions. It opens at 12:30 PM on weekends. ⊠ *Exit 49 off I-10 (follow signs), Fabens* ☎ *915/544–3200* ⌂ *Reservations not accepted* ⊟ *AE, D, MC, V* ⊘ *No lunch Mon.–Fri.*

¢–$
✕ **Leo's.** The Mexican food at Leo's four El Paso locations is repeatedly voted a favorite by locals. Enchiladas, tacos, combination plates, and fluffy sopapillas are served in helpings that will leave you stuffed— that is, if you can elbow your way through the crowds and get a table. ⊠ *5103 Montana St.* ☎ *915/566–4972* ⊠ *5315 Hondo Pass* ☎ *915/757–9025* ⊠ *315 Mills Ave.* ☎ *915/544–1001* ⊠ *7520 Remcon Circle* ☎ *915/833–1189* ⊟ *AE, D, MC, V.*

> ### OVER RAMPARTS THEY WATCHED
>
> The Franklin Mountains that frame El Paso, bending it into its familiar horseshoe shape, are iconic at sunset, when the sky blushes then bursts into bloody color behind them. Sometimes called the northern ramparts of El Paso Del Norte, the mountains are similar to a range located nearby in Mexico but separated by the river valley. More than 24,000 acres of the arid, bald mountains—which fold, lava-like, into the landscape—are protected within Franklin Mountains State Park.

$$–$$$ ✕**The Magic Pan.** They've got the magic stick—or, the magic touch at
★ least. The chefs at the Magic Pan dish up fusion cuisine, like Tex/Italian blend mesquite chicken penne. However, they also serve classy Asian standbys such as sesame-crusted ahi tuna and distinctly domestic selections like Angus rib eye. A strong Southwestern current underlies many of the dishes. Dine outside and take in the desert breeze. ✉*5034 Doniphan, inside Placita Santa Fe* ☎*915/581–2121* ⊕*www. magicpanrestaurant.com* ⌕*Reservations required for dinner* ▤*AE, D, MC, V* ⊙*No lunch Tues.–Sun., no dinner Wed.–Sat.*

WHERE TO STAY

$–$$ 🏨**Holiday Inn Sunland Park.** This Holiday Inn, on a hill with 6.5 acres
Fodor'sChoice near Sunland Park Racetrack, has outdoor courtyards; the Southwest-
★ ern-style rooms have ironing boards, hair dryers, and coffeemakers. Breakfast buffets are served in the Sierra Grille Restaurant, and a Sunday brunch is available from 11 to 2. The service from the staff is attentive and noteworthy. **Pros:** There's a nice, well-maintained gym, and room service. **Cons:** Some rooms are on the small side. ✉*900 Sunland Park Dr.,* ☎*915/833–2900 or 800/658–2744* ⊕*www.holidayinn.com* ⌂*178 rooms* ⌕*In-room: dial-up. In-hotel: restaurant, bar, pool, no-smoking rooms* ▤*AE, D, DC, MC, V.*

$ 🏨**El Paso Marriott.** This clean, spacious hotel is a free shuttle trip away
★ from the airport and near plenty of restaurants. Though not fancy, it's a great place to stay for a couple of nights, and offers an in-hotel bar and restaurant. **Pros:** Free airport shuttle and free newspaper in the morning. **Cons:** You have to pay to use the Internet. ✉*1600 Airway Blvd.,* ☎*915/779–3300* ⊕*www.marriott.com* ⌂*296 rooms* ⌕*In-room: Ethernet. In-hotel: restaurant, bar, pool, no-smoking rooms* ▤*AE, D, DC, MC, V.*

CIUDAD JUÁREZ, MEXICO

Across the Rio Grande from El Paso.

If what you want is a quick and easy Mexican experience, Juárez is worth a day's excursion. There are any number of goods to buy, and tastes to taste, but it's a border town at the very end of it, with all the good and bad that title entails. Walking across the border is easy enough, but taking the trolley makes it all so much easier. At the end of a hot day of exploring, eating, and drinking margaritas, hopping on the trolley to take you back across the border is a welcome respite. Avoid driving in Juárez if you can, as it tends to be stressful, and parking your car isn't always safe. ■TIP➡**The more than a decade-long string of serial murders of women (hundreds since 1993) has caused a great deal of legitimate concern. Travelers of all genders should be mindful of this and *women should not travel alone at all.* Also note that at the time of this writing, drug violence is wreaking havoc with safety and tourism here. Please exercise great caution, and check travel warnings on the Department of State Web site about visiting Mexico (⊕*www.state.gov*).**

10

GETTING THERE

Due to the stricter border crossing rules, lines of cars now clog entrance checkpoints. Crossing on foot is substantially quicker, especially since there are three bridges that allow pedestrian traffic—the Sante Fe Bridge in downtown El Paso, the Zaragosa Bridge in far east El Paso, and The Bridge of the Americas, which is located close to museums, shopping, and a visitor center. The Bridge of the Americas doesn't charge a toll, but does have the longest lines because of the free pass. The other pedestrian bridges only charge a pittance, though, due to a favorable exchange rate. There are parking lots near the Santa Fe Bridge, but it's easier to bypass driving alltogether by taking a taxi to the bridges.

If you don't want to walk to Juárez, catch a ride with the **El Paso–Juárez Trolley Co.** (⊠ *1 Civic Center Plaza, El Paso* ☎ *915/544–0061*). Its Border Jumper trolley leaves hourly from 10 AM to 5 PM. For a $12.50 ticket you have a day's worth of transportation along the route weaving through Juárez's shopping areas and restaurants. Juárez is a sprawling city, and not necessarily a pretty one. The trolley stops keep you moving toward the areas most worth visiting.■TIP➜ **No matter which route you take, stow your passport in a safe place.**

SHOPPING

West Texans, New Mexicans, and visitors cross the border in Juárez for beautiful handicrafts as well as dental procedures, eyeglasses, and even cheap prescription drugs. A warning, however: buying prescription drugs is not a good idea, as regulations are much more lax in Mexico, and possession of some controlled medications will land the bearer in jail on the U.S. side.

It's entertaining to browse the outdoor stalls here with their attendant tchotchkes. Outdoor stalls and indoor markets feature wares as diverse as velvet paintings, leather saddles, turquoise jewelry, and cheap, poorly painted wood carvings—along with better-made handicrafts. The Sante Fe Bridge may be the best port of entry; it's near copious shopping opportunities, including the Mexican government–owned, bustling and touristy Mercado Juárez near Avenida Juárez. The market offers a diverse selection of handicrafts and other items as well as several outdoor cafés.

FodorśChoice
★ **Avenida de Juárez** features artisan-oriented shops where you can find handwoven shawls or hand-embroidered *huipiles,* the traditional blouses worn by indigenous Mexican women. There are also duty-free stores here.

FodorśChoice
★ One avenue in town, **Avenida Lincoln,** provides the pathway to a well-rounded afternoon. Nicer shops line its length, which eventually gives way to a shopping district featuring the bustling and modern Plaza de las Americas Mall and Museo de Instituto Nacional de Bellas Artes (Museum of Fine Art). Though there are bridal shops throughout the major shopping areas in Juárez, they cluster densely in the **"Bridal district"** (⊠ *Av. Lerdo, near the main drag*). It isn't a well-defined district, per se, just a concentration of fancy-dress stores. One of the safest and most touristy sectors of Ciudad Juárez, **City Market Juarez** (⊠ *Av. 16 de*

Septiembre) is just a stroll from where the Sante Fe Bridge spills foot travelers. It's on September 16 Street, named after Mexican Independence Day. At the **Mercado** (⊠*Av. 16 de Septiembre*) merchants sell wares in a labyrinth of booths carrying piñatas (papier-mâché animals stuffed with candy, or left empty for you to stuff), wooden figurines, belts, and jewelry. *Please* try your hand at bartering with the vendors! They really, really do expect you to haggle about the price, and you'll look like a rube if you don't.

WHERE TO EAT

Food is everywhere in Juárez—in carts alongside the road, in storefront kitchen stalls open to the air, and in fine restaurants with all the trappings of civility. A lot of the food here is very, very good and very, very authentic. Americans should keep in mind that food safety and sanitation are not regulated and enforced as aggressively as in the States. And yes, it's true about the water: Don't drink it unless bottled.

¢–$$ ✕**Ajuua!** Built in the style of a *pueblito* (small pueblo), this restaurant
★ is a popular stopover for passengers aboard the El Paso–Juárez Trolley Co.'s Border Jumper. The traditional Mexican dishes are reliably good, as are the margaritas. On weekend evenings, expect mariachi bands and colorfully costumed dancers. It's customary to tip the mariachi's leader a dollar or two. (You'll need to dial 011 plus 52 for the country code if calling from El Paso.) ⊠*162 N. Efren Ornelas, Av. Lincoln and Av. 16 de Septiembre* ☎*52–656/616–6935* ⊟*AE, MC, V.*

¢–$$ ✕**Barrigas.** There are Barrigas sites throughout the sister cities, and all of them serve traditional Mexican food and live music. The chicken mole (a rich sauce made with chocolate) is wonderful, and so is the *ribojo,* or rib-eye steak. ⊠*4850 Av. Triunfo de la República* ☎*915/611–4840* ⊟*AE, MC, V.*

ALPINE, MARFA & THE DAVIS MOUNTAINS

Nestled amid the plum and tan beauty of the Davis Mountains is a duo of cities increasingly known for their hipness as much as for their oddity. Originally ranching towns, Marfa and Alpine have held on to their deep Southwestern roots while getting a facelift from wealthy East Coasters who have established an incredibly influential arts foundation in the area and who continue to trickle in.

In Marfa the Chinati Foundation (founded by Donald Judd) attracts thousands of New Yorkers during its open house every year, creating a demand for book stores, coffee shops, art galleries, and bistros that wouldn't look out of place in Manhattan or Los Angeles. In nearby Alpine there isn't quite as much urban foot traffic, but there are enough visitors to elicit fine Southwestern eateries. Historic Alpine is also a place that gubernatorial and senatorial hopefuls come to stump in. Maybe it's because their venue of choice—Railroad Blues—has to be one of the quirkiest and most laid-back bars you'll ever hope to find.

Seeing the Lights

Nobody knows what they are. Nobody knows where they came from. And, to many's frustration, nobody knows when they'll appear.

There are folks who have lived in the 2,100-soul town of Marfa all their lives and never once seen the famous Marfa lights. Meanwhile, some visitors have happened upon the spectacle their very first night in town.

Those who have seen the lights all share similar accounts. They're balls that glimmer and glow along the horizon or on mountainsides. They float and they grow and they shrink, seeming almost to breathe. They split apart and merge together. And they change colors many times before disappearing into wherever it is they've come from.

Though the lights have been here for hundreds of years, scientists have yet to offer a viable explanation for what causes the ghostly lights. They've proffered ideas such as swamp gas, moonlight on minerals in the earth, or atmospheric conditions that play on the eye. Marfa residents have long ceased to care, however; they'd rather just enjoy the mystery and continue to celebrate it annually with their well-attended Marfa Lights Festival (☎432/729–4942 or 800/650–9696, www.marfacc.com/marfa_lights.htm), which is during Labor Day weekend.

—Jennifer Edwards

ALPINE & MARFA

Marfa is about 200 mi southeast of El Paso; Alpine is about 80 mi north of Big Bend National Park.

WHAT TO SEE

Museum of the Big Bend. This West Texas haven for art lovers and cowboy poets is under renovation and expansion, but it remains open, with 5,000 feet of space holding exhibits on cowboys and conquistadors. There's also an annual show of ranching handiwork (like saddles, reins, and spurs) held in conjunction with the Cowboy Poetry Gathering each February. ⊠*Sul Ross State University Campus, just off the westbound lane of Holland Avenue, the city's (two-way) main drag. Alpine* ☎*432/837–8143* ⊕*www.sulross.edu/~museum* ⊠*Donations accepted* ⊙*Tues.–Sat. 9–5, Sun. 1–5.*

ARTS & ENTERTAINMENT

ART GALLERIES

Young, hip, modern, and undeniably cool, the **Ballroom Marfa** (⊠*198 E. San Antonio St., Marfa* ☎*432/729–3600.* ⊕*www.ballroommarfa.org* ⊠*$5, sometimes more for certain events* ⊙*Thurs.–Sun. noon–6 (later when there's a live performance)* is part gallery, part performance-art and live-music venue. The **Chinati Foundation** (✉*Box 1135, Marfa* ☎*432/729–4362* ⊕*www.chinati.org* ⊠*$10* ⊙*By guided tour only, Wed.–Sun. at 10 AM and 2 PM*) changes its exhibits regularly. People fly from all over the country to see the collection, and the foundation conducts tours of its huge contemporary-art holdings by appointment. Getting to the museum is tricky; get directions by phone or online.

NIGHTLIFE

FodorsChoice **Railroad Blues** (⊠*504 W. Holland Ave., Alpine* ☎*432/837–3103*
★ ⊕*www.railroadblues.com*), a cozy wooden bar thick with atmosphere
and Texas music, is home to live music artists, kooky characters, and
live, spontaneous dancing. Watch couples two-step and see if you can
pick up the moves. Acts generally go on at 10 PM on weekends.

SHOPPING

Alpine's main drag, **Holland Avenue**, is lined with shops. You can have
a triple shot of espresso, pick up a local painting, browse books, and
shop for groceries. Nearby, Marfa offers shopping downtown, but the
best finds are off the town square. **The Brown Recluse** (⊠*111 W. San
Antonio, Marfa* ☎*866/731–1811*) is a used bookstore that serenades
shoppers with music on vinyl and offers some killer *juevos con nopali-
tos* (eggs and cactus) and coffee that's roasted in the store.

WHERE TO EAT

¢–$$ ✕**Edelweiss Restaurant.** Opened in 2003 by a native German brewmeis-
☻ ter, the restaurant in the Holland Hotel offers ales that are as authentic
as the spaetzle and schnitzel. There are standard choices like ham-
burgers, plus there's a kids' menu. ⊠*209 W. Holland Ave., Alpine*
☎*800/535–8040* ▤*AE, D, DC, MC, V.*

¢–$$ ✕**Pizza Foundation.** This funky gas station turned hip pizza joint will
☻ appeal to most park visitors, and especially families, because of its
★ casual atmosphere, good-smelling interior, and, most of all, the quality pizza the Rhode Island–native owners turn out. Kids will dig the
fun pizza names such as the Faux Caeser, as well as several varieties
of limeade, including blueberry and melon. ⊠*100 E. San Antonio St.,
Marfa* ☎*432/729–3377* ▤*AE, D, DC, MC, V.*

$–$$ ✕**Reata.** This is a favorite eatery for many West Texans spending the
day in Alpine. The restaurant feels both welcoming and upscale, with
lots of wood, big tables, and an overall rustic feel. The menu features
Tex-Mex touches such as tortilla soup and tenderloin tamales, and
reflects its Texas roots with dishes like calf fries and gravy. ⊠*203 N.
Fifth St., Alpine* ☎*432/424–3471* ▤*AE, D, DC, MC, V.*

WHERE TO STAY

$ ⌂**Holland Hotel.** Once a stop on the transcontinental railroad, the
★ Holland Hotel is now a historic landmark in downtown Alpine. Still
hung with its original sign, the hotel is set on the town's main, bustling
drag. Choose from a light-filled penthouse at the top of the motel, a
1,000-square-foot loft, and basic rooms on the second and third floors.
Higher-priced suites and more luxurious accommodations are available. **Pros:** Interesting furnishings. **Cons:** It's near the train track, so it's
noisy (you can request complimentary ear plugs from management).
⊠*207–209 W. Holland Ave.,* ☎*800/535–8040* ⊕*www.hollandhotel.
net* ⇆*14 rooms* &*In-room: no phone (some), kitchen (some), Ethernet. In-hotel: Internet* ▤*AE, D, MC, V* ��*BP.*

$–$$$$ ⌂**Hotel Paisano.** Once the playground of Liz Taylor, Rock Hudson, and
FodorsChoice James Dean, who stayed here while filming *Giant,* the Paisano has kept
★ its glamour with beautiful Mediterranean architecture and a fountain
in the center. It's located amid downtown Marfa's quirky buildings

and just down the street from the historic courthouse. **Pros:** It's quiet and well-maintained. **Cons:** The elevator is not operational (there are plans to resuscitate it in 2009). ⊠*207 N. Highland St.,* ☎*432/729–3669* ⊕*www.hotelpaisano.com* ✐*41 rooms* ⟡*In-room: no phone. In-hotel: public Wi-Fi, pool, no elevator* ⊟*AE, D, MC, V.*

FORT DAVIS AREA

24 mi south of Alpine.

WHAT TO SEE

☾ **McDonald Observatory Visitors Center.** There's plenty to do here: check
★ out exhibits, examine sunspots and flares safely via film, or peer into the research telescopes. After nightfall, the observatory offers "star parties." Kids get a discount on admission. ⊠*Hwy. 118 north through Alpine and Fort Davis, Fort Davis* ☎*432/426–3540* ⊕*www.mcdonaldobservatory.org* ✉*$8 ($10 for star party).*

Fort Davis National Historic Site. Tucked snug in the Davis Mountains, Fort Davis is regarded as one of the best surviving examples of Old West frontier posts. Troops were garrisoned here to protect travelers and mail coaches from American Indian depredations. There's no lodging or camping. ⊠*Off Hwy. 118, Fort Davis* ☎*432/426–3224, Ext. 20* ⊕*www.nps.gov/foda* ⊙*Daily 8–5* ✉*$3 for a 7-day pass.*

SPORTS & THE OUTDOORS

☾ **Balmorhea State Park.** Slide out of the broiling sun and into the waters
★ of Solomon Spring in this paved artesian pool. The park, just outside Balmorhea, is open seven days a week year-round, 8 AM to sunset (and later for pre-arranged night-scuba diving). ⊠*Box 15, Toyahvale* ☎*432/375–2370* ⊕*www.tpwd.state.tx.us* ✉*$5 Oct.–Apr.; $7 May–Sept.*

Davis Mountains State Park. More than 2,700 acres in size, the park celebrates the Davis Mountains, the largest range in Texas. Horseback riding is allowed, and so are camping, hiking, mountain biking, and picnicking. It's very close to the little town of Fort Davis. ⌂*Box 1707, Fort Davis* ☎*432/426–3337* ⊕*www.tpwd.state.tx.us* ✉*$3.*

MIDLAND-ODESSA

284 mi east of El Paso via I–10 and I–20, and 76 mi east of Pecos via I–20, and 350 mi west of Fort Worth via I—20.

The oil crazy city of Midland during the '80s could well have been the setting for TV's "Dallas." Many of its surrounding fields are lined with pumpjacks, iron devices that resemble sipping-bird toys as they pull the oil from the earth. Midland is considered the hometown of the Bush family, who frequently come back to visit. Often grouped with Midland as a sort of West Texas metroplex (albeit on a much smaller scale than the Big D metroplex), the football-manic city of Odessa lies just 20 mi west of Midland. It is the origin of the Friday Night Lights book

CLOSE UP

Friday Night Lights: Football as Religion

The Red Raiders of Texas Tech University.

There are two main ways to socialize in the Panhandle. No, make that three. There's church. There's football. Then there's the church of football—one faith in these parts on which most everyone can agree.

That's a bit of a stereotype, agreed, but one reinforced with glee throughout the small towns and large cities of Texas. Fall's a time of great expectation, and not just because of the changing of the leaves or the cooling of the sizzle. Let the season begin! Parents of players or parents who know the parents of high-school and college football players often schedule their weekends around attending the game. Texans are staunchly patriotic, and are wholeheartedly devoted to their state, their hometowns, and their families. Attending the game is a way for them to show support for all four.

In this part of the world high-school football is as important as NFL, and college football is pretty up there, too. Little Joey playing first string or the Cowboys' Tony Romo getting distracted by his girlfriend is equally big news. Sportswriters are assigned exclusively to cover high-school football games, and journalists from all over the state will travel to attend the state finals if their team is in them; so will families and supporters.

Football can also be political. As in other places, mayoral hopefuls and those running for office know the games are a good time to network, but it goes beyond that. Rooting for an NFL team from "up north" that's playing a Texas team seems disrespectful somehow. And tensions arise between family members rooting for, say, the Texas Tech Red Raiders over the University of Texas Longhorns (That liberal city! It isn't even *part* of Texas!).

But in the end, it's all in good fun, and Texans will good-naturedly make fun of their football obsession. Just don't block the view.

—Jennifer Edwards

and movie, and the hometown of the "Heroes" TV show cheerleader character Claire Bennet. Texas native Tommy Lee Jones often comes to West Texas to film his epics about life along the border.

There's more to the story, however. In 1880 the Texas and Pacific Railroad decided it was high time to construct a railroad from Marshall, Texas, near the Louisiana border, clear through to El Paso by way of the vast Llano Estacado—a land far, far away from all metropolitan areas (and also from water, buildings, and civilization in general). (Llano Estacado means staked plains. It's been known as the Llano ever since conquistadors placed wooden markers in the ground here so they could find their way back through this seemingly endless region.)

By 1881, railroad workers had reached the site now known as Odessa, and founded the town. Rumor and legend have it that the town's name was a bit of a joke. Russian railroad workers surveyed the stark, flat-as-a-pancake desert covered with scrub and cactus and decided, snidely, to name it Odessa, after a famous and beautifully wooded resort area in the Ukraine. Halfway between Dallas and El Paso, the town of Midland was founded in the same year and in a similar fashion, but named without the sarcasm.

When oil was discovered in the 1920s, it brought in workers by the thousands, and, later, the tens of thousands. From those origins grew two closely related, highly populated cities that, as all twins must, developed distinctly different personalities. During the three huge oil booms of the 1950s, 1970s, and now the '00s (naughts), Midland got, and maintained, a reputation as the white-collar, well-groomed twin, while Odessans have steeped themselves in a blue-collar, rough and rowdy culture. Midland got the skyscrapers and the nickname "The Tall City," while Odessa got the nightlife, the university, and the rodeo. Both got to host presidents 41 and 43.

Both cities have a lot to offer in terms of theater, museums, shopping, and culture—from rodeos and barn dances to lively Mexican events like the Ballet Folklorico, Fiesta West Texas, Cinco de Mayo, and Diez y Seis de Septiembre, as well as mariachi competitions. There's also a richly entrenched Tex-Mex cuisine tradition that will make it hard to eat Mexican food anywhere else.

WHAT TO SEE IN MIDLAND

5 Bush Childhood Home. In 1948, George H. W. and Barbara Bush moved with two-year-old George W. to Odessa, Texas. They lived there for a brief spell, moved to California briefly, and then returned to Texas, only this time settling in Midland. Though they lived in several homes, this one, measuring 1,655 square feet and inhabited in 1951, is one of the area's best-preserved. Daily tours are offered. Hear and read interpretive information such as interviews culled from childhood friends of the Bushes, and view photo exhibits and original furnishings in the home's museum. ⊠1412 W. Ohio Ave., Midland ☎866/684–4380 ⊕www.bushchildhoodhome.org ▨Donations accepted ☉Tues.–Sat. 10–5, Sun. 2–5; tour times vary.

6 Petroleum Museum. The 60,000 square feet of this multi-stage museum make for a pleasant afternoon viewing murals of early oil-field life, taking in an explanation of the origins of the vast oil reserves in West Texas, and enjoying lots of award-winning artwork. The cherry on top: the Chapparal cars—the cutting edge, mostly 1960s racers that were named after the fleet bird commonly known as the roadrunner. One of the models on display won the Indy 500 in 1980. ⊠1500 I–20 W, Midland ☎432/683–4403 ⊕www.petroleummuseum.org ▨$8 ☉Mon.–Sat. 10–5, Sun. 2–5.

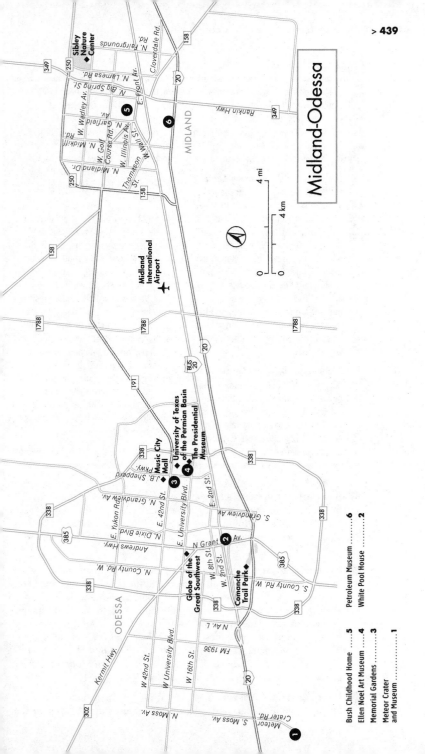

Midland-Odessa

Sibley Nature Center

N. Fairgrounds Rd.

Cloverdale Rd.

158

MIDLAND

Rankin Hwy.

349

W. Wadley Av.
N. Big Spring St.
W. Garfield Av.
E. Front Av.
N. Lamesa Rd.
N. Mickff
N. Golf Course Rd.
W. Illinois Av.
N. Wall St.
Thomason St.
W. Midland Dr.
158
250

Midland International Airport

158

1788

158

1788

1788

20

BUS 20

191

20

338

University of Texas of the Permian Basin
The Presidential Museum
Music City Mall
J.B. Shepperd Pkwy.
338

E. Yukon Av.
N. Grandview Av.
E. 42nd St.
E. University Blvd.
E. 2nd St.
S. Grandview Av.

338

N. County Rd. W.
Andrews Hwy.
N. Dixie Blvd.

385

338

ODESSA

Globe of the Great Southwest

N. Grant Av.
W. 8th St.
W. 2nd St.
N Av. L
W. County Rd. W.

Comanche Trail Park

385

338

Kermit Hwy.
W. University Blvd.
W. 16th St.
FM 1936
S. Moss Av.
N. Moss Av.
W. 42nd St.

Meteor Crater Rd.

302

20

0   4 mi

0   4 km

Bush Childhood Home **5**
Ellen Noel Art Museum **4**
Memorial Gardens **3**
Meteor Crater
and Museum **1**

Petroleum Museum **6**
White Pool House **2**

Bush Country

Despite a fierce rivalry between the similar-sized and closely spaced cities of Midland and Odessa, there's no denying that the histories of both oil burgs are entwined, and the Bush family legacy is just one example.

Beginning in 1948, a young George H.W. and Barbara lived for many years in both cities, though they stayed longer in Midland. It was also in Midland that they reared current president George W. Bush, and also where "Little Bush" met Laura Welch, his now wife of 30 years. The entire Bush family keeps close ties to the area, with George W., Laura, and her mother, Jenna Welch, returning often to attend church at First United Methodist in Midland, where the couple was married.

The Bush family is said to have occupied six Midland/Odessa homes between 1948 and 1958—three in Odessa and three in Midland. From 1948 to 1949, the young family lived at 1319, 1523, and 916 E. 17th St. in Odessa before moving to Midland

in 1950, where they inhabited 405 E. Maple, 1412 W. Ohio, and 2703 E. Sentinel Dr., before moving to New England. The oldest child, George W., returned with Laura and from 1975 to 1986 lived in four Midland homes: 2008-A Bedford, 1405 W. Golf Course Road, 2006-A Harvard, and 910 Harvard.

Not all homes are still standing, and many are inhabited; two, however, have been preserved for visitors: the George W. Bush Childhood home at 1412 W. Ohio in Midland and the Bush Home in Odessa, formerly at 916 E. 17th St. and now behind the Presidential Museum and Law Library, located at 4919 E. University. In January 2008 an intentionally set fire damaged the property, which remained closed at the time of this writing but was due to reopen in the future. For directions and additional information on these homes, check out online driving-tour directions at ⊕ www.odessacvb.com/presidential_drivetour.html.

—Jennifer Edwards

WHAT TO SEE IN ODESSA

❹ ☺ **Ellen Noel Art Museum.** Right next door to the presidential museum, this big museum features several galleries and a beautiful outdoor "sensory garden." ✉ *4909 E. University Blvd., Odessa* ☎ *432/550–9696* ⊕ *www.noelartmuseum.org* ✉ *Donations accepted* ☉ *Tues.–Sat. 10–5, Sun. 2–5.*

❸ **Memorial Gardens.** Once known as Buffalo Wallow, in commemoration of the great, wooly mammals who created the lake by wallowing here, these gardens have paved trails ringing the wallow, which now has beautiful sculptures, a fountain, a waterfall, and restrooms. In September, volunteers place thousands of full-size flags around the rippling waters to commemorate those that lost their lives on September 11th. ✉ *4730 E. 42nd St. (near the intersection of John Ben Shepperd Parkway and 42nd St.), Odessa* ☎ *432/368–3548* ⊕ *www.odessa-tx.gov/public/parks-recreation/parks.asp* ✉ *Free.*

❶ **Meteor Crater and Museum.** Yeah, it's a hole in the ground. But it's a *HUGE* hole in the ground—the second-largest impact crater in the

United States and the sixth-largest meteor crater in the world. Tours of the crater are self-guided; a museum about the attraction is also on-site. ✉ *Exit 108 off I–20/3100 Meteor Crater Rd., Odessa* ☎ *432/381–0946* 🖂 *Donations accepted* ⊘ *Daily 9–6 (crater); Mon.–Sat. 10–5, Sun. 1–5 (museum).*

❷ White Pool House. Charles and Lucy White built this two-story Victorian-era home just a few years after the railroad broke ground in the region. Then, during the oil boom of the 1920s, Oso Pool bought the home and turned it into an apartment building. These days, visitors can take in rotating exhibits and original furnishings—including old-style glasses—during a tour of the well-preserved home. ✉ *112 E. Murphy St., Odessa* ☎ *432/333–4072* ⊕ *www.odessahistory.com/whitpool.htm* 🖂 *Donations accepted* ⊘ *Tues.–Sat. 10–3.*

ARTS & ENTERTAINMENT

THEATER

The Globe of the Great Southwest. This beautiful, full-scale replica recalls Shakespeare's Globe Theatre, built on the River Thames but lost to fire. There are just a few replicas like this one, and they are scattered throughout the world. This theater features a well-attended Shakespeare festival each year, and visitors will sigh over its writer's garden and cute little Anne Hathaway Cottage, which recalls Shakespeare's wife's childhood home. Plays are generally staged on weekends. ✉ *2308 Shakespeare Rd., Odessa* ☎ *432/580–3177* ⊕ *www.globesw.org* 🖂 *$12.*

NIGHTLIFE

The Ranch. The Ranch is in many ways Dos Amigos's Midland counterpart, except that the fare on its stage is almost always cowboy hat–wearing country artists—and some of the best in Texas at that. Drinks are also cheaper here, and make for a nice accompaniment to a nice, authentic Texan ballad. ✉ *4400 N. Big Spring St., Midland* ☎ *432/620–0114* ⊕ *www.theranchmidland.com* 🖂 *Concert prices vary; no cover on non-music nights.*

Dos Amigos Cantina. A combination rodeo ring and rock-'n-roll stage, Dos Amigos is the place to go for outdoor and indoor concerts, a Bud, and some interesting local action. The area's strategic location along the long stretch from Dallas to El Paso helps it net a wide range of performers, on the road to larger cities, including Morrissey, Deftones, Chevelle, and other popular acts. It also hosts a lot of Texas country-and-western artists and indy artists still on the make. ✉ *4700 Golder Ave., Odessa* ☎ *432/368–7556/* ⊕ *www.dosamigoscantina. com* 🖂 *Concert prices vary; no cover on non-music nights.*

10

SPORTS & THE OUTDOORS

⟳ **Sibley Nature Center.** The sere lands that make up the Staked Plains may not, at first glance, seem to be teeming with wildlife. But first impressions aren't always correct, because it happens to be home to the only ground-nesting owl in West Texas, bands of prairie dogs and ground squirrels, and the archetypical horned lizards immortalized by Yosemite Sam as "horney toads." The nearly 50 acres of Sibley pay homage to the flora and fauna of the region with a natural trail, amphitheater, libraries, and an herbarium and insect collection. ✉*1307 E. Wadley, Midland* ☎*432/684–6827* ⊕*www.sibleynaturecenter.org* ☜*$1* ☾*Mon.–Fri. 8–5.*

WHERE TO EAT

MIDLAND

¢–$$ ✕ **Doña Anita's.** Despite the plain decor, the cooks serve fantastic, homey food. It's said that this is a favorite eatery when the Bush family's in town. Maybe that's because there are a ton of Tex-Mex faves on the menu, from fajitas to flautas, and even the waitresses complain about getting plump from trying them all. ✉*305 W. Florida Ave., Midland* ☎*432/683–6727* ☾*No dinner Sun.* ⊟*AE, D, MC, V.*

FodorsChoice ★

¢–$$ ✕ **The King and I.** No one can live on Tex-Mex alone, and this is a nice break from the norm. The Thai owners serve up an extensive menu of soups, spring rolls, curries, and entrées. ✉*801 N. Big Spring St., Midland* ☾*Closed Sun.* ☎*432/682–0988* ⊟*AE, D, MC, V.*

ODESSA

$–$$$ ✕ **Barn Door.** The Barn Door, with its tall windmill, is an easily spotted Odessa tradition. Each meal begins with a free hunk of cheese that looks, at first, only slightly smaller than the hood of a car. The restaurant specializes in steaks. ✉*2140 Andrews Hwy., Odessa* ☎*432/337–4142* ⊕*www.odessabarndoor.com* ☾*Closed Sun.* ⊟*AE, D, MC, V.*

¢–$ ✕ **Delicias.** Delicias is, in a word, delicious. Period. Every dish, from the *menudo* (that quintessential, spicy Mexican stew made with beef tripe and hominy) to fajitas, is well prepared and maybe just a little deliciously greasy. Locals, including native and first-generation Mexican families, fill up the restaurant at lunch and dinner. ✉*716 W. 8th St., Odessa* ☾*Closed Sun.* ☎*432/580–8306* ⊟*D, MC, V.*

WHERE TO STAY

$$ ★ 🏨 **Holiday Inn & Holiday Inn Express.** Tidy, quiet, and comfortable, locations in Midland (Holiday Inn Express) and Odessa (Holiday Inn) are consistently some of the most popular. **Pros:** Near shopping in both Midland and Odessa. **Cons:** As with most chains, rooms don't have much personality. ✉*5309 W. Loop 250,* ☎*432/520–3600* ⊕*www.holidayinn.com* 📞*94 rooms (Midland), 102 rooms (Odessa)* ♿*In-hotel: pool, no-smoking rooms. In-room: Ethernet, Wi-Fi* ✉*5275 E. 42nd St.,* ☎*432/366–5900.*

$–$$$$ 🏨 **MCM Eleganté.** In a town with a lot of options, the Eleganté stands out—and not just because it's a local landmark. The service is friendly and the restaurant and lobby are elegant. The beds are comfortable and rooms are pretty. **Pros:** Good drinks at the bar. **Cons:** Because of the local worker shortage, the quality of service in the area has dipped, including that offered in this hotel. ✉*5200 E. University Blvd., Odessa* ☎*915/544–1743* ⊕*www.mcmelegante.com* 📞*191 rooms* ♿*Pool, cable, data ports for high-speed Internet.*

SAN ANGELO

112 mi southeast of Midland.

In the late 1800s the all-black regiments known respectfully by American Indians as the Buffalo Soldiers kept travelers and settlers in West Texas safe from attack by hostile Indian tribes. The protection they provided from Fort Concho was effective enough that a rowdy town sprang up on the opposite bank of the Concho River. In those days, the frontier town that would later become San Angelo was known for prostitution, gambling, and illicit revelry in general.

Immortalized in gunslinger ballads and given nods in Old West novels, the town has grown up. These days the fort has become a historic landmark and the town is home to a university, Angelo State, a beautiful fine arts museum, a bordello museum, and fun little shops along the Concho River. It also has some hidden gems, like the artists' commune known as the Chicken Farm and a colony of Mexican free-tail bats that fly in clouds from the Foster Road Bridge. It's also known for native sons Los Lonely Boys, who snagged a Grammy in 2005.

WHAT TO SEE

The Chicken Farm Arts Center. Perhaps one of San Angelo's most singular attractions, the Chicken Farm Arts Center has neither chickens nor farms, but rather a clutch of artists creating beautiful works in a compound that houses the Silo Restaurant, a bed-and-breakfast, 15 artists' studios, multiple kilns, and on some days, blacksmiths and musicians. ⊠*2505 Martin Luther King Blvd.* ☎*325/653–4936* ⊕*www.chickenfarmartcenter.com* ⊙*Tues.–Sat. 8–5.*

San Angelo Museum of Fine Arts. The organic, sway-backed shape of this top-notch art museum blends into the terrain and houses 40-foot ceilings, a rooftop exhibit and rotating collections that in the past have included original works by Georgia O'Keefe, Norman Rockwell, and entries into the National Ceramic Competition. ⊠*1 Love St.* ☎*325/653–3333* ⊕*www.samfa.org* 🖾*$2* ⊙*Tues.–Sat. 10–4.*

Miss Hattie's Bordello Museum. San Angelo's cleaned up its image since the late 1800s, when it was known for boozing, gambling, and prostitution. But it hasn't let the past die completely. Miss Hattie's provides a peek into one of West Texas's most famous brothels—which didn't turn off the red light until 1949. A café and saloon next door fit hand-in-glove with the theme. ⊠*1331 McKelligon Canyon Rd.* ☎*325/653–0112* ⊕*www.misshatties.com* 🖾*$5* ⊙*Thurs.–Sat. 1–4 (tours leave at the top of the hour).*

SPORTS & THE OUTDOORS

Fort Concho National Historic Landmark. An important frontier post, Fort Concho protected settlers and travelers in West Texas from hostile American Indian tribes. It was also home to the Buffalo Soldiers until it was decommissioned in 1889 after decades of service. The museum preserves many of the fort's original 28 buildings, which face each other in a square shape. ⊠*630 S. Oakes St.* ☎*325/657–4444*

10

⊕*www.fortconcho.com* ✉*$3 (self-guided tour), $5 (guided tour)* ☽*Mon.–Sat. 9–5, Sun. 1–5 (museum), Mon.–Fri. 8–5 (trading post).*

Angelo State Park. Home to part of the Texas State Longhorn herd, which preserves the iconic cattle, this nearly 8,000-acre park has a rich history, as seen in American Indian petroglyphs and tracks left by ancient animals. Sightseeing tours are available, although hikers, joggers, and mountain bikers can do their own thing. Hunting for native deer and wild turkey is allowed, but only with a permit and only during certain times. Bird-watching, fishing, camping, and horseback riding are also available. Swimming is allowed but not recommended (the lake is quite shallow). ✉*3900-2 Mercedes St.* ☎*325/949–8935 (reservations), 325/949–4757 (headquarters)* ⊕*www.tpwd.state.tx.us* ☽*Daily dawn–dusk.*

SHOPPING

The well-preserved Concho Avenue historic shopping district is the place for little jewelry stores, along with shops featuring wooden crosses, stained glass, and furniture made with native mesquite.

WHERE TO EAT & STAY

¢–$$ ✕**Franco's Cafe.** Franco's is one of those holes-in-the-wall you might pass right by if you didn't know what tasty burritos, *caldo de res* (an incredibly tasty, Mexican beef stew), and guiso (stewed meat) they serve. With chubby breakfast burritos fetching just $1.50, it's also awe-inspiringly inexpensive. ✉*2218 Martin Luther King Blvd., San Angelo* ☎*325/623–8010* ⊕*www.francoscafe.org* ▭*AE, D, MC, V* ☽*Closed Mon.*

$–$$$$ ✕**Zentner's Daughter.** This comfy steak house is a San Angelo institu-
Fodor's Choice   tion, and often one of the first places residents return to after they've
★   moved away. It doesn't look like much on the outside, but the inside is both comfortable and elegant, and the steaks melt in your mouth. ✉*1901 Knickerbocker Rd., San Angelo* ☎*325/949–2821* ▭*AE, D, DC, MC, V.*

$–$$ ▦**Inn at the Arts Center.** This cozy B&B is set amid a complex known
Fodor's Choice   as the Chicken Farm, which houses artists' studios and the Silo Res-
★   taurant. Rooms are built into old coops and grain silos; the structures influence the rooms' shapes. **Pros:** Shopping right outside the door. **Cons:** Some rooms are a little small. ✉*2503 Martin Luther King Blvd.,* ☎*866/557–5337* ⊕*www.hollandhotel.net* ⇆*3 rooms* ♿*In-hotel: no-smoking rooms. In-room: no phone, no elevator* ▭*AE, D, MC, V* ⊺◎⊺*BP.*

EN ROUTE   In a state peppered with caverns, limestone caves, and sinkholes, many remain undiscovered, others are still being explored. Many of them, particularly those open to the public, contain rock twisted by water into beautiful shapes and eerily lifelike clusters of forms that can resemble faces, mushrooms, waves, or—in the case of the **Caverns of Sonora**—a beautiful and diaphanous butterfly. It's partly for this reason that many consider these caverns the most beautiful in the world. In fact, the founder of the National Speleological Society has quipped that its beauty can't be exaggerated, "not even by a Texan."

Guides conduct a nearly two-hour-long tour, as well as special classes for kids that feature real fossil digs. The caverns, dubbed a National Natural Landmark, are located 10 mi outside of Sonora, Texas.

DEL RIO & LAKE AMISTAD NATIONAL RECREATIONAL AREA

DEL RIO

204 mi east of Alpine via Hwy. 90, 157 mi south of San Angelo via Hwy. 87/277.

The town of Del Rio has always lived on the edge—the edge of the Texas–Mexico border, the edge of Texas's Hill Country, and on the corner of the natural-spring brightened Edwards Plateau. This town also gained edginess—and notoriety—when it became the American address for XERA, an ground-breaking and popular Mexican radio station that blasted waves all the way to Canada during the 1930s.

West Texans often come to Del Rio to enjoy the historic downtown museums, shops, and restaurants, while outdoorsy types get a kick out of the beautiful rock paintings preserved in nearby Seminole Canyon, or bike on paths that skirt desert wildlife and river ecosystems. There's also a local winery.

When you get here, be prepared for a change from the rest of West Texas. There are many more trees, many more river trails, and fewer people who speak English. It's an excellent introduction to the rich mélange that is Tex-Mex border culture and history.

WHAT TO SEE

Alamo Village—It's not possible to run out of activities on this huge, historic movie set surrounded by miles of ranch. There's a museum commemorating John Wayne, who filmed *The Alamo* here in 1959, and the goings-on for guests include horse races, gunfighter skits, and an Indian museum flush with artifacts. Plus, to drink there's ice-cold sarsaparilla. Kids only pay $5 for admission. ⊠ *7 mi north of Brackettville on Hwy. 674, Brackettville* ☎*325/653–4936* ⊕*www.thealamovillage. homestead.com/alamovillage.html* 🔖*$10.75* ⊙*Daily 9–6.*

Fodor'sChoice
★

SPORTS & THE OUTDOORS

Seminole Canyon State Park and Historic Site. Most folks come to Seminole Canyon in order to take in some of the oldest cave paintings in the nation, left thousands of years ago by ancient hunters. A challenging hike to the Fate Bell Shelter, which houses some of the best examples, is conducted several days a week. Mountain biking is available, and so is hiking, but hikers must go with a guide (to protect the aging cave art). ⌂ *Box 820 (40 mi west of Del Rio on Hwy. 90), Comstock 78337* ☎*432/292–4664* 🔖*$3* ⊙*Daily except during public hunts.*

10

FRITO PIE

What is it? We don't know. But we surely like it. In drive-through lanes and laid-back restaurants throughout the Southwest, visitors are sure to notice a little, inexpensive dish called Frito pie. No one knows exactly where the dish (if we can call it that) originated, though apocryphal stories say that Frito-Lay's founder Elmer Doolin's mother concocted it after her son produced his first Frito.

Generally, the construction of the messy dish begins by dumping a "mess" of Frito corn chips into a dish or Styrofoam container, then lavishing them with chili, mounds of melted cheddar, and, often, sliced fresh onions, jalepeños and, in some places, salsa or even sour cream, and guacamole. The result is a delicious, sense-assaulting merge of crisp corn, silky sauce, and particles of meat.

WHERE TO EAT

¢–$$$ ✕ **Wright's Steak House.** Even though Del Rio flirts with the border, it's
★ still in Texas—and that means steak's on the table. Locals especially like this steak house, located just a smidge outside of town. The salad bar is constricted, but you're most likely here for the beef anyway. The crispy, golden onion rings are a do-not-miss side, and the tangy margaritas are a plus. ⊠*8116 Hwy. 90, Del Rio* ☎*830/775–2621* ▤*AE, D, DC, MC, V.*

LAKE AMISTAD

8 mi north of Del Rio via Hwy. 90, 150 mi west of San Antonio via Hwy. 90

In a West Texas/Mexico heat that sizzles, it's comforting to slip into the silken waters of Lake Amistad, or simply to picnic along the waters. Surrounded by sheer limestone cliffs that sheltered waves of prehistoric visitors, the lake is known for excellent fishing.

Like many things in the Del Rio/Acuña border area, the 89,000-acre Lake Amistad Reservoir was created by a cooperative effort between the United States and Mexico. In 1964, work began on a strong dam that corralled the mingled waters of the Rio Grande and the Devil's River—resulting in millions of feet of surface water and thousands of feet of visitors. The lake's name is a symbol of the two countries' cooperation and even fond regards; it mean "Friendship."

The lake is the focal point of the Lake Amistad National Recreation Area (*see below*), located in a rich transition area between desert, shrub land, and plateau. And though the landscape looks hardscrabble, with its cacti and spiny plants, it's host to tons of signature wildlife like bristly porcupines, long-eared jackrabbits, ever-present deer, and an amazing variety of birds during the winter migration.

On Set in Brackettville

Most have never heard of a little burg called Brackettville, Texas, but movie producers and hallmark Western actors like John Wayne and Tommy Lee Jones clearly have. That's because they've chosen a sprawling ranch near this 1,800-soul town to film more than 200 productions on the most extensive outdoor set in the country. Since 1959, films from The Good Old Boys (starring Jones and Frances McDormand) to Bad Girls (starring Drew Barrymore and Andie McDowell) have captured the beautifully maintained ersatz glory of the ranch and set.

Among a long list is John Wayne's 1960 flick The Alamo, which also featured Frankie Avalon and Laurence Harvey; and Barbarosa, a film about feuding families starring Willie Nelson and Gary Busey. Creators of the incredibly popular TV miniseries "Lonesome Dove" also chose the ranch to weave their tale of cowboys trying to drive their herd through the state despite various challenges.

The $12 million set was worked on by as many as 400 workers at once. Many of them roamed the huge ranch, collecting cow and horse manure to make the adobe-style dwellings in the traditional way. Apparently, the dirty work paid off; more than a million bricks were made, more than 200,000 square feet were lofted, and the film became an icon. These days, strollers don't find a single false front among the buildings on the monumental set. They find a John Wayne museum, a mariachi band and folklorico dancers, line dancing, and even cattle drives. Live entertainment is served up alongside cheeseburgers and barbecue in the Alamo Village Cantina, and a stagecoach carries riders on a careening ride through the streets.

Surrounding the Alamo set is almost 30 mi of working ranch, complete with longhorns, horses, and goats. The ranch is still used for filming. For about 11 bucks the public can tour the famous full-scale Alamo Village set or take in the periodic horse races and the gunslinger competitions, where contenders try for the fastest draw.

—Jennifer Edwards

Nearby is Panther Cave, famous for its large, leaping-cat pictograph, and Parides Cave, an excellent place for rock-art viewing.

WHAT TO SEE

☼ **Lake Amistad National Recreation Area.** Miles of turquoise waters north
★ of the Del Rio and Acuña border towns beckon for boaters and skiers, and those who just want to cool off their toes at this visitor-friendly area between the shores of the United States and the banks of Mexico. Eagles fly overhead. Fishing enthusiasts will love the plump bass, which have measured up to 15 pounds. Campsites are available and so are tours of the ancient rock art in Paridas and nearby Panther caves. Boats can be rented, but you must have a permit (pick one up at the visitor center. ⊠ *4121 Veterans Blvd.* ☎ *830/775–7491* ⊕ *www.nps.gov/amis* ⊠ *$4* ⊙ *Daily 8–5.*

10

WEST TEXAS ESSENTIALS

Research prices, get travel advice, and book your trip at fodors.com.

TRANSPORTATION

BY AIR

The El Paso and Midland airports keep West Texas serviced and hopping. Most of the major airlines fly to the El Paso Airport, 7 mi from downtown. The petite but busy Midland Airport is served by Southwest, American Eagle, and Continental Express. Continental has thrice daily flights between Del Rio and Houston.

Contacts **Del Rio International Airport** (✉ *1104 W. 10th St., Del Rio* ☎ *830/774–8538*). **El Paso International Airport** (✉ *6701 Convair Rd., El Paso* ☎ *915/780–4749* ⊕ *www.elpasointernationalairport.com*). **Midland International Airport** (✉ *9506 LaForce Blvd., Midland* ☎ *432/560–2200* ⊕ *www.flymaf.com*).

BY BUS

Through this remote region, Greyhound (☎ *800/231–2222* ⊕ *www.greyhound.com*) connects Alpine, Big Spring, Del Rio, El Paso, Marfa, Midland, Odessa, and Pecos.

BY TRAIN

Amtrak (☎ *800/872–7245* ⊕ *www.amtrak.com*) operates two lines, the Texas Eagle and the Sunset Limited, with stops in Del Rio, Sanderson, Alpine, and El Paso; they bypass the rest of the region.

CONTACTS & RESOURCES

EMERGENCIES

In an emergency, dial 911 (from Mexico dial 066). Each of the following facilities has an emergency room open 24/7.

Hospitals **Midland Memorial Hospital** (✉ *2200 W. Illinois Ave.* ☎ *432/685–1111*).**Sierra Providence** ✉ *4815 Alameda, El Paso* ☎ *915/544–1200*.

VISITOR INFORMATION

Alpine Chamber of Commerce (✉ *106 N. 3rd St., Alpine* ☎ *800/561–3735 or 432/837–2326* ⊕ *www.alpinetexas.com*). **Del Rio Chamber of Commerce** (✉ *1915 Veterans Blvd., Del Rio* ☎ *800/889–8149* ⊕ *www.drchamber.com*). **El Paso Convention and Visitors Bureau** (✉ *1 Civic Center Plaza, El Paso* ☎ *915/534–0601 or 800/351–6024* ⊕ *www.elpasocvb.com*). **Marfa Chamber of Commerce** (✉ *207 N. Highland St., Marfa* ☎ *800/650–9696* ⊕ *www.marfacc.com*). **Midland Chamber of Commerce** (✉ *109 N. Main St., Midland* ☎ *800/624–6435* ⊕ *www.midlandtxchamber.com*). **Odessa Convention and Visitors Bureau** (✉ *700 N. Grant St., Ste. 200, Odessa* ☎ *800/780–4678* ⊕ *www.odessacvb.com*). **San Angelo Chamber of Commerce** (✉ *418 W. Ave. B, San Angelo* ☎ *325/655–4136* ⊕ *www.sanangelo.org*).

1

Big Bend National Park

WORD OF MOUTH

"I'd rather be broke down and lost in the wilds of Big Bend, any day, than wake up some morning in a penthouse suite high above the megalomania of Dallas or Houston."

—Environmental writer Edward Abbey

WELCOME TO BIG BEND

TOP REASONS TO GO

★ **Varied Terrain:** Visit gilded desert, a fabled river, bird-filled woods, and mountain spirals all in the same day.

★ **Wonderful Wildlife:** Catch sight of the park's extremely diverse number of animals, including several dozen shy mountain lions and about the same number of lumbering bears.

★ **Bird-watching:** Spy a pied-billed grebe or another member of the park's more than 400 bird species, including the Lucifer hummingbird and the unique-to-this-area pato Mexicano (Mexican duck).

★ **Hot spots:** Dip into the natural hot springs (105°F) near Rio Grande Village.

★ **Mile-high Mountains:** Lace up those hiking boots and climb the Chisos Mountains, reaching 8,000 feet skyward in some places and remaining cool even during the most scorching Southern summer.

Bobcat

1 North Rosillos. Dinosaur fossils have been found in this remote, northern portion of the park. Made up primarily of back roads, this is where nomadic warriors traveled into Mexico via the Comanche Trail.

2 Chisos Basin. This bowl-shaped canyon amid the Chisos Mountains is at the heart of Big Bend. It's the place to watch a sunset and begin a hike.

3 Castolon. Just east of Santa Elena Canyon, this historic district was once used by ranchers and the U.S. military, earning it a place on the National Register of Historic Places.

4 Rio Grande Village. Tall, shady cottonwoods highlight the park's eastern entrance along the Mexican border and Rio Grande. It's popular with RVers and bird-watchers.

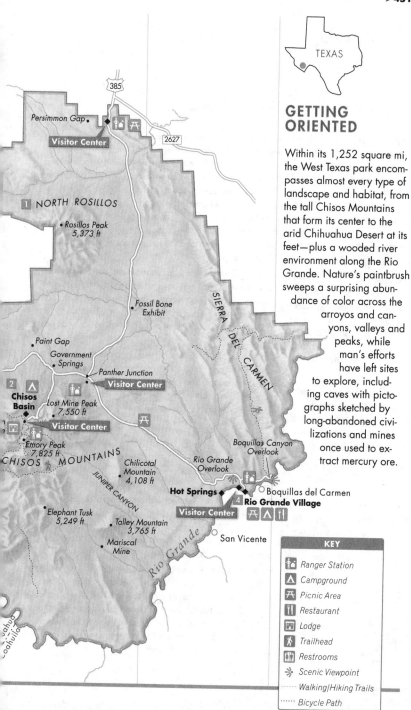

TEXAS

GETTING ORIENTED

Within its 1,252 square mi, the West Texas park encompasses almost every type of landscape and habitat, from the tall Chisos Mountains that form its center to the arid Chihuahua Desert at its feet—plus a wooded river environment along the Rio Grande. Nature's paintbrush sweeps a surprising abundance of color across the arroyos and canyons, valleys and peaks, while man's efforts have left sites to explore, including caves with pictographs sketched by long-abandoned civilizations and mines once used to extract mercury ore.

385

Persimmon Gap

Visitor Center

2627

1 NORTH ROSILLOS

Rosillos Peak
5,373 ft

Fossil Bone
Exhibit

SIERRA DEL CARMEN

Paint Gap

Government
Springs

Panther Junction

Visitor Center

2

**Chisos
Basin**

Lost Mine Peak
7,550 ft

Visitor Center

Emory Peak
7,825 ft

CHISOS MOUNTAINS

Chilicotal
Mountain
4,108 ft

Rio Grande
Overlook

Boquillas Canyon
Overlook

JUNIPER CANYON

Hot Springs

Boquillas del Carmen

4 Rio Grande Village

Visitor Center

Elephant Tusk
5,249 ft

Talley Mountain
3,765 ft

Mariscal
Mine

Rio Grande

San Vicente

Chihuahua
Coahuila

KEY	
🚻	Ranger Station
🔺	Campground
⛱	Picnic Area
🍴	Restaurant
🏨	Lodge
🚶	Trailhead
🚻	Restrooms
⚹	Scenic Viewpoint
-----	Walking/Hiking Trails
⋯⋯⋯	Bicycle Path

BIG BEND PLANNER

When to Go

There is never a bad time to make a Big Bend foray—except during Thanksgiving, Christmas, and Spring Break. During these holidays, competition for rooms at the Chisos Mountain Lodge and campsites is fierce—with reservations for campsites and rooms needed up to a year in advance.

Depending on the season, Big Bend sizzles or drizzles, steams up collars or chills fingertips. Many shun the park in the summer, because temperatures skyrocket (up to 120°F in some areas), and the Rio Grande dips.

In winter, temperatures rarely dip below 30°F. During those few times the mercury takes a dive, visitors might be rewarded with a rare snowfall.

Temperatures vary throughout the park, the mountains routinely 5–10 degrees cooler than the rest of the park, and the sweltering stretches of Rio Grande 5–10 degrees warmer.

AVG. HIGH/LOW TEMPS

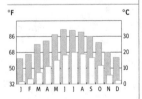

Flora & Fauna

Because Big Bend contains habitats as diverse as spent volcanoes, slick-sided canyons, and the Rio Grande, it follows that species here are extremely diverse, too. Among the park's most notable residents are endangered species like the agave cactus–eating Mexican long-nosed bat, shadow-dappled peregrine falcon, and fat-bellied horned lizard (Texans call them "horney toads"). More than 400 species of birds wing throughout the park, including the black-capped vireo and the turkey vulture, which boasts a 6-foot wingspan.

In the highlands several dozen mountain lions lurk, while black bears loll in the crags and valleys. Your chances of spotting the reclusive creatures are rare, though greater in the early morning. If you do encounter either, don't run away. Instead, stand tall, shout, and look as scary as possible.

If the winged, furred, and legged denizens of Big Bend are watch-worthy, so, too, are the plants populating the region. Supremely adapted to the arroyos, valleys, and slopes, the plants range from the brightly colored hedgehog cactus (found only in the Chisos) to the towering rasp of the giant dagger yucca. Also here are 65 types of cacti—so be careful where you tread.

Getting There & Around

Big Bend is 39 mi south of Marathon, off U.S. 385; 76 mi south of Alpine, off Route 118; and 50 mi east of Presidio, off Route 170. The nearest airport is in Midland, 3½ hours north of the park. The bus takes you as far as Marathon, and the train as far as Alpine.

Paved park roads have twists and turns, some very extreme in higher elevations; RVs and trailers longer than 20 feet should avoid the Ross Maxwell Scenic Drive on the park's west side and the Chisos Basin Road into higher elevations in Big Bend's central portion. Four-wheel-drive vehicles are needed for many of the backcountry roads. At parking areas take valuables with you.

By Jennifer Edwards

CRADLED IN THE WARM, SOUTHWESTERN elbow of Texas, the 801,163 acres of Big Bend National Park hang suspended above the deserts of northern Mexico. From the craggy, bald Chisos Mountains rising up to 8,000 feet to the flat and stark plains of the Chihuahua Desert, Big Bend is one of the nation's most geographically diverse parks, with the kind of territory that inspired Hollywood's first Western sets. Visitors can ride the rapids of the Rio Grande, trek through the classic, Old West landscape, and marvel at the moonscape that skirts Boquillas, Mexico.

SCENIC DRIVES

Chisos Basin Road. This road leads south from Chisos Basin Junction. By driving into higher elevations (the heart of Big Bend), you're likely to spot lions and bears as well as white-tailed deer amid juniper trees and pinyon pines. You'll also see lovely, red-barked Texas madrone along with some Chisos oaks and Douglas fir trees. Avoid this drive, however, if you are in an RV longer than 24 feet because of sharp curves.

Fodor's Choice ★ **Ross Maxwell Scenic Drive.** This route takes you 30 mi through pyramid-shaped volcanic mountains. If you don't mind a little grate in your gait from the gravel that blankets the road, you can make this drive a loop by starting out at the west park entrance and turning southwest onto Old Maverick Road (unpaved) for 12.8 mi to the Santa Elena Canyon overlook—where you can get a taste of the lowland desert. (*Note: If you're in an RV, don't even attempt Old Maverick Road. The road isn't paved and is rough going in some spots.*)

WHAT TO SEE

HISTORIC SITES

Castolon Historic District. Adobe buildings and wooden shacks serve as reminders of the farming and military community of Castolon. The Magdalena House has historical exhibits. ⊠*At the end of the Ross Maxwell Scenic Dr., southwest portion of the park* ☎*432/477–2225 ranger station.*

☺ **Hot Springs.** Hikers soak themselves in the 105°F waters alongside the Rio Grande, while petroglyphs (rock paintings) coat the canyon walls nearby. The remains of a post office, motel, and bathhouse point to the old commercial establishment operating here in the early 1900s. ⊠*15 mi southeast of Panther Junction, near Rio Grande Village.*

Mariscal Mine. Hardy, hard-working men and women once coaxed cinnabar, or mercury ore, from the Mariscal Mine, located at the north end of Mariscal mountain. They left the mines and surrounding stone buildings behind for visitors to explore. If you stop here, take care not to touch the timeworn stones, as they may contain poisonous mercury residue. ⊠*5 mi west of Rio Grande Village, on River Rd. East.*

BIG BEND IN ONE DAY

You can drive the paved roads of the park in a day, but don't short yourself; you miss the most striking parts if you don't get out and hike. Two not-to-miss trails are those through the rifts and boulders of **Santa Elena Canyon** and the rocky pinnacles of the **Chisos Mountain Basin**.

Access the Santa Elena trailhead from the junction of **Ross Maxwell Scenic Drive** and **Old Maverick Road**, at the northwestern rim of the park. From there, take the **Santa Elena Canyon Trail**. You need to wade Terlingua Creek, and then enter the canyon, where you'll see gargantuan rocks, singular rock formations, and the Rio Grande sandwiched between sheer cliffs. Back at the trailhead take **Ross Maxwell Scenic Drive** 30 mi back north and turn east at Santa Elena Junction.

Drive to the **Chisos Mountains Basin Junction** and turn south. This will take you to the heart of Big Bend, where you can linger for a quick hike along the **Window View Trail.** Have lunch at the restaurant or picnic at a campground table near the **Chisos Basin Visitor Center.**

Drive north back to the junction, turn east, and drive 23 mi to **Rio Grande Village.** Stroll through the tall, shady cottonwoods in the picnic area and you'll likely see many varieties of birds, including speedy roadrunners. If you have the time, follow the signs to the natural hot spring and take a dip.

Before calling it a day, drive east to the **Boquillas Canyon** overlook and view the Mexican village of Boquillas on the south side of the Rio Grande.

SCENIC STOPS

★ **Chisos Basin.** Panoramic vistas, a restaurant with an up-close view of the mountains, and glimpses of the Colima warbler (found only in Big Bend) await in the forested Chisos Basin. This central site also has hiking trails, a lodge, a campground, a grocery store, and a gift shop. ⊠ *Off Chisos Basin Rd., 7 mi southwest of Chisos Basin Junction and 9 mi southwest of Panther Junction.*

Dugout Wells. A windmill using the restless desert winds continues to siphon water from the lowlands, creating a shady oasis amid cactus and sand. The trees and foliage that drink from the well attract several varieties of birds, especially white-winged doves. A picnic table is available, along with a ½-mi nature trail. Guided walks are sometimes led here. ⊠ *6 mi southeast of Panther Junction.*

Rio Grande Village. Don't be fooled by the name—there's no real village here. There is, however, a campground, RV park, and amphitheater, as well as a boat launch on the Rio Grande. A grove of giant cottonwood trees alongside the river makes for cooling shadows in this hot, southern area of the park, and the grassy picnic area is highly recommended for birders. A visitor center (with a small bookstore), gasoline, and groceries are available. Note: this area is closed during summer's leaf-curling heat. ⊠ *22 mi southeast of Panther Junction.*

★ **Santa Elena Canyon.** The finale of a short hike (1.7 mi round-trip), is a spectacular view of the Rio Grande and cliffs that rise 1,500 feet to create a natural box. ⊠ *30 mi southwest of Santa Elena Junction via Ross Maxwell Scenic Dr.; 14 mi southwest of Rte. 118 via Old Maverick Rd.*.

VISITOR CENTERS

Castolon Visitor Center. Here you'll find some of the most hands-on exhibits the park has to offer, with touchable fossils, plants, and implements used by the farmers and miners who settled here in the 1800s and early 1900s. ⊠ *In the Castolon Historic District, southwest side of the park, at the end of the Ross Maxwell Scenic Dr.* ☎ *432/477–2271* ☉ *Nov.–May, daily 10–noon and 1–5.*

Fodor's Choice **Chisos Basin Visitor Center.** The center is one of the bettter-equipped, as
★ it offers an interactive computer exhibit, a bookstore, camping supplies, picnic fare, and some produce. There are plenty of nods to the wild, with natural resource and geology exhibits and a larger-than-life representation of a mountain lion. ⊠ *Off Chisos Basin Rd., 7 mi southwest of Chisos Basin Junction and 9 mi southwest of Panther Junction* ☎ *432/477–2264* ☉ *Nov.–Mar., daily 9–3:30, closed for lunch; Apr.–Oct., daily 9 AM–4:30 PM, closed for lunch.*

Panther Junction Visitor Center. At this writing, the park's main visitor center was undergoing renovations that were expected to continue well into 2008; however, the center will remain open throughout the construction. Planned improvements include an enlarged bookstore and new, touchable exhibits on the park's mountain, river, and desert environments. Nearby, a gas station offers limited groceries such as chips, premade sandwiches, and picnic items. ⊠ *30 mi south of U.S. 385 junction leading to north park boundary* ☎ *432/477–1158* ☉ *Daily 8–6.*

Persimmon Gap Visitor Center. Complete with exhibits and a bookstore, this visitor center is the northern boundary gateway into miles of flatlands that surround the more scenic heart of Big Bend. Dinosaur fossils have been found here; none are on display in the center, but the **Fossil Bone Exhibit** is located on the road between Persimmon Gap and Panther Junction. ⊠ *3 mi south of U.S. 385 junction* ☎ *432/477–2393* ☉ *Daily 9–4:30, closed for lunch.*

Rio Grande Village Visitor Center. Opening days and hours are sporadic here, but if you do find this center open, then view videos of Big Bend's geological and natural features at its minitheater. There are also exhibits dealing with the Rio Grande. ⊠ *22 mi southeast of Panther Junction* ☎ *432/477–2271* ☉ *Daily 8:30–4. Closed May through Oct.*

SPORTS & THE OUTDOORS

Spectacular and varied scenery plus nearly 300 mi of road spell adventure for hikers, bikers, horseback riders, or those simply in need of a ramble on foot or by Jeep. A web of dusty, unpaved roads lures experienced hikers deep into the back country, while paved roads make casual walks easier. Because the park has over half of the bird species in North

America, birding ranks high. Boating is also popular, since some of the park's most striking features are accessible only via the Rio Grande.

BICYCLING

Mountain biking the backcountry roads can be so solitary that you're unlikely to encounter another human being. However, the solitude also means you should be extraordinarily prepared for the unexpected with ample supplies, especially water (summer heat is brutal, and you're unlikely to find shade except in forested areas of Chisos Basin). Biking is recommended only during the cooler months (Oct.–April).

On paved roads, a regular road bike should suffice, but you'll have to bring your own—outfitters tend to only stock mountain bikes. Off-road cycling is not allowed in the park. For an easy ride on mostly level ground, try the 14-mi (one way) unpaved **Old Maverick Road** on the west side of the park off Route 118. For a challenge, take the unpaved **Old Ore Road,** for 26.4 mi from the park's north area to near Rio Grande Village on the east side. ⇨ *Multisport Outfitters box for bike rentals and expeditions.*

BIRD-WATCHING

Situated on north–south migratory pathways, Big Bend is home to at least 434 different species of birds—more than any other national park. In fact, the birds that flit, waddle, soar, and swim in the park represent more than half the bird species found in North America, including the Colima warbler, found nowhere else. To glimpse darting humming-birds, turkey vultures, and golden eagles, look to the Chisos Moun-tains. To spy woodpeckers, scaled quail (distinctive for dangling crests), and the famous Colima, look to the desert scrub. And for cuckoos, car-dinals, and screech owls, you must prowl along the river. Rangers lead birding talks; ⇨ *Ranger Programs under Educational Offerings.*

Chisos Basin. You'll have to hike trails of higher elevations (5,400 feet or higher) and canyons to spy the Colima warbler and Lucifer humming-bird, but don't go in June or July, when bird activity is at a minimum. ✉ *Off Chisos Basin Rd., 9 mi southwest of Panther Junction.*

Rio Grande Village. Considered the best birding habitat in Big Bend, this river wetland has summer tanagers and vermilion flycatchers among many other species. The trail's a good one for kids, and a portion is wheelchair accessible. ✉ *22 mi southeast of Panther Junction.*

Fodor'sChoice ★

OUTFITTERS & EXPEDITIONS

Mark Smith Nature Tours. The nine-day April trip, which includes the Texas Hill Country as well as Big Bend, runs $1,885. One of the two annual tours begins in El Paso and concludes in San Antonio; the other goes from San Antonia to El Paso. ✆ *Box 3831, Portland, OR 97208* ☎ *800/821–0401, Willamette International Travel* ⊕ *www.marksmith naturetours.com/destinations/bigbend.html.*

WINGS Birding Tours Worldwide. This Arizona-based company offers an 11-day trip that encompasses Big Bend and the Davis Mountains. It's offered in the spring, and 2008 prices begin at $2,920. ✉ *1643 N. Alvernon, Suite 109, Tucson,* ☎ *888/293–6443* ⊕ *www.wingsbirds. com/tours.*

BOATING & RAFTING

Much is made of the park's hiking trails and the exquisite views they offer. Likewise, the watery pathway that is the Rio Grande should be mentioned for the spectacular views it affords. The 118 mi of the Rio Grande that border the park form its backbone, defining the vegetation, landforms, and animals found at the park's southern rim. By turns shallow and deep, the river flows through stunning canyons and picks up speed over small and large rapids.

By turns exciting (Class II and III rapids develop here, particularly after the summer rains) and soothing, the river can be traversed in several ways, from guided rafting tours to more strenuous kayak and canoe expeditions. In general, rafting trips spell smoother sailing for families, though thrills are inherent when soaring over the river's meringue-like tips and troughs. It's also pretty safe; no fatalities have been reported in several years. ■ TIP➔ **Be sure to check the river levels before planning an outing—many times during the year the river's too low to get a decent rafting experience.**

You can bring your own raft to the boat launch at the Rio Grande, but a river-use permit is required. The permits are free and you can obtain them from a visitor center or at the self-administered station at Lajitas (Barton Warnock Environmental Education Center); they allow you to camp at sites along the river. Also, leave the Jet Skis at home; no motorized vehicles are allowed on the river. For less fuss, go with a tour guide or outfitter on trips that range from a few hours to several days. ■ TIP➔ **Whichever route you decide on, definitely bring your passport—new border laws are much stricter than in the past.**

Most outfitters are in the communities of Study Butte, Terlingua, and Lajitas just west of the park boundary, off Route 170. They rent rafts, canoes, kayaks, and inflatable kayaks (nicknamed "duckies") for when the river is low. Their guided trips last anywhere from a couple of hours to several days, and cost in the tens of dollars to thousands of dollars. Personalized river tours are available all year long, and since this is the Lone Star State, they might include gourmet rafting tours that end with beef Wellington and live country music. Though many of the rafting trips are relatively smooth, thus safe for younger boaters, be sure to tell the equipment-rental agent or guide if a party member weighs less that 100 pounds or more that 200, since special life jackets may be needed. *For area outfitters,* ⇨ *Multisport Outfitters box.*

FISHING

You can cast a line into the Rio Grande all year long for free, as long as you obtain a permit from one of the park's visitor centers. You cannot use jug lines, traps, or other nontraditional fishing methods.

HIKING

Each of the park's zones has its own appeal. The east side offers easy mountain hikes, border canyons, lush vegetation, limestone aplenty, and sandy washes with geographic spectacles. West-side trails go down into striking scenery in the Santa Elena Canyon and up into towering volcanic land forms. Descend into gorges and springs or ascend into

CLOSE UP

Big Bend's Buffalo Soldiers

During the Indian Wars of 1866 through 1892, the U.S. government enlisted vast numbers of African-American soldiers to serve in its cavalry. Those that entered the Army were confined to all-black regiments led by white officers, and were treated as third-rate citizens. Despite many hardships—including poor rations, little respect, and cavalry mounts sometimes described as "old and half-dead"—soldiers in two Texas all-black regiments persevered and became known as the Buffalo Soldiers. (Yep, the same Buffalo Soldiers immortalized in the popular Bob Marley song.)

Explanations diverge for how these brave men (and one, barely-documented woman) of the 9th and 10th cavalry units received their unique name. Some say it was because their thick, curly hair resembled buffalo hair. Others contend that the American Indians they fought—and also protected—gave them this name out of respect for their courage and fortitude, traits their culture associated with that animal.

These units were given the toughest, most inhospitable terrain to guard—including the severe, cactus-covered desert plains that comprise modern-day Big Bend National Park. They protected this land, fought the natives, wrestled rustlers, and even strung telegraph lines. In West Texas, the government put them to work rounding up the intractable Apaches and Comanche Indians that inhabited the region.

Despite adversity from the natives, the weather, the terrain, and racist attitudes, the Buffalo Soldiers' units are said to have had the lowest desertion rates in the Army. They were eventually rewarded for their contribution in

Buffalo soldiers of the 25th infantry regiment pose in 1890.

the late 1880s, when several became the first African-Americans to receive the Congressional Medal of Honor—only 30-plus years after the Civil War, and nearly a century before the civil rights movement.

The all-black units were finally dissolved in the late 1950s. The last living Buffalo Soldier, Mark Mathews, died in 2005 at the age of 111 and was interred in Arlington National Cemetery.

While there are no longer any living soldiers to recall the wild, harsh time of the Indian Wars, Texas strives to keep their memory alive through events, plaques, signs, and demonstrations at the forts where they served. Visitors to West Texas can explore this history through events at Fort Concho in San Angelo, The Frontier Texas Museum in Abilene, Texas Buffalo Soldiers Heritage Trail/Trails of the Last Frontier corridor in Levelland, and through pamphlets and information in the visitor centers of Big Bend National Park.

—Jennifer Edwards

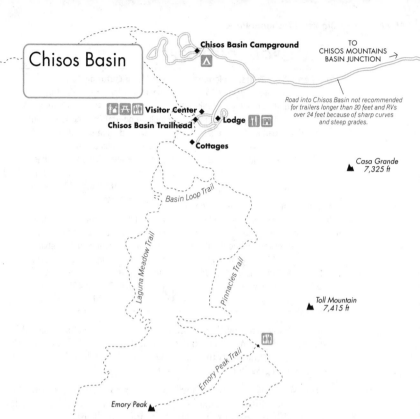

Chisos Basin

Chisos Basin Campground

TO CHISOS MOUNTAINS BASIN JUNCTION

Visitor Center
Chisos Basin Trailhead
Lodge
Cottages

Road into Chisos Basin not recommended for trailers longer than 20 feet and RVs over 24 feet because of sharp curves and steep grades.

Casa Grande
7,325 ft

Basin Loop Trail

Laguna Meadow Trail

Pinnacles Trail

Toll Mountain
7,415 ft

Emory Peak Trail

Emory Peak

the must-see scenic windows of Grapevine Hills. The heart of the park has abandoned mines, scrub vegetation around the Chisos, and deserts lying just below soaring Chisos Mountain aeries. **Carry enough drinking water—a gallon per person daily (more when extremely hot).** ⇨ *Multisport Outfitters box for guided hiking expeditions.*

EASY **Chihuahuan Desert Nature Trail.** A windmill and spring form a desert ☽ oasis, a refreshing backdrop to a ½-mi, hot and flat nature trail; wild ★ doves are abundant, the hike is pleasant, and kids will do just fine. While you're there, keep an eye out for the elf owl, one of the sought-after birds on the Big Bend's "Top 10" list. ✉*Dugout Wells, 5 mi southeast of Panther Junction.*

☽ **Rio Grande Village Nature Trail.** This ¾-mi trail is short and easy yet packs a powerful wildlife punch. The village is considered one of the best spots in the park to see rare birds, and the variety of other wildlife isn't in short supply either. Keep a lookout for coyotes, javelinas (they look like wild pigs), and other mammals. Although this is a good trail for kids to lay their tootsies on, it isn't the most remote, so expect higher traffic. Nearby facilities are closed in the summer. Restrooms (open year-round) are nearby, and the trail can be done in less than an hour, even when lingering. The first ¼ mi is wheelchair accessible. ✉*22 mi southeast of Panther Junction.*

MULTISPORT OUTFITTERS

Big Bend River Tours. Exploring the Rio Grande is their specialty. Tours include rafting, canoeing, and hiking and horseback trips combined with a river float. Rafting tours include gourmet or music themes. ⌂ *Box 317, Terlingua, TX 79852* ☎ *800/545–4240* ⊕ *www.bigbendrivertours.com.*

Desert Sports. From rentals—mountain bikes, boats, rafts, and inflatable kayaks—to experienced guides for mountain-bike touring, boating, and hiking, this outfitter has it covered. ⊠ *Box 448, Terlingua* ☎ *432/371–2727 or 888/989–6900* ⊕ *www.desertsportstx.com.*

Far Flung Outdoor Center. Call these pros for personalized trips via rafts and 4x4s. Tailored trips include gourmet rafting tours with cheese and wine served on checkered tablecloths alongside the river, and sometimes spectacular star-viewing at night. ⊠ *Box 377, Terlingua* ☎ *800/839–7238* ⊕ *www.farflungoutdoorcenter.com.*

Red Rock Outfitters. This outfitter sells clothing and gear, and leads river-rafting, canoeing, horseback-riding, and mountain-biking excursions, as well as Jeep and ATV tours. ⊠ *HC 70 Box 400, Lajitas* ☎ *432/424–5170.*

☾ **Window View Nature Trail.** This .3-mi nature trail is wheelchair accessible and great for little ones. Take in the beautiful, craggy-sided Chisos with ease, as this self-guiding trail is easily accomplished in less than an hour. ⊠ *The trail begins in the Chisos Basin.*

MODERATE **The Lost Mine Trail.** Set aside about two hours to leisurely explore the nature of the Chisos Mountains along this elevation-climbing trail. It starts at 5,400 feet, one of the highest elevations in the park, and climbs to an even higher vantage point. Though the air is thinner, all but the smallest kids should enjoy this trail because of the sweeping cliff view at the end of the first mile. The entire length of the trail is 4.8 mi round-trip. ⊠ *Begin at mile marker 5 on the Basin Rd..*

DIFFICULT **Chisos Basin Loop Trail.** A forested area and higher elevations give you
★ some sweeping views of the lower desert and distant volcanic mountains on this 1.6-mi round-trip. The elevation in the pass where the trail begins is 5,400 feet; the highest point on the trail is 7,825 feet. What makes this trail difficult is not the length, but the climb. Set aside about an hour. ⊠ *7 mi southwest of Chisos Basin Junction.*

Hot Springs Trail. An abandoned motel and a bathhouse foundation are among the sights along this 2-mi hike. The Rio Grande is heard at every turn, and trees shelter the walkway. Temperatures can soar to 120°F, so hike it during cooler months. ⊠ *22 mi southeast of Panther Junction.*

Fodor'sChoice **Santa Elena Canyon Trail.** A 1.7-mi round-trip crosses Terlingua Creek
★ and takes hikers to a view of steep cliffs jutting above the Rio Grande. Try to end up there near sunset, when the dying sun stains the cliffs a rich red-brown chestnut—its beauty can inspire poetry. It's a moderate-to-difficult trail, and worth every bead of sweat. ⊠ *8 mi west of Castolon, accessible via Ross Maxwell Scenic Dr. or Old Maverick Rd..*

HORSEBACK RIDING

At Big Bend, guides give horseback tours, and visitors can bring their own horses. The going might be slow in some parts, as horses aren't allowed on paved roads. Trips range from two hours to several days. If you're bringing your own horses, call any visitor center at least a day ahead of time to get a permit. You may camp with your horse at any of the park's primitive campsites, but not in the developed areas. A campsite with corrals near Panther Junction may be reserved (no longer than 10 weeks' notice) by calling ☎432/477–1158.

OUTFITTERS &
EXPEDITIONS

Lajitas Stables. Guided horseback-riding tours include participation in an honest-to-goodness, brand-to-hide cattle drive. You can also foray into the Mexican state of Chihuahua, via horse, on a 4- to 5-day trip. ⊠ *Box 6, Terlingua* ☎*888/508–7667* ⊕*www.lajitasstables.com.*

> **FAMILY PICKS**
>
> ■ **Cowboy Poetry.** Cowboys and cowgirls regale with tales at the Museum of the Big Bend's annual event.
>
> ■ **McDonald Observatory's Star Parties.** Guides lead observers on a tour of the celestial bodies.
>
> ■ **Haunted Trails.** In October an old movie set in Big Bend Ranch State Park is transformed into a ghost town. Come in costume.
>
> ■ **Overnight Rafting Trips.** Far Flung Outdoor Center sometimes offers Spring Break trips only for families with kids under 12. Trips include short hikes, goggles for stargazing, and canoeing.

JEEP TOURS

Wheeled traffic is welcome in the park, up to a point. RVs, trucks, cars, and Jeeps are allowed in designated areas, though personal ATV use is prohibited. Jeep rental isn't available inside the park, but Jeep and ATV tours are given by outfitters just outside the park, and often include lunch and interpretive talks. Jeep tours can cost as little as $40 for a two-hour tour, while ATV tours ring up at about $120 for the first person, with reduced rates for accompanying riders.

SWIMMING

Though it might be tempting to doff sweat-drenched T-shirts in favor of bathing suits, be careful where you take your dips. The Rio Grande has ample waters, but swimming isn't recommended due to dangerous currents and high pollution levels.

EDUCATIONAL OFFERINGS

CLASSES & SEMINARS

Big Bend Seminars. The Big Bend National History Association offers one- to two-day seminars covering subjects such as wildflowers, geology, and desert survival. Class size is limited, generally from 5 to 15, and the seminars are operated by a group called Far Flung Adventures. ⊠ *Held at locations throughout the park* ☎*877/839–5337* ⊕*bbnha@ nps.gov* ✉ *Fees vary.*

RANGER PROGRAMS

Birding Talks. Rangers lead two-hour birding tours; binoculars are needed. ⊠ *Chisos Basin Visitor Center* ☎ *432/477–2264* ⊙ *Daily 9–4:30 (varies by season), closed for lunch.*

Interpretive Activities. Ranger-guided activities include daily slide shows, talks, and walks on natural and cultural history. Check visitor centers and campground bulletin boards for event postings. ☎ *432/477–2251.*

Junior Ranger Program. This self-guiding program for kids 7 to 15 is taught via a $2 booklet of nature-based activities (available at visitor centers). Upon completion of the course, kids are given a Junior Ranger badge or patch, a certificate, and a bookmark. ☎ *432/477–2251.*

> **FUN FESTIVAL**
>
> **Terlingua International Chili Championship**—Each November, top chili chefs spice up cooling weather with four days of chili cooking, bragging, and gathering at Rancho CASI, on the north side of Highway 170, 11 mi east of Lajitas. Some of the prize-winning cooks dole out samples. ⊠ *Terlingua* ☎ *214/392–3499* ⊕ *www.chili.org/terlingua.html.*

WHAT'S NEARBY

Just as many of Big Bend's zones are geographically isolated, the park itself is isolated among hundreds upon hundreds of miles of West Texas desert and scrub. The nearest metropolis is El Paso, about 320 mi away, while the nearest sizable cities are Odessa and Midland, 210 and 240 mi to the northeast. Those who fancy a border crossing can also choose from a couple of Mexican destinations.

NEARBY TOWNS

Marathon, just 50 mi to the north, is one of the closest towns to Big Bend. Once a shipping hub, the population-500 town still contains reminders of its Old West railroad days. **Alpine,** a town of about 6,000, hunkers down among the Davis Mountains, about 70 mi north of the park. The town is known for its extensive college agriculture program at Sul Ross University. It also attracts celebrities like Will and Jada Pinkett-Smith, who have been spotted at its historic Holland Hotel. About 26 mi west of Alpine is **Marfa,** a population-2,000, middle-of-nowhere West Texas city known for its spooky, unexplained "Marfa lights," attributed to everything from atmospheric disturbances to imagination. Once the headquarters of quicksilver mining (now defunct), **Terlingua,** population 25, is just 5 mi from the park's west entrance on Highway 118. To the east 5 mi is **Study Butte** (pop. 100), which also has its roots in the old quicksilver mining industry. Follow Highway 170 west from Terlingua for 13 mi and you come upon the flat-rock formations of the tiny (pop. 50) **Lajitas.** Once a U.S. Cavalry outpost, Lajitas, which means (loosely) "tableland with little flat stones," has been converted to a resort area offering plenty of golf and tennis. The border town of **Presidio,** 70 mi from the park's west exit, is regarded as the gateway to northern

Mexico. Across the border from Presidio is a Spring Break favorite, **Ojinaga, Mexico,** famous for its party-like atmosphere. A railroad beginning in Ojinaga can take you to Copper Canyon, a striking series of canyons that runs down the west side of the Sierra Tarahumara.

> **CAUTION**
>
> ⚠ If you try to enter the U.S. through Big Bend National Park, you're subject to thousands in fines and/or one year's imprisonment.

From Presidio it's easy to cross the border. You can hop a bus, hail a cab, park and walk, or drive your vehicle across. Many people choose public transportation or walking, because in order to drive your car into Mexico, you must have a permit ($15 per person). Bring your passport. For details, see the Department of State's Web site (⊕ *www.travel.state.gov). For more information on visiting Mexico, ⇨ the Travel into Mexico section in Texas Essentials at the back of the book.*

NEARBY ATTRACTIONS

Barton Warnock Environmental Education Center. A self-guided walking tour takes you through indoor and outdoor exhibits providing insight into cultural history and natural resources of the Big Bend area. It's a good way to become oriented to Chihuahua Desert plant life before touring Big Bend. In the summer, the center offers desert garden tours. ⊠ *Off Rte. 170, 1 mi east of Lajitas, Terlingua* ☎ *432/424–3327* ⊕ *www. tpwd.state.tx.us/park/barton/barton.htm* ✉ *$3; $14 per group for the Desert Garden Tours* ⊙ *Daily 8–4:30.*

Big Bend Ranch State Park. As a southwest buffer to Big Bend National Park, this rugged desert wilderness extends along the Rio Grande across more than 300,000 acres from southeast of Lajitas to Presidio. You can hike, backpack, raft, and even round up longhorn steers on the annual cattle drive put on by the park in March or April of each year. ⊠ *Entrance road at Fort Leaton, 4 mi southeast of Presidio off Rte. 170, Presidio* ☎ *432/229–3416* ⊕ *www.tpwd.state.tx.us/park/ bigbend/bigbend.htm* ✉ *$3 entrance fee, $3 activity fee* ⊙ *24/7, year-round; centers are open daily 8–5.*

☺ **Fort Leaton State Historic Site** The 23-acre site in Presidio County contains a thick-walled adobe trading post that dates back to pioneer days. There are exhibits, a ½-mi trail, picnic sites, and a store. The park is day use only—no camping is available. ⊠ *4 mi south of Presidio on Hwy. 170, Presidio* ☎ *432/229–3416* ⊕ *www.tpwd.state.tx.us/spdest/ findadest/parks/fort_leaton* ✉ *$3* ⊙ *Daily 8–4:30.*

AREA ACTIVITIES

SPORTS & THE OUTDOORS

GOLFING Golfing opportunities in general are few and far between in the spread-out towns of West Texas—with the exception of Lajitas. The little resort town offers the **Ambush Golf Course** (⊠ *HC 70 Box 400, Lajitas*

☎432/424–5080), a public, 18-hole course set into the banks of the Rio Grande, about 12 mi from the center of town. Golf lessons are offered. Greens fees at this par-72 course are $45 Monday through Thursday, then $55 Friday through Sunday.

WHERE TO EAT & STAY

ABOUT THE RESTAURANTS

One word can sum up the fare available in the park: casual. You can wear jeans and sneakers to the one park restaurant, which has American-style fare. Outside the park, Alpine and Marfa in West Texas (⇨ West Texas chapter)have the biggest selection.

ABOUT THE HOTELS

At the only hotel in the park, the Chisos Basin Mountain Lodge, visitors can select from a freestanding cabin or a hotel room, both within a pace or two of spectacular views—Chisos sunsets are not to be missed. It's fun to stay here because it's close to trails, and has a nice little gift shop and the park's only restaurant. Even if you don't stay here, go just to see the stunning view through the wall-sized dining room windows. Outside the park, the area boasts the Lajitas Resort and some more moderately priced hotels, especially farther north in Alpine and Marfa (⇨ West Texas chapter).

ABOUT THE CAMPGROUNDS

The park's copious campsites are separated, roughly, into two categories—front country and backcountry. Each of its four front-country sites has toilet facilities at a minimum. You can reserve a spot at these popular places from November 15 to April 15, and rangers recommend doing so as far in advance as possible. During the off-season, sites are given on a first-come, first-served basis. Make reservations by phone at ☎877/444–6777 or online at ⊕www.reserveusa.com.

Far more numerous are the primitive backcountry sites, which have no amenities and are generally inaccessible via RV. Free permits, obtained from the visitor center, are needed to camp there.

WHAT IT COSTS					
	¢	$	$$	$$$	$$$$
RESTAURANTS	under $8	$8–$12	$13–$20	$21–$30	over $30
HOTELS	under $50	$50–$100	$101–$150	$151–$200	over $200
CAMP-GROUNDS	under $10	$10–$17	$18–$35	$36–$49	over $50

Restaurant prices are per person for a main course at dinner. Hotel prices are per night for two people in a standard double room in high season, excluding taxes and service charges. Camping prices are for a standard (no hookups, pit toilets, fire grates, picnic tables) campsite per night.

WHERE TO EAT

IN THE PARK

¢–$$ ✕**Chisos Mountains Lodge Restaurant.** Views of the imposing Chisos Mountains are a pleasant accompaniment to nicely prepared (but not fancy) fare such as chicken-fried steak and hamburgers. The view is great and the salad bar isn't bad, and there is a takeout hiker's lunch. Try the firm Imperial shrimp, raised not far from the park. ⊠*7 mi southwest of Chisos Basin Junction and 9 mi southwest of Panther Junction* ☎*432/477–2291* ☐*AE, D, DC, MC, V.*

PICNIC AREAS **Rio Grande Village Area.** Half a dozen picnic tables are scattered under cottonwoods south of the store. Half a mile away at Daniels Ranch there are two tables and a grill. Wood fires aren't allowed (charcoal and propane okay). ⊠*2 mi southeast of Panther Junction.*

Dugout Wells Area. There is a picnic table under the shady cottonwoods off the Dugout Wells Trail loop. There is also a vault toilet here (these type of facilities are more pleasant than pit toilets). However, as with all vault toilets in the park, there is no running water to wash your hands. We suggest bringing some hand wipes. ⊠*5 mi southeast of Panther Junction.*

Santa Elena Canyon Area. Two tables sit in the shade next to the parking lot at the trailhead. There is a vault toilet. ⊠*8 mi west of Castolon, accessible via Ross Maxwell scenic drive or Old Maverick Rd..*

Castolon Area. There are two tables here next to the store parking lot.

Chisos Basin Area. There are about half a dozen tables scattered near the parking lot, as well as a few grills. The tables provide an awesome view of the Chisos Mountains. ⊠*Off Chisos Basin Rd., 7 mi southwest of Chisos Basin Junction and 9 mi southwest of Panther Junction.*

Persimmon Gap Area. Quiet and remote, this new picnic area has tables shaded by metal roofs called ramadas. There are no grills; there is a pit toilet. ⊠*North Big Bend, 4 mi south of U.S. 385 junction.*

OUTSIDE THE PARK

$–$$$ ✕**Candelilla Cafe and Thirsty Goat Saloon.** Steaks, Southwestern dishes, and Mexican-inspired fare are Candelilla's specialties. Glass walls give you unobstructed views of sunsets and the nearby golf course, and a quick stroll next door finds you a nightcap at the Thirsty Goat Saloon. ⊠*Lajitas Resort, off Rte. 170, 25 mi west of park entrance, Lajitas* ☎*432/424–5010* ☐*AE, D, DC, MC, V.*

WHERE TO STAY

IN THE PARK

$$ ▭**Chisos Mountains Lodge.** Views of desert peaks and staying in the cooler, forested section of Big Bend's higher elevations more than make up for the spartan rooms. With ranger talks just next door at the visitor center, miles of easy hiking paths, and plenty of wildlife, this is a great place for kids. Make advance reservations during busy times,

such as Thanksgiving and Spring Break—up to a year's lead time is not out of the question. Guests can rent a TV/VCR and movies. ⊠ *7 mi southwest of Chisos Basin Junction and 9 mi southwest of Panther Junction* ☎ *432/477–2291* ⮐ *72 rooms* ♿ *In-room: no phone, no TV. In-hotel: restaurant, some pets allowed, no-smoking rooms* ▤ *AE, D, DC, MC, V.*

$ ⚠ **Chisos Basin Campground.** Scenic views and cool shade are the highlights here. Steep grades and twisting curves mean trailers longer than 20 feet and RVs longer than 25 feet are not recommended. ⊠ *7 mi southwest of Chisos Basin Junction* ☎ *432/477–2251* ⮐ *65 sites* ♿ *Flush toilets, drinking water, grills, picnic tables, food service, public telephone, general store, ranger station* ▤ *No credit cards.*

$ ⚠ **Cottonwood Campground.** This Castolon-area campground is a popular bird-watching spot. The grounds are generator free. ⊠ *Off Ross Maxwell Scenic Dr., 22 mi southwest of Santa Elena Junction* ☎ *432/477–2251* ⮐ *31 sites* ♿ *Pit toilets, drinking water, grills, picnic tables, general store, ranger station* ▤ *No credit cards.*

$ ⚠ **Rio Grande Village Campground.** A shady oasis, this campground is
☼ a birding "hot spot." It's also a great site for kids and seniors, due to
★ the ease of accessing facilities. RV parking is available. ⊠ *22 mi southeast of Panther Junction* ☎ *432/477–2251* ⮐ *100 RV and tent sites* ♿ *Flush toilets, dump station, drinking water, guest laundry, showers, grills, picnic tables, public telephone, general store, service station, ranger station* ▤ *No credit cards.*

$ ⚠ **Rio Grande Village RV Park.** Often full during holidays, this is one of
☼ the best sites for families because of the toilet facilities, minitheater, and proximity to the hot spring, which is fun to swim in at night. Register at the Rio Grande Village Store (22 mi southeast of Panther Junction). Only 30-amp electrical connections are available. You must have a 3-inch sewer connection to stay here. ⊠ *22 mi southeast of Panther Junction* ☎ *432/477–2293* ⮐ *25 RV sites* ♿ *Flush toilets, dump station, drinking water, guest laundry, grills, picnic tables, electricity, public telephone, general store, service station, ranger station* ▤ *AE, D, MC, V* ♿ *Reservations not accepted.*

¢ ⚠ **Backcountry camping.** Primitive campsites with spectacular views
★ are accessed via the following backcountry roads: River Road, Glenn Springs, Old Ore Road, Paint Gap, Old Maverick Road, Grapevine Hills, Pine Canyon, and Croton Springs. There are also some along these main roads: Nine Point Draw, Hannold Draw, and K-Bar. ⊠ *Throughout the park* ☎ *432/477–2251.*

OUTSIDE THE PARK

$$$–$$$$ ⊡ **Lajitas Resort.** This is the nicest place to eat, shop, and overnight
Fodor's Choice within 25 mi of the park. Various theme motels and lodging options
★ are available (under the same ownership) in this revived ghost town converted into a classy, Old West–style resort community alongside the Rio Grande. Conveniences within walking distance of Lajitas include a restaurant, lounge, and golf course. Make reservations well in advance of holidays and Spring Break. Some visitors have noted that service here can lag behind the reputation. **Pros:** Resort is a town unto itself,

many luxury activities, full spa, golf course. **Cons:** Quite expensive, property may be sold soon. ⊠*Highway 170, 17 mi west of Highway 118,* ⌂*HC 70, Box 400, Lajitas* ☎*432/424–5000, 877/525–4827 reservations* ⊕*www.lajitas.com* ↩*72 rooms, 16 suites, 2 cottages* ⌂*In-room: kitchen (some), refrigerator (some). In-hotel: 3 restaurants, bar, golf course, tennis court, pool, spa, bicycles, laundry service, nosmoking rooms* ⊟*AE, D, DC, MC, V.*

¢ 🏕️**Big Bend Motor Inn and RV Campground.** Shade trees and a scenic setting make this a nice RV roosting place within 3 mi of the west park entrance. But the motel rooms are overpriced for spartan accommodations, and service can be less than cordial here and at the grocery store and restaurant near the premises. Convenience may outweigh disadvantages. **Pros:** Full-service campground. **Cons:** Service can be hit or miss. ⊠*Hwy. 118, 3 mi west of west park entrance, Terlingua* ☎*800/848–2363* ⊕*www.texbesthotels.com/bigbend_motorinn.htm* ↩*84 motel rooms, 126 RV sites, separate informal tent area* ⌂*Flush toilets, full hookups, drinking water, guest laundry, showers, grills, picnic tables, food service, electricity, public telephone, general store, service station* ⊟*AE, D, DC, MC, V.*

BIG BEND ESSENTIALS

For more information on visiting national parks, go to ⊕*fodors. com/parks.*

ACCESSIBILITY

Visitor centers and some campsites and restrooms at Rio Grande Village and Chisos Basin are wheelchair accessible. A TDD line (☎432/477–2370) is available at park headquarters at Panther Junction Visitor Center. Wheelchair-accessible hiking trails include the Founder's Walk and Panther Path at Panther Junction; Window View Trail at Chisos Basin; and Rio Grande Village Nature Trail boardwalk. The Rio Grande and Chisos Basin amphitheaters also are accessible.

ADMISSION FEES

It costs $20 to enter at the gate, and your pass is good for seven days. Camping fees in developed campgrounds are $14 per night; it's free to camp in primitive areas (backcountry permits required).

ADMISSION HOURS

The park never closes. Visitor centers may be closed Christmas Day. The park is in the Central time zone.

ATMS/BANKS

The park has no ATMs.

Contacts Quicksilver Branch Bank and ATM (⊠*At intersection of Rte. 118 and Rte. 170, Study Butte/Terlingua* ☎*432/371–2211).*

AUTOMOBILE SERVICE STATIONS

There are two Chevron gas stations in the park: the one at Panther Junction does minor work (oil and tires), and the Rio Grande Village one offers gas, and propane for camp stoves.

Contacts **Panther Junction FINA** (✉ *26 mi south of north park entrance* ☎ *432/477–2294*). **Rio Grande Village FINA** (✉ *22 mi southeast of Panther Junction* ☎ *432/477–2293*). **Terlingua Auto** (✉ *Off Hwy. 170 in the Terlingua business district, Terlingua,* ☎ *432/371–2223*).

EMERGENCIES

Dial 911 or 432/477–1188. Medical services are just outside the park in tiny communities along Route 170.

Contacts **Big Bend Regional Medical Center** (✉ *2600 N. Highway 118Alpine,* ☎ *432/837–3447*). **Terlingua Medics** (✉ *Terlingua* ☎ *432/371–2536*).

LOST AND FOUND

The park's lost-and-found is at Panther Junction Visitor Center.

PERMITS

Mandatory backcountry camping, boating, and fishing permits are available for free at visitor centers.

POST OFFICES

Visitors can post letters and cards weekdays at the Panther Junction post office. There's also a mail drop at the Chisos Basin store.

PUBLIC TELEPHONES

Public telephones can be found at the visitor centers. Cell phones do not often work in the park.

SHOPS & GROCERS

Two shops at the Chisos Basin Junction in the park sell some of the basics for meals and camping.

Contacts **Chisos Basin Store and Post Office** (✉ *7 mi south of Chisos Basin Junction* ☎ *432/477–2291* ☉ *Daily 9–9*). **Chisos Mountain Lodge Gift and Photo Shop** (✉ *7 mi south of Chisos Basin Junction* ☎ *432/477–2291* ☉ *Daily, 7–9*). **La Harmonia Company Store** (✉ *35 mi southwest of Panther Junction at Castolon, 22 mi southwest of Santa Elena Junction* ☎ *432/477–2222* ☉ *Daily 10–6*). **Rio Grande Village Store** (✉ *22 mi southeast of Panther Junction* ☎ *432/477–2293* ☉ *Daily 9–6*).

NEARBY TOWN INFORMATION

Contacts **Big Bend Chamber of Commerce** ✉ *Hwy. 170 at Terlingua Creek (Box 607), Terlingua* ☎ *432/371–2427* ⊕ *www.bigbendchamber.com.*

Presidio Chamber of Commerce ✉ *Box 2497, Presidio, 79845* ☎ *432/229–3199* ⊕ *www.presidiotex.com.*

VISITOR INFORMATION

Contacts **Big Bend National Park** ✉ *Box 129, Big Bend National Park, 79834* ☎ *432/477–2251* ⊕ *www.nps.gov/bibe.*

Guadalupe Mountains National Park

WORD OF MOUTH

"May your trails be crooked, winding, lonesome, dangerous, leading to the most amazing view. May your mountains rise into and above the clouds."

—Edward Abbey,
environmental writer and activist

WELCOME TO GUADALUPE MOUNTAINS

El Capitan

Cutoff Mountain
6,933 ft

TOP REASONS TO GO

★ **Tower over Texas:** The park is home to 8,749-foot Guadalupe Peak, the highest point in the state.

★ **Fall for fiery foliage:** Though surrounded by arid desert and rocky soil, the park has miles of beautiful foliage in McKittrick Canyon. In late October you can watch it burst into flaming colors.

★ **Hike unhindered:** The main activity at the park is hiking its rugged, remote, and often challenging trails: 80 mi worth will keep you captivated and spry—and far away from civilization.

★ **Eat with elk, loll with lions:** Despite the surrounding arid region, a variety of wildlife—including shaggy brown elk, sneaky mountain lions, and shy black bears—traipses the mountains, woods, and desert here.

★ **Catch a (ghost) stagecoach:** In the late 1830s a stagecoach line ran from St. Louis and San Francisco with a stop at what's now Guadalupe Mountains National Park. The stages are long gone, but ruins of an old station still remain in the park, along with old ranch houses.

1 Guadalupe Peak. This crude, rocky pinnacle tops 8,700 feet and towers over the rest of the park's peaks. Those who brave the seven hour–plus round-trip to the summit are rewarded with breathtaking views of New Mexico and southwestern Texas.

2 McKittrick Canyon. In late October and early November, the lush green foliage along McKittrick Canyon's trout-filled desert stream bursts into russet, amber, and gold hues. An easy, handicapped-accessible ramble takes visitors through this geological wonder.

3 El Capitan. Not to be confused with equally impressive El Capitan in Yosemite National Park, this 3,000-foot cliff dominates the view at the southern end of the Guadalupe Range. It has visitors talking and hikers walking: a 6- to 11-mi–plus trail winds around the base of this massive limestone formation.

Texas Madrone

4 Manzanita Spring. The area around this idyllic stream and picnic spot has a little bit of everything: a spring feeds lush grasses and trees, giving life to hundreds of wildflowers. Birds hang out here to enjoy the tasty seeds and insects that the water, shade, and vegetation provide. Plus, it's only a 0.2-mi, paved ramble from here to the Frijole Ranch Museum.

5 Frijole Ranch Museum. This easily accessible historic ranch site houses the stone ruins of the oldest structure in the park. The recently restored ranch-house museum injects a bit of man-made history into the natural surroundings. Five nearby springs are just a refreshing stroll away.

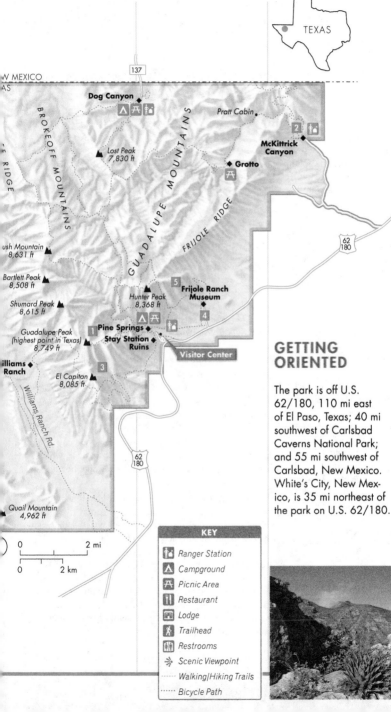

TEXAS

12

W MEXICO
AS

137

Dog Canyon 🏕️🏞️🚻

BROKEOFF MOUNTAINS

RIDGE

Lost Peak
7,830 ft ▲

Pratt Cabin

2 🚻

McKittrick Canyon

♦ **Grotto**
🏞️

GUADALUPE MOUNTAINS

FRIJOLE RIDGE

62
180

ush Mountain ▲
8,631 ft

Bartlett Peak ▲
8,508 ft

Shumard Peak ▲▲
8,615 ft

Hunter Peak ▲
8,368 ft

5 ♦ **Frijole Ranch Museum**

4

Guadalupe Peak
(highest point in Texas) ▲
8,749 ft

1 **Pine Springs** ♦ 🏕️🏞️🚻
Stay Station Ruins ♦

iliams
Ranch ♦

El Capitan ▲
8,085 ft

3

Williams Ranch Rd.

Visitor Center

GETTING ORIENTED

The park is off U.S. 62/180, 110 mi east of El Paso, Texas; 40 mi southwest of Carlsbad Caverns National Park; and 55 mi southwest of Carlsbad, New Mexico. White's City, New Mexico, is 35 mi northeast of the park on U.S. 62/180.

62
180

Quail Mountain
4,962 ft

0 — 2 mi
0 — 2 km

KEY	
🚻	Ranger Station
🏕️	Campground
🏞️	Picnic Area
🍴	Restaurant
🏠	Lodge
🚶	Trailhead
🚻	Restrooms
🔭	Scenic Viewpoint
----	Walking/Hiking Trails
......	Bicycle Path

GUADALUPE MOUNTAINS NATIONAL PARK

When to Go

Trails here are rarely crowded, except in fall, when foliage changes colors in McKittrick Canyon, and during Spring Break in March. Still, this is a very remote area, and you probably won't find too much congestion at any time. Hikers are more apt to explore back-country trails in spring and fall, when it's cooler but not too cold. Snow, not uncommon in the winter months, can linger in the higher elevations.

Getting There & Around

Since about half of the Guadalupe Mountains is a designated wilderness, few roadways penetrate the park. Most sites are accessible off U.S. 62/180. Dog Canyon Campground on the north end of the park can be reached via Route 137, which traverses the woodlands of Lincoln National Forest.

AVG. HIGH/LOW TEMPS

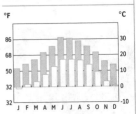

Flora & Fauna

Despite the constant wind and the arid conditions, more than a thousand species of plants populate the mountains, chasms, and salt dunes that make up the park's different geologic zones. Some grow many feet in a single night; others bloom so infrequently they're called "century plants." Some of the most spectacular sights, however, are seasonal. In fall, McKittrick Canyon's oaks, bigtooth maples, and velvet ashes go Technicolor above the little stream that traverses it. Barren-looking cacti burst into yellow, red, and purple bloom in spring, and wildflowers can carpet the park for thousands of acres after unusually heavy rains.

Hundreds of animal species haunt the diverse environments of the Guadalupes. At last count there were nearly 300 different bird species, 90 types of butterflies, and 16 species of bats alone. The park's furry residents include coyotes, black bears, and badgers. You may also spot elk, which were reintroduced here in the late 1920s after nearly becoming wiped out here.

Plenty of reptiles and insects make their homes here too: coachwhip snakes, diamondback rattlers, and lovelorn tarantulas (the only time you'll spy them is in the fall, when they search for mates), to name a few. Texas's famous horned lizards—affectionately called "horny toads"—can also be seen waddling across the soil in search of ants and other insects. Rangers caution parents not to let little ones run too far ahead on the trails. ■TIP➔ **Be mindful that rattlesnakes are common in the park. They aren't aggressive, but be sure to give a wide berth to any snakes your hear or spot.**

By Jennifer
Edwards

GUADALUPE MOUNTAINS NATIONAL PARK IS a study in extremes: it has mountaintop forests but also rocky canyons; arid deserts and yet a stream that winds through verdant woods. The park is home to the Texas madrone tree, found commonly only here and in Big Bend National Park. Guadalupe Mountains National Park also has the distinction of hosting the loftiest spot in Texas: 8,749-foot Guadalupe Peak. The mountain dominates the view from every approach, but it's just one member of a rugged range carved by wind, water, and time.

More than 86,000 acres of mountains, chasms, canyons, woods, and deserts house an incredible diversity of wildlife, including hallmark Southwestern species like roadrunners and long-limbed jackrabbits, which run so fast they appear to float on their enormous, black-tipped ears.

SCENIC DRIVE

Williams Ranch Road. You'll take in panoramic views and get an up-close look at limestone cliffs on this 7¼-mi, one-way drive over what was once the Bitterfield Overland Mail Stage Line. The closest highway, U.S. 180, parallels the old trail. The rough route—you'll need a high-clearance, four-wheel-drive vehicle or a mountain bike—is enjoyable. To drive it, get a gate key at the visitor center and drive west on U.S. 62/180 for 8.25 mi until you see a brown metal gate on the north side with a National Park Service sign. Drive through two locked gates (be sure to lock them behind you), and follow the road to an old, lonely ranch house. James "Dolph" Williams operated this spread with his partner, an Indian named Geronimo (no relation to the historical figure). The road closes at night, though, so don't tarry too long.

WHAT TO SEE

HISTORIC SITES

✪ **Frijole Ranch Museum.** You'll find displays and photographs depicting ranch life and early park history inside this old ranch-house museum. Hiking trails are adjacent to the shady, tree-lined grounds. Some of the trails, which are easy to travel and great for kids, lead to the **Manzanita Spring.** ⊠ *Access road 1 mi northeast of Headquarters Visitors Center* ☎ *915/828–3251* ☜ *Free* ☾ *Call for hours.*

★ **Pinery Bitterfield Stage Station Ruins.** In the mid-1800s passengers en route from St. Louis or San Francisco would stop for rest and refreshment this structure, one of the stops along the old Bitterfield Overland Mail stagecoach route. A paved ¾-mi round-trip trail leads here from the Headquarters Visitors Center, or you can drive directly here. ⊠ *½ mi east of Headquarters Visitors Center.*

SCENIC STOP

Fodor'sChoice **McKittrick Canyon.** A desert creek flows through this canyon, which is
★ lined with walnut, maple, and other trees that explode into brilliant colors each fall. Call the visitor center to find out the progress of the colorful fall foliage; the spectacular changing of the leaves can often

GUADALUPE MOUNTAINS IN ONE DAY

Start your tour at **Headquarters Visitor Center,** where a year-round exhibit and slide show will introduce the park's wildlife and geology. Nearby is the ¾-mi round-trip, handicapped-accessible **Pinery Trail,** which rambles to the Pinery Bitterfield Stage Station ruins. Take in the sites, but be sure not to touch the fragile walls; the site is more vulnerable than most. Next, head to the **Frijole Ranch Museum,** built in 1876 and preserved through several renovations.

Once you're done gawking at the old structures, stroll to the calming waters of **Manzanita Spring.** Turn onto the paved trailhead behind the ranch house for the 0.2-mi trek to the spring. Manzanita is one of five springs that gurgle within a couple of miles of the museum. Park staff call such areas riparian zones. These oases supply the fragile wildlife here, and can sometimes look like Pre-Raphaelite paintings, with mirrored-surface ponds and delicate flowers and greenery.

Afterward, pay a visit to the famed **McKittrick Canyon.** Regardless of the season, the dense foliage and basin stream are worth the hike—though it's best to visit it in late October and early November when the trees burst into color. There isn't a direct route, but you can get here quickly by driving northeast from the visitor center on U.S. 62/180. Follow it to the gate at the western turnoff, which is locked at sunset. Head northwest through the gate (ignoring the service road) in your car, and you'll arrive at the canyon.

Take your time walking the **McKittrick Canyon Trail** that leads to Pratt Lodge, or the strenuous but rewarding 8.4-mi **Permian Reef Trail,** which takes you up thousands of feet, past monumental geological formations. Or traverse the easy, short (less than 1 mi) **McKittrick Canyon Nature Trail.**

take until November, depending on the weather. You're likely to spot mule deer heading for the water here. ⊠4 mi off U.S. 62/180, about 7 mi northeast of Headquarters Visitor Center ☉ Highway gate open Nov.–Apr., daily 8–4:30; May–Sept., daily 8–6.

VISITOR CENTERS

Headquarters Visitors Center. Exhibits and a slide show here give you a quick introduction to the park, half of which is a wilderness area. Some nicely crafted exhibits depict typical wildlife and plant scenes. ⊠U.S. 62/180, 55 mi southwest of Carlsbad, 110 mi east of El Paso ☎915/828–3251 ☉June–Aug., daily 8–6; Sept.–May, daily 8–4:30.

McKittrick Contact Station. Poster-size illustrations in a shaded, outdoor patio area tell the geological story of the Guadalupe Mountains, believed to have been carved from an ancient sea. You can also hear the recorded memoirs of oilman Wallace Pratt, who donated his ranch and surrounding area to the federal government for preservation. ⊠4 mi off U.S. 62/180, 7 mi northeast of Headquarters Visitor Center ☎915/828–3251 (Headquarters Visitor Center) ☉June–Aug., daily 8–6; Sept.–May, daily 8–4:30.

SPORTS & THE OUTDOORS

BIRD-WATCHING

More than 300 species of birds have been spotted in the park, including the ladder-backed woodpecker, Scott's oriole, Say's phoebe, and white-throated swift. Many non-native birds—such as fleeting humming birds and larger but less graceful turkey vultures—stop at Guadalupe during spring and fall migrations. **Manzanita Springs**, located near the Frijole Ranch Museum, is an excellent birding spot. As with hiking, there aren't any local guides, but rangers at the Dog Canyon and Pine Springs stations can help you spot some native species. Books on birding are available at the Pine Springs station; visitors might find the Natural History Association's birding checklist for Guadalupe Mountains National Park especially helpful. It will be easy to spot the larger birds of prey circling overhead, such as keen-beaked golden eagles and swift, red-tailed hawks. Be on the lookout for owls in the **Bowl** area, and watch for swift-footed roadrunners in the desert areas (they're quick, but not as speedy as their cartoon counterpart).

HIKING

No matter which trail you select, be sure to pack wisely—the park doesn't sell anything. This includes the recommended gallon of water per day per person, as well as sunscreen and hats. (Bring a five, too—that's the additional cost to use the trails, payable at the visitor centers.) The area has a triple-whammy as far as sun ailments are concerned: it's very open, very sunny, and has a high altitude (which makes sunburns more likely). Slather up. And be sure to leave Fido at home—few of the park's trails allow pets. The staff at the **Dog Canyon ranger station** (☎ *505/981–2418*) can help you plan your hike. The bookstore at the **Pine Springs ranger station** also sells hiking guides. These and other guides can also be found at ⊕*www.ccgma.org.*

EASY
The **Indian Meadows Nature Trail** in Dog Canyon is a very easy, mostly level ½-mi hike that crosses an arroyo into meadowlands. It's a good way to spend about 45 minutes savoring the countryside.

Fodor's Choice
★
The easiest McKittrick trail is the 1-mi **McKittrick Nature Loop.** Signs along the way explain the geological and biological history of the area. The trail is handicapped accessible and great for little ones. Plus, you can see the canyon's signature foliage in the late fall.

MODERATE
Bush Mountain, a moderate 4.5-mi round-trip, rewards you with a panoramic view of West Dog Canyon. It will take about half a day to complete. ⊠*Rte. 137, 60 mi southwest of U.S. 285.*

The moderate **Devil's Hall Trail** runs through about 4 mi of Chihuahua Desert habitat, thick with spiked agave plants, prickly pear cacti, and giant boulders, and Devil's Hall, a narrow canyon about 10 feet wide and 100 feet deep. This moderate hike, which begins at the Pine Springs trailhead, will take about a day if you travel at a leisurely pace.

★
The **El Capitan/Salt Basin Overlook Trails** form a popular loop through the low desert. El Capitan skirts the base of El Capitan peak for about 3.5 mi, leading to a junction with Salt Basin Overlook. The 4.5-mi Salt

Basin Overlook trail begins at the Pine Springs trailhead and has views of the stark, white salt flat below and loops back onto the El Capitan Trail. Though moderate, the 11.3-mi round-trip is not recommended during the intense heat of summer, since there is absolutely no shade. ⊠*Behind Headquarters Visitor Center at Pine Springs campground.*

The **Frijole/Foothills Trail,** which branches off the Frijole Ranch trailhead, leads to the Pine Springs campground behind Headquarters Visitors Center. The moderate, 5.5-mi round-trip route through desert vistas takes about five hours.

The 6.75-mi round-trip to the **Grotto Picnic Area** starts at the McKittrick Contact Station. It affords views of a flowing stream and surface rock that resembles formations in an underground cave, with jagged overhangs. Plan on about five hours for a leisurely walk.

You can view stream and canyon woodland areas along the **Pratt Lodge Trail,** a 4.5-mi round-trip excursion that leads to the now vacant Pratt Lodge. Plan on at least two hours if you walk at a fast pace, but give yourself another hour or two if you want to take your time. ⊠*4 mi off U.S. 62/180, about 7 mi northeast of Headquarters Visitor Center.*

The **Smith Spring Trail** also departs from the Frijole Ranch trailhead. The trail, a round-trip walk of 2.2 mi, takes you through a shady oasis where you're likely to spot mule deer alongside a spring and a small waterfall. Allow 1½ hours to complete the walk. This is a good hike for older kids, whose legs won't tire as easily. ⊠*Access road 1 mi northeast of Headquarters Visitors Center.*

DIFFICULT
★

Cutting through forests of pine and Douglas fir, **The Bowl** is considered one of the most gorgeous trails in the park. The strenuous 9-mi round-trip—which can take up to 10 hours, depending on your pace—begins at the Pine Springs trailhead. This is where rangers go when they want to enjoy themselves. Don't forget to drink (and bring) lots of water!

The 8.5-mi **Guadalupe Peak Trail** is a strenuous workout over a steep grade, but it offers some great views of exposed cliff faces. The hike begins at the Pine Springs trailhead and can take up to eight hours to complete.

The somewhat strenuous **Lost Peak Trail** in Dog Canyon is 6.5-mi round-trip, which will take about six hours to complete if your pace is slower; it leads from Dog Canyon into a coniferous forest.

If you're in shape and have a serious geological bent, you may want to hike the **Permian Ridge Geology Trail.** The 8.5-mi round-trip climb heads through open, expansive desert country to a forested ridge with Douglas fir and ponderosa pines. Panoramic views of McKittrick Canyon and the surrounding mountain ranges will allow you to see the many rock layers that have been built up over the millennia. Begin at the McKittrick Contact Station, and set aside at least eight hours for this trek.

MOUNTAIN BIKING

If you've got a mountain bike or a high-clearance, four-wheel-drive vehicle, cruise to the **Williams Ranch Trail**. Skittering down it will only take about an hour one way (for vehicles) and will lead you to the **Williams Ranch House**, which sits alone at the base of a 3,000-foot cliff. ■TIP→ Before you set out, check out the gate key at the Headquarters Visitor Center. Then head west on Highway 62/180. Drive 8¼ mi to the brown metal gate with National Park signs; be sure to lock the gate behind you once you're through. Proceed for another ¾ mi to another gate; lock this one as well once you're through it. Follow the worn dirt road—which runs past arid scenery and cacti that bloom in the spring months—to the Ranch House, and enjoy a great view of El Capitan. Be sure to leave before sundown, and don't forget to return the key to the visitor center.

> **OUTFITTERS**
>
> The staff at **Dog Canyon Ranger Station** can help you plan your hikes. ⊠ Box 400, Pine Canyon Rd., Salt Flat ☎ 915/825–3251.
>
> Visit **Headquarters Visitor Center** for hiking advice. ☐ HC 60, Box 400, Salt Flat, 79847 ☎ 915/828–3251.

EDUCATIONAL OFFERINGS

RANGER PROGRAM

☾ ★ **Junior Ranger Program.** The park offers a self-guided Junior Ranger program: kids choose activities from a workbook—including taking nature hikes and answering questions based on park exhibits—and earn a patch and certificate once they've completed three. If they complete six, they earn an additional patch. ⊠ Headquarters Visitor Center ☎ 915/828–3251 Ext. 118 ☞ Free ☉ June–Aug., daily 8–6; Sept.–May, daily 8–4:30.

WHAT'S NEARBY

NEARBY U.S. TOWNS

Tiny **White's City, New Mexico**, 35 mi to the northeast off U.S. 62/180, is more of a crossroads than a town. The town of **Carlsbad, New Mexico**, 55 mi northeast of the park, has more amenities. For more information about both cities, including dining, lodging, and attractions, ⇨ Chapter 13, Carlsbad Caverns National Park.

WHERE TO STAY & EAT

ABOUT THE RESTAURANTS

Dining in the park is a do-it-yourself affair. Ranger stations don't serve meals or sell picnic items, though nearby White's City offers some basics—sodas, snacks, and the like.

ABOUT THE HOTELS

The Best Western in White's City, New Mexico, is your best local option (⇨ *Chapter 13, Carlsbad Caverns National Park*).

ABOUT THE CAMPGROUNDS

Visitors haul their supplies across miles to stretch out on the unsoiled land of several backcountry sites, but there are only two developed campsites in the park, Pine Springs and Dog Canyon.

WHAT IT COSTS					
	¢	$	$$	$$$	$$$$
RESTAURANTS	under $8	$8–$12	$13–$20	$21–$30	over $30
HOTELS	under $50	$50–$100	$101–$150	$151–$200	over $200
CAMP-GROUNDS	under $10	$10–$17	$18–$35	$36–$49	over $50

Restaurant prices are per person for a main course at dinner. Hotel prices are per night for two people in a standard double room in high season, excluding taxes and service charges. Camping prices are for a standard (no hookups, pit toilets, fire grates, picnic tables) campsite per night.

WHERE TO EAT

IN GUADALUPE MOUNTAINS

The park has no snack bars or restaurants, but several picnic areas are available. Wood and charcoal fires are not allowed anywhere in the park. If you want to cook a hot meal, bring a camp stove.

Dog Canyon Campground. Thirteen campsites have picnic tables, which you can use during the day for free. This is a lovely shaded area where you're very likely to see mule deer. Drinking water and restrooms are available at the site. This area is about a 2½-hour hike from the Headquarters Visitor Center (you can also drive there). ⊠ *Off Rte. 137, 65 mi southwest of Carlsbad.*

Frijole Ranch Museum. This area is much cooler than nearby Pine Springs Campground. Two picnic tables are set up under tall trees; restrooms are available at the ranch-house Housemuseum. ⊠ *Access road 1 mi northeast of Headquarters Visitor Center.*

Pine Springs Campground. Shade varies depending on the time of day, and it can be hard to find a cool spot in hot summer. You will find drinking water and restrooms here, though. ⊠ *Behind Headquarters Visitor Center.*

OUTSIDE THE PARK

For dining options in the nearby area, ⇨ *Chapter 13, Carlsbad Caverns National Park or Chapter 10, West Texas.*

WHERE TO STAY

The park has two developed campgrounds that charge fees, and a number of designated primitive, backcountry sites where you can camp for free (check with the visitor center about using primitive sites). Wood and charcoal fires are prohibited throughout the park, but you can use your camp stove. The same rules apply for backcountry sites; however, no restrooms are provided. Visitors may dig their own privies, but toilet paper and other paper waste should be packed out. There are no hotels within the park. *For information on lodging near the park, see Chapter 13, Carlsbad Caverns National Park.*

IN THE PARK

¢ **Dog Canyon Campground.** This campground is remote and a little tricky to find, but well worth the effort. Located on the north side of Guadalupe National Park, it can be accessed by turning west on County Road 408 off U.S. 62/180, about 9 mi south of Carlsbad. Drive 23 mi on this county road; then turn south on Highway 137. Travel 43 mi through Lincoln National Forest until the road dead-ends just at the park boundary, at the New Mexico–Texas state line. The very well-maintained camping area is located in a coniferous forest, with hiking trails nearby. ⊠ *Guadalupe Mountains National Park, off Rte. 137, 65 mi southwest of Carlsbad* ☎ *505/981–2418* ⤳ *4 RV sites, 9 tent sites* �½ *Flush toilets, drinking water, picnic tables, public telephone, ranger station* ▭ *AE, D, MC, V.*

¢ **Pine Springs Campground.** You'll be snuggled amid piñon and juniper trees at the base of a tall mountain peak at this site behind the Guadalupe Mountains National Park Visitor Center. Wood and charcoal fires are prohibited, although camp stoves are allowed. Shade here can be a bit sparse in the intense summer heat. Advance reservations are accepted for group sites only. ⊠ *Guadalupe Mountains National Park, off U.S. 62/180* ☎ *915/828–3251* ⤳ *20 tent sites, 18 RV sites, 1 wheelchair-accessible site, 2 group sites* �½ *Flush toilets, drinking water, picnic tables, public telephone, ranger station* ▭ *AE, D, MC, V.*

OUTSIDE THE PARK

For lodging and camping options in the nearby area, ⇨ *Chapter 13, Carlsbad Caverns National Park or Chapter 10, West Texas.*

GUADALUPE MOUNTAINS ESSENTIALS

For more information on visiting national parks, go to ⊕ *fodors.com/parks. Also, for more basic services in the town of Carlsbad, see Chapter 13, Carlsbad Caverns National Park.*

ACCESSIBILITY

The wheelchair-accessible Headquarters Visitor Center has a wheelchair available for use. The ¾-mi round-trip Pinery Trail from the visitor center to Butterfield Stage Ruins is wheelchair accessible, as is McKittrick Contact Station.

ADMISSION HOURS
The park is open 24 hours daily, year-round; some sites, like McKittrick Canyon, are day-use only.

ADMISSION FEES
An admission fee of $8 per camping site ($5 per day-use person) is collected at the visitor center.

ATMS/BANKS
Contacts **Best Western Cavern Inn** (⊠ *17 Carlsbad Caverns Hwy., White's City* ☎ *505/785–2291*).

AUTOMOBILE SERVICE STATION
Contacts **White's City 24-Hour Shell** (⊠ *17 Carlsbad Caverns Hwy., White's City* ☎ *505/785–2291*).

EMERGENCIES
There are no fire boxes in this largely wilderness park, but cell phones with far-reaching service can pick up signals at key points along trails. Rangers have emergency medical technician training and are also law-enforcement officers. To reach them, call 911 or contact Headquarters Visitor Center or Dog Canyon Ranger Station.

LOST AND FOUND
The park's lost-and-found is at Headquarters Visitor Center.

PARK PUBLICATIONS
The Guadalupe Mountains' natural features and history are the subjects of the illustrated **The Guadalupes,** by Dan Murphy, a booklet published by the Carlsbad Caverns Guadalupe Mountains Association. Other booklets include **Trails of the Guadalupes,** by Don Kurtz and William D. Goran, and **Hiking Carlsbad Caverns and Guadalupe Mountains National Parks,** by Bill Schneider. These and other publications are available at the visitor center.

PERMITS
For overnight backpacking trips, you must get a free permit from either Headquarters Visitor Center or Dog Canyon Ranger Station.

POST OFFICE
Contacts **Dell City Post Office** (⊠ *Ranch Rd. 1437, 13 mi north of junction with Rte. 62, Dell City* ☎ *915/964–2626* ⊙ *Weekdays 7–11:30 and 12:30–3*).

PUBLIC TELEPHONES AND RESTROOMS
Dog Canyon Ranger Station, Headquarters Visitor Center, McKittrick Contact Station, and Pine Springs Campground all have public phones and restrooms.

VISITOR INFORMATION
Contacts **Headquarters Visitor Center** ⊓ *HC 60, Box 400, Salt Flat, 79847* ☎ *915/828–3251* ⊕ *www.nps.gov/gumo*.

Carlsbad Caverns National Park

WORD OF MOUTH

"The more I thought of it the more I realized that any hole in the ground which could house such a gigantic army of bats must be a whale of a big cave."

—Jim White, cowboy, from *Jim White's Own Story: The Discovery and History of Carlsbad Caverns*

WELCOME TO CARLSBAD CAVERNS

TOP REASONS TO GO

★ **300,000 hungry bats:** Every night and every day, bats wing to and from the caverns in a swirling, visible tornado.

★ **Take a guided tour through the underworld:** Plummet 75 stories underground, and step into enormous caves hung with stalactites and bristling with stalagmites.

★ **Living Desert Zoo and Gardens:** More preserve than zoo, this 1,500-acre park houses scores of rare species, including endangered Mexican wolves and Bolson tortoises, and now boasts a new black bear exhibit.

★ **Birding at Rattlesnake Springs:** Nine-tenths of the park's 330 bird species, including roadrunners, golden eagles, and acrobatic cave swallows, visit this green desert oasis.

★ **Pecos River:** The Pecos River, a Southwest landmark, flows through the nearby town of Carlsbad. The river is always soothing, but gets festive for holiday floaters when riverside homeowners lavishly decorate their homes.

1 Bat Flight. Cowboy Jim White discovered the caverns after noticing that a swirling smokestack of bats appeared there each morning and evening. White is long gone, but the 300,000-member bat colony is still here, snatching up 3 tons of bugs a night. Watch them leave at dusk from the amphitheater located near the park visitor center.

2 Carlsbad Caverns Big Room Tour. Travel 75 stories below the surface to visit the Big Room, where you can traipse beneath a 255-foot-tall ceiling and take in immense and eerie cave formations. Situated directly beneath the park visitor center, the room can be accessed via quick-moving elevator or the natural cave entrance.

3 Living Desert Zoo and Gardens. Endangered river cooters, Bolson tortoises, and Mexican wolves all roam in the Living Desert Zoo and Gardens. You can also skip alongside roadrunners and slim wild turkeys in the park's aviary, or visit a small group of cougars. The Living Desert is located within the town of Carlsbad, New Mexico, 23 mi to the north of the park.

GUADALUPE

Yucca Canyon Tr

MOUNTAINS

NEW MEXICO
TEXAS

4 The Pecos River. In the town of Carlsbad, a river runs through it—the Pecos River, that is. The river, a landmark of the Southwest, skims through town and makes for excellent boating, waterskiing, and fishing in some places. In the winter, residents gussy up dozens of riverside homes for the holiday season.

5 Rattlesnake Springs. Despite 30,000-plus acres in which to roam, nine-tenths of the park's 330-plus species of birds show up at Rattlesnake Springs at one time or another—probably because it's one of the very few water sources in this area.

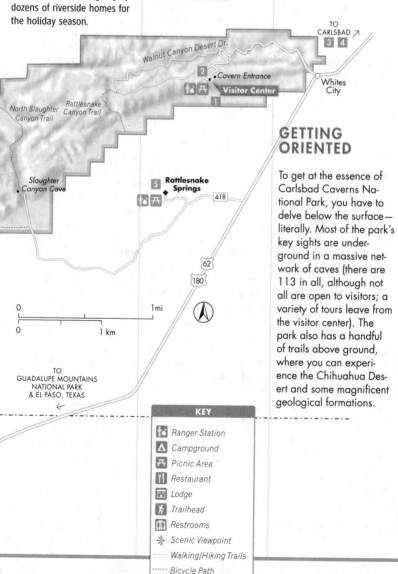

NEW MEXICO

TO CARLSBAD ↗
3 4

Walnut Canyon Desert Dr.

2 Cavern Entrance

Visitor Center
1

Whites City

North Slaughter Canyon Trail

Rattlesnake Canyon Trail

Slaughter Canyon Cave

5 Rattlesnake Springs
418

62
180

| 0 | | 1 mi |
| 0 | | 1 km |

TO GUADALUPE MOUNTAINS NATIONAL PARK & EL PASO, TEXAS
←

GETTING ORIENTED

To get at the essence of Carlsbad Caverns National Park, you have to delve below the surface—literally. Most of the park's key sights are underground in a massive network of caves (there are 113 in all, although not all are open to visitors; a variety of tours leave from the visitor center). The park also has a handful of trails above ground, where you can experience the Chihuahua Desert and some magnificent geological formations.

KEY

- 🏠 Ranger Station
- ▲ Campground
- 🏕 Picnic Area
- 🍴 Restaurant
- 🏨 Lodge
- 🥾 Trailhead
- 🚻 Restrooms
- ⇗ Scenic Viewpoint
- ···· Walking/Hiking Trails
- ···· Bicycle Path

1

CARLSBAD CAVERNS PLANNER

When to Go

While the desert above may alternately bake or freeze, the caverns remain in the mid-50s; the fantastic formations don't change with the seasons either. If you're coming to see the Mexican free-tailed bat, however, come between spring and late fall.

Getting There & Around

Carlsbad Caverns is 27 mi southwest of Carlsbad, New Mexico, and 35 mi north of Guadalupe Mountains National Park via U.S. 62/180. The nearest full-service airport is in El Paso, 154 mi away. The 9.5-mi Walnut Canyon Desert Drive loop is one-way. It's a curvy, gravel road and is not recommended for motor homes or trailers. Be alert for wildlife such as mule deer crossing roadways, especially in early morning and at night.

AVG. HIGH/LOW TEMPS

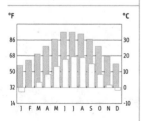

Flora & Fauna

Without a doubt, the park's most prominent and popular residents are Mexican free-tailed bats. These bats have bodies that barely span a woman's hand, yet sport wings that would cover a workingman's boot. Female bats give birth to a single pup each year, which usually weighs more than a quarter of what an adult bat does. Their tiny noses and big ears enable them to search for the many tons of bugs they consume over their lifetime. Numbering nearly a third of a million, these tiny creatures are the park's mascot.

Famous fanged flyers aside, there is much more wildlife to recommend in the park. One of New Mexico's best birding areas is at Rattlesnake Springs. Summer and fall migrations give you the best chance of spotting the most varieties of the more than 330 species of birds. Lucky visitors may spot a golden eagle, a rare visitor, or get the thrill of glimpsing a brilliant, gray-and-crimson vermilion flycatcher.

Snakes generally appear in summer. ■TIP➔ **If you're out walking, be wary of different rattlesnake species, such as banded-rock and diamondbacks. If you see one, don't panic. Rangers say they are more scared of us than we are of them. Just don't make any sudden moves, and slowly walk away or back around the vipers.**

This area is also remarkable because of its location in the Chihuahua Desert, which sprouts unique plant life. There are thick stands of raspy-leaved yuccas, as well as the agave (mescal) plants that were once a food source for early Apache tribes. The leaves of this leggy plant are still roasted in sand pits by Apache elders during traditional celebrations.

In spring, thick stands of yucca plants unfold yellow flowers on their tall stalks. Blossoming cacti and desert wildflowers are one of the natural wonders of Walnut Canyon. You'll see bright red blossoms adorning ocotillo plants, and sunny yellow blooms sprouting from prickly pear cactus.

By Jennifer
Edwards

ON THE SURFACE, CARLSBAD CAVERNS National Park is deceptively normal—but all bets are off once visitors set foot in the elevator, which plunges 75 stories underground. The country beneath the surface is part silky darkness, part subterranean hallucination. The snaky, illuminated walkway seems less like a trail and more like a foray across the river Styx and into the Underworld. Within more than 14 football fields of subterranean space are hundreds of formations that alternately resemble cakes, soda straws, ocean waves, and the large, leering face of a mountain troll.

WHAT TO SEE

SCENIC STOPS

The Big Room. With a floor space equal to about 14 football fields, this underground focal point of Carlsbad Caverns clues visitors in to just how large the caverns really are. Its caverns are close enough to the trail to cause voices to echo, but the chamber itself is so vast voices don't echo far; the White House could fit in just one corner of the Big Room, and wouldn't come close to grazing the 255-foot ceiling. The 1-mi loop walk on a mostly level, paved trail is self-guided. An audio guide is also available from park rangers for a few dollars. ⊠*At the visitor center* 🔲*$6; free for kids under 15* ☉*Memorial Day–Labor Day, daily 8–5 (last entry into the Natural Entrance is at 3:30; last entry into the elevator is at 5); Labor Day–Memorial Day, daily 8:30–3:30 (last entry into the Natural Entrance at 2; last entry into the elevator at 3:30).*

Natural Entrance. A self-guided, paved trail leads from the natural cave entrance. The route is winding and sometimes slick from water seepage aboveground. A steep descent of about 750 feet takes you about a mile through the main corridor and past features such as the Bat Cave and the Boneyard. (Despite its eerie name, the formations here don't look much like femurs and fibulas; they're more like spongy bone insides.) Iceberg Rock is a 200,000-ton boulder that dropped from the cave ceiling some millennia ago. After about a mile, you'll link up underground with the 1-mi Big Room trail and return to the surface via elevator. ⊠*At the visitor center* 🔲*$6* ☉*Memorial Day–Labor Day, daily 8:30–3:30; Labor Day–Memorial Day, daily 9–2.*

Rattlesnake Springs. Enormous cottonwood trees shade the picnic and recreation area at this cool oasis near Black River. The rare desert wetland harbors butterflies, mammals, and reptiles, as well as 90% of the park's 330 bird species. Don't let its name scare you; there may be rattlesnakes here, but not more than at any other similar site in the Southwest. Overnight camping and parking are not allowed. Take U.S. 62/180 5.5 mi south of White's City and turn west onto Highway 418 for 2.5 mi. ⊠*Hwy. 418.*

VISITOR CENTER

A 75-seat theater offers an engrossing film about the different types of caves, as well as an orientation video that explains cave etiquette. Some of the rules include staying on paths so you don't get lost; keeping objects and trash in your pockets and not on the ground; and not

CARLSBAD CAVERNS IN ONE DAY

In a single day, visitors can easily view both the eerie, exotic caverns and the volcano of bats that erupts from the caverns each morning and evening. Unless you're attending the annual Bat Breakfast, when visitors have the morning meal with rangers and then view the early morning bat return, you'll probably want to sleep past sunrise and then stroll into the caves first.

For the full experience, begin by taking the **Natural Entrance Route Tour,** which allows visitors to trek into the cave from surface level. This tour winds past the Boneyard, with its intricate ossifications, and a 200,000-ton boulder called the Iceberg. After 1.25 mi, or about an hour, the route links up with the **Big Room Route.** If you're not in good health or are traveling with young children, you might want to skip the Natural Entrance and start with the Big Room Route, which begins at the foot of the elevator. This underground walk extends 1.25 mi on level, paved ground, and takes about 1½ hours to complete. If you have made reservations in advance or happen upon some openings, you also can take the additional **King's Palace** guided tour for 1 mi and an additional 1½ hours. At 83 stories deep, the Palace is the lowest rung the public can visit. By this time, you will have spent four hours in the cave. Take the elevator back up to the top. If you're not yet tuckered out, consider a short hike along the sunny, self-guided ½-mi **Desert Nature Walk** by the visitor center.

To picnic by the birds, bees, and water of **Rattlesnake Springs,** take U.S. 62/180 south from White's City 5.5 mi, and turn back west onto Route 418. You'll find old-growth shade trees, grass, picnic tables, and water. Many varieties of birds flit from tree to tree. Return to the Carlsbad Caverns entrance road and take the 9.5-mi Walnut Canyon Desert Drive loop. Leave yourself enough time to return to the **visitor center** for the evening bat flight.

touching the formations. Besides laying down the ground rules, visitor center exhibits offer a primer on bats, geology, wildlife, and the early tribes and nomads that once lived in and passed through the Carlsbad Caverns area. Friendly rangers staff an information desk, where tickets and maps are sold. Two gift shops also are on the premises. ⊠ *7 mi west of park entrance at White's City, off U.S. 62/180* ☎ *505/785–2232* ☉ *Labor Day–Memorial Day, daily 8–5; Memorial Day–late Aug., daily 8–7.*

SPORTS & THE OUTDOORS

BIRD-WATCHING

From warty-headed turkey vultures to svelte golden eagles, about 330 species of birds have been identified in Carlsbad Caverns National Park. Ask for a checklist at the visitor center and then start looking for greater roadrunners, red-winged blackbirds, white-throated swifts, northern flickers, and pygmy nuthatches.

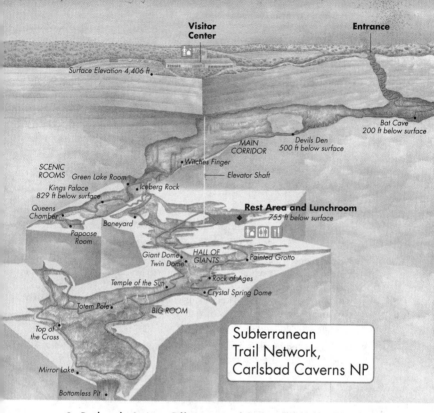

Subterranean
Trail Network,
Carlsbad Caverns NP

Visitor Center

Entrance

Surface Elevation 4,406 ft

Bat Cave
200 ft below surface

Devils Den
500 ft below surface

MAIN
CORRIDOR

Witches Finger

Elevator Shaft

SCENIC
ROOMS   Green Lake Room

Kings Palace
829 ft below surface

Iceberg Rock

Queens
Chamber

Boneyard

Papoose
Room

Rest Area and Lunchroom
755 ft below surface

Giant Dome
Twin Dome

HALL OF
GIANTS

Painted Grotto

Temple of the Sun

Rock of Ages

Crystal Spring Dome

Totem Pole

BIG ROOM

Top of
the Cross

Mirror Lake

Bottomless Pit

C **Rattlesnake Springs.** Offering one of the best bird habitats in New Mex-
Fodor'sChoice ico, this is a natural wetland with old-growth cottonwoods. Because
★ southern New Mexico is in the northernmost region of the Chihuahua
Desert, you're likely to see birds that can't be found anywhere else in
the United States outside extreme southern Texas and Arizona. If you
see a flash of crimson, you might have spotted a vermilion flycatcher.
Wild turkeys also flap around this oasis. ⊠ Hwy. 418, 2.5 mi west of
U.S. 62/180, 5.5 mi south of White's City.

HIKING

Deep, dark, and mysterious, the Carlsbad Caverns are such a park focal
point that the 30,000-plus acres of wilderness above them have gone
largely undeveloped. This is great news for people who pull on their
hiking boots when they're looking for solitude. What you'll find are
rudimentary trails that crisscross the dry, textured terrain and lead up
to elevations of 6,000 feet or more. These routes often take a half day
or more to travel; at least one, **Guadalupe Ridge Trail**, is long enough that
it calls for an overnight stay. Walkers who just want a little dusty taste
of desert flowers and wildlife should try the **Desert Nature Walk**.

Finding the older, less well-maintained trails can be difficult. Pick up a
topographical map at the visitor center bookstore, and be sure to pack
a lot of water. There's none out in the desert, and you'll need at least

a gallon per person per day. The high elevation coupled with a potent sunshine punch can deliver a nasty sunburn, so be sure to pack SPF 30 (or higher) sunblock and a hat, even in winter. You can't bring a pet or a gun, but you do have to bring a backcountry permit if you're camping. They're free at the visitor center.

EASY   **Desert Nature Walk.** While waiting for the night bat-flight program, try taking the ½-mi self-guided hike. The tagged and identified flowers and plants make this a good place to get acquainted with much of the local desert flora. The paved trail is wheelchair accessible and an easy jaunt for even the littlest ones. The payoff is great for everyone, too: a big, vivid view of the desert basin. ⊠ *Off the cavern entrance trail, 200 yards east of the visitor center.*

Rattlesnake Canyon Overlook Trail. A ¼-mi stroll off Walnut Canyon Desert Drive offers a nice overlook of the greenery of Rattlesnake Canyon. ⊠ *Mile marker 9 on Walnut Canyon Desert Dr..*

MODERATE   **Juniper Ridge Trail.** Climb up in elevation as you head north on this nearly 3-mi trail, which leads to the northern edge of the park and then turns toward Crooked Canyon. While not the most notable trail, it's challenging enough to keep things interesting. Allow yourself half a day, and be sure to bring lots of water, especially when the temperature is high. ⊠ *Trailhead at 8.8 mi marker of Desert Loop Dr..*

Old Guano Road Trail. Meandering a little more than 3.5 mi one-way on mostly flat terrain, the trail dips sharply toward White's City campground, where the trail ends. Give yourself about half a day to complete the walk. Depending on the temperature, this walk can be taxing. Drink lots of water. ⊠ *The trailhead is at the Bat Flight Amphitheater, near the Natural Cave Entrance and visitor center.*

Rattlesnake Canyon Trail. Rock cairns loom over this trail, which descends from 4,570 to 3,900 feet as it winds into the canyon. Allow half a day to trek down into the canyon and make the somewhat strenuous climb out; the total trip is about 6 mi. ⊠ *Mile marker 9 on Walnut Canyon Desert Dr..*

Fodor's Choice   **Yucca Canyon Trail.** Sweeping views of the Guadalupe Mountains and ★   El Capitan give allure to this trail. Drive past Rattlesnake Springs and stop at the park boundary before reaching the Slaughter Canyon Cave parking lot. Turn west along the boundary fence line to the trailhead. The 6-mi round-trip begins at the mouth of Yucca Canyon, and climbs up to the top of the escarpment. Here you'll find the panoramic view. Most people turn around at this point; the hearty can continue along a poorly maintained route that follows the top of the ridge. The first part of the hike takes half a day. If you continue on, the hike takes a full day. ⊠ *Hwy. 418, 10 mi west of U.S. 62/180.*

DIFFICULT   **Guadalupe Ridge Trail.** This long, winding ramble follows an old road all the way to the west edge of the park. Because of its length (about 12 mi), an overnight stay in the backcountry is suggested. The hike may be long, but for serious hikers the up-close-and-personal views into Rattlesnake and Slaughter canyons are more than worth it—not to mention the serenity of being miles and miles away from civilization. ⊠*Follow Desert Loop Dr. 4.8 mi to the trailhead.*

North Slaughter Canyon Trail. Beginning at the Slaughter Canyon parking lot, the trail traverses a heavily vegetated canyon bottom into a remote part of the park. As you begin hiking, look off to the east (to your right) to see the dun-colored ridges and wrinkles of the Elephant Back formation, the first of many dramatic limestone formations visible from the trail. The route travels 5.5 mi one way, the last 3 mi steeply climbing onto a limestone ridge escarpment. Allow a full day for the round-trip. ⊠*Hwy. 418, 10 mi west of U.S. 62/180.*

> ### A LONG WAY DOWN
>
> The newest discovery in Carlsbad Caverns National Park is **Lechuguilla Cave,** the deepest limestone cave in the United States. Scientists began mapping the cave network in 1986, and though they've located more than 112 mi of caverns extending to a depth of more than 1,600 feet, much more of this area along the park's northern border remains to be investigated. Lechuguilla is not open to the public, but an exhibit describing it can be viewed at the visitor center.

SPELUNKING

Carlsbad Caverns is famous for the beauty and breadth of its inky depths, as well as for the accessibility of some of its largest caves. All cave tours are ranger led, so safety is rarely an issue in the caves, no matter how remote. There are no other tour guides in the area, nor is there an equipment retailer other than the Wal-Mart located in Carlsbad, 23 mi away. Depending on the difficulty of your cave selection (Spider Cave is the hardest to navigate), you'll need at most knee pads, flashlight batteries, sturdy pants, hiking boots with ankle support, and some water.

Hall of the White Giant. Plan to squirm through some tight passages for long distances to access a very remote chamber, where you'll see towering, glistening white formations that explain the name of this feature. This strenuous, ranger-led tour lasts about four hours. Steep drop-offs might elate you—or make you queasy. Wear sturdy hiking shoes, and pick up four AA batteries for your flashlight before you come. Visitors must be at least 12 years old. ⊠*At the visitor center* ☎*800/967–2283* ⊠*$20* ⌁*Reservations essential* ☉*Tour Sat. at 1.*

King's Palace. Throughout King's Palace, you'll see leggy "soda straws" large enough for a giant to sip and multi-tiered curtains of stone—sometimes by the light of just a few flashlights. The mile-long walk is on a paved trail, but there's one very steep hill. This ranger-guided tour lasts about 1½ hours and gives you the chance to experience a blackout, when all lights are extinguished. While advance reservations are highly recommended, this is the one tour you might be able to sign up for on the spot. Children under 4 aren't allowed on this tour. ⊠*At the visitor center* ☎*800/967–2283* ⊠*$8* ☉*Tours Labor Day–Memo-*

CAVEMEN SPEAK

Sound like a serious spelunker with this cavemen cheat-sheet. These *Speleothems* (cave formations) are ones you may see at Carlsbad Caverns.

Cave balloons: Thin-walled formations resembling partially deflated balloons, usually composed of hydromagnesite.

Boxwork: Composed of interconnecting thin blades that were left in relief on cave walls when the bedrock was dissolved away.

Flowstone: Consists of thin layers of a mineral deposited on a sloping surface by flowing or seeping water.

Frostwork: Sprays of needles that radiate from a central point that are usually made of aragonite.

Gypsum beard: Composed of bundles of gypsum fibers that resemble a human beard.

Logomites: Consists of popcorn and superficially resembles a hollowed-out stalagmite.

Pool Fingers: Deposited underneath water around organic filaments.

Ribbons: Thin, layered formations found on sloping ceilings or walls that resemble curtains or scarves.

Stalagmites: Mineral deposits that build up on a cave floor from dripping water.

Stalactites: Carrot-shaped formations that hang down from a cave ceiling and are formed from dripping water.

rial Day, daily 10 and 2; Memorial Day–Labor Day, daily 10, 11, 2, and 3.

Left Hand Tunnel. Lantern light illuminates the easy walk on this detour in the main Carlsbad Cavern, which leads to Permian Age fossils—indicating that these caves were hollowed from the Permian Reef that still underlies the Guadalupe Mountain range above. The guided tour over a packed, dirt trail lasts about two hours. It's a moderate trek that older kids can easily negotiate, but children under 6 aren't allowed. ⊠ *At the visitor center* ☎ *800/967–2283* 🖃 *$8* ⊙ *Tour daily at 9.*

Lower Cave. Fifty-foot vertical ladders and a dirt path will take you into undeveloped portions of Carlsbad Caverns. It takes about half a day to negotiate this moderately strenuous side trip led by a knowledgeable ranger. Children younger than 12 are not allowed on this tour. ⊠ *At the visitor center* ☎ *800/967–2283* 🖃 *$20* ⚲ *Reservations essential* ⊙ *Tour weekdays at 1.*

★ **Slaughter Canyon Cave.** Discovered in the 1930s by a local goatherd, this cave is one of the most popular secondary sites in the park, about 23 mi southwest of the main Carlsbad Caverns and visitor center. Both the hike to the cave mouth and the tour will take about half a day, but it's worth it to view the deep cavern darkness as it's punctuated only by flashlights and, sometimes, headlamps. From the Slaughter Canyon parking area, give yourself 45 minutes to make the steep ½-mi climb up a trail leading to the mouth of the cave. Arrange to be there a quarter of an hour earlier than the appointed time. You'll find that the cave consists primarily of a single corridor, 1,140 feet long, with numerous side passages.

You can take some worthwhile pictures of this cave. Wear hiking shoes with ankle support, and carry plenty of water. You're also expected to bring your own two-D-cell flashlight. Children under age 6 are not permitted. It's a great adventure if you're in shape and love caving. ⊠ *End of Hwy. 418, 10 mi west of U.S. 62/180* ☎ *800/967–2283* 💲 *$15* 🔑 *Reservations essential* ⊙ *Tours Memorial Day–Labor Day, daily 10 and 1; post–Labor Day–Dec., weekends at 10; Jan.–Memorial Day, weekends 10 and 1.*

> ### FLYING BLIND
>
> Bats use a type of sonar system called echolocation to orient themselves and locate their insect dinners at night. About 15 species of bats live in Carlsbad Caverns, although the Mexican free-tailed is the most predominant.

13

Spider Cave. Visitors may not expect to have an adventure in a cavern system as developed and well stocked as Carlsbad Caverns, but serious cavers and energetic types have the chance to clamber up tight tunnels, stoop under overhangs, and climb up steep, rocky pitches. This backcountry cave is listed as "wild," a clue that you might need a similar nature to attempt a visit. Plan to wear your warm, but least-favorite clothes, as they'll probably get streaked with grime. You'll also need soft knee pads, 4 AA batteries, leather gloves, and water. The gloves and pads are to protect you on long, craggy clambers and the batteries are for your flashlight. It will take you half a day to complete this ranger-led tour noted for its adventure. Visitors must be at least 12 years old and absolutely not claustrophobic. ⊠ *Meet at visitor center* ☎ *800/967–2283* 💲 *$20* 🔑 *Reservations essential* ⊙ *Tour Sun. at 1.*

OUTFITTERS & EXPEDITIONS Spelunkers who wish to explore both developed and wild caves are in luck; park rangers lead visitors on six different tours, including the **The Hall of the White Giant** and **Spider Cave,** known for its tight twists and grimy climbs. Reservations are required at least a day in advance. If you're making reservations 21 days or more before your visit, you can send a check; 20 days or less, and you must pay by credit card over the phone or online. ☎ *800/967–2283* ⊕ *www.nps.gov/archive/cave/tour-gui.htm.* Those who want to go it alone outside the more established caverns can get permits and information about 10 backcountry caves from the **Cave Resources Office** (☎ *505/785–2232 Ext. 363*). Heed rangers' advice for these remote, undeveloped, nearly unexplored caves.

EDUCATIONAL OFFERINGS

RANGER PROGRAMS

Fodor's Choice ★ **Evening Bat Flight Program.** In the amphitheater at the Natural Cave Entrance (off a short trail from main parking lot) a ranger discusses the park's batty residents before the creatures begin their sundown exodus. The bats aren't on any predictable schedule, so times are a little iffy. ⊠ *Natural Cave Entrance, at the visitor center* 💲 *Free* ⊙ *Mid-May–mid-Oct., nightly at sundown.*

WHAT'S NEARBY

NEARBY TOWNS

On the Pecos River, with 2¾ mi of beaches and picturesque riverside pathways, **Carlsbad, New Mexico,** seems suspended between the past and the present. It's part university town, part Old West, with a robust Mexican kick. The Territorial town square, a block from the river, encircles a Pueblo-style country courthouse designed by New Mexican architect John Gaw Meem. Seven miles east of the caverns is **White's City,** grown from a tiny outpost to a small outpost. This privately owned town is the nearest place to Carlsbad Caverns and contains dining and lodging options, plus the essentials.

NEARBY ATTRACTIONS

Living Desert Zoo and Gardens State Park. The park contains impressive plants and animals native to the Chihuahua Desert. The Desert Arboretum has hundreds of exotic cacti and succulents, and the Living Desert Zoo—more a reserve than a traditional zoo—is home to mountain lions, deer, elk, wolves, bison, and endangered Mexican wolves, which are more petite than their snarly kin. Nocturnal exhibits and dioramas let you in on the area's nighttime wildlife, too. Though there are shaded rest areas, restrooms, and water fountains, in hot weather it's best to visit during the early morning or early evening, when it's cooler. ⊠*1504 Miehls Dr., off U.S. 285* ☎*505/887–5516* ⊠*$5 tour* ⊙*Late May–early Sept., daily 8–8; early Sept.–late May, daily 9–5; last admission 1½ hrs before closing.*

AREA ACTIVITIES

SPORTS & THE OUTDOORS

BOATING & FISHING

The **Lake Carlsbad Recreation Area** offers boat ramps, boating, and fishing; there are no admission fees. ⊠*Along Riverside and Park drives in Carlsbad* ☎*505/885–6262* ⊙*Open daily; swimming area open Memorial Day weekend through Labor Day.*

ARTS & ENTERTAINMENT

The **Fiesta Drive-In Theater** (⊠*401 W. Fiesta, Carlsbad* ☎*505/885–4126* ⊕*www.fiestadrivein.com*) offers three reasonably current movie selections. During the school year the theater is open Friday–Monday; in summer, it's open every night.

WHERE TO EAT & STAY

ABOUT THE RESTAURANTS

Choice isn't an issue inside Carlsbad Caverns National Park because there are just three dining options—the surface-level café, the underground restaurant, and the bring-it-in-yourself option. Luckily, everything is reasonably priced (especially for national park eateries).

ABOUT THE HOTELS

The only overnight option within the arid, rugged park is to make your own campsite in the backcountry, at least half a mile from any trail.

Outside the park, however, options expand. White's City, which is less than 10 mi to the east of the park, contains two motels. Both are near the boardwalk that connects shopping and entertainment options.

In Carlsbad there are even more choices, but many of them aren't as appealing as they once were. The hotels here are aging and not particularly well maintained, so don't expect a mint on your pillow. Still, most are clean, if less than opulent.

ABOUT THE CAMPGROUNDS

Backcountry camping is by permit only (no campfires allowed) in the park; free permits can be obtained at the visitor center, where you can also pick up a map of areas closed to camping. You'll need to hike to campsites. There are no vehicle or RV camping areas in the park. Commercial sites can be found in White's City and Carlsbad.

WHAT IT COSTS					
	¢	$	$$	$$$	$$$$
RESTAURANTS	under $8	$8–$12	$13–$20	$21–$30	over $30
HOTELS	under $50	$50–$100	$101–$150	$151–$200	over $200
CAMP-GROUNDS	under $10	$10–$17	$18–$35	$36–$49	over $50

Restaurant prices are per person for a main course at dinner. Hotel prices are per night for two people in a standard double room in high season, excluding taxes and service charges. Camping prices are for a standard (no hookups, pit toilets, fire grates, picnic tables) campsite per night.

WHERE TO EAT

IN THE PARK

¢–$ ✕**Carlsbad Caverns Restaurant.** This comfy, diner-style restaurant has the essentials—hamburgers, sandwiches, and hot roast beef. ⊠ *Visitor center, 7 mi west of U.S. 62/180 at the end of the main park road* ☎ *505/785–2281* ▤ *AE, D, MC, V* ☼ *Closes at 6:30 Memorial Day weekend–Labor Day, then at 5 after Labor Day.*

¢–$ ✕**Underground Lunchroom.** Grab a treat, soft drink, or club sandwich for a quick break. Service is quick, even when there's a crowd. ⊠ *Visitor center, 7 mi west of U.S. 62/180 at the end of the main park road*

☎ *505/785–2281* ▭ *AE, D, MC, V* ⊗ *No dinner. Closes at 5 Memorial Day weekend–Labor Day, then at 3:30 after Labor Day.*

OUTSIDE THE PARK

$–$$ ✕ **Velvet Garter Restaurant and Saloon.** This eatery dishes up steaks, chicken, shrimp, and Mexican food in an Old West atmosphere, and a newly added Italian menu with pasta and luscious sauces has proven to be a hit. You won't find gourmet meals here, but it's a convenient place for a decent meal if you don't want to drive an additional 20 mi north to Carlsbad. There's also a full-service bar. ✉ *26 Carlsbad Caverns Hwy., White's City* ☎ *505/785–2291* ▭ *AE, D, MC, V.*

¢–$ ✕ **Bamboo Garden Restaurant.** Possibly the best Chinese food in south-
★ ern New Mexico. Kung pao chicken is among the highlights, but there are also favorites like sweet-and-sour pork and cashew shrimp. Surroundings are pleasant but not elegant. ✉ *1511 N. Canal St., Carlsbad* ☎ *505/887–5145* ▭ *MC, V* ⊗ *Closed Mon.*

¢–$ ✕ **Jack's.** A good spot to have a hearty breakfast before heading off to the caverns, this fast-food favorite shares an adobe-style building with the Velvet Garter Restaurant. Grab a booth and order eggs, a burger, Mexican food, or pizza. ✉ *26 Carlsbad Caverns Hwy., White's City* ☎ *505/785–2291* ▭ *No credit cards.*

¢–$ ✕ **La Fonda.** For decades, residents of Carlsbad and Roswell have driven
★ to this modest Mexican restaurant to dine on celebrated specialties like the Guadalajara (beef, cheese, and guacamole on a corn tortilla). Artesia is 26 mi north of the park. ✉ *206 W. Main St., Artesia* ☎ *505/746–9377* ▭ *AE, D, MC, V.*

¢–$ ✕ **Lucy's Mexicali Restaurant & Entertainment Club.** "The best margaritas
★ and hottest chile in the world" is the motto of this family-owned Mexican food oasis. All the New Mexican staples are prepared here, plus some not-so-standard items such as chicken fajita burritos and enchiladas served the New Mexico way—that is, flat with an egg on top. Try the Tucson-style chimichangas and brisket *carnitas* (beef brisket or chicken sautéed with chilies and seasonings). Low-fat and fat-free Mexican dishes and 12 microbrewery beers are served—or try Lucy's original Mexicali beer with a slice of orange. Live entertainment on weekends. ✉ *701 S. Canal St., Carlsbad* ☎ *505/887–7714* ▭ *AE, D, DC, MC, V.*

WHERE TO STAY

IN THE PARK

Backcountry camping only is allowed. ⇨ *About the Campgrounds.*

OUTSIDE THE PARK

$ ▦ **Best Western Cavern Inn.** This Territorial-style, two-story motor inn just outside the Carlsbad Caverns entrance has rooms with Southwestern decor. Under the same ownership next door is the hacienda-style **Best Western Guadalupe Inn,** notable for its tidy landscaping and private spa; it has 42 rooms and Southwestern furnishings. All guests are free to use the water park, open May through September, which features two 150-foot waterslides. **Pros:** Both properties are close to the park, water park at Best Western Guadalupe is a boon in summer.

Cons: Rooms and service are fairly bare-bones. ✉ *17 Carlsbad Caverns Hwy., look for large registration sign on south side of road, White's City* ☎ *505/785–2291 or 800/228–3767* ⤳ *63 rooms* ♿ *In-room: Wi-Fi. In-hotel: pool, spa, some pets allowed, no-smoking rooms* ▤ *AE, D, DC, MC, V* ⏏ *BP.*

$ ★ ⊞ **Best Western Stevens Inn.** This is widely known as the best-maintained hotel in town. To be honest, it needs a little updating, but until the brand-new Holiday Inn is finished, it is arguably the best bet in Carlsbad and in White's City. Etched glass and carved wooden doors add a touch of elegance, and prints of Western landscapes decorate the spacious rooms while prime rib and steaks are served in the evening at the motel's Flume Room Restaurant and Coffee Shop, which opens at 5:30 AM daily. **Pros:** Long considered the best lodging option in Carlsbad. **Cons:** Aging property. ✉ *1829 S. Canal St., Box 580, Carlsbad* ☎ *505/887–2851 or 800/730–2851* ⤳ *222 rooms* ♿ *In-room: kitchen (some), refrigerator (some), Wi-Fi. In-hotel: no elevator, restaurant, bar, pool, laundry facilities, airport shuttle, some pets allowed, no-smoking rooms* ▤ *AE, D, DC, MC, V* ⏏ *BP.*

CAMPING & RV PARKS $–$$ ⚠ **Carlsbad RV Park & Campgrounds.** This full-service campground inside the city limits has level gravel sites and an indoor swimming pool. Camping cabins with heating and air-conditioning are available, as are phone hookups and a meeting room. Reservations are recommended in summer. A professional RV service center where repairs can be made is next door. **Pros:** Full-service campground, free Wi-Fi. **Cons:** Sites are close together. ✉ *4301 National Parks Hwy., Carlsbad* ☎ *505/885–6333* ⊕ *www.carlsbadrvpark.com* ⤳ *96 RV sites, 41 tent sites* ♿ *Flush toilets, full hookups, partial hookups, dump station, drinking water, guest laundry, showers, grills, picnic tables, electricity, public telephone, general store, play area, swimming (pool)* ▤ *MC, V.*

CARLSBAD CAVERNS ESSENTIALS

For more information on visiting national parks, go to ⊕ fodors.com/parks.

ACCESSIBILITY
Portions of the paved Big Room trails in Carlsbad Caverns are accessible to wheelchairs. A map defining appropriate routes is available at the visitor center information desk. Strollers are not permitted on trails (use a baby pack instead). Individuals who may have difficulty walking should access the Big Room via elevator. The TDD number is 888/530–9796.

ADMISSION FEES
No fee is charged for parking or to enter the aboveground portion of the park. It costs $6 to descend into Carlsbad Cavern either by elevator or through the Natural Entrance. Costs for special tours range from $7 to $20 plus general admission.

ADMISSION HOURS

The park is open year-round, except Christmas Day. From Memorial Day weekend through Labor Day, tours are conducted from 8:30 to 5; the last entry into the cave via the Natural Entrance is at 3:30, and the last entry into the cave via the elevator is at 5. From Labor Day until Memorial Day weekend tours are conducted from 8:30 to 3:30; the last entry into the cave via the Natural Entrance is at 2, and the last entry into the cave via the elevator is 3:30. Carlsbad Caverns is in the Mountain Time Zone.

ATMS/BANKS

No ATMs are in the park—but there are plenty in Carlsbad, New Mexico.

AUTOMOBILE SERVICE STATIONS

Contacts **White's City 24-Hour Texaco** (⊠ *17 Carlsbad Caverns Hwy., White's City* ☎ *505/785-2291).*

EMERGENCIES

In the event of a medical emergency, dial 911, contact a park ranger, or report to the visitor center. To contact park police dial 505/785-2232, locate a park ranger, or report to the visitor center. Carlsbad Caverns has trained emergency medical technicians on duty and a first-aid room. White's City has emergency medical technicians available to respond to medical emergencies. A full-service hospital is in nearby Carlsbad.

LOST AND FOUND

The park's lost-and-found is at the visitor center information desk

PERMITS

All hikers are advised to stop at the visitor center information desk for current information about trails; those planning overnight hikes must obtain a free backcountry permit. Trails are poorly defined, but can be followed with a topographic map. Dogs are not allowed in the park, but a kennel is available at the park visitor center.

POST OFFICES

There is a mailbox at the visitor center; purchase stamps in the gift shops.

Contacts **White's City Post Office** (⊠ *Carlsbad Caverns Hwy., White's City* ☎ *505/785-2220* ⊙ *Weekdays 8–noon and 12:30–4:30, Sat. 8–noon).*

PUBLIC TELEPHONES

Public telephones are at the visitor center—handy, because cell phones only work about 10% of the time.

VISITOR INFORMATION

Contacts **Carlsbad Caverns National Park** ⊠ *3225 National Parks Hwy., Carlsbad,* ☎ *505/785-2232, 800/967-2283 reservations for special cave tours, 800/388-2733 cancellations* ⊕ *www.nps.gov/cave.*

The Panhandle

WORD OF MOUTH

"Especially in January, the only thing between the Panhandle and the North Pole is a barbed wire fence . . . and that's blown down. It's the land of the horizontal snows."

—JimM

By Jennifer
Edwards

THE RUGGED TEXAS PANHANDLE, PART of the Llano Estacado ("Staked Plain"), is a huge region, even for a state as big as Texas. At 256,601 square mi it's almost twice the size of California and bigger than neighboring New Mexico, Oklahoma, and Louisiana combined.

This is a land where American Indians roamed free and confident, astride fine horses, over seemingly limitless hunting grounds, and where cowboys cooked over their campfires on long, wearying cattle drives—which are still practiced today. Cotton farming, ranching, and oil are the ballast that has stabilized the region, and still does despite the many hardships over the years: the Dust Bowl, the oil busts, and the severe winds and climate—tornadoes, hail, and snow are all common here. It follows, then, that the people who live here now (many of whom have one or two American Indian ancestors) pride themselves on their hardiness in facing the extremities and their relative isolation.

Visitors come to the Panhandle to experience the cowboy culture and florid, striated beauty of Palo Duro canyon, second in size only to the Grand Canyon. They also trek here for the live entertainment, the authentic cowboy boots and hats, and some of the best steaks in Texas, all of which mingle to create a pervasive Old West atmosphere.

EXPLORING THE PANHANDLE

The Panhandle stretches from the state's border with Oklahoma south to U.S. 180, Amarillo and Lubbock being its main towns. Though not technically the Panhandle, also included for the purposes of this chapter is the section north (and just a bit south) of U.S. 180 going east to the west side of Fort Worth; Abilene and Wichita Falls are here. Though it's a big region, it's surprisingly simple to putter from town to town and city to city. Once visitors arrive here via Abilene, Lubbock, or Wichita Falls, they find a network of interlacing highways to follow. There are plenty of smaller, meandering roads, too, but it's best to stick with the larger ones in the interest of time—not to mention, the byways can be disorienting in a terrain spread with a constellation of small towns and interrupted by long patches of bald desert and oilfield equipment. Gas up in the larger towns.

The Panhandle region is often called the High Plains because it is composed of what's called the North Plains (anchored by Amarillo) and the South Plains (anchored by Lubbock). The North Plains' crops are wheat, corn, and sugar beets, and the planting and harvesting schedule is like that of most of the Plains states; while in the South Plains, cotton is king (half of the state's cotton comes from here), and it's harvested well into December.

ABOUT THE RESTAURANTS

With cattle ranches covering the region, the Panhandle is a wonderful, truly authentic place to try some of the best beef and Southern cooking in the nation. Texans don't joke about their fajitas and T-bones. The people of this area are big fans of home cooking, including Soul Food, chicken-fried steak, and the beloved dish known as steak fingers—think chicken fingers, only battered, tenderized steak instead and served with "cream" (white gravy).

A deep tradition of authentic Mexican and Tex-Mex cooking continues here, too. It's not quite as ubiquitous up here as it is nearer to the border, but it's a spicy, sumptuous presence. A must-not-miss dish is the sloppy, artery-busting delight known as Frito pie—a mess of corn chips, home-cooked chili, cheese, and sometimes even jalepeños and onions. No matter where you sup, prepare to do so in jeans and T-shirts. Most restaurants are closed on Sundays.

ABOUT THE HOTELS

Finding a place to stay won't be difficult, but choosing from so many options might be. Lubbock and Amarillo offer the most options,

THE PANHANDLE TOP 5

■ **Oh Say Canyon See:** Visit beautiful Palo Duro Canyon, second in grandeur only to the Grand Canyon.

■ **Ranch Dressing:** Slip into some cowboy boots and chaps. Several ranches host guests.

■ **Steak It Out:** Thousands of cattle yards supply superlative steaks here, while wineries include award-winning Llano Estacado.

■ **Get Your Kicks:** Route 66 winds through these parts; its halfway point is near Adrian.

■ **Wallow in the Weird:** Check out Amarillo's Cadillac Ranch, neither a ranch nor an auto maker.

but all of the major towns host major, reliable hotel chains—everything from the humble motor lodge to semi high-rises and extended-stay lodging. There are great RV options, too, from more basic parks to "ranches" offering pools, wireless Internet, and cable. Camping in Palo Duro Canyon outside of Amarillo is awe-inspiring but requires reservations.

There are off-beat choices for the more adventurous, too—like the smattering of bed-and-breakfasts, usually built into historic homes evoking the Victorian era, Texas-style. There are also some dude ranches here—that is, working ranches that host guests and include them in ranching activities like horseback riding and the occasional cattle drive. Giddy up!

WHAT IT COSTS					
	¢	$	$$	$$$	$$$$
RESTAURANTS	under $8	$8–$12	$13–$20	$21–$30	over $30
HOTELS	under $50	$50–$100	$101–$150	$151–$200	over $200
CAMPING	under $10	$10–$17	$18–$35	$36–$50	over $50

Restaurant prices are per person for a main course at dinner. Hotel prices are per night for two people in a standard double room in high season, excluding taxes and service charges. Lodging taxes are some of the highest in the country, ranging from 13 percent in Lubbock and Wichita Falls to 15 percent in Amarillo and Abilene. Camping prices are for a standard (no hookups, pit toilets, fire grates, picnic tables) campsite per night.

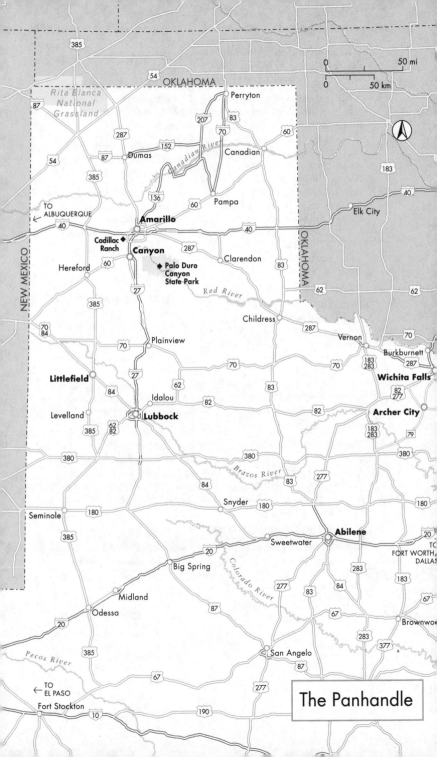

The Panhandle

NORTH PLAINS

AMARILLO

341 mi northwest of Fort Worth via Hwy. 81 and U.S. 287, 124 mi north of Lubbock via I–27.

Amarillo is one of those legendary Old West towns where cowboys-and-Indians culture has morphed into a softer, more modern version of Western tenacity and hospitality. The people still hold on to their hardiness and homespun values, and celebrate the rich mix of culture in the region, including a strong Tex-Mex feel. Folks are proud of their assorted histories and the city that settlers, businessmen, and railroads carved from this dry, flat grassland.

Located about two hours south of the Oklahoma border, Amarillo celebrates other richly historical themes with several museums. These include the capacious Panhandle–Plains Historical Museum, nicknamed by some "The Smithsonian of Texas." It's also home to the famous and hyperbolic Big Texan Steak Ranch, where diners can park their cars or their horses, swim in the pool, or stay the night after trying to tackle the famous 72-ounce steak. Continuing the tongue-in-cheek and over-the-top trend, eccentric millionaire Stanley Marsh III ("It's 3, not the third," he's quoted as saying) has continued to sow mischief throughout the lands with random and visually striking public art.

WHAT TO SEE

8 **American Quarter Horse Hall of Fame & Museum.** Did you know that the quarter horse got its name because it runs a faster quarter-mile than all other horses? This museum celebrates quarter horses with a hall of fame, exhibits, theater, paintings, and live demonstrations of feeding and saddling during summer camp. (And in case you're wondering just how fast quarter horses run, they can do 50 mph or more for short distances.) ⊠*2601 I–40 E.* ☎*806/376–5181* ⊕*www.aqha.com/foundation/halloffame* ⊠*$4* ⊙ *Early Sept.–late May, Mon.–Sat. 9–5; Memorial Day–Labor Day, Mon.–Sat. 9–5, Sun. noon–5.*

4 **Amarillo Botanical Gardens.** Lush outdoor trails lead visitors through acres filled with roses, native plants, and arbors, and there's a huge tropical greenroom. Kids get half-off admission. ⊠*1400 Streight Dr.* ☎*806/352–6513* ⊕*www.amarillobotanicalgardens.org* ⊠*$4* ⊙*Tues.–Fri. 9–5.*

6 **Amarillo Zoo.** Lions, tigers, bison, and wallabies are just a few of the animals populating the city zoo, along with hissing cockroaches, scorpions, and a slew of snakes. The highlights are the native Texas creatures, including the chukar (pronounced chuck-er) partridge. ⊠*N.E. 24th Ave. and Dumas Hwy. (in Thompson Park)* ☎*806/381–7911* ⊕*www.amarillozoo.org* ⊠*Free* ⊙*Tues.–Sun. 9:30–5:30.*

3 **Don Harrington Discovery Center.** It's all about the juniors at this fun educational center featuring badge workshops, a space theater, a play area for young children, and exhibits exploring the universe. ⊠*1200*

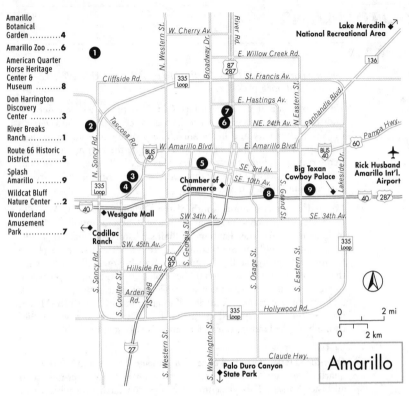

Streight Dr. ☎*806/355–9547* ⊕*www.dhdc.org* ✉*$5.50* ☉*Tues.–Sat. 9:30–4:30, Sun. noon–4:30.*

① **River Breaks Ranch.** Ride a covered wagon, clap for the ropers, and ☼ watch all of the pretty horses race while betting on 'em with funny ★ money. Afterward, savor some succulent barbecue and sourdough biscuits, chuck-wagon style. Late April through September is the high season. *⌖612 S. Van Buren* ☎*806/374–0357* ⊕*www.riverbreaks. com* ⚓*Reservations essential* ✉*$20–$40 for everything.*

⑤ **Route 66 Historic District.** This old part of Amarillo is located in the his-
Fodor'sChoice toric neighborhood of San Jacinto. The district affords an enjoyable
★ stroll through history with modern shops built in historic places that once lined the old Route 66. Set among homes from the early 1900s, some of which are admittedly a bit run-down), the mile-long strip offers cute little antiques stores and restaurants with several types of cuisine—locals love the hamburgers at Golden Light, dishing up American classics for half a century. Check out the live music in the summer, too, and be sure to stop by "The Nat," a huge ballroom where famous musicians played in the heyday of Route 66. This is a great place for antiques. ✉*Sixth Street.*

PLANNING YOUR TRIP

WHEN TO GO

The Panhandle bursts with life regardless of the season. No matter how chill the wind is, or how broiling the summer climax, Texans will seize reasons to celebrate and congregate. That said, your best bet is to skip the wind-scoured depths of winter, particularly November through January. When folks say there's no barrier to Canada in the winter, they're not joking; residents of Amarillo will regale you with stories about how a Nor'easter froze their door shut one night. The cold nights probably won't kill you, but they will make it uncomfortable to traipse around. The Panhandle's northern part, which is a mere 80 mi from southern Colorado, sees an annual average snowfall of 15.6 inches.

In terms of the weather, it's best to visit during the more temperate months of March, April, and especially May, when Cinco de Mayo festivals hit full swing, and early summer, before the late-July and August tongue-hanging heat waves. But all summer long could be your pick if you're looking for a party. Summer is the only time many attractions open up, and when live music and several fun events take place. The month of September is cooler, and it's time Lubbock musically celebrates native son Buddy Holly. Festivals also explode elsewhere in September, as towns and cities festively commemorate their Hispanic heritage on the Mexican Independence Day from Spain. Called Diez y Seis de Septiembre, it translates to September 16 and is a historic event equal in weight to the Fourth of July.

GETTING THERE & AROUND

Though the cities are widely spaced, most of them offer easily accessible airports. Amarillo, Lubbock, and Abilene all have smallish but busy airports. Nearby Midland International Airport, in West Texas, is also a good option. Wichita Falls has a municipal airport, but it's used mostly by the military, though American Eagle flies in from the DFW airport. There's a shuttle service between DFW and the city of Wichita Falls. It's about $65 and is faster than taking the bus. Greyhound connects the region's larger cities as well as several small ones.

❾ **Splash Amarillo.** Cool off at the Panhandle's only water park. Among its amusements are half-a-dozen slides, a wave pool, and an arcade. The price is significantly less if you're coming as a chaperone and aren't going to be getting in the water (and you're not in swimwear). ✉1415 Sunrise Dr. ☎806/376–4477 ⊕www.splashamarillo.com ✉$17 ⊙May 31–Aug. 24. Mon.–Sat. noon–7, Sun. noon–6.

❷ **Wildcat Bluff Nature Center.** See the prairie-dog town, porcupines, butterfly garden, cottonwood trees, and the rugged scenery along 5 mi of trails near what once was the Santa Fe Trail. Wagon ruts from early trail crossers can still be seen. ■TIP→Exercise caution where you step, because prairie rattlesnakes and the Texas brown tarantula are among the wildlife. ✉2301 N. Soncy Rd. ☎806/352–6007 ⊕www.wildcatbluff.org ✉$3 ⊙Tues.–Sat. 9–5.

Cadillac Ranch

This is a car wreck.

Well, at least that's what it looks like at first, this line of paint-embroidered Cadillacs, half-buried in a cow pasture near Amarillo. The Caddies, which number 10, stand straight up with their tails in the air and spray paint cans nearby for scrawling. It's a surreal sight in the Texas desert, which is probably exactly what eccentric artist Stanley Marsh had in mind. Marsh, who made millions by harnessing the natural helium of the region, owns the cow pasture they're sunk into, and originally built the "ranch" in 1974. He had to move them in 1997 due to development and in order to keep the

disjointed, eye-candy image going. It's located west of Amarillo on old Route 66 south of I-40 and is open 24/7. You're encouraged to bring spray paint and gussy up the Cadillacs.

These days Marsh keeps himself occupied by manufacturing mischievous and random road signs that residents clamor to display in their yards, and there's a long waiting list. You'll undoubtedly see them throughout Amarillo, but don't mess with them and don't spray paint them at Cadillac Ranch. Marsh gets testy about that, and just like Texas, you don't mess with him.

—Jennifer Edwards

7 **Wonderland Amusement Park.** An arcade, roller coasters, miniature golf, bumper cars, and more make this attraction in Thompson Park a whirlwind of fun for kids and the parents who love them (and the ones who love coasters, too!). ⊠*2601 Dumas Dr.* ☎*432/426-3540* ⊕*www.wonderlandpark.com* ☎*$12.95–$21.95 (miniature golf and some rides extra).*

ARTS & ENTERTAINMENT

NIGHTLIFE **Big Texan Cowboy Palace.** Located inside the Big Texan Steak Ranch, the Western-themed Palace rounds up an assortment of entertainment throughout the week. Some events, such as the Big Texan Opry, are held only during summer months. Dinner and dancing—the Texas two-step, of course—can be had every Friday and Saturday nights. ⊠*7701 E. I–40* ☎*800/657-7177* ⊕*www.bigtexan.com/entertainment.htm.*

Artist Georgia O'Keeffe was inspired by the endless sky of the Panhandle, and she lived here on and off from 1912 to 1918. She taught in the Panhandle for four years, first in an Amarillo elementary school and later for two years at West Texas A&M in nearby Canyon. Residents thought she was strange because of her odd personality and weird way of dressing—including her tendancy to wear pants decades before doing so became okay for women.

WHERE TO EAT

$–$$$$ ✕**Big Texan Steak Ranch.** A sprawling, almost over-the-top landmark along what was once U.S. Route 66, the Big Texan is famous for its
Fodor's Choice   Texas-shaped pool, live entertainment, and, most of all, its legend-
★   ary 72-ounce slab o' beef. If you can consume the entire 4.5-pound

fillet, you get it free—but note: 8,000 have succeeded, while 34,000 have tried and failed. (No word on how many got sick afterward.) You might try the flavorful Frito pie instead. The Big Texan offers a free limousine service to and from hotels in the area. ✉ *7701 E. I–40,* ☎ *800/657–7177* ☰ *AE, D, MC, V.*

$–$$ ✕ **La Fiesta Grande.** Meaning "the Big Party," this local Mexican favorite has a long menu (from chimichangas to chipotle shrimp), big portions, and cold margaritas that add up to a party-worthy experience. Many of the city's multitudinous fajita lovers think the fajitas here are the best. ✉ *2201 S. Ross Ave.* ☎ *806/374–3689* ☰ *AE, D, DC, MC, V* ✉ *7415 S. 45th Ave.* ☎ *806/352–1330.*

WHERE TO STAY

$ 🏨 **Bar H Dude Ranch.** The ranch offers what few hotels can claim to—the ☾ chance to gallop on a horse, sleep outdoors, and go on a cattle drive Fodor's Choice (if you choose). Guests can also take in the sights on this 5,500-acre ★ property via Jeep or wagon and eat chuck-wagon style. The owners and staff treat visitors the way the best people in Texas tend to—like they already know you and hope to know you better. People come from all over the country and abroad to eat the rib eye, participate in ranch life, bird-watch, and hunt anything from buffalo to wild pigs to mule deer. The ranch is an hour or so south of Amarillo. Rooms must be rented in blocks. **Pros:** Many kids programs, satellite TV, and free Wi-Fi. **Cons:** Rooms are basic, but this *is* a ranch, after all. ✍ *Box 1191, Clarendon, 79226* ☎ *800/627–9871* ⊕ *www.barhduderanch.com* ↩ *2 houses, 4 cabins, 10 bunkhouses* ⚒ *In room: Wi-Fi, no phone (some). In hotel: Wi-Fi, no elevator, no-smoking rooms* ⦿ *MAP* ☰ *AE, D, MC, V.*

$–$$ 🏨 **Historical Parkview House Bed and Breakfast.** A wonderful example of an Old West home during the Victorian period, this B&B is crammed with antique knickknacks. It has a strong country feel, reflecting the early 1900s in the West. Because there are so few rooms, the owner is able to welcome her guests personally, and the price is reasonable. The hot breakfast isn't exactly Western, but it's rib-sticking regardless. **Pros:** A claw-foot bathtub is an option; there's also a hammock for relaxing, and a hot tub. **Cons:** Bathrooms are down the hall, not in the rooms. ✉ *1311 S. Jefferson St.,* ☎ *806/373–9464* ⊕ *www.parkviewhousebb. com* ↩ *6 rooms* ⚒ *In-room: VCR (some). In-hotel: no elevator, no-smoking rooms* ☰ *AE, MC, V* ⦿ *CP.*

$ 🏨 **Big Texan Motel.** A little exaggerated but a lot of fun, this hotel takes ☾ the Texas spirit way past even the Texas-sized level. There are a Texas-shaped pool, an oversized rocking chair, a great steakhouse with an it's-free-if-you-can-finish-it 4.5-pound steak, and even a horse hotel for parking your filly (should you have happened to ride into town on one). Rooms feature colorful lit-up "false fronts." While you're in residence, check out the shooting gallery or full-of-Texas-souvenirs gift shop. There are free rides from the hotel to the airport in the Big Texan limo, which, we kid you not, has steer horns affixed to the hood. This is Texas in the extreme, and it makes for a darn good time. **Pros:** The famous steak house is next door, in-room hot tubs (some), natural scenery surrounds you. **Cons:** No in-room Internet. ✉ *7701 E. I–40* ☎ *800/657–7177* ⊕ *www.bigtexan.com* ↩ *50 rooms* ⚒ *In-hotel: Wi-*

14

CLOSE UP

Get Your Kicks...

It's easy to forget how young the concept of interstates is, now that ours have morphed into slick, Information Age versions with six and eight lanes fenced in by traffic signs and digital billboards, paved as slickly and thickly with asphalt as our own arteries are by the fast-food joints that flank them.

The U.S. interstate highway system actually had its genesis in legislation in the 1920s, and its early childhood during the Great Depression, when the government financed massive public works. But it didn't have its great, adolescent awakening until U.S. Route 66 was constructed, connecting untold capillaries in small towns that otherwise were isolated from any national highway. Finally completed in 1938, it became the major east–west route through America. When World War II broke out, traffic exploded with trucks moving supplies, moving people, moving concepts, and culture. The route also breathed new life into the town as it created gas stations, motor inns, campgrounds, and even the rock-'n'-roll scene one cow town at a time.

Amarillo got a sizeable share of Texas's scant 178 mi of Route 66, much of which the city has preserved and glorified. Touring it can be confusing, though. The project that snuffed its life—a major interstate and intrastate system (more on that later)—used parts of the road in its projects and averted other parts. In the city, two roads are associated with it—Sixth Street (also called Mother Road) and Amarillo Boulevard. On both are the scuttled remains of old hotels; distinctive, vintage signs from the '50s; and ruins of once-profitable mom-and-pop businesses. The Sixth Street stretch is set in downtown Amarillo and is full of dance halls, restaurants, bars, and shops, taking visitors through the historic district. Along the other section, Amarillo Boulevard, are the ruins of an old airport and airport museum, the Triangle Motel, and the famous Cadillac Ranch.

In the Panhandle, Amarillo's the only major city the road plugged into the matrix. The rest were handfuls of towns as small as monopoly houses on the vast plains. Many turned into ghost towns after the road was declared deceased. The town of Adrian commemorates its claim to be the halfway mark on the route with a café called The Midpoint.

In the mid-1950s, Route 66 was increasingly unable to keep up with the high traffic demands placed on it. Dwight D. Eisenhower proposed a vast new interstate system. By 1970 Route 66 had been severed from hometown America and bypassed by the new highways. In the Depression novel *The Grapes of Wrath,* Steinbeck called it *The Mother Road.* In Amarillo as elsewhere, to history buffs it will always remain just that.

—Jennifer Edwards

Fi, pool, restaurant, bar, laundry, no elevator, no-smoking rooms ▭AE, D, MC, V.

CANYON & PALO DURO CANYON STATE PARK

19 mi south of Amarillo.

More than 13,000 residents occupy the trim, tidy town of Canyon. Built on bulls, blood, sweat, and agriculture, Canyon was founded in 1889 by businessman Lincoln Guy Conner. The coming of a railway about a decade later established it as a cattle and cotton shipping hub, while the opening of a university in 1910 helped tame, educate, and grow the town. Today Canyon's revitalized downtown has lovely rose-colored paving stones and a very strange but eye-catching historic courthouse. There's also a serene wildlife refuge set squarely in the migration flyway, providing an awesome vantage point for bird-viewing.

> **FRITO PIE**
>
> You've heard of the Texas two-step, but when it comes to Texas food, here's a four-step routine you need to give a whirl:
>
> 1. Fill a bowl with Fritos.
>
> 2. Pour some chili on top.
>
> 3. Add shredded cheese, diced onions (optional), sliced jalapeños (optional), salsa (optional), and sour cream (optional).
>
> 4. Dig in!

But the area's main draw is Palo Duro Canyon, located 15 mi east of town on Highway 217. The canyon's name comes from the copious mesquites growing throughout its ridges and pinnacles—Palo Duro means "hard wood" in Spanish. The canyon reaches into two counties, and the state park that contains it covers 16,402 acres. If that sounds like a lot, it is, but get this: the canyon was once in private hands!

Visitors to Palo Duro Canyon come from across the state, across the nation, and across the world to take in the "TEXAS!" musical, explore via Jeep and horse-drawn wagons, take ranch tours, and pitch tents in the bottom of the canyon (RVs are welcome in some spots, too). The long, winding drive down into the canyon affords some beautiful, beautiful—did we mention beautiful?—vistas, particularly when the morning or evening sun casts the colors in gold. The thin pillars of rock called hoodoos are especially amazing.

DID YOU KNOW? Ranches that host guests are known as dude ranches because Westerners referred to Easterners, especially those from major cities, as "dudes." The word came from New York slang in the 1880s.

WHAT TO SEE

★ **Panhandle Plains Historical Museum.** The state's largest historical museum, this extensive, multi-department "Smithsonian of Texas" explores the geological and cultural history of the Panhandle, from 19th-century pioneers to 1960s hot rods. It's located on West Texas A&M University's campus. Families receive a discount on admission. ✉ *2503 4th Ave.* ☎ *806/651–2250* ⊕ *www.panhandleplains.org* 💲*$7* ⏲ *June–Aug., Mon.–Sat. 9–6, Sun. 1–6; Sept.–May, Mon.–Sat. 9–5 Sun. 1–6.*

SPORTS & THE OUTDOORS

Buffalo Lake National Wildlife Refuge. Lots of wildlife roam—or soar, as the case may be—in this 7,664-acre refuge in Umbarger, a small town outside of Canyon. Bald eagles, bobcats, coyotes, and prairie dogs are among them. The refuge is an excellent place for bird-watching due to its location on the migratory flyway. Various habitats on the grounds include river, marsh, and plains. ⊠ *On FM 168, 1.5 mi off U.S. 60 between Hereford and Canyon, Umbarger* ☎ *806/499-3382* 🖾 *Free* ⊙ *Daily 8–6 Oct.–Mar., daily 8–8 May–Sept.*

Palo Duro Canyon State Park. At 120 mi long, 20 mi wide, and 800 feet

Fodor's Choice ★

deep in places, the "Grand Canyon of Texas" is one of those awe-inspiring parks that hikers and campers rhapsodize about and revisit over and over. The blood-colored walls and spires, spectacular at sunset, are iconic of the West both visually and historically. It's where the last American Indian tribes surrendered to the U.S. government during the Red River wars. The park's very busy in the summer. The gift store sells stadium-type food such as nachos, candy, and burgers. ⊠ *11450 Park Rd. 5* ☎ *806/488-2227, Ext. 100* ⊕ *www.tpwd.state.tx.us* 🖾 *$4 (day use), $12/$20 (camping; reservation required)* ⊙ *Mar.–Oct., daily 8 AM–10 PM; Nov.–Feb., daily 8–5.*

■ DID YOU KNOW?

The closing scenes of the 1989 movie *Indiana Jones and the Last Crusade* were filmed at a ranch near the eastern edge of Palo Duro Canyon. (Nearby Claude was the site for a Paul Newman movie).

ARTS & ENTERTAINMENT

Elkins Ranch. A small ranch on the cusp of the gorgeous scenery in Palo Duro, offers an 8:30 AM chuck-wagon breakfast for booked-ahead guests, plus Old West entertainment that includes cowboy poets and pickers, as well as short to long canyon Jeep tours. There's also a dinner option with campfire tales, cowboy music, and tale-tellers dressed in period costume; it's available only to groups of 40 or more. An interesting note is the ranch's staff, which includes at least two full-blooded American Indians from different tribes (Comanche and Kiowa) as well as an engaging "mountain man" with a hippie beard and an incredible knowledge of local and natural lore. Try the cowboy coffee—coffee grounds are simmered with water without the benefit of a filter. It's not what you're used to, but it's a fun experience. ⊠ *Hwy. 2, Box 289 (near the entrance to Palo Duro)* ☎ *806/488-2100* ⊕ *www.theelkinsranch. com* 🖾 *$20–35 (Jeep tours), $25 (breakfast, entertainment, and canyon tour)* ⊙ *By appointment.*

"TEXAS!". Famed, family friendly, and going strong for more than 40

Fodor's Choice ★

years, the musical "TEXAS!" is the official state play. Each summer a troupe of 60 actors re-enacts the great battles of Texas history, as the state went from being part of Mexico to setting up its own country. The much-loved spectacle is staged in an amphitheater set in the cleft of stunning Palo Duro Canyon—a spectacular natural backdrop. Fireworks and music add to the lively atmosphere. Buy tickets in advance, in person or online. The ticket office is at 1514 5th Avenue in Canyon.

PANHANDLE FESTIVALS

MAY **Cinco de Mayo.** Each year around May 5, Panhandle towns burst into color and explode with sound as Texans celebrate their Hispanic roots. The day marks the Battle of Puebla, an amazing victory for Mexicans fighting a much larger, better equipped force of French soldiers. Amarillo's celebration is one of the region's biggest and features live music, food, Mexican dancing and costumes, vendors, and a parade. ⊠ *Downtown Amarillo* ☎ *800/735–1288.*

SEPT. **Lubbock Music Festival.** For years, this annual event in mid- to late September celebrated rock music and native son Buddy Holly—in fact, until 2007, it was known as the Buddy Holly Music Festival. The name changed following a lawsuit by Holly's widow, Maria Elena Holly (she wanted more money for the use of his name). The live-music festival continues with the focus now on local musicians. ⊠ *Depot Entertainment District, Lubbock* ☎ *800/735–1288.*

14

⊠ *11450 Park Rd. 5, Palo Duro Canyon State Park* ☎ *806/655–2181* ⊕ *www.texas-show.com* ⊠ *$7.50–$43.45* ⊙ *June–July.*

WHERE TO EAT & STAY

¢–$ × **Pepito's Mexican Restaurant.** Bright, colorful, and probably the most popular sit-down Mexican place in Canyon, Pepito's serves up *carne guisada* (beef strips simmered for a long time in a spicy sauce), plus sour-cream chicken enchiladas and quesadillas by the boatload. They also do an interesting twist on stir-fry by substituting in veggies like squash and tomatoes. Pepito's also makes its own tortillas. ⊠ *408 23rd St.* ☎ *806/655–4736* ⊟ *AE, D, DC, MC, V* ⊙ *Closed Sun.*

$–$$ ⊞ **Hudspeth House Bed and Breakfast.** In Canyon's historic downtown square, the beautifully kept, multi-story Hudspeth House is part of the scenery. It's within walking distance of the university and skipping distance of the antiques shops on the square. Built in 1909 from a mail-order kit from Sears, this B&B is a community landmark where weddings and murder mysteries are sometimes conducted. With the patina of nearly a century of history, this a place for an evening spent Southern-style in the breezes of the porch or asleep in one of the comfy beds. **Pros:** Rooms are large, with options galore. **Cons:** Noisy sometimes due to university's proximity. ⊠ *1905 4th Ave.,* ☎ *806/655–9800* ⊕ *www.hudspethinn.com* ⇆ *8 rooms* ⌂ *In-room: Wi-Fi. In-hotel: no elevator, no-smoking rooms* ⊟ *D, MC, V* ⊙ *open year-round* ⟡ *BP.*

Fodor's Choice
★

SOUTH PLAINS

The South Plains have been a center for cattle and cotton for more than 100 years. The United States produces about a quarter of the world's supply of cotton; Texas produces more than any other state, and about half the Texas yield comes from the South Plains.

LUBBOCK

123 mi south of Amarillo, 347 mi northwest of Dallas.

Larger than Amarillo, probably by virtue of the nearly 30,000 students who attend Texas Tech University, Lubbock's history is wed to Amarillo and the other towns in the area by a shared Western history and frontier culture. Like Amarillo and Abilene, Lubbock also hosted rock musicians during the Route 66 heyday. It also reared some of its own, namely the dark-rimmed-glasses-wearing, pompadour-sporting Buddy Holly and his band, the Crickets.

> ### CONFUSING QUAFFING
>
> Those looking to wet their whistles inside Lubbock County or the city itself will have to navigate some of the most head-rubbing alcohol laws in the state. The area's nearly dry, with a few wet spots. Inside the city, alcohol can be sold by the glass but not by the "package"—except at an assembly of stores known as the Strip. Outside city limits, it's the reverse: alcohol can be bought at a liquor store but not sold by the glass.

These days Lubbock's as famous for its rousing Texas Tech and Lubbock Christian University games and unique history as it is for its Buddy Holly Walk of Fame and Texas-sized Holly statue. West Texans travel from miles around to party in the district formerly known as the Depot, fill in the Red Raider stands (Texas Tech games are usually at 97 percent or greater capacity), or to pop into the bevy of museums immortalizing Lubbock's wartime and agricultural heritage. Luckily, a lot of the landmarks are situated close together near the Depot Entertainment District, while others are clustered on the northern side of Texas Tech.

WHAT TO SEE

❶ Apple Country Hi-Plains Orchards. Make like Dorothy and enter this refreshing 6,000-tree, 30-variety apple grove. The fruit is pick-your-own (during July when the apples ripen) and so fresh no one will want to chuck a single one. The apples you bring back are just a dollar a pound. There's also a bakery serving apple-centric pastries and a cider mill (try the apple spice wine). Each September you can celebrate the beloved fruit during the orchard's Apple Butter Festival, a mix of live music and kids' activities. ✉ *12206 E. U.S. 62, 4 mi east of Idalou* ☎ *806/892–2961* ⊕ *www.applecountryorchards.com* ⊙ *Mon.–Sat. 9–6 Sun. 9–4.*

❷ American Museum of Agriculture. Nothing runs like a Deere, dear, and this homey museum's here to tell the story of just what those famous tractors were used for. This museum unfolds a rich story about agriculture and survival in the Panhandle—through more than 700 models, artifacts, and restored pieces of farm equipment. Interesting to behold, this collection of physical history includes horse-drawn equipment and machines that made it through the devastation of the Dust Bowl. ✉ *1501 Canyon Lake Dr.* ☎ *806/239–5796* ⊕ *www.agriculture history.org* ✉ *$3 donation suggested* ⊙ *Wed.–Sat. 10–5.*

3 The American Wind Power Center and Museum. The shiny silver windmills that populate this area have long been used to pump water from the ground for "stock tanks," drinking containers for cattle, horses, and other critters. Many cities in Texas, however, are attempting to harness the restless, eternal winds to produce energy. This museum immortalizes that history with scores of windmills and paintings, too. ✉ *1701 Canyon Lake Dr.* ☎ *806/747–8734* ⊕ *www.windmill.com* ✐ *$5 or $10 (per family) donation suggested* ⊙ *Tues.–Sat. 10–5, Sun. 2–5.*

14

5 The Buddy Holly Center. Despite its name, the center doesn't simply eulogize its famous, enormously influential native son Buddy Holly. It also recognizes excellence in Texas artists, including Waylon Jennings and Roy Orbison, both from the Panhandle. The collection features Holly's early childhood artifacts and legendary Fender as well as his thick-rimmed glasses. ✉ *1801 Crickets Ave. (formerly Ave. G)* ☎ *806/775–3560* ⊕ *www.buddyhollycenter.org* ✐ *$5* ⊙ *Mon.–Sat. 10–5, Sun. 1–5.*

6 The Buddy Holly Statue and Walk of Fame. Pewter-colored plaques pave the street thoroughfare, commemorating great Texas artist and native son Buddy Holly, plus other influential musicians such as Mac Davis and Tanya Tucker. ✉ *7th St. and Ave. Q.*

7 National Ranching Heritage Center. Two hundred years of ranching life is re-created on this 30-acre park adjacent to the Texas Tech campus through nearly 40 relocated historical ranching structures that include barns, an old train, and a smithy. It's fun during the holidays because buildings and grounds are festively lit. Kids can join the "Junior Rough Riders" program; it provides invitations to special kids' events. ✉ *3121 4th St.* ☎ *806/742–0498* ⊕ *www.depts.ttu.edu/ranchhc/home.htm* ✐ *Free* ⊙ *Mon.–Sat. 10–5, Sun. 1–5.*

8 Museum of Texas Tech University. Texas Tech is one of the most important educational institutions in all of the Panhandle and West Texas, attracting nearly 30,000 students a year to its diverse programs. How it came about is an interesting story, and the museum will give you your fill. There's also a "stellar" planetarium with daily shows, and other museums as part of the complex. ✉ *3301 Fourth St.* ☎ *806/381–7911* ⊕ *www.mottua.org* ✐ *Free* ⊙ *Mon.–Fri. 8–5.*

9 Science Spectrum and Omni Theatre. Fun. Lots of fun. Is this learning? Housing dozens of interactive exhibits, amphibians and reptiles, dinosaur re-creations, and a huge hot-air balloon, this place is a delight. ✉ *2579 S. Loop 289, Ste. 250* ☎ *806/745–2525* ⊕ *www.sciencespectrum.com* ✐ *$11 (including theater)* ⊙ *Mon.–Sat. 10–5, Sun. 1–5.*

4 Mackenzie Park. Though it began as a humble city project, this Brazos River–laced park has grown to accommodate adventurous undertakings like the Joyland Amusement Park (⇨ *Arts & Entertainment)* as

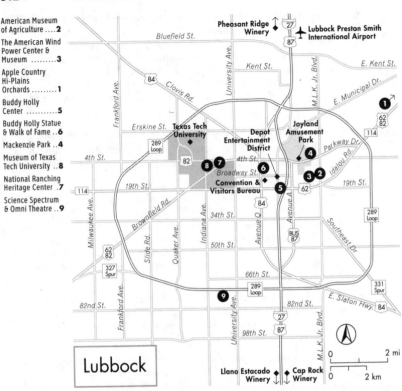

Lubbock

well as a traditional golf course and disc golf course. Several museums like the American Wind Power Center and American Museum of Agriculture call the soft green grass of this area home. So, too, does a sleek colony of chattering, hole-digging prairie dogs. ⊠*302 N. I–27 not far from 4th St.* ☎*806/376–4477* ⊠*Free (museums and theme parks extra)* ⊙ *Daily, dawn to dusk.*

OFF THE BEATEN PATH

About 38 mi northwest of Lubbock, in Littlefield, stands a replica of the **World's Tallest Windmill.** The original, built in 1887, was 132 feet high, sitting in a canyon (the reason it had to be built so high) on XIT Ranch. It blew over in 1926. Located at U.S. 84 and XIT Avenue, the replica is 114 feet tall.

DID YOU KNOW?

You might have some Texas "jeans" in your family. Each year the American Cotton Growers mill in Littlefield, Texas, transforms cotton from the state into enough yards of denim to create 19 million pairs of blue jeans.

ARTS & ENTERTAINMENT

Joyland Amusement Park. Despite the hokey name, this is an orderly park with lots of rides to offer, including bumper cars, a carousel, Tilt-a-Whirls, roller coasters, and three water coasters. Visitors can pay one price to ride however many rides they can fit in before the park closes at 7 or 10 PM, depending on the day of the week. Families can expect a

CLOSE UP

Buddy Holly: When the Music Lived

Though he only had five or so years of recording (1954–59), Buddy Holly changed the face of rock 'n' roll. In the process, he established the rock-band prototype: guitar, bass, drums, and vocals.

Born in Lubbock on Sept. 7, 1936, Holly was a dyed-in-the-straw hick, playing bluegrass and country music, working at transforming the music into something rawer, more exciting—until he heard Elvis Presley, and the seed was planted for a life of rock 'n' roll. He formed a group called the Crickets, the players all Lubbock boys. In early 1957 the quartet set to wax "That'll Be the Day" and "I'm Lookin' for Someone to Love," both major hits.

Holly was a perfectionist, and the results were heard on the singles "Peggy Sue," "Not Fade Away," "Everyday," and "Oh Boy!" All released in short succession from September to November 1957, each track is a rock classic: simple, clear, powerful.

"Maybe" and "Rave On" followed in early 1958, and by the middle of that year Holly and the Crickets were superstars with number-one,

Lorem ipsum dolor sit amet,

million-selling records. They went on European tours and the popular Ed Sullivan TV show.

In January 1959 Holly headed out on a tour with Ritchie Valens, the Big Bopper, and the Belmonts. The plane carrying them went down in a snowstorm on February 3rd near Mason City, Iowa, killing all aboard. Holly's fame continued to grow in his death, with songs like Don McLean's "Miss American Pie" recalling "the day the music died."

—Robert Wilonsky, excerpted from a piece in *Fodor's Compass American Guides: Texas 3rd edition*

14

well-behaved crowd, as operators don't tolerate funny business. ⊠ *In Mackenzie Park* ☎ *806/763–2719* ⊕ *www.joylandpark.com* ⌨ *$11.50 to $16.50* ⊙ *Late-Mar.–early Sept. Hours can vary widely, however, it's never open before 2 PM or past 10 PM; it's open earlier on early summer weekends.*

NIGHTLIFE

Fodor's Choice
★ **Depot Entertainment District.** Barbecues, breakfast, breweries, and a darn good time can be had in Lubbock's Depot District, built around an old railroad depot. Pub entertainment, grub, and good conversation are on tap in this buzzing area. It feels a little outlawish, too, because Lubbock is a mostly dry city, where beer, wine, and liquor can't be sold except by the glass. There are upscale restaurants, a live theater, and dance halls. La Diosa serves up atmospheric fun and dispenses boutique wines

from this area. The district's also a good place for shopping. ⊠*19th St. and I-27.*

WHERE TO EAT

$–$$$$ ✕ **Las Brisas Southwest Steakhouse.** Residents serious about their steak
Fodors Choice but in quest of a casual atmosphere return again and again to this
★ steak house, with its succulent Black Angus beef, long wine list, and
live music on summer weekends. The blackened salmon is to die for
(or, at least trek for) if you're a fish fan, and you gotta try some of the
melt-in-your-mouth mashed potatoes with jalapeño. ⊠*4701 112th St.*
☎*806/687–6050* ▤*AE, D, MC, V.*

$–$$ ✕ **Abuelo's Mexican Food Embassy.** Though this is a chain restaurant, it's
a darn fine chain restaurant, with good service and great diversity in its
menu, from starters to the tequila—and the enchiladas are a stand-out.
It's a gorgeous restaurant, with beautiful walls and a colonial Spanish theme. ⊠*4401 82nd St.* ☎*806/374–3689* ▤*AE, D, DC, MC, V*
⊙*Closed Sun.* ☎*806/794–1762.*

¢–$ ✕ **Rudy's Country Store and Bar-B-Q.** Locals love Rudy's, and it's one of
the first places they turn to when they get that barbecue craving. In
this laid-back, patriotic restaurant, Rudy's treats its meat to a spice rub
and offers piquant, homey spicy sauces to top it—the way it's done in
many old-school Texas barbecue joints. Brisket's the standby, though
turkey's the healthier option. ⊠*4930 S. Loop 289* ☎*806/797–1777*
▤*AE, V, MC.*

WHERE TO STAY

$–$$ ▦ **Woodrow House Bed and Breakfast.** Located across from Texas Tech
☾ and its attendant sights, this three-story house is a spectacle in itself.
The house contains some rooms with 1800s-furniture, while others
are decked out in—what else?—Texas Tech regalia. Kids are awed by
the bright red Caboose, a suite in the back yard. **Pros:** Within walking distance of the major sights **Cons:** No elevator. ⊠*2620 19th St.,
Clarendon,* ☎*806/793–3330* ⊕*www.woodrowhouse.com* ⮑*7 rooms*
☾*In-room: Wi-Fi, Ethernet, TV (some), DVD (some), VHS (some) In-
hotel: no elevator, no-smoking rooms* ▤*AE, MC, V* ⊙|*BP.*

ABILENE

*164 mi southeast of Lubbock via U.S. 84 and I–20 or U.S. 82 and U.S.
83, 154 mi west of Forth Worth via I–20*

A dusty domicile of more than 116,000 people, Abilene boasts some
noteworthy attractions: a historic fort, three lakes, several museums,
a zoo (where visitors can feed almost all the animals—even the elephants), a re-created frontier village, and a stately old theater. Abilene
also has a few claims to fame. Pop star Jessica Simpson was born and
reared here, while runners like Bobby Morrow, the Olympics champion, were incubated in this sports-centric area.

It's Time to Wine

There's no shame in admitting it. The words "Texas" and "wine" seem mutually exclusive, don't they? After all, the state's known for some of the best beef in the country, a meat and potatoes culture, and a definite overall aversion to the California lifestyle, famous for its sumptuous vino.

But wine lovers are in for a pleasant surprise in—of all places—Lubbock. This conservative, family-values town is near to several wineries, some of which continue to garner awards in national and international contests. Llano Estacado led the charge when it opened in 1977, and has grown to become the biggest premium winery in the state. It's netted tons of awards in state and international competitions and features tours, wine tastings, and a gift shop. The Cabernet Sauvignon is one of the winery's best offerings.

Another award-winning producer, Cap+Rock has also scored state and international awards. Its wines are delicious and its grounds are (arguably) more so. High ceilings, commodious adobe-style structures, and Spanish tile welcome guests before the first hello. Try the sweet, tingling wash of its award-winning Orange Muscat, especially if you're new to wine. (An aside: the winery is named after the impenetrable stone beneath the Panhandle strata.) A much smaller winery, family-owned Pheasant Ridge,

produces highly regarded wines that have also won many awards.

WINERIES

Llano Estacado. The winery is capable of producing 125,000 cases a year, and it likes to share its knowledge with other winemakers. A complimentary tour and tasting take about 40 minutes. Tours run every 30 minutes. ■**TIP**➜ **If you can, come during October's Grape Day, which celebrates the harvest and Lubbock.** ✉ *3426 E. FM 1585 (3.2 mi east of U.S. 87)* ☎ *806/745–2258* ⊕ *www. llanowine.com* ⊗ *Mon.–Sat. 10–4, Sun. noon–4.*

Cap+Rock. In the winter, warm yourself by the natural stone fireplaces. In the summer, dance in a ballroom at your wedding or anniversary. This upscale winery with beautiful surroundings offers free tastings of some of its 15 wines and free tours of the large grounds (call for tour hours). ✉ *408 E. Woodrow Rd.* ☎ *806/863–2704* ⊕ *www.caprockwinery.com* ⊗ *Mon.–Sat. 10–5, Sun. noon–5.*

Pheasant Ridge. Complimentary tastings are available in the tasting room during business hours. This winery is less accessible than other wineries in the area, so call for directions. ✉ *Off U.S. 287 on RR 3* ☎ *806/746–6003* ⊕ *www.pheasantridgewinery.com* ⊗ *Fri. and Sat. noon–6, Sun. 1–5.*

—Jennifer Edwards

14

WHAT TO SEE

⟲ ★ **Abilene Zoo.** People travel from miles around to see this small but popular zoo, which features African creatures like zebras alongside Texan critters like buffalo. The somewhat small zoo, located in Nelson Park, is a great place to interact because you can buy inexpensive food for the animals and then feed them by hand. ✉ *2070 Zoo La.* ☎ *325/672–9771* ⊕ *www.abilenetx.com/zoo* ✉ *$4* ⊗ *Memorial Day weekend–Labor Day, daily 9–9; early Sept.–late May, daily 9–5.*

♻ **Buffalo Gap Historic Village.** Located 14 mi south of Abilene, Buffalo Gap

Fodor'sChoice tells the story of frontier Texas as much through wood and stone as it

★ does through words. Several structures are clustered around the original limestone Taylor County Courthouse and Jail, completed in 1879. These structures re-create life during three important periods—1883, 1905, and 1925—with such buildings as pioneer homes, a parsonage, and an old country store. Exhibits range from frontier firearms to American Indian artifacts. ⊠*14 mi south of Abilene on Loop 89/ Buffalo Gap Rd.* ☎*325/572-3365* ⊕*www.buffalogap.com* ⊠*$5-$12* ⊙*Mon.-Sat. 10-5, Sun. noon-5.*

♻ **Fort Phantom Hill.** In the 1850s the U.S. government was fortifying its

★ frontiers with a second string of forts designed to protect travelers and residents from Indian attacks. Fort Phantom Hill was one of those forts, but only occupied for three years and damaged by fire. Today three of the originals structures and lots of chimneys remain to give visitors a visual clue about what life was like in wild and wooly Texas. ⊠*On FM 600, 11 mi north of I-20* ☎*325/677-1309* ⊕*www.fort phantom.org* ⊠*Free* ⊙*Daily, dawn to dusk.*

SPORTS & THE OUTDOORS

♻ **Abilene State Park.** People gather at this cool, oak- and pecan-shaded

Fodor'sChoice park to fish in the pond, swim in the central pool, camp beneath the

★ leaves, and hike the trails. Though small (530 acres) for a state park, it's a welcome respite full of activities and has room for soccer and football playing, and even kite flying. There are sites for both tent campers and RVers, plus the park rents neat, Mongolian-style yurts. The park is located 16 mi southwest of Abilene. ⊠*150 Park Rd. 32* ☎*325/572-3204* ⊠*Free* ⊙*Daily, dawn to dusk, plus camping.*

WHERE TO EAT & STAY

¢-$$ ✕ **Spaghetti Warehouse.** This little-bit upscale restaurant in the Mall of Abilene is a cozy venue for a romantic dinner or even a nice place to treat the kids to some hearty lasagna. The menu isn't big on experimental dishes, but rather sticks with what its kitchen does best—lasagna, fettuccini Alfredo, and its trademark, mouth-watering, build-your-own spaghetti. ⊠*4310 Buffalo Gap Rd.* ☎*325/695-8616* ⊟*AE, D, DC, MC, V* ⊙*Closed Sun.*

$$-$$$ 🏨 **MCM Eleganté.** One of seven Eleganté properties scattered through

♻ Texas and New Mexico, this hotel comes highly recommended by locals and passers-through. With an elegant Spanish-style decor, a good restaurant (Remington's Restaurant/American fare) and excellent bar area, it offers guests more comfort than the average chain hotel. There's an indoor pool, sauna, game room, and cooked-to-order breakfast. **Pros:** Near the mall and restaurants; airport shuttle. **Cons:** Because locals often come in to the bar for a nightcap, it can get a little noisy. ⊠*4250 Ridgemont Dr.* ☎*325/698-1234* ⊕*www.mcmelegantesuites. com* ⇄*65 rooms* ⏦*In-room: Ethernet, kitchenettes (some). In hotel: bar, restaurant, pool, no-smoking rooms* ⊟*AE, D, MC, V* ⏦*BP.*

WICHITA FALLS & ENVIRONS

WICHITA FALLS

123 mi southeast of Amarillo, 347 mi northwest of Dallas.

Serenely parked on the high plains just 15 mi south of Oklahoma, Wichita Falls is an earnest and family-friendly city. The town was founded in the 1800s by cattle ranchers and the railroads that later sustained them—before the all-important discovery of oil in the early 1900s. The Wichita River once did contain the city's titular waterfall, but an 1886 flood destroyed the landscape that created it. In 1987 the city erected an artificial waterfall that rises more than five stories.

With more than 100,000 residents, Wichita Falls qualifies as a city but still feels like a small town—and it's one that can boast of noteworthy natives like the band Bowling for Soup and soccer star Mia Hamm.

WHAT TO SEE

☺ **Littlest Skyscraper.** The rumored work of a scam artist, the Littlest Skyscraper was supposed to be at least 12 times larger—some say it was supposed to be 50 stories—than it turned out to be. It was a $200,000 swindle (a huge amount in the early 20th century) that resulted in a well-preserved but only four-floor, one-room-wide building. It's said that the boondoggle happened when the speculator presented a plan measured in inches not feet. Nowadays visitors can scale a narrow staircase or shop at the antiques store within the building. ⊠ *Corner of 7th St. and LaSalle* ☾ *Tues.–Sat. 10:30–5.*

★ **Museum of North Texas History.** This University of North Texas museum collects the lore, legend, and lure of Wichita Falls, and helps visitors understand this Old West town through rotating exhibits. One charming 2008 exhibition, for instance, is "Aprons," complete with actual frontier specimens. This museum is intensely, delightfully local. ⊠ *720 Indiana Ave.* ☎ *940/322–7628* ⊕ *www.month-ntx.org* ☞ *Free, but donations accepted* ☾ *Tues.–Thurs. 10–noon, 1–4; Sat. 10–2.*

☺ **Wichita Falls Museum of Art.** On the Midwestern State University campus, this museum glorifies fine arts on a tight budget and manages to do it very well. Rotating exhibits range in scope and medium. There's a planetarium, too. ⊠ *2 Eureka Circle* ☎ *940/692–0923* ⊕ *www. sciencespectrum.com* ☞ *Free* ☾ *Tues.–Fri. 9:30–5, Sat. 10–5.*

SPORTS & THE OUTDOORS

☺ **Riverbend Nature Center.** These gorgeous grounds wind through varied
★ ecological systems not normally preserved in the Panhandle, from wetlands with singing baby frogs (depending on the season) to thick stands of trees and a brand-spanking new conservatory with lots of local, fluttering guests. The facilities will soon include butterfly gardens and a bigger gift shop. ⊠ *2200 Third St.* ☎ *940/767–0843* ⊕ *www.river bendnaturecenter.org* ☞ *$5* ☾ *Fri.–Sat. 10–4, Sun. noon–4.*

Larry McMurtry: Writing the West

The West portrayed by native Texan Larry McMurtry is a gritty one, not the romantic one of Louis L'Amour or Zane Grey. Perhaps that's because his father and eight uncles were real cowboys and ranchers.

McMurtry's characters can be dark and thoroughly unlovable, like Hud Bannon from his debut novel, Horseman, Pass By, or Sam the Lion, called "a hell of a man" in The Last Picture Show. But they're palpably true.

In 1970 the prolific novelist added bookseller to his accomplishments, opening a rare-book store in Wash-ington and following in 1988 with a huge, four-building complex in little Archer City, Texas, used as a model for fictional towns in his book and where The Last Picture Show was set. In between establishing these book businesses, McMurtry won a Pulitzer Prize for the epic novel Lonesome Dove.

In 2006 he added to his awards an Oscar for Best Adapted Screenplay for Brokeback Mountain, which he wrote with Diana Ossana. Now in his seventies, McMurtry shows no sign of slowing down.

—Lisa Miller

ARTS & ENTERTAINMENT

★ **Kemp Center for the Arts.** Located within sanguine brick and Greek-revival columns, the landmark center contains performance space, galleries, studios, rotating exhibits, an outdoor sculpture garden, and a gift shop. Come for tours, to view the art, and to hear the symphony. ✉ *1300 Lamar St.* ☎ *940/767–2787* ⊕ *www.kempcenter.org* ✉ *Free but donations appreciated.* ⊙ *Mon.–Fri. 9–5, Sat. 10–4.*

WHERE TO EAT

¢–$ ✕ **Branding Iron.** This is almost an exclusively locals-only place, and residents love it so much that they overlook the bare decor and haphazard hours. This is a good spot for a lunch that may not be placid: the taste of it overwhelms the noise. Try the Texas barbecue, especially the beef brisket, and you'll feel like an insider. It's lunch and brunch only, except for Fridays. ✉ *104 E. Scott Ave.* ☎ *940/723–0338* ⊙ *No dinner Sat.–Thurs. Closed Sun.* ▭ *No credit cards.*

ARCHER CITY

25 mi south of Wichita Falls via Hwy. 79

Known for its two rare and used bookstores, Archer City also attracts film aficionados. This small town has made it to the big screen not once, but twice, and has often been the model for author Larry McMurtry's fictional towns. Two movies based on books by McMurtry, *The Last Picture Show* (1971) and *Texasville* (1990), were filmed here.

SHOPPING

BOOKSTORES For awhile the downward economy was about to put the breaks on Larry McMurtry's **Booked Up, Inc.** (✉ *216 S. Center St.* ☎ *940/574–2511* ⊕ *www.bookedupac.com* ⊙ *Mon.–Sat. 10–5*), but at the time of this printing, the bookstore specializing in antiquarian books is still open and selling its vast collection of fine, rare, and scholarly titles. **Three Dogs Books** (✉ *107 E. Main St.* ☎ *940/733–2157* ⊕ *www.three dogbooks.com* ⊙ *Mon.–Sat. by appointment only*) carries an assortment of rare and unusual books. To set up an appointment to visit the store, you can e-mail owners Cody and Julie Ressell at *threedogbooks@ sbcglobal.net.*

THE PANHANDLE ESSENTIALS

Research prices, get travel advice, and book your trip at fodors.com.

TRANSPORTATION

BY AIR

The area's fortunate enough to be serviced by airports in the four largest towns: Amarillo, Lubbock, Abilene, and (very limited) Wichita Falls.

Information **Rick Husband Amarillo International Airport** (✉ *10801 Airport Blvd., 10.5 mi east of downtown off I-40, Amarillo* ☎ *806/335–1671* ⊕ *www. ci.amarillo.tx.us/departments/airport/flightinfo.htm*). **Lubbock Preston Smith International Airport** (✉ *5401 N. Martin Luther King Blvd., 5 mi northeast of downtown off Hwy. 240, Wichita Falls* ☎ *806/775–2044* ⊕ *www.flylia.com*). **Abilene Regional Airport** (✉ *2933 Airport Blvd., 6 mi east of downtown, Abilene* ☎ *325/676–6367* ⊕ *www.abilenetx.com/Airport*). **Wichita Falls Municipal Airport** (✉ *4000 Armstrong Dr., Ste. 8, 12 mi northwest of downtown off I-5, Wichita Falls* ☎ *940/855–3621*).

BY BUS

Getting to and from the Panhandle cities (even the little ones) can be accomplished via **Greyhound** (☎ *800/231–2222* ⊕ *www.greyhound. com*). City buses are available in Amarillo, Lubbock, Abilene, and Wichita Falls for a pittance.

CONTACTS & RESOURCES

EMERGENCIES

In an emergency, dial 911. Each of the following medical facilities has an emergency room open 24 hours a day.

Hospitals **Baptist St. Anthony's Health System** (✉ *1600 Wallace Blvd., Amarillo* ☎ *806/212–1000*). **Covenant Health System 19th St. Campus** (✉ *3615 19th St., Lubbock* ☎ *806/725–1011*). **Covenant Health System Lakeside Campus** (✉ *4000 24th St., Lubbock* ☎ *806/725–6000*). **Covenant Children's Hospital** (✉ *3610 21st St., Lubbock* ☎ *806/725–1011*). **Lubbock Heart Hospital** (✉ *4810 N. Loop 289., Lubbock* ☎ *806/687–7777*). **University Medical Center** (✉ *602 Indiana Ave., Lubbock* ☎ *806/775–8200*). **Abilene Regional Medical Center** (✉ *6250 Hwy. 83-84 at Antilley Rd., Abilene* ☎ *325/428–1000*). **United Regional Health Care** (✉ *52nd and F Sts., Wichita Falls* ☎ *916/733–1000*).

VISITOR INFORMATION

Abilene Chamber of Commerce (✉ *1101 N. First St., Abilene* ☎ *325/676–2556 or 800/727–7704* ⊕ *www.abilenevisitors.com*). **Amarillo Chamber of Commerce** (✉ *1000 S. Polk St., Amarillo* ☎ *806/373–7800* ⊕ *www.amarillo-chamber.org*). **Canyon Chamber of Commerce** (✉ *1518 Fifth Ave., Canyon* ☎ *806/655–7815* ⊕ *www.canyonchamber.org*). **Lubbock Chamber of Commerce** (✉ *15000 Broadway, Sixth Flr., Lubbock* ☎ *806/747–5232* ⊕ *www.visitlubbock.org*). **Wichita Falls Convention & Visitors Bureau** (✆ *P.O. Box 630, Wichita Falls* ☎ *940/716–5500* ⊕ *www.wichitafalls.org*).

Texas
Essentials

There are planners and there are those who, excuse the pun, fly by the seat of their pants. We happily place ourselves among the planners. Our writers and editors try to anticipate all the issues you may face before and during any journey, and then they do their research. This section is the product of their efforts. Use it to get excited about your trip to Texas, to inform your travel planning, or to guide you on the road should the seat of your pants start to feel threadbare.

GETTING STARTED

We're really proud of our Web site: fodors.com is a great place to begin any journey. Scan Travel Wire for suggested itineraries, travel deals, new openings, and other up-to-the-minute info. Check out Booking to research prices and book flights, hotel rooms, rental cars, and vacation packages. Head to Talk for on-the-ground pointers from other travelers.

■ RESOURCES

ONLINE TRAVEL TOOLS

All About Texas Texas Tourism's Web site, ⊕www.traveltex.com, has wonderful driving tours and trip-planning tools as well as an extensive events calendar.

Billing itself as the "National Magazine of Texas," **Texas Monthly** (⊕www.texasmonthly.com) has its finger on the state's pulse, with coverage on politics, shopping, arts and culture, and Texas travel

Texas Highways at (⊕www.texashighways.com) focuses on exploring the Lone Star State.

The Texas Governor's office (⊕www.governor.state.tx.us) covers far more than politics—it's devoted to promoting music and the arts throughout Texas.

The Texas Commission on the Arts (⊕www.artonart.com) maintains an events calendar.

The Texas Historical Commission (⊕www.thc.state.tx.us) has a wealth of information on the rich history of the Lone Star State.

The Handbook of Texas Online (⊕www.tshaonline.org), by the Texas State Historical Association, is an incredible resource for information about any Texas hamlet, town, or city (from Abbott to Zybach)—and pretty much any other topic about Texas you can think of.

The Texas Parks and Wildlife Department (⊕www.tpwd.state.tx.us) is a source for nature-lovers. The **National Park Service** (⊕www.nps.gov) provides insight into its parks.

■ TRAVEL INTO MEXICO

GOVERNMENT ADVISORIES

■TIP➔If you decide to take an extended trip into Mexico from Texas, consider registering with the State Department (⊕*https://travelregistration.state.gov*), so the government will know to look for you should a crisis occur in Mexico while you're visiting.

Other than long lines, crossing into Mexico isn't much of a hassle—just bring your passport. Don't carry a single bullet or even a pocketknife into the country; Mexican law is harsh on weapons possession. U.S. driver's licenses are valid in Mexico, but cars must be driven only by their owners or by those with signed documents from a rental agency. (Do *not* bring a rental car into Mexico without your rental agency's blessing—this can void your contract, making you personally responsible for any damages that occur on the other side of the border—Taking public transportation or walking are your best options.

Keep in mind that when you travel in Mexico you're under Mexican law and fully liable. Things that seem minor here—like insulting someone, littering, being tipsy in public, or making a rude gesture—can be criminal south of the border. Just be respectful, and you'll probably be okay.

Re-entering the United States is more vigorous than crossing the border into Mexico. If you're traveling with children, keep in mind that both parents must consent to the travel. If one is not present, the child must have a notarized permission letter, preferably with times and itinerary of travel, and proof of their relationship to the child. (This precaution is meant to safeguard children from abduction.)

TRAVEL TO MEXICO	
Passport	Must be valid at the time of re-entry.
Visa	Tourists and business travelers staying more than 3 days and 6 months, respectively, require an application.
Vaccinations	Hepatitis A, typhoid, and even rabies shots have been recommended (but are rarely needed) in border towns. If venturing farther south, anti-malarial drugs may be needed.
Driving	U.S. driver's license is fine. Temporary Mexican insurance should be purchased.
Departure Tax	None if walking or on a bus. If you're driving, you'll need to pay $15 for a permit, which should be displayed in the windshield. (Some areas also require a tourist card.)

DRIVING IN MEXICO

If you go south of the border, be aware that your American insurance probably won't cut it in Mexico—no matter how great your coverage is—since Mexican law requires insurance that covers personal injury. Credit cards often provide some coverage, as does AAA, but your best bet is to get a tourist card for identification purposes, and to buy Mexican insurance either online or at the stores on the border. That way, you can drive with a clear conscience and no worries.

If you have an accident in Mexico, be aware that you might go to jail while authorities try to figure out who is at fault. Also, keep in mind that Mexican insurance won't spring you from jail if you're found to be criminally at fault (for example, if you were deemed to be drinking and driving or criminally negligent).

ROADSIDE EMERGENCIES

Green federal repair trucks are paid to cruise the Mexican highways. Services from the "Green Angels" is free (and you can call them from anywhere in Mexico), but you'll have to pay if your car needs supplies or parts.

Emergency Services (Mexico) Green Angels (☎English-speaking, 01-55-5250-8221).

INSURANCE

Driving in Mexico requires Mexican insurance—period. Getting in a minor fender bender without it can result in your car's getting impounded, and you might even get arrested. Also, be aware that driving while intoxicated or under the influence of any drug automatically invalidates your insurance in Mexico!

SHOTS & MEDICATIONS

Everyone entering Mexico should be up-to-date on their booster shots, regardless of age. This isn't a requirement, but it's a good precaution. The Centers for Disease Control maintains pertinent updates and requirements for Mexico on their Web site—consult it and speak with your physician before a long trip south of the border. All visitors should pay attention to how their food is cooked and drink only bottled water.

Health Warnings National Centers for Disease Control & Prevention (CDC ☎877/394–8747 international travelers' health line ⊕www.cdc.gov/travel). World Health Organization (WHO ⊕www.who.int).

PASSPORTS & VISAS

U.S. Passport Information U.S. Department of State (☎877/487–2778 ⊕http://travel.state.gov/passport).

TRANSPORTATION

▌BY AIR

The go-to airports in Texas are, hands-down, Dallas (DFW) and Houston (George Bush Intercontinental). Dallas is about four hours away from New York City by air, and about six from Los Angeles; it takes about the same amount of time to reach Houston.

Airline Contacts Alaska Airlines (☎800/252–7522 ⊕www.alaskaair.com). **American Airlines** (☎800/433–7300 ⊕www.aa.com). **ATA** (☎800/435–9282 ⊕www.ata.com). **Continental Airlines** (☎800/523–3273 ⊕www.continental.com). **Delta Air Lines** (☎800/221–1212 for U.S. reservations ⊕www.delta.com). **Frontier Airlines** (☎800/432–1359 ⊕www.frontierairlines.com). **jetBlue** (☎800/538–2583 ⊕www.jetblue.com). **Northwest Airlines** (☎800/225–2525 ⊕www.nwa.com). **Southwest Airlines** (☎800/435–9792 ⊕www.southwest.com). **Spirit Airlines** (☎800/772–7117 ⊕www.spiritair.com). **United Airlines** (☎800/864–8331 ⊕www.united.com). **USAirways** (☎800/428–4322 ⊕www.usairways.com).

▌BY BUS

All sizable cities in Texas are connected by bus, but the time it takes to get from point to point can vary widely depending on the time of day and the date. For instance, a trip from Dallas to El Paso can take a little over 11 hours—or 16½ hours—depending on the route you pick. The same trip by car (without stops) takes about 9 hours. On the plus side, the bus can cost less than half as much as an intra-state flight—purchase your ticket ahead of time for the best deal. Only one major bus line goes to every Texas city: Greyhound.

Bus Information Greyhound (☎800/231–2222 ⊕www.greyhound.com).

▌BY CAR

The state has a fantastic network of interlacing highways and smaller, meandering roads. Just be aware that distances are great here—Texas is the largest state in the lower 48. The drive from Houston, in the east, to El Paso, in the west, is 745 mi—about the distance from New York City to Charleston, South Carolina!

GASOLINE

In Texas, if you see a sign warning you that the next gas station is 75 mi away, take heed and gas up—they're not kidding! There are some desolate stretches of Texas highway, especially out west, where you can go for miles without seeing signs of civilization, save the road you're driving on. Be sure you have a full tank before tackling long stretches between towns like Alpine and Terlingua; the more remote the road, the fewer the gas stations. Also, despite Texas's plethora of oil fields, prices at the pump are not much cheaper here elsewhere in the country.

ROAD CONDITIONS

Most roads in Texas are smooth and well maintained. Frontage roads run parallel to many highways, which makes it easy to merge into and out of traffic. Be aware that U-turns are a way of life in Texas—lanes on some Texas highways will lead you to a U-turn, and U-turns are permitted from most left-turn lanes. As you motor along, you'll see abbreviations like FM (which means Farm-to-Market; most of these routes were originally in rural areas); RM means Ranch-to-Market (and springs from the same roots); IH means Interstate Highway; and Loop (LP) means a bypass around a city.

In rural areas, traffic tends to move quite a bit more slowly. This is a law-and-order culture, and that attitude even bleeds into the way people drive—it's not uncommon for commuters to drive a steady five miles under the speed limit. Take a deep breath and wave when you pass. (Whatever you do, don't make rude gestures—that'll get you a ticket in Texas.)

Note that some highways have two posted speed limits—one for during the day (the white sign with black lettering), and one for after dark (the black sign with white lettering that says "Night"). The night speed limit is usually 5 mph below the daytime speed limit.

TRAVEL TIMES BY CAR

From	To	Distance, Est. Travel Time
Austin	San Antonio	79 mi, 1¼ hr
Austin	Houston	165 mi, 3 hrs
San Antonio	Houston	197 mi, 3 hrs
San Antonio	El Paso	580 mi, 8 hrs
San Antonio	Laredo	159 mi, 2 hrs
San Antonio	South Padre Island	291 mi, 5 hrs
Dallas	Houston	197 mi, 3 hrs
Dallas	Amarillo	362 mi, 6 hrs
Dallas	El Paso	636 mi, 9 hrs
Houston	Corpus Christi	222 mi, 4 hrs
Corpus Christi	South Padre Island	178 mi, 3 hrs

ROADSIDE EMERGENCIES

In Texas, help is just a 911 call away. The highway patrol is always cruising the highways and byways and will likely spot you, depending on where you are.

Emergency Services Texas Highway Patrol (☎512/424–2000 ⊕www.txdps.state.tx.us).

RULES OF THE ROAD

In Texas, littering is verboten (thanks to decades of the "Don't Mess with Texas" ad campaign), so don't throw anything out of your car window. (Even a flicked cigarette butt can spell big trouble, particularly if there's a drought on.)

All front-seat passengers must wear seat belts, and children younger than 5 or under 36 inches tall must be restrained in a car- or booster seat firmly secured in the back seat of the vehicle. The state further recommends that children shorter than 4 feet 9 inches be secured in booster seats in the back seat. Also, be aware that some parts of Texas have passed laws against using cell phones while driving.

Standard driving laws apply. A right on red is okay (after a full stop), as long as there's no sign telling you not to.

Police are scrupulous about enforcing the drinking and driving laws; a blood alcohol level of .08 or higher (sometimes less, if you're driving erratically) will result in your arrest. Police stage checkpoints at certain times of year (mainly holidays known for heavy drinking, like New Year's Eve). Not every town or city does this, but plenty do across the state. If you're caught driving under the influence (even if it's a first offense), you can lose your license for a year, spend six months in jail, and/or pay a $2,000 fine. A third offense can get you two to ten in the pen. And if you're under 21 and have any alcohol in your system, you'll automatically lose your license.

▌ BY TRAIN

Amtrak provides rail service to several parts of Texas, though the state isn't completely covered. The Texas Eagle line runs between Chicago and Dallas, Fort Worth, Austin, and San Antonio, with links to other parts of the state; service does not extend to the Panhandle and many parts of West Texas.

Information Amtrak's Texas Eagle (☎800/222-4357 ⊕www.texaseagle.com).

Austin-Bergstrom International Airport

Airlines	Gates
ExpressJet Airlines	1 & 4
AeroMexico	2
Northwest Airlines	3
Delta Air Lines	5 & 6
Southwest Airlines	7–12
American Airlines	13–15, 17 & 25
Continental Airlines	16, 18 & 22
JetBlue Airways	19
US Airways	20
United Airlines & United Express	21 & 23
Frontier Airlines	24
Midwest Airlines	24

Lot F
Lot E
Lot G
Lot D
Lot B
Lot C
Lot A
Lot A

Parking Garage

Terminal

Parking Garage

24 22 20 18 16
26 23 21 19 17 15 14
13 12 11 10 9 8 7 6 5 4 3
1 2

TICKET COUNTERS:
American Airlines
Continental Airlines
United Airlines
US Airways
JetBlue Airways
Frontier Airlines
Midwest Airlines

TICKET COUNTERS:
Southwest Airlines
Delta Air Lines
Northwest Airlines
AeroMexico
ExpressJet Airlines

San Antonio International Airport

TERMINAL 2
American Airlines
Continental Airlines
US Airways

TERMINAL 1
Aerolitoral
Comair
Delta Air Lines
Express Jet
Frontier Airlines
Mexicana
Midwest Airlines
Northwest Airlines
SkyWest Airlines
Southwest Airlines
United Airlines

HOURLY PARKING

LONG TERM PARKING

Airport Blvd.

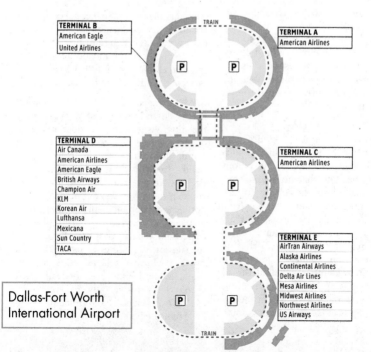

George Bush Intercontinental Airport/Houston

NORTH CONCOURSE

TERMINAL LINK

P

Hotel

TO →
TERMINAL C

TERMINAL A
Air Canada
American Airlines
Continental Airlines
Delta Air Lines
Frontier Airlines
Northwest Airlines
United Airlines
US Airways

SOUTH CONCOURSE

TERMINAL B
Continental Airlines

TERMINAL E
Continental Airlines

NORTH CONCOURSE

← TO
TERMINAL B

TERMINAL LINK

P

Hotel

TERMINAL D
AeroMexico
Air France
British Airways
Emirates Airline
KLM
Lufthansa
Singapore Airlines
TACA

SOUTH CONCOURSE

TERMINAL C
Continental Airlines

TRAIN

TERMINAL B
American Eagle
United Airlines

TERMINAL A
American Airlines

P **P**

TERMINAL D
Air Canada
American Airlines
American Eagle
British Airways
Champion Air
KLM
Korean Air
Lufthansa
Mexicana
Sun Country
TACA

TERMINAL C
American Airlines

P **P**

TERMINAL E
AirTran Airways
Alaska Airlines
Continental Airlines
Delta Air Lines
Mesa Airlines
Midwest Airlines
Northwest Airlines
US Airways

P **P**

Dallas-Fort Worth International Airport

TRAIN

ON THE GROUND

▍ BUSINESS HOURS

Business hours in urban areas of Texas and in Mexico can stretch after sunset, particularly at chain stores and shopping malls. Even in the smallest towns, the malls close at a decent hour (usually 9 PM, unless it's Sunday), but the smaller shops often close as early as 5 PM. Some shops in Texas close for lunch (usually from noon to 1 or 2 PM). Religious holidays above and below the border are stringently observed; these include Easter, Christmas, and sometimes Ash Wednesday and Good Friday.

▍ EATING OUT

RESERVATIONS & DRESS

Regardless of where you are, it's a good idea to make a reservation if you can. We only mention them specifically when reservations are essential (there's no other way you'll ever get a table) or when they are not accepted. For popular restaurants, book as far ahead as you can (often 30 days), and reconfirm as soon as you arrive. (Large parties should always call ahead to check the reservations policy.) We mention dress in our listings only when men are required to wear a jacket or a jacket and tie.

WINES, BEER & SPIRITS

Of Texas's 254 counties, 42 are completely dry (including Angelina County, home to Lufkin, and Smith County, home to Tyler), meaning that no alcohol may be purchased within the county borders. Most off those dry counties are located in the Panhandle and West Texas, but many of Texas's non-dry counties have confusing laws (called "Blue Laws") that are inconsistent from county to county. For instance, some counties will allow the sale of liquor—but not the sale of alcoholic beverages by the glass; in some counties, the opposite is true. Other counties restrict the sale of alcohol to beverages below a certain alcohol percentage, and some areas require you to join a club to drink. Because these laws are impossible to briefly codify here, it's a good idea to do a little research before coming. Most affected areas are rural.

▍ FISHING PERMITS

Texas stores, sporting-goods shops, and hunting outlets all sell fishing permits, and they are also available online. The only time you won't need one when fishing is on the first Saturday in June, or if you're a non-resident under 17 or mentally disabled. Otherwise, fees start at $15. The **Texas Parks and Wildlife Department** (☎713/948–3350 ⊕www.tpwd.state.tx.us) has a list of businesses that vend the licenses.

▍ HEALTH

Ailments that might strike, depending on the time of year, include sunstroke, heat exhaustion, and dehydration. These are easy to prevent by simply donning hats in the sun, slathering on SPF 30 regardless of season, and packing bottled water.

In Mexico, malarial insects tend to infest deeper down in the country, so generally the most visitors have to fear is a case of incontinence due to lower sanitation standards for water and food. Wash your hands frequently, and use hand-sanitizer. Make sure your food is thoroughly cooked, don't buy food from street vendors whose cooking methods you haven't watched, and avoid any meat product (particularly pork) that may have sat in the sun for 30 minutes or longer. Do not buy any Mexican folk remedies, as they might contain high levels of lead. Stick with what's proven—bring your own aspirin or Tylenol, cold remedies, and headache medicines.

▮ MONEY

Prices in this guide are given for adults. Reduced fees are often available for children, students, and seniors.

Mexican–American border towns are linked by an umbilical cord born of trade. Siblings, the twin towns are often bilingual and generally accept currencies of both countries. Pesos will be necessary in small, less frequented Mexican towns.

ATMS & BANKS

If you travel across the border, you can easily get pesos by using an automatic teller machine (ATM) at a Mexican bank. Note, however, that your own bank will probably charge a fee for using ATMs abroad, and the foreign bank may also charge a fee. Nevertheless, you'll usually get a better rate of exchange at an ATM than at a currency-exchange office—or even when changing money in a bank. And extracting funds as you need them is a safer option than carrying around a large amount of cash.

CREDIT CARDS

Throughout this guide, the following abbreviations are used: **AE**, American Express; **D**, Discover; **DC**, Diners Club; **MC**, MasterCard; and **V**, Visa.

It's a good idea to inform your credit-card company before you travel, especially if you're going into Mexico and don't travel internationally very often. If you don't, the credit-card company might put a hold on your card owing to unusual activity—not a good thing to find out halfway through your trip.

Reporting Lost Cards **American Express** (☎800/528–4800 in the U.S. or 336/393–1111 collect from abroad ⊕www.american-express.com). **Diners Club** (☎800/234–6377 in the U.S. or 303/799–1504 collect from abroad ⊕www.dinersclub.com). **Discover** (☎800/347–2683 in the U.S. or 801/902–3100 collect from abroad ⊕www.discovercard.com). **MasterCard** (☎800/627–8372 in the U.S. or 636/722–7111 collect from abroad

⊕www.mastercard.com). **Visa** (☎800/847–2911 in the U.S. or 410/581–9994 collect from abroad ⊕www.visa.com).

▮ SAFETY

Some border towns are troubled by violence, much of it drug-related—especially Nuevo Laredo (which tourists should steer clear of) and nearby border towns. Juárez, which has more than 1 million residents, reported 200 homicides by the end of April 2008; most were suspected to be drug-related. (the U.S. government is not advising tourists to steer clear of the popular shopping destination, however.) Juárez has also been the subject of numerous documentaries because of the "Women of Juárez"—hundreds of women who have gone missing over the past ten years and were later found sexually assaulted and murdered. Police have made arrests in connection with the murders, but women shouldn't travel alone there, period.

For further information, check out **www.Travel.state.gov**, the U.S. government's travel Web site. The site posts travel warnings and alerts should dangerous conditions arise in another country.

▮ TIME

Unlike the rest of Texas and of Mexico, El Paso and Juárez are on Mountain Time; most of the rest of the state of Texas and Mexico are on Central Time (except for a part of Mexico's Baja California, Norte, which uses Pacific Standard Time).

INDEX

PHOTO CREDITS

NOTES

NOTES

ACKNOWLEDGMENTS

There are many we wish to thank for assistance during the research and reporting of this guide. The writers and editors gratefully acknowledge the many convention and visitors bureau representatives, like Dee Dee Poteete and Tonya Hope from the San Antonio CVB, Daryl Whitworth of the Fredericksburg CVB, Lou Hollander of the Brenham Chamber of Commerce, Pattie Sears of the Bryan-College Station CVB, and Beth Krauss of the Austin CVB; Meredith Spurgeon Michelson, who handles public relations for the state; the many restaurant and hotel employees who took the time to show us their properties; those who gave us tours of some of Texas's noteworthy attractions, such as Fran Stephenson at Sea World Texas and Bill Weiss at Blue Bell Creameries; and last but definitely not least, we thank the many residents of Texas who shared with us their insights on the land they love.

ABOUT OUR WRITERS

While he now calls the Big Apple home, **Tony Carnes** (*Texas Mega-churches*), a senior writer at *Christianity Today* magazine, was born in the Hill Country. He and his wife Darilyn go back often to, as President LBJ called it, this "special corner of God's real estate."

Stewart Coerver (*South Texas & the Coast*) is a freelance writer based in Corpus Christi—for now. He has also lived in Dallas, Chicago, Atlanta, Austin, and St. Louis. He has visited some two dozen countries (and counting) and works part-time for ExpressJet Airlines.

Dallas native and lifelong Texan **Tyra Damm** (*Dallas & Fort Worth*) has lived in tiny towns, big cities, and middle-sized suburbs all over the state. A graduate of the University of North Texas, she worked for daily newspapers in Bryan, Lubbock, Fort Worth, and Dallas before tackling freelance journalism. She and her husband Steve enjoy traveling with their two adventurous children.

Jessica Norman Dupuy (*The Hill Country, Austin's Arts & Entertainment*) is an Austin-based freelance writer specializing in food and travel. Raised in the Texas Hill Country, she enjoys the outdoors, savoring different cuisines, and any chance to travel abroad—or to the Rocky Mountains in a pinch. She is a contributor to *Texas Monthly*.

Jennifer Edwards (*Big Bend, Guadalupe Mountains, and Carlsbad Caverns National Parks; West Texas; The Panhandle; Texas Essentials*) is the assistant lifestyle editor at the *Midland Reporter-Telegram*. She's won multiple Associated Press awards for her work as a journalist, and her articles have appeared in dozens of newspapers, including the *Dallas Morning News* and the *New York Sun*. She loves the smell of morning in the West Texas outdoors.

Specializing in the arts and travel, **Wes Eichenwald** (*Austin*) is a freelance writer and editor who has lived in Austin since 2002 (following previous lives in New York, Boston, and Ljubljana, Slovenia). His writing has appeared in numerous outlets, including the *Chicago Tribune* and the *Los Angeles Times*. Along with their two young children, Wes and his wife enjoy discovering hidden corners and new places to eat, shop, and explore in the Texas capital.

Writers **Lisa Miller & Larry Neal** (*Famous Texans close-ups*) usually save their pithy writing for press releases and op-eds. But these two Texans, who work together in the nation's capital, had fun writing up the bios of some of the state's most famous characters, from renegades like Bonnie & Clyde to genteel souls like Lady Bird Johnson.

Tim Moloney (*Houston & Galveston*) has called Houston home for 20 years, and has no plans to leave any time soon. When he's not working away furiously at his keyboard, you can usually find him eating and drinking his way across town, or driving around aimlessly, looking for new things to discover.

An Arkansas-based travel writer, **Michael Ream** (*East Texas*) once upon a time wore the hat of newspaper reporter. In that capacity he traveled extensively in Europe and South America. In addition to East Texas, he has covered Memphis and the Ozarks for Fodor's guides and Web site.

Born and raised in Texas, **Kevin Tankersley** (*North-Central Texas, San Antonio Sports & the Outdoors*) roots for the Bears of Baylor University, his alma mater and where he teaches writing in the journalism department. He has worked as a photographer, writer, reporter, and sports information director. He and his wife Abby have a daughter, Sophie, and a son, Brazos. They live in Waco.